THE SPANISH REPUBLIC AND
THE CIVIL WAR
1931–1939

The
Spanish Republic
and the
Civil War

1931-1939

BY GABRIEL JACKSON

PRINCETON UNIVERSITY PRESS
PRINCETON, NEW JERSEY

PREFACE

AT THE time of its occurrence, the Spanish Civil War epitomized for the Western world the confrontation of democracy,
fascism, and communism. An entire generation of Englishmen
and Americans felt a deeper emotional involvement in that
war than in any other world event of their lifetimes, including
the Second World War. On the Continent, its "lessons," as
interpreted by participants of many nationalities, have played
an important role in the politics of both Western Europe
and the People's Democracies. Everywhere in the Western
world, readers of history have noted parallels between the
Spanish Republic of 1931 and the revolutionary governments which existed in France and Central Europe during
the year 1848. The Asturian revolt of October 1934, reminded
participants and observers alike of the Paris Commune of
1871, and even the most politically unsophisticated observers
could see in the Spain of 1936 all the ideological and class
conflicts which had characterized revolutionary France of
1789 and revolutionary Russia of 1917.

It is not surprising, therefore, that the worthwhile books on
the Spanish Civil War have almost all emphasized its international ramifications and have discussed its political crises
entirely in the vocabulary of the French and Russian revolutions. Relatively few of the foreign participants realized
that the Civil War had arisen out of specifically Spanish circumstances. Few of them knew the history of the Second
Spanish Republic, which for five years prior to the war had
been grappling with the problems of what we now call an
"underdeveloped nation." A George Orwell, a Pietro Nenni, a
Gustav Regler, an André Malraux understood the issues in
terms of evident analogies to contemporary situations in
England, Italy, Germany, France. Since they were intelligent,
literate observers, interpretation of the Civil War has remained strongly colored by their impressions and by those
of other foreign writers.

In the present work I have tried to expound the history of

the Second Republic and the Civil War primarily as seen from within Spain. In this respect I have depended heavily on memoir literature and on the free, and politically variegated, Spanish press for the years 1931 to 1936. For events in the provinces during the Republican era, and for many aspects of the Civil War, I have supplemented my printed sources with interviews. In Spain I had the opportunity for serious, lengthy conversations with more than 120 persons who had lived through the entire period I was studying. Some of these conversations were with leading political figures, but most of them, by my own choice, were with civil servants, military and professional men, and random witnesses, many of whom had no political commitments—past or present—and no public reputations to defend. I tried to make these conversations as concrete as possible. If my companion was a doctor, I asked him about hospital conditions, medical supplies, and public health problems in the cities where he had lived or on the battlefronts where he had served. If he was a municipal official I asked him about strikes, political demonstrations, public works programs of which he knew from personal experience.

There were two general questions which I always posed because they could not help but be central to everyone's memories, and because they were crucial to an understanding of the eight-year period. I always asked to what extent the maintenance of public order had been a problem and in what manner the Church had been persecuted. These conversations shaped to a considerable degree my preoccupations in writing. Almost always, I found my interlocutor asking me why the Republic had failed, and why Spaniards could not live in peace with one another. Such questions came incessantly from people who had fought on opposite sides, from people who today support the government, and from people who hate it. I made those questions my own, the more especially as the Spanish experience can throw much light on the difficulties of Western-style democracy in Latin America and on the relationship of military to civil power throughout the world.

I wish to acknowledge specifically the following aids to my work. The Social Science Research Council and the

Commission for Educational Exchange Between the United States and Spain gave me the fellowships which enabled me to devote to the preparation of this book the entire academic years 1960–1962. Professor Jacques Godechot of the University of Toulouse, under whom I had worked as a graduate student, Professor Pierre Vilar of the Ecole des Hautes Etudes in Paris, and my dear friend and Wellesley colleague, the poet Jorge Guillén, aided me greatly with personal introductions and bibliographical suggestions; as did also the late Professor Jaime Vicens Vives of the University of Barcelona. Dr. Howard Cline, Director of the Hispanic Foundation of the Library of Congress, and Professors C. J. Bishko of the University of Virginia and Lewis Hanke of Columbia University, took the lead in urging the fellowship committees that the time had come to attempt a scholarly study of the Spanish Republic and the Civil War. During my research in France, all manner of intricate problems were handled for me by my friends Tomás and Antonia Quérol, Ricardo and Olga Hernández Alvariño, and by the French hispanist Marie Laffranque. I wish also to acknowledge the kindness of Mme. Eléna de la Souchère in permitting me to consult her valuable unpublished notes on several phases of the history of the Republic.

The work of completion and revision has been greatly facilitated by grants-in-aid from the American Council of Learned Societies and from the Knox College Faculty Research Fund. I owe several valuable corrections to Professor Juan Linz of Columbia University, and many helpful suggestions in the final preparation of the manuscript to two Knox undergraduate history majors, Mr. Thomas Schmidt and Miss Jo Ann Ooiman. I owe to my wife Elizabeth the shared enthusiasm which makes the whole work spiritually hers as well as my own. The aid of dozens of Spaniards who gave me their time and confidence at some risk to themselves I can only acknowledge by the book itself, in the hope that it will appear to them a worthy history of the hopeful, and later tragic, years through which they lived.

Knox College, Galesburg, Illinois GABRIEL JACKSON
January, 1964

The publication of a paperback edition has given me the opportunity to include a number of factual additions and corrections. I owe these to the letters of several colleagues: Professors Stanley Payne and Edward Malefakis, Mr. Antonio Ramos Oliveira of UNESCO, and Mr. Herbert Southworth.

University of California at San Diego   GABRIEL JACKSON
August, 1966

ORGANIZATIONS AND POLITICAL TERMS

Acción Española organization of royalist intellectuals, both Carlist and Alphonsine, editing a journal of that name.

Acción Popular political organization defending the rights of the Church against laic legislation.

Acción Republicana the party of Manuel Azaña; fused in 1934 with several other small parties and known thereafter as Izquierda Republicana (Republican Left).

CEDA Confederación Española de Derechas Autónomas; a federation of small independent rightist parties grouped in the Cortes under the leadership of José María Gil Robles, strongly Catholic, and uncommitted as to the form of government.

chekas Kangaroo courts formed by the various far left parties in the summer of 1936; also used to refer to the private prisons operated by the Communists during the Civil War.

CNT Confederación Nacional de Trabajo; the labor federation of the anarchists.

Carlists The partisans of the younger branch of the royal family, strongest in Navarre, and in parts of the Levant, preaching a traditionalist, Catholic monarchy as against the Liberal Monarchy of the years 1875–1923. Their official name was Communión Tradicionalista.

Casa del Pueblo A workers' club, with free lending library and meeting rooms. Those of the Socialist Party were the most numerous and the most important as political-educational centers.

CTV Corpo Truppe Volontarie; the Italian troops serving in Spain from early 1937 to the end of the war.

Esquerra The Catalan Left, led by Luis Companys and corresponding in political complexion to the Azaña-Prieto forces in Madrid.

Euzkadi The medieval name of the Basque country, and widely used as a term for the Basque Nationalist movement.

FAI Federación Anarquista Ibérica; organization of theoreticians and pistoleros who controlled the CNT and rural anarchist masses.

Falange-Española A small, quasi-fascist political party founded and led by José Antonio Primo de Rivera from October 1933 to July 1936.

FALANGE ESPAÑOLA TRADICIONALISTA Y DE LAS JONS   The fusion of the Falange and the Carlists in April 1937 to form the sole authorized political party in Nationalist Spain; headed by General Franco.

GENERALITAT   The autonomous Catalan government under the statute of September 1932, named after the medieval parliament of Aragon-Catalonia.

IRC   International Red Cross, entirely Swiss in personnel.

IZQUIERDA REPUBLICANA   Republican Left; the fusion in early 1934 of the Azaña, Marcelino Domingo, and Casares Quiroga forces; led by Manuel Azaña.

JAP   Juventud de Acción Popular; the youth organization of the CEDA.

JONS   Juntas de Ofensiva Nacional-Sindicalista; small, militant fascist party centered in Valladolid, fused with the Falange in early 1934.

JSU   Juventud Socialista Unificada; the combined Socialist and Communist youth groups after their fusion in April 1936.

LLIGA CATALANA   Catalan conservative party led by Francisco Cambó.

NKVD   The initials of the Soviet secret police (also GPU).

PASEO   An unauthorized political assassination; the term is equivalent in flavor to the English "being taken for a ride."

PISTOLERO   A gunman hired for strikebreaking, or in inter-union struggles of the UGT, CNT, and Communists.

POUM   Partido Obrero de Unificación Marxista; a small anti-Stalinist communist party important in Lérida, led by Andrés Nin and Joaquín Maurín.

PSUC   Partido Socialista Unificado de Cataluña; the united Socialist and Communist parties of Catalonia, fused in the spring of 1936.

RENOVACIÓN ESPAÑOLA   The Alphonsine monarchist party led by Antonio Goicoechea and José Calvo Sotelo.

REQUETÉS   The Carlist militia units.

UGT   Unión General de Trabajadores; the trade-union federation of the Socialist Party.

UHP   Unión, Hermanos Proletarios (proletarian brothers); slogan of the Asturian miners in October 1934, and symbol of the hope for working-class unity.

UNIÓN REPUBLICANA   The party of Martínez Barrio after his split with Lerroux in the summer of 1934.

UME   Unión Militar Española; organization of officers opposed to the Azaña reforms and plotting during the spring of 1936.

UMRA   Unión Militar Republicana Antifascista; founded in early 1936 to combat the UME.

CONTENTS

CONTENTS

ILLUSTRATIONS

MAPS

CARTOONS

PHOTOGRAPHS
(following page 210)

Azaña Cabinet, June 1933
Conservative Republican Leaders
Insurgent Generals, Burgos, August 1936
Defense of Madrid, November 1936
Nationalist Cabinet, October 1938
President Azaña and Prime Minister Juan Negrín
Nationalist Army in Barcelona, January 1939
Refugees Crossing the French Border, February 1939

THE SPANISH REPUBLIC AND
THE CIVIL WAR
1931–1939

1

THE BACKGROUND OF THE
SPANISH REPUBLIC

THE Spanish Republic of 1931 was born of a unique set of circumstances: a long-term political crisis, the conjunction of domestic economic problems with the world depression, and an intellectual renaissance of great vigor and optimism. Another way of stating the situation is to say that Spain in 1930 was simultaneously a moribund monarchy, a country of very uneven economic development, and a battleground of ardent political and intellectual crosscurrents. Each of these elements must be understood, both separately and in relation to one another. In determining the republican form of the new government, however, the political crisis was the primary factor, and I shall therefore outline first the political background of the Republic.

From the days of Ferdinand and Isabella to the end of the Napoleonic era, the national consciousness and the national unity of the Spanish people were indissolubly bound up with the institution of the monarchy. This factor remained constant despite the weak character of many kings, and despite the dynastic struggle involved in the War of the Spanish Succession at the opening of the eighteenth century. But upon the death of Ferdinand VII, in 1833, a seven-year civil war began between the partisans of his infant daughter, the future Queen Isabella II, and the partisans of the late King's brother, Carlos de Borbón. Underlying the dynastic quarrel in this "Carlist" uprising was the deeper question of the role of the Spanish monarchy. Should it welcome the growth of capitalism, centralize and standardize its governing methods, permit a certain degree of liberty in the press and the universities, and avail itself of the accumulated wealth of the Church—all of which things had occurred in France? Or should the monarchy reaffirm the exclusively Catholic, predominantly agrarian and

3

decentralized character of traditional Spain? Successive Isabeline governments contained the Carlist forces, but the civil war sputtered on even after the establishment of general peace in 1840. The deeper issues were never resolved. The Queen as a grown woman turned out to be only a lascivious mediocrity, and the coincidence of her character with the always latent civil war produced three very serious results: the person of the monarch no longer commanded respect; the monarchy as an institution no longer was the symbol of national unity; and most important, the government was forced to depend entirely on the generals who had saved Isabella's throne from the Carlists. Between 1833, the opening of the Carlist War, and 1875, when the Constitutional Monarchy was established, the Spanish Army directed the political destinies of the country. The only method of changing governments was that of *pronunciamiento,* a brief, and by common consent relatively bloodless, uprising by a general around whom the opposition forces had gathered as their only hope of change.

In 1868 Isabella II was dethroned as the result of one such pronunciamiento. In the seven years that followed, the nation experimented with a Liberal Monarchy under a conscientious but not very strong Italian prince, Amadeo of Savoy; and with a short-lived First Republic in which four presidents served in a period of less than twelve months. Neither a new dynasty nor a republic was able to establish its authority, its "legitimacy," in the existing circumstances. At the same time, it was perfectly evident that no one would again accept the irresponsible absolutism, punctuated by pronunciamientos, which had been characteristic of the decades prior to 1868.

A practical solution to the immediate problem was worked out by the able conservative statesman Cánovas del Castillo. Cánovas believed that only the Bourbon dynasty could be considered the legitimate fountainhead of authority in Spain. But he was convinced also that civil peace would depend upon at least a measure of political liberty, and upon the removal of the army from the center of the political stage. He was a great admirer of the British monarchy, but at the same time, he believed that the period 1868–74 had amply

4

demonstrated that Spaniards were not ready for any such degree of self-government as existed in England. Possessing the full confidence of the royal family in exile, he also gained sufficient military backing so that a successful pronunciamiento at Sagunto, in December 1874, restored the Bourbon monarchy in the person of Alfonso XII.

The constitution of 1876 was the personal creation of Cánovas. Under this constitution Spain possessed an elective Cortes. Genuine freedom of speech existed in that Cortes, independent political parties could be formed, and for the most part, the press enjoyed complete liberty. However, the Cortes was in no sense a responsible governing body comparable to the British Parliament. The Prime Minister was freely named and removed by the King, and legislative initiative remained almost entirely the royal prerogative. Limitations of suffrage, and the process of counting the votes in advance, deprived elections of all real meaning until the early twentieth century. Governors and mayors were appointed rather than elected; rural politics was controlled by local bosses known as *caciques,* from the Indian word for the chieftains through whom the Spaniards had ruled their American empire. The term is indicative of the political psychology of the Spanish ruling class. Having lost their American empire early in the nineteenth century, they ruled rural Spain, especially in the south, as they had once ruled naïve and ignorant Indians.

Two fairly coherent parties developed under the Restoration: the Conservative Party, led by Cánovas; and the Liberal Party, which was distinguished principally by its more secular orientation, under Sagasta. An informal pact, jocularly known as the *turno político,* existed between Cánovas and Sagasta. On their initiative, with the consent of the King—and with the necessary cooperation of the Minister of the Interior, the caciques, and the Civil Guard—elections were arranged in such manner as to alternate the two parties in power. It was probably Cánovas' intent that gradually the system should evolve into a true constitutional monarchy, just as the rotten boroughs and arbitrary prerogatives of eighteenth-century England had evolved toward responsible parliamentary government. But a two-party system involving fixed elections

5

ultimately undermined rather than developed the sense of political responsibility in Spain. Each change of party involved a large turnover in government jobs. Besides interfering with the already mediocre performance of public services, this Spanish version of the "spoils system" created a whole new class of unemployed civil servants, the *cesantes*, living on pitiful commissions, and on influence peddling, while waiting for the next turn of the political wheel.

In 1897 Cánovas was assassinated by an anarchist, and in 1898 Spain lost the vestiges of her overseas empire in the brief war with the United States. From that time until 1917, the Conservative and Liberal parties steadily disintegrated. The Monarchy seemed incapable either of asserting its authority under the existing system or of evolving genuinely representative institutions. Once again the Army, but recently humiliated in Cuba and the Philippines, became a protagonist in Spanish politics. Its only remaining field of military action was Spanish Morocco. The young Alfonso XIII salved the wounded pride of his officers, made sure that the Parliament voted them large budgets, and followed with keen interest the never-ending "mopping up" operations in the Atlas mountains. Three times during his reign, King and Army found themselves under simultaneous attack. In 1909 anarchist agitation, and popular protests set off by exaggerated reports of casualties in Morocco, led to the famous "Tragic Week" in Barcelona. After anarchist terrorists and *agents provocateurs* had committed bombings and arson, the intellectual anarchist and educator Francisco Ferrer was executed for "moral responsibility." In 1917, following the overthrow of the Czarist autocracy in Russia, a series of revolutionary strikes, clearly directed against the Monarchy, broke out. The Army, as the apostle of order, broke the strikes and saved the throne. In 1921 a disastrous defeat in Morocco led to a parliamentary investigation which implicated the King personally in the military debacle. By late 1923 the frequently changing coalition cabinets were completely paralyzed, and the Monarchy seemed about to collapse. Once again a military coup, by General Miguel Primo de Rivera, gave the Monarchy its last reprieve.

Primo de Rivera was a man of considerable intelligence and generous instincts. He dealt successfully with the acute military problems in Morocco; he encouraged public works and industrial development; and in contrast with Mussolini, he cooperated with socialist labor unions. But with his rise to power, Spain lost the considerable intellectual and slight parliamentary liberty she had achieved since 1875. Corruption, inefficiency, and military influence in politics expanded steadily. Primo's highly personal regime lasted through the prosperous 1920's, but when the world depression struck Spain at the end of 1929, King Alfonso, always agile but never generous, dropped Primo de Rivera. For fifteen inglorious months the King experimented with another military dictator, General Berenguer, and finally with a "government of concentration." On April 12, 1931, municipal elections in the large cities—the only unfixed elections in Spain at the time—showed a strong antimonarchical trend. Discreet inquiries by the King indicated that the Army would not take up arms to save him as in 1917. In one of the more dignified episodes of his career, Alfonso XIII decided quietly and quickly to leave Spain. The Republic was proclaimed in the streets of Madrid during the very hours that he pondered his decision.

From even so brief an outline of the political history of the century preceding 1931, it will be clear that the Bourbon Monarchy had lost its authority, and a large share of its sentimental hold over the Spanish people. When we ask why the Constitutional Monarchy was unable to preserve its authority, why it feared truly to become a parliamentary monarchy, why, by 1917, there seemed to be no middle ground between a thoroughgoing social revolution and a military dictatorship, we approach the deeper problems of Spanish life in the late nineteenth and twentieth centuries.

The critical economic problems of Spain provided the second set of factors underlying the revolution of the 1930's. The vast majority of the people depended on the land for their living, but favorable geographic and social conditions for agriculture existed only on the northern and Mediterranean peripheries of the peninsula. In Galicia, in the narrow provinces north of the Cantabrican mountains, and in the

Basque country, rainfall is plentiful and the soil satisfactory, if not rich. The farmers either own their land, or work it on long-term leases at low rentals. Most of the terrain is too hilly for the use of machinery, but prosperous truck gardens, orchards, and dairy farms cover the countryside. Along the Mediterranean coast of Catalonia and the Levant provinces, truck farming, vineyards, rice, olives and citrus fruits all flourish. Rainfall is scanty. However, Catalonia is watered by the Ebro river and its many branches descending from the Pyrenees mountains. Further south, long-established water tribunals in the communes of the Levant regulate the intricate irrigation systems in the regions of Valencia and Alicante. Here, as along the northern coast, land is widely distributed. The sunny climate and the careful use of water resources make this Mediterranean coast the most prosperous agricultural area of Spain.

These favored regions constitute less than 10 per cent of the surface of the country. Central Spain is dominated by a great *meseta* covering León, Old and New Castile, and large parts of Aragon and Extremadura. A land of harsh wind and sun, of dramatic sierras, of thin soil and scattered rainfall. Wherever water flows there are well-kept farms and neat rows of poplar trees. But much of the countryside is bare and empty. The southern-most province, Andalusia, possesses all the natural prerequisites for agricultural prosperity, but in this area, history, race prejudice, absentee landlordism and economic errors of the nineteenth century have combined to produce a venomous social context. This was the portion of Spain longest ruled by the Arabs, and until the late Middle Ages it was the wealthiest part of Spain. When the Reconquest moved forward swiftly in the twelfth and thirteenth centuries, the kings of Castile distributed huge tracts of land—and the population working that land—to military Orders and to leading war captains. From that time on, these landed estates were entailed, and a master class of Castilian warriors and descendants of warriors lived on the labor of a despised mass of half-Berber, frequently Moslem, peasants.

This form of land ownership, the *latifundia* system, re-mained stable until the nineteenth century, at which time the beginnings of capitalism and the influence of Liberal economic doctrine altered the situation. The Liberals wished to reduce the institutional power of the Church and also believed that the latifundia were uneconomic units. In 1837 a Liberal ministry decreed the disentailment of the estates belonging to the Church Orders. They placed the land on public sale, hoping thereby to encourage the development of a class of small independent farmers such as constituted the leading element in French society. But the land was bought by the only people who had the money to pay for it—a relatively small group of businessmen and wealthy landlords. Thus, in the late nineteenth century, land ownership was perhaps even more concentrated than in previous centuries.

The steady population increase during the nineteenth and twentieth centuries had several important effects on Spanish agriculture. The growth of the industrial regions of Catalonia and Bilbao, and of the capital, Madrid, provided larger markets for the farmers of those regions. The rising European standard of living, and the availability of transport, led to greatly increased exports of wine and citrus fruits. The farmers of the already-prosperous northern and Mediterranean provinces, along with the new businessmen-farmers of Andalusia, were the principal beneficiaries of this development.

In Galicia, and generally along the Atlantic coast, where farms were already small, the population increase created the problem of *minimifundia*—farms so subdivided that they could not support the families living on them. To some extent the pressure was relieved by emigration to industrial cities and to America, but the availability of arable land became a most serious problem in the north.

Another response to the population growth was the increase in commercial wheat production on the central *meseta*. This meant that new lands were brought under cultivation in an area already suffering from water shortages. High costs of production brought a demand for heavy tariff protection, without which Argentine and American wheat would have been cheaper in Madrid than Castilian. Increasingly in the decades preceding 1931, the Spanish government chose to protect the wheat growers at the expense of the Spanish consumer. The high cost of bread represented a permanent obstacle to raising living standards, and the wheat tariff encouraged the uneconomical use of thousands of acres of tableland.

Much more important in Spanish consciousness, however, than either the problem of minimifundia or of uneconomic wheat production was the steadily growing number of landless peons in Andalusia. By 1900 the royal governments, Conservative and Liberal alike, recognized the gravity of the land question. Population and land statistics were compiled, presumably with a view toward initiating a gradual, compensated land reform. No actual change followed the taking of the land census. But the people of northern and central Spain became aware that in the south a growing landless proletariat eked out a miserable existence with about forty days' poorly paid work per year, that debilitating diseases undermined the health of the entire working population, that the caciques controlled all available employment, and that the Civil Guard kept order as in an occupied territory. In a country of idyllic climate, such a situation could not possibly be justified. In 1931 the question of land reform in Andalusia bulked larger than any other single issue in the political consciousness of the public.

Exclusive concentration on land questions, however, paints an unnecessarily dark picture of the Spanish economy. In the peripheral provinces of Catalonia and Viscaya, commercial capitalism and the industrial revolution made swift progress. Barcelona and its suburbs developed a large textile industry catering to Spanish and Latin American markets. Typically, the Catalan factories were small enterprises, family owned, and hence used mostly Spanish capital. In Vizcaya the steel industry, and such natural accompaniments as shipbuilding and locomotive manufacturing, developed rapidly in the late nineteenth century. Here the industries combined local management and capital with considerable foreign investment, principally British. But the necessary capital and skills were present in sufficient measure in Bilbao so that Basque industry never was subordinated in colonial fashion to the interests of foreign capital. Mining also developed steadily, and the twentieth century saw the growth of chemical and electrical industries, these latter being far more heavily dependent on foreign capital and technology than the earlier-developed industries.

Both agricultural and industrial production rose steadily from 1860 to 1914, with the exception of temporary slumps which coincided with world depressions and with the aftermath of the Spanish-American War. The export of rice, olives, and citrus fruits also increased steadily during this period. World War I created boom conditions for neutral Spain. But Spanish industry failed to use its wartime profits for modernization and replacement of machinery, and after 1918, Spain was unable to hold her wartime markets in the face of renewed competition from more advanced industrial powers. In the 1920's neither industrial nor agricultural production and export maintained their pre-1914 rate of growth. In addition, almost from the beginning, Spanish industries depended on the highest protectionist tariffs in Europe. Such tariffs, and world prosperity in the twenties, tended to obscure the inefficiency and high production costs of Spanish industry until the depression of 1929.

Nevertheless, despite its weaknesses, and its geographical concentration in two outlying provinces, Spanish industry was supplying employment opportunities, producing consumer goods, and slowly raising the urban standard of living in the seventy-odd years prior to 1931. In terms of economic development, the Republic came at a time when Spain had accumulated considerable industrial progress, but also at a time when the pace of progress had clearly been declining for a decade, even before the occurrence of the worst depression in modern times. It is worth repeating that Spanish public opinion was not nearly so conscious of industrial problems as it was of the land question.

The decades of economic and demographic growth also witnessed a tremendous cultural renaissance in Spain, a period of accomplishment in the arts and sciences comparable only to the *siglo de oro* in splendor. The novelists Galdós and Pio Baroja; the philosophers Unamuno and Ortega y Gasset; the poets Antonio Machado, Federico García Lorca, Vicente

Aleixandre, and Jorge Guillén; the composer Manuel de Falla; the painters Picasso, Miró, Dali; the philologists Menéndez Pidal and Américo Castro; the historians Menéndez y Pelayo and Claudio Sánchez Albornoz; the physicians Ramón y Cajal and Gregorio Marañon—all these men belonged in the very front rank of European civilization. And many critics would claim that no nation in the twentieth century could boast such a Pleiad of poets as Spain.

The reasons for such an upsurge of cultural vitality can never be precisely formulated, but even an approximation will serve to illuminate the background of the Spanish Revolution. In Restoration Spain two great intellectual currents confronted each other; Krausism, which was European, liberal, and secular in its general orientation; and a revived Catholicism, drawing its strength from the Spanish past and from a defensive reaction against the rapid secularization of European civilization in the nineteenth century. The ideas of the early nineteenth-century German philosopher Krause became influential in Spain through his disciple, Julián Sanz del Río, who during the 1850's expounded his own freely modified version of Krause's doctrines from his chair as professor of philosophy in Madrid. The strength of Krausism lay more in its general philosophical and religious outlook than in its technical coherence. Its major doctrine, "harmonious rationalism," combined the most optimistic elements of the eighteenth century Enlightenment and German Idealism. It embraced both Reason and Evolution. The Krausists praised the natural sciences as the key to understanding the intellectual harmony of the universe. They interested themselves even more in the new social sciences and in the history of law. If the universe was fundamentally harmonious, or at least evolving in that direction, then the solution to Carlist wars, and to revolutionary agitation by landless laborers, was to seek in the human past the natural forms of *convivencia* and to revise the political-legal system so as to conform to that convivencia. The Krausists were not theologians, but many were practicing Catholics, and none were atheists. For them, Man was the highest product thus far of the divine intelligence, and Man, like the rest of the universe, was constantly evolving toward the goal of harmonious rationalism. They considered education to be the most important field of human activity, and in 1876 Francisco Giner de los Ríos, professor of law and disciple of Sanz del Río, founded what was to be, until 1936, the most influential secondary school in Spain: the *Institución Libre de Enseñanza*. The ideal school should encourage intellectual curiosity through the informal contact of students with the most brilliant and creative minds. Giner, a man of great magnetism and organizational ability, obtained the enthusiastic services of leading university professors. Education should inculcate the love of beauty and of nature as manifestations of God; the Institución emphasized field trips and art history. Education should form the whole man, and so manual labor and artistic skills were given equal dignity with purely intellectual accomplishment. The Institución published a *Boletín* in which leading Spanish scientists and literary men discussed their work in progress, and to which world figures like Emile Durkheim, Bertrand Russell, and John Dewey sent contributions. Francisco Giner and his collaborators pressed the royal government to provide generous scholarships for graduate study in Europe and were thus largely responsible for the creation of the *Junta para Ampliación de Estudios*, founded in 1907 and increasingly active until the outbreak of the Civil War in 1936. The influence of the Institución was paramount for the creation in the present century of Spain's Pleiad of scientists, philologists, archaeologists, and historians.

The second great intellectual current in late nineteenth-century Spain was Catholicism. The Spanish Church drew on the strength of its universality, of its long line of poets and saints, of its magnificent ritual, and of its historic identification with the Reconquest and the unification of Spain. But the very power of its traditions inhibited its response to new ideas. The Krausists could glory in their eclecticism, identifying themselves with the best of European thought, whatever its source or its theological implications. The Catholics had to be sure that anything new was consistent with accepted canons. The preparation of histories and commentaries on a corpus of revered writings could not possibly have the audacity and savor of original thought. The Catholic historian Marcelino Menéndez y Pelayo was an intellectual giant, but the literary renaissance took place outside the Church.

The principal fields of the Catholic revival were social action and education. Until the time of Leo XIII, the Church had adopted a purely defensive position in regard to the new currents of the nineteenth century. Pius IX had condemned Liberalism, Materialism, and Socialism without formulating a positive response to the effects of the industrial revolution. It was all very well to warn the faithful against error, but how should the Church respond to the brutal exploitation of the early factory system and to the overcrowded, unhealthy conditions of life in the industrial areas? Leo XIII, in the 1890's, elaborated the ideal of Social Justice as the basis of Catholic political and social action in the industrial era. He favored the founding of Catholic trade-unions, of mutual insurance societies, and of rural credit cooperatives. The masses had the right to a more equitable distribution of wealth rather than to mere charity, and the socialists must not be permitted to monopolize this just demand. The Church should also extend its school and hospital systems, lest these areas of properly Catholic activity be taken over entirely by the secular state.

The program of Leo XIII achieved a strong response in northern Spain and Catalonia. The French and Italian anti-clerical laws of this era brought to Spain many new Orders and a consequent expansion, for that reason alone, of Church-sponsored hospitals and schools. Some of the teaching Orders, notably the Marianistas (of French origin) and the Salesianos (of Italian origin), introduced more modern teaching methods than those practiced by their Spanish brethren. Both the competition of the Krausist schools, and the increased rivalry among the Orders, tended to improve the quality of Catholic education.

The great limitation of the cultural efforts of the Krausists and the Catholics was that it touched only the middle classes. With very few exceptions, the graduates of the Institución Libre and of schools with a similar program, came from families already possessing considerable economic and cultural standing. Many Church schools granted scholarships, but the vast majority of their students came from the traditionally Catholic middle classes of northern Spain and Catalonia.

While Krausism and Catholicism were the major philosophical currents among the middle classes of Spain as a whole, there were also several regional movements of combined middle-class and peasant character: Catalan nationalism, Basque nationalism, and Carlism. The Catalan and Basque movements had much in common for both arose in areas which enjoyed a higher level of prosperity than was typical of the Peninsula. Both regions had close historical connections with France. They each possessed a linguistic tradition of their own, and they were the only areas in Spain to develop modern industry.

In the nineteenth century the Catalans, like many of the smaller nationalities of Europe, rediscovered their past. The Catalan language, which for centuries had enjoyed the status of a peasant dialect, became the vehicle of an impressive literature. With the revival of the language came a study of the medieval glory of the Catalan Mediterranean empire and an emphasis on its historic and cultural separateness from the rest of the Peninsula. Catalanism created a new link between the peasants, who had continued to speak Catalan during the long centuries since the days of an independent Catalonia, and the *bourgeoisie,* who created the philological, literary, and artistic revival. In political and economic matters, Catalanism was a predominantly conservative movement until 1917. During the presidency of Francisco Cambó, the *Lliga Catalana* was on the whole satisfied with the Restoration Monarchy. Its leadership of businessmen pressed Madrid for high tariffs in favor of Catalan industry, which tariffs were granted; they also agitated for a measure of local self-government, which was achieved in the *Mancomunidad* of 1914.

The Catalanism of these decades was predominantly Catholic. The Church contributed to the literary revival, and as in other European countries, willingly preached in the language of the local population. Choruses, folk-dance societies, and mutual insurance schemes all cemented the connections between Catalan nationalism, Catholicism, and the peasantry.

There was always an element of doubt, however, whether the ultimate goal of Catalanism was regional autonomy within the Spanish monarchy or complete separation from the Spanish state. In the struggles over tariffs and local government, the Catalan leaders did not hesitate to threaten Madrid with the specter of separatism. During and after World War I, their own control of Catalan politics was increasingly threatened by radical peasant groups and anarcho-syndicalist labor unions. The tone of political life became less Catholic and more class conscious. Then the pronunciamiento of Primo de Rivera in 1923 destroyed the Mancomunidad, and with it the leadership of the moderates. Catalan nationalism was forced underground, and in 1931 no one knew whether in conditions of unrestricted political liberty Catalans would lean toward moderate regionalism, separatism, or anarcho-syndicalism.

Basque nationalism, like Catalan nationalism, was based on the sense of a separate language and culture, and on an increasing consciousness of these elements under the impact of romanticism and industrialization. The Basques gloried in the remote mystery of their origins, for whereas Catalan was merely one more among many romance languages, Basque was utterly unrelated to any European language except Magyar and Finnish—with some philologists contesting even the latter relationship. The Basque movement was more political and religious than literary. Until 1837 the Basque provinces had been largely self-governing, under *fueros* dating back to the early Middle Ages. When the northern provinces rose against the Liberal government in the name of traditional Catholic monarchy, thereby initiating the first Carlist War, Madrid deprived the Basque provinces of their ancient fueros. The restoration of those fueros was a major political demand of the Basque Nationalist Party in the twentieth century. In 1912 a group of Basque priests founded *Jaungoika-Zale Bazkuna,* an organization devoted to Catholic instruction in the Basque language; and in Vizcaya generally there were an increasing number of mutual insurance societies and folkloric celebrations of strongly Catholic character during the last decades of the Monarchy.

The growth of Basque nationalism produced a strong

countercurrent in the renewed strength of Carlism. Historically speaking, Navarre and Vizcaya had enjoyed the same fueros, and in 1837 the entire region had supported the Carlists. But in the twentieth century, Basque nationalism developed in industrial Bilbao, and in the provinces of Guipúzcoa and Vizcaya, immediately contiguous to the industrial center; these were also the two provinces in which a substantial majority of the peasants spoke Basque. In Navarre, which remained agricultural, and where most of the peasants spoke Castilian, traditional Carlism reaffirmed itself against the bourgeois, urban leadership of the Basque Nationalists. After the fall of the Monarchy, the Basque Nationalists were preparing home-rule demands including separatism if necessary, while the Carlists were preparing the paramilitary units, known as *Requetés*, which rose against the Republic in 1936. Both groups were intensely Catholic.

Historians will long debate the extent to which Krausism and the regional movements undermined the Spanish Monarchy, but the greatest threat undoubtedly came from the two mass working-class movements: anarcho-syndicalism and socialism. It was a significant, though sometimes exaggerated, coincidence, that the Revolution of 1868 occurred precisely at the time of the great debate between Marx and Bakunin within the First International. Young, militant unions already existed in the Barcelona textile industry and in certain skilled trades in Madrid when the representatives of the competing tendencies arrived in Spain. But whereas in Europe generally the Marxist tendency was clearly the stronger by about 1900, in Spain the anarcho-syndicalists remained stronger than the Socialists right down to the time of the Second Republic in 1931.

Anarcho-syndicalism and socialism shared the same purpose: the creation of a world-collectivist commonwealth; and they shared a messianic faith in the industrial working class as the vehicle of the revolutionary transformation. Socialists believed in both careful, centrally directed trade-union organization, and in political action. Strikes were to be conducted to obtain specific economic advantages. Suffrage, and the parliamentary system, were important means toward the political revolution. Anarcho-syndicalists, however, considered parliamentary activity a waste of time, opposed centralized direction of the labor movement, and expected to accomplish the revolution largely by means of the general strike—a total, politically motivated stoppage of work which would demonstrate the power of the proletariat and paralyze the capitalist class and its government.

The naïvely millenary character of anarcho-syndicalism resulted not only from the doctrine of the general strike, but from the largely anarchist background of the majority of Catalan industrial workers. Indeed, to understand the Spanish working class, it is necessary first to understand the rural anarchism of Andalusia and the Levant.

Anarchism, by its very nature, was a less systematic doctrine than socialism; but fundamental to all anarchist thought was the destruction of the modern centralized state. The anarchists proposed the decentralization of government, insisting that the state be the servant of the commune rather than the master. The nation of the future would be composed of freely federated communes, and the world order would consist of freely federated nations. Authority must flow up from the local unit, not down from the center. Such an idea was appropriate to regions which resented the authority of the central government in Madrid, and it was appropriate to a country with strong communal traditions.

In nineteenth- and twentieth-century Spain there were still mountain villages governing themselves under ancient fueros, with customs including annual redistribution of arable land, and collective rights to firewood, and pasture land. Some of the more isolated villages coined their own money for local use. Many of the fishing villages of Catalonia and the Levant practiced collective ownership of boats and nets and collective sale of their catch. Levant farmers were accustomed to communal regulation of their water resources.

Rural anarchism made a quasi-religious, as well as a historically grounded appeal. In the late nineteenth century the communal cultivation of monastic lands was still a living memory in Andalusia. Many of the early anarchist leaders resembled in personality the mendicant friars of former centuries: abstemious wanderers, proud to possess few worldly goods, inured to physical hardship, motivated by an inner certainty which could manifest itself in legendary kindness as well as in utopian ideals. Psychologically, rural Spanish anarchism was closely akin to primitive Christianity, to the Gnostic and Montanist communities, and to seventeenth-century utopian sects such as the Levellers, Diggers, and Anabaptists.

It was largely people of this background who flowed into the Barcelona factories in the late nineteenth and twentieth centuries, and who formed the mass membership of the *Confederación Nacional de Trabajo* (CNT) founded in 1911. Once exposed to the doctrines of syndicalism, they conceived of the general strike as a kind of Judgment Day on which the wicked capitalists would be struck down and the world-collectivist commonwealth inaugurated. Simplicity of organization, and a spirit of sacrifice, characterized the anarcho-syndicalist unions. They grouped all the workers of a given industry in one union, regardless of skills; they asked relatively small dues, and remitted even these in the case of the poorer workers. They collected no strike funds, paid no salaries to their officers, and kept no written records. Their refusal of craft distinctions and their system of unpaid leadership testified to their belief in human equality and a classless society. But the loose organization and the lack of funds also lent itself to easy corruption. In addition, there was a wing of the anarchist movement which, as in Russia and Italy during the same decades, believed in the efficacy of individual terrorism. Three Spanish Prime Ministers were the victims of anarchist bombs: Cánovas in 1897, Canalejas in 1912, and Dato in 1921. While these assassinations were the work of a minority wing, the fact remains that the anarcho-syndicalist movement as a whole tolerated such actions as possible contributions to the revolution. Hence it was easy for police and employer organizations to infiltrate the CNT. No one knows how many anarchist bombings were actually the work of *agents provocateurs,* but no one doubts that they were responsible for a considerable number of the wartime outrages in Barcelona. It was some measure of the royal government's desperation after 1917 to suppose that it could maintain the respect of the Spanish people while dabbling in paid assassination.

The years 1919–23 witnessed a swift rise in the number of terrorist acts in Catalonia. Within the syndicates, a crucial struggle for leadership took place between the partisans of violence and the partisans of strict industrial unionism. The latter proposed an extension of peaceful, disciplined strikes for specific objectives such as better wage rates and the 8-hour day. Their concepts of organization and their objectives were much like those of the later CIO unions in the United States. But this group was defeated by the partisans of the revolutionary strike and terrorism. The victory of the extremists was sealed in 1923 by the action of the dictatorship in suppressing both the Mancomunidad and the Catalan labor unions. The CNT went underground, and as of 1927 was to be dominated by the newly founded secret society, the *Federación Anarchista Ibérica,* known by its initials as the FAI. One of the more tragic coincidences of the history of the Spanish Revolution is the domination of Catalan labor by its extremist wing during the 1930's.

Spanish socialism developed somewhat more slowly than did anarchosyndicalism. Its areas of great strength were Madrid, the Basque industrial cities, and the mining areas of Asturias and Huelva. Founded in 1879 and long led by the Madrid typographer Pablo Iglesias, the Socialist Party in its early days concentrated on organization of its labor federation, the *Unión General de Trabajadores* (UGT) and on worker education. Characteristic of socialist organization were the *Casas del Pueblo,* with their libraries of popularly written works on science, mechanics and health and their reprints of great novelists such as Tolstoy and Dickens. The class-conscious socialist worker could also follow, through the Casa library, the great debate within the French party, between Jules Guesde and Jean Jaurès, the one an advocate of revolutionary combativeness, the other of gradualism.

Spanish socialism believed in political action, and in the use of parliamentary methods. But it had also to achieve immediate benefits for the workers—especially since it found itself in competition with the larger, and more revolutionary, anarcho-syndicalist unions. It was a red-letter day for the Party when in 1902 Pablo Iglesias took his seat as the first Socialist deputy to be elected to the Cortes; and Spanish

Socialists were proud of the increasing number of university intellectuals who joined the Party in the twentieth century. But the UGT had to demonstrate its combativeness and effectiveness in the day-to-day struggle. The militants in Bilbao, in the Asturian mines and in the railroad unions proved in numerous strikes that they were as tough, as class

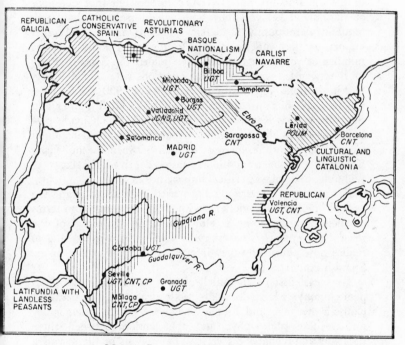

MAP 1. Regional Political geography

conscious, and as combative as the anarcho-syndicalists of Barcelona.

The breaking of the revolutionary strikes by the Army in 1917, followed by the Bolshevik revolution in Russia, led to renewed debate within the party and the UGT over methods. In 1921 the party voted by a small majority not to join the Third International, and the consequent foundation of the

Communist Party by the defeated minority, left the Socialist Party more reformist in orientation. When Primo de Rivera, early in his dictatorship, sought the cooperation of Francisco Largo Caballero, head of the UGT, his offer was accepted. When in 1926 a number of republican intellectuals joined in the so-called Night of St. John conspiracy against the dictatorship, the Socialists stood aside. Not that they were supporters of the dictatorship, but the UGT leaders felt that questions of parliamentary monarchy, mild dictatorship, or bourgeois republic were purely academic questions and not of great import to the working class. On the other hand, a large number of young professional men joined the Socialist Party in the twenties, and for them, questions of political liberty and institutions were very important. As of 1930, the Socialist intellectuals constituted a link between the UGT masses and the middle-class Republican parties, a link which made possible the Republican-Socialist coalition in the Constituent Cortes. But the differences of outlook between the university Socialists and the trade-union masses deprived the Party of real unity and were of critical importance in 1936.

For purposes of clarity, I have tried thus far to define the several intellectual, regional, and political movements in terms of their separate content. However, while definition of the several movements is necessary to start with, it is essential to realize how powerfully they interacted with each other in the Spanish context.

To speak first of the intellectual crosscurrents: the great poet Antonio Machado was equally drawn to the Castilian Catholic heritage and to the Europe of political democracy and secular philosophy; and the tension between these polarities impregnates his verse. The essayists of the so-called Generation of 1898 oscillate between proud nostalgia for a stoic, militant, Castilian past and an inferiority complex with regard to European industry, education, and standards of living. The philosophers Unamuno and Ortega, while glorying in the regional variety of Spanish culture, conclude by insisting proudly on the primacy of Castile. The Catholic historian Menéndez y Pelayo reaffirms his orthodoxy while writing, often with marked sympathy and admiration, the history of heterodox religious trends. The young communist poet Miguel Hernández acquires much of his vocabulary and his deep spiritual tone from his Catholic background. Underlying the most fruitful research into the Spanish past is a polemic over the meaning of Spanish history: those of conservative political outlook emphasize the importance of the Church, of the Castilian monarchy, of *hidalgismo,* of the Catholic Kings and of the Counter-Reformation, in the formation of Spanish civilization; those of liberal political outlook emphasize the variety of communal traditions, the contributions of the Arabs and the Jews, the more humane Catholicism of the Erasmists as against that of Isabella or Cardinal Cisneros, and the enlightened despotism of Charles III in the eighteenth century.

Moving from intellectual currents to mass movements: Catalan nationalism and anarcho-syndicalism mutually influenced one another—the former moving markedly to the left after 1917, the latter thinking of itself frequently as a specifically Catalan rather than Spanish phenomenon. The Socialist Party, always weak in Catalonia, could cooperate with Primo de Rivera without being too disturbed by his suppression of both labor unions and civil liberty in Catalonia. The UGT, though predominantly reformist, could adopt at times the tactic of the general strike and the militant street demonstration. And the Socialist intellectuals, while Marxist in their theoretical analysis, were deeply influenced by the Krausists. The anarchists and anarcho-syndicalists, though apolitical in principle, decided to vote in certain elections so as not to allow only the Socialists and Communists to speak for labor. In 1917, and again from 1930 on, the UGT and the CNT competed bitterly in the organization of the landless proletariat of Andalusia.

The intellectual and political ferment, taken together with the institutional decomposition of the Monarchy after the death of Cánovas in 1897, led to the formation of many small parties, held together more often by a particular leader than by a clear program or strong organization. At no time before 1917 were there more than a handful of convinced republicans. But the revolutionary events of that year suddenly revealed that only the Army could save the Monarchy. Then when the King interfered, with dire results, in the conduct of the Moroccan War, and when in 1923 he himself destroyed what was left of the constitution by welcoming the pronunciamiento of Primo de Rivera, his personal credit, if not that of his dynasty, was exhausted. The Second Republic became inevitable through the bankruptcy of the Monarchy rather than through the strength of a republican movement. Between roughly 1927 and 1931, a large number of liberals who would formerly have settled for a restoration of the Constitutional Monarchy, became Republicans. When the depression struck Spain at the end of 1929, the King dismissed Primo and attempted without success to find a substitute dictator. On August 17, 1930, a number of political personalities signed at San Sebastián (where many of them were spending the summer holidays) the political pact which was to usher in the Second Republic. They agreed to establish a republic, by force if necessary; to guarantee religious and political liberty; to proceed to the election of a Constituent Cortes; and to permit the regions so desiring to frame autonomy statutes and submit them to the Cortes. Among the signers were the half-dozen principal Republican leaders, three Catalan Republicans, and the moderate Socialist, Indalecio Prieto.

In December, a brief military rising failed to overthrow the Monarchy, but the cause of the republic received two martyrs in the persons of Captains Galán and García Hernández, executed for military rebellion. On April 12, 1931, municipal elections went overwhelmingly against the Monarchy in the major cities and the King decided to leave Spain rather than risk a civil war. Though he did not formally abdicate, the day of the Republican liberals had clearly arrived.

THE FIRST DAYS OF THE
SPANISH REPUBLIC

APRIL 14 was a day of joyous celebration and anticipation in the major cities of Spain. Immediately after the municipal elections of the 12th, the Count of Romanones, faithful friend and counsellor of the King, and Dr. Gregorio Marañon, his personal physician, a liberal and a man of wide general culture, had advised the King to recognize the strongly republican trend of the voting.[1] Alfonso XIII, loath to quit his throne, asked the opinion also of the military, who made it clear to him that he could maintain his position only at the cost of a civil war.[2] Meanwhile, Romanones and Marañon negotiated the transfer of power with the Prime Minister of the provisional government, Niceto Alcalá-Zamora. In the months since the Pact of San Sebastián, the Republicans had formed their entire shadow cabinet. On April 14 these gentlemen emerged from the Model Prison in Madrid, or returned from exile in France, while the King packed his bags and the people shouted "vivas" for the Republic, and for the new ministers as their names were read off in the Puerta del Sol. In city squares and on military parade grounds the strains of the Marseillaise mingled with those of the traditional republican anthem, the "Himno de Riego." The example of the French Revolution dominated all minds, and by contrast, the Spanish Republicans pointed proudly to the fact that the King had left in peace and that the revolutionaries had agreed beforehand on the distribution of power and the naming of ministers.

Actually, many a dangerous situation arose, and a number

[1] Conde de Romanones, *Las últimas horas de una monarquía* (Madrid, 1931), p. 81 and *passim*.

[2] Emilio Mola Vidal, "Lo que yo supe," in *Obras completas* (Valladolid, 1940). General Mola was the last Director General of Security under the Monarchy.

of lucky coincidences were responsible for the peaceful transition. The attitude of the masses ranged from goodhumored iconoclasm to revolutionary bloodlust. In Madrid a boisterous crowd toppled the statue of Isabella II from its pedestal

EL PRIMER GOBIERNO DE LA REPUBLICA, por Bagaría

THE FIRST REPUBLICAN GOVERNMENT
Como Puede Comprobarse, de Aqui Salieron "Estrellas" y Estrellados

Lerroux		Domingo		Azaña		Maura		De los Ríos
	D'Olwer			Alcalá-Zamora				Largo
Casares	Quiroga		Albornoz			Martínez Barrio		Prieto

El Sol, 14 April 1936

and carted it off to the Convento de las Arrepentidas (Convent of the Penitents). During the same afternoon, April 14, a less friendly crowd gathered in front of the Palacio de Oriente, where the Queen and her children were to pass an anxious night. Alcalá-Zamora had specified that the King should leave the city "before sundown" precisely because he feared violence if he did not leave quickly. At the palace itself, dozens of young men with red armlets, most of them Socialist workers from the Madrid Casa del Pueblo, linked arms to prevent the crowd from approaching closer, and stayed on guard throughout the night.[3]

In many villages the Civil Guard broke up republican demonstrations in the hours before the change of regime was officially known. In the port city of Huelva the Socialist leader Ramón González Peña was in jail awaiting trial for his part in the abortive Jaca rising. A crowd of stevedores came to release him during the afternoon, and he found himself amid a revolutionary mass demanding the head of the civil governor because a worker had been killed in a clash between police and demonstrators. González Peña took it upon himself to persuade the crowd not to engage in a lynching which would immediately discredit the new Republic.[4] In Barcelona the provisional government faced the challenge of Catalan nationalism. Colonel Macià, fresh from his surprise victory in the Barcelona election, proclaimed in a radio broadcast—in the Catalan language—a Catalan state and Catalan republic, after which he cordially invited the other Iberian peoples to associate themselves with Catalonia in the formation of an Iberian Federation. Three members of the provisional cabinet—Marcelino Domingo, a long-time Catalan Republican, Nicolau D'Olwer, a Catalan Republican and Minister of Economy, and Fernando de los Ríos, the Socialist Minister of Justice—rushed to Barcelona to remind the exalted old gentleman that the new constitution had not yet been written. Pleading for patience and for the necessary recognition of central authority, they won his agreement to a formula whereby the Catalans would submit a projected statute of autonomy to the Cortes. In turn, they promised that the Cortes would act with the minimum possible delay. In

[3] Luis de Zulueta, *El Sol,* April 14, 1935; article commemorating the founding of the Republic.

[4] *ABC,* April 16, 1931; *El Sol,* Feb. 16, 1935. The latter reference gives the statement of González Peña on this incident at his military trial following the Asturian revolution.

working out the temporary agreement, the Madrid ministers depended largely on the good offices of Luis Companys, second only to Colonel Macià himself in the victorious Esquerra. Companys, a labor lawyer, and an old associate of Marcelino Domingo, was an autonomist rather than a separatist. Quickly appointed civil governor of Barcelona, he co-operated loyally with the Madrid authorities during the first touchy weeks of the new regime.[5]

Generally speaking, while April 14 was indeed a day of celebration, it is equally true that Spaniards of all political shadings heaved a sigh of relief when the day had in fact passed without widespread violence. The atmosphere of the following weeks was a mixture of euphoria, incredulity, and anxiety. From abroad, the King counseled his followers to accept the new Republic, which he recognized as having come by the choice of the people. The Church counseled respect for constituted authority. The anarchists stated that a bourgeois republic was no affair of theirs, but they did not attack it.

The Pact of San Sebastián had dealt exclusively with political organization, and with the need to call a Constituent Cortes. But many Republicans, and all the Socialists, knew that the Republic must take quick action on behalf of the rural masses if the new regime were to take root outside the urban middle classes and the aristocracy of organized labor. Francisco Largo Caballero, head of the UGT, had joined the revolutionary committee in late 1930, despite the opposition of other high officials, notably Julián Besteiro and Andrés Saborit. In Barcelona Colonel Macià had stayed up all night on April 14 in an unsuccessful effort to get Angel Pestaña, the most moderate of the CNT leaders, to accept a post in the Catalan cabinet.[6] It was evident that the CNT as a whole, and a large proportion of the UGT, did not con-

[5] Miguel Maura, who was Minister of the Interior in the Provisional Government, and with whom I had a detailed conversation in April, 1961 concerning the first months of the regime, highly praised the conduct of Companys with regard to Madrid.

[6] Francisco Madrid, *Ocho meses y un día en el gobierno civil de Barcelona* (Barcelona, 1932), p. 133.

sider it opportune for labor to participate in the new Republican government. Caballero, pressed by the revolutionary committee on grounds that the Republic could not succeed without the active cooperation of the Socialist labor federation, had agreed to serve as Minister of Labor. He moved quickly in the area of rural relief. On April 29 a cabinet decree protected small farmers against mortgage foreclosures, and on May 8 municipal authorities were authorized to oblige landowners to cultivate their unused lands. On April 28 Caballero announced a decree intended to combat rural unemployment: no workers were to be hired outside a given municipality until all the local farm laborers had been employed. On June 12 the government extended to agricultural workers the benefits of the existing industrial accident legislation.

These laws challenged an established rural order which had not been directly affected by the mere change of regime. In the rural areas the election had been dominated, as always, by the caciques; outside the large cities, Spain had voted royalist. Some 22,000 royalist municipal councillors were elected as against 5,800 republicans. On April 14 everyone from the King down recognized that only the large city vote was free enough to reflect public opinion; but the new government in Madrid had, nevertheless, to deal with royalist municipal governments in practically all of rural Spain. In order to carry his revolutionary decrees into effect, Largo Caballero depended upon the officials of the Federation of Land Workers. He had already served as a labor councillor during the dictatorship of Primo de Rivera. In 1926 the dictator had established *comités paritarios,* mixed commissions representing equally the landlords and the workers in agricultural Spain, and the UGT had used the commissions to begin the organization of the rural proletariat. In April 1931, there were perhaps 100,000 members in the Federation of Land Workers. Its principal organizer, Lucio Martínez Gil, was a follower of Besteiro. No one knew better than he the primitive psychology of the largely illiterate land workers. He and Besteiro had opposed Socialist participation in the revolutionary committee precisely because they feared a premature republic in which they would have to share the governing responsibility before labor had grown to sufficient maturity. The rural labor decrees of Largo Caballero now brought the rival social forces of Spain face to face in the villages. On the one side was the royalist municipality, representing the landlords, and counting on the support of the Civil Guard, the majority of lawyers, bailiffs, pharmacists, and priests. On the other was the Casa del Pueblo, headquarters of the local trade-unionists and the minority of professional men and priests who sympathized with the Left. In the villages the first weeks of the Republic inevitably brought with them a sense of class warfare. The liberal middle class which had voted for the Republic in the cities was almost entirely absent. The forces of the *ancien régime* faced the inexperienced, but newly militant, workers.

The proclamation of the Republic also produced an immediate test of wills between the new government and the Roman Catholic Church. The Republicans announced their determination to build a laic school system, introduce divorce, secularize cemeteries and hospitals, and greatly reduce, if not eliminate, the number of religious Orders housed in Spain. For its part, the Vatican did not follow the great majority of world governments in quickly recognizing the Republic. The bishops counseled obedience to established authority, but they also justified nonrecognition, on the grounds that the government called itself "provisional," and that the King had only absented himself from Spain, and had not abdicated.[7] During the first week in May, the Madrid Catholic press carried on a bitter debate between those who wished to accept the Republic and those who insisted on identifying Catholicism with the Monarchy. *El Debate* expounded the view that the fundamental Catholic principles of family, property, and social order could be guaranteed by different forms of government. The Church was eternal; political forms were "accidental." (*El Debate* was the organ of *Acción Católica,* and after recovering from the first surprise of the revolution, its leadership sought consistently to defend the Church's material and spiritual interests within the new

[7] The *New York Times,* May 26, 1931; Rhea Marsh Smith, *The Day of the Liberals in Spain* (Philadelphia, 1938), p. 90.

framework.) The Monarchist journal *ABC,* on the other hand, accused *Debate* of cowardice and hair-splitting. It stated unambiguously that in Spain, at least, only the Monarchy could guarantee a Catholic social order.

Meanwhile, the government published plans for the construction of thousands of new primary schools. The Minister of Education, Marcelino Domingo, was the leader of a small Radical Socialist Party whose program was frankly inspired by the example of the Jules Ferry and the Clemenceau Radicals in the French Third Republic. The Director of Primary Education was Rodolfo Llopis, a Socialist and a professor in one of the normal schools of the state. Under existing rules of April 1931, religious instruction was obligatory in the public schools. On May 6 the government decreed that such instruction would no longer be obligatory but would be offered to those children whose parents requested it. Finally, during the same week in which this decree appeared and in which *ABC* and *El Debate* were conducting their polemic, *ABC* was carrying daily announcements of the opening of a *Círculo Monárquico* (Monarchist Club), registration for which would take place on Sunday morning, May 10.

On the seventh of May the newspapers published a pastoral letter of Pedro Cardinal Segura, Archbishop of Toledo, and hence, head of the Church hierarchy in Spain. This was the Cardinal's first public pronouncement since the proclamation of the Republic. In it he referred repeatedly to the grave commotions and the threats of anarchy to which Spain was exposed. Although the Church was not concerned with forms of governments, he wished to express the Church's gratitude to His Majesty for having dedicated Spain to the Sacred Heart and for having preserved the traditions and piety of his ancestors. He called upon the women of Spain to organize a crusade of prayers and sacrifices to defend the Church against the many attacks on her rights. He recalled the example of Bavaria in 1919, where the Catholic population had rescued the country from a brief Bolshevik occupation, thereby suggesting, through this analogy, that the provisional government of the Second Republic fell in the same category as the Communist government during

31

Bavaria's brief revolution. By attacks on the Church's rights, the Cardinal meant the well-known determination of the new regime to separate Church and state, build a laic school system, secularize marriage, and introduce divorce. The publication of his letter coincided with floods of street-corner oratory calling for the expulsion of the Orders, as well as with the publicity over the newly organized Círculo Monárquico.

On the morning of May 10 a brief scuffle took place in front of the Círculo headquarters, and the rumor ran through the city that a taxi driver had been killed by a monarchist señorito. An orator in the Puerta del Sol demanded, among other things, the expulsion of the Orders, the dissolution of the Civil Guard, and the removal of the Minister of the Interior, D. Miguel Maura. Maura had anticipated trouble with the opening of the Círculo Monárquico and had also received reports threatening a general strike for Monday May 11. At an afternoon cabinet meeting which lasted long into the night, Maura demanded permission of his colleagues to call out the Civil Guard. The cabinet refused, but decided to meet early Monday morning so as to follow events from minute to minute. Before noon came the news of a Jesuit building being burned in the Calle de la Flor. Maura threatened to resign if not granted permission to use the Guard immediately. The cabinet refused to call out the Guard or to accept Maura's resignation.[8]

Meanwhile, in Madrid, 6 of the city's 170 convents were set on fire by small bands composed mostly of teen-agers. The police, the firemen, and the crowds watched passively, the only organized activity being to assist the evacuation of the frightened nuns from the buildings. In the southern cities of Málaga, Seville, Cádiz, and Alicante some 15 convents were attacked in the same manner. There, as in Madrid,

[8] Joaquín Arrarás, *Historia de la segunda república española* (Madrid, 1956), I, 77, 96–7. This work covers the first two years of the Republic only. It is especially useful for detailed accounts of social conflicts and of the Sanjurjo revolt. Its selection of data and emphasis reflect strongly the Rightist preoccupation with public order and the reputation of the military.

taxis were organized to evacuate the nuns, some of whom, in leaving the convent grounds, were riding in automobiles for the first time in their lives. In Barcelona Colonel Macià slept in the Generalitat so as to be on hand if any attempt were made on church buildings in that city. In Saragossa and Valencia, republican organizations posted guards at church doors when the news of the Madrid burnings arrived. Since very few persons attacked the churches, very few could also defend them, as in these latter cities.[9]

In Madrid the cabinet reversed its position on the 12th. Not only did Maura receive permission to use the Civil Guard; Alcalá-Zamora proclaimed an *estado de guerra* (martial law) throughout Spain and gave Maura permission to use the Army in restoring order. Spain was quiet within 48 hours. Roughly two dozen churches in all had been attacked. No priests or nuns had been killed, but the laboratories of the Jesuit industrial and technical school in Madrid, and many art works of variable value, had been destroyed.

The shock effect of these events on the Spanish middle class was tremendous. Less than a month after the founding

[9] Regarding the number of church burnings, I have accepted the figures offered by *El Sol* and by The *New York Times* in their reports during the week following May 10. Antonio Montero Moreno, *Historia de la persecución religiosa en España* (Madrid, 1961), p. 25, lists some 119 attacks. In the presence of such discrepancies the historian can only admit that numerical accuracy is impossible. At the same time, simply to choose a figure halfway between the reports of the time and the research of Catholic authors would be an easy compromise, but not an answer. Having talked with many priests and Catholic laymen in Spain in 1960, I am convinced that they suffer from the most exaggerated persecution complex, and that—in all sincerity—priests studying the May events in recent years have listed churches as having been "sacked" if a witness to the events of 30 years ago says that he heard that such and such a building was to be attacked. It is quite possible that the journalists of the time may have missed a few incidents, but such sensational news was not likely to be minimized either by *El Sol* or by the *NYT,* both of which were jealous of their reputations for accuracy and fair play. I have therefore based my account on their reports.

of the Republic, the country was forcibly reminded of all the complex issues of public order and religious attitudes running throughout her modern history. Mobs had burned churches in Madrid in 1835 and in Barcelona in 1909. Had nothing changed in Spain? Who were the incendiaries? Maura and the government press, in 1931, like their forbears in the earlier instances, insisted that reactionary *provocateurs* had stirred elemental hatreds and paid the actual perpetrators.[10] The evidence was always circumstantial, never conclusive. For several days after May 12, the Madrid and Barcelona police received anonymous telephone calls warning them of further incidents to come, calls which in virtually every case turned out to be false alarms.[11] Provocation by monarchists, by anarchists, or by the nonpolitical lunatic fringe? An accurate answer is impossible. More important was the question why the Catholic population of Spain allowed such incidents to occur. Cardinal Segura had referred to Spain as a country in which virtually the entire population professed the Catholic religion. Everyone knew, of course, that church attendance figures were very low, especially in the large cities. But most Spaniards did baptize their children, did marry and die within the Church. How many of those large crowds standing around watching the fires, how many of the firemen and policemen watching with them, were professing Catholics? If handfuls of republicans, knowing how easily the Republic could be discredited, dissuaded or shamed would-be arsonists, where were the millions of Catholics who could have prevented all but the first surprise attacks? Clearly, in the Spanish urban public there was a large measure of tolerance, more, of secret pleasure, in seeing the Church attacked.

How could one explain the passivity of the government for almost 48 hours? The Minister of Justice had qualified the Cardinal's letter by the phrase "veiled bellicosity." The government knew very well that the opening of the Círculo Monárquico could occasion riots. And the government knew that the First Republic of 1873, as well as the Liberal govern-

[10] *El Sol*, May 14, 1931; also its report on June 16 of a speech of Miguel Maura in Zamora.

[11] F. Madrid, *Ocho meses*, pp. 146–48.

ments of 1812 and 1820, had been discredited by their failure to maintain public order. Spanish fathers, even republican fathers, when they found their children quarreling noisily or beating each other up, were in the habit of saying: "This is a republic." Why then did they refuse Maura's request to call out the Civil Guard, especially when the problem turned out to be not one of simple public order, but of attacks on the Church?

The most important single factor was undoubtedly the determination of the majority of ministers that the new government should not begin its career by shooting Spaniards. Better that a few lunatics burn a few churches than that the Republic order the Civil Guard into action. The Socialists in particular identified the Guard as the enemy of the working class, a worse enemy, as a matter of fact, than the Monarchy itself. The liberals felt that the Spanish people, even in their most deplorable actions, had been far more sinned against than sinning. The Republic must lead the people by persuasion only. Against the idea that earlier liberal governments had been discredited by their failure to maintain public order, they placed the certainty that the masses would hate a government which called out the Civil Guard at the first sign of riot. Thus for two days they hoped in vain that no repressive measures would be necessary. When this hope was exhausted they gave Maura the full powers he had demanded.

Many Spaniards have exaggerated the importance of the May 11 church burnings, seeing in these events nothing less than the origin of the Civil War. In sober fact, the Socialist Party, the UGT, and the middle-class Republican parties, no matter how anticlerical, joined in the most unequivocal condemnation of the church burnings. The passivity of the population, Catholic and non-Catholic, cannot be attributed to any one government or ideology, and if the main economic and social problems of Spain had been more successfully dealt with in the following years, the May 11 burnings would have left but a slight memory in history.

At the time of their occurrence, the incidents hardened both the Church and the anticlericals in the positions already adopted. The government blamed Cardinal Segura for provoking anticlerical violence and declared him *persona non grata*. The Cardinal himself left Spain for Rome on May 13, stating that the government was unwilling to guarantee his personal safety. On May 22, the government proclaimed complete religious liberty. It also forbade the exhibition in schoolrooms of images of the saints, on the grounds that the practice of kissing these images was unsanitary. And on the same day, it issued a decree authorizing the Minister of Education to remove art objects from religious buildings if he judged that there was risk of their deterioration. On May 30 the Vatican refused its placet to the newly appointed Republican ambassador, Luis Zulueta. The next day, in Madrid, the government temporarily suspended *El Debate* and *ABC* for their violent diatribes against the government's recent measures.

On June 3 the Spanish bishops sent a collective letter of protest to the Prime Minister. Among other things, they protested the plans to secularize cemeteries and to separate Church and state. They asserted that the "liberty of cults" which had been decreed was a violation of the existing Concordat and of the fundamental laws of Spain. They protested the suppression of obligatory religious instruction and the decrees prohibiting high civil and military officials from participating as officials in public religious ceremonies. A week later Cardinal Segura reentered Spain incognito. His car was stopped by the police in Guadalajara and he was escorted to the border. On June 14, in the bull ring of Pamplona, Catholics gathered from all over northern Spain to protest the ouster of the Cardinal.[12] During the month of June, there were scattered incidents in which republican town councils threatened to confiscate Catholic schools. Before the meeting of the Constituent Cortes, the religious question was the most bitterly contested issue in Spanish politics.

The provisional government also initiated military reforms before the meeting of the Cortes. The Minister of War,

[12] J. Arrarás, *Historia*, i, 102–105; *The Times*, London, June 16, 1931.

Manuel Azaña, was known primarily as a literary man. In 1930 he had been elected President of the Ateneo, the Madrid literary club. But Azaña had also, as a journalist, observed the French Army during the First World War. He had become interested in military history at that time. He had also come to believe, by observing the Spanish Monarchy and the dictatorship, that Spain needed, above all, government by experts—men of integrity who had been carefully trained. In 1931 the Spanish Army consisted of 16 skeleton divisions which normally would have been served by 80 general officers. In fact, there were almost 800 general officers, and there were more majors and captains than there were sergeants. The first problem was to reduce the Army to a sensible size without offending a caste-conscious officer corps which had suffered repeated humiliations and which had a long tradition of conspiratorial politics and of pronunciamientos.

On May 26 Azaña announced the first of his reforms. He cut the number of divisions from 16 to 8, reduced to one year the term of compulsory military service, and eliminated the rank of Captain General. The last item was a political as well as military reform since the Captain Generalcy was a jurisdiction dating from colonial times which permitted the subordination of the civil government in moments of tension or disorder. The highest rank in the peacetime forces would now be General of Division, one for each of the 8 military districts into which the country was divided, and his functions would be strictly military. There were some 26,000 officers in the *escalafón* in 1930. The new Army was to consist of 7,600 officers with 105,000 troops in the Peninsula; and an African contingent of 1,700 officers with 42,000 troops.[13] To the surplus officers, Azaña offered retirement at full pay. Indeed not only did he offer full pay—the decree stated that those accepting retirement would also be promoted to the salaries they would have received in the course of a normal promotion within ranks. In short, the professional officer could retire without the slightest financial sacrifice, present or future.

[13] Luis Jiménez de Asúa, *La constitución de la democracia española y el problema regional* (Buenos Aires, 1946), 57–8.

Military circles reacted to the Azaña decree with mixed emotions. Almost everyone acknowledged that the Army was top heavy with brass, but many a proud career officer felt that Azaña simply wished to destroy the officer corps by buying it off. On the other hand, thousands of professionals immediately pulled every string available to be certain that their names were accepted for retirement. On June 3 the Minister announced that all promotions for merit made during the dictatorship would be reviewed, and on July 14, the very day the new Cortes was to meet, the government closed the Academía General in Saragossa. These two moves distinctly roused the suspicions of the conservative, and largely anti-republican, officers. The first decree implied that promotions during the last years of the Moroccan War had been based on political rather than professional criteria. They interpreted the closing of the Academía General as a blow at the *esprit de corps* of the Army, since this was the only institution in which officers of different branches of service trained together.

The change of regime was also accompanied by a species of financial panic. The peseta had never been a strong currency, and it had depreciated slowly throughout the rule of Primo de Rivera. The last government of the Monarchy, however, had succeeded in obtaining a $60 million loan from a combination of Morgan and Dutch banking interests. The Aznar government had pledged the restoration of the Constitutional Monarchy, and the conservative Catalan banker Juan Ventosa had inspired confidence as Minister of Finance. Between February and April, 1931, the peseta had begun to recover.

The provisional government contained no financial expert, and Indalecio Prieto accepted appointment as Minister of Finance more in a spirit of solidarity than out of enthusiasm for the job. Prieto was a self-made businessman, the proprietor of the influential newspaper, *El Liberal,* of Bilbao. He was highly intelligent and pragmatic, and he counted many friends among Basque and Catalan business leaders. But Prieto was also a Socialist, pledged, as were all the Socialists, to reforms which would unquestionably be expensive. In any event, the combination of a sudden change of regime with the appointment of a Socialist to the Ministry of Finance, led to the immediate cancellation of the Morgan loan, to the export of private wealth, and to a 20 per cent drop, within the first month, in the international quotation of the peseta.[14]

Prieto was not the man to appease either the Spanish reactionaries or the international financial world. He required government licenses for the purchase of foreign equipment and for the possession of bank accounts in foreign currencies. He threatened fines and confiscation for those engaged in the massive export of capital. He negotiated with the Soviet Union to buy gasoline at prices 18 per cent lower than those offered at the same period by British and American oil companies. He insisted on the right to trade freely with all countries, and in early May he reopened negotiations with the same bankers who had arranged the canceled loan to the Aznar government.[15] But the church burning on May 11 led the banks to break off negotiations; he then turned to the Bank of France, in which he deposited 257,000,000 pesetas in gold (about $20,000,000) in order to guarantee a loan intended to protect the peseta against further depreciation. Generally speaking, in these first weeks, the international financial community indicated its lack of confidence, and a large proportion of Spain's wealthy declared war on the Republic; the new regime returned the challenge in kind.

In accordance with the Pact of San Sebastián, the provisional government intended to hold elections as soon as possible for a Constituent Cortes. In order to make these elections fully free and representative, they decreed on May 8 that all persons over twenty-three years of age could vote, including

[14] Juan Ventosa y Calvell, *La situación política y los problemas económicas de España* (Barcelona, 1932), pp. 10–14, on the peseta decline; pp. 142–49 on the Morgan loan.

[15] *New York Times,* May 31, 1931. On the problem of the export of capital see Charles Lefaucheux, *La peseta et l'économie espagnole depuis 1928* (Paris, 1935), pp. 54–6, and Elli Lindner, *El derecho arancelario español* (Barcelona, 1934), 137ff. Lindner accepts the estimate of the Banca Soler y Torra Hermanos of Barcelona that roughly $250,000,000 worth of pesetas was exported illegally from March to December, 1931.

39

women and clergy. In order to prevent the municipal caciques from dominating the campaign, they also prescribed that deputies would be chosen from provincial rather than local electoral districts, assigning one deputy for each 50,000 persons. At the same time, responsible leaders feared to elect a chamber without a working majority. In Italy the parliamentary monarchy had often been paralyzed, and was eventually discredited by the lack of such a majority; and the same problem appeared repeatedly in the experience of the French Third Republic and the young German Republic. In Spain itself, only the Socialists possessed a coherent party organization. Hence the May 8 decree called for the preparation of coalition lists and stipulated that in each province the majority list would receive 80 per cent of the seats and the minority 20 per cent. The procedure was not obligatory, and a complex arrangement was made for distributing seats where several parties entered candidates; but the decree obviously encouraged the formation of coalitions and made it theoretically possible for a slender majority to hold four-fifths of the seats.

The elections were set for June 28, and the campaign aroused far greater interest and passion than any previous electoral contest in Spain. Conservative leaders were frightened by the radical groundswell of a long-repressed public opinion. In Oviedo Melquiades Alvarez, leader of the Reformist Party and a prestigious figure in the parliamentary opposition before 1923, threatened to withdraw his candidacy on the grounds that "Reds" were breaking up his party's rallies. Friends of Alcalá-Zamora urged him to accept a place on the Valencia list because it was quite possible that the Left would defeat him in his home province of Córdoba. In the Levant many individual anarchists were tempted to vote, despite the official abstention of their organizations. Knowing this, the Radicals of Alejandro Lerroux and the Radical Socialists of Marcelino Domingo both appealed for anarchist votes, with demagogic promises largely of an anticlerical nature.

The campaign was simultaneously a release of pent-up passions and a sober political education, depending on the personalities of the candidates and the maturity of their audiences.

In Catalonia, the Basque country, and Galicia autonomist candidates appealed for home rule, sometimes on reasoned economic and historical grounds, sometimes with chauvinist demagogy. There were almost no avowed monarchist candidates, but the candidates grouped under the banner of "Agrarians" were considered by friends and enemies alike to be, in fact, monarchists. Socialist orators spoke for everything from a liberal parliamentary regime to a proletarian dictatorship. In the mining provinces and the seaport towns, militant workers made themselves heard in a political campaign for almost the first time in Spanish history. There was much heckling and a certain amount of street fighting. In the voting, the Left undoubtedly benefitted from the sense of disarray among not only the monarchists but also the moderates who saw even such figures as Alcalá-Zamora in danger of defeat.

In analyzing the result of the voting, only approximate figures can be given. Most parties had very little formal organization. In the case of coalitions, the leaders decided on the distribution of seats, and many important individuals represented "tendencies" but were not formally affiliated with parties. The expectation of change, the atmosphere of the campaign, and the provisions of the electoral law produced a strong victory for the coalition of Left Republicans and Socialists. They held about 250 seats, of which 120 were Socialist and 80 attributed to the parties of Manuel Azaña, Marcelino Domingo, and Alvaro de Albornoz. This working majority also counted on the votes of perhaps 30 Catalan deputies of the Esquerra and 20 Federal Republicans from Galicia. Forming the center of the new chamber were some 100 Radicals, the followers of the "historic republican" Alejandro Lerroux. The Radicals were both anti-Socialist and anticlerical, and represented largely the middle-class elements which resented the older order but had no fixed program of their own. There were roughly 80 deputies to be classified on the Right: some 30 conservative republicans divided among the followers of Alcalá-Zamora, Miguel Maura, and Melquiades Alvarez; some 25 Agrarians, representing the landlords of both the wheat districts and Andalusia, and considered anti-Republican; about 10 conservative deputies of the *Lliga Catalana;* and 14 ardently Catholic Basques, of whom 8 were Basque Nationalists.[16]

The new Cortes was thus heavily weighted to the left. It included many men without political experience, and many who were almost unknown to the leaders of their respective parties. But all the known leaders of all the organized political parties were present, and both conservative and leftist regional sentiment was represented. The assembly also included a distinguished group of nonparty intellectuals who were anxious to contribute to the building of a new Spain; the philosopher Ortega y Gasset, the leading writers Unamuno and Pérez de Ayala; Dr. Gregorio Marañon; the famous jurists Felipe Sánchez Román and Angel Ossorio y Gallardo. The representation of the Socialist Party also included some of the nation's leading academicians: Jiménez de Asúa, specialist in constitutional law on the faculty at Madrid; Julián Besteiro, professor of logic at Madrid; Juan Negrín, internationally known professor of physiology and the chairman of the new University City being constructed northwest of the capital. Allowing for the fact that conservative Spain was underrepresented, proportionately speaking, it may truly be said that the new Cortes included able spokesmen of every political tendency and a distinguished cross section of the nation's intellectual elite.

[16] I have deliberately used only round figures. The difficulty of labeling both parties and individuals may be appreciated by comparing the efforts of various scholars to analyze the composition of the Constituent Cortes. See R. M. Smith, *The Day of the Liberals,* pp. 116–17; E. Allison Peers, *The Spanish Tragedy, 1930–36* (New York, 1936), p. 61; Frank E. Manuel, *The Politics of Modern Spain* (New York, 1938), p. 66; and Gerald Brenan, *The Spanish Labyrinth* (Cambridge, Engl., 1943), pp. 232–34. While in Spain, I discussed the problem with several former deputies of the Cortes, all of whom agreed that the Cortes had been composed of numerous *personalista* groups rather than of political parties in the British, or even French, meaning of the term.

THE CREATION OF A CONSTITUTION

WITH the collapse of the Monarchy and the peaceful proclamation of the Republic, everyone was aware of a unique
opportunity to transform Spain. At the same time, the church
burnings and the sporadic violence of the electoral campaign
created a sense both of urgency and of uneasiness. In early
July, just before the Cortes was to meet, the country experienced its first major labor struggle since April 14. The telephone strike of July 4 was called by the anarchists and was
clearly intended to embarrass the Socialist ministers in the
provisional government. The Spanish Telephone Company
was a subsidiary of the American Telephone and Telegraph
Company. A long-term contract had been negotiated a few
years earlier with the government of Primo de Rivera and, at
the time of signing, the Socialists had accused the King of
selling out to American capitalism while receiving free stock
in the bargain. In July, 1931, the Socialist Minister of Finance,
Indalecio Prieto, was bending every effort to reassure Spain's
creditors, to stem the export of wealth, and to arrest the down-
ward trend of the peseta.

The telephone workers, affiliated with the CNT, chose this
moment to challenge the American-managed company. The
strike cut most of the service in Barcelona and Seville but was
only sporadically successful in other provinces. The Socialists
supported the government's determination to maintain service,
and UGT workers substituted for striking CNT workers in
Madrid and Córdoba. The Socialist press qualified the
anarchist tactics as infantile and provocative and accused the
CNT of being controlled by *pistoleros* (gunmen).[1] In efforts to
negotiate a settlement, Colonel Macià claimed jurisdiction in

[1] *El Socialista,* June 13, 1931. The accusation was repeated in late
July and August.

43

Catalonia, while Largo Caballero insisted that the Ministry of Labor was the sole competent authority for all of Spain.

Failing to achieve a nationwide stoppage, the anarchists called for general strikes to support the telephone workers. They were successful in Seville on July 20. With the double justification that pistoleros were running the strike and that telephones were an essential public service, Miguel Maura declared martial law in Seville on the 22nd. Artillery reduced the headquarters of the CNT, heavily armed police patrolled the city streets; by July 29 the strike had been broken and order restored, at the cost of 30 dead and 200 wounded. Meanwhile, in Barcelona the strike slowly petered out. Colonel Macià stated that he would never treat strikers with such severity as had the central government, and Luis Companys, head of the *Esquerra* delegation in the Cortes, refused to join the vote of confidence in the government after order had been restored in Seville.[2]

The telephone strike resulted from the rivalry between Socialist and anarchist unions, from the impatience of naïve workers who had for years been hearing that the Company was a wicked foreign monopoly, and from the equally naïve desire of the anarchists to test the temper of the new government. The anarchists found out that a republic would treat them as severely as had the royal government. At the same time, they were tempted to play off Madrid against Barcelona, the Catalan officials having expressed strong criticism of Maura. The Socialists found themselves in the uncomfortable position of defending a foreign company, whose contract they had bitterly criticized, and of acting as strikebreakers against fellow workers.

The newly chosen Cortes began their labors against the dramatic background of the telephone strike. They also honored the memory of the French Revolution by holding their first session on July 14, Bastille Day. The preparation of a draft constitution was entrusted to a committee whose leading members were Luis Jiménez de Asúa and Angel Ossorio y Gallardo. Jiménez de Asúa belonged to the moderate wing

[2] J. Arrarás, *Historia*, I, 125–26; *New York Times*, July 7, 1931; *El Sol*, July 23–30, 1931.

of the Socialist Party. As a professor of law at Madrid University, he was widely known for studies of both constitutional and criminal jurisprudence. Ossorio had been a practicing lawyer and an important political figure for almost thirty years. In the Cortes of the Constitutional Monarchy he had been a follower of the great Conservative Prime Minister, Antonio Maura, and had served from 1903 to 1908 as civil governor of Barcelona. He had been a Minister of Public Works, and also President of the *colegio de abogados* (lawyers' guild) in Madrid. Like the President of the provisional government, Alcalá-Zamora, he had remained a Monarchist until he was convinced that Alfonso XIII would never restore the constitutional norms which had prevailed from 1876 to 1923. In 1930 he served as defending lawyer for Alcalá-Zamora and the other imprisoned Republican leaders. To the task of preparing a constitution, he thus brought long political experience and a moderately conservative viewpoint.

The constitutional committee presented its draft to the Cortes on August 18, and between that date and December 9 the deputies hammered out the charter of a thoroughly democratic, laic, potentially decentralized republic. Spain was declared to be a "Republic of workers of all categories," a statement which reflected the egalitarian ardor of the Socialists. Legislative and ministerial power were concentrated in a single-chamber parliament. All elections to the Cortes and to municipal governments were to be conducted by universal, direct, secret suffrage. Article 29 guaranteed the right of habeas corpus and Article 94 promised free justice for the needy by an independent judiciary. The Cortes favored a single chamber because of the strong tendency of upper houses toward conservatism. They provided a check on the abuse of legislative power by the creation of a Tribunal of Constitutional Guarantees, charged with the duty of determining the constitutionality of laws and with jurisdiction over conflicts between the central government and the autonomous regions. The Constitution protected property as well as individual rights, but at the same time it stated, in Article 44, that the wealth of the nation would be subject to indemnified

45

expropriation for purposes of social utility, thereby making possible an evolution towards socialism.

The Cortes agreed easily on the principles of legislative supremacy and the independence of the judiciary. The definition of executive power, however, was more difficult. The deputies feared the abuses of a strong executive. Everyone knew how Alfonso XIII had made and unmade cabinets in accordance with his personal feelings toward leading politicians, and how he had seen to it that his favorites rose rapidly in the Army and in the Church. A majority of the deputies held him responsible for the *coup d'état* of 1923 in which the constitution had been suspended and a military dictatorship established. Thus it was essential to limit clearly the President's powers, but on the other hand, he must not be a mere ceremonial figure. The constitutional lawyers, many of whom had studied in Germany, borrowed from the Weimar Constitution the notion of a presidential moderating power, all the more necessary in Spain because of the lack of a senate.

According to Article 71, the President would be chosen by an electoral college for a six-year term and would not be immediately eligible for reelection. Article 75 allowed him to appoint and remove the Prime Minister freely. Article 76 stated that, in accord with the cabinet, he could ask the Cortes to reconsider projected laws which in his opinion would contravene the constitution. Article 81 authorized him to dissolve the Cortes twice, and Article 83 gave him a veto power equivalent to that of the American President. Each of these rather broad powers was quite carefully limited by other clauses. The power to name the Prime Minister was his strongest positive function, and in a country with many small political parties it was a difficult task which would greatly affect the stability of the regime. In order to avoid any possible abuse of the initiative, the Constitution made it clear that only a Prime Minister enjoying the support of the majority of the deputies could hold office. Article 87 also stated that "the acts and mandates of the President" would not be valid unless countersigned by a cabinet minister. The power to dissolve the Cortes included a powerful check: in the case of a second dissolution, the first act of the new Cortes would be to determine the necessity for that dissolution. If the new chamber decided unfavorably on the President's action, he would automatically be removed from office. The deputies inserted this clause in Article 81 to ensure themselves against a strong-minded President who might defeat the will of the voters by repeatedly calling new elections. Finally, the veto power enabled the President to inhibit the passage of laws he found repugnant. But between 1876 and 1923 the constitutional Kings of Spain had never exercised that power, and their precedent could be counted on to restrain the President as well.

Thus the Spanish President had important, but carefully limited, responsibilities. He was to choose the person best qualified to govern with a given Cortes. He had advisory power in the matter of the constitutionality of proposed laws. If willing to break precedent, he could veto laws, and he could once in his six-year term dissolve the Cortes on his personal responsibility. In so carefully hedging the President's initiative, the writers of the Constitution thought entirely in terms of European precedents, principally those of the Third Republic in France, with whom the liberal republicans identified themselves emotionally, and the Weimar Republic of Germany, admired particularly by the constitutional lawyers. They did not consider the possible analogies between their situation and that of the Spanish-speaking republics of Latin America. The Mexican revolutions of 1858 and 1911–20, the experiences of Irigoyen in Argentina from 1916 on, and of Alessandri in Chile from 1920 on, had all indicated that in the Hispanic world the advance of both political and economic democracy required a strong, affirmative presidential power.[3]

[3] L. Jiménez de Asúa, *La constitución de la democracia española y el problema regional* gives the full text of the constitution and contains a critical analysis. See R. M. Smith, *The Day of the Liberals,* for a daily account of the deliberations from July 14 to December 9. For the debates themselves, *Diario de sesiones de las Cortes Constituyentes, 1931–33,* 25 vols. (Madrid, 1933). The *Diario* is available in the Library of Congress. Useful, and more widely available excerpts were edited by Arturo Mori, *Crónica de las cortes constituyentes de la segunda república española,* 12 vols. (Madrid, 1931 and 1934).

The most important conflict in the elaboration of the Constitution concerned the new relations between Church and state. Under the Concordat of 1851, Roman Catholicism was recognized as the official religion of Spain. The provisional government had proclaimed religious liberty by decree, and Article 3 of the Constitution declared that the state had no official religion. The Vatican protested both these measures as unilateral violations of the Concordat. However, the formal separation of Church and state would doubtless have been negotiable, and a large proportion of Catholics themselves favored it. The critical dissension arose over the many future restrictions that were to be placed on all aspects of the Church's activity. Article 26 stated that the budget for the support of the secular clergy was to be eliminated within two years. The many Orders, which in 1931 housed approximately 45,000 monks and nuns, were to register their property as well as their income and investment figures. They were to be permitted to hold only such property as was directly necessary to their functions, and they were to submit to the normal tax laws.

Strictly speaking, these clauses were no more radical than those which had separated Church and state in France in 1905; and the attempt to control the activities of the Regular clergy merely repeated the efforts made by several royal governments since 1887 to register the Orders through a Law of Associations. Article 26 also proclaimed, however, that the Orders were not to engage in commerce, industry, or non-confessional teaching. If this clause had been carried out, the Regular clergy would have been reduced to charitable and medical functions, the training of priests, and subsistence farming.

The debate over Article 26 was the first revolutionary conflict in the history of the young Republic. For over a thousand years the Church had been, aside from the Monarchy, the most powerful single institution in Spain. Its right to control education had been barely contested before the late nineteenth century. It had always engaged in large economic enterprises. A Liberal government in 1837 had deprived it of its landed estates, but the Church continued to engage in commercial and industrial activities. Its schools, particularly at the level of secondary education, were, in 1931, a tremendous source of income. Actually no one could measure precisely either the importance of Church schools or the extent of its wealth, and no one seemed to notice the fact that the number of monks and nuns in Spain had been declining for some decades. The impassioned but carefully thought out speeches of Fernando de los Ríos (Socialist) and Alvaro de Albornoz (Radical Socialist) on one side, and those of Gil Robles (Catholic) and Antonio de Pildaín (lectoral canon of Vitoria and a Basque deputy) on the other, ranged over the history of the Spanish Church from Visigothic days to the present. The Republic was identified with the struggle against the Inquisition, with the *erasmistas* of the sixteenth century, the *afrancesados* of the eighteenth, the *krausistas* of the nineteenth and twentieth. The defense of the Church was identified with the national mission of Spain in the *Reconquista,* and with the defense of contemporary Spain against the sins of liberalism and materialism. Once the floodgates had been opened, no one could consider calmly the need for a new relationship between Church and state.

Meanwhile, the Church assumed that she was to be despoiled by the Republic. Cardinal Segura, still Primate of Spain, sent directions from France for the sale of Church properties—directions which were discovered when the emissary passed the frontier. The government responded on August 20 with a decree prohibiting the sale, transfer, or mortgage of property belonging to the Church, and followed the decree with a formal demand for the removal of the Cardinal from the Archbishopric of Toledo.[4] Pope Pius XI, who had been nuncio in Poland just after the Russian Revolution, and who had been struggling for almost a decade with the rulers of revolutionary Mexico, was anxious to minimize the damage to the Church that might occur in Spain. He was also advised by his nuncio in Madrid, Bishop Tedeschini, that Cardinal Segura was too intransigent and too royalist to deal reasonably with the republican authorities. The Pope then asked the Cardinal to resign; the latter replied that he could not in

[4] Frank Kluckhohn in The *New York Times,* Aug. 21 and 22, 1931.

49

conscience voluntarily resign, but that the Pope's wishes were for him commands. His resignation was announced at the end of September.[5]

In the first week of October the debate in the Cortes over Article 26 came to a climax. The Socialist Minister of Justice, Fernando de los Ríos, himself disturbed by the violence of anticlerical oratory in the chamber, rose to remind the deputies in emotional terms of the selfless medical and charitable work done by many of the Orders. In the presence of such communities, he said, one forgets all differences of dogma and sees only the grandeur of souls fired by love. A few days later, Manuel Azaña, treating the entire religious problem, questioned in somewhat ironical tones the ideal picture drawn by de los Ríos and asked whether his colleague was unaware of the proselytizing function of these nurses and sisters of charity. What was true in hospitals was of course still more the case in schools. The Republic, said Azaña, could not permit the Church to continue in nonreligious teaching. This was not, he insisted, a question of liberty but of public health!

Azaña, however, argued the necessity of Article 26 on much wider grounds. In defending the right of the Church to control education, clericals always claimed that Spain was overwhelmingly a Catholic country. But, said Azaña, "what constitutes the religious situation of a country . . . is not the numerical sum of beliefs and believers, but the creative effort of its spirit, the direction followed by its culture." In this sense Spain had been Catholic in the sixteenth century, though with many and important exceptions; and Spain today was no longer Catholic, although there were millions of believers. The task of the Cortes was to organize institutions corresponding to this truth. In present circumstances the Church had no right to use the state as its "secular arm" to pay the costs of the cult, impose its spiritual vision on the young, and control such functions as marriage and burial. Article 26 was not intended to despoil the Church, but to deprive it of the special privileges it had enjoyed. It would be ridiculous, said Azaña, to drive out the many minor Orders, but the immense

[5] Juan de Iturralde, *El catolicismo y la cruzada de Franco,* 2 vols. (Vienne, France, 1955 and 1960), I, 339–48.

educational influence of the Church must be broken if a democratic, laic Republic were to be built.[6]

The deputies as a whole recognized the revolutionary nature of Article 26, and almost half of them avoided participating in the final vote. Whereas they had approved Article 3, separating Church and state, by a vote of 278 to 41, in the case of Article 26 the vote was 178 to 59.[7] Many who voted for Article 26 felt as did the Catalan moderate, and Minister of Economy, Nicolau d'Olwer. He had voted for a bad law, he told the newspapers, but he was afraid that if he did not accept Article 26, an increasingly anticlerical Cortes might later have voted a still harsher law.

The passage of Article 26 opened the first cabinet crisis of the new regime. The two practicing Catholics in the provisional government, Prime Minister Alcalá-Zamora and Interior Minister Miguel Maura, resigned. There were proclerical demonstrations in the Basque and Navarrese towns and anticlerical parades in Madrid and many southern towns. The Vatican commented that in its opinion the Republic was a "transitory regime." In the Cortes the young Catholic deputy for Salamanca, José María Gil Robles, considered Article 26 a frontal assault on the best Spanish traditions and called for a complete revision of the Constitution. Maura, interviewed by the newspapers, took pains to clarify his own position. He had not resigned, he said, with the intention of attacking the work of the provisional government as a whole. He could not, as a matter of personal conscience, approve Article 26, and in a parliamentary regime it was important that the cabinet be unified on all major issues. He had resigned in order to facilitate that unity. He considered Article 26 unworkable and felt sure that the Cortes itself would realize the fact in due time. The phraseology of Gil Robles was, in his opinion, a call for religious warfare which would do incalculable harm to the country. The crisis over Article 26 crystallized two

[6] Manuel Azaña, *Una política* (Madrid, 1932) contains the slightly corrected text of his October 13 speech in the Cortes. The debates on Article 26 which I have summarized appear in vol. III of the Mori *Crónica* and vols. 5 and 6 of the *Diario*.

[7] *New York Times*, Oct. 14 and 16, 1931.

different forms of opposition to the anticlerical majority. One was the "loyal opposition" of Maura, accepting the institutions and the good faith of the Republic; the other was a generalized attack on the laic, reformist Republic as such.[8]

Meanwhile, Manuel Azaña emerged as the natural leader of the majority coalition of liberal Republicans, Socialists, and anticlericals. He had achieved a reputation for clarity and technical competence as Minister of War. His ideas, and his great eloquence, had made a tremendous impression during the debate over Article 26. He was an advocate of political democracy and civilian supremacy in government. Economic problems for him were important, but secondary, and his approach to them was pragmatic, making it possible for him to work well with both economic liberals and moderate Socialists. He became Prime Minister on October 16, and two early laws of his ministry were thoroughly characteristic of the man. On October 29 the Cortes passed a Law for the Defense of the Republic, a law designed to punish violence in political, social, and religious strife, and news casting a slur on the Republic. The new regime, with its constitution still incomplete, was being violently attacked by Carlists and clericals in the north, and by anarchists in the east and south. Even when rioters were arrested, there were many instances of complicity with them by anti-Republican police and judges. Admittedly there was an element of self-contradiction in a democratic regime seeking exceptional police powers, but the alternative, argued Azaña, was to put a scrupulously pacifist government at the mercy of reactionary and revolutionary opponents. The law he requested was to be limited in application to the life of the Constituent Cortes. It gave the government power to impose fines up to 10,000 pesetas and to deport individuals within the Peninsula or to the African provinces. The next week the government decreed a cut of 50 per cent in the personnel of the civil service and a 20 per cent general salary increase for the reduced force. With these two acts, Azaña indicated his determination to govern strongly, to cut down administrative waste, and to offer better pay for better work.

[8] *El Sol*, Oct. 15, 1931, for the Maura interview. *El Debate,* Oct. 15 and 16 for Gil Robles' reactions.

During the final weeks of constitution writing, the Cortes also tried the former King *in absentia*. The commission preparing the charges accused Alfonso of *lèse-majesté* on the following grounds: neglect of his duties as a constitutional sovereign, complicity in administrative immorality, and complicity in the *coup d'état* which established the Primo de Rivera dictatorship. The Count of Romanones spoke in the King's defense. The Cortes majority altered *lèse-majesté* to high treason. Since they also were abolishing capital punishment in the new constitution, they sentenced the absent King, not to death, but to perpetual banishment. On December 9 the completed text of the new constitution was approved by a vote of 368 to 38, with several dozen abstentions. The next week, Don Niceto Alcalá-Zamora, who had resigned as provisional Prime Minister in October, accepted election as the first President of the Spanish Republic, and after consultation with the party leaders in the chamber, called upon Manuel Azaña to continue as Prime Minister.

The new charter accurately reflected the wishes of the Cortes' majority. It was democratic and laic. It made the legislature the supreme branch of the government. It would be compatible with a mixed economy containing both capitalist and socialist elements. The debates, however, had also indicated that the Constitution as it stood would be unacceptable to Catholic opinion, not only on grounds of the clauses concerning the Orders in Article 26, but also because of Article 48, which stated that education at all levels was to be laic. Some of the leading intellectuals who had welcomed the Republic were also disenchanted. On December 6, just a few days before the final vote, Ortega y Gasset delivered a resounding public lecture entitled *Rectificación de la República*. He welcomed the social clauses of the Constitution. Indeed, if anything, he said, the working class was not sufficiently represented in the new regime. But he was worried to see the Republic undermined by a spirit of faction. Exaggerated regionalism, exaggerated anticlericalism, and the shortsighted defense of privilege by the reactionaries threatened to stifle the new regime in its infancy. He called for an "estado integral, superior a todo partidismo," and for a "partido de amplitud nacional" which would direct from above the necessary national revolution. His phraseology clearly suggested a disillusionment with the results of universal suffrage, and a need for intelligent, paternalist authority in the hands of an elite.[9] Ortega had already published his famous work *The Revolt of the Masses,* in which he spoke apprehensively of the irruption of the uncultured masses into European political life in the twentieth century. As a member of the Constituent Cortes, he had now personally witnessed some of the manifestations of that irruption. He and other writers, notably Unamuno, were deeply troubled. They had been leading intellectual opponents of Primo de Rivera. Unamuno had frequently visited the Casa del Pueblo in Salamanca and had marched arm in arm with Largo Caballero in the 1931 May Day parade. Consciously or not, these men had expected to be listened to as elder statesmen by the new generation of republicans. Instead, they found themselves swamped in the Cortes by anticlerical demagogy; by bad grammar, by offensive Catalan, Galician and Andalusian accents; by all the jealousy, meanness, and irrational passion of the underprivileged. As university intellectuals, they were not prepared for the crude demands or the uncultured manners. They had known Azaña as a moderately successful writer and as the President of the Madrid Ateneo, but he had cut a decidedly minor figure in the intellectual firmament. Now he had emerged as the leader of the parliamentary majority, putting his literary and oratorical gifts at the service of anticlerical and antinational forces. They did not attack him. They did not withdraw from the Cortes. But by December of 1931 they had lost their initial enthusiasm for the Republic. In his speech, Ortega set forth his opinion that Miguel Maura was the man who could successfully form and lead the "partido de amplitud nacional." But Maura was anathema to the monarchists. In their opinion the son of Antonio Maura had become a republican simply out of resentment at the King's treatment of his father. Don Miguel was a *resentido* and a betrayor of his class; far from accepting his leadership, they boycotted his law office,

[9] José Ortega y Gasset, *Rectificación de la república* (Madrid, 1931).

which from father to son had handled the affairs of many of the leading aristocrats of Spain.[10] To Catholics, Maura was the Minister of the Interior who had failed to prevent the burning of the churches on May 11. His political prospects were therefore discouraging.

At the end of 1931, the Azaña government could count on the support of the liberal Republicans and Socialists, the opposition of the monarchists and Catholics, the hostility of the anarchists, and the disenchantment of important intellectuals. The principal parliamentary conflicts had turned upon Church-state relations. The new President was a Catholic and his Prime Minister an anticlerical. The problem of the future would be to consolidate the Republic in these circumstances.

[10] Conversation with Miguel Maura, April, 1961.

THE POLITICS OF THE
AZAÑA GOVERNMENT

MANUEL AZAÑA served as Prime Minister from October 1931 until September 1933. During 1933 a rising tide of opposition obstructed the government's program, but in the late months of 1931 and throughout the following year the Azaña cabinet held the initiative. Azaña had become Prime Minister largely as a result of his role in the passage of Article 26. In January 1932, the Cortes passed new laic legislation: Spain's first divorce law, and the secularization of the cemeteries. There were a few well-publicized cases of divorce, such as that of Constancia de la Mora, granddaughter of Antonio Maura, who ended a thoroughly unhappy society marriage and soon remarried (this time in a civil ceremony) the young aviation officer Hidalgo de Cisneros. But the striking fact was the relative infrequence of divorce. Spaniards of all classes were intensely conservative in this matter. The middle class in Madrid and Barcelona used the new law sparingly, and in many provinces there were no applications at all. Secular control of cemeteries took place without fanfare in most areas, but there were some towns in which the Republican mayor, accompanied by the municipal band playing the Marseillaise, made a public ceremony of the change. In many cities there was a small, walled-off portion of the cemetery reserved for the few stubborn citizens who had desired a civil burial. The secularization ceremony often included an ostentatious destruction of the wall, and cases were reported of municipal authorities proselytizing the citizens to request civil marriage and burial now that Spain had achieved religious liberty.[1]

Such actions were both offensive and illegal from the Church's point of view. In theoretical terms, at least, Church-

[1] A Montero, *Historia de la persecución religiosa*, 34–5.

¿Cómo reacciona usted cuando se le posa una mosca en la oreja?

LERROUX (the "historic republican" waiting for Azaña's majority to dissolve): When that happens I pull down my hood and maintain 15 or 20 years of silence.

AZAÑA (Minister of War as well as Prime Minister): There's no relief for it. The moment I feel the fly I start kicking the tables.

PRIETO (Minister of Public Works and Socialist leader): I let off a string of oaths, for which reason we Socialists are losing votes. [Pun on the word *voto*]

GALARZA (Director General of Security): Instinctively I cover my fat cheeks because some jokers think they were made for playing dumbledore.

LARGO CABALLERO (Minister of Labor and Socialist trade union head): I decree civil war and that's that.

MACIA (President of the Generalitat): If the fly is Mediterranean I do nothing, but if it comes from Castile I declare war on the Spaniards.

from the rightist satirical magazine *Gracia y Justicia*, May 21, 1932

THE AZAÑA GOVERNMENT SEEN FROM THE RIGHT
How do you react when a fly settles in your ear?

state relations in Spain were still being governed by the Concordat of 1851, according to which the Catholic religion was to be maintained as the official religion of Spain. In conformity with Church precepts generally, marriage must be a sacrament, not merely a civil ceremony, and all education, public and private, should conform to Church doctrine.

Even in the nineteenth century, however, the state had felt itself cramped by the rigidity of the Concordat. A number of nonreligious private schools appeared in the large cities, civil marriage and burial became possible for those specifically requesting them, and in 1913 the government decreed that religious instruction in the public schools would no longer be obligatory for children whose parents professed another religion. The Primo de Rivera dictatorship, on the other hand, had restored obligatory religious instruction, and a royal decree of 1924 had threatened to suspend teachers who expressed ideas offensive to the Catholic religion.[2]

Whenever the governments of the Constitutional Monarchy had reduced the Church's monopoly, the hierarchy had cried persecution. Secularization of any of the functions under discussion constituted both a violation of the Concordat and an attack on religious liberty, i.e., in this context, the liberty of the Church to monopolize these functions with the aid of the state. When the Republic immediately ended obligatory religious instruction and announced its intention to introduce laic legislation, the Church responded as in the past: the government was violating the Concordat and attacking religious liberty.[3]

The laws of January 1932 were consequently extremely important in principle, even if few persons applied for divorce and few desired a civil burial. For the deputies, these laws continued the liberal tradition of the Constitutional Monarchy and reversed the clerical trend of the recent dictatorship. Republicans identified the principle of neutral state control with the far greater individual liberty enjoyed by the peoples

[2] Rodolfo Llopis, *Hacia una escuela más humana* (Madrid, 1934), pp. 26–30.

[3] Alfonso Iniesta Corredor, *Educación española* (Madrid, 1942), pp. 31–40, 68–9, states passionately and succinctly the griefs of the Church regarding the secularization of Spanish life under both Monarchy and Republic. There are many similar references in the Cortes speeches of Gil Robles and in Antonio de Pildaín y Zapaín, *En defensa de la Iglesia y la libertad de enseñanza* (Madrid, 1935). The latter is a collection of Cortes speeches by a Basque priest and deputy who has since become the Bishop of the Canary Islands.

of western and northern Europe, the United States, and the British dominions. They identified it also with the writings of the French Enlightenment and the Jacobin tradition. Hence the ceremonial destruction of walls, the playing of the Marseillaise, and the propaganda to the effect that civil marriage and burial were signs of "culture," whereas the religious ceremonies were signs of superstition.

Article 26 called for the dissolution of all Orders constituting a danger to the state, as well as those Orders requiring a special oath in addition to the normal canonical vows. The first of these provisions applied principally, and the second exclusively, to the Jesuits. In January 1932 the Azaña government decreed the dissolution of the Order and the sequestration of its property. The Jesuits had been expelled repeatedly by French, Spanish, and Italian governments in the eighteenth and nineteenth centuries. As a particularly disciplined Order, and as the leading defenders of the papacy during the Counter-Reformation, the Jesuits had become traditional scape-goats for anti-Catholic action in the northern countries and for anticlerical action in the Catholic countries. The stated grounds for their dissolution reflected this extraordinary historical animus. In the Spain of 1931 the famous special oath meant only that the Jesuits placed themselves unconditionally at the Pope's service for foreign missionary work.[4] As for the question of danger to the state, Vatican references to the transitory nature of the Republic, and the evident royalism of most of the high dignitaries, might well be considered a potential danger to the state, but these factors had no greater reference to the Jesuits than to any other branch of the Church. In fact, the Jesuit disciples who edited *El Debate* were the first leading Spanish Catholics to argue that a Catholic society could be compatible with the Republic, and to recall the example of Leo XIII in urging the *ralliement* of French Catholics to the Third Republic in the 1890's.

[4] Alfred Mendizábal, *Aux origines d'une tragédie* (Paris, 1937), p. 168. This work, published in English as *The Martyrdom of Spain* (London, 1937) offers a liberal Catholic view of the entire Church-state problem under the Republic. Mendizábal was a professor of law.

The more rational causes for dissolution of the Jesuits were their educational influence, their tremendous hidden wealth, and the economic power consequent to that wealth. They ran two engineering schools which were known to have higher standards and better equipment than those of the state. It was widely assumed that these schools filled the most coveted posts in the expanding industries of the early twentieth century, if only because the royal government did not recognize the Jesuit degree for civil service posts.[5] The Order was known to have vast real estate and industrial interests, including a large bloc of preferred stock in the Telephone Company, considerable holdings in government bonds, and controlling shares in the electric and street railway companies of the big cities. But these, and many other forms of corporate property, could never be numerically assessed because they were not held in the name of the Jesuits. The Liberal ministry of Canalejas in 1910 had proposed to tax the property of the Orders, and more extreme anticlericals had called for their dissolution. In view of that threat, the Jesuits had begun an orderly transfer of their properties to strawmen—individuals or businesses which became the legal owners but which in fact continued to administer the property for the Order. The threat did not materialize in 1910, but the Jesuits had continued to act on the assumption that a stronger anticlerical government might one day take office, and at the time of the 1932 dissolution, no one but their own lawyers, one of whom was the leading young Catholic deputy Gil Robles, knew exactly what the Jesuits possessed in the way of stocks and real estate.[6]

[5] Ilsa and Arturo Barea, *Spain in the Postwar World* (London, 1945), p. 14. As a patent agent before the Civil War, Barea had considerable knowledge of the banking and industrial structure. Nevertheless, according to a careful sociological analysis of the Spanish business community now being prepared by Juan Linz, it appears that Jesuit graduates do not by any means hold a disproportionate number of the directorships in Spanish private industry. I owe this information to the kindness of Professor Linz.

[6] Regarding the wealth of the Jesuits and their means of camouflaging it, I depended on the following sources: J. Torrubiano Ripoll, *Beatería y religión* (Madrid, 1930); Alvaro de Albornoz,

When the government attempted to sequester Jesuit property, it became involved in a labyrinth of detail. The question of strawmen was only one aspect of the problem. It proved impossible to separate gifts, sacramental fees, charitable collections, and tuition fees from the income of properties and investments. It was equally impossible to determine the true cost of normal upkeep of buildings, expenses of the cult, and amounts of money assigned to overseas missions. The government was able, however, to identify some 33 schools, in addition to 47 residences and 79 other urban buildings which it hoped to use as schools. In some cases the government was frustrated by legal action showing that the Jesuits were not the owners, but only the tenants, of the given buildings. In certain instances the government established public school classes, in others, it faced lockouts and pupil strikes. Sometimes the Jesuits simply dissolved as the law bade them do, but continued running their schools as private educational corporations in the same category as any other private school. Since so much has been said of "expulsion" and "persecution," it is important to realize that in the vast majority of cases the government was punctilious about legal procedures, and the Jesuits had every opportunity to evade the force of the decree by dissolving in form only. The principal concrete result of the dissolution order was that the government acquired the use of a few dozen buildings pending decision of the courts as to the legality of their occupation and the eventual compensation

---

La política religiosa de la república (Madrid, 1935), particularly the appendix, which contains letters illustrating several techniques of camouflage; articles in *El Liberal* of Madrid for June 1 and 12, 1935, and in *Política* for August 15, 1935. Torrubiano Ripoll, whose book consists of a compilation of articles which appeared in *El Liberal* during the twenties, was a member of Alcalá-Zamora's party. Albornoz was one of the leaders of the Radical Socialist party and took a leading part in the parliamentary struggle on behalf of Article 26. I checked the above material with several priests and lawyers in Spain, all of whom confirmed the facts as given. In these conversations, indeed, I received the impression that many a priest and Catholic layman were more inimical to the Jesuits than was the Azaña government.

to be paid. The Jesuits decided of their own accord to withdraw many of their younger priests and teachers from Spain, but the departure of these men was reported in the world press as the expulsion of the Jesuits.[7]

For republicans and clericals alike, though for opposite motives, the implementation of Article 26 and the fate of the Orders was intimately connected with the struggle to build a laic school system. From April 14 on, the provisional government had considered that one of its most pressing tasks was the rapid expansion of the state primary schools. Estimates of Spanish illiteracy in 1931 varied between 30 and 50 per cent of the total population. No dependable figures were available for the number of children in school or the grades they had completed. The quality of materials and instruction varied widely. The only fixed data from which to start were the existence of some 35,000 state schools served by an official corps of 36,680 *maestros* and *maestras*. As Spain was a predominantly rural country, most of these were one-room schoolhouses, and for purposes of estimating capacities, the planners counted 50 students per school with maestro. Assuming then that the existing 35,000 schools served between one and a half and two million children, the Ministry of Education estimated that Spain needed another 27,000 schools to serve between one and one and a half million children currently lacking schools.

The first year of the Republic was a year of school-building fever. While Prieto struggled with the falling peseta and Miguel Maura with problems of public order, Marcelino Domingo and Rodolfo Llopis rolled up their sleeves in the Ministry of Education—Domingo as Minister and Llopis, a Socialist and normal school professor, as Director of Primary Education. Knowing the determination of the Republic to build schools, they went ahead with the confident assurance that their cabinet colleagues, and later the Constituent Cortes, would confirm their initiative. The municipal governments were to provide the sites and help finance the building. The central government would provide between 50 and 75 per

[7] *The Times*, London, Jan. 27 and 28, Feb. 6, 1932; Indalecio Prieto in *El Socialista*, Toulouse, Dec. 13, 1951.

cent of the construction costs, and pay the salary of the *maestro* once the school was in operation. When municipal officials, following old habits, would come to Madrid to ask the government to help them build a new bridge, the Ministry of Public Works would say that unfortunately they had no money to offer, but that if the town wished to build a school, the Ministry of Education would be delighted to help. Marcelino Domingo spent the happiest months of his life getting the construction program under way and wept bitter tears when in October, 1931, he was asked to yield the Ministry to Fernando de los Ríos, the Socialist professor of law who was technically better qualified, who was not a little jealous of the credit going to Domingo, and who was undoubtedly anxious to leave the Ministry of Justice after the grueling debate over Article 26.

In March 1932 de los Ríos contrasted for the Cortes the progress of school construction under the Monarchy and under the Republic. From 1909 to 1931 the state had built 11,128 schools, or about 500 per year. In the first 10 months the Republic had built 7,000 schools, a rate then, ten times as rapid as that of the Monarchy. By the end of the year he could announce the completion of some 9,600 primary schools, and a five-year plan had been elaborated to provide the remainder of the necessary 27,000. With average cost of construction at 25,000 pesetas per classroom, the government reasoned that a 400,000,000 peseta loan to help the municipalities during the following 4 years would complete the construction of the minimum buildings necessary to put all the children of Spain into public primary schools.

In order to provide the necessary teachers, the Ministry had set up refresher courses for the many adults who had acquired the title of *maestro* but who had been working in other branches of government service. Some 15,000 men and women with teaching degrees applied for refresher courses in the first year, with only 7,000 appointments to be made, so that in this instance considerable selectivity was possible. The average teaching salary rose about 15 per cent between 1931 and 1933, at a time when the cost of living remained stable. On grounds then both of economic improvement and of public enthusiasm, teaching became a more attractive career, and it seemed reasonable to believe that in the four or five years of intensive construction to come, the normal schools and universities could also provide another 20,000 teachers.

But for a number of reasons the intensive pace of school construction was not to extend beyond the end of 1932. One major objection concerned the budget. The provisional government had begun by giving full priority to human rather than financial considerations. But as the months passed, a balanced budget seemed increasingly important, not only to establish the new regime's international credit, but to fulfill the pledges of republican economists who had considered the annual deficits of the dictatorship a national scandal. Besides advancing general arguments for economy, the critics could point to many specific examples of waste, in which faulty architectural plans and corruption in the letting of contracts had doubled and tripled the original cost estimates for a given building.

The laic-religious dispute also became an increasing drag on the construction program. The very figure of 7,000 used by Fernando de los Ríos for the number of schools created in the first 10 months became a battle cry. One of the first moves of the Ministry of Education had been to ask the municipalities to report the number of children attending religious primary schools. The total for all Spain came to some 350,000, and once again on the basis of 50 pupils per school, this figure meant that the Republic needed 7,000 new schools in order to *replace* those being run by the Orders. The Ministry also planned its total program on the basis of a province-by-province survey, and the response of the municipalities varied greatly. In Alicante, Llopis' home district, and an area of great Republican-Socialist strength, some 130 new schools were needed according to the survey. The municipal authorities provided 104 furnished buildings even without government aid. In Madrid, with a municipal government of the same complexion as the Cortes majority, the government and the city cooperated to build 174 schools which by the end of 1932 housed 12,500 pupils. But in the highly prosperous, Catholic province of Vizcaya, the municipalities only offered 106 buildings, where the survey called for 219; and in neighboring Guipúzcoa, where the survey recommended 355 new schools, the municipalities opened 56. In many rural areas, and in a few cities, parents objected to coeducation; when the government decreed that crucifixes were no longer to be hung in the classrooms, many families responded by having their children wear large crucifixes. They also tried—by intimidating them—to force the maestros and maestras to attend mass.

Finally, important criticisms were raised concerning the qualifications of teachers. The Cortes minority, and many critics outside the government, did not accept the qualifications of those who had passed the refresher courses. Why had those people not been teaching all these years? They must have been those who just barely managed to get through, or who had taken a teaching degree because it was the easiest way in which to acquire a "title," and hence a better job. Government supporters replied that they had not been teaching because the Monarchy had not created the necessary schools; and they pointed out that more than half the teachers in the religious primary schools held no academic titles of any sort. This in turn led to bitter exchanges concerning the intellectual level of the laic as against the religious schools. In early 1933, almost 10,000 new primary schools stood as the great accomplishment of two years' efforts, but further progress was paralyzed by the pervasive religious controversy in which almost everyone appeared to lose sight of the original objective of providing a minimum education for all Spain's children.[8]

[8] My discussion of the primary schools is based upon the following sources: Fernando de los Ríos' speech to the Cortes, printed in *El Sol,* March 1, 1932; an editorial survey of the school program of Madrid in *El Sol,* December 27, 1932; Rodolfo Llopis, *La revolución en la escuela* (Madrid, 1933), and also his article in *Leviathan,* July, 1934, no. 3; E. Allison Peers, *Spain, the Church and the Orders* (London, 1939), pp. 150–52; Alfred Mendizábal, *Aux origines,* pp. 170–71. I had the benefit also of personal conversations with Sr. Llopis and with four former primary school teachers in Madrid and Seville.

During his first year as Prime Minister, Azaña extended considerably the Army reforms which he had begun in May 1931 as Minister of War. In December he created a Corps of Noncommissioned Officers, giving them greater responsibility than their ranks had previously exercised, and increasing their opportunities to become officers. This measure, intended to democratize and republicanize the Army, also narrowed the professional gap between "noncoms" and officers. And by recruiting officer candidates among the noncoms, the government hoped to broaden the social base of the officer corps. As a matter of fact, the Spanish officer corps was traditionally open to all social classes. The upper ranks of the French and German armies in the early twentieth century were far more dominated by birth and family connections than were those of Spain. The law of December 1931 was therefore not a break with Spanish practice but the extension of a democratic tendency already present.[9]

In March 1932 the Minister of War received authority to pass to the reserve any general for whom an appointment had not been found within six months. Some such measure was absolutely necessary since the reformed Army would have place for only about one-third the number of officers on active duty in early 1932. The government also intended by this means to force the retirement of generals unfriendly to the Republic. Among those liable to be retired by the terms of this law at the moment of its passage were a number of the generals who in 1936 were most actively involved in the planning of the military revolt: Mola, Saliquet, Orgaz, Millán Astray, and González de Lara.[10] The same law provided that officers who had accepted retirement under the May 1931 decree would lose their pension if convicted of defamation under the Law for the Defense of the Republic. This measure produced a lively debate in the Cortes, with General Fanjul leading the opposition. Miguel Maura and Angel Ossorio y Gallardo also opposed the clause, fearing the

[9] Manuel Azaña, *Una política,* pp. 142ff., a discussion which in its essentials repeats his Cortes speech of December 2, 1931, introducing the new corps.

[10] *El Sol,* Feb. 25, 1932.

obvious injustice that might occur to the persons and families of some 5,000 recently retired officers who might at one time or another have publicly criticized the government. Azaña pledged the government to restraint in the use of the law but insisted that it was intolerable for the Republic to have to subsidize its enemies.[11]

Pursuing the technical improvement of military supply, Azaña created in May 1932 an auxiliary corps of technicians, the *Cuerpo Auxiliar Subalterno del Ejército* (CASE). Previously there had been no table of organization and no standard wages for civilian employees. The new law provided standard pay and job security for administrative personnel, armorers, typists, mechanics, and building-maintenance workers. Another law of September 1932 affected both organization and training. It created a *Cuerpo de Tren* for more rapid delivery of supplies, and greatly increased the budget for aviation. All candidates for the professional officer corps were to serve six months' active duty before entering a specialized academy and were to take a certain number of liberal arts courses in the regular university. At the same time, Azaña reduced from five to two the academies for training the different specialties. The military courts, formerly constituting a jurisdiction of their own, were subordinated to the civil courts by the creation of a *Cuerpo Jurídico* of civilian lawyers to act in military cases and by making the Supreme Court the highest court of appeal for military as well as civil cases.

Military opinion accepted the active service for officer candidates, the *Cuerpo de Tren,* and the aviation budget as sensible forms of modernization. Opinion was divided on the wisdom of reducing the number of academies. For some it was a logical economy when the entire Army was being reduced by more than half; for others it threatened the quality of special technical training. The majority of professional officers disliked the rest of the law. In their opinion the requirement of university studies was an attempt to dilute the military spirit of the new generation of officers; the subordination of military to civilian courts would have the same effect. The

[11] *Diario* of the Cortes for Feb. 25–March 1, 1932. Azaña's interventions also given in *Una política.*

motive of the government was indeed to break the old barriers of caste and mutual ignorance by bringing future officers into contact for part of their education with future members of the liberal professions.[12]

Structural changes in the Army (and less important but similar reforms in the Navy) were only one aspect, and probably the less controversial aspect, of the entire role of military forces in Spanish life. Just as the questions of Church and public schools were always intimately related, so too were the questions of Army reform and public order. To a greater extent than most people cared to acknowledge, public order in Spain depended upon the *Guardia Civil,* the militarized police force created in the 1840's to end highway robbery. The Civil Guard were armed with rifles; they always traveled in pairs; their companies were headed by career officers, and the national chief of the Guard was always a general officer of the Army. For its efficiency in clearing the roads of rural Spain, the Guard became known among the landlords and the middle class as *La Benemérita.* With the rise of anarchism in the second half of the nineteenth century, the Guard was used increasingly to break up peasant demonstrations and to prevent or break strikes. It was a frequent practice for the Guard to fire point-blank at strikers, and the Ministry of the Interior invariably protected the anonymity of the marksmen if it could not entirely suppress the news. If for the landlords the Guard was indeed La Benemérita, for the landless peasants it was an army of occupation composed of 25,000 well-armed servants of the rich.

In April 1931 the head of the Civil Guard was also one of the most prestigious generals of the Spanish Army: José Sanjurjo, Marqués del Rif for his role in the pacification of Morocco. General Sanjurjo had been a key figure in the

[12] An article by Mildred Adams, *New York Times,* June 25, 1933, sums up a favorable view of the several reforms. For more technical and critical analysis, see Emilio Mola, *Obras,* pp. 1078–89, and in general the entire section: "El pasado, Azaña, y el porvenir." I also benefitted from several conversations with a retired general staff officer who had been a conservative deputy of the Alcalá-Zamora party and was one of the authors of the legislation.

successful *coup d'état* of 1923. As a personal friend of Primo de Rivera, and as a *caballero,* he had resented the King's treatment of Primo in 1930. When, after the municipal elections, the King asked him whether the Guard would defend his throne, General Sanjurjo had advised His Majesty to leave Spain, thereby playing an important role in the peaceful transition to the Republican regime. But while the General himself was encouraging Miguel Maura to take possession of the Ministry of the Interior on April 14, crowds all over Spain were shouting "Down with the Civil Guard." His proclamation of loyalty to the new regime, undoubtedly sincere, could not immediately wipe out decades of resentment by the masses. Nor did it, indeed, alter the sentiments of the largely monarchist guards themselves.

Winters in rural Spain were times of heavy unemployment, and hence of social tension, and the last day of 1931 witnessed a tragic clash between the peasants and the Civil Guard at Castilblanco, a fairly sizeable village in the valley of the Guadiana, close to the provincial border between Badajoz and Cáceres. On December 20, under the leadership of the Federation of Land Workers, the unemployed peasants conducted a peaceful demonstration demanding work. The Civil Guard dissolved the demonstration, as it had dissolved all such demonstrations for decades. Their action in this instance was pacific, but it also denied the peasants any effective right of assembly.

The Federation then called a two-day general strike, whose objective was to force the transfer of the head of the local Guard, whom they regarded as particularly unfriendly. The mayor refused a permit for the December 30 parade, but the demonstration nevertheless occurred, without incident. On the 31st he sent the Civil Guard to the Casa del Pueblo to ask its president to call off the intended demonstration for that day. While the negotiations were going on, a group of women taunted the four guards and attempted to enter the Casa. In preventing them, one of the guards fired a shot. A mob of angry peasants closed in on the four. They were murdered on the spot, by means of knives and shovels. Their eyes were gouged out, their skulls crushed, and the women performed a dance over the corpses, after which the peasants left the bodies in the street and shut themselves in their homes.

A thrill of horror passed through the country. General Sanjurjo commented that never among the most primitive tribes of Morocco had he seen corpses so savagely mutilated. The Minister of the Interior, Casares Quiroga, attended the funeral of the four guards and publicly stated that their conduct had been unexceptionable. Dr. Marañon, writing in *El Sol,* compared the situation with the famous Lope de Vega play, *Fuenteovejuna,* in which a group of villagers murdered a particularly cruel and hated cacique. When questioned by the royal judges as to who had committed the deed, the villagers replied unanimously: "Fuenteovejuna." For Dr. Marañon, all Spain—every landlord, every businessman, every teacher, every priest, who knew the misery of rural Spain, and who had not acted to relieve that misery—was guilty of the horrible crime at Castilblanco. The murder was the result of inhuman social conditions, and only the change of those social conditions could expiate the collective guilt of the Spanish nation. In the later trial of the village leaders their defense attorney, the Socialist lawyer Jiménez de Asúa, appealed to reasoning of the same type. Arguing the deplorable social conditions in the village, and the explosive, mob nature of the act, he asked the court to punish his clients for illegal possession of arms only. Actually, the court handed down six death sentences, later commuted to life imprisonment.[13]

Another clash between the populace and the Civil Guard occurred on January 5, 1932, this time in the northern Castilian town of Arnedo. A crowd of workers was accompanying a strike delegation to a meeting with the employers. At the sight of the Civil Guard they shouted slogans calling for the dissolution of the Guard and referring to them as the lackeys of the capitalists. The guards, especially nervous after what had happened in Castilblanco, fired into the crowd,

[13] My account of the events at Castilblanco is based upon both the prosecution and defense cases, cited at considerable length, though not in their entirety, in Luis Jiménez de Asúa, *Castilblanco* (Madrid, 1933).

killing six (of whom four were women and one a child) and wounding sixteen.

The public reaction of sympathy in favor of La Benemérita at Castilblanco was now reversed. Here was another case, like so many in the past, of the Civil Guard firing point-blank at hostile but unarmed peasants. The Cortes demanded the removal of General Sanjurjo. The government refused to act under pressure and knew in any event that there was no point in holding Sanjurjo personally responsible for a historic problem. But a month later General Cabanellas replaced him as head of the Civil Guard.

Military dislike of the Azaña laws and public criticism of the Army and Civil Guard produced a number of incidents in the spring of 1932, the most serious of which took place at a military review of the Madrid garrison at Carabanchel. A lieutenant colonel of infantry, Julio Mangada, took umbrage at certain remarks by General Villegas, in command of the Madrid Division, and of General Goded, Chief of the General Staff. When the latter concluded his brief speech with the traditional phrase, "Viva España," and invited the officers present to join him in that toast, Colonel Mangada voiced his resentment of the scarcely veiled antirepublican sentiments of General Villegas in particular, and insisted on crying "Viva la República." In the circumstances his act was both rude and insubordinate. The government arrested him and turned the case over to the courts. But it also replaced General Villegas as head of the First Division and accepted the resignation of General Goded, who had committed no offense, but whose known personal feelings were such that confidence could hardly exist in the future between him and the Azaña government. The entire incident involved nothing but "words, words, words." But "Viva España" already symbolized one set of loyalties, and "Viva la República" another. If Mangada was legally in the wrong, he had not been unprovoked. Generals Goded and Villegas were among those who rose in July 1936. Colonel Mangada fought for the Republic, as did General Masquelet, appointed by Azaña at this time to succeed Goded as Chief of Staff.

During these same months, the Cortes was actively debating

the question of a Catalan autonomy statute. Catalonia posed particular problems and opportunities for the Republic. It was a region of small farms and relatively well-distributed property. It was also the most industrialized and urbanized area of Spain, its typical business unit being the family firm, as in France during the same period. There were few large banks and corporations. There was considerable foreign capital invested in Catalonia, but Catalan industry did not depend upon foreign managers and technicians.

Catalonia also had a strong cultural life of its own. In the nineteenth century it had produced a series of eminent writers and philosophers, and neither Krausism nor Marxism, crucial intellectual currents in Castile, were particularly influential in Catalonia. The Catalans were industrious and culturally alert; they had better roads, better street lighting, more attractive shops, more theater and music than the rest of Spain. These contrasts had existed in 1830 as well as in 1930, but modern transportation and communication had made people far more aware of the differences in the twentieth century. The many small peoples of central Europe had achieved nationhood by the provisions of the Treaty of Versailles. The more ardent Catalan nationalists saw themselves as the victims of Castilian "imperialism" and compared their situation to that of the Poles seeking freedom from Russia and the Czechs throwing off the Austrian yoke.

Catalan literacy, prosperity, and middle-class economic structure represented a great opportunity for the Republic, since it was axiomatic that democracy flourishes most readily where property is widely distributed and the middle class is strong. The political conjuncture favored the Republicans also. The conservative *Lliga Catalana* had lost heavily in the elections of 1931. Its chief, Francisco Cambó, had chosen in 1930 to help the King reestablish the Constitutional Monarchy, and so the heavily republican sentiment of the Catalans had resulted in the victory of the *Esquerra*. The Esquerra chief, Colonel Macià, had originally demanded a Catalan Republic; however, more able, if less flamboyant, Catalan Republicans such as Luis Companys, Nicolau d'Olwer, and Jaime Carner were the personal friends of the Left Republican leaders in Spain, and they brought enthusiasm and technical competence to the service of the provisional, and later the Azaña government—d'Olwer as Minister of Economy and Carner as Minister of Finance.

During June and July 1931, the Catalans elaborated their projected statute in accordance with the principal restrictions accepted by Colonel Macià in his conference with the three Madrid ministers. The project referred to Catalonia as an autonomous state within the Spanish Republic and said nothing about an Iberian federation. It clearly stated that defense, foreign affairs, tariffs and customs, and relations between Church and state were to be controlled exclusively by the Madrid government. However, it also stated that the public power in Catalonia emanated from the people, pre-sumably the Catalan people, though no adjective was em-ployed. It made Catalan the official language of the state, and it demanded full control of the schools and the Uni-versity of Barcelona. In the plebiscite held August 3, of 208,000 eligible voters in the province of Barcelona, 175,000 voted in favor of the projected statute and 2,127 against. Similar overwhelming majorities favored the Statute in the three other Catalan provinces: Gerona, Lérida, and Tar-ragona.[14]

In the Cortes, strong unitary republicans, like the con-servative Melquiades Alvarez and the liberal law professor Felipe Sánchez Román, opposed the entire project as opening the way to an unworkable federal regime. The Castilian intellectuals Unamuno and Ortega y Gasset were most con-cerned about the school and language clauses, though Ortega y Gasset eventually voted for the statute as revised by the Cortes. Angel Ossorio y Gallardo, the self-styled "monárquico sin rey" of the dictatorship, and one of the principal architects of the new constitution, favored Catalan autonomy on grounds of the strong local sentiment and the advanced cultural pat-tern of Catalonia. Dr. Marañon and Miguel Maura recog-nized the dangers of the project as originally submitted, but

[14] *El Sol,* Aug. 4 and 7, 1931, gives the detailed electoral returns.

CAMBIOS, por Cañavete

COLONEL MACIÀ IN THE ROLE OF QUEEN ISABELLA
Monument to be erected by popular subscription to replace that
of Isabel la Católica as soon as the autonomy statute is approved
(Colonel Macià, with the poet Ventura Gassol in the foreground).
Gracia y Justicia, 14 May, 1932

insisted also that if the Cortes were to refuse autonomy to Catalonia, the most economically advanced region of Spain would inevitably be disaffected from the Republic.

Manuel Azaña staked the life of his government, and his personal prestige, on the passage of the statute. He rejected the federal formula, and any such reasoning as would compare the Catalans to the oppressed nationalities of central Europe. Catalonia was geographically, economically, and historically an integral part of Spain. The peculiar problem for Azaña, as an intelligent Spanish nationalist, was to build the unity of Spain around its less populous, less advanced geographical center. The autonomy statute was a calculated gamble in the construction of a Spain united by mutual interests rather than by military force. General Primo de Rivera had attempted to solve the Catalan problem by abolishing the Mancomunidad and prohibiting the use of the language. Azaña would try to solve it by granting a large measure of linguistic and administrative autonomy to the most advanced region in Spain, in the hope also that a reconciled Catalonia would exercise a healthy influence in the economy and the civil service of Spain as a whole.[15]

The elaboration of the statute was interrupted by the first military revolt against the Republic. General Sanjurjo had been deeply offended when the government had transferred him from the Civil Guard to the much less important Carabineros (frontier police). In several public statements he had affirmed his loyalty to the Republic while condemning extremes of Right and Left and warning against any tampering with the organization of the Civil Guard. He was a hearty, likeable, sentimental man, but not one of great discretion or clear ideas. In the summer of 1932 he permitted a number of personal friends and prominent monarchists to convince him that the country was on the verge of anarchy and that the people would rise to his standard the moment he unfurled it.

[15] *Diario* of the Cortes for June–Sept., 1932. The course of the debate is excellently summarized in the *Bulletin of Spanish Studies,* Oct., 1932 and Jan., 1933. The editor, Professor E. Allison Peers of the University of Liverpool, was particularly concerned with Catalan politics and culture.

Sanjurjo came from the north, and his father had been a captain in the Carlist army. Among those who urged him to lead a pronunciamiento were the Carlist chiefs Fal Conde and the Conde de Rodezno. Among his military collaborators were a number of antirepublican officers who were also to play prominent roles in the rising of July, 1936: Generals González Carrasco and Ponte; Colonels Varela, Martín Alonso, Valentín Galarza, and Heli Rolando de Tella. The conspirators had also counted upon General Francisco Franco to rise in Coruña, but he had decided a few days earlier that the pronunciamiento was unlikely to succeed.

The Sanjurjo revolt was not well planned. The government had ample advance warning, and there was no popular response. In Madrid the local garrison easily defeated the attempted seizure of the War Ministry. At his headquarters in Seville, General Sanjurjo acted indecisively. Either because his backers had told him that the whole country was with him, or because inwardly he doubted the popular response, he kept the troops in the barracks when, on the morning of August 10, he declared martial law. His manifesto announced that he was not rising against the Republic as such, but it referred to the present "illegitimate" Cortes, convoked by a "regimen of terror," and stated that the future form of state power would be determined by freely elected representatives. He emphasized the problems of unemployment, disorder, the destruction of the Army by ill-conceived reforms, and the dangers of exaggerated regionalism. Though edited by monarchists, the manifesto made no mention of the King, and referred only indirectly to the religious question.

The workers of Seville responded to the *estado de guerra* by an immediate general strike. Sanjurjo fled the city, but he was arrested in Huelva on his way to the Portuguese border and brought to Madrid to face court-martial. He was condemned to death for military rebellion, but the President, upon the immediate recommendation of the cabinet, commuted the sentence to life imprisonment. A small sector of the Cortes majority thought that the government should serve a severe warning to military conspirators by shooting Sanjurjo, but Alcalá-Zamora, Azaña, all the Socialists, and most of the

76

Republicans agreed that leniency would better serve the cause of the Republic. No lives had been lost in Seville, and only a few in Madrid; from lack of public support, the revolt had collapsed by itself. It would have been foolish under such circumstances to make a martyr of the man who had been the senior general of the Spanish Army on August 10. Sanjurjo went to jail, and some 145 of his monarchist supporters were deported to Villa Cisneros.[16]

The failure of the Sanjurjo rising redounded to the prestige of the Azaña government and made possible the quick passage of the long-debated autonomy statute. The final version eliminated all phrases implying sovereignty for the regional government. It rejected also the federal formula and the demand for complete control of the schools. It granted the equality of the Castilian and Catalan languages, shared the control of the schools, and granted specific control of municipal government, local courts and civil law, public works, public order, museums, and mines. Catalonia would have its own parliament, named the *Generalitat*, after the medieval parliament of the Kingdom of Aragon-Catalonia. It would also receive control of local finances, of the radio, of interior railroads, roads, and harbors.

At the urging of Azaña, the entire Republican-Socialist majority voted favorably, and most of Alejandro Lerroux's Radical deputies joined the majority. The statute was less than what the Catalan nationalists had hoped for, but when the Prime Minister traveled to Barcelona for the presentation ceremony, he received a tremendous ovation. In September 1932 Azaña stood at the high point of his political career. He was the head of a government which was building schools and remodeling the Army. He had successfully dealt with a military revolt, and he had piloted through the Cortes an autonomy statute which would bind Catalonia to the democratic Republic.

[16] J. Arrarás, *Historia, I,* chs. 18–20, for the factual account. My view of Sanjurjo's motives is based more upon conversations with officers who knew him and civilians connected with his trial. See also his interview with *El Sol,* Nov. 29, 1931, and with the *Revenue Hebdomadaire,* April 9, 1932.

ECONOMIC PROBLEMS DURING
THE AZAÑA ERA

THE proclamation of the Republic had in itself caused a grave financial crisis in Spain. Wealthy Spaniards had immediately begun to transfer their capital to foreign banks, and the international financial community reacted skeptically to the new regime. Both the first Finance Minister, Prieto, and his successor, the Catalan Republican Jaime Carner, made it a cardinal objective to stabilize the peseta as a prelude toward restoring the international credit of Spain. They followed conservative, deflationary methods, restricting imports, cutting the size of administrative staffs, and moving toward a balanced budget. By mid-1932 the peseta had achieved stability, and the deficits of the 1932 and 1933 budgets of Carner were considerably smaller than those of the dictatorship.

In meeting the long-standing issue of land reform, and in facing the many problems of the world depression, the government followed pragmatic, and often inconsistent policies, which were due in part to the novelty of the problems, in part to the indecisive character of the cabinet's economic thinking, and in part to the fact that the Cortes majority consisted of middle-class Republicans and Socialists.

Because of its long history, and because of the acuteness of peasant dissatisfaction, land reform was the most crucial of the economic questions. At the same time, it involved complex social and economic problems which varied from province to province, often from village to village. No serious revision could be accomplished without the expropriation of large estates, in other words, without attacking some of the most powerful vested interests in the country. The Socialist Minister of Labor, Largo Caballero, had moved quickly to establish mixed juries and to offer rent relief and accident insurance to sharecroppers and landless laborers. The provisional government also appointed a committee of technicians, under the chairmanship of the liberal law professor, Felipe Sánchez-Román, to work out a colonization scheme for landless families of Extremadura, Andalusia, Ciudad Real, and Toledo. In mid-July this commission presented to the Cortes a plan to settle between 60 and 75 thousand families in the first year of operations. But protests on behalf of existing property interests were so strong that the commission was dissolved and all action left to the future decision of the Cortes.[1]

Largo Caballero remained as Minister of Labor in the several Azaña cabinets. In November the Cortes passed a Law of Mixed Juries to deal with problems of wages and work contracts in each industry and branch of agriculture. The appropriate union and employer associations were to elect their own jurors, and a chairman was to be chosen by the unanimous consent of the jurors. If they could not agree on the choice of a chairman, as occurred frequently, the Minister of Labor would name him. Also, the Ministry would name the secretary of each jury and the provincial labor delegate (representing the central government)—a power that placed tremendous authority in the hands of the Minister of Labor. With Caballero in office, the institution of rural mixed juries worked simultaneously to reduce the power of the local caciques and to increase that of the Socialists. Precisely in those areas of greatest social tension, the chairman and the secretary were likely to be members of the Federation of Land Workers. Under the experienced, moderate trade-unionist, Lucio Martínez Gil, the Federation had numbered about 100,000 in early 1931, as a result of almost five years' organizational work. By the summer of 1932 it boasted 445,000 members, with most of the new recruits being radical, landless laborers who felt beholden to the Socialists for their first opportunity to participate in economic decisions. The new union now constituted numerically almost half the UGT, and it changed the tone of what had been—under Pablo Iglesias, and later under Largo

[1] Marcelino Domingo, *La experiencia del poder* (Madrid, 1934), pp. 218–35.

79

Caballero and Julián Besteiro—a disciplined and gradualist organization representing the aristocracy of Spanish labor.[2]

The Cortes also passed, at the urging of Largo Caballero, a Law of Municipal Boundaries, intended to protect local agricultural labor and to end the massive migration of landless families eking out a miserable existence through seasonal harvesting. The law required agricultural workers to register in the municipality where they lived and wished to work, and the lists became a function of the Casa del Pueblo. The effect of mixed jury decisions roughly doubled agricultural wages between the summers of 1931 and 1932, and the several decrees and laws of 1931 promised to rural labor the same forms of legal protection and social insurance as were enjoyed by industrial labor. For the first time in Spanish history, the most poverty-stricken class in the entire population felt itself protected by the government. However, these laws did not attack the fundamental question of land reform, and the Law of Municipal Boundaries turned out, to use an expressive Spanish adjective, to be *contraproducente*. Without greatly affecting the problem of underemployment, it did interfere measurably with the collection of the harvest, and deprived the migrant workers of their usual employment.[3]

Bitter conflicts over mixed jury decisions kept the deputies well aware of rural discontent, and land reform was the subject of frequent debate through the first eight months of 1932. There was no lack of technical data. The royal government

[2] *Anuario español de política social* (Madrid, 1934), pp. 112–14. The *Anuario* supplies not only the annual figures on the size of the Federation of Land Workers, but also the texts of the important agrarian, labor, and social security laws of both the Monarchy and the Republic. Gerald Brenan, *The Spanish Labyrinth*, p. 273 and *passim* discusses the expansion of the UGT. See also Jules Moch and Germaine Picard-Moch, *L'Espagne républicaine* (Paris, 1933), pp. 228–30, 281ff. for Socialist Party views of the rural organization and agrarian reform question. The authors visited Spain in the summer of 1932 and as French Socialists enjoyed the confidence of their Spanish colleagues.

[3] *El Sol,* July 9, 1933.

had made a careful census of rural property in the first decade of the century, with both tax purposes and land reform in mind. Irrigation plans dating from 1902, and greatly expanded during the 1920's by Spain's leading irrigation engineer, Manuel Lorenzo Pardo, provided detailed information on types of soil, gradients, and potentially available water. The difficulties arose in the interpretation of the data, and from differing ideas of what was socially desirable. The many different views may be placed in three general categories.

The Agrarians, often supported by the deputies of the Lliga Catalana, argued that most of the available land was too dry and not sufficiently fertile for agricultural use. By available, they meant land which was not currently being profitably farmed, and if on the map they pointed to certain portions of Extremadura and New Castile, the soil involved was indeed mediocre. As for the question of water, no one doubted the integrity of Lorenzo Pardo, but dams and canals were very expensive to build, and the problem of the extreme irregularity of rainfall would not be resolved, even if it were mitigated, by hydraulic development. In addition, it was doubtful whether the half-million landless families of southern Spain necessarily wanted to become landowning peasants, and if they did, they could only be successful farmers after receiving heavy subsidies for equipment and the technical education necessary to use that equipment.

A second group of deputies, mainly the Radicals and Radical Socialists, were anxious to create a class of peasant proprietors in the areas dominated by the latifundia. Their arguments were more social than economic. The small landowning farmers of France were the backbone of prosperity and social stability in the French Republic. As defenders of property rights, these Republican deputies were opposed to confiscation of the great estates; but they were also loath to face the tremendous taxes that would be required to buy out the great landlords in favor of their tenants and landless laborers. On the other hand, while recognizing the initial expense of the reform, they argued that the small farmer—with a personal incentive he had previously lacked—

81

would cultivate the land far more intensively than in the past, thereby making it possible over a few decades to pay a fair price for the expropriated estates.

A third group, comprising most, but by no means all, of the Socialists, believed in collective solutions. They argued that machines, fertilizers, and technical services of all sorts could be more efficiently used by groups of peasants than by individual small holders; and also that the initial investment per family would be much smaller if technical services were pooled. There were many existing, successful precedents in Levantine and Pyrennean Spain for the collective management of water rights and the common use of tools and storage facilities.[4]

All these views could be buttressed with technical data and made sense in particular areas. But since each group inevitably chose their data with a political bias, deputies of different political and social views could not accept the truth in the mouths of their opponents. The Agrarians, who emphasized insufficient fertility and absence of water, were clearly the representatives of the large landlords. The proponents of the small family farm were the middle-class Republicans, and the proponents of collective solutions were Socialists.[5]

The debate took place against a background of rising agitation in the countryside. Due to improved wages and excellent weather conditions, Andalusia in 1932 anticipated the best early grain harvest in many years. As the harvest time approached, the workers threatened to leave the grain standing in the fields unless new wage demands were granted.

[4] Brenan, *The Spanish Labyrinth,* pp. 336–40, and J. Langdon-Davies, *Behind the Spanish Barricades* (London, 1936), pp. 66–8, 78–80 discuss several traditional Spanish collectives. The monumental pioneer work on the subject is Joaquín Costa, *Colectivismo agrario en España* (Madrid, 1898).

[5] The most complete and objective study, covering geographical and social conditions, and summarizing past reform plans, is Pascual Carrión, *Los latifundios en España* (Madrid, 1932). It was the source of data for many deputies of widely differing viewpoints.

Justifying his action on the grounds of national emergency, the Minister of the Interior, Casares Quiroga, established in Seville a special technical jury and ordered the employer and labor representatives to appear before that jury forthwith. All the employer and most of the labor groups responded, with the anarcho-syndicalist unions abstaining. The special jury established wages and working conditions for the spring harvest; the strike threat was broken and the harvest saved.[6]

But uncertainty concerning the future affected the whole pattern of Spanish agriculture. As early as 1931, many large landlords had left their estates uncultivated. A few of them feared immediate revolutionary confiscations, to be accompanied by the lynching of the rich. The cooler-headed ones considered simply that it would be well to await developments and perhaps discipline the workers by a salutary increase in unemployment. Some, anticipating that a new period was opening in which there would probably be many readjustments, preferred to sell their land and put the money in foreign banks. Thus cultivation declined and much land went on sale, both developments contributing to the uneasiness of the rural population.

In the summer of 1932 an increasing number of *arrendatarios* deserted the countryside. They were an intermediate, and very important, class of farmers who were neither landlords nor proletarians. Technically they might be called sharecroppers, but this term in English suggests a poorer class of farmer than the Spanish arrendatarios of the western and southern provinces. They were commercial farmers employing wage laborers and paying rents, partly in money and partly in kind, to the landlords. Many arrendatarios simply found that the wages which the mixed juries required them to pay made their farms unprofitable, even when allowance was made for the degree of rent relief they had received. Psychologically they identified themselves far more with the owner class than with the rural proletariat. Between questions of technical feasibility, the increasing social conflicts, the decline of cultivation, the drop in land values, and the danger of attacking vested interests, the whole project of land re-

[6] *El Sol,* June 14, 1936.

form appeared to be stymied in the summer of 1932. Then the Sanjurjo rebellion renewed the Jacobin and Socialist revolutionary impulses within the Cortes and provided a justification for the confiscation of the latifundia belonging to the Grandees of Spain, the Grandees as a class being considered morally implicated in the unsuccessful pronunciamiento. Even at this moment of revolutionary fervor, however, the government stated that confiscation would only proceed as justified by social utility under Article 44 of the Constitution. The determination of social utility in individual cases would still take a long time.

The Agrarian Law as passed in September 1932, authorized the expropriation of millions of acres belonging to the nobility and provided in theory for both collective and individual exploitation of the land. That it was excessively legal in formulation, however, may be well illustrated by reference to a single provision. According to Article 5, paragraph 12, estates exploited for a fixed rent were subject to expropriation. Exception was made, however, for those rented in the names of minors, and for properties held as portions of unappraised dowries. Also, if the owner were not exploiting the land directly out of respect for a prior contract and could show that he intended in the future to cultivate the land directly, such an estate would not be subject to expropriation.

In addition to exceptions of this kind, the law provided for several stages of appraisal to determine a fair price for land that was subject to expropriation. Anticipating considerable litigation, Article 9 provided a means of temporary occupation of the land during the transaction of legal formalities. The settlers in such case were to pay a rent of 4 per cent of the assessed value of the land, and their occupancy would cease after 9 years in case the land finally was not expropriated. Imagine the position of the semiliterate, poverty-stricken peasant in the face of such a law, awaiting the action of local, provincial, and national courts, paying rent and lawyer's fees for a maximum of nine years without being certain whether or not he would finally acquire title. One would have thought the law written for an association of unemployed lawyers who wished to assure not only their own, but their sons' futures, rather than a law written for the peasants of Spain.

The law satisfied no one. During the two years of its operation, until late 1934, only 12,260 families received land, according to the figures of the Institute of Agrarian Reform.[7] In the summer of 1933 both large estates and arrendatario holdings were being auctioned at perhaps 20 per cent of their 1930 value. In Extremadura the landless peasants burned harvests, villas, and the casinos of the rich in the rural towns. In Andalusia less violent forms of sabotage occurred. When some of the farms of the Duke of Medinaceli were to be distributed, local clerks placed the names of long-deceased peasants on the list of those to receive land. At the same time, anarchists tore up the explanatory leaflets of the Institute of Agrarian Reform and explained to journalists that if the government gave land to the peasants they would lose their revolutionary fervor.[8]

Meanwhile, in the Cortes the government tried in vain to pass a law for the benefit of the small arrendatarios. The project provided that they would have the right to buy land which they had rented for at least fifteen years. In the original version, they would capitalize the farm at 5 per cent, that is, pay 20 times the annual rental in order to acquire title. The owners claimed that this would be extremely unjust, that the traditional rentals were nothing like 5 per cent of the actual value of the farms. Another formula then proposed that the sale value be determined by a mixed jury, a method equally objectionable to the landlords. The mixed jury would naturally refer to the existing assessment for taxes, which had always been kept very low by the landlord interests under the Monarchy. The Azaña government fell in September, 1933, without having completed a law of arrendamientos.[9]

Aside from the matter of land reform, the government faced a number of serious economic problems, all of them aggravated by the world depression, all of them requiring experimental solutions in the context of the time. Three problems of particular gravity concerned the production and mar-

[7] *Agrarian Reform in Spain* (London, 1937), p. 29.
[8] *El Sol*, Aug. 30 and Sept. 20, 1933.
[9] *El Sol*, Sept. 1, 1933, for the text of the proposed law.

keting of wheat, coal, and citrus fruits. Cereals were grown in almost all regions, but their production was concentrated in Castile and Aragon, the heart of the Spanish *meseta*. As mentioned earlier, production costs were high, and, without tariff protection, Spanish wheat could never have competed with American or Argentine wheat in the home market. Grain farms were of all sizes and types: latifundia, medium sized rented farms, and small family farms. The population as a whole was traditionally conservative and Catholic, and the arrendatarios and small individual farmers identified their interests by and large with those of the landlords.

. In early 1932, it appeared that the autumn grain harvest in Castile would be small. The price of wheat was rising. The 1931 harvest had been reduced somewhat by the uncertainties attending the first year of the Republican regime. Wages had risen, and the anarchists could be expected to push further wage demands in the harvest season. From the moment that Marcelino Domingo became Minister of Agriculture, Commerce, and Industry in October 1931, the grain growers had been pressing him to raise the minimum market price, the *tasa,* from 46 to 49 pesetas per metric quintal. The Minister had each provincial agronomy office send him information on local production costs. Learning from this survey that such costs varied between 33 and 42 pesetas, he decided that a *tasa* of 46 was sufficient.

In March the newspapers began to talk of a wheat shortage and of the possible need to resort to imports. Wheat had been imported frequently in the past, but since the peseta had declined on the foreign exchange market, and since the Republic was pledged to a policy of balancing the budget, it would be awkward politically to have to import grain in 1932. Marcelino Domingo then appealed, through the newspapers and over the radio, for a voluntary estimate by the wheat growers of their anticipated harvest. The reports sent in indicated a shortage. At the same time, the price continued to rise, and the government received anguished telegrams from civil governors pleading for an immediate importation to avoid further increases in the cost of bread.

In these circumstances, and allowing for a measure of

exaggeration in the telegrams, the Minister decreed the import of some 250,000 tons of wheat during late April and May. The price of wheat reached its high point in June, at which time the arrival of the foreign grain brought on to the market about 250,000 tons of Spanish wheat which had not figured in the survey reports. Then, as luck would have it, the weather was fine, there were few strikes, and the harvest was the largest in several decades. Through the autumn the price of wheat dropped steadily, and a storm broke over the Minister's head. The very same deputies and governors who had appealed for imports in March now accused him of ruining the wheat growers of Spain. The Cortes wanted to know why the harvest had been so poorly estimated. The Left accused the big grain dealers of hiding their reserves so as to speculate on a price rise and the Right laughed at a former newspaper man and Freemason who was of course incapable of finding out the true situation in the grain country.

Attention was also focused on the fact that the imports were being paid for at higher than world market prices. On this point the Minister, in consultation with the treasury, had had to make a difficult choice. If he paid cash for the wheat, the peseta, which had reached its low point in March, 1932, might fall still further, whereas in April and May it was beginning to show signs of recovery. If he paid in installments, so as not to upset the foreign exchange situation, he would have to pay interest. The two ministries decided jointly that it would be preferable to pay the interest, thereby opening themselves later to the charge of paying higher than world prices for the imported wheat.[10]

Difficulties of another sort arose in connection with the coal mining industry. Coal was a declining industry all over the world, due to the exhaustion of the best grades and to the competition offered by new sources of energy: oil, gas, and electricity. The Asturian miners, most of whom were members of the UGT, were among the most militant of Spanish workers. These men worked in the pits only four days a week in 1932, and coal was accumulating at the mine heads. The

[10] M. Domingo, *La experiencia del poder*, pp. 237–52. *El Sol*, Jan. 30, June 12, July 7, 1932, and Feb. 18, 1933.

Spanish ore was qualitatively too poor for economical use in the steel industry and for railroad locomotives, the two uses accounting for 75 per cent of Spanish coal consumption. The better grade of coal was being imported from England, and these imports in turn aided the sale of a large percentage of Spanish citrus fruits in the United Kingdom.

In October 1932 some 350,000 tons of unsold ore had accumulated at the pit heads. The government was a Republican-Socialist coalition, and the Minister of Industry was a Republican whose party depended largely on working-class votes. The UGT miners, led by Ramón González Peña, demanded that the government buy the surplus coal, and that Spanish railways and ships use Spanish coal. They also threatened a mine strike, to be combined if necessary with a sympathy strike by the stevedores of the northern coastal ports. In the course of painful negotiations, punctuated by a four-day surprise strike, the government contracted to buy 100,000 tons of Asturian coal immediately. The coal would be used by the Ministries of War, Navy, and Public Works; the government would also import tar so as to manufacture briquets which would make the Asturian coal usable in Spanish locomotives. On this occasion the press and the opposition criticized the "coddling" of the Socialists, the prospect of new imports, and the fact that the ministries involved had no real use for any such amounts of coal as they would be buying now and in the future.[11]

The coal problem was only incidentally related to that of citrus exports, but politically the two were bound to affect each other. Citrus fruits were one of the main commercial interests of eastern Spain, particularly in the region around Valencia. Regional feeling was strong here. It did not take the nationalist form that it took in the Basque country and Catalonia; but as in those areas, there was in Valencia a local language, the memory of medieval independence, a resentment against the military-centralizing spirit of Castile, and a

[11] Both technical and social aspects of the coal question are covered in articles in *El Sol,* Oct. 22, Nov. 15 and 19, 1932. On the problem of coal quality, see Manuel Fuentes Irurozqui, *Síntesis de la economía española* (Madrid, 1946), p. 38.

feeling of superiority based upon a wealthy agricultural economy and a fairer distribution of income than in Castile and Andalusia. In the nineteenth century the regional, anti-Castilian feeling had taken the form of Carlism. In recent decades the farmers had in large numbers joined the republican party of the famous novelist and newspaperman Blasco Ibañez. As of 1932, the majority of the Valencian farmers belonged to a conservative regional party, led by Luis Lucía, and the minority, to the Radical Socialist party of Marcelino Domingo.

During the 1920's the world market for citrus fruits was growing, and Valencian farmers had greatly expanded their cultivation. The export trade was controlled by the fleet owners rather than by the farmers, though of course many of the wealthier growers were also part owners of the fleet. The crop was sold to the shippers while still on the tree, at prices set by the shippers. Most of it went to northern Europe and England, and the citrus farmers paid both the outbound and the return voyages, even in cases where the ships returned with a part cargo from German or British ports. The depression coincided with the coming of the Republic, and the worst years were 1932 and 1933. All countries at that time reacted to the contraction of foreign markets by policies of economic nationalism. Even England abandoned free trade, and, in particular, the Ottawa Imperial agreements of 1932 pledged England to give the preference in her purchases to her dominions and colonies. In these circumstances Palestine, then a British Mandate under the League of Nations, substituted largely for Spain in the British orange market.

Although the principal reason for the loss of the English market was perfectly clear, the political picture was complicated by the coincidence of the Asturian coal crisis with the citrus problem. When the miners demanded that Asturian coal be bought in preference to British coal, the Valencian Chambers of Commerce immediately opposed the demand, fearing that the British might retaliate by cutting still further their imports of Spanish fruit. The government recognized the gravity of the citrus export question at the same time that it denied any cause-and-effect relation between it and the coal problem. Foreign buyers had indicated the uneven quality of Spanish fruit. In the late 1920's quality had been sacrificed to quantity, and indeed, the first reaction of the growers to falling prices in 1931 had been to expand their cultivation still further. Exporters had also falsified brand names in an attempt to have less known companies benefit from the reputation of established ones.

The Minister of Agriculture made two major proposals: a technical committee should separate the different grades of fruit so as to avoid abuses of quality, and the government should build a fleet which would break the shipping monopoly and end the dependence of the small growers on the prices offered by the large private interests. Neither of these proposals, made in the spring of 1933, went into effect, but they added substantially to the political difficulties of the government. The large growers and the shippers resented the publicity given to their several shortcomings. The small growers received no immediate aid. The government was once again criticized for readiness to unbalance the budget, and for the socialistic aspect of the proposal to build a national freighter fleet.[12]

Throughout the Republican era, the Basque steel industry suffered a severe depression, partly due to world conditions and partly to government policies. The industry had expanded and had enjoyed good prices and tariff protection during the 1920's. Armaments for the Moroccan War had long been an important source of income, and when that war ended, Primo undertook a modernization and expansion of the railway network which continued to offer a large market for Basque steel. The Republic, however, reversed the dictator's railroad policy. Largely on the advice of Indalecio Prieto, the government decided to expand road construction, and thus brought railroad construction to a virtual halt. The change was motivated mainly by Prieto's conviction that trucks were going to be the more efficient and economical transport of the future, but the new policy also had important political implications. Many Basque industrialists tended to favor the Republic be-

[12] *El Sol,* Oct. 21, 1932, April 11 and 20, 1933.

cause of the republican promise of autonomy statutes. Prieto himself, though born in Oviedo, had lived almost all his life in Bilbao, where he owned the influential newspaper *El Liberal,* and he counted on the cooperation of the Basque and Catalan middle class to develop the economy of republican Spain. Needless to say, the Basque industrialists blamed the Republic for the steel depression, when their market for railroad equipment was drastically cut. Their statute hopes kept them in the republican camp, but without great enthusiasm.

The Republic also had trouble with the railroad workers, traditionally organized by the UGT but influenced now by the CNT. With the coming of the Republic, they expected large raises as well as an eight-hour day, and in the summer of 1931 they were ready to strike. Prieto, as Finance Minister of the provisional government, risked his prestige with the workers by refusing the wage demands. Using specific figures, he showed how the railroads had been operating at a deficit for years, how the granting of the eight-hour day in itself would increase costs, and how it would be impossible simultaneously to finance a general wage increase even if the government were to authorize fare increases, a move which in itself would hit the consumer. The workers settled for the eight-hour day and for various improvements in working conditions, but they also began from that time on to consider Prieto as having "sold out" to the capitalists.[13]

In the fall of 1931 Prieto moved from Finance to Public Works, where he directed for two years the major constructive economic efforts of the Republic. In política hidráulica he carried forward the work of the dictatorship. Primo de Rivera had called upon Manuel Lorenzo Pardo to direct a national program of dam building and irrigation. Between 1926 and 1930 a number of dams were completed along the Ebro River, and detailed plans made for the Levant and the valley of the Guadalquiver. Prieto reappointed Lorenzo Pardo, moved ahead with the existing Ebro projects, built two dams on the

[13] *El Sol,* Jan. 7 and 10, 1934, carried articles reviewing the tangled railroad problem from the early 1920's on. An editorial of June 9, 1936 recalled Prieto's forthright handling of the workers' demands in the summer of 1931.

Guadalquivir, and inaugurated a new project in Extremadura (the *Obras de Cíjara*), which was interrupted by the Civil War and completed in 1957 under the new name of *Plan de Badajoz*. Prieto believed irrigation would be a more effective answer to the land problem of Spain than the expropriation of the existing estates, because it could be done without additional social conflict and because much of the land tied up in great estates was too dry to be successfully farmed by small holders. Irrigation would increase greatly the cultivable surface of Spain and would yield subsidiary benefits in the form of electric power and reforestation. In the Ebro valley, where the main dams and canals had been built in the late twenties, Prieto concentrated on the building of power plants. Wherever ground was being broken or a dam completed, Prieto harangued the local population on the importance of water, trees, and electricity. In the summer of 1932 he accompanied the President of the Republic on a tour of the Guadalquivir works—D. Niceto Alcalá-Zamora representing the dignity of the social-minded Republic, and his chubby minister preaching the doctrines of Joaquín Costa and singing the praises of the Republic's corps of irrigation engineers.[14]

Second only to the importance of hydraulic works were railroad and road projects. Here Prieto carried forward certain plans of the dictatorship and radically altered others. Primo de Rivera had begun the Guadarrama tunnel which would cut considerably the rail distance between Madrid and Irún. Prieto completed this project in 1933. But where Primo had begun extending rail mileage in various provinces, Prieto preferred to concentrate on the electrification of existing lines and

[14] My information on hydraulic works accomplished comes principally from the private papers of the late Manuel Lorenzo Pardo, in whose office I had several valuable conversations. Sr. Lorenzo Pardo's testimony to the effectiveness of Prieto's administration was all the more impressive as he was strongly conservative in political outlook, and an ardent admirer of the Portuguese dictator Salazar. Concerning the *Obras de Cíjara*, later renamed *Plan de Badajoz*, see the articles by Manuel Díaz Marta in *El Socialista* (Toulouse), March 21 and August 29, 1957. Sr. Díaz Marta was one of the original team of hydraulic engineers on the project.

the creation of underground central terminals in Madrid and Barcelona. Much of the electrification of the Madrid-Segovia stretch dates from this period. In Barcelona, the central government, the Generalitat, and the municipality cooperated to finance the construction of the underground terminal in the Plaza de Catalunya. In Madrid the government began the still-uncompleted central terminal under the capital's main thoroughfare, the Castellana.

As in the case of school construction, there was an increasing chorus of criticism from a budget-conscious Cortes and press. Primo had spent an average of 50 to 60 million pesetas a year on hydraulic works. The 1932 budget called for 80 million, and the 1933 budget for 175 million. On top of this came the construction of secondary roads, the lengthening of the Castellana, the construction of a new group of government ministry buildings, and an underground railway terminus. Opponents claimed that the projects were tailored to take care of unemployed Socialist workers, that the ministries and the terminus were unnecessary, that wages on the projects were too high. Government supporters replied that the expansion of Madrid, and the improvement of its transport network were, like irrigation works, investments in the economic future of all Spain.[15]

In 1933 the cabinet was painfully conscious of the contradiction between a budget-balancing effort and large, publicly financed construction projects. Jaime Carner had resigned as Finance Minister (stricken by the throat cancer of which he was to die a year later). He was succeeded by another Catalan, Viñuelas, who in cooperation with Prieto proposed a new method of financing hydraulic works. Speaking to a meeting of the directors of Spain's principal savings banks, they suggested that the banks undertake together the formation of an autonomous company to finance dam construction. The banks in turn would rent the irrigated land and sell the electric

[15] In late March, 1935, a full-dress Cortes debate over the Azaña regime produced high praise of Prieto's public works program by his two principal successors in the Ministry, José María Cid of the CEDA and Rafael Guerra del Río of the Radical Party. See *Política,* March 28 and April 11, 1935.

power produced as a result of their investment. The government would supervise the rents and electric rates in the public interest. This proposal, so similar to the actual investment pattern of many large American insurance companies, was much too bold for the assembled bankers. In any event, the Azaña government fell two months later, and there was no further opportunity to pursue the idea.[16]

There are several important elements common to the various economic problems discussed above. For each of the years from 1932 to 1935, the total of Spain's foreign trade averaged only about 30 per cent of its 1928 value. The areas most dependent upon international commerce were simultaneously making the most articulate demands on the new regime: the Basque country, with its strong autonomy movement; and Andalusia, with its newly organized rural proletariat. Under the new government, Spain enjoyed an unprecedented degree of freedom of the press, and problems were therefore well ventilated in the newspapers. The issues had important political implications which were thoroughly exploited in the Cortes. It was fine politics in conservative Catholic Castile to be able to blame the wheat problem on a Catalan Republican. With the Socialist Party in the government, Agrarians and Radicals suddenly became the champions of oppressed UGT miners and railroad workers. The true cause of the citrus export crisis might be the world depression and the Ottawa agreements, but it was fine politics to blame everything on a Republican minister who could be accused, however inaccurately, of coddling the miners at the expense of Valencian business interests. The fall of the peseta would have been likely in similar economic circumstances under any new government, but it was good politics to claim that a revolutionary government of intellectuals, Krausists, Masons, and Socialists was ruining the Spanish economy through its ineptitude.

If the observer were to take the excitement and publicity at face value, he would give a greatly exaggerated importance to these criticisms. In 1931 no government had yet employed Keynesian pump-priming methods. No governments except those of fascist Italy and communist Russia had yet employed

[16] Prieto in *El Socialista*, May 27, 1954.

the police power of the state to control currency. Beginning in the late 1930's—but more especially since the Second World War—governments of all kinds have established currency, price, export and import, and investment controls of a sort that at the time of the Spanish Republic automatically raised the cry "communism." Prieto's public works program was very similar in content to that of the American New Deal launched two years later; it also resembled many programs labeled "economic development" in the mid-twentieth century. But deficit financing and public investment for the sake of future public welfare were not easily accepted doctrines in the Europe of 1931. It is also true that no matter what Prieto and Carner and Domingo might have done, they would have been attacked for their affiliations regardless of the policies pursued. In Spain during the 1940's and 1950's, problems of exactly the same sort arose in fully as grave a form, but with a censored press and a powerful police force, the issues were not aired in public. With wealthy nations subsidizing the governments of weaker allies, there are economic supports today which were never available to the Republic.

Actually, in many of the aspects most important for the ordinary citizen, the Spanish economy prospered despite the general world depression. In part, this prosperity resulted from its relative isolation; in part, it resulted from the policies adopted. During the years from 1931 to 1935, wages rose generally while the cost-of-living index remained stable. Food was among the cheapest items in the family budget, and per capita production of grains, vegetables, and fish was higher than at any time before or since. The textile industry, largest single employer of labor among Spanish industries, maintained its 1920–30 level of production and volume of sales. Electric industries, commercial fishing, and food processing all expanded. There was a continuous high level of activity in the building trades, due first to the school construction and public works programs, and then to a boom in housing. Contrary to the impression one might receive from the strong criticism of deficit financing, the budgetary deficits were smaller than during the years of the Primo de Rivera dictatorship. Government revenue rose as a result of new industrial and real estate taxes and increases in the alcohol, tobacco, and gasoline excises.[17]

At the worst moments of the depression there were about a half-million unemployed, proportionately one-fourth the extent of the unemployment suffered in the United States and Germany in 1932. The first years of the Republic did indeed witness a tremendous rise in strikes. For 1933 the total number of workdays lost had increased threefold by comparison with 1931 and tenfold by comparison with 1928. It is true also that 1933, the maximum year for strike activity, was the year of deepest depression for the Spanish economy taken as a whole.[18] But a close analysis of the figures, industry by industry and province by province, shows, nevertheless, that political motives played a far larger role than did economic demands. For one thing, the percentage of days lost in economically motivated strikes dropped steadily for the period 1930 to 1933, during which years the total strike time rose steeply. For another, wide variations in local behavior did not correspond to any discernible economic pattern. Thus agricultural strikes in the province of Málaga cost 81,600 workdays in 1932 and

[17] My information concerning favorable aspects of the economic picture is drawn from the statistical data on wages, prices, and production in Fuentes Irurozqui, *Síntesis de la economía española*, which information I then discussed with several economists now working for Madrid banks. Regarding budgetary deficits of the dictatorship and of the Republic, the Cortes on May 18, 1934, heard a detailed debate on the question between José Calvo Sotelo, Finance Minister under Primo de Rivera, and Indalecio Prieto, defending the record of the Azaña period. In this debate the Radicals, the Mauristas, and the *Lliga Catalana* all supported Prieto's analysis, upon which my conclusion is based.

[18] The financial pages of *La Vanguardia* of Barcelona, and most statistical sources, support the general statement that 1933 was the worst year of the depression. However, a highly competent analysis by Antonio de Miguel, in *Economía Española*, Oct., 1933, pp. 81–8, argues that mining industries have improved their condition over 1932 and that the rate of new investment is rising. The unreliability of Spanish statistics and the great variety of local conditions make it impossible to state with certainty just how severe the depression was in Spain.

only 13,000 in 1933; whereas Jaén lost a mere 27,000 work-days in 1932 as against 485,000 in 1933. The metallurgical in-dustries of Vizcaya lost 162,839 workdays in 1930; 4,149 in 1931; and 91,942 in 1932. No pattern of prices, wages, or total sales remotely corresponded to the strike pattern. The year 1932 was the maximum strike year for construction industries in Valencia. For Barcelona 1933 was the maximum year, with construction strike losses four times greater than those of Madrid in the same period.[19]

All the available evidence tends to show that the social agitation of the Republican era was more political than economic in motivation. In the years of Azaña's ministry, the young Republic failed to solve the land question, but in regard to the various economic problems resulting from the world depression, the record of the Spanish government can be com-pared very favorably with that of many a more stable and experienced democratic state.[20]

---

[19] Casimir Martí, Jordi Nadal, and Jaume Vicens Vives, "El moviment obrer a Espanya de 1929 a 1936 en relació amb la crisi econòmica," *Serra D'Or*, Feb., 1961. In this excellent three-man study the analysis of strikes is by Father Martí, who kindly allowed me also to see unpublished materials of his own, from which I have drawn the statistical data given immediately above. The portion prepared by the late Jaume Vicens reinforces my conclusion arrived at earlier that the social conflicts of the Republican era were more political and *passional* than economic in origin.

[20] The special difficulties of land reform become very clear from a reading of the excellent doctoral thesis of Professor Edward Malefakis of Columbia University. The Republic could find no arable state or municipal lands to distribute. There were no Church estates, such as had been available in the revolutionary France of 1789. Nor were there foreign-owned estates to confiscate, as in Rumania in 1918 and Algeria in 1963. Confiscation of 97 estates would have been insufficient, since the nobility owned only 10–12% of the land. Thus any major land reform in Spain would in-evitably have had to strike at the interests of powerful *middle-class* absentee landlords, a class which the Republican government could not afford to alienate.

97

THE DEFEAT OF THE LEFT

IN THE autumn of 1932 the Azaña government enjoyed its maximum prestige. The Prime Minister had molded a dependable majority out of the several republican fractions and the Socialist Party. The government had contained the anarchist opposition and had suppressed, without difficulty, the military-monarchist rising in August. The UGT was supporting the government despite the impatience of thousands of its most militant affiliates and the growing, mass influence of the anarchist-dominated CNT. The Republic had initiated Army reform, public school construction, and a greatly expanded public works program. It had finally passed an agrarian reform law and granted a statute of autonomy to Catalonia.

Throughout the year, however, the Republic had been subjected to a crossfire of violent opposition from both the Right and the Left. On January 10, following on the heels of the Castilblanco and Arnedo affairs, Traditionalist and Socialist youth clashed in Bilbao. And at a Carlist meeting—where shouts of "Gora Euzkadi" (the Basque nationalist slogan) competed with shouts of "Viva España"—Socialist youth paraded outside to the tune of the *Internationale*. As the Carlists emerged from their meeting, they fired shots into the crowd, killing three persons and wounding several, including a Civil Guard. Upon investigation, the Minister of the Interior closed the Convento de Las Madres Reparadoras, because some of the shots were proven to have come from within that building, and fined the Colegio del Sagrado Corazón (an aristocratic girls' school) after finding rifles and cartridges there.[1]

During the week of January 20, a minor anarchist uprising in the suburbs of Barcelona cost several lives. The revolution-

[1] *El Sol,* Jan. 10, 21, and 22, 1932.

aries derailed trains at Manresa and Berga, troops occupied Barcelona, and the government closed the headquarters of the Communist Party and the anarchists in the city. The Cortes gave the Minister of the Interior a vote of confidence covering both the Bilbao and Barcelona incidents; a call for a general strike in Catalonia failed, and the revolutionaries avoided a direct clash with the troops.[2]

In mid-April in Pamplona, capital of Carlist Navarre, a street-corner debate between Socialist and Traditionalist youth degenerated into a general brawl, with one of each band killed and eight others wounded by gunfire. During the same month in Madrid, one Manuel Lahoz was arrested in a bar with a pistol and 1,000 pesetas on his person. Judge Luis Amado held him in jail for 72 hours, then released him provisionally without bail after preferring a charge of illegal possession of arms. Casares Quiroga, invoking the Law for the Defense of the Republic, slapped a two-month suspension on the judge for negligence in not requiring bail for an identifiable gunman. The colegio de abogados (the lawyers' guild) saw the matter differently and formally protested the Minister's interference with the independence of the judiciary.[3]

The sporadic violence did not constitute a threat to the stability of the government, but the Republican leaders, men of humane and pacific temperament, were anxious to adopt gentler methods for the maintenance of public order than those used by the Civil Guard. They therefore created a new urban security force, the *Guardia de Asalto,* candidates for which were to be chosen for their athletic prowess and their Republican loyalty. In principle, they were not armed, and they were trained to break up demonstrations without shedding blood, but they were as nervous as other Spanish police, particularly in newly autonomous Catalonia. Thus on November 2, 1932, when the medical students of Barcelona held an impromptu farewell demonstration for some of their professors about to depart to a conference in France, the Assault Guards

[2] F. G. Bruguera, *Histoire contemporaine de l'Espagne* (Paris, 1953), pp. 400–401. See also the interview of Casares Quiroga with The *New York Times,* Jan. 18, 1932.

[3] J. Arrarás, *Historia,* I, 333–34.

beat them up, on the assumption that they had happened upon an illegal nationalist parade.[4]

On November 30 Prieto, speaking in the Cortes about various problems of the public-works budget, charged that numerous anarchists were on the payroll of the Huelva port authority, receiving salaries for no visible function. Their names had been inscribed by higher officials who were prominent members of conservative parties. Prieto emphasized the element of reactionary-anarchist cooperation. He might, just as truthfully, have recognized the need felt by many employers and officials for simple physical protection, especially in Barcelona, Saragossa, and the Andalusian cities where the anarchist pistoleros were strongest. Those pistoleros who were arrested in late 1932 carried the most up-to-date machine pistols and often had as much as 2,000 pesetas on their person (about $200 at the exchange rates of the time, or about six months' wages in a unionized factory). The money came from union dues, shakedowns of small shopkeepers, and subsidies of the *agent-provocateur* type. Many of these gunmen wandered from city to city, exploiting labor tension, now in Barcelona, now in Seville. They were often well known to the police but rarely remained more than a few hours under arrest.[5] In fact, in the Amado case, many liberals felt that the government had made a scapegoat of one of the few judges who would hold a pistolero in jail for as long as 72 hours. In Huelva the authorities had perhaps hoped to reduce violence by placing some of their toughest customers on the public payroll. The practice is not unknown in other seaports.

Early in January 1933 the Ministry of the Interior alerted the national security forces to the imminent likelihood of an anarchist rising in the name of *comunismo libertario*, i.e., the complete collectivization of the economy and the abolition of central government. On January 8 several Aragonese and Andalusian villages burned their town halls and tore out the telephone wires. In the industrial suburbs of Barcelona there were serious clashes between police and workers. Newspaper

[4] *El Sol,* Nov. 3, 1932.

[5] Article in *El Sol,* Jan. 10, 1933, summarizing the arrests of late 1932.

reports listed 37 dead and 300 injured in the course of three days, after which order was restored.

In the following few weeks, increasingly shocking reports were published of the events in the southern Andalusian village of Casas Viejas, where the villagers had declared *comunismo libertario* and unsuccessfully besieged the barracks of the Civil Guards. The latter, reinforced by a group of Assault Guards, had then beset a group of five anarchists in the home of the leader, "Seisdedos" ("Six Fingers," a sobriquet frequently attached to alleged thieves). When the anarchists refused a surrender order, the soldiers had fired (killing all the defenders); they then burned the house, and according to later reports, deliberately left the partially burned corpses for the villagers to see as an example.[6] Liberal and Left papers, and the monarchist journal *ABC*, sent in reporters who vied with each other in supplying sensational details. In some of the later accounts, the Guards were supposed not only to have killed Seisdedos and his companions, but to have rounded up other villagers and forced them into the house to share the fate of the chiefs.

It was also discovered that fourteen prisoners had been shot in cold blood by a platoon of Assault Guards under one Captain Rojas. Then came the most sensational news: Captain Rojas told reporters that he had received orders to take "neither wounded nor prisoners," and that Prime Minister Azaña had used the crude phrase "Shoot them in the belly" (*tiros a la barriga*). Azaña immediately ordered a government investigation of the events while denying flatly that any such orders had been given or that he had used any such phrase. Meanwhile, he confided to his diary that deputies of three different parties were proposing a dictatorship as the only solution to continued anarchist risings, and that the friends as well as the enemies of the Republic were saying that things could not go on this way indefinitely.

In the Cortes debate the leading Radical deputy Diego Martínez Barrio characterized the Azaña regime as a govern-

[6] Ramon J. Sender, *Viaje a la aldea del crimen* (Madrid, 1934), tells the story in detail and quotes liberally from the depositions later made by the peasants to parliamentary investigators.

ment of "mud, blood, and tears." What shocked public opinion was the harsh treatment of obviously ignorant, miserable peasants. When Carlist and Socialist youth clashed, they were persons of political consciousness who knew what they were doing and who deliberately challenged each other, and the government. In such cases it was inevitable, if regrettable, that the government should respond with force. Likewise, majority opinion would back the government if it handled roughly the professional gunmen who exploited the anarchist unions. But the public conscience reacted strongly against the shooting of primitive, poverty-stricken peasants, and the worst crime in this instance had been committed by the new Republican Assault Guard.

The results of the parliamentary investigation were inconclusive. General Cabanellas of the Civil Guard, and other police officials, stated that there had been absolutely nothing extraordinary about the orders they had received. Their testimony implied either that Captain Rojas was a liar, or that the Madrid government orders had been "interpreted" in the course of transmission, so as to give the Captain the impression that he really was meant to shoot his prisoners. In early March the Radicals, led by Alejandro Lerroux, withdrew their motion of censure against the government, and a week later the official Cortes report concluded that "there exists no proof whatsoever which would permit the insinuation that the police acted in the repression according to orders given by members of the government." But public opinion nevertheless held the government morally responsible, and the events of Casas Viejas were to become the cornerstone of a "black legend" against the Republic.[7]

Even without a Casas Viejas tragedy to dramatize the political situation, there were various signs in early 1933 of a more conservative mood in the country. In late January the *Confederación Patronal Española,* an important businessmen's association, addressed an open letter to Azaña. They noted the "vertiginous rapidity" with which new social legislation had been passed and complained that mixed juries, through the

[7] See Appendix B for a detailed discussion of Captain Rojas' accusations.

vote of the chairman appointed by the Minister of Labor, practically always decided for the workers. At the same time, the workers, especially those of the CNT, felt no obligation to abide by an agreement for the calendar period thereof. They asked the government to compel the workers to abide by the jury agreements for the full term and demanded also that the chairmen and secretaries of the mixed juries be chosen through *oposiciones* rather than by ministerial appointment: in other words, that these posts be treated as technical, competitive nonpolitical civil service jobs.[8]

In late March the *Unión Económica,* representing a combination of businessmen and academic economists, complained to the government that its "socializing" tendencies had created an atmosphere of insecurity in industry. They pointed out that the coalition lists presented in the June 1931 election had not given the voters a choice between Republicans and Socialists, and they demanded a new election before the government proceed to any further measures of a socialist nature.[9] In July more than a hundred local businessmen's organizations joined the Madrid *Círculo de la Unión Mercantil e Industrial* in attacking the operation of the mixed juries in industry.[10]

The dissatisfaction of the business community was an important indication of rising opposition to the Azaña government. The Spanish middle class had always been largely apolitical, and their nonparticipation had been one of the great weaknesses of the First Republic and of Liberal governments during the Restoration. In general, they had welcomed the Second Republic, and the liberal minority among them were the financial supporters of Azaña's *Acción Republicana* and of the Radical Socialist Party. But most of those who rallied actively to the Republic were the friends of Lerroux rather than of Azaña, not so much on grounds of program as

[8] *El Sol,* Jan. 27, 1933.

[9] *Economía Española,* March, 1933, pp. 63–5.

[10] *El Sol,* July 19, 1933. From the internal evidence of the various newspaper reports, it is clear that the *Unión Económica* and other groups functioned as important pressure groups in Spanish politics. But none of the economic journals available to me provided information on their numbers, wealth, etc.

of personality. Azaña represented the Ateneo and the intellectuals, Lerroux the more earthy, "self-made," nonintellectual type of politician.

Another indication came with the municipal elections of April, 1933. The Constitution called for the renewal of municipal councilorships every two years, and these were the first elections in which republican candidates ran in the hundreds of villages which had been purely cacique-controlled in the elections of April 12, 1931. Of some 16,000 councilors chosen, 9,802 were committed republicans and 4,954 were avowed monarchists or far Right candidates whose attitude to the Republic was equivocal. The results then indicated a solid republican majority in the country, but the number of monarchist victories was a disagreeable surprise to the government. In addition, within the republican fold, the Radicals of Alejandro Lerroux advanced at the expense of the Socialists. Whereas in the election of June 1931 for the Constituent Cortes, Socialists had outnumbered Radicals in a proportion of roughly four to three, this ratio was reversed in the municipal election of 1933.

The opposition demanded Azaña's resignation, and the caustic-tongued Prime Minister replied by qualifying as *burgos podridos* ("rotten boroughs") the towns which had elected monarchists. The President, however, considered the municipal elections a swing to the Right and hoped that Azaña himself, having shown great skill in leading his majority, would slow the tempo of reform legislation while continuing as Prime Minister. The Cortes was again occupied at this time with the religious question. Article 26 of the Constitution was a statement of intentions which required "complementary laws" for its fulfillment. The first of these laws had been the dissolution of the Jesuits in January 1932. The government now pressed for a Law of Congregations which would fulfill the constitutional clauses forbidding the Orders to engage in commerce, industry, and teaching. Even more than in the earlier debates, education was the crux of the conflict.

In the past half-century, secondary schools had become one of the most important activities of the Orders, in terms both of their material prosperity and their sense of social mission.

In 1933 they were running 259 secondary schools served by 2,050 teachers, of whom 1,150 had university degrees. Their leading institutions of this type were the Exeters and Andovers of Spain—schools which cultivated good social tone, which were meeting-grounds for the sons and daughters of the wealthy, which provided "connections" in the professional and business worlds, and which provided a work discipline absent in the public schools. They also provided a certain number of scholarships, and although most of the students came from the moneyed class, the Church itself emphasized this charitable-educational function. Many a Spanish business-man, lawyer, engineer, and civil servant who never went to mass and didn't care if the secular clergy starved, was ambitious to place his children in a reputable Church secondary school.[11]

The terms of the problem were different from those in the case of primary education, in that the state was in no position immediately to substitute for the existing religious schools. There had been a pool of potential primary school teachers with the necessary degrees in education, but there was no such surplus of university-trained personnel. One of the first acts of the Azaña government in October 1931 (just after the battle over Article 26) had been to order the religious schools to remain open. At that time, what the government feared was a school strike by the Church, of the sort which had caused sporadic civil war in Mexico in the late 1920's. Also, in the two years of republican experience the government had had ample evidence at all levels of resistance to the total laicization of the school system.

The Cortes in the spring of 1933 received numerous petitions from parent groups urging the government not to close the religious schools. However, pressure on the Cortes in this matter seemed to reinforce its anticlerical sentiments, and a majority, which had been falling apart on economic legislation,

[11] Figures on the number of Church secondary schools and their faculties from Mendizábal, *Aux origines d'une tragédie,* p. 171. A most interesting discussion of the historic role of those schools appeared over the signature of Américo Castro in *El Sol,* Aug. 13, 1933.

reunited to pass the Law of Congregations in May by a vote of 278 to 50. The secondary schools were ordered closed by the first of October, and the primary schools by early 1934. As voting time approached, many bishops talked of excommunication for those voting the law. But the papal nuncio, Bishop Tedeschini, counseled patience. He was in close touch with the government and knew that Alcalá-Zamora eagerly desired a new Concordat, and that Azaña also favored such a solution.[12]

Generally speaking, two distinct lines of opinion had appeared within the Church since the proclamation of the Republic. The majority of bishops felt, and in private spoke, as did the exiled Cardinal Segura. Catholicism in Spain was for them consubstantial with the Monarchy. A republic was by definition the child of the impious French Revolution, surreptitiously imposed upon Catholic Spain by the Masons. In addition, all of them had owed their advancement to the favor of Alfonso XIII, and they regarded as ungrateful opportunists those churchmen who showed a readiness to accept the Republic. A minority of the bishops favored a temporizing policy. In their view the anticlerical laws resulted from momentary passions. As in France and Italy, these passions would cool, and new arrangements could then be made to defend the essential interests of the Church. These men could also acknowledge that the Church had failed in its social mission among the proletariat, and that a properly defined separation of Church and state might well benefit both parties. The leading exponents of this position were Angel Herrera, editor of *El Debate*, Cardinal Vidal y Barraquer of Tarragona, and the nuncio, Bishop Tedeschini.

Pope Pius XI was personally inclined to the moderate position. Unfortunately, during the intense lobbying over the appointment of a new Primate, he was forced to realize that the majority of Spanish prelates snickered at Angel Herrera, with his reasonings concerning the "lesser evil" and the "possible good"; that they regarded Cardinal Vidal as a Catalan nationalist with a scandalous taste for jazz; that

[12] The *New York Times*, June 11 and July 30, 1933, carried excellent articles by Frank L. Kluckhohn on the significance of the Law of Congregations debate and the Church reaction thereto.

Bishop Tedeschini had no business intervening in the internal affairs of the Spanish Church, and that his entire reasoning resulted simply from his well-known personal animosity towards Cardinal Segura. Meanwhile, the nuncio's friends in the government repeated to him the official position that the Republic, in distinction from the Monarchy, had no desire to intervene in the naming of the hierarchy, a position which indicated to the Pope one of the potential advantages, from Rome's point of view, of a separation of Church and state.

Seeking a middle way, the Pope in April 1932 appointed Bishop Gomá y Tomás of Tarazona as the new Cardinal-Archbishop of Toledo. Gomá was a highly intelligent, literate, energetic prelate. He was not closely associated with either the intransigent monarchists or the social Catholics. He was politically ambitious, ready to take a strong position in defense of the Church's historic rights, but not given to impolitic outbursts of personal feeling like those of Segura. He waited until July 1933 to publish his first pastoral letter, a measured reply to the Law of Congregations, in which he restrained the militants while holding doggedly to the full claims of the Church. Thus he reminded the faithful of their duty to accept the constituted civil power, even as in pagan Rome. But he repeated firmly that it was the duty of Catholic parents to send their children to Catholic schools and stated that the Church would continue in its educational functions. The Cardinal's unmistakable determination was an important factor in President Alcalá-Zamora's decision to dissolve the Cortes and call new elections before October 1, the date on which the Azaña government, if still in office, presumably would have closed the religious secondary schools.[13]

---

[13] My discussion of the internal divisions of the hierarchy with regard to the Republic is based upon Juan de Iturralde, *El Catolicismo y la cruzada de Franco,* I, 313–54. This is the work of an exiled Basque priest whose pseudonym "Iturralde" means "close to the source," and whose documentation includes, among other things, letters and memoranda of Cardinals Segura and Gomá. Spanish churchmen tried to persuade the author not to publish the book, but were unable to challenge its authenticity. I also checked Iturralde's interpretations with the memories of persons in Madrid who knew both the nuncio and the Spanish prelates.

The Republican-Socialist insistence on closing the Church schools was a self-defeating sectarian policy. The majority had taken as their guide the French separation of Church and state, but the French government had not ultimately deprived the Church of the right to have private schools. The Republic was unable to substitute for the existing secondary schools, so that a government which had, in fact, done more for primary education than any other in Spanish history nevertheless put itself in the position of trying to destroy secondary facilities. Finally, prohibiting the Orders from teaching made it impossible to arrange the separation of Church and state in a way that the majority of Spanish Catholics, and the Vatican, would probably have accepted. Other clauses of the law had to do with appointment of priests, their nationality, the nationalization of church buildings, the taxation of their revenues, the inspection of their hospitals, orphanages, and colleges for the training of clergy. The peaceful settlement of these questions was lost through the government's determination to carry through the maximum program of laicizing all schools.

In the summer of 1933 the Republic launched one of the noblest of its experiments. Ever since 1882, the great art critic and biographer of El Greco, Manuel B. Cossío, had dreamed of bringing the backward, isolated villages of Spain into cultural contact with the nation. Cossío was a colleague of Giner de los Ríos in the Institución Libre. Like Francisco Giner, he was a great walker, a lover of the country, and a pedagogue for whom the aesthetic education of his pupils was fully as important as their intellectual and technical education. The Institución emphasized the appreciation of the national artistic heritage, and Cossío conceived the idea that even the most illiterate and isolated villagers could fruitfully enjoy contact with this aspect of modern culture. In 1922, at a time when it appeared that the King was encouraging a greater participation by liberal intellectuals in the governing process, Cossío had proposed that the government send *misiones ambulantes* to the villages. The Republic seized upon his idea. By 1931 Cossío, who was then a very old man, was too ill to take active leadership, but under the direction of Luis Santullano, and with the cooperation of professors and students, mostly from the University of Madrid, the first *misiones pedagógicas* were organized in the summer of 1933.

Imbued with the faith of Cossío, that beauty could be appreciated even by the most primitive souls, the students went to the villages with reproductions of great paintings, and with movies. On improvised stages they produced the plays of Lope de Vega and Calderón. They brought medicines and books, and in cooperation with the villagers built schools. The reactions of the people were mixed. In many villages the peasants had never seen an auto, much less heard a phonograph or seen a movie, and they reacted like the interior tribesmen of Africa and South America in their first contacts with twentieth-century explorers. All was wonder, fear, curiosity, a reaction as if to magic. In slightly more sophisticated villages the response would be friendly if the attitude of the priest were sympathetic, hostile if not. In some villages the women, dressed in black, giggled and disappeared into their houses, as in the Orient. In others, the sense of wonder took a more skeptical, contemporary form. The peasants gazed quietly, noncommittally at the young men and women from Madrid. Not tax collectors? Not agents looking for real estate bargains, nor come to draft soldiers? Slowly, they realized that the strangers had come to give something to the village: books, medicines, pictures.

In the few days' contact between the stone age and the twentieth century, between illiterate peasants and middle-class university students, few concrete practical achievements resulted. But a living, sentimental contact of tremendous potential importance was established. These students would have been the future governing generation of Spain, if the Civil War had not intervened. Out of a naïve, generous desire to help the peasants, they had come face to face with the poverty, the ignorance, the fear, and the dignity of the Spanish *pueblo*. Here were the people who had conquered America and risen against Napoleon. Here, too, were the people who had trampled the corpses of the Civil Guard in an orgiastic dance at Castilblanco. Here was the untapped, undirected energy of Spain, a human group which had never been assimilated into the life of the nation in modern times. Through the theater, through the handshakes and embraces and gentlemanly courtesies common to all classes of Spaniards, a contact was established across a cultural gap of thousands of years. The misiones, product of the nineteenth-century Krausist renaissance, could have signaled the start of a far more profound awakening in the Spanish people as a whole.[14]

In the summer of 1933 labor disaffection and interunion rivalries further undermined the stability of the Azaña coalition. The Socialists had always been divided on the question of participation in the Republican government. After the passage of a very timid Agrarian Law, and especially after the Casas Viejas affair, an increasing proportion of their deputies felt that the time had come to withdraw from the government. At the same time, no majority was possible without them, a fact that was quickly demonstrated just after the passage of the Law of Congregations. President Alcalá-Zamora, convinced that public opinion was moving to the Right, dismissed Azaña and called upon Lerroux. The latter was unable to form a government in the face of Socialist opposition, and so after a few days the President recalled Azaña. The Socialists then had to decide whether to support Azaña once more or to force the dissolution of the Cortes. Faced with the possibility of elections in conditions unfavorable to them, they decided to maintain the coalition.

An important reason for the restlessness of the Socialists was the disaffection of the UGT. The Socialist labor federation had been a carefully disciplined, and, on the whole, a gradualist organization through most of its history. It was traditionally strongest in Madrid and Bilbao, and its oldest unions were made up of skilled laborers. But during the first two years of the Republic, the Federation of Land Workers had

[14] *Patronato de misiones pedagógicas,* 2 vols. (Madrid, 1934 and 1935), contain numerous photographs and detailed personal accounts. G. Somolinos D'Ardois, "Las misiones pedagógicas de España (1931–36)," *Cuadernos Americanos,* Sept.–Oct. 1953, summarized the background and purposes. See also Juan Guixé, *Le vrai visage de la république espagnole* (Paris, 1938), pp. 122ff., and the interviews with participating students in *El Sol,* Aug. 6, 1933.

come to total almost half the entire membership of the UGT. These workers, largely illiterate, were the most primitive of the Spanish proletariat, and their political psychology was much closer to that of the anarchists than to Marxism. In 1932 the Socialists had supported, however unhappily, the strong action of Casares Quiroga in assuring the Andalusian wheat harvest. In 1933, after the disappointment of the Agrarian Law, they were in no mood to sacrifice the loyalty of their militant land workers in order to maintain public order for the republican government. As the price of their participation in the last Azaña cabinet, they insisted on the immediate repeal of the Law for the Defense of the Republic.

The other large labor federation, the anarchist-dominated CNT, had been opposed to the Republican government from the start. The telephone strike, the Seville general strike, the uprisings of January, 1932 and January, 1933, had been the work of the CNT. Within three months the anarchists had proclaimed that the Republic was no improvement on the Monarchy, and they had placed the Socialists in the role of strikebreakers. The debate over the Catalan Statute gave them the opportunity to win favored treatment in Catalonia. Castilian-Catalan tension was doubled by UGT-CNT rivalry. Freedom of the press gave them unprecedented propaganda opportunities. Both their opposition posture and their philosophy found greater resonance among the hitherto unorganized workers than did Socialist ideas. When the UGT leaders observed the more rapid growth of their rivals, they attributed the anarchist success to the fact that the anarchists were not compromised by participation in a bourgeois government.

Generally speaking, the expansion of the UGT was concentrated in the western provinces, while the CNT dominated Catalonia and the Levant. They had roughly equal strength in Andalusia, and Seville was the focal point of their rivalry. The Andalusian capital was also the one significant area of communist activity. At the proclamation of the Republic, the Spanish Communist Party had numbered about 1,000 members.[15] This minuscule group had been deeply split in 1932 by the defection of its principal intellectual leaders, Andrés Nín

[15] David T. Cattell, *Communism and the Spanish Civil War* (Berkeley, 1955), p. 20.

and Joaquín Maurín, both of whom had collaborated with Lenin in founding the Third International. Without sharing all of Trotsky's theories, they had been much troubled by his expulsion from the Soviet Union in 1928 and had become increasingly anti-Stalinist in proportion as Stalin had consolidated his dictatorship. In 1933 the reorganized Party in the Seville area called itself the "Committee of Reconstruction." It was led by an energetic young port worker who was destined to be the General Secretary of the Communist Party during the Civil War—José Díaz.

Altogether then, three militant labor groups were struggling for power in the Andalusian capital: the CNT, the UGT, and the "Committee of Reconstruction." Most of the urban workers belonged to CNT unions. The communists were strongest among the port workers. The UGT Federation of Land Workers had been growing in the villages, and the UGT was challenging the communists for control of the stevedores. Each of these groups, plus the employer organization, the Economic Federation of Andalusia, hired pistoleros on occasion. There were perhaps a dozen clashes leading to death or serious injury in the course of the year. The secretary of the Economic Federation and a brilliant young communist doctor were the best-known victims of assassination. The pistoleros were hired at a rate of ten pesetas per day, at a time when the average daily wage in unionized factories was about twelve. Each organization reduced the individual risk to its strong-arm men by maintaining hideouts, supplying false papers, and forming prisoner welfare committees to aid those unfortunate enough to see the inside of a jail. The occasional violence was localized in the port area, and if cases came to court, they usually led to acquittal, since none of the witnesses could remember anything.[16]

The newspapers gave tremendous publicity to these events. The *Junta de Obras del Puerto* (port authority) was largely

[16] *El Sol*, Aug. 4, 6, and 15, 1933, carried special articles on union rivalries and waterfront violence in Seville. I had the opportunity in Seville in 1961 to check the contents of these articles and also to learn about the first efforts of the "Committee of Reconstruction" in conversation with two former municipal officials.

controlled by the Luca de Tena family, owners and publishers of the monarchist daily *ABC*. If a CNT worker punched a communist in a waterfront bar, the Seville edition of *ABC* reported an outbreak of lawlessness. If one of the syndicates called a general strike, and a few prudent shopkeepers pulled down their shutters in case anyone might throw a rock, *ABC* had the city paralyzed. Actually, life was normal outside the port area, and the harbor districts of all the world's seaports were the scenes of union rivalry and sporadic violence in the 1930's.

The violence in Seville was significant mainly for its political overtones. While the Spanish middle class had welcomed the Republic, they associated this form of government historically with disorder and were obsessed by the question of *orden público*. Police might be unable to solve underworld crime in France or the United States, but the stability of governments in those countries was not tied so delicately to the question of police efficiency. The emotions of the liberal Republicans were sorely tried by labor violence. On the one hand they were determined to prove the authority of the Republic. On the other hand, they felt that this violence was a reaction against the governmental violence to which the Spanish working class had always been exposed. During most of the two-year Azaña regime, the Galician liberal—and personal friend of Azaña—Santiago Casares Quiroga, was the Minister of the Interior. Time after time he stated that the government was not going to make martyrs of the anarchists, and time after time he had to call out the Civil Guard and the Assault Guard, temporarily close CNT headquarters, and suspend anarchist newspapers.

The Socialists in 1933 were particularly sensitive to events in the countryside of Extremadura and parts of Andalusia. There were a number of fires set in July and August, as well as several fatal bombings of casinos and isolated private farmhouses. The civil governor of Badajoz, a member of Azaña's party, resigned because dozens of Socialist mayors refused to cooperate with him. When moderate and conservative deputies accused the Socialists of fomenting violence in the countryside, the latter indignantly denied supporting incendiarism.

The point, unfortunately, was not whether Socialists believed in burning harvests, but whether they had sufficient control of the terribly poor and uneducated workers who had joined the Federation of Land Workers and had in 1932 expected an agrarian reform which would put land in their hands immediately.[17]

During the first half of 1933, the President of the Cortes, Julián Besteiro, tried to restrain the exaggerated passions of the Left, not only in the Cortes, but face to face with the increasingly radical workers. In mid-April he spoke in the Casa del Pueblo of one of the most militant suburbs of Seville. He told the workers that a responsible radical does not choose innovation for its own sake. He also warned against anticlerical excess, adding that if some people insist that the voice of the people is the voice of God, it is not surprising that others should brand as false such a definition of democracy. In July, speaking to the national congress of the railroad unions, he told his audience that the Spanish proletariat retained too much of the destructive spirit of the early industrial era; that a modern economy was too complex for the workers to achieve their ends by such actions as the factory occupations in Italy, which had led to fascism; that the Socialist Party must bend every effort to provide a constructive, nonviolent program for the disoriented peasants who were now becoming factory workers. Because Besteiro had the courage to say things he knew would not be popular with his audiences, and because of his decades of service as an officer of the UGT, he was applauded. But his position was unacceptable to the UGT workers, confident of their increasing numbers, disillusioned with the slowness of Republican reform, and feeling the pressure of the anarchists to their left.[18]

The breakdown of the Constituent Cortes majority was

[17] The number of burnings was greatly exaggerated in the debate. The year 1933 was a poorer agricultural year than either 1932 or 1934, but the statistics in Fuentes Irurozqui, *Síntesis de la economía,* indicate that the harvests in Extremadura and Andalusia were proportionately as good as those of the two Castiles.

[18] *El Sol,* April 19 and July 27, 1933.

completed by the movement of the Radicals into full opposition. Though often critical and obstructive in the debates
of 1932, they had nevertheless voted with the government
on the major bills—the Catalan Statute and the Agrarian Law.
Their anticlerical sentiment held them in line for the passage
of the Law of Congregations in May. But they were increasingly opposed to Socialist participation in the cabinet and
believed, after their victory in the municipal elections, that
the time had come for Alejandro Lerroux to head the government. When the debate over harvest burnings had completely embittered relations between the Azaña Republicans
and the Socialists, the President called upon Lerroux to form
a government.

In September the first elections for the Tribunal of Constitutional Guarantees confirmed the conservative trend of
opinion. The Tribunal, designed to act as a kind of Supreme
Court in constitutional conflicts, was chosen principally by the
municipal concilors, with two seats also reserved for the
colegio de abogados and several for the university law faculties. The municipalities, themselves elected in April 1933
by the freest vote thus far in Spanish history, chose anti-
government personalities in the proportion of two and a half
to one. They elected, among others, the financier Juan March,
who at the time was in jail, having been recently convicted on smuggling charges. The lawyers elected José Calvo
Sotelo, Monarchist and former Finance Minister of Primo
de Rivera, who was at this time in exile. The municipalities
and the lawyers showed their disgust with the government, and
incidentally deprived the Tribunal, from the outset, of the
dignified, nonpartisan character which was absolutely essential to its function. Socialist opposition now prevented
Lerroux from governing, and the President decided to dissolve the Constituent Cortes and proceed to general elections.

The election campaign revealed the importance of several
new political forces, the most important of which was the
Confederation of Autonomous Right parties, known by its
Spanish initials as the CEDA. At least since 1917, if not
earlier, Catholic conservatives of a parliamentary persuasion
had been groping unsuccessfully for leadership. They had been

frightened by the revolutionary strikes of 1917 and disappointed by the short-lived National Government of Antonio Maura in 1918. In the spring of 1923 they had formed the Partido Social Popular, an imitation of the ill-fated Don Sturzo party in Italy. In September 1923 the Primo de Rivera coup had destroyed normal political activity just as had Mussolini's assumption of power in Italy a year earlier. Some had joined Primo's *Unión Patriótica* in the late twenties while others had refused all collaboration with a dictatorial regime. In May 1931 the elections for the Constituent Cortes had occurred before they had had time to reorganize politically.

In the course of 1931 the newspaper *El Debate* became the leading organ of those Catholics willing to accept provisionally the new Republican regime and to defend Catholic interests within the context of Republican legality. Its founder and editor, Angel Herrera, also headed the Church's social and charitable organization, *Acción Católica*. Herrera himself avoided direct political activity, but in the columns of *El Debate* and through the local chapters of *Acción Católica*, he very ably helped to organize a new party, *Acción Popular*, under the chairmanship of the young deputy from Salamanca, José María Gil Robles. *Acción Popular* was strongest in northern Spain. With the approach of the electoral campaign in 1933, the party sought to broaden its base by including as many small Catholic political forces as were willing to merge with it, most notably the regional Valencian Catholic party led by Luis Lucía.

The common denominator of the parties forming the CEDA was the defense of Catholic sentiments and interests against the anticlerical attitudes and laws of the Constituent Cortes. It had no coherent economic program, representing as it did the large landlords of Castile, the small farmers of northern Spain, and the Catholic labor unions and cooperatives. It was inspired by the Social Catholicism of Pope Leo XIII and campaigned for the principles of Religion, Fatherland, Family, Order, Work, and Property. It advocated a corporate organization of society in the terms used by Pope Pius XI in his 1931 encyclical, *Quadrogesimo Anno*. In the

Spanish context, it avoided the question of republic versus monarchy, preaching the accidentality of forms of government.

Combining with the CEDA for electoral purposes were two small, but militant monarchist parties; the Traditionalists, strong in the North and espousing Carlist principles; and *Renovación Española,* founded by Antonio Goicoechea in March 1933, representing mainly the Alfonsine monarchists. Both parties stressed that what they were seeking was not a *restauración,* but an *instauración.* The Monarchy had failed, in their opinion, not because the Spanish people were no longer monarchical in sentiment, but because the dynasty after 1875 had sponsored liberal ideas which were incompatible with Spanish tradition. The Carlists considered the main branch of the Bourbon family to have compromised hopelessly with liberalism. *Renovación* preferred to postpone the dynastic question, since in any case Spain was not yet ready to accept the Monarchy again, but it defended the person of Alfonso XIII. Both groups desired an authoritarian monarchy, which would rest upon the traditional religion and institutions rather than upon the guns of a fascist party. Both groups made up in wealth and aristocratic social connections what they lacked in numbers. In the electoral alliance the CEDA represented the Catholic masses and that wing of the Church which was provisionally willing to accept the Republic. The monarchist parties represented Catholic wealth and aristocracy, and the intransigent elements of the Church.[19]

The year 1933 also witnessed the first significant activities of small, fascist-style parties. As early as October, 1931, Ramiro Ledesma Ramos and Onésimo Redondo Ortega had founded the *Juntas de Ofensiva Nacional Sindicalista* (JONS). Ledesma, a philosophy student and son of a village schoolmaster in Zamora, was an anticlerical and an admirer of both Mussolini and Hitler. Onésimo, of peasant background, was an ardent Catholic and an organizer of the

[19] Santiago Galindo Herrero, *Los partidos monárquicos bajo la segunda república,* 2d. ed. (Madrid, 1956), pp. 167–220. In telling the history of the monarchical parties, the author, who is strongly monarchist, analyses the relation between these parties and the CEDA.

small sugar-beet farmers of Valladolid province. Though differing in their religious positions, the two leaders shared a strong feeling for the grandeur of the Spanish past under the Catholic Kings, a hatred of Marxism, and a belief in some form of "popular dictatorship."[20] As of late 1933 they claimed to have organized some 400 Madrid University students into a new anti-Marxist syndicate, and to have some 500 other members organized in small syndicates in other Spanish cities. They were not taken seriously by CEDA or monarchist leaders, but they received small subsidies from such figures as Juan March and Antonio Goicoechea, and from various Basque bankers.[21] They did not present candidates for election to the Cortes.

Another fringe rightist group which did enter the campaign of 1933 was the *Falange Española,* founded on October 29 by three men: José Antonio Primo de Rivera, son of the late dictator; Julio Ruiz de Alda, famous as one of the aviators who took part in the first transatlantic flight from Spain to South America; and Alfonso García Valdecasas, a deputy associated in the Constituent Cortes with the group *Al Servicio de la República.* The Falange did not present a list of candidates. It was significant primarily for the entrance upon the national political stage of a young Primo de Rivera who, without specific program or proven ability, nevertheless aroused feelings of intense personal loyalty among both university and nonuniversity youth.

With the greatly increased participation of a reorganized Right, the 1933 elections were more hotly contested than those of 1931. Diego Martínez Barrio, chosen by the President to preside over the elections, was a Mason who had taken as his sobriquet the name "Vergniaud," after the Girondist deputy who had coined the phrase "Sooner death than crime." Martínez Barrio was an excellent choice, because he was a man of unquestioned integrity, and because he represented almost the absolute center in the political spectrum.

[20] Charles Foltz, *Masquerade in Spain* (Boston, 1948), pp. 61–5, and Stanley G. Payne, *Falange, a History of Spanish Fascism* (Stanford, 1961), pp. 11–16.
[21] Payne, *Falange,* p. 45.

There was sporadic violence and much crisis oratory in the six-week electoral campaign. José Antonio Primo de Rivera, a candidate of the Right in the province of Cádiz, spoke with scorn of general elections and of parliaments savoring of cheap taverns. An attempt was made to assassinate him on the occasion of one of his campaign speeches.[22] José Calvo Sotelo, speaking on the Paris radio, stated: "I consider it evident that this Parliament will be the last elected by universal suffrage for many years. I am persuaded that the Republic is more endangered by being parliamentary than by being a Republic." A Communist streetcar conductor and candidate for the Cortes was assassinated in his tram, and a conservative speaker was beaten unconscious in a normally peaceful Basque village. The Socialists accused the government of permitting anarchist pistoleros to walk the streets with impunity.

But the Prime Minister refused to meet provocative agitation with police intervention. He had led in the denunciation of brutality at Casas Viejas, and he believed that the Minister of the Interior had abused his powers of intervention in municipal politics. The election meetings were the principal form of political education reaching the masses. Democracy must be learned in action, even at the cost of many an error. He took the calculated risk that sporadic violence would not falsify the results of the vote to the extent that government intervention would.

On November 19, with some 8,000,000 persons voting, the Right won a substantial victory. As a result of the electoral pact, the Traditionalists and Renovación received a total of 40 seats. The CEDA, with 110 seats, became the largest single minority in the chamber, benefitting both from the provisions of the electoral law and from its powerful and well-financed campaign. The formerly apolitical Catholic middle class rallied to a party which preached the accidentality of forms of government while guaranteeing the protection of property and religion. The wheat farmers of Castile voted heavily for the CEDA, spurred equally by their Catholic-

[22] *New York Times,* Nov. 13, 1933.

THE DEFEAT OF THE LEFT

conservative outlook and the successful smear campaign against Marcelino Domingo and the wheat import program of 1932. In the cities, taxis carried the nuns to the polls to vote for the CEDA.

The Radical Party, with about 100 deputies, achieved the second largest minority, garnering thousands of urban middle-class votes which were both anti-Socialist and anticlerical. The parties of Manuel Azaña and Marcelino Domingo were virtually wiped out, and the Socialist representation was halved. A portion of the Republican losses was attributable to the mass abstention of the anarchists, many of whom had voted for Left Republicans in 1931. But the major factor was the breakup of the Republican-Socialist coalition in which the Left Republicans had been overrepresented on the combined lists by virtue of their agreements with the Socialists. In the second Cortes their numerical weakness was patent, and the Socialists themselves, without having lost votes, lost half their seats. Similarly, as a result of the electoral law, the CEDA was overrepresented in relation to its proportionate voting strength.

The representation of parties which did not enter coalitions in either 1931 or 1933 did not vary greatly. The moderate conservative groups of Miguel Maura and Alcalá-Zamora had 28 deputies in the first Cortes and 21 in the second. At the same time, the Liberal Democrats of Melquiades Alvarez rose from 2 to 8 deputies, and the Radicals increased their representation by roughly 10 per cent. The Basque Nationalists had 14 deputies in both Cortes. If public opinion had altered radically, it is reasonable to suppose that the numbers of these noncoalition parties would have changed more than they did. The election result as a whole indicated a moderate trend to the Right, characterized particularly by anarchist abstention and strong Catholic participation.[23]

[23] See Appendix C for a detailed discussion of the significance of both Cortes and local elections during the Republic.

7

GOVERNMENT BY THE CENTER-RIGHT

⁞⁞⁞

FROM the returns, it was clear that coalition governments would again be necessary in the new Cortes. Even if the entire Right were to vote under CEDA leadership, they would still constitute less than half the chamber. If the CEDA combined with the Center rather than the far Right, a disciplined alliance of the CEDA and the Radicals would also fall short of a majority. The question was further complicated by personal attitudes. President Alcalá-Zamora had always respected Manuel Azaña, however much he might oppose him politically. The leaders of the principal minorities in the new Cortes were Alejandro Lerroux of the Radical party and José María Gil Robles of the CEDA. The President, in common with many conservatives as well as with the whole Left, distrusted Lerroux because of his past. Lerroux had begun his political career as an anti-Catalanist demagogue, and in the early years of the century he had been known as "the Emperor of the Paralelo," the main street in the working-class district of Barcelona. In its evolution toward republicanism, his party had won the municipal elections in Barcelona; however, it had then been found guilty of considerable corruption along the lines familiar in American big-city politics. Lerroux was a "gran señor" without a university education and without any regular income. He was famous for mollifying his creditors, who would burst into his apartment demanding instant payment, spend a half-hour with the great man, and emerge (having made him a new loan) saying that they had met the man who was going to save Spain. In the course of his political activities, he became friendly with the wealthy tobacco smuggler Juan March; and when he was over sixty years of age, he acquired a law degree in order decorously to collect his retainer fees as an adviser to several businesses controlled by March. Nevertheless, Lerroux had won a certain prestige in the 1920's as a "historic republican" during years when Alcalá-Zamora was a royal official and when Azaña belonged to the Reformist Party of Melquiades Alvarez.

The President was a man of great personal culture, relative timidity, and extreme moral scruples. He was never comfortable with the gregarious, free-and-easy Lerroux, and like the majority of the republican intellectuals, he half-feared, half-scorned the quick sense of realities that made Lerroux a successful politician. On the other hand, he could not trust the leader of the CEDA. Gil Robles had served as defending lawyer for a number of the military involved in the Sanjurjo rebellion, and he was also one of the main lawyers of the Jesuits. Neither of these facts disqualified him to lead a conservative party under the Republic, but they understandably chagrined the President when taken together with the fact that at no time during or after the electoral campaign would Gil Robles affirm his loyalty to the Republic as such. He insisted on his parliamentarism, on his respect for constituted authority. He acknowledged that the Republic had arrived by the will of the Spanish people. But he continued to speak of the accidental quality of forms of government. Since the Republic was only two years old, since much of its social legislation and many articles of the Constitution were under attack, the President, even though he was himself a devout Catholic and a conservative, would not hand power to Gil Robles. Faced with the unpleasant choice, he preferred Alejandro Lerroux.

Lerroux conceived his mission to be one of rectification and pacification. He believed the Constituent Cortes had moved too far to the left, particularly in labor legislation and anticlerical laws. As a "historic republican," he knew better than anyone else how few truly committed republicans there were in Spain. He felt that the Socialists had dominated the Constituent Cortes through Azaña's dependence at all times on their cooperation. He proposed to win over the mass of Catholics and monarchists by showing that the Republic could protect the Church and the rights of property. He reasoned that the CEDA and its voters would in a few years willingly accept the Republic when they no longer automatically identified it with threats of social and religious revolution.

Lerroux's first government (in office from November 1933 to April 1934), although composed entirely of Radicals, was dependent on the votes of the CEDA and the monarchists. It was thus not a coalition government in the sense that Azaña's had been. But just as Azaña had depended on Socialist votes, Lerroux depended on the Right. Without being repealed, the most objectionable laws of the first Cortes were simply suspended: the Law of Congregations was ignored, and the Church schools operated normally. Agrarian reform, always slow, came to a halt. Largo Caballero, in the Ministry of Labor had used his power to appoint pro-labor chairmen of mixed juries, and now the new minister, José Estadella, used the same power to appoint chairmen favorable to the proprietors.[1] Agricultural wages, which had risen to an average of ten to twelve pesetas daily during Largo Caballero's ministry, were brought back to the four to six peseta average of 1930. These changes naturally increased tension in the countryside. In March the Cortes voted to increase the Civil Guard by one thousand. Martínez Barrio resigned as Minister of the Interior, and his successor, Rafael Salazar Alonso, announced that the Socialists were subverting the Republic and that every major strike constituted a public-order problem as well as a labor problem. The cabinet also approved, in April, a project for the restoration of the death penalty, ostensibly as a deterrent to social crimes, but quite evidently, in the political context, to strengthen the repressive force available to the government. But the Cortes, including a large number of the Radical deputies as well as the Left, refused to vote the death penalty.

The Constituent Cortes had ruled that the state budget for the payment of priests' salaries was to be discontinued within two years, and that as part of the separation of Church and state under Article 26, the expenses of the clergy should be paid by the faithful. This had caused consternation among the hierarchy, who knew very well that with the exception of

[1] *Economía Española,* Dec., 1933, pp. 111ff.

Navarre and the Basque country the clergy would probably starve if obliged to depend on the voluntary contributions of the faithful. In 1934 the Cortes voted to pay roughly two-thirds of the costs of the secular clergy. They also passed, after applying cloture to a bitter debate, a law for the restoration of such property of the Orders as had already been confiscated.

While the Radicals governed on behalf of the Right, a number of important party realignments took place. From the moment of the election, Azaña and Prieto had begun preaching the need for a renewed Republican-Socialist coalition. At the same time, Azaña's party, *Acción Repúblicana,* fused with the Radical Socialists of Marcelino Domingo to form *Izquierda Repúblicana* (Republican Left). The Agrarian Party of Martínez Velasco, socially conservative and allied with the CEDA, nevertheless made a declaration of republican loyalty, while Gil Robles maintained his uncommitted position. Martínez Barrio, Lerroux's principal lieutenant in the Radical Party, split with his chief, largely over the restoration of Church property and the toughening public-order policies.[2] All these changes were symptomatic of the uneasiness of moderate, and even conservative, republicans at the sight of a Lerroux government moving rapidly to the Right.

Equally important changes were taking place among working-class political forces. Immediately after the Right's electoral victory, Largo Caballero began to speak in revolutionary terms, charging that the workers were no better off under the Republic than under the Monarchy. Caballero had been a trade-union official and a reformist Socialist for decades, but several converging influences now determined his leftward evolution. He saw the appointment of Estadella as Minister of Labor, followed by the rapid revision of mixed jury decisions, as treason to the working class. The rise of Hitler to full

[2] Alejandro Lerroux, *La pequeña historia* (Buenos Aires, 1945), pp. 271–75. This book is extremely valuable for insight into Lerroux's personal feelings and for details of political maneuvering within the cabinets of 1934 and 1935.

power in Germany, with the clear support of the traditional Right, showed how readily the conservatives might collaborate in the destruction of a republic whose constitution had been modeled principally on that of republican Germany. In addition, Caballero was jealous of the great praise bestowed upon Julián Besteiro as President of the Cortes, and upon Prieto as Minister of Public Works, by many of the same people who opposed his work in the Ministry of Labor. Early in 1934 younger radicals within the party, particularly Carlos Baraibar and Luis Araquistáin, encouraged Largo Caballero to break with "reformist" tendencies and remodel the Socialist Party as a revolutionary party.

Caballero had long been troubled by the rivalry of anarchist and Marxist unions and was anxious to take the lead of a united working-class front that would avoid such conflicts as the 1931 telephone strike or the violent rivalries of the Seville waterfront. Under the name *Alianza Obrera*, he established the beginnings of cooperation between the UGT and the moderate minority group within the CNT, led by Angel Pestaña. He also negotiated with Joaquín Maurín, the leader of a small anti-Stalinist communist party in Catalonia. Pestaña's influence within the CNT was very slight, and both political theories and the Catalan autonomous tendency separated Caballero from Maurín; thus his efforts at this time bore little fruit.[3]

Militant activity without unified direction marked the early months of the new Cortes. In December 1933 the anarchists rose against Lerroux, as they had a year earlier against Azaña. Once again, there were declarations of *comunismo libertario,* scattered church burnings, and industrial sabotage. The government, with Martínez Barrio as Minister of the In-

[3] Brenan, *Spanish Labyrinth,* pp. 274–75. In a conversation in New York in 1960, Mr. Maurín did not recall feeling the enthusiasm attributed to him in the Brenan passage. He spoke of the Alianza as having been crippled from the start by antipathy between Caballero and the Catalans. Nor does *El Socialista* for the spring and summer of 1934 give the impression that the new movement was very important.

terior, restored order in four days, with a minimum of force and fortunately no repetition of Casas Viejas.[4] In March the newly elected radical leadership of the UGT printers union in Madrid called a strike, and the new Interior Minister, Salazar Alonso, immediately declared the state of alarm. The strike was a failure but illustrated the militant mood of the new UGT leaders and the readiness of Salazar Alonso to apply his theory that strikes were public order problems.

In late March, the CNT in Saragossa called a general strike which tied up the city for the better part of six weeks. Saragossa, even more than Barcelona, was the spiritual center of anarcho-syndicalism, unadulterated by Catalan nationalism. It was the most powerful center of the Iberian Anarchist Federation (FAI), the militant, tightly organized elite which since 1927 had dominated the CNT masses. It was the home of the principal FAI leaders—the Ascaso brothers, Buenaventura Durruti, and Juan García Oliver. The FAI combined anarchist idealism with gangsterism, often in the same persons. They collected the dues of the CNT unions, forming prisoner funds, buying arms, "protecting" the workers from the police. In 1923 the Ascaso brothers had struck a blow for their conceptions of freedom by assassinating Cardinal Soldevila of Saragossa, considered by them to be a pillar both of clericalism and of political reaction. Sentenced to thirty years in capitalist jails, they had nevertheless been amnestied in 1931 by the bourgeois Republic. Masons by trade, they had then taken jobs on the restoration of the Basilica of Pilar, in the course of which work they daily passed the tomb of their distinguished victim.

The Saragossa anarchists could be divided roughly into three types. There were a handful of self-educated idealists, readers of Bakunin and Tolstoy, sometimes mystical pacifists, sometimes vegetarians or nudists. They lived ascetically, on the proceeds of their own proud but ill-paid labor, and believed literally that the declaration of *comunismo libertario* throughout the Peninsula would lead immediately to a peace-

[4] In *El Sol,* Jan. 17, 1934, Dr. Marañon praised as exemplary Martínez Barrio's handling both of the November, 1933 elections and of the December anarchist risings.

ful, prosperous, egalitarian society. Then there were the mass of unskilled and semiskilled workers, proud of their physical resistance to hunger and police beatings, convinced of the moral superiority inherent in being a proletarian rather than a bourgeois, and identifying spiritual liberation with atheism. Before the days of the FAI, these people easily might have been cajoled into settling their strikes. Most of the shops in which they worked were small, and the relation between boss and worker therefore was intimate. But the class consciousness and the revolutionary mystique which had been inculcated by the FAI, made them determined to show the bosses that society depended upon them, the workers. They enjoyed demonstrating that power by tying up the city and looked upon their general strikes as rehearsals for the eventual revolutionary achievement of *comunismo libertario*.

Finally there were a small but important group of professional gunmen, by no means all Spaniards. When the residents of Saragossa observed 20 or 30 strangers with foreign accents selling ties on the streets, they knew that another general strike was coming. The demands which aroused the enthusiasm of the anarchist masses were more often political than economic. In 1933 they called effective one-day strikes for the freeing of Thaelmann, the imprisoned chairman of the German Communist Party, and ended meetings with the cry: "Viva Sacco and Vanzetti." No matter that the Communists were in reality their mortal enemies, that Hitler could not care less what the workers of Saragossa thought, that Sacco and Vanzetti had been electrocuted six years before, and that very few of them could afford to lose a day's pay.[5]

The principal motive of the March 1934 general strike was to free the prisoners taken in the unsuccessful December rising. It also protested the action of the civil governor in depriving some local bus drivers of their licenses. The national government did not negotiate with the strikers concerning

[5] The perhaps improbable-sounding details in the above paragraphs are drawn from conversations in Saragossa in 1961 with several owners of small businesses who had had repeated experiences with CNT and FAI men through the twenties and early thirties.

prisoners, and the governor restored most of the licenses in question, but the strike went on for almost six weeks, and created the legendary, national reputation of Durruti. Toward the end, with the workers' families facing starvation, Durruti organized a spectacular bus caravan to evacuate children of the strikers to the homes of fellow anarchists in Catalonia.[6]

The Right as well as the Left showed a mood of new militancy in these months. *Acción Popular,* the Catholic youth organization associated with the CEDA, wanted to know why their idol, Gil Robles, had not taken power after the November 1933 election. Gil Robles' public position was indeed difficult. He could not expect to become Prime Minister without declaring his loyalty to the Republic, but the financial backing of his party was overwhelmingly monarchist, so that he could not afford to declare himself a republican. He insisted on his parliamentarism.[7] But the Catholic Center Party in Germany had voted full powers to Hitler, and the Vatican had signed a Concordat with Hitler in July 1933. This occurred at a time when many governments were attempting at least to exercise moral pressure against the first anti-Semitic outrages and were protesting the wholesale imprisonment of the opposition. In February 1934 a Catholic Prime Minister, Dollfuss, took dictatorial power in Austria and put down in blood the Socialist protest against the suspension of Parliament. Under these circumstances, how many liberals and Socialists in Spain would believe in Gil Robles' declarations of parliamentarism? And how many of his militant followers, mouthing anti-Semitic slogans and generally aping the fascist and nazi youth movements, would be satisfied with the "correct" attitude of their chief?

[6] *El Sol* and *La Vanguardia,* March and April, 1934. An interesting article on the evacuation of the children appeared in *Humanitat* (Barcelona), May 9, 1934.

[7] Galindo Herrero, *Partidos monárquicos,* pp. 212–17 illustrates the type of pressure put on Gil Robles by the reactionary monarchists. The liberal Catholic professor Alfred Mendizábal, on the other hand, criticizes him bitterly for failing to make a declaration of republican loyalty. See *Aux origines,* pp. 190, 195.

On April 22, 1934, the Catholic youth movement held a mass meeting at the Escorial, in which militancy and caution were carefully combined. The choice of site could not but remind the public of its builder, the stern King Phillip II, who had dedicated the monastery to San Lorenzo in gratitude for the victory of St. Quentin and had supplied it with the immense crypt in which the Kings of Spain lay buried. Thirty thousand youth, some of them having walked all the way from Madrid, gathered to hear Gil Robles tell them that they would take power in their own good time, that they were the defenders of legality against the Revolution, that if the Revolution "descended into the streets," they would be there to meet it heroically. The crowd cheered wildly as the speaker refused the shelter of an umbrella against the cold rain sweeping the plaza.

Heroic postures and fascist phrases did not come easily to Gil Robles, but in April 1934 he knew that his followers' eyes were not only turned toward Austria and Germany, but that the radical Right was growing in Spain. In February the Falange and the JONS had merged. They counted less than 3,000 members at the time, but José Antonio Primo de Rivera was a young man of magnetic personality who might well make inroads on the JAP. In the first months of the Falange's existence, he had preached against violence in the streets. But the monarchist press had laughed at him for the unavenged shootings of several Falange students, and for a brief but significant period, from April to July 1934, the monarchist terrorist Juan Antonio Ansaldo joined the Falange specifically to train its reprisal squads.[8]

Gil Robles, speaking at the Escorial, took pains to distinguish his movement from fascism and nazism. "I am not afraid that in Spain this national movement will take the path of violence; I do not believe that, as in other nations, the national sentiment will claim to revive pagan Rome or engage in a morbid exaltation of race . . . We are an army of citizens, not an army which needs uniforms and martial parades."

[8] Payne, *Falange,* pp. 48, 57.

While he spoke, the city of Madrid was tied up by a one-day general strike. No trams, buses, or taxis ran; few bars or cafés were open that Sunday.[9] The working class of Madrid demonstrated with virtual unanimity its distrust of the CEDA chief. A parliamentary crisis was in the making, and the workers were notifying the government that they would never accept the participation of the CEDA in the cabinet. The principal cause of that crisis was bound to arouse the hostility of the Left; the Cortes had passed a bill giving amnesty to General Sanjurjo and his companions for their part in the August, 1932 military revolt; at the same time, the cabinet was proposing the restoration of the death penalty.

The April cabinet crisis was as much a conflict between the President and the ministry as it was a conflict between the Right and the Left. Article 83 of the Constitution gave the President the power, by means of a "reasoned message," to ask the Cortes to reconsider a law within fifteen days of its passage. This was the equivalent of the American President's veto power, since the Cortes would have to muster a two-thirds majority on the second vote if the law were to override the President's objections. Alcalá-Zamora felt very strongly that the amnesty would set a dangerous precedent, but he also had strong scruples about the use of his presidential authority. Article 84 of the same Constitution stated that all "acts and mandates" of the President would be null unless countersigned by a minister. Article 83 said nothing about a countersignature. Was the President then free to veto a law by himself, or did the Constitution mean to include the veto among his "acts and mandates" requiring such signature? The constitutional vagueness illustrated the mixed motives of its authors. On the one hand they wished to give the President a moderating power; on the other, they wished the cabinet, representing legislative supremacy, to have a controlling hand over his initiative.

Alcalá-Zamora, during the fifteen-day period available to him, exposed to the cabinet both his objections to the amnesty

[9] *El Debate*, April 24, 1934, for the text of Gil Robles' speech. *La Vanguardia*, April 24, for description of the crowd at El Escorial and of the Madrid general strike.

and his scruples about the veto. He hoped to avoid the legal issue by having a countersignature, but the cabinet unanimously supported Lerroux, brushed aside his worries over Article 84, and told him either to sign the law or veto it under Article 83.[10] Meanwhile, the conservative press was repeating that the constitutional monarchs had also enjoyed the power of veto, but that they had never exercised it. The Cortes under the Monarchy had never been representative of actual opinion and would never have inconvenienced the Monarch by passing a law he would have to veto. But Alcalá-Zamora was extremely sensitive to any suggestion that he might be overstepping the limits of his just power.

He tried, in effect, to have it both ways: signing the law while writing simultaneously his objections thereto. In a 34-page memorandum he argued that any reincorporation into the Army of officers who had revolted would inevitably encourage future plotters to act with the virtual assurance of impunity and reintegration in case of failure. He also argued that while technically he was asking for a second consideration, in reality he was asking for a first consideration, since the clauses he objected to had not formed part of the original law and had been added without debate. But he desired also to satisfy the families who had counted on the amnesty, and he signed the bill as a lesser evil.[11]

This was one of several political crises in which the unfortunate President satisfied no one. Lerroux resigned in fury, feeling that Alcalá-Zamora had withdrawn his confidence in the cabinet without having had the candor to say so. The Left, while applauding his reasoning concerning the amnesty itself, felt irritated and scornful at his exaggerated scrupulosity. He ought to have had the courage to veto the law rather than to split hairs about what constituted a "first" or a "second" consideration. Opinion generally found his conduct unbecoming the dignity of a head of state. Meanwhile, the amnesty went into effect, and a new cabinet, headed by Ricardo Samper, but very similar in composition to the

[10] Lerroux, *La pequeña historia*, pp. 248–52.

[11] *El Sol*, April 25, gives the text of the President's message. *El Sol*, April 25–9 and *El Debate*, April 26–7 on the cabinet crisis.

recent one, took office—"the same dogs with different collars," as they used to say of many a cabinet change in the nineteenth century.

National attention during March and April was occupied principally with the amnesty debate and the militant strikes going on in Madrid and Saragossa. The Samper government was destined to face the first important crisis in the relationship between the central government and the autonomous province of Catalonia. In November 1933 the conservatives had won the majority bloc of Cortes seats in Catalonia as well as in the rest of Spain. Francisco Cambó's *Lliga Catalana* (which cooperated in the chamber with the CEDA) had 25 seats, as against 19 for the *Esquerra*. However, in the elections for the *Generalitat* in January 1934, the Esquerra won a large majority, the difference probably being due to the abstention of anarchists in the first election and their participation in the second.

Colonel Macià, hero of the struggle for the autonomy statute, had died suddenly in December. The new leader of the Esquerra, Luis Companys, was less a Catalan nationalist and more a Left Republican than Macià. Companys had been associated with Marcelino Domingo in leading the revolutionary strikes of 1917. He had been the defending lawyer for the anarcho-syndicalists during the 1920's, and in the course of his work had defended both the saints and the pistoleros of the Barcelona working class. In 1931 he had proclaimed a federal republic within which Catalonia would enjoy autonomy, whereas the formula of Colonel Macià had been separatist in effect if not in immediate wording. The victory of the Esquerra in January, and the leadership of Companys, meant that Catalonia was being governed by a parliament and cabinet of the same complexion as the Azaña coalition, but enjoying greater unity than that coalition since the Esquerra itself included most of the tendencies represented in the Azaña cabinet. While Madrid had a Radical government heavily dependent on the Right, Catalonia had a Left government.

One of the principal aims of Companys was the enactment of an agrarian reform tailored to the specific needs of Catalonia, where there were thousands of small farmers whose principal commercial crop was grapes. Most of them did not own the land, but cultivated their vines under long-term contracts which depended upon the life of the vine. During the nineteenth century, the average life of the vines was about fifty years. Owner and tenant divided the proceeds fifty-fifty, and tenancy lasted until three-quarters of the vines had died; from this feature of the contract, the *rabassa morta,* the farmers were known as *rabassaires.* In the 1890's a phylloxera plague had killed off the predominant species of vine, and the new type lasted only about twenty-five years. After the World War I, the shorter tenancy, combined with a drop in wine prices, created much hardship.[12] Luis Companys, among his other activities, had founded and led the *Unió de Rabassaires,* whose program was to acquire title to the vineyards for the farmers now working them as tenants.

On April 11, 1934, the Generalitat passed a law empowering tenants to acquire title to land which they had cultivated for at least fifteen years, and setting up tribunals for the determination of boundaries and prices. This *ley de cultivos* was the Catalan equivalent of the projected *ley de arrendamientos,* which had failed to pass the Cortes in the summer of 1933. The landlords immediately challenged the constitutionality of the law and asked the Samper government to place the issue before the Tribunal of Constitutional Guarantees. They claimed that the law violated Article 15, which reserved to Madrid all laws affecting the bases of contractual obligations. The Generalitat claimed that under Article 12 of the autonomy statute, it had the right to legislate in matters of agrarian social policy.[13]

The law certainly concerned agrarian social policy, and its effects were limited to the territory of Catalonia; but the law

[12] Brenan, *Spanish Labyrinth,* pp. 277–78.

[13] *La Vanguardia,* April 22, 1934. André Lubac, *Le tribunal espagnole des garanties constitutionnelles* (Montpellier, 1936), pp. 83–96. The Lubac volume is a doctoral thesis in law and provides a clear account of the complex role of the Tribunal.

with equal certainty affected the bases of contractual obligations. Thus the court's decision was bound to be political
rather than legal. On June 8, by a 13 to 10 vote, without an
absolute majority of the court having heard the case, the
Tribunal affirmed the objections of the landlords. It was a
vote in favor of centralism and conservative vested interests
against regionalism and land reform. As such, the Generalitat
refused to accept it, and proceeded to pass a virtually identical
new law.[14] But Luis Companys was not a separatist, and
Ricardo Samper was not a fascist, for all that an excited press
said about each of them. The two men negotiated quietly
during the summer in search of a formula that would permit
the land reform without contravening the Constitution.

The *rabassaire* issue coincided with rising agitation among
the agricultural proletariat of western and southern Spain. As
the Socialist Party moved to the left after losing the November
elections, the moderate founders of the Federation of Land
Workers were replaced by a younger generation of leaders
committed to the new revolutionary trend represented by
Largo Caballero. In the spring of 1934 wage levels were being
reduced, and the repeal of the Law of Municipal Boundaries
had deprived the Casa del Pueblo of its control of the local
labor supply. Landlords, spurred by two years of class conflict
and rising wages, had begun to introduce harvesting machines
in the grain country. The new Federation leaders established
a united front with the anarchist leadership in Andalusia, and
a combined UGT-CNT committee announced on May 25
that the agricultural workers would strike on June 5 if their
demands were not met. At the same time, they publicized the
already well-known prospect of the most abundant wheat
harvest yet in Spanish history.

The Federation demanded wage rates of 12 to 13 pesetas
daily, similar to those of the Azaña period. In order to compensate for the repeal of the Law of Municipal Boundaries,
they demanded guarantees that all available workers be employed, and that no one be denied work because of political
affiliation. By the second of June they had won these conces-

[14] *La Vanguardia,* June 9 and 10, 1934. Manuel Azaña, *Mi
rebelión en Barcelona* (Madrid, 1935), p. 235.

sions in government-supervised bargaining, but some of the leaders now required that the agreed-upon wage rates for the harvest be applied to the entire year. This demand alone would have more than doubled the annual wage bill, since the agricultural proletariat were employed only about 150 days each year in planting and harvesting. The moderates in effect withdrew from the apparently militant united front, so that when June 5 arrived, only a scattering of villages took part and not more than 20 per cent of the workers went out on strike in any given area. By the tenth of June it was clear that the strike was a total failure, although isolated incidents were reported as late as the eighteenth.[15]

The Minister of the Interior firmly believed that he had on his hands a revolutionary strike. He called out the Civil and Assault Guards, clamped censorship on the affected provinces, deported hundreds of peasants to jail in distant provinces, and arrested various teachers, doctors, lawyers, and Socialist deputies whom he accused of fomenting the Revolution. Before the Cortes, he read incendiary passages calling for attacks on the Civil Guard, praising the burning of harvests and the murder (on earlier occasions) of a half-dozen particularly hated landlords of Jaén province. He stated that confidential reports indicated that the Socialist leaders had lost control to the Communists and the FAI. He justified the heavy censorship by saying that without it, workers who had already returned to the fields would go out on strike again at false rumors of success in other provinces. He justified the arrest of professional and political personalities on grounds that they were guilty of revolutionary propaganda and that Spain had become a fertile area for the Marxist Revolution.[16]

The Cortes debates were violent. The Socialists were always especially sensitive to charges that Communists or anarchists were pushing them to extreme positions, and Largo Caballero rose angrily to refuse all responsibility, direct or indirect, for the incendiary phrases of "provocateurs." The Socialists particularly hated Salazar Alonso. In the twenties he had been a

[15] *El Sol,* May 26 and 27, June 1, 3, 6, and 18, 1934.

[16] Rafael Salazar Alonso, *Bajo el signo de la revolución* (Madrid, 1935), pp. 142–44, 151–53, and *passim.*

liberal journalist, a city councilor in Madrid, and a friend if not an intimate, of many of his present opponents. Authority seemed to have gone to his head. He saw revolutionary plots in every incident, and the contrast between his restraint during the Saragossa general strike and his heavy hand against the agricultural workers in June appeared to indicate a particular animus against the Socialists.[17]

During the week of the peasants' strike, a melodramatic incident occurred in Madrid between Socialist workers and Falangists. Both groups were devoting Sunday afternoons in 1934 to para-military exercises in the Casa de Campo park west of the city. Between the hostile parties defiant shouts and fistfights were common, and occasional shots were fired. On June 10, in one such clash, a young Falangist was beaten to death. His eyes were gouged out, and a girl worker urinated in the empty sockets. The news spread rapidly across the city, and a posse of young Falangists, using the automobile of Sr. Alfonsito Merry del Val, drove to the working class district where they fired at random at a group of workers returning from the Casa de Campo. Their burst of gunfire fatally wounded a girl and inflicted serious leg wounds on two of the young men accompanying her. By an extraordinary coincidence, it turned out that the girl, Juana Rico, according to her own dying statement in the clinic, was the one who had desecrated the corpse of the young Falangist. Merry del Val was tried that summer, but acquitted for lack of evidence.[18]

The repression of the peasants' strike continued, its most serious aspects being the deportation of workers and the arrests of deputies. On July 3, a full-dress debate took place

[17] *El Sol*, June 23, 1934.

[18] *El Sol*, June 11, for the incident, Aug. 20 and 21 for the trial. On September 26 it also reported that a lawyer had informed the Supreme Court that friends of Merry del Val had offered him an indemnity to desist from efforts to reopen the case. The facts of the incident were reported to me in virtually identical terms by Falangists and Socialists who were living in Madrid at the time. See also Payne, *Falange,* pp. 57–8, for an account including the admission of Merry del Val's responsibility by David Jato of the *Sindicato Español Universitario,* the Falange student organization.

over the arrest of the deputies, against a background of the passage through Madrid of trainloads of campesinos, on the way home from the Burgos jail to the villages of Extremadura. The Left press carried pathetic stories of the unsanitary conditions in which the campesinos had been hustled off without food, and in the railway terminals Socialist committees served meals and distributed tobacco to handsome, illiterate, fist-saluting peasants who could have stepped out of Goya's canvases of 1808 or out of the heroic *Episodios Nacionales* of Galdós.

Indalecio Prieto took the lead in the Cortes debate. A man of powerful memory and clear expository style, he had served in monarchical times on the parliamentary committee which had handled all criminal accusations against deputies. He noted to begin with, that prior to June, 1934, the government had never deported peasants and had never arrested deputies. Articles 55 and 56 of the Constitution of 1931, drawn almost word for word from the text of the monarchical constitution, dealt with the rights of deputies. Under Article 55, they enjoyed immunity to engage in political propaganda. Article 56 stated that a deputy could be arrested only in case of "flagrante delito" of a common crime, and even then, only if the crime in question carried with it a "pena aflictiva," that is to say, a specific fine or jail sentence. It had been a tradition of the Parliament never to prosecute deputies for political crimes.

In the first days of the peasants' strike, the Socialist deputy, Rubio Herrera of Badajoz, had been ordered out of the district by the civil governor and escorted out of town by the Civil Guard. Challenged in the Cortes, Salazar Alonso had pointed out that Rubio had not been arrested, but went on to say that the government would have backed the Guard even if they had arrested him. During the following two weeks, three deputies were arrested and held overnight in jail. The only Communist deputy in the Cortes, Doctor Cayetano Bolívar, was arrested while visiting campesinos held in the jail at Jaén. Ideologically Dr. Bolívar stood far closer to the primitive Christians than to the functionaries of the Third International. He was a man consumed by the sense of social injustice, idealizing the *pueblo* among whom he lived, charging nothing to the vast majority of his patients. And in his examination room there hung a crucifix. A few days later the Socialist deputy, Carlos Hernández Zancajo, was arrested by the Civil Guard in Pozuelo, ostensibly for carrying arms. Practically all government officials carried small arms, and Hernández told the guards he was armed. They nevertheless searched him, handcuffed him, and held him overnight. He was released upon the demand of two fellow Socialists, one of whom was the future wartime Prime Minister, Juan Negrín. In the Cortes the Socialists contended that these arrests had taken place because of Salazar Alonso's remarks in the discussion of the Rubio case. The Minister of the Interior stated that he would inquire whether there had been any extra-legal treatment of Hernández but refused to make any policy statement.

The case of the Socialist deputy, Juan Lozano, was more serious. The police had found in his home a package which he claimed contained leaflets and which turned out to contain pistols. The government had not only arrested him, but had laid the evidence before the appropriate parliamentary committee, and the committee had handed down an indictment against Lozano for having an illegal "deposit of arms." Along with the indictment against Lozano the committee also brought in one against José Antonio Primo de Rivera. On June 3, some 500 Falangists had gathered at an airport without government permission. The Civil Guard had dissolved the meeting, and young José Antonio had gallantly assumed personal responsibility for the illegal demonstration. The guards did not arrest anyone, and they did not search the Falangists for arms. José Antonio also confessed personally, however, to the possession of a deposit of arms in his home. In his case the government was asking a fine of 10,000 pesetas, not too difficult for a young man of his means to pay.

Prieto's announced purpose in the debate was to defend both Juan Lozano and José Antonio against the parliamentary indictments. In his view, both men had committed political crimes, and the Spanish Parliament had never prosecuted deputies for *delitos políticos*. His real aim was to contrast the treatment of the Socialists with that accorded young Primo. Three deputies had been physically arrested while visiting their constituents, and a fourth was being charged with a *delito común* in having received a package of arms. In all these cases the police had searched the individuals as they would have any criminal suspect. While Lozano was out on bail, the Ministry of the Interior had telegraphed the frontier posts to anticipate his possible flight from justice. On the other hand Primo de Rivera had been found at the head of an illegal concentration of men belonging to a para-military organization. No searches, no handcuffs, no arrests; and the Cortes commission, quite properly, in Prieto's view, treated the Primo case as a purely political offense.

The debate did not yield any concrete result. The Cortes recessed for the summer two days later, and when they met again in early October, far more serious problems absorbed their attention. But the debate was symptomatic. The Socialists saw fascism in the heavy hand of Salazar Alonso against landless peasants and the handful of deputies who represented them. The spokesmen of the CEDA and of the monarchist parties argued that parliamentary immunity under Article 55 did not include the right to make revolutionary propaganda. Prime Minister Samper was more conciliatory than his Minister of the Interior, but the government would make no clear policy statement on how it might handle similar cases in the future. The Socialists reiterated that they would not be cowed like the German Social Democrats in 1933, or cornered and shelled into submission like the Vienna Socialists in 1934. At one dramatic moment Prieto, imagining that he saw a rightist deputy draw a pistol, rushed across the aisle flourishing a new (and doubtless unfired) one of his own, to be hurriedly surrounded by friends and taken out to the corridor to cool off. Melodramatic words and gestures, but behind them, the somber conviction of the Right that a communist revolution was in the making and the somber conviction of the Left that Spain was going fascist. An interesting sidelight of the debate, which might have become meaningful in later years if not for the tragic war, was the obvious current of mutual affection between Prieto and José Antonio Primo de Rivera.[19]

During the summer recess of 1934, the question of Basque autonomy suddenly became prominent. The four provinces of Navarre, Vizcaya, Alava, and Guipúzcoa had a long history of special economic and administrative privileges. Until 1876 they had possessed a *fuero*, entitling them to their own parliament, courts, and mint. As a punishment for their participation in the Carlist uprising, the central government had deprived them of the *fuero* but had substituted for it a *concierto económico* under which they retained the right to assess their own taxes through their municipal governments and pay a fixed sum to Madrid. In the late nineteenth and early twentieth centuries the provinces of Vizcaya and Guipúzcoa in particular had become centers of industry and banking. The Basques, with their face to the sea, with their iron and steel industry and their commercial relations with England, were the only people in Spain to develop modern corporate enterprise. In Catalonia the textile mills were family affairs. But the banks and steel industries of Bilbao were corporations with stockholders, boards of directors, capital pooled from different sources and impersonally managed. On the other hand, while corporate organization was strong, the directorships were carefully kept in the hands of Basques, even when the Bilbao-centered banks had become, through their activities, nationwide banks.

The Basques were proud of their high living standards, their capitalist efficiency, their better roads, schools, and hospitals. Their society was a unique amalgam of social Catholicism with English influences. Land was well distributed, Catholic co-ops and credit unions flourished in the towns, the Church was in fact as well as theory the social center of village life; the educational level of the Basque clergy, and consequently of their schools, was high. English influence was most apparent in business organization, outdoor sports, and a less rhetorical

[19] *El Sol* and *El Socialista,* July 4, 1934, for the Cortes debate on the arrests of deputies.

manner of conducting their affairs. Many sons of Basque businessmen went to English schools.

The Atlantic orientation of the Basques gave them in reality a psychology very different from that of the agricultural, mountain-bound Navarrese. This fact became apparent in the planning of the autonomy statute. Originally it was intended for the four provinces, but in June 1932 the Navarrese delegates had walked out of the conference in which delegates from the other three provinces had approved the draft statute by large majorities. On November 5, 1933, the voters of Vizcaya, Alava, and Guipúzcoa approved the proposed law by the same overwhelming majorities as the Catalan voters had given their draft statute in 1931.

In the new Cortes of November 1933 the Basque Nationalists had jointed the CEDA bloc. As social and economic conservatives, and as ardent Catholics, it was indeed logical for them to work with the CEDA. However, they were abruptly disillusioned when it became clear that neither Lerroux nor Gil Robles would support the introduction of a Basque autonomy statute. In the spring of 1934 they supported the Catalan Left in the struggle over the *rabassaire* law. In the summer they decided to force the issue of their own autonomy. They knew that a Cortes dominated by Gil Robles would not give them satisfaction. But Prime Minister Samper had demonstrated his willingness to compromise with the Catalans. Perhaps they could get a commitment from him in their favor.

According to Article 10 of the Constitution, a new Law of Municipalities was to be drawn up to regulate tax collections throughout Spain. This was one of a number of complementary laws which had not been completed when the Constituent Cortes was dissolved. The Basques announced that on grounds of the traditional *concierto económico* and of the wording of Article 10, it was imperative that the government grant the new law. They proposed to hold elections in the towns of the three provinces on August 12, elections to choose municipal delegates who would negotiate with the Madrid government about the entire tax question.

On August 3 the civil governor forbade them to hold the

elections, and Madrid sent troops to Bilbao, Vitoria, and San Sebastián. Some 50 out of 180 towns defied the government and held the elections in nearby fields while the police occupied the town halls. There was no violence, but about 50 aldermen were arrested, and more than half the municipal officials in the Basque provinces resigned in protest at the government's action. Samper averted a more serious crisis by acknowledging that the Law of Municipalities was long over-due and promising to introduce in the Cortes a specific bill permitting the Basques to elect delegates to negotiate the modalities of the tax system with the government. He pointed out at the same time that not just the Basque municipalities, but those of all Spain, were awaiting the new law.[20]

The Basque action in August 1934 was a bald political move not spurred by any such groundswell of popular suffering as the peasants' strike or of long-standing economic need as in the case of the *rabassaires*. The Nationalists were angry at what they regarded as a CEDA betrayal, and it seemed politically appropriate to push their demands at the same time that the Catalan issue was being fought out publicly. The bankers and businessmen of Bilbao and San Sebastián generally invited the titled aristocracy aboard their yachts. But on September 4, they held a well-publicized picnic with deputies of the Esquerra, the Socialists and the Republican Left. Monarchists, the CEDA, and the "smart set" of the San Sebastián summer colony fumed while the Catholic Basques courted the "red rabble."

Life proceeded normally in the summer of 1934 for the vast majority of Spaniards. Farmers all over the country enjoyed the best harvest of the century. Industry and business were relieved to begin recovery from the bottom depression years of 1932 and 1933. Vacation resorts were full. This summer

[20] My account of the conflict over Article 10 and of the municipal elections is based on *El Sol*, Aug. 1934. An excellent article on the subject appeared in *Current History*, Nov., 1934. On the Basque question as a whole see *Le clergé basque* (Paris, 1938). Important data on the linguistic division of the four provinces and their municipal structure appeared in Arnold Toynbee, ed., *Survey of International Affairs*, 1937, vol. II (London, 1938), 38, 41.

witnessed also the maximum activity of the *misiones pedagógicas*.

But the political tension of the spring did not subside. On July 11, barely a week after the Cortes debate involving José Antonio Primo de Rivera's illegal deposit of arms, the young founder of the Falange was surprised by the police in another meeting of para-military character. The police confiscated a quantity of pistols, inflammables, and clubs. A week later, Rafael Salazar Alonso announced that the government would consider illegal any meeting in which the fascist or the raised fist salute were used.

In a newspaper interview, Julián Besteiro hoped that the government would not push the Catalan Generalitat into a corner. In his opinion the *rabassaire* law was a legitimately handled internal affair of the Catalans which should never have been brought before the Tribunal of Guarantees. He went further, stating that if Madrid coerced the Catalans the rest of Spain would be justified in revolting. In his opinion also, the CEDA was not qualified to govern the Republic, having refused to state its unequivocal loyalty toward the regime.[21]

Late in August, on the occasion of a brief visit by Gil Robles to a steel mill in Bilbao, the workers spontaneously dropped tools while he was present. Such was the near universal hatred of the industrial proletariat for the man whom they considered the leader of Spanish fascism. At the same time, one of the oldest and most respected of the UGT leaders, Andrés Saborit, a contemporary and friend of Pablo Iglesias, feared for the radicalization of Spanish socialism. In an interview he stated that not even the discipline of the Socialist Party could force him to give the raised fist salute, and he protested vehemently against its use in the summer children's camps of the UGT.[22]

When the Cortes adjourned in July, it was generally assumed that there would be a parliamentary crisis when it reconvened on October 1. Gil Robles, pressed by his wealthy monarchist friends during the summer season at San Sebastián, announced his intentions in a public address at Covadonga on

[21] *El Sol,* July 10, 1934.
[22] *Ibid.,* Aug. 4, 1934.

September 9. As in April he had chosen the Escorial, so in September he chose the birthplace of the Reconquista, the tiny valley in which the Christian kingdom of Asturias had successfully prevented the Moslems from conquering the mountainous northwest of Spain. From the victory of Covadonga, Christian Spain had dated the beginning of its eight-century struggle to wrest Spain from Islam.

The workers of Oviedo and Gijón protested with effective one-day general strikes. The road to Covadonga was covered with tacks, and the CEDA caravan proceeded slowly, with brooms attached to the front fenders of the cars. In his speech, the chief referred to the Socialists as traitors and warned that he would never accept the dismemberment of the national territory implied by the concessions Samper had made to the Catalans and the Basques. He explained once again that the CEDA group in the Cortes had been too small to govern and too large to act merely as an opposition. They had sacrificed themselves for the good of Spain, but tomorrow they would govern. While carefully avoiding any incitement to violence, he stated that they would take the "trenches" to power one by one.[23]

Meanwhile, Indalecio Prieto was attempting to prove his own proletarian militance by smuggling arms to the Asturias. This feat was made possible by his unrivaled knowledge of backstairs politics in Spain and by the almost ludicrous inefficiency of government records. In 1931, shortly after the establishment of the Spanish Republic, a group of Portugese revolutionaries had tried to buy small arms from Spanish arsenals in the hope of overthrowing the Salazar dictatorship. They had worked through a wealthy Basque industrialist who was a friend of Prieto, but they had been unable ultimately to buy the arms, and these had been impounded at Cádiz in 1932 by the government of which Manuel Azaña was Prime Minister and Minister of War, and of which his friend Casares Quiroga was Minister of the Interior. In 1934 Prieto, knowing of the existence of this consignment, arranged to buy it—ostensibly for shipment to Ethiopia, which at that time was

[23] *La Vanguardia* and *El Debate,* Sept. 10, 1934.

---

anticipating invasion by Italy. In order to ship the arms, his agents bought a seagoing yacht, the *Turquesa,* from no less a person than the retired Admiral and royalist deputy Ramón Carranza.

The arms were loaded at Cádiz in the presence of a general staff officer bearing a "Clear Urgently" order from Prime Minister Samper.[24] The *Turquesa* then set its course for the Asturias where it made a brief nocturnal visit to the tiny fishing port of Ría Pravia. In the presence of Prieto, several cases of cartridges, eight pistols, three revolvers, and two muskets were unloaded.[25] Then, sensing the approach of the police, the vessel weighed anchor for Bordeaux, where the Spanish consul impounded the ship and the vast majority of its cargo. Meanwhile, the Socialist chief had run into a pair of suspicious carabineros but had managed to convince them that he loved nothing so much as walking along the seashore by night. Several days later he fled to France, where he was to remain until late 1935.

The whole month of September 1934 was punctuated by violent words and acts. In several Asturian villages, miners protesting the Covadonga rally and singing the *Internationale* clashed with police. In San Sebastián, in the heart of the moderate-mannered Basque country, two political assassinations occurred. Unknown revolutionaries killed Manuel Carrión, a wealthy industrialist of Falange sympathies, and on the day of his funeral, unidentified pistoleros shot Manuel Andrés Casaus, a member of Azaña's *Izquierda Republicana* and the former Director General of Security.[26] In Catalonia the rabassaires, against the advice of their leaders, were seizing harvests, and hotheads among them set fire to the Instituto Agrícola de San Isidro, the Barcelona headquarters of the hated landlords. Two days later, in Madrid, Gil Robles and

[24] Prieto in *El Socialista* (Toulouse), October 15, 1953. J. Alvarez del Vayo, *The Last Optimist* (New York, 1949), pp. 261–62.

[25] The figures are those of Salazar Alonso, *Bajo el signo,* pp. 259–62. For information on other small seizures of hidden weapons, see *La Vanguardia,* Sept. 20, 1934, and *Economía Española,* Sept., 1934, p. 111.

[26] *El Sol,* Sept. 11 and 12, 1934.

Martínez de Velasco addressed an assembly of Catalan landlords while the UGT called a general strike and the Minister of the Interior closed the Casa del Pueblo.

In the province of León, the Assault Guards mistakenly killed one man and seriously wounded two others. They were patrolling the Madrid-León highway on the night of September 16, watching for contraband arms. At intervals of a few minutes, they had challenged a truck, and then a car; however, they had done this without appearing on the road. In each case the drivers had speeded on, supposing that they were being attacked by bandits; and in each case the guards had kept out of sight, supposing that they were dealing with desperadoes, and had shot at the moving vehicles. The one fatality was a Catholic, and at his funeral in León spectators sang the Internationale and cried "death to Fascism."[27]

Late in the month, Salazar Alonso, addressing the Círculo Mercantil in Madrid, repeated his oft-spoken warnings concerning the imminence of a revolution and asked his audience to consider whether it might not be advantageous to provoke, and hence crush, the revolution.[28] The former King Alfonso intervened openly in Spanish politics for the first time with a letter to Antonio Goicoechea (printed later in *ABC*), offering his services to preserve Spain from revolutionary plots. The royalist leader Calvo Sotelo chose this moment to visit the exiled General Sanjurjo in Portugal.

Against this background of violence and threats, the Cortes convened on October 1. The CEDA refused its confidence to the Prime Minister, and the cabinet fell. For ten months the Radicals had governed with the support of the CEDA. Gil Robles now demanded CEDA participation in the cabinet. President Alcalá-Zamora remained profoundly suspicious of the "accidentalism" preached by Gil Robles. He was also jealous of the young man who had succeeded in organizing the conservative masses of the Republic, a role which Alcalá-

[27] *Ibid.*, Sept. 18, 1934.

[28] *La Vanguardia,* June 1, 1935. The speech had been referred to in several newspapers. Its direct quotation by Angel Ossorio y Gallardo was part of the defense of the Catalan government when it was tried in May, 1935 for the events of October 6, 1934.

Zamora had pictured as being his. He was well aware of the Socialist threat to rise against the legally constituted regime if power were handed to the CEDA. "Better Vienna than Berlin," cried the Socialists; meaning that however hopeless the odds, they would fight fascism as the Viennese workers had done rather than be destroyed without a struggle as in Hitler's Germany.

But the CEDA represented the largest single bloc of votes in the chamber. It had won its seats in a free election. Its leader insisted on his loyalty to the parliamentary system, if not to the Spanish Republic. While his party were admirers of the Austrian Chancellor Dollfuss, while their youth groups frequently mouthed fascist slogans, there was no evidence that Gil Robles personally was preparing a fascist regime. The President decided that in spite of his fears and distrusts, he could not forever exclude the CEDA. He called upon Alejandro Lerroux to form a coalition cabinet in which the CEDA would receive three ministries.

The reaction of other Republican leaders was immediate. In almost identical notes, Manuel Azaña, Diego Martínez Barrio, Felipe Sánchez Román, and Miguel Maura wrote the President saying that they were breaking all relations with the "existing institutions" of the country, and that the President was guilty of handing over the Republic to its enemies. The Socialists had hoped to the end that Alcalá-Zamora would refuse power to the CEDA. Now, in a divided vote, with the followers of Julián Besteiro and Andrés Saborit voting no, the Party decided to call a general strike throughout all Spain. In Valencia, on October 1, *El Pueblo,* organ of the outgoing Radical Prime Minister, Samper, defended the legality of the new Catalan *ley de cultivos* and went on to say: "Faced with a period of oppression and shame, no exit remains except a revolutionary outbreak. If the Right forces of Gil Robles are not understanding [in their attitudes] the road of legality will disappear."

THE REVOLUTION OF OCTOBER 1934

THE October revolution was intended to prevent the CEDA from participating in the government, a participation which appeared both to the middle-class liberals and to the revolutionary Left as equivalent to fascism in Spain. The revolt included three major phases. There was a series of unco-ordinated and unsuccessful general strikes in the large cities on the fifth of October. Then on the sixth, Luis Companys proclaimed the "Republic of Catalonia within the Federal Republic of Spain" and invited a democratic "government in exile" to establish itself in Barcelona. Meanwhile, in the mining province of Oviedo the united proletarian forces began an armed struggle against the government, the Army, and the existing capitalist regime.[1]

[1] The truth concerning the Catalan and Asturian risings is extremely difficult to determine. Political passions prevented most observers from acknowledging unpalatable truths about the side with which they sympathized. Press censorship lasted through the year 1935. Various agents of the Army, the Civil Guard, and the Assault Guard were a law unto themselves in the investigations after the event. Spanish, French, and English liberals who were moved by the fate of the miners nevertheless often knew very little about what had actually occurred. The forces of repression reacted violently to any civilian questioning of their conduct. Censorship was lifted in early 1936, but journalistic treatment at that time was entirely a function of the electoral campaign. Since the Civil War, only the victors' version has been documented in Spain. Needless to say, the thousands of knowledgeable leftists who fled Spain at the close of the Civil War did not carry documents in their baggage. With these facts in mind I have tried as far as possible to base my account on the most professionally competent journalism of the time and on the direct testimony of participants, particularly when that testimony comes from official investigations and trials in which the witness is under oath and liable to confrontation.

The general strikes failed for a number of reasons. First of all, the anarchists abstained almost entirely. In Aragon they were exhausted from the extraordinary efforts of the Saragossa general strike of March-April. In Catalonia they looked upon the Companys government as a purely "bourgeois" affair of no interest to them. In addition, the politically conscious workers, anarchist and Marxist alike, were confused by the divisions in their leadership. CNT Moderates like Angel Pestaña were evolving toward the notion of political participation in democratic governments. The anti-Stalinist leaders Andrés Nin and Joaquín Maurín, influential particularly in the province of Lérida, preached a communist revolution which would be less naïve and more organized than the *comunismo libertario* of the anarchists, but which would equally avoid the bureaucracy and centralism characteristic of both the Spanish Socialist and Communist parties. At the same time, Francisco Largo Caballero, disillusioned with the Republic, was organizing an *Alianza Obrera* (Workers' Alliance) which was to group all the nonanarchist elements of the proletariat in eastern Spain. Such a multiplicity of consigns tended to neutralize the force of the working class in Aragon and Catalonia.

In Andalusia and Extremadura the peasants were exhausted and confused after the failure of the June strike. The politically active ones knew that the Socialists had been divided as to the advisability of the strike, and all of them knew that the strike had been a costly failure. Again in October, the Socialists were divided on the best manner of combatting the entry of the CEDA into the government. Most of the intellectuals and the old-line trade-union leaders opposed the revolutionary talk of Largo Caballero and the arms-landing venture in Asturias. Largo himself called the general strike for the fifth in Madrid, but led it indecisively—the first of a number of occasions in which he was to show that his bark was worse than his bite. A final important reason for the failure of the strike calls was the prompt reaction of the government in declaring the *estado de guerra* throughout Spain.

The first important events took place in Catalonia. The

specific issue between the Generalitat and the central government was still the *ley de cultivos,* but several other circumstances added to the tension. The transfer of powers under the
Statute of Autonomy was going too slowly for Catalan taste,
and the delays naturally caused confusion as to who was
responsible for policy, management, salaries, and budgetary
costs in the existing provincial services. Crime increases in
1933 were attributed by the Barcelona press to the deliberate
negligence of the Madrid-controlled police.[2] When in April
1934, the transfer of authority took place, virtually the
entire police force resigned in ostentatious protest. The Civil
Guard, on the other hand, offered immediate cooperation to
the new Catalan authorities. The latter, however, were determined to create a rural police of their own and established the *Mossos d'Esquadra* to patrol the villages in sandals
and gold-braided blouses.[3]

Despite the Statute and the great personal popularity of
Companys, a wave of uncontrollable nationalism was sweeping Catalonia. Castilian professors at the university felt that
their students and their Catalan colleagues were deliberately
hostile to the continued use of Castilian in the lecture halls.
Leaflets appeared exhorting Catalans not to defile their blood
by marrying Castilians. More serious than such symptoms
was the growth of a quasi-fascist movement within the
younger ranks of the Esquerra. Wearing green shirts, calling
themselves *escamots* (squads), and naming their movement
Estat Català, they drilled in military formation with obsolete,

[2] *El Sol,* March 29 and July 1, 1933, articles on the problems
arising with regard to the transfer of powers, by the moderate
Catalanist historian A. Rovira i Virgili. Also Jesús Pérez Salas,
Guerra en España (Mexico, D. F., 1947), pp. 59–60. The author
headed the Barcelona municipal police during part of 1933.

[3] *New York Times,* Oct. 23 and 26, Nov. 6, 1933; April 29 and
Sept. 30, 1934. Lawrence Fernsworth, the *NYT* correspondent in
Barcelona, was particularly well informed. To understand the
tremendous impetus of Catalan national feeling, see E. Allison
Peers, *Catalonia Infelix* (London, 1937), Anton Sieberer, *Katalonien gegen Kastilien* (Vienna, 1936), and Brenan, *Spanish Labyrinth,* ch. 2.

nonserviceable rifles, and acknowledged as their chief José Dencás, councilor of public order in the Generalitat.

When the UGT called for a general strike against the entrance of the CEDA into the cabinet, Dencás thought he saw the perfect opportunity to achieve an independent Catalonia under his own leadership. On the morning of October 5 anarchist workers, and also most of the Socialist railway employees, reported for work. The escamots, sometimes at pistol point, stopped trolleys, told subway ticket agents to go home, and threatened to smash the windows of shops which did not close. They were reported also to be tearing up railroad lines west of Lérida so as to separate "Catalonia" from "Spain."[4]

President Companys found himself in the eye of a gathering storm. To his left, the impatient rabassaires threatened to expropriate the land now that the very men who had annulled the ley de cultivos were in full power in Madrid. To his right, the escamots prepared a fascist coup on Catalan soil. Meanwhile, throughout Spain the liberals and the Left were pressing for unity of action to forestall what they regarded as incipient fascism under Lerroux. If a clash should occur, there were no less than eight forces in Catalonia capable of armed violence: the Fourth Division of the Spanish Army, the municipal police of Barcelona, the Civil Guard and the Assault Guards, the Catalan Mossos, the escamots, the rabassaires, and the FAI.

Throughout October 5, and into the late afternoon of October 6, Companys repeatedly ordered the insubordinate Dencás not to bring his escamots into the streets. Since the municipal police chief, Miguel Badía, was a loyal lieutenant of Dencás, Companys could not enforce his orders. Meanwhile, he tried by telephone to reach Alcalá-Zamora in Madrid in order to warn the President that he could not contain either leftist or nationalist reactions against the new central government. The President's secretary read him a reassuring general message, but Companys made no direct contact with the

[4] Enrique de Angulo, *Diez horas de estat català* (Barcelona, 1935), pp. 30–3. This work is a detailed account by a competent Barcelona journalist not sympathetic to Catalan nationalism.

President himself.[5] On the morning of the sixth came the Prime Minister's announcement of the estado de guerra. That afternoon Companys telephoned General Batet, a Catalan and a known moderate, who was in charge of the Barcelona military district. He invited Batet to place himself at the service of "the federal Republic" and the General tried to calm his interlocutor's fears by pointing out that the proclamation of martial law applied to all Spain and was not directed against Catalonia.

All Barcelona anticipated a climax on the evening of the sixth. The councilors of the Generalitat appeared on the balcony of the government palace at 7:30, prepared to address the dense crowd on the Square of St. James below them and the radio audience of Catalonia as a whole. Exalted nationalists awaited the proclamation of full Catalan independence. Liberals awaited a declaration of resistance to Madrid fascism. Dencás planned to proclaim the *Estat Català* himself. Companys, caught between the several crossfires, grabbed the microphone from Dencás' hands and proclaimed the "Catalan state within the Federal Spanish Republic." He and his cabinet then barricaded themselves in the Generalitat, in downtown Barcelona, depending for their defense on about 100 Mossos, and hoping desperately that General Batet would remain neutral.

The wisdom of General Batet averted a major tragedy. He of course refused to place himself at the service of the Generalitat. But when the Minister of War called impatiently on the telephone at 2 a.m. to ask him why he had not crushed resistance, he replied that he preferred to await dawn so as to save lives.[6] Dencás, scenting failure, fled Barcelona that night. At five a.m. Companys arranged over the telephone the modalities of the surrender. General Batet ordered the gates to be opened and the Mossos to walk out with their hands up. Companys replied that this would be extremely

[5] *Ibid.*, pp. 36–41. Also testimony of Companys and of Rafael Sánchez-Guerra, secretary to President Alcalá-Zamora, at the 1935 trial of the Generalitat, *El Sol*, May 29, 1935.

[6] Diego Hidalgo, ¿ *Por qué fuí lanzado del Ministerio de la Guerra?* (Madrid, 1934), pp. 67–8.

dangerous because of the excited crowd waiting outside and because of the fact that a boy had been wounded in the very act of raising the white flag over the Generalitat. The General then revised his order. The gates were to be opened and he would send in his representative to receive the surrender. In this manner the Generalitat was enabled to surrender in dignity and without further bloodshed. The Catalan October revolution had cost a few deaths in the skirmishes during the night of October 6–7, and at dawn the Companys government went off to prison to await trial on charges of rebellion against the duly constituted authority.[7]

In the Asturias the course of events was determined largely by the geographical and psychological isolation of the mining towns. Nestling in the mountain valleys south and southeast of Oviedo, along the Aller and Nalón rivers, lay a series of mining communities, most of them numbering less than 10,000 inhabitants. Their conditions of life included dangerous work, constant police surveillance, an almost total absence of national newspapers, autos, radios, and household amenities, and a thirst for the minimum dignity and education which they could achieve through their labor unions. The UGT had the largest following, particularly in the provincial capital itself. The CNT, the Communists, and the Trotskyites all were represented in varying strength throughout the province.[8]

[7] Angulo, *Diez horas, passim,* and the testimony of General Batet and the members of the Generalitat, given in full in *La Vanguardia,* May 28, 1935. The trial is well summarized from a sympathetic point of view in Alardo Prats, *El gobierno de la generalidad en el banquillo* (Madrid, 1935).

[8] The Minister of War spoke of 20–30,000 revolutionaries, and Professor Mendizábal, who lived in Oviedo, speaks, in *Aux origines d'une tragédie,* pp. 201–204, of 20,000 Socialist and 6,000 Communist militants. Both Mendizábal and another eyewitness, a German emigré communist, Hans Theodore Joel, writing in *Living Age,* Feb., 1935, pp. 493ff., speak of 8,000 militants fighting their way into Oviedo. In view of these figures, I am inclined to think that Brenan, in *The Spanish Labyrinth,* pp. 284–88, overestimates when he speaks of 70,000 rising. However, this is only one of many factors that have been so long blanketed by censorship and propaganda that assured figures will probably never be available.

Years of Marxist and anarchist propaganda had created a sense of mission among the miners. Even as the Christian Reconquest of Spain had started from Covadonga, deep in the Cantabrican Mountains, so the proletarian revolution would be born in the Asturias. Sectarian quarrels had frequently prevented unity of action in the past, but in 1934, mindful of Hitler's triumph in Germany and of Dollfuss' triumph in Austria, they had achieved a considerable degree of unity. Taking the slogan *Unión, Hermanos Proletarios* (UHP) as

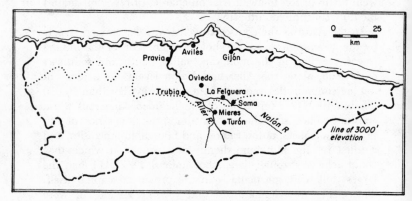

MAP 2. The Province of Asturias,
with Place Names Important in the October, 1934 Revolution

the name for their groups, the several working-class organizations had united in village revolutionary committees.[9]

On the night of October 4, when word of the new cabinet

[9] Except where otherwise specified, the following account of the days October 5–13 is based on Manuel Grossi, *La insurrección de Asturias* (Barcelona, 1935), and José Canel (pseud.) *Octubre rojo en Asturias* (Madrid, 1935). The first is the work of a thirty-year old miner who belonged to the *Bloque Obrero y Campesino* (non-Stalinist communists) and was a member of the Oviedo committee. He writes without literary flourishes, and with obvious candor. The second is the work of an experienced journalist and an evident admirer of the moderate Socialists Teodomiro Menéndez and Julián Besteiro. The two accounts are generally consistent throughout and are completely consistent in the details I have used.

arrived, the committees decided immediately to call a general strike. In Mieres, where Communist miners predominated, 200 militants, armed with about 30 rifles, surrounded the town hall and the barracks. Through a combination of surprise, terror, and exaggeration of their numbers (by firing the same rifles from different positions), they obtained the surrender of the Civil and Assault Guards. The next day they easily occupied several other mining towns between Mieres and Oviedo, sometimes using the Red Cross flag for their signalling, and on the sixth attacked the provincial capital itself. The population of Oviedo totaled about 80,000. In contrast to the mining centers, the city possessed a considerable middle class, a university, various government offices, and a garrison of 1,000 soldiers. About 8,000 militants marched on the city, with a few small arms and no artillery, but with quantities of dynamite. With the majority of the population keeping behind closed shutters, the miners captured the greater part of the city, occupying the lower floors of office and government buildings and hugging the walls to avoid being shot at from the upper stories.

The next day, news arrived of the failures in Madrid and Barcelona, and the Prime Minister mounted a radio and leaflet campaign to convince the miners that the government controlled the situation throughout the country. But the miners were not in the habit of believing Alejandro Lerroux, and the exaltation of their quick success, plus the large measure of popular backing which they felt in the mining and factory towns, increased their ardor. They occupied the Trubia and La Vega arms factories, confiscated numerous businesses, and established rationing of food and raw materials. For the best of the militant elements, the revolutionary regime was to be a demonstration of proletarian morality. Bourgeois received the same food rations as did workers. In the hospital, doctors were instructed to treat equally the government wounded and the revolutionary wounded. Nonpolitical middle-class and professional people were to be protected, even at the risk of life, by the revolutionary militia.[10]

[10] Mendizábal, *Aux origines,* pp. 207–209.

In Oviedo the Socialists and the Communists shared authority. The UGT was the strongest element numerically, and in Ramón Gonzáles Peña and Belarmino Tomás it possessed moderate leaders who enjoyed considerable prestige among middle-class liberals as well as among the proletariat. Communist prestige was based upon their capture of Mieres, and upon their prowess with dynamite in the capture of Oviedo. Both parties prided themselves on their discipline, and were anxious to prevent looting. The Oviedo committee looked with suspicion upon those who specifically requested night guard duty. They welcomed the opportunity to place political prisoners in private homes and counted for this purpose on the good offices of Teodomiro Menéndez, a Socialist deputy who had refused to take any part in the rising and had been briefly arrested by the militants.

However, for many of the revolutionary workers the looting of bourgeois shops did not constitute robbery. They were so accustomed to thinking of both the Civil and the Assault Guards as their class enemies that the temporary disappearance of these forces seemed a glorious opportunity simply to appropriate goods of all sorts. Also, for a tiny, primitive minority who had learned class hatred without learning "revolutionary discipline," physical liquidation of the enemy was in order. At Mieres, on the morning of October 5, when the Assault Guards had surrendered, the crowd demanded the death of two particularly hated Guards. The committee had refused, forming a circle with their own bodies to protect their prisoners. One of the Guards, crazed with fright, had broken out of the circle and been shot down.

In the two weeks following October 5 a total of perhaps 40 persons were murdered. A handful were engineers and businessmen, killed for motives of personal vengeance rationalized as class hatred. The principal victims, however, were priests. Several convents were searched unsuccessfully for arms, and priests trying to escape through the windows were shot at like rabbits. In Turón a half-dozen monks were arrested on the morning of the fifth, without mistreatment. During the next two days, their guards, who had separated them from their other prisoners, repeatedly asked them whether they would not join the revolutionary forces. The monks replied that they could not go to the front except in their religious capacity. On the eighth a group of soldiers, who did not belong to their guard, entered and marched them off on the pretext that they were going to the front. They took them instead to the village cemetery, and shot them. In the village of Sama, the corpse of an Assault Guard was trampled in a manner reminiscent of Castilblanco. It is equally true, however, that many a surviving soldier and priest testified to the efforts of the committee leaders to prevent the assassination of priests and prisoners, interventions which had saved dozens of lives.[11]

The government was taken aback by the revolutionary capture of Oviedo. It feared to send in the regular Army because of the strong possibility that the Spanish conscripts would refuse to fire on the revolutionaries—or even desert to them. The War Minister, Diego Hidalgo, acting on the advice of Generals Franco and Goded, sent in contingents of the Moorish *regulares* and of the Foreign Legion.[12] Arriving at the ports of Avilés and Gijón on October 8, these troops were able quickly to overcome the resistance of the local fishermen and stevedores.[13] The revolutionary committees here were anarchist-dominated. Though they had joined the rising and accepted the slogan UHP, the Socialists and Communists of Oviedo clearly distrusted them and had refused arms to their delegate the day before.

As of October 9, the revolutionaries knew that they were isolated, completely on the defensive, and that the Foreign Legion had landed. In Oviedo González Peña had difficulty restraining the desperate miners from blowing up the Cathedral, from which building they claimed to have been shot at. Between the tenth and the twelfth, he and other leaders advising surrender were accused of cowardice and threatened with death. By nightfall of October 12, General López Ochoa had recaptured all of Oviedo except the railway station. As a

[11] *El Sol,* Oct. 23, 28, and 30, for reports of both terror and prevention of terror among the revolutionaries.

[12] Hidalgo, *op. cit.,* pp. 83–8.

[13] Fernando Solano Palacio, *La tragedia del norte* (Barcelona, 1938), p. 90.

result of artillery bombardments by the Army and dynamiting by the miners, the city had neither water nor light. The university library and hundreds of houses had been destroyed.

González Peña, worn out by efforts to prevent unnecessary destruction, and unable to convince the miners of the hopelessness of continued resistance, resigned. The Communists (as they were to do in March, 1939) came forward as the spokesmen of continued resistance, regardless of the odds. A new, Communist-dominated committee was formed, and all the parties pledged to continue the struggle. The new committee could make gestures, but not exercise authority. It arrested Teodomiro Menéndez for a few hours. The next morning, October 13, it dispatched a six-car "armored train" with some 200 men to the village of Campomanes. The railway workers cooperated most unwillingly. A few miles out of the capital a three-hour halt was necessary for boiler repairs, after which the train happened upon an enemy patrol, and the boiler was pierced by gunfire. The leader of the expedition had difficulty preventing his men from killing the engine driver for presumed sabotage.

Meanwhile, from October 10 to October 18, the Moors and Legionaries took the mining villages house by house. General López Ochoa, an enlightened officer and a Freemason, did what he could to prevent murder and rape—including the shooting of four Moorish soldiers guilty of atrocities. Colonel Yagüe of the Legion preferred to use salutary terror as a weapon and did not inhibit his troops. The last days were characterized by acts of desperate bravado, with unarmed miners baring their breasts defiantly at the advancing troops.

Mieres, from which the revolutionaries had started on October 5, was their last remaining stronghold by October 18. Belarmino Tomás, Socialist delegate on the committee, negotiated terms of surrender with General López Ochoa. The revolutionaries demanded that the Moors not be allowed to enter the villages. Tomás related how on October 13 he and a handful of miners had probed the outskirts of Oviedo. In the cemetery they had seen 18 corpses which had been tied together and mutilated, and in a miner's home they had found the body of a girl who had been raped and whose two arms had been cut off. The General was anxious to avoid further bloodshed, and acknowledged that if the miners were to fight on in suicidal desperation, it might take weeks and months to pacify the Asturias. He agreed that the Moors and the Legion were not to enter the villages unless they were sniped at, in which case he would put them in the vanguard.[14]

Sniping was the real or alleged reason for the frequent shooting of prisoners during the ten days of the military "cleanup." A small contingent of soldiers would be marching a large group of prisoners through hostile, hilly territory. An isolated shot, or imprecation, would ring out from a wooded mountainside. Supposing that this shot might be the prelude to a general attack in the effort to liberate the prisoners, their guards would shoot them. It is impossible to know just how many men were killed in this fashion, since the method was not readily acknowledged.

During the two weeks of fighting the Spanish public knew very little concerning the methods employed by the government forces. Many had admired the dignity with which Prime Minister Lerroux had gone on the radio the night of October 5, simultaneously announcing the estado de guerra and promising a swift, just return to normality. The collapse of the general strikes and the Catalan revolt added considerably to the government's prestige. Even for a large proportion of the Left, the Asturian revolution constituted a disastrous political error, and it was admitted that any government would have had to repress the miners' commune. But in the following weeks the government, dependent upon the military and the far Right, lost control of the situation in the Asturias. The Civil and Assault Guards vied with one another in prying lurid confessions from the prisoners. The right-wing press printed tales of nuns having been raped and of children whose eyes had been gouged out. The Cortes, which had refused to restore the death penalty at the time of the Saragossa general strike, now voted it quickly.

[14] *Le Populaire,* Jan. 5 and 6, 1935. The French Socialist daily interviewed Tomás in prison where he awaited trial, and at a time when censorship prevented discussion in the Spanish papers.

In Oviedo a liberal journalist, Luis Sirval, was shot dead in the street by a Legionary who had taken umbrage at his articles. The murder of Sirval was no more brutal than many another committed by the forces of repression, but the name Sirval was well known and highly respected. The government imposed censorship on all news from Asturias, but a parliamentary investigation group went to Oviedo: Alvarez del Vayo and Fernando de los Ríos for the Socialists; Félix Gordón Ordás and Clara Campoamor for the Republicans, both of them supporters, up to that time, of Lerroux. These investigators established the falsity of the stories concerning nuns and children. At the same time, they amassed the most damaging evidence of torture in the prisons, and many middle-class witnesses in Oviedo lauded the nobility of the miners, who for the most part had strictly respected noncombattant persons during the siege of the city. The Cortes delegation was joined by a British Parliamentary group. The latter were unable to do more than confirm the evidence of their Spanish colleagues, but their presence in Spain was considered an insult by the Right, while their reports abroad created a wave of international sympathy for the miners.

The principal instigator of sadistic torture was Major Doval of the Civil Guard, who employed, among other techniques, pressure on the sexual organs, and the thrusting of pins and splinters under the fingernails. He also had an ingenious method of binding the victim's wrists and legs to the stock of a rifle and then lifting him off the floor by a pulley. By such means his men had obtained several confessions for the same crime. Félix Gordón Ordás, professor of veterinary medicine, a Mason, and a deputy of the Radical Party, after collecting evidence of Doval's activities, wrote a denunciatory letter to Prime Minister Lerroux. Lerroux was under intense pressure from the Right to "crush" the revolution, and from the Left to amnesty the thousands of prisoners taken during the cleanup. He telephoned Doval's superior, General Velarde, ordering the latter to restrain and control the Major's activities. Doval somehow learned the text of the telephone conversation and sent copies of it to the Monarchist leaders Antonio Goicoechea and Luca de Tena. Goicoechea showed his to friends in the Cortes corridors, and when Lerroux learned of this he immediately ordered Doval removed for insubordination.[15] Luca de Tena's newspaper, *ABC*, then prepared an editorial excoriating Lerroux, which was prevented by the censor from appearing. Lerroux's action was characteristic, in that he desired to act humanely, but in order to avoid a confrontation with his reactionary supporters, he seized the pretext of insubordination to remove Doval rather than face the issue of police torture. The Right howled that the government was betraying Spain by retreating before International Masonic Marxism, and the Left compared the Asturian commune with the Spartacus revolt, the Paris Revolution of 1848, the Paris Commune, the resistance of the Vienna workers to Dollfuss, and other heroic episodes in the struggle of the international proletariat.

The "liquidation" of the October revolt occupied the government well into the year 1935. Hundreds of mixed juries and municipal governments, including those of Madrid, Barcelona, and Valencia, were suspended; the estado de alarma and the press censorship were extended month after month. Between 30–40,000 prisoners awaited trial all over Spain. The vast majority of these prisoners, and of the suspended municipal councilors, could at most be accused of belonging to the same political parties or being colleagues on friendly terms with one or another of the leaders directly involved in the Catalan or Asturian risings.

A number of military and political trials revealed the uncertainty of the government and the embitterment of public opinion. Major Pérez Farras, the professional officer who had led the Catalan Mossos in their resistance to General Batet's troops during the night of October 6, was court-martialed and condemned to death for military rebellion. Under Article 102 of the Constitution, the President had the power to commute death sentences "following review by the Supreme Court and upon the proposal of the cabinet." President Alcalá-Zamora was loath to create martyrs in the cause of Catalan autonomy, and he was convinced that a pro-

[15] *Ibid.*, and Brenan, *Spanish Labyrinth,* pp. 287–89.

tracted campaign of repression would destroy the Republic. The members of the Cabinet were unwilling to recommend a commutation but agreed to a review by the High Court. The Court confirmed the fatal verdict, and Alcalá-Zamora threw the entire weight of his prestige into a now successful effort to have the Cabinet permit him to commute the death sentence. Lerroux took the position that Major Pérez, a professional officer and a university-educated engineer, had been guilty of flagrant military rebellion. The President reminded his ministers that the death sentence for General Sanjurjo had been immediately commuted, to the universal satisfaction of all those now demanding the death of Major Pérez Farras. The President won his point, at the cost of worsening personal relations between himself and the Lerroux ministry.[16]

In Oviedo on February 1, 1935, two men were shot after courtmartial: a Sergeant Vásquez who had deserted, arms in hand, to the revolutionary militia, and a miner who had commanded the firing squad at the execution of 8 Civil Guards. In this case Alcalá-Zamora refused to commute, though pressed by the Left to do so. Vásquez and Argüelles indeed had blood on their hands, but many people felt that it was unjust to commute the sentence of an educated man who knew precisely what he was doing and to execute two poor devils swept away by emotions and vaguely understood ideologies. The President was accused of appeasing Catalan nationalism rather than of acting out of disinterested humanity.

In mid-February came the trials of the principal Socialist deputies involved in the Asturian revolt: Teodomiro Menéndez and Ramón González Peña. Menéndez had been one of the small group of Socialist deputies during the Monarchy and had belonged always to the moderate sector of his party. The rising had caught him at his house in Oviedo and the entering army arrested him there. Lined up among several hundred prisoners, he counted 27 men shot before his turn came and attributed his momentary survival to the fact that he had been on friendly personal terms with General López Ochoa. During the first weeks of his imprisonment, he

[16] Lerroux, *La pequeña historia,* pp. 330–36, 362–64.

showed symptoms of nervous collapse. The sounds of torture could be heard clearly, and the news of irregular executions arrived constantly. In late December he apparently attempted to commit suicide by jumping from a balcony to the concrete floor of the prison. (The word "apparently" is necessary because censorship made it impossible for anyone to obtain the full story). In any event, he suffered severe skull and back injuries. On December 20, during the parliamentary investigation of prison tortures, his old friend Fernando de los Ríos visited him, and the latter reported that Menéndez recognized him but spoke incoherently, and in evident delirium.[17]

By the time of his trial, in February, he was still both physically and mentally incapacitated. Local testimony indicated that he had stayed in his house all week, that his only activity had been to try to have various prisoners released, and that he had refused an invitation to address the crowd which was about to march on the La Vega arms factory. The case against him rested on his "being seen" with several revolutionary leaders, and his signature appeared on one document, which turned out to concern the transfer of prisoners to private homes. There were affidavits signed by persons who had been released through his efforts, and a letter from Julián Besteiro affirming that in the Socialist Party caucas Menéndez had voted against the rising. At the end, he was wheeled into court on a stretcher and asked whether he wished to speak in his own defense, to which he replied in the negative.[18]

A few days later, without sentence having been passed yet on Menéndez, the trial of González Peña began. He had been a member of the revolutionary committee and had handled funds robbed from the Bank of Spain. Many witnesses testified to his having "given orders," though significantly none accused him of violence or cruelty to prisoners. In his own testimony, González Peña stated that he had indeed received 15,000 pesetas with which to flee. (He had remained successfully hidden until December 4). But upon his capture he had returned 15,500 pesetas. He said that

[17] *El Sol,* Dec. 30, 1934, for the suicide report. *Le Populaire,* Jan. 13, 1935, for De los Ríos' report of his visit to the prison hospital.
[18] *El Sol* and *Le Populaire,* Feb. 10, 1935.

he had saved 100 guards from being shot at the Pelayo Barracks, and there were several witnesses to his efforts to prevent incendiarism and terrorism. On trial for his life two weeks after the executions of Vásquez and Argüelles, he delivered to the court an autobiographical justification of his solidarity with the revolutionaries. Among other things, since he was accused of robbing the Bank of Spain, he described his personal income. As an electrician he had been making between twenty and sixty thousand pesetas a year under the Republic. Of this income, he lived on 5,000, spent 4,000 on books, loaned 9,000 to friends, and gave the rest to the unemployed.[19]

In the interval between the Menéndez and González Peña trials, the French Socialist Party collected thousands of signatures on amnesty petitions, and the French Socialist deputy, Vincent Auriol, visited Lerroux on behalf of the League of the Rights of Man. A group of Spanish intellectuals simultaneously wrote to President Alcalá-Zamora, protesting the tortures in the Oviedo prison as revealed in a document signed by some 564 prisoners in late January. Among those signing the letter to the President were the famous writers Unamuno and Valle-Inclán, and Francisco Bergamín, the lawyer who had defended General Sanjurjo in 1932.[20]

On February 16 the military court announced the death sentences of both Menéndez and González Peña, followed in the next few days by condemnation of 17 other members of the revolutionary committees. This succession of death penalties caused a crisis within the Center-Right government. Prime Minister Lerroux, though he had favored the death penalty for Pérez Farras, was not a vengeful man. His own reputation rested not on any program, but on his ability to appease extremists. He was humorously known as "the commissioner (contratista) of public tranquility." Partly out of his own humanity and partly out of desire not to let Alcalá-Zamora receive the credit, Lerroux recommended a commuta-

[19] *El Sol,* Feb. 16, 1935.
[20] *Le Populaire,* Feb. 11 and 16, 1935. Events not mentioned in the Spanish press.

tion of the sentence against the revolutionary political chiefs. Immediately, Gil Robles for the CEDA and Melquiades Alvarez for the Reformist Party announced that they would no longer collaborate with the government.[21]

The Right hoped to use the Asturian crisis not only to execute the Socialist leaders but to discredit the Left Republicans. In the courts and in Parliament they attempted repeatedly to make Manuel Azaña co-responsible personally for both the Catalan and Asturian risings. Azaña had come to Barcelona at the end of September 1934 to attend the funeral of Jaime Carner, who had been Minister of Finance in his government. The tribute to Carner naturally brought together many leading personalities of the 1931–33 era, and there were several conversations involving Left Republicans, Socialists, and members of the Generalitat. Azaña had planned to return to Madrid on October 4, but over the telephone several friends had pleaded with him not to leave Barcelona. All of them feared a military coup and considered that Azaña's life would be endangered if he were to return. The next day, the general strike was virtually complete in Catalonia, and he was thus obliged to remain where he was.

On the 6th, while the Esquerra were debating whether or not to declare the *Estat Català*, a member of Companys' cabinet, Juan Lluhí, came to see Azaña at the Hotel Colón. In an obviously agitated frame of mind, he told the former Prime Minister that the Generalitat could not restrain the masses, and that they would either have to channel the nationalist movement or fire on their own supporters. Azaña reminded him that he had voted against a federal republic, and that no matter what the actual motive of the Generalitat might be, any declaration against the central government would appear to be separatist. Azaña was sure also that the move would fail. Lluhí taxed him with pessimism and suggested hopefully an analogy with the events of 1931. Colonel Macià had gone too far in declaring the Catalan Republic. Madrid had hurried to negotiate with him. In the resulting

[21] Lerroux, *op. cit.*, pp. 372–75. See also the tribute to Lerroux's motives by Indalecio Prieto in *El Socialista* (Toulouse), May 10, 1956.

compromise the Catalans had yielded their separate republic in return for the firm pledge of an autonomy statute. Lluhí suggested that what the Generalitat really hoped for was a similar bargain. After declaring the federal republic they would negotiate with Madrid, conceding the *Estat Català* against a satisfactory settlement of the *ley de cultivos* issue.

Aware of the puerility of any such hope, and knowing that by his mere presence in Barcelona he would be implicated in whatever occurred, Azaña immediately called to his hotel the Catalan committee of Izquierda Republicana. He related to them his conversation and received their unanimous approval for his expression of opposition to any such rising as Lluhí hinted at. About eight o'clock that evening he left the hotel, accompanied by several friends and by the plain-clothes policeman assigned by the Madrid government to guard and watch him. He spent the night in the home of a personal friend, Dr. Rafael Gubern.

At about the time Azaña was checking out of the Hotel Colón, Alejandro Lerroux was speaking with General Batet over the telephone. Among other things, he told the General that Azaña was at that moment writing a manifesto for Companys "which presumably will have a seditious character." On the morning of the 7th, when all was over, the Director General of Security announced to the journalists in Madrid that "Azaña and his band" had fled through a sewer in the basement of the Generalitat. Had the Director checked with his own agent assigned to watch Azaña he would have known that the latter had never gone to the Generalitat, and had he checked with the Barcelona police he would have known that no such sewer existed. Had he asked his agent about Azaña's activities the afternoon of the 6th, he would have known that Azaña had tried to dissuade Lluhí, and that his party had gone on record against any attempted rising.

Azaña was arrested on the 7th and interned on a prison ship in the harbor of Barcelona. After three days' examination, the military investigator in charge, General Pozas, was completely convinced of Azaña's innocence and made no secret of the fact to anyone. But the government refused to release him. On November 14 a group of prominent intellectuals addressed an open letter to the government protesting the senseless persecution of the former Prime Minister. Censorship prevented the letter from appearing in the newspapers.[22] Azaña was provisionally released late in December while the case went to the Supreme Court. During January and February, public attention was concentrated on the torture revelations in Oviedo and on the trials of Menéndez and González Peña. Then on March 21, when it appeared likely that the death 'sentences would be commuted, the Monarchists initiated a full-dress Cortes debate. Antonio Goicoechea held Azaña responsible for the entire civil discord reigning in Spain. He repeated all the unproven and disproven charges made at the time of Casas Viejas; he went on to accuse Azaña of having initiated the Catalan rising, and then attributed to him the arms landings in the Asturias.

In its attempt to destroy Azaña, the Right virtually created the Popular Front. Public opinion would probably have supported the Center-Right government if after the revolution it had singled out for punishment the perpetrators of atrocities among both the revolutionaries and the military. But the Monarchist press and deputies were determined to identify the entire liberal Republic with the most militant revolutionary miners. The CEDA and the Lerroux government, though they knew better, meekly followed the lead of Antonio Goicoechea.

In point of fact, every form of fanaticism and cruelty which was to characterize the Civil War occurred during the October revolution and its aftermath: utopian revolution marred by sporadic red terror; systematically bloody repression by the "forces of order"; confusion and demoralization of the moderate Left; fanatical vengefulness on the part of the Right. After the restoration of order, the President and the Prime Minister had tried, fumblingly but sincerely, to limit the repression. But press censorship prevented the Spanish people ever from knowing what had happened in the Asturias, and therefore from learning the lessons of that tragic prologue to civil war.

[22] Manuel Azaña, *Mi rebelión en Barcelona* (Madrid, 1935), pp. 5–6, for the text of the letter; pp. 90–125 and *passim* for his conversation with Lluhí and his arrest. See also Frank Sedwick,

When in March 1935, the Right attempted, against the overwhelming weight of the evidence, to equate Azaña with Sergeant Vásquez, they forged the unity of the moderate and the extreme Left. They disgusted the honest conservatives and went far toward making Azaña the idol of the masses. During the day of the debate, large, friendly crowds gathered to cheer Azaña as he entered and left the Cortes. When the balloting took place in the evening the Carlists, *Renovación,* and the CEDA voted against Azaña. The conservative republicans, the Basque Nationalists, the Esquerra, and the entire Left voted for him.[23] The lineup was much that of Spain on July 18, 1936. It came almost as an anticlimax when the Supreme Court on April 6 cleared Azaña of all charges in connection with the October revolution. Even then, the Right did not accept the verdict, and in July the Cortes was once more to hear all the old charges repeated.

The Tragedy of Manuel Azaña (Columbus, Ohio, 1963), pp. 137–39 and 251–60 for details on the imprisonment of Azaña, including a hitherto unpublished letter by Angel Ossorio, Azaña's defending lawyer.

[23] *La Vanguardia,* March 21, 22, and 26, 1935. *Política,* March 28, 1935 (organ of *Izquierda Republicana*).

POLITICS AND IDEOLOGIES IN 1935

WITH the Asturian revolt over and the Lerroux government firmly in power, the Center-Right coalition had one more opportunity to govern Spain. The Minister of Agriculture, Manuel Giménez Fernández, was determined to transform latifundia Spain according to Catholic social principles. Lawyer and historian, an energetic speaker, and lieutenant to Gil Robles within the CEDA, he sponsored three laws intended to encourage the development of individual family farms in Andalusia and Extremadura. The law passed in March was designed to improve the conditions of those who rented small parcels of land. They were to receive long-term leases and to be compensated for improvements which they made on the land and buildings. The land they worked was not to be sold without their agreeing to the sale price. The law of August was intended to give arrendatarios the opportunity to buy a parcel of land. And the law of November specifically obliged the landlords of Extremadura to rent their uncultivated lands during the following year.

However, the Minister's own party insisted on clauses in these laws which effectively prevented them from leading to any fundamental change in rural property relations. The March law gave the proprietor the choice of meeting the new rental conditions or cultivating the land himself. Its passage was followed by a wave of evictions on the part of landowners who simply announced to their helpless tenants that they now intended to work the land themselves.[1] The August law stated that peasants should have the opportunity to buy *some* land, not necessarily the land they were currently living on. The property available would be that which the landlords were willing to sell. Numerous legal steps were necessary before title was acquired, and the peasant settling

[1] *El Sol*, April 20, 1935.

on a given parcel was to pay a rent of 4 per cent of the assessed value during the years of legal transactions.[2] As under the 1932 law, the peasant faced an indefinite period of litigation, during which time he paid rent without knowing whether he would secure title. In 1932 at least the government had subjected a great deal of land to expropriation, but in 1935 the available acreage would be that which the landlords themselves wished to dispose of.

The problem of surplus wheat arose in 1935 as it had in the two previous years. In June the Cortes authorized the government to buy the surplus but stated that preference should be given to farmers who held loans of the agricultural credit banks. Thus the prosperity of the banks became the first criterion in deciding which farmers needed the most rapid relief. When this measure proved totally inadequate, the Ministry of War bought large quantities and provided a 200 million peseta credit to keep the mills operating despite unfavorable market conditions.[3]

As in the Azaña period, the school question occupied the Cortes frequently and passionately. From April to December 1934 the Minister of Public Instruction had been Filiberto Villalobos, a member of the Melquiades Alvarez party. Villalobos, though with reduced budgets in comparison with the years 1931–33, had continued building primary schools in the villages and had attacked the housing problem for teachers by offering a 3,000 peseta subsidy to each village that built a house for the *maestro*. The CEDA charged him with promoting laic education, and he was removed at the end of the year. During 1935, the pretext of economy brought school construction to a virtual halt. The government drastically cut the budgets for foreign scholarships, the Center of Arabic studies, the summer school of the University of Madrid in Santander, the *misiones pedagógicas,* and the medical faculty Madrid.[4] In some of these cases a plausible argument could

[2] The *New York Times,* March 2 and Oct. 27, 1935. *El Sol,* Dec. 1, 1935, in which "un agricultor" offered a full-page technical analysis of the effects of the three agrarian laws of 1935.

[3] *El Sol,* Oct. 8, 1935. *Economía Española,* Sept., 1935, pp. 60–62.

[4] Américo Castro in *El Sol,* June 30, 1934, and Claudio Sánchez Albornoz in *Política,* Oct. 17, 1935.

be made for economy, but the real motive was to hamper the work of those institutions in which the influence of the *Institución Libre de Enseñanza* was the strongest. In November came a decree ending the independence of primary school inspectors. Since 1913, they had enjoyed long tenure in office, but now they could be transferred or removed at the request of local authorities.[5]

Together with the starvation of the budget for public education came the restitution of confiscated Jesuit properties. The government restored some 25 buildings which had been taken over by the municipalities of Barcelona and Valencia as schools, and prepared to pay an additional indemnity to the Order. Lerroux made no secret of the fact that his government intended to appease the Church, and the CEDA insisted that all schools, public and private, should be Catholic.[6]

Gil Robles had brought down the government in March by his refusal to accept the commutation of the death sentences of the Asturian leaders. The Monarchist press had praised him for this intransigeance. In early May the CEDA reentered the cabinet, this time with Gil Robles himself as Minister of War, and with the Monarchists accusing him of betrayal by his "acceptance" of the Republic. As War Minister Gil Robles retained most of the structural reforms made by Azaña. He considered that the reduction in size—and much of the reorganization—had been necessary, but that Azaña's personal appointments had offended the majority of the officer corps: that Azaña had chosen his friends rather than the most prestigious professional officers, to carry out his reforms. In 1935, however, appointing the officers of greatest corps prestige meant appointing officers who either hated the Republic, such as Generals Fanjul and Goded, or who were indifferent to political forms, like General Francisco Franco, the able, ambitious career officer who had trained the Foreign Legion to its high pitch of efficiency and discipline.

Even before the Asturian revolt, Spanish liberals had feared the Legion. After October they saw it as the perfect instrument for a *coup d'état:* disciplined, well armed, as cruel as it

[5] *El Sol,* Nov. 30, 1935.

[6] *El Liberal,* Madrid, May 25 and 30, June 1–12, 1935. The *New York Times,* Sept. 8, 1935.

needed to be in any given situation, and without any inhibiting ties to the Spanish population. On April 14, 1935, at the ceremony commemorating the fourth anniversary of the Republic, President Alcalá-Zamora had decorated Generals Batet and López Ochoa, thus singling out the military men who had shown humanity during the October revolt. The right-wing press had preferred to praise Franco and the work of the Legion in the Asturias, and in early May, Gil Robles appointed him chief of staff. During the summer he made another move which seemed to portend a military coup. He attempted to have the Civil Guard transferred from the Ministry of the Interior to the Ministry of War in order to remove it from "leftist" influence. Since the Minister of the Interior was the very respectable and conservative Manuel Portela Valladares, Gil Robles' own colleagues in the cabinet began to fear him.

At various intervals during 1935 Gil Robles repeated publicly his opposition to military coups. Popular distrust of him was artfully satirized in a prizewinning comedy by Juan Ignacio Luca de Tena, son of the founder of *ABC*. The hero of ? *Quien soy yo?*, (*Who am I?*) Mario Colomer, is a young minister whose brilliant career has caused the Prime Minister and the President to be jealous of him, but whose efficacy and party backing are such that everyone expects him shortly to achieve full power. Now, a certain general has placed himself entirely at the Minister's disposition. Yet Mario Colomer says he will never consent to a *coup d'état*. However, he has a double, who has been heard talking of just such a move. In the last act, the general, understandably confused, seizes power on his own responsibility and hands it to Mario Colomer. Like the general in the play, the Spanish public were confused about Gil Robles' true intentions.[7]

[7] In the course of my research in Spain I asked Sr. Gil Robles about the repeated rumors that he had contemplated a *coup d'état* during his tenure as Minister of War, May 8–Dec. 14, 1935. He flatly denied all these rumors, and I personally accept his denials so far as he himself is concerned. However, I posed the same questions independently to several of his personal and party collaborators, and every one of them believed that he had

Alejandro Lerroux still desired to bring moderate and able men into his cabinet. His best appointment along these lines was the choice of Joaquín Chapaprieta, a wealthy lawyer of high reputation, as Minister of Finance. Before the Primo dictatorship, he had served as sub-secretary of Finance under Santiago Alba, who was now President of the Cortes. He was a technical expert without political ambitions, and among the collaborators of Lerroux he stood out as being beyond the reach of temptation. Chapaprieta wished to balance the budget through honesty, economy, and new taxation. He planned to reduce departmental staffs and called for a general 10–15 per cent cut in civil service salaries. At the same time, he planned to raise inheritance taxes and to increase various charges on the transfer of large properties. The CEDA informed Chapaprieta that they would not support his budget if it included the new inheritance and transfer taxes. As in the case of Giménez Fernández' land reform efforts, Gil Robles placed the interests of his wealthy backers above those of social justice, whether conceived in Catholic or nonreligious terms.

Exception made for certain nuances, the government in 1935 was unabashedly reactionary. It refused land reform and starved public education. It restored the Jesuit properties, favored the anti-Republican sector of the professional Army, and refused to approve taxes which would in any way strike the rich. Its unpopularity and lack of program forced it constantly to depend upon powers of exception. In the summer of 1933 the Law for the Defense of the Republic had been repealed, and in its place the Cortes had passed a more

---

indeed considered a coup, giving me names and dates to support their contention. Needless to say, in these latter cases, the persons interviewed either would have approved, or at least "understood," such a coup.

See also the unfavorable interpretations of Gil Robles as Minister of War in Mendizábal, *Aux origines,* pp. 214–22, and Brenan, *Spanish Labyrinth,* pp. 291–93. Salvador de Madariaga, *Spain* (New York, 1958), p. 439, defends him strongly, pointing to the number of opportunities he had to seize power if that was what he wished to do.

detailed, graduated Law of Public Order. The new law defined the states of prevention, alarm, and war. In the first case, police would be alerted and preventive arrests made. In the second the government might apply broad measures of censorship and close the headquarters of organizations deemed to be threatening public order. In the third case the government could declare martial law. On October 5, 1934, Prime Minister Lerroux had declared the state of war. Two months later the government had felt confident enough to begin the return to normal civilian government by substituting the state of alarm for the state of war. But no further progress was made. Throughout 1935 the *estado de alarma* was extended month by month; the municipal governments, the mixed juries, the Catalan Generalitat, all remained suspended. The thirty to forty thousand political prisoners taken in October remained in jail.

At the same time, however, the press, despite frequent censorship, expressed bitter and fearless criticism of the government. Since the government's existence depended at all times on its maintaining a majority in the Cortes, it would be a gross exaggeration to label the Lerroux governments of 1935 "fascist." On the contrary, the entire Right felt that they had twice been cheated of their victories: once after winning the elections in November 1933 and again after the failure of the Catalan and Asturian revolts. Following the electoral victory, Gil Robles had spoken in the Cortes of cooperation between his party and the Republican government. *ABC* immediately had cried betrayal, since in their view the majority of the CEDA votes were Monarchist votes. *El Debate* replied by quoting texts of Leo XIII on the compatibility of all forms of government with the Church. After a bit of research, *ABC* was quick to point out that the Pope's statements had referred specifically to France of the late 1890's, where the Third Republic had already been established for twenty years, and where there were no monarchist candidates standing for election. Thus while the Left considered Gil Robles the leader of a clerical-facist movement on the model of the Dollfuss regime in Austria, the Monarchists accused him of selling out to the Republic.

After the amnesty of General Sanjurjo in April 1934 the reactionary monarchist organization *Acción Española* was permitted to reopen. Its avowed purpose was to revitalize Spain's traditional values which had been undermined by the republicans and Krausists. Among the lecture courses it offered was one on *Antiparlamentarismo,* by Ramón Serrano Suñer, brother-in-law of General Franco and himself head of the CEDA youth.[8] The Monarchist exiles also returned now to Spain. José Calvo Sotelo, who had become an ardent admirer of Charles Maurras while living in France, formed the *Bloque Nacional,* with a program calling for a corporative and totalitarian state. In public speeches he asked repeatedly, with ironic reference to the CEDA: why consolidate a republic without republicans? At the end of the year, the Monarchists were disgusted by what they considered to be the relatively mild repression in the Asturias. In a newspaper polemic between the two leaders, Calvo Sotelo complained that the results achieved by the CEDA were totally disproportionate to the great electoral triumph of 1933, and stated that the Monarchists could not understand what "mysterious formula" permitted the Catholic CEDA to maintain an alliance with the "unbelieving positivism" represented by Lerroux's Radicals. Gil Robles avoided specific argument in his reply but expressed his grief that the Monarchist press had begun attacking him the moment the election had been won; he reminded his respected colleague that the latter was sitting in the Cortes and publishing a newspaper because of the Sanjurjo amnesty obtained by the CEDA.[9]

Throughout 1935 Gil Robles labored to hold together his disparate coalition. He demanded the death penalty for González Peña in February and March in order to appease the Monarchists. In May he joined a new Center-Right cabinet, and in June he sealed the alliance at a Salamanca banquet in honor of Alejandro Lerroux. He spoke of the honored worker and the small farmer, but his party emasculated land reform and extended the suspension of municipal governments in which the Left had gained a majority in 1933.

[8] Galindo Herrero, *Los partidos monárquicos,* pp. 230–34.
[9] *Ibid.,* 246–65.

The press of *Acción Católica* frequently printed violent attacks on the Masons and the Jews. Gil Robles disavowed these phrases, but on November 9, 1935, speaking to an audience of Catholic youth in Salamanca, he assailed the "revolutionary spirit" which had been "the fruit of many generations of teachers" and "the work of a de-christianized university" and of the foreign scholarship program. His audience was delighted, but the moderate republican newspaper *El Sol* attacked him editorially for such demagogy. Gil Robles knew very well, wrote *El Sol*, that the majority of the Salamanca faculty were practicing Catholics, and that many of the most highly praised professors of the Centro Católico de Estudios Universitarios had received foreign scholarships.

The internal quarrels of the Right eroded the personal prestige of Gil Robles and were largely responsible for the legislative sterility of the years 1934–35. But the working alliance between the Radicals and the CEDA might well have survived Monarchist and quasi-fascist criticism in the Cortes. It was destroyed by two major political scandals which broke in the fall of 1935. The first concerned a variant form of roulette known as *straperlo*. The new game was supposed to introduce an element of skill into the operation of roulette. A government license was necessary to install the straperlo in Spanish cafés, and its Dutch promoter had sought the influence of government personalities to obtain the license. Within a few hours of his opening the first game in San Sebastián, the police withdrew his permit.[10] He now sought financial compensation for his lost investment, and, failing to get what he felt he deserved, he embarked on a campaign of simple blackmail. Among his "friends" were the nephew of Prime Minister Lerroux, the former Interior Minister Salazar Alonso, and the Lerroux-appointed governor of Catalonia, Pich y Pon. In a letter to President Alcalá-Zamora he intimated that these men had accepted money from him when he was first applying for

[10] *El Socialista*, Sept. 16, 1934, named the promoter, Strauss, and spoke of the license having been obtained through the nephew or the son of a person in high office. The indirect reference to Lerroux was clear, and the makings of the scandal were thus present even before the October revolution.

the license. The President, always suspicious of Lerroux's morality, forced him to resign and gave the denunciatory materials to the new Prime Minister, Chapaprieta. The Constitution required that criminal charges against a member of the government be heard in the Cortes, but the ensuing debate was more political than judicial, and nothing was proven. But since Lerroux personally, and the Radicals as a party, enjoyed a shady reputation, the formal vote exonerating them could not restore their credit. Furthermore, the Cortes debate concerned only the Radical ministers and was discreetly silent on the question whether Lerroux's nephew and a number of lesser personalities had received bribes. Public opinion concluded that they had.[11]

The straperlo scandal broke in October and added to the Spanish vocabulary a new and frequently used sobriquet for the black market. Then in December came the Nombela affair, in which it appeared that several friends of Lerroux had taken an improper interest in Army supply contracts for Morocco.[12] By now the credit of the "historic republican" and his party was completely destroyed. Under Azaña the Radicals had combined anticlericalism with fear of social reform. Under Lerroux they had appeased the Church and governed on behalf of the Right. Admirers and clients of the pirate-capitalist Juan March, they had now made themselves ridiculous in minor bribery scandals.

The effective political life of Spain now took on new and ominous forms outside the Cortes. Each of the mass parties, the CEDA and the Socialists, had a youth organization, and the striking common denominator of those organizations was their rejection of the moderate leaders of the older generation. The Juventud de Acción Popular (JAP) used the anti-Semitic vocabulary of the Nazis and dreamed of a St. Bartholemew of Masons and Marxists. The Juventud Socialista adopted the Communist analysis of Social Democrats as "social fascists" and applied the phrase to the Prietos and Besteiros. In the principal universities the Federation of University Students (FUE), founded in the 1920's to combat the dictatorship, was

[11] Lerroux, *op. cit.,* pp. 419–22, 445–55.

[12] *Economía Española,* Dec. 1935, pp. 45–6.

dominated by militant Marxist officers in 1935, and Catholic students were founding equally militant organizations of their own. In addition to all these, there were the small but ardent Falange Española, whose principal chief was José Antonio Primo de Rivera, and the Juntas de Ofensivas Nacional-Sindicalista (JONS) of Ramiro Ledesma Ramos.

Typical of the ideals and the confusions of a whole generation of youth was José Antonio, son of the late dictator. As a law student he had made many friends among the liberals and had considered himself a disciple of Ortega y Gasset. The gallantry and loyalty which were always characteristic of him had led him to defend his father's memory, but when in October 1933, he took part in the founding of the Falange, he defended neither the Monarchy nor the dictatorship. Spain needed a revolution, a far more profound revolution, in fact, than that being attempted by the Republic. He referred to socialism as just in its origins and aspirations, and he favored the separation of Church and state. The trouble with socialism, he said, was its dependence on foreign models and its atheism. In his speeches and writings José Antonio propounded no specific program but called for a spirit of sacrifice, of national unity. He paid homage to Mussolini's energy and oratorical prowess, without being particularly impressed with the corporative state. He admired Imperial England and loved to quote Kipling's "If," but he was convinced of the decline of the West. He had many personal friends and social connections among the Monarchists, but he did not think them capable of leading the regenerated Spain of which he dreamed. He and his followers liked to work with their sleeves rolled up, a posture which symbolized their energy, their display of muscle, their impatience with fussy routines and bourgeois inhibitions. José Antonio could never feel any warmth toward Gil Robles, with his soft, pudgy, unheroic face and verbal subtleties. In principle he was opposed to violence, but in fact, he collected arms for the Falange and more than once defended Falange gunmen in court. He admired the leadership principle, and like most leaders with a penchant for the authoritarian style, he could not cooperate with equals. He quarreled with his fellow-founder, Ruíz de Alda. In February

1934 he merged the Falange with the JONS of Ramiro Ledesma, but in January 1935 Ledesma was expelled and José Antonio remained the uncontested chief. The Falange literature emphasized theoretical and political differences in explaining these quarrels, but fundamentally they resulted from competitive personal ambitions on both sides.

There were several José Antonios—all dramatic, personally attractive, and naïvely egotistical. There was the José Antonio of legal robes who defended one of his father's ministers at the Cortes trial for the *responsabilidades* of the dictatorship. There was the shirtsleeved José Antonio calling for heroism and sacrifice. There was the impish José Antonio who mimicked the old-time politicians and cried "viva el straperlo" during a debate on political corruption. There was the hero-worshipping José Antonio who revered his father's memory and Ortega's intellect. There was a José Antonio who admired Prieto, and who thought similarly of the need for industrialization and irrigation in Spain. And there was a José Antonio who despised the materialism of the modern West and the Marxists, and who shared the fascist mystiques of elitism, hierarchy, tradition.[13]

In all these qualities he was typical of his generation in Spain. Class feelings and religious loyalties determined which of the organizations a student or young worker would join. If his Catholicism were fundamental, and he had no strong monarchist leanings, he joined the JAP. If the ideals of hierarchy and legitimacy were as strong as Catholicism, he joined the Carlists or *Renovación*. If he admired Mussolini and Hitler, hated the Marxists, and also the old privileged classes, he joined the JONS or the Falange. If he were attracted by the dialectic of Marxism, and had rejected Christianity, he joined the Juventud Socialista, or the Communist Party. But in all instances he rejected the bourgeois

[13] Payne, *Falange,* chs. 3 and 4. Felipe Ximénez de Sandoval, *José Antonio* (Barcelona, 1941), *passim.* The first is a scholarly study, the second a sentimental and anecdotal biography, valuable, however, precisely for showing the adoration aroused by its subject. See also Gumersindo Montes Agudo, *Vieja Guardia* (Madrid, 1939) for excellent photos of the original Falange and JONS leaders.

Republic, and he either scorned, or unconsciously undervalued, the virtues of parliamentary democracy. Of these organizations only the JAP and the Socialist Youth represented substantial numbers, but all of them were preparing for heroic violence, conceived not as a brute test of strength, but as a necessary ingredient of political activity. In the Casa de Campo, west of Madrid, the JAP, the Falange, and the Socialist Youth engaged in para-military training on Sundays. In Valladolid, the JONS squads imitated the Italian fascists with lightning terrorist raids on working-class districts and ostentatious street brawls with leftist students. In Valencia Carlist and JAP youth organizations guarded convents at moments of political tension, just in case.

The thinking of both Right and Left youth groups was dominated by the memory of the Asturian revolution and its aftermath. With the press heavily censored, each had no choice but to believe their own myths. JAP and Falange youth, believing that the miners had raped nuns and massacred the Oviedo middle class, were outraged by the commutation of death sentences. It also seemed typical, to them, of the shame and muddle of democratic government to let the leaders escape the death penalty while the glorious Army bore the opprobrium of the necessary clean up of the revolutionaries. Socialist youth, on the other hand, looked upon Asturias as a heroic defeat. Believing that atrocities had been committed only by the forces of repression, and convinced that the industrial working class was destined to lead humanity toward a better future, they brushed aside the responsibility of the Left in the origin of the tragedy. The revolt had been a tactical error, not a political crime, and it had failed through poor organization and insufficient armament. For both sides, the October revolution pointed not to the need for moderate, democratic government, but to the inevitability of a better-prepared test of force between the Right and the Left.

In July 1935 the younger intellectuals of Largo Caballero's following revolted against the "reformism" of the party organ, *El Socialista,* and founded a new weekly (and later daily) newspaper, *Claridad.* Their aim was to convince the Socialist masses that Besteiro and Prieto had deformed the revolutionary tradition of the Spanish Socialist Party. Each week they printed citations from Pablo Iglesias, the revered founder of the Party, pointing to the eventual necessity of a revolutionary seizure of power. Iglesias had always been a moderate in action and had in 1921 fought against a majority tendency to take the Party into the Third International. But Iglesias, like Marx, could be made to say very different things when quoted out of context. *Claridad* also analyzed various texts of Lenin on tactics, all of them indicating the naïveté, if not the treason, of those comrades who expected to achieve socialism by purely parliamentary means. Margarita Nelken, Socialist deputy for Badajoz and a champion of the Federation of Land Workers, visited the Soviet Union and returned to write a series of laudatory articles concerning the Second Five Year Plan, with particular emphasis on the presumed success of the collective farms.

During these same months, thirty thousand leftist prisoners were sitting in jail, with much time to read and many friends to bring them books. The last years of the dictatorship and the first years of the Republic had witnessed several mass publishing ventures. There was a series of popular, inexpensive political primers whose titles all began with *Al servicio de . . .* and which outlined the programs of the several political parties from moderate Right to far Left. There was Editorial Maucci of Barcelona, selling cheap editions of Kropotkin, Bakunin, Tolstoy, Nietzsche, and offering guides to health and happiness which combined useful medical knowledge, vegetarian and health food fads, and pornography. In Madrid Ignacio Bauer, a secondary school professor, a friend of Manuel Azaña, and a distant relative of the Rothschilds, bought up a number of small publishers and paid fabulous wages for the preparation of a series of excellently edited, little-known Spanish masterpieces: *Los Clásicos Olvidados.* Through Editorials Zeus and Cenit he issued superior translations of the best Russian and German literature, as well as Marx, Engels, Lenin and their principal commentators. In the course of the depression, most of these ventures went bankrupt. A generation of workers and students bought books by the armload from pushcarts lined up around the Puerta del Sol and along

POLITICS AND IDEOLOGIES IN 1935

the Carrera de San Jerónimo. And many of these books in turn constituted the literary fare of the political prisoners.

Books by moderate republicans, written before the depression and before the Asturian revolt, seemed to such readers to have little connection with reality. The novels of Zola, Dreiser, and Upton Sinclair struck closer to home; but most widely read of all were the works of Marx and Lenin, who had analyzed scientifically, and had forecast, the economic crisis and the brutal class struggles in which the readers found themselves involved. Among the prisoners in Madrid, Francisco Largo Caballero held a special place of honor. A skilled plasterer and lifelong trade-unionist, he was a man of completely proletarian origin who had devoted his entire life to the betterment of his class. In October Professor Besteiro had opposed the rising; the bourgeois Prieto had fled to France; and the bourgeois Azaña had carefully established his non-involvement with the revolutionaries. But Caballero had gone to jail and had refused to say anything that could conceivably have aided the police in their pursuit of his party comrades. Caballero had been moving left since 1933, and now he read Marx for the first time, in the company of ardent young intellectuals who regretted their own bourgeois background and who idolized him doubly, as an authentic proletarian, and as the spiritual successor of "el abuelo"—the equally proletarian, equally austere, equally honorable Pablo Iglesias.

The year 1935 was by no means completely dominated by the political failures of the Cortes or the political emotions of the youth. It was a climactic year in Spain's cultural renaissance. In fact, at almost no time in the past half-century had the contrast been so great between the stagnation of Spanish politics and the vitality of Spanish culture. No less than three new plays of Federico García Lorca received their premières in the first four months of the year. Vicente Aleixandre published *La destrucción o el amor* and Rafael Alberti his *Verte y no verte*. The poet's poet Jorge Guillén achieved his first wide recognition with the second edition of *Cántico*. The Murcian shepherd and self-taught poet Miguel Hernández settled in Madrid and contributed poems to Alberti's review

Octubre. Luis Buñuel produced his documentary masterwork, *Tierra sin Pan,* concerning Las Hurdes, the poverty-stricken area north of Cáceres which had first been brought to the attention of the Spanish public by the then Bishop of Coria and later Cardinal-Archbishop Segura.

Ramón Menéndez Pidal launched the publication of a new multi-volume, scholarly history of Spain, and in September the world famous entomologist Ignacio Bolívar presided over the International Congress of Entomology in Madrid. The *misiones pedagógicas* continued undiminished, with private enthusiasts filling the gap left by the government's drastic cut in their budget. Miguel de Unamuno, liberal opponent of the Primo dictatorship, and now an outspoken critic of much that the Republic had done, was named Honorary Citizen for 1935. In Barcelona Pablo Casals, world-famous cellist and fiery Catalan patriot, subsidized from his own concert earnings a symphony orchestra and a choral society; and Dr. Juan Negrín, son of a wealthy Canary Islands merchant, continued to spend his private income building the magnificent medical library which he placed at the disposal of the Madrid medical students. The political passions, the literary genius, the cultural vitality, the individual idealism and generosity of all classes of Spaniards were fully engaged in the year 1935.

10

THE POPULAR FRONT ELECTION

THROUGHOUT 1935 the President of the Republic was weighing the advisability of new elections. If the Constituent Cortes had tried to carry the country too far to the left, the present Cortes was simply sterile. Like most Spaniards, he felt that the October revolt had been "badly liquidated," but whereas the Right meant by this phrase that the government had been criminally lenient, the President felt that the repression had been unnecessarily harsh. He feared to weaken the Republic, and to bring down bitter criticism on his own head, by dissolving the Cortes in less than two years. But he feared equally for a democratic republic which could maintain itself only by the constant extension of the *estado de alarma*.

After the straperlo and Nombela scandals, he decided that new elections were imperative, and he hoped that they might take place in conditions that would produce a moderate, middle-of-the-road majority rather than a Left or Right majority. In the past year the quarrels between the Monarchists and the CEDA had undermined the unity of the Right, and the increasing strength of the Caballero faction within the Socialist Party made most unlikely a renewal of the Republican-Socialist coalition as it had existed in the Constituent Cortes. Against a disunited Right and a disunited Left, a strong Center might emerge. Thus, at any rate, reasoned the President. Everything depended upon finding the right Prime Minister for the electoral period. With this in mind he offered the dissolution power first to Chapaprieta, who refused, and then to Manuel Portela Valladares, who had been the first governor appointed in Barcelona after the sixth of October, and who in May 1935 had entered the Lerroux cabinet as Minister of the Interior. In both roles he had been widely praised for his combination of firmness and moderation. Within the cabinet he had successfully opposed Gil Robles' effort to have the Guardia Civil transferred to the Ministry of War. Appointed on December 14, Portela lifted the remaining press censorship during the following three weeks. On January 7, he dissolved the Cortes and announced elections for February 16.

But no strong Center was to emerge during the campaign, in large part because of two major political developments of 1935, which resulted in the formation of the Popular Front. The Cortes trial of Azaña had increased the warmth of personal relations among the liberal Left leaders and had put them all on notice that the Monarchist Right would stop at nothing to destroy them. The parties of Azaña and Marcelino Domingo had already fused to form *Izquierda Republicana,* and the Galician liberals of Casares Quiroga also joined them. Martínez Barrio had formed a party of his own, *Unión Republicana,* and many Radicals who disagreed with Lerroux's pro-clerical policy and were shocked by the repression in Asturias now followed Martínez Barrio. Professor Felipe Sánchez Román had also launched his *Partido Nacional Republicano,* small in numbers but with considerable influence in academic circles. In April, 1935, Azaña, Martínez Barrio and Felipe Sánchez Román agreed upon a general program of cooperation for their three parties. Azaña made a series of public speeches to increasingly large audiences, proposing a return to the program of the first biennium, together with a more rapid land reform; a union of the liberal and left political forces; and an end to the corruption and repression which were the principal characteristics of the Lerroux era.

The second new development affected all of Western Europe. In the summer of 1935 the Communist International reversed its policy of constant struggle against the Social Democrats, and with great energy and publicity launched the slogan of a "Popular Front" of all liberal and left forces against the threat of fascism. In the years preceeding 1933, the German Communist Party had stigmatized the Social Democrats as "social fascists," had fought street battles with them, and had on occasion joined the Nazis and other reactionary parties to vote against them in the Reichstag. Hitler had always been fanatically anti-Communist, but the Communists themselves underestimated his strength until he had largely destroyed them. With the principal leaders either dead or in concentration camps, and the membership decimated, the Kremlin decided that fascism was a more immediate and virulent enemy than capitalism, and that it would serve both the foreign policy interests of Russia and the well-being of the international proletariat to seek an alliance of all democratic, Socialist, and Communist forces against fascism. The campaign for a "Popular Front" of all anti-fascist elements was officially opened by the Communist International in the summer of 1935.

It thus happened that the Azaña republicans and the Communist Party were both seeking for a political understanding among all liberal-left forces. The Communist Party had polled less than 5 per cent of the vote and had elected only one deputy in 1933, but they were a major force in France, where the Popular Front was being rapidly formed, and French example always carried great weight with the Spanish Left. In October Prieto, who had been living in France since the failure of the Asturian revolt, returned to Madrid clandestinely. Exerting his personal influence within the Socialist Party, he persuaded the executive committee on December 20 to vote a renewed coalition with the Left Republicans. Meanwhile, the revolutionary wing of the Party, increasingly impressed by the accomplishment of the Soviet five year plans and the collectivization of agriculture, drew closer spiritually to their former enemies, and many of the younger leaders of both the Socialist and Communist parties were talking of fusion. The end of the year thus witnessed a general *rapprochement* between the Azaña and Prieto forces on the one hand, and the revolutionary Socialists and the Communists on the other. When Portela dismissed the Cortes and announced new elections on January 7, only one more week of negotiation was required to produce the Popular Front pact of January 15. *Izquierda Republicana* (Azaña), *Unión Republicana* (Martínez Barrio), the Catalan *Esquerra,* the Socialist and Communist parties formed an electoral alliance with a minimum program demanding a return to the religious, educational, and regional policies of the first biennium, a more rapid land reform, and an amnesty for the 30,000 political prisoners. They established a coalition list for the election to the Cortes, alloting in advance the proportion of seats to go to each party. They agreed also that the government should be composed only of republicans, while the Socialists and Communists were pledged to support that government for the purpose of fulfilling the announced "bourgeois democratic" program.

The decision of the Socialists not to enter the cabinet was a concession to the revolutionary wing. Largo Caballero had resigned from the executive committee when the latter had voted for a renewed coalition with Azaña.[1] Largo refused to be compromised again by participation in a bourgeois government. His wing of the party (like the Communists in both the French and Spanish Popular Fronts) proposed to support the government in the fulfillment of a minimum program, but refused to share executive responsibility with bourgeois parties. Indeed, at this time the younger Socialists considered themselves more "advanced" than the Communists. With the latter doing everything possible to reassure their middle-class allies, "Caballeristas" coined the delightful slogan: "To save Spain from Marxism, vote Communist." As for Largo Caballero himself, the proud old fighter did not forget a decade of Communist policy toward his and brother Socialist parties, but he counted on Socialist numbers, and on the loyalty of the young revolutionaries to him personally, to keep his new allies under control.

The leading personalities in the Left's campaign were Azaña and Largo Caballero. The former spoke of representative democracy and nonrevolutionary reform. The latter made vague, but intoxicating prophecies of a Socialist revolution looking beyond the immediate future. The two men were hardly on speaking terms, and no one could fail to see how different were their aims. But the Popular Front, during the month of intense campaigning, remained united by the fear of fascism and the prospect of the amnesty.

The Right also entered the campaign with great confidence and energy. Tremendous funds were collected among businessmen and in door-to-door campaigns by the local chapters of

[1] *Claridad*, Dec. 21, 1935.

Acción Popular. Automobiles with loudspeakers circulated the main streets. Larger-than-life portraits of Gil Robles stared down at passersby in the Puerta del Sol, and everywhere, his mass meetings shouted "All power to the Chief." He could not, however, bridge the gap between social Catholics like Giménez Fernández and Luis Lucía on the one side, and the Carlists and Goicoechea Monarchists on the other. In most instances the CEDA and the Monarchist leaders at the local level agreed to support a single candidate so as not to commit political suicide. There was thus a considerable measure of electoral unity on the Right, but there was no unity at the top. Caught between the majority of his CEDA partisans and the national Monarchist leaders, Gil Robles chose to base his campaign on the social Catholic program of a CEDA which was prepared to accept, and was supremely confident that it would soon govern, the Republic.

The Right was further handicapped by the many divisions within the Catholic camp. Generally speaking, ever since April 1931 the Catholics had been divided between monarchists and "accidentalists." Under the Center-Right coalition the Church had retained its schools, and the Jesuits had recovered most of their property. A representative of the government and member of the CEDA, Sr. Pita Romero, had begun negotiations in Rome looking toward a new Concordat. In December 1935 the nuncio Tedeschini was to become a cardinal, receiving the red hat from the President of the Republic. But at the investiture ceremony, neither the Primate, Cardinal Gomá, nor any leading member of the CEDA or a monarchist party was present. The guests were Cardinal Vidal of Tarragona, Cardinal Ilundáin of Seville, a half-dozen bishops, including those of Madrid and Barcelona, two Basque Nationalist deputies, and several liberal Catholic friends of the President and the new Cardinal.[2] At the end of 1935 the Church counted at least five factions, none of which felt truly cordial toward any of the others: Carlists, Alfonsine Monarchists, accidentalists, partisans of Alcalá-Zamora and Miguel Maura, and Basque Nationalists.

The President and the Prime Minister tried unsuccessfully

[2] *El Sol,* Dec. 22, 1935.

to form a Center coalition. But even the most moderate CEDA deputies could not forgive Alcalá-Zamora his treatment of Gil Robles and they were inimical to Portela as a leading Mason. Among the moderate Left, memories of October created unity around Azaña and against the President. While unable to form a strong Center, Portela nevertheless presided over the electoral campaign with justice and dignity.

He lifted all newspaper censorship and preferred the risk of sporadic violence to the heavy use of the police. He warned the Left against "direct action" and bitterly criticized the wealthy conservatives, who would of course not engage in brawls themselves but who did not hesitate to subsidize fascist gunmen to break up Popular Front rallies. The campaign was marked by less violence than in 1933, largely because the unity of the Left had brought about a truce between Socialist, Communist, and anarchist rivals in local situations. The latter took almost no part in the campaign, but whereas in 1933 they had considered Azaña the butcher of the proletariat, in 1936 they were as sympathetic as their apolitical outlook would permit them to be toward a coalition which promised amnesty for the Asturian prisoners.

Every major theme in Spanish political life was vigorously debated, and local issues were particularly important. In Andalusia and Extremadura the Popular Front candidates promised quick, uncomplicated land reform. In Catalonia the Companys government (in prison at the time) would be restored to power and the transfer of functions to the Generalitat speeded. In the Basque country, too, the campaign turned on the autonomy question. Though pressed by the hierarchy to ally with the CEDA, the Basque Nationalists chose to run independently and to maintain a provisionally friendly attitude toward the Popular Front which promised them an autonomy statute. In Guipúzcoa Carlist landlords threatened to dispossess long-time tenants who were Catholic, conservative, but also Basque Nationalist.

Without any doubt, however, the memories of Asturias were fundamental. *El Socialista* ran a series of articles on the horrors of the military repression, and *La Nación* (the organ of Calvo Sotelo) ran a series on Red atrocities in which they

¿QUE LES GUSTARIA A LOS POLITICOS QUE LES TRAJERAN LOS REYES?, por Bagaría

LERROUX: Instead of bringing me a present I wish they would whisk away this Republic which has been my ruin.

PORTELA: For me, medicinal tea to distribute among the cedistas.

GOICOECHEA: More motive power for my drooping eyes.

CAMBO (head of the conservative Lliga Catalana): Let them get the Esquerra off my back!

GIL ROBLES: a suit of armor to resist so much "golpe" (pun on a word which means kicks and punches in general, and also coup d'état).

SAMPER (former Radical Prime Minister, negotiating with Portela concerning the proposed Center coalition): A smile from Portela.

BARCIA (presumptive Foreign Minister in the next Azaña cabinet): A portrait of Lord Brummel, dedicated with his seal and autograph.

MELQUIADES (head of the minuscule Reformist Party, but a distinguished opposition leader in the last years of the Monarchy): The seat this year for Asturias.

MARTINEZ DE VELASCO (Agrarian leader rallied to the Republic): Let them send me whatever they want, so long as they don't make me think too hard.

EL PUEBLO: I am more modest; all I ask is that they don't take my shoes away.

El Sol, 5 January, 1936

EL SOL ANTICIPATES THE POPULAR FRONT ELECTION

What would the politicians like to get for Three Kings? (January 6, day of the 3 Kings who worshipped the infant Jesus, a children's holiday more important than Xmas itself).

191

claimed that the revolutionaries had assassinated 1,335 persons. This figure was higher than the total number of deaths from all causes reported by the Ministry of the Interior. But then no one in either camp believed what the government had said in trying vainly to minimize the entire episode. Those who believed that the Foreign Legion had saved Spain from a bloody communist upheaval prepared to vote for the Right. Those who believed that a clerical-fascist government had driven the Left to desperation and then repressed it sadistically, prepared to vote for the Popular Front.

The specific conditions under which the voting took place are of considerable importance, inasmuch as official versions of Spanish history since 1939 have claimed that the Popular Front victory was fraudulent. The Centrist Prime Minister, Portela Valladares, was also Minister of the Interior. The civil governors of the vast majority of the provinces were either those who had come into office with the electoral victory of the Right in 1933 or who had been appointed to replace Left governors after the Asturian revolt. In 52 out of the country's 70 electoral districts, the voters had a clear choice between two lists: one for the Center-Right and one for the Popular Front. In each of the districts the juntas counting the votes included representatives of all parties.

On Sunday, February 16, the atmosphere was calmer than most people had anticipated. The voting was heavy from the first hours of the morning, and the polls closed at 4 P.M. The quickly counted city returns indicated the likelihood of a Left victory. The Prime Minister, perhaps self-deceived, perhaps wishing to slow down the news so as to forestall early victory demonstrations, went on the air at 6 P.M. to say that the electoral process had been normal, and that a Center-Right victory appeared likely. At 10 P.M. his secretary took the microphone, saying that the general picture was not clear yet, but acknowledging a Left victory in Catalonia.[3] On Monday afternoon, and through Tuesday, the 18th, papers of all political persuasions printed returns crediting the Popular Front with 220 to 270 deputies out of a potential total of 473.

[3] José Venegas, *Las elecciones del frente popular* (Beunos Aires, 1942), pp. 68–9.

At the same time, the civil governors were congratulating the government on the orderly nature of the election.[4] When the official figures were reported by the provincial electoral juntas on February 20, the Popular Front had elected 257 deputies, the Right 139, and the Center 57. This came to a total of 453, with some 20 seats still to be accounted for through runoff elections. But regardless of what might happen in the runoffs, the Popular Front had obtained more than the 237 seats which would constitute an absolute majority of 473. In these circumstances all parties recognized the Left victory, and between February 18 and February 22 the principal CEDA and Monarchist leaders made public statements interpreting the significance of their defeat.

If the figures reported by the juntas on February 20 are rounded off, the Left had obtained 4,700,000 votes, the Right 3,997,000, the Center 449,000, and the Basque Nationalists (concentrated in 4 electoral districts) 130,000. Since a higher proportion of the people voted than in either 1931 or 1933, the Left and the Right had each increased their absolute vote total, the Right by about 600,000 (perhaps half of whom had voted for Radicals in 1933) and the Left by over 700,000 (most of them probably anarchists who had abstained in 1933). As many commentators have pointed out, the figures show an increase in the absolute strength of the Right, and they show a non-Popular Front total of 4,576,000. From these facts many arguments have been developed alleging the injustice of the solid majority of seats awarded to the Popular Front.[5]

[4] *El Sol,* Feb. 17 and 18, 1936. Mendizábal, *Aux origines,* pp. 233–38.

[5] All the figures used in the above paragraphs come from Venegas, *op. cit.,* pp. 31–2, 46–7, 65, and *passim.* These are the figures of the juntas, undoctored by post-electoral polemics. Brenan, *Spanish Labyrinth,* p. 298, also uses these as the most nearly reliable figures available. Mendizábal, *op. cit.,* p. 239, uses the figures of *El Debate,* which, by en'arging the definition of Center, yield a Center-Right total of 4,910,000 as against 4,356,000 which he recognizes as legitimate Popular Front votes. Madariaga, *Spain* (1958 ed.), pp. 445–46, limits the Popular Front to 4,206,000 by refusing to award them the runoff votes reported on Feb. 20. Since these

But the Popular Front election, like those of 1931 and 1933, was held under a law written specifically to encourage the formation of coalitions and to avoid a fragmented parliament. In each electoral district, 80 per cent of the seats went to any list obtaining over 50 per cent of the vote. Many of the seats which had been won by the Right in 1933 against the divided opposition of Republicans and Socialists, now went to a Popular Front coalition candidate, without there having been any notable change in the political sentiments of the individual voters. And of course, the Popular Front received 80 per cent of the seats wherever it won over 50 per cent of the votes.

In February 1936 all these things were clear to politically conscious Spaniards. However, the very fact of an indubitable victory for the Left sowed panic among both the government and the defeated Right. According to CEDA personalities of the time, General Franco was invited by emissaries of the Right to launch a coup which would annul the elections (a technique which has several times been employed in the histories of Argentina, Chile, Mexico, and Peru). The General is said to have refused, for a variety of reasons.[6] Sources close

---

votes were counted by the juntas appointed under Portela, and since all the complaints registered at that time concerning fraud and terror came from the Left, his procedure seems rather arbitrarily to minimize the Left vote total.

[6] Brenan, *op. cit.*, p. 300, reports the speech of Portela to the Cortes in Valencia, Oct. 1, 1937, accusing Gil Robles and Franco of proposing a military coup. See also José María Iribarren, *Con el General Mola* (Zaragoza, 1937), pp. 9–13, for a version of Franco's initiative. Gil Robles told Stanley Payne in Madrid, in 1959, that "frightened conservative politicians" urged Franco and other generals to act, but that Franco refused (*Falange*, p. 94). I do not know whether Gil Robles intended to include himself in the above category, but he assured me in 1961 that he had *always* opposed military coups. Several officers who fought on the Nationalist side in the Civil War believed, for reasons I find convincing myself, that Franco was too cool and too intelligent to become involved in a panic move. Such a conclusion contradicts the account in Iribarren, but is made more plausible by the notorious fact of Franco's long hesitation before joining the military plot in the spring of 1936.

to the Portela government have been equally emphatic in stating that—through confidential emissaries—General Franco offered his services to Portela for the purpose of annulling the elections, but that Portela and President Alcalá-Zamora were determined to respect the popular will, regardless of their anxieties concerning the future. Whatever the truth concerning Franco and Portela may be, the city of Madrid on February 17 was filled with rumors of a coming pronunciamiento. Loyal officers such as General Pozas of the Civil Guard and General Nuñez del Prado of the Air Force, warned Portela of widespread nervousness in the barracks. In the cafés reactionary officers called for the simple annulment of the elections.

On the morning of February 18 Portela begged Azaña to assume power immediately in the name of the Popular Front. Azaña wished to await the opening of the Cortes, scheduled for March 16, in order to prepare his legislative program. The President also believed that Portela should stay in office at least for the week necessary to complete the count of votes and to be positive, given the closeness of the vote, of the exact distribution of seats in the new Cortes. Portela was terror-stricken, however, and in the face of his refusal to remain in office a day longer, Alcalá-Zamora called upon Azaña to assume power immediately as the only possible alternative to chaos.[7]

[7] My version of the transfer of power is based upon an article by Diego Martínez Barrio in *ABC* (Madrid edition), Feb. 23, 1937. This article was recommended to me as absolutely correct by a member of the Portela government who had been present in Portela's office throughout the 18th, and who had read the article while in the Madrid jail where he spent the Civil War years. Without mentioning the article, I once asked Sr. Martínez Barrio in Paris about this incident. His oral version corresponded completely with what he had written 23 years earlier. Reassured by the evidence of such a powerful memory and such honesty, I depended upon him for a number of other details which I have not footnoted separately.

11

FROM FEBRUARY TO JUNE 1936

THE first act of the new Prime Minister, Manuel Azaña, was to appoint a cabinet composed entirely of Left Republicans and men enjoying his personal confidence: as Minister of War, General Masquelet, who had greatly aided him with the Army reforms of the first biennium; as Minister of the Interior, his personal friend, the architect Amós Salvador; as Minister of Education Marcelino Domingo; as Minister of Agriculture the Murcian liberal and respected personal friend Mariano Ruiz Funes. On February 22 the 30,000 political prisoners were amnestied, and on the 23rd, payment of rents was suspended in Extremadura and Andalusia as the first step toward renewed, and more rapid, land distribution. At the same time the Basque municipal governments which had been suspended in the summer of 1934 were restored to their functions; likewise the Companys government in Catalonia and the many Socialist municipalities which had been suspended since October 1934. Azaña also removed from Madrid the two generals whose names had come up most persistently in connection with military plots. General Franco was assigned to the Canary Islands and General Goded to the Balearics.

These first moves not only satisfied the mass of liberal urban voters who were Azaña's personal following, but they evoked the unstinted praise of the conservative republican Miguel Maura and the liberal secondary leaders of the CEDA, Giménez Fernández and Luis Lucía. It was equally apparent, however, that victory had intoxicated the left wing of the Popular Front, and that the Azaña government was *desbordado,* "swamped," by its own masses. In dozens of cities, victory parades were accompanied by clashes with the police, marches on the prisons, and attacks, or threats of attack, on churches. Extra police were assigned to guard churches in the main cities, and to guard the buildings of *El Debate* and *ABC* in Madrid. The *estado de alarma,* which had been proclaimed by Portela on February 17, was maintained by Azaña. The censored press carried not a word of violence outside the capital, but the Ministry of the Interior received constant reports of land seizures accompanied by clashes with the Civil or Assault Guards.

In Madrid, and in the large industrial cities, each week witnessed several large parades demanding proletarian rule, and the left Socialists talked of parallels between the Russia of 1917 and the Spain of 1936, with Azaña cast in the role of Kerensky, and Largo Caballero in the role of Lenin. Azaña hoped that in the month following the election, the fever would diminish, but with the Cortes due to meet on March 16, he summoned Largo Caballero on the 11th to demand an end of the victory parades. On March 13, a group of Falangist students attempted to assassinate the Socialist deputy Jiménez de Asúa and succeeded in killing one of the policemen assigned to guard him. The next day, mobs partially burned two churches and the printing plant of Calvo Sotelo's newspaper, *La Nación.* On March 15 Azaña forbade all further victory demonstrations and arrested José Antonio Primo de Rivera and eight other directors of the Falange. A few days previously, in Logroño, a clash had occurred between peasants and the Army, with four deaths resulting; a group of officers now sent Azaña a virtual ultimatum regarding leftist provocations against the armed forces. Meanwhile, at the opening session of the Cortes, the Left challenged the outspoken Monarchist deputy, Admiral Carranza, to shout "Viva la República," which the old gentleman refused to do, whereat the Left deputies sang the *Internationale.*

At the very least, dozens of political shootings and bombings occurred in the spring months, of which only a small proportion can be specifically dated. On March 19, shots were fired at Caballero's home. On the 24th, in Oviedo, the rightist deputy Alfredo Martínez was assassinated. In early April a bomb was discovered in the home of the republican deputy Eduardo Ortega y Gasset, and several mayors and civil governors barely escaped assassination. These are only the best-known instances, since press censorship and the sheer inability of the police to check on every instance of violence made it impossible to know in detail what was happening throughout the country.[1]

The para-military exercises of the last two years now overflowed into constant street violence. The Falange had long suffered the taunts of a Monarchist press, which referred to them as "more Franciscans than fascists." Recruiting members rapidly among the Catholic Youth and the anti-Marxist workers, they formed motorized squads which drove through the working-class districts firing haphazardly at "reds." The violence obeyed no logical pattern. It could begin with a shouted insult, a shove on a street corner, or the tearing of a poster off a wall. With almost total freedom of the press—following two years of censorship—the resultant competition among newspapers led to daily encounters. Vendors of *Claridad* and *Mundo Obrero* (the Communist organ which had been suppressed entirely from October, 1934, until January 2, 1936) fought pitched battles with newsboys hawking *ABC* and *La Nación*. The funerals for the occasional dead of each camp became the occasion of huge political demonstrations and sometimes fighting was renewed in the cemetery itself. Ideologically speaking, heroic violence belonged more to the fascist spirit than to the Left, but the Socialist Youth, meditating the fate of the German Socialists in 1933 and the Austrians in 1934, chose to fight fire with fire. Neither side expected to achieve a specific political end by street fighting, but the atmosphere of violence went far to destroy the remaining chances of the democratic Republic.[2]

[1] The *New York Times* and the London *Times* were my principal day-to-day sources concerning street violence in the early spring of 1936. For particularly detailed reports and major incidents, see The *New York Times,* Feb. 21; March 2, 12–17, 19, and 25; April 4 and 8; *The Times,* London, March 16. The difficulties of an inadequate, and not always loyal, police force were explained to me in some detail by D. Amós Salvador in Madrid in 1960.

[2] The vast polemical literature on the Civil War might easily lead readers to conclude that the street fights were indeed part of a coherent fascist or communist plot. My conclusion to the contrary is based upon numerous conversations with men who were

By the end of March the Cortes had still not been able to get legislative work under way. On the 31st the parliamentary commission charged with reviewing the elections refused to seat some dozen rightist deputies on the grounds that they had secured their majorities through terrorism and by stuffing the ballot boxes. The Monarchist and CEDA deputies immediately withdrew from the chamber in protest. Debates on the subjects of public order and the legitimacy of the elections were thereupon postponed.

On April 4 Prime Minister Azaña announced to the Cortes his legislative program. The preelectoral program of the Popular Front was to be fulfilled literally; renewed land reform and school construction, greater autonomy for the municipalities, a statute of autonomy for the Basque provinces, and the reemployment of all workers dismissed for political or union activity since late 1933. Also, as indicated in the preelectoral pact, there was to be no socialization of land, banks, or industry. Men of the moderate Right, such as Miguel Maura and Giménez Fernández, immediately pledged their support of such a program. Calvo Sotelo had no strong objections, but questioned whether the Socialist and anarchist masses would permit the Republicans to govern.[3] Azaña coupled with the announcement of his plans an appeal to the Right to accept the results of a democratic election and an appeal to the Left to cooperate with the moderate program which had formed the basis of the Popular Front. He asked the Right to condemn Falange terrorism as vigorously as they

---

members of the Falange, the JAP, or the JSU in 1936. As for the number of victims, Payne, *Falange,* p. 104, estimates on the basis of a careful sifting of Falange reports that some 40 Falangists, "well over" 50 Leftists, and several conservatives were killed in the three months following the February election. The techniques of pre-Civil War Falange violence, not always approved by José Antonio, may be seen in Luis Moure-Mariño, *Galicia en la guerra* (Madrid, 1939), pp. 202–27; also in an article entitled "Las cruzadas de España" in *Living Age,* Oct., 1936, by a young Englishman who had belonged to a terrorist squad in Valencia just after the February election.

[3] *El Sol,* April 4, 1936.

condemned attacks on churches. At the request of the Right, he postponed the municipal elections that were scheduled for the second week in April, acknowledging explicitly that in the present state of public turbulence fair elections would be impossible.

Three days later the Cortes complicated an already tense situation by deposing President Alcalá-Zamora and thereby opening a constitutional crisis. The unfortunate President had indeed alienated almost everyone during the previous two years. The liberal Left had broken with him when he had permitted the CEDA to enter the government; the CEDA in turn could never forgive him for refusing to offer the position of Prime Minister to Gil Robles when he was the designated leader of the largest single party in the Cortes. Lerroux felt that the President's distrust of him had ruined his chance to govern Spain. Everyone was tired of his constant legal scruples, his attention to petty details, his consultation of dozens of deputies on the occasion of each crisis. Everyone knew that he aspired to lead the moderate sector of opinion, which was neither Marxist nor Monarchist, and suspected that he was motivated largely by jealousy in his treatment of Gil Robles. He was accused of trying to split the parties so that no strong leaders might emerge, of encouraging a Samper against Lerroux, of offering power to Giménez Fernández rather than Gil Robles, and so forth. Right and Left laughed at his discomfiture when the Center failed so miserably in the February election.

In point of fact, he had had good reasons for many of his actions but was in no position to state them publicly. Spain lacked men with the experience to govern, and the President, in offering the Prime Ministership to many different persons, was attempting in part to provide the Republic rapidly with a choice of experienced political executives.[4] His instincts for loyalty to the regime were shrewd. Lerroux complained bitterly of Alcalá-Zamora's objections to many of the military promotions of 1935. But the men to whom the President objected were precisely those who most eagerly attacked the Republic

[4] Explanation offered to me by a former "Nicetista" deputy and personal friend of the President.

in 1936. The men of the Center-Right whom he preferred to Lerroux and Gil Robles—Martínez Barrio, Ricardo Samper, Manuel Giménez Fernández, Miguel Maura—were men who remained loyal to the Republic at the outbreak of the Civil War.

The Constitution provided that the President could twice dissolve the Cortes, but, as stated earlier, the framers had added the provision that after the second dissolution, it would be the immediate duty of the new Cortes to examine the President's reasons. If they were found unsatisfactory, the President would be automatically removed from office. In the interpretation of Alcalá-Zamora, the dissolution of January, 1936, was only the first dissolution of a regular Cortes, the Constitutent Cortes having been convoked for that task alone. But the Left insisted on debating what they called the second dissolution. Since they had won the resulting elections, they attacked him for dissolving the Cortes "too late," and Prieto aroused a vengeful enthusiasm with his excoriation of the sterile biennium and the Asturian repression. The debate took the Right by surprise. Rather than defend a President who they thought had constantly appeased the Left, they abstained, and Alcalá-Zamora was deposed by a vote of 238 to 5. In the corridors the old Count of Romanones, sole avowed Monarchist in the Constituent Cortes, chuckled to himself. The provisional Prime Minister, who had demanded that King Alfonso leave Madrid "before sundown," had, less than five years later, been unceremoniously booted out of office. Martínez Barrio, President of the Cortes, now became temporary President of the Republic in accordance with the Constitution.

On April 13 Judge Manuel Pedregal, who had sentenced a Falangist to thirty years in jail for the murder of a leftist newsboy, was murdered. On the 14th, the anniversary of the Republic, a Civil Guard was murdered by an Assault Guard, and a crude bomb exploded, without doing serious damage, under the Presidential reviewing stand. In the Cortes on the 15th the first of two important debates on public order occurred. Calvo Sotelo, speaking for the Monarchists, charged that the government, whatever its intent, was being over-

whelmed by the Left. He read Socialist texts on the nationalization of land and banks, quoted articles by Alvarez Del Vayo
which said that the Popular Front was proceeding too slowly,
and charged Largo Caballero with threatening to make generals out of corporals. The Socialist Party, he declared, aimed
at nothing less than implanting communism in Spain. Gil
Robles spoke more moderately and more specifically. He
reminded the Left that his party had organized the middle-
class masses, that they commanded a number of votes equal
to that of the Left, that he had aimed always to channel these
masses toward the acceptance of republican legality, and that
the Left had cut off his legal path to power by the October
revolution of 1934. He warned the Cortes that because of the
reigning atmosphere of violence, he was losing followers to
organizations which promised to meet violence with violence—
an announcement, in effect, that the CEDA youth organization was rapidly losing members in favor of the Falange.[5]

Neither speaker made an impression on the majority. Calvo
Sotelo was already marked as the principal civilian leader
of both open and clandestine attacks against the Republic.
Since his return from France in 1934, he had never hidden
his contempt for parliamentary government. During the campaign he had referred to the Army as "the spinal column of
the nation," and since February 16 he had privately sounded
out numerous deputies about their attitude toward a military
coup. He had also tried through friends of the President to
reach Alcalá-Zamora with a proposition for a presidential
dictatorship. As for Gil Robles, the Left considered him to be
a Dollfuss who had missed his chance to seize power, and they
never credited his repeated professions of faith in parliamentary government.

During the second half of April the Popular Front had to
supply the Republic with a new President. Immediately after
the ouster of Alcalá-Zamora, Martínez Barrio seemed the
logical choice. However, his role as President of the Cortes was
by no means negligible. Azaña appeared to favor the choice
of Felipe Sánchez Román, a professor of law (intimately

[5] *El Sol,* April 16, 1936.

associated with the writing of the agrarian reform and the Constitution), a moderate liberal, and an intellectual of considerable prestige. But Sánchez Román had at the last minute refused to sign the Popular Front manifesto, although he was in every other respect the political ally of Azaña and Martínez Barrio. The Left therefore would not accept him. By late April it looked as though Azaña himself would be the new President.

In the spring of 1936, as in the years from 1931 to 1933, Azaña was the only Republican leader with sufficient executive capacity to lead a liberal-Left government. But the Popular Front, an uneasy coalition at best, threatened to break up over the question of the presidential succession. From the moment it became clear that only Azaña would receive the unanimous vote of the Popular Front deputies, he became the only possible candidate. Other considerations entered into the choice at this moment. Many deputies talked of revising the Constitution. In their distrust of executive power the Constituent Cortes had strictly limited the President's functions. With a man of Azaña's stature and integrity in the office, its authority could be expanded. There was also talk of a "deal" between Azaña and Prieto, the two "strong men" of the old Republican-Socialist coalition. Azaña as President would be the guarantee to the Right and the Center of a moderate regime. Renewed Socialist participation would end the unstable situation in which only Republicans governed while everyone knew that the votes behind them were Socialist and anarchist votes. Also, after three years of the American "New Deal," the international atmosphere might be more favorable than in 1931.[6]

Azaña's complex personality was an important factor in the situation. He had been a strong Prime Minister in the first biennium, and in matters of public order and the fulfillment of the Popular Front program he had begun once again to follow a firm line. But at heart Azaña did not enjoy the exercise of power; he was by temper more a literary man than a man of action. He had always considered that he could

[6] *El Sol,* April 25 and May 6, 1936.

govern successfully only if he could count on the full support, if not the actual cabinet participation, of the Socialists. In the spring of 1936 most of the Socialists had moved far left in relation to their position of 1933. Azaña's stormy interviews with Largo Caballero in the first two weeks of March had been fundamental tests. Would Caballero restrain the masses so that the government could assert its authority and proceed to its program in orderly fashion, or would he harass the government, waiting to play Lenin to Azaña's Kerensky? Caballero wanted to have it both ways. He promised to restrain his followers and insisted on his loyalty to the Popular Front program. At the same time, he demanded speed and refused to commit himself as to how long the Socialists would support Azaña and as to just what was meant by repeated calls in *Claridad* for proletarian government. During the remainder of March and April, Azaña had to suppose, regardless of what weight he gave to Caballero's professions, that the latter was unable or unwilling to control the masses, since the strikes and disorders continued without pause.

Lack of assured Socialist support meant, in turn, that Azaña could not govern. By late April both the practical situation and the underlying temperament of Azaña urged him to accept the Presidency. He would be able still to serve the Republic, and he might be, hopefully, "above the battle" as President. He was the only figure around whom the Popular Front could unite. With his literary gifts he might infuse greater dignity into the ceremonial functions of the Presidency. As President he might be better able than as Prime Minister to communicate his Republican and democratic faith to the masses who were still politically illiterate. He was also, of course, not immune to the flattery of being sought out as the most representative figure available to the Republicans and the Left.

On May 1, Indalecio Prieto made one of the most important speeches of his career at Cuenca. Both the date and the place were significant. May 1 was International Labor Day, an occasion of class consciousness and proletarian fraternity for labor unions and left political parties the world over. Cuenca was one of the few provinces in which a three-way electoral struggle had taken place in Feburary. All candidates had reported threats of death and the use of strongarm squads to break up their meetings, and none of the lists had obtained the minimum 40 per cent necessary to elect a deputy. The necessary special election had been several times postponed. The Right, presenting new candidates in all-out effort to win the province, named José Antonio Primo de Rivera to their list, and would have named Francisco Franco if the General had been willing to run. In the special election held in April, the Left had won the majority, but the Right had not accepted the legitimacy of the second election, and national attention had been focused on the tense electoral contest in Cuenca.[7]

Prieto had played no public role in Spanish politics from October 1934 until after the Popular Front electoral victory. When the October 5 general strikes had failed, he had fled to France. In October 1935 he had reentered Spain incognito and taken part in the Socialist Party executive deliberations, but he could not appear in public until after the February 22 amnesty. The Asturian tragedy had marked him deeply. Though always in the reformist wing of the Party, he had nevertheless engineered the *Turquesa* arms landing and voted for the nationwide general strike, motivated in large part by the desire not to be isolated from the leftward moving UGT workers. After Asturias, he swore to his intimate friends that he would never let himself again be responsible for an adventure he knew would likely fail. In early 1936 the Caballero wing was taxing him with cowardice as well as reformism. He had been living in Paris while the miners died and the 30,000 sat in jail. In April he had sought to recover prestige among the workers by leading the attack on Alcalá-Zamora. By May 1 he saw civil war in the offing, and the Cuenca speech was not a grandstand play for the revolutionaries but the statement of a sober program by a candidate for the post of Prime Minister.

He told his audience that violence would consolidate nothing: neither democracy, nor socialism, nor communism; that church burnings and street brawls would lead only to

[7] *El Sol,* April 28, and José Venegas, *Las elecciones del frente popular,* p. 50. *El Sol,* June 3, 1936, for the final retrospective debate in the Cortes over the Cuenca election.

fascism; and that the young and professionally competent General Franco would be the natural candidate of the forces seeking a military dictatorship in Spain. He spoke also of the pressing economic needs of Spain: agrarian reform, hydraulic works, and industrialization. And he insisted that capitalism had an essential role to play in this economic program.

The election of the new President took place on May 8. The Monarchists and the CEDA officially decided to boycott the election. However, Azaña received not only the unanimous support of the Popular Front parties, but the votes of the Basque Nationalists, the *Lliga Catalana,* the handful of Lerrouxistas and Mauristas.[8] The first person to whom the new President offered the Prime Ministership was Indalecio Prieto, but the latter, in the face of the absolute opposition of the majority of the Socialist Party, declined to form a cabinet. Prieto's decision was the expression of a crisis which had been long brewing in the Socialist Party between the moderate and the revolutionary elements.

Thoroughout 1934 and 1935 Largo Caballero had been talking increasingly of a Socialist revolution, while Prieto had been preaching the renewal of the Republican-Socialist coalition. At the end of 1935 the great majority of the UGT workers and the Socialist Youth favored Caballero over Prieto. Local party elections in Madrid, Murcia, and Badajoz gave overwhelming victories to the pro-Caballero slates.[9] On December 21 *Claridad* published an analysis of the current situation and a program. The minimum program called for the nationalization of banks and land; small farmers were to be protected, but preference in distribution was to be given to collectives. The maximum program called for the dictatorship of the proletariat. Largo Caballero himself waxed sarcastic concerning so-called socialists who feared dictatorship above all else in a world where dictatorships were becoming so frequent and successful. The editors of *Claridad* stated that the task of the moment was to consolidate the bourgeois Republic, but that inevitably the class struggle would sharpen

[8] Venegas, *op. cit.,* pp. 70–71.
[9] *Claridad,* Jan. 18 and 30, 1936.

under that regime, and that the Party must prepare for the advance to socialism.

In March, after the Popular Front electoral victory, *Claridad* published a new program. They called now for unification of the Socialist and Communist parties and the unification of the UGT and the CNT. Spain was to become a "confederation" of the Iberian peoples, including Morocco, with the right of self-determination for each people. Their phraseology had become virtually indistinguishable from that of the Communist Party organ *Mundo Obrero*. The Communists, with less than 50,000 party members and an expanding youth organization (but one which also numbered less than 50,000, in comparison with the 200,000 affiliates of the Socialist Youth) stood to gain far more than did the Socialists from any program of unification.[10] Largo Caballero refused the Communist calls for fusion of the parties and of the UGT and CNT. He preferred to maintain the looser cooperation of the existing Popular Front. But his close adviser, Julio Alvarez del Vayo, and the most active youth leaders in Madrid such as Santiago Carrillo, Carlos de Baraibar, and the naturalized Italian Fernando de Rosa, all favored fusion. On April 1 they announced the creation of the Unified Socialist and Communist Youth (JSU), and during the spring, Rafael Vidiella, a Caballerist leader of the small Socialist unit in Barcelona, worked for the creation of the Unified Socialist-Communist Party of Catalonia (PSUC). On May Day, while Prieto at Cuenca proposed a reformist government with Socialist participation, the JSU in Madrid carried placards calling for proletarian government and the formation of a Red Army.

The young Caballerist leaders were intoxicated with the assurance that they represented "the wave of the future."[11] They expected that in the proposed fusions they would dominate the Communists and educate the CNT masses to their way of thinking. They proposed to expel Besteiro from

[10] Cattell, *Communism and the Spanish Civil War*, pp. 31–3.

[11] My analysis is based principally on *Claridad*. See also the interview given by Luis Araquistáin to Frederick Birchall, *New York Times*, June 26, 1936.

the Party on the grounds that he was not Marxist. Prieto was at best a "reformist," at worst a would-be Mussolini, planning an "Azaña-Prieto coup" to arrest the onward march of the revolution. For them, the middle class and the peasantry who had voted for the Right were not half the voters of Spain, but simply the remnant of a doomed *bourgeoisie*. They were sufficiently confident of mass support, and thus, alongside the program for socialized industry, collectivized agriculture, and a Red Army, were planks which guaranteed freedom of the press and secret suffrage. The predestined leader of the coming revolution would be the dignified, experienced, thoroughly proletarian head of the UGT, Francisco Largo Caballero. The old man himself, with a lifetime of cautious trade-union politics behind him, and mixed memories of his days in the Azaña cabinet, was both confused and flattered by the exalted terminology of *Claridad*. Somewhat to his embarrassment, and to that of the Communist Party (which at this time was seeking to reassure the *bourgeoisie*), the young Socialists began referring to Largo Caballero as "the Spanish Lenin."

During the crucial months from late 1935 into the spring of 1936, the mass of the Socialist voters looked upon Caballero as their chief. At the same time, the executive committee of the Socialist Party continued to be dominated by Prieto. In the intraparty struggle Prieto was supported strongly by the veterans of the Asturian revolt. Thousands of Socialist youth in the north had dropped their membership when the JSU was founded in Madrid.[12] To a considerable extent, those who had seen the sufferings of the Asturian miners and villagers at close range supported Prieto, while those who had read about it supported Caballero. Prieto also enjoyed the solid support of the leading Socialist intellectuals such as Jiménez de Asúa and Juan Negrín, and that of Julián Zugazagoitia, editor of *El Socialista*, the official party organ.[13]

In order to maintain the fragile unity of the Popular Front, Prieto had urged Manuel Azaña to accept the Presidency. Now, in the name of that same unity, he himself refused to

[12] Cattell, *op. cit.*, p. 33.
[13] *El Socialista,* Jan. 4, 1936.

become Prime Minister. He continued, in public speeches and in his personal newspaper, *El Liberal* of Bilbao, to denounce the infantile leftism of the UGT and CNT masses and the irresponsibility of the Caballerist leaders, who let themselves be swept along by this current. To those who insisted on interpreting the Asturian revolution as the first step toward a proletarian dictatorship, he replied that the document signed by the UGT and Socialist Party executive before the October rising had called for a program very similar to that of the present Popular Front. In October the workers had sacrificed their lives to prevent fascism. With the February electoral victory they had won a chance to effect peacefully and legally the same social program they had formulated in 1934. It was sheer madness to risk civil war for a premature revolution now.

At Cuenca and elsewhere, Prieto had been almost shouted down by hostile elements in his audience. Socialist students, sometimes accompanied by Professor Negrín, constituted an informal bodyguard on his speaking tours. On May 31 at Ecija, in the province of Seville, shots greeted him as he came out on the platform accompanied by the Asturian mine leaders González Peña and Belarmino Tomás. Just who fired the shots has never been determined. Certain Andalusian Falangists have claimed credit for the act, but their boasts must be treated skeptically. The larger truth is that in the spring of 1936 the revolutionary Socialists, the anarchists, and the Falangists would all have been fully capable of assassinating Prieto. Shortly after the Ecija incident, the Socialist Party's national convention, which had been scheduled for June, was postponed until September. The Prieto-Caballero struggle had virtually split the largest political party in Spain, and when the Party rejected Azaña's offer of a Prieto ministry, they virtually paralyzed the Popular Front government. In demanding that the Republicans govern alone, they were standing on the letter of the Popular Front pact. But everyone knew that without the Socialists, Azaña's *Izquierda Republicana* was, to use the pungent Spanish phrase, "cosa de cuatro gatos" (a matter of four cats). From *Claridad,* and from café gossip,

NOTICIA DE ULTIMA HORA, por Bagaría

AZAÑA CONSIDERS THE PRESIDENCY

It seems that there are only two roads, as in [Don Juan] Tenorio: either break my heart or love me, because I adore you; either Manuel Azaña or Azaña (Don Manuel).

El Sol, April 30, 1936

it was abundantly clear that the revolutionary Socialists assumed that by blocking an Azaña-Prieto government they were clearing the path for themselves.

The new President confided power to his faithful personal friend and political ally, Santiago Casares Quiroga. Casares had proven his ability, and his willingness to undertake difficult jobs, as Minister of the Interior during the first

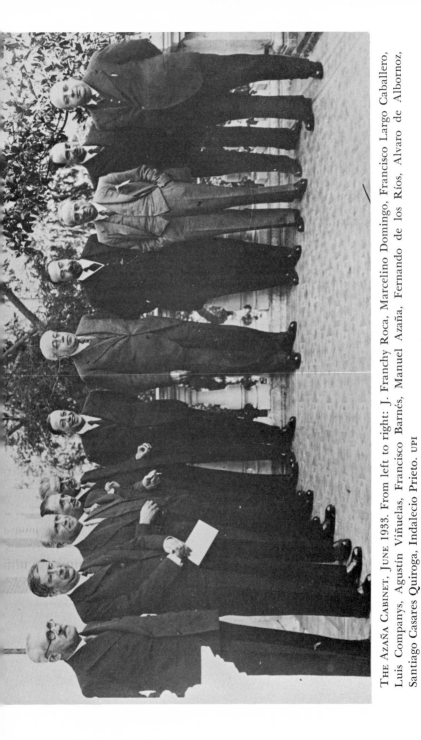

THE AZAÑA CABINET, JUNE 1933. From left to right: J. Franchy Roca, Marcelino Domingo, Francisco Largo Caballero, Luis Companys, Agustín Viñuelas, Francisco Barnés, Manuel Azaña, Fernando de los Ríos, Alvaro de Albornoz, Santiago Casares Quiroga, Indalecio Prieto. UPI

CONSERVATIVE REPUBLICAN LEADERS

José María Gil Robles   WIDE WORLD   Alejandro Lerroux   UPI

THE INSURGENT GENERALS, BURGOS, AUGUST 1936. From left to right: Generals Mola, Saliquet, Franco, Queipo de Llano, and Cabanellas. UPI

The Defense of Madrid, November 1936. Militia firing from behind a barricade of dirt-filled suitcases near

THE NATIONALIST CABINET, OCTOBER 1938. From left to right: Ramón Serrano Suñer, Gen. Martínez Anido, Gen. Fidel Dávila, Conde de Rodezno, Gen. Gómez Jordana, Gen. Franco, Pedro González Bueno, Alfonso Peña y Boef, Pedro Sáinz Rodríguez, Raimundo Fernández Cuesta, Andrés Amado, Juan Antonio Suances. UPI

PRESIDENT AZAÑA AND PRIME MINISTER JUAN NEGRÍN. Photo taken at the farewell parade of the International Brigades, Barcelona, November 1, 1938

THE NATIONALIST ARMY IN BARCELONA, JANUARY 1939. Gen. Yagüe (in front with glasses) and his troops hear Mass in the Plaza Catalunya. UPI

REFUGEES CROSSING THE FRENCH BORDER, FEBRUARY 1939. UPI

biennium. The landlords, the anarchists, the professional civil servants, and the various police forces under his command had all made life unpleasant for him during that period. No one knew better from personal experience how many elements of Spanish society would be happy to wreck the Republic. He was also suffering from tuberculosis and often took part in the Cortes debates while running a fever. Only through loyalty to Azaña did he consent to accept the assignment as Prime Minister on May 10, 1936.

Despite the hectic political agitation of the spring, the Republican cabinet made strong efforts to fulfill the Popular Front program. On February 29 the government suspended the eviction of agricultural tenants, a process which had been gathering momentum in late 1935. On March 16 Azaña announced once again the confiscation of the estates of the grandees involved in the Sanjurjo revolt, estates which had been confiscated in September 1932, and then restored in April 1934, as part of the Sanjurjo amnesty law. The Minister of Agriculture, Mariano Ruiz Funes, traveled constantly in the western and southern provinces, intervening where he could to prevent clashes between the peasants and the Civil Guard and formalizing by his presence the position of thousands of squatters.[14] The landlords cried that the government was simply legalizing robbery, but the Minister was doing the only thing that might still preserve peace in the country-side. He was pledging the government to distribute land as rapidly as possible and giving a measure of orderly procedure to actions which absolutely could not be postponed for the months that would be required to produce legislation.

In the matter of regional autonomy, the Catalan Generalitat was immediately reestablished with the powers it had exercised before October 6, and, in the course of the spring, the Madrid government transferred to it authority over public order, hydraulic works, and ports. In the Basque country the suspended municipal governments were restored, and specific discussion of a Basque autonomy statute begun. The principal difficulties to be worked out were financial. Under

[14] *El Sol*, March 4 and April 12, 1936.

AL REVES, por Bagaría

THE DILEMMA OF CASARES QUIROGA

BULLFIGHTER: Either you settle our grievance or we go out on strike.

MINISTER (Casares Quiroga): No, hombre, no. The other way around. You give me the grievance settled or you go out on strike, whether you want to or not.

El Sol, 22 May, 1936

the *concierto económico* dating back to 1878, the central government levied an agreed sum of taxes from the Basque provinces but permitted the Basques to distribute the tax burden at home as they saw fit. Articles 40 and 41 of the proposed statute guaranteed to continue this system. But in the opinion of government economic experts the Basque quota was proportionately much lower than it should have been, and the Basques of course were not ready to have the Madrid government raise their taxes. Relatively speaking, the Basques were paying smaller taxes than other Spaniards and this, together with their superior economic efficiency, tended to draw new industry to an already highly industrial area. Even Castilian liberals were not anxious to grant a statute of autonomy which would at the same time confirm a privileged position in regard to taxes.[15]

The Popular Front pledge to restore to their jobs all workers who had been dismissed for political reasons since 1934 created serious problems. It was no easy matter to determine just who had been dismissed and for what reason. The rehiring of workers who had been fired more than a year previously inevitably meant expansion of the employer's pay-rolls if they were not to dismiss the more recently hired workers. Anarchist pistoleros occasionally forced employers to take on men who had never been their employees, and the general atmosphere of political tension did not ease the re-lationship between recent prisoners or unemployed and those who had replaced them over a period of some eighteen months. The situation was further complicated by the rivalry of UGT and CNT unions for credit in obtaining jobs for their re-spective clients.

In Catalonia the metal workers had won a 44-hour week shortly before the October revolt. Through 1935 they had had to work a 48-hour week without a compensating wage raise. After the February elections they demanded to be paid for all the unpaid hours of the past 15 months and turned down a Generalitat offer to compensate them by a 40-hour week at the 44-hour wage rate.[16] The railway workers all over Spain renewed their wage demands of the years 1931–33. Railway revenues were low in 1936, as they had been in 1933. Some companies offered to show their books to prove the impossibility of meeting the demands. Many reduced their services and were glad to be taken over by the government. In Spain as in other countries the business community tolerated

[15] *El Sol,* July 9, 1936.
[16] *Economía Española,* March, 1936, pp. 323–37.

a measure of socialization, provided the industries taken over were those about to go bankrupt. In the spring of 1936 the Azaña and Casares governments did what they could to keep the railways in operation regardless of budgetary difficulties to be faced later.[17]

Marcelino Domingo again was Minister of Education, as he had been in the provisional government of 1931. He restored coeducation, which had been repudiated during the second biennium, and renewed the school-building program which had come to a virtual halt in 1935. The teaching community at this time was greatly perturbed about the problem of textbooks. In the first flush of enthusiasm in 1932, the Ministry had suppressed the use of required textbooks in secondary schools. The students were to have a range of choice, and instead of taking standardized examinations, they were to submit their notebooks to the teachers. This move reflected the influence of Swiss and American progressive education in the thinking of the republicans and was also posited in part on the notion that classes would be limited to about 30 pupils. But in fact they had averaged more than 60. The teachers had clamored for the restoration of textbooks, and the conservative trend of the second biennium had favored the older methods in any case. Meanwhile, the suppression of required texts had led to the publication of many new ones. The teachers were urged to make use of the new facilities, and publishers lobbied among the Radical deputies known to be friendly to business. As a result, the students in urban high schools were forced to buy many books for the sake of a few chapters in each, and in early 1936 there were many well-substantiated complaints about profiteering in textbooks.[18]

The clerical issue inevitably arose in connection with schools. The conservative deputies opposed coeducation and accepted with ill grace the renewal of a school-building program. However, both the Church and the government were anxious to avoid a renewal of the anticlerical passions of 1931. The Holy Week processions in Seville proceeded quietly—with

[17] *The Times,* London, May 29, 1936.
[18] *El Sol,* Jun. 17, 1936.

extra police assigned to assure tranquility.[19] When the temporary President, Martínez Barrio, departed for Madrid, Cardinal Ilundáin was among the dignitaries who accompanied him to the train. Using the limited information and the limited forces at its command, the government throughout the spring sent police to protect churches which the anti-clericals had threatened to burn. On its side, the Church scrupulously avoided political statements of the sort made by Cardinal Segura in 1931, and the Vatican, which had not received Luis Zulueta as ambassador in 1931, accepted him promptly in 1936 when he was reappointed by Azaña. Church schools operated during the spring without interference except from occasional hooligans, but on May 20 they were ordered closed. The government claimed it was doing this to prevent the schools from being burned, an explanation which in effect admitted to a rising tide of anticlerical sentiment and to the inability of the government to control the situation. Final examinations were interrupted by the order, and Catholic parents flooded the government with letters of protest.[20]

Prominent personalities outside the government also exerted their influence to maintain civil peace and legal forms of political action. In March, Gil Robles, explaining his electoral defeat, condemned the employers who, during the second biennium, had reduced wages vengefully. In April Manuel Giménez Fernández demanded in a caucus of the CEDA minority that the deputies take their stand for or against loyal cooperation with the Republican government. Of the 115 deputies, 101 pledged their republican loyalty, and that 101 included those who were the personal followers of Gil Robles.[21]

On June 2 Dr. Gregorio Marañon published a long, front-page article in *El Sol*. He deplored the exaggerated reports in the foreign press of disorders in Spain and attributed those reports to frightened reactionaries who had fled abroad after February 16 and now felt they must justify their precipitous

[19] *The Times,* London, April 11 and 13, 1936.
[20] *Ibid.,* May 22, 1936.
[21] Information from Sr. Giménez Fernández.

action. He condemned the Right for having identified conservatism with the defense of every vested interest during their two years in power. He admonished the Left against the "antinational" tone of its propaganda, an indirect reference to the glorification of the Soviet Union. He warned Spaniards generally that the reforms of the Azaña government were absolutely necessary to the modernization of Spain. He predicted months of "astringent, and at times violent, friction" while this modernization proceeded, and he warned that if Azaña were defeated, all Spain would be divided between reaction and Marxism.

Miguel Maura also came forward with considered criticisms and proposals. In the June 18th issue of *El Sol* he began a series of articles, the first of which, concerning the Lerroux-Gil Robles governments, was unambiguously entitled *Una política de suicidas*. He excoriated the Right for the purely negative policy of undoing the work of the Constituent Cortes. He credited his political opponents, Azaña and Izquierda Republicana, with having saved Spain from anarchy at the end of 1935 by getting the workers to accept a Popular Front program of moderate reform. But now, five months later, Spain was suffering from an unprecedented degree of internal anarchy. "Jacobin committees" in the countryside were checkmating the best efforts of the Cortes and the civil governors. The frightened *bourgeoisie* were deserting their own parties [those of Gil Robles, Martínez de Velasco, Lerroux, the *Lliga Catalana*] and beginning to support a youthful group [the Falange] whose members were valiant and idealistic, but who lacked any precise ideal, who were wasting their energies in street battles, and who could not hope to triumph except as the result of a civil war. In view of the gravity of this situation, Maura called for a "republican dictatorship." The President should appoint a cabinet representing all tendencies from reformist socialism to conservative republicanism. That government should reestablish public order by the use of the Civil Guard, permit the highest salaries compatible with production costs and market conditions, proceed rapidly with agrarian reform, modernize the military forces, and finally, proceed to constitutional reform.

216

Both the gentle Dr. Marañon and the vigorous Miguel Maura were prophets without honor in the spring of 1936. Their specific proposals depended on a strengthening of the presidential power which neither the defeated Right nor the revolutionary Left would grant to Azaña. Many moderates, though they approved the Popular Front program and feared the "infantile leftism" of the young Socialists, nevertheless could not conceive a government of national union. Thus Julián Besteiro, when asked whether he would support Azaña if the latter sought CEDA votes in a struggle against a communist revolution, replied that he would never accept union with Gil Robles.[22] Neither the Right nor the Left was in any mood to listen to the criticism offered of their general conduct. The Right, far from feeling that they had been mistaken simply to undo the work of the Constituent Cortes, felt on the contrary that they ought to have rewritten the entire document, and that if they had shot the leaders of the Asturian revolt the Popular Front would never have had the opportunity to organize. As for the Left, they were intoxicated by the notion that History was on their side. They would use the Republican government as long as it enacted the reforms they desired and then take power in the name of the proletariat, when in their eyes the time seemed ripe. They had promoted Azaña to the presidency, not to strengthen the office, but to remove from active politics the most able "bourgeois" leader. The Casares government, and any succeeding Republican government, would exist solely by grace of Socialist and Communist support in the Cortes. While the Marañons and the Mauras, the Besteiros and the Prietos, talked of ending useless strikes, stopping attacks on churches, restoring public order, the *exaltados* of both the Right and the Left rolled up their sleeves. When the feeble parliamentary bourgeois government had been discredited, the future would be theirs.

[22] *El Sol*, May 14, 1936.

THE APPROACH OF THE CIVIL WAR

WHEN on June 2 Dr. Marañon publicly criticized the *émigrés* who were exaggerating the disorders in Spain, he was correct with regard to those whose overheated imaginations were picturing the rape of nuns, the paralysis of commerce, and the sacking of wealthy apartments. But President Azaña himself assigned police to guard major political figures, and many conservative deputies found rural hotel managers afraid to lodge them as they traveled to and from the capital. Clashes between CNT and UGT workers, between Falangists and leftists, between police and peasants, were daily occurrences. Responsible figures might deny the facts in a sincere effort to tranquilize public opinion and to protect Spain's international reputation. Certain areas, notably Catalonia, enjoyed greater public order in the spring of 1936 than at other times in the past five years. But all over central and southern Spain the atmosphere of class hatred was almost palpable.

On June 16 the Cortes heard a second series of charges and countercharges concerning the state of public order. Gil Robles presented a statistical summary of the disorders which had occurred in the four months since February 16. He listed, among other things, 170 churches destroyed by fire and 251 unsuccessful attempts at burning; 269 deaths and 1,287 wounded through assassination and street fighting; 133 general strikes and 218 partial general strikes; various other aggressions, assaults, burnings, and attempts within each category of crime. The speaker weakened his case, and maddened the Popular Front deputies to whom he addressed himself, by applying numbers in a situation where neither he nor anyone else could possibly have achieved accuracy. The figure for general strikes was incredible, given the inter-union rivalries, the general indiscipline of labor, and the catastrophic results which any such number of effectively realized general strikes would have produced on the economy. The figures for churches destroyed and those partially destroyed by fire were almost as difficult to accept. The destruction of a stone church by fire is a formidable task, and there had been too many examples in the past of churches being reported burned when some hooligan had lit a pile of newspapers on the steps. On these, and on many less reasonable grounds, the Left rejected his entire summary with accusations of fascism. They claimed that all the dead were defenseless workers or hired gunmen, and charged that he had initiated the entire debate in order to slander the Republic.

In clarifying his motives, Gil Robles referred to his daily visits to the Ministry of the Interior to obtain the release of CEDA and JAP personnel falsely arrested, and to the press censorship by which the government tried to prevent the public from knowing the constant state of disorder in which the country was living. Lashing back at constant Left epithets of "fascist," he warned the Popular Front majority that there would never be peace in Spain as long as they cut off all rational discussion by labeling their opponents fascists.

Calvo Sotelo also spoke at length, emphasizing anarchist provocations to the government, chaotic land seizures, and what he claimed were 100 per cent wage raises in the countryside. He criticized the antimilitary spirit of the government, in particular the decree which permitted the Minister of War to shift officers and fill vacancies at will. He assured the Cortes that he did not know a single officer who was disposed to rise against the Republican regime, but he did not wish to deny the possibility that some patriotic officers might indeed try to save Spain from anarchy. At one point he referred to the Republican governor of Oviedo as a "blue ribbon anarchist" (*anarquista de fajín*) and to Asturias as a Russian province. After several further insulting personal references to Republican officials, the President of the Cortes interrupted to remind him of the decorum appropriate to a parliament. In replying to Calvo Sotelo on behalf of the government, Casares Quiroga accused him of wild exaggerations and incitements to rebellion and then added that, in view of the words just pronounced by the deputy, "if anything happens (which it will not) I hold Your Excellency responsible for all." To which Calvo Sotelo replied that like Santo Domingo de Silos, he was a man of broad shoulders, and proud to accept the responsibility attributed to him.[1] Calvo Sotelo was to be assassinated one month later. Official historians of the Civil War have universally interpreted Casares' statement as a threat of assassination and Calvo Sotelo's reply as a heroic anticipation of martyrdom.

The months of June and July witnessed truly revolutionary events in both city and countryside. On June 1, in Madrid, some 40,000 construction workers and 30,000 electricians and elevator repairmen went out on strike.[2] Both UGT and CNT unions were involved, and the strike was in large measure a test of strength between the two union groups. Madrid had historically been UGT territory, but in the past year the CNT had made many converts among Madrid workers. With the strike continuing, and no pay coming in, the CNT leaders encouraged their followers to act out the principles of comunismo libertario. The workers ate in restaurants and collected groceries without paying while the UGT officials stood by in embarrassed silence and the shopkeepers wondered whether the Revolution had indeed arrived.[3] The government had named a special mixed jury to arbitrate the specific demands. By June 20, the majority of the employers had accepted the jury, and in the Casa del Pueblo the UGT workers voted to do likewise, by the immense majority of 17,164 to 510.[4]

But the CNT decided to continue the strike, and the UGT leaders, despite the vote of their own workers, followed the CNT line. Behind the scenes, the struggle continued. Eduardo Domínguez (for the UGT) argued that the con-

[1] *El Sol*, June 17 and 18, 1936.
[2] The *New York Times*, July 9, 1936.
[3] *El Sol*, June 3 and 12, 1936. *El Socialista, Claridad,* and *Mundo Obrero* all criticized these tactics as "anarchist provocations." On June 23 *Solidaridad Obrera* in Barcelona editorialized that the accumulation of strikes was injuring the interests of the working class, and that workers should seek lower prices rather than wage increases.
[4] *El Sol*, June 24.

tinuance of the strike imperiled the regime, while the CNT chiefs David Antona and Cipriano Mera (the latter to become the most important military commander produced by the anarchists) argued for revolutionary unity and pressure on both the employers and the government. On July 4, with the strike six weeks old, the UGT and *Claridad* publicly accepted the arbitration of the mixed jury. The anarchists stayed out, and the Socialist workers, to avoid clashes with their fellow proletarians, reported to their jobs but did not actually work.[5] Even so, during the following week there were a handful of deaths in clashes between UGT and CNT workers, and the janitors of Madrid office buildings refused to run the elevators on grounds that they had been threatened with death if they did so.

The construction and elevator strike was a great blow to the prestige of Largo Caballero. He had made himself the spokesman of UGT-CNT unity, and had talked all through the spring of proletarian government. The tactics of the CNT in the building strike had frightened the Left Socialists. Their hesitations over the arbitration offer showed their fear of losing influence to the anarchists, and their eventual decision to accept arbitration acknowledged the split in the revolutionary front. For the anarchists, Largo had backed off from a revolutionary test of power. For the Republicans and Socialists, he had shown himself incapable of controlling his followers and afraid either to collaborate with the government or to attack it frontally. On June 30 the Socialist Party held elections to fill various party offices. The Prieto and Caballero groups claimed quite different results for the voting, but if one totals all the votes which both factions claimed as valid, it still becomes clear that the tide had turned against Caballero and back toward the Prieto moderates.[6] The Spanish middle

[5] *El Sol,* July 7.

[6] *El Sol,* July 1 and 2, reported the votes as listed by the executive committee (Prietista) and by the *agrupaciones* (district clubs, strongly pro-Caballero). Totaling the two reports yields a 6 to 5 victory margin for the executive, in addition to which, allowance must be made for Communist votes on the agrupación list. Thus José Díaz, chairman of the Communist Party, was elected by the agrupaciones.

class had been thoroughly frightened by talk of a Caballero dictatorship. One of the many tragic ironies of the outbreak of the Civil War is that it occurred a few weeks after the first tangible evidence that the revolutionary tide within the Socialist Party was beginning to ebb.

The construction strike, because it took place in the capital, captured national attention. During the same period, less-publicized revolutionary events were occurring in the fields of Salamanca, Extremadura, and Andalusia. Renewed, and faster, land reform had been a major point in the Popular Front electoral program. After the victory of February 16, the left Socialist leadership of the Federation of Land Workers encouraged the peasants to seize the land in anticipation of a legal reform. In all the latifundia provinces squatters moved onto the land, occupying some 250,000 hectares in March; about 150,000 in April; and about 46,000 hectares each in May and June. Almost always they came without seeds, tools, or knowledge of what the land could produce. Cattle production was disorganized; landlords and arrendatarios, remembering the burnings and killings of 1933, moved to the city; federation locals promised work to the unemployed. By mid-June thousands of peasant families were roaming the roads. Gypsies and bootblacks had registered to work in the harvest, knowing of the 7½-hour day and the 30 per cent wage raise over the year before. In Badajoz the census of reapers available rose from 200 in 1935 to 1,800 in July 1936. The use of machines was forbidden as long as there were workers awaiting employment. Proprietors were forced to accept larger numbers than they needed and to provide housing for the thousands of wanderers. Peasants decided on their own which fields to harvest, showed no resistance when the Civil Guard moved them off the land, and filtered back the next day. Property lines and authority melted. An elemental land hunger and a pathetic faith in the coming land distribution swept the Spanish peasantry in the spring of 1936, as it had the "Zapatistas" in Mexico in 1917, the Ukrainian peasants in the same year, and the Cuban peasants in 1959. On the eve of the Civil War there existed no such Communist plot as most official historians in Spain have claimed. But in the countryside of western and southern Spain, a profound agrarian revolution had indeed begun in March, 1936.[7]

From the moment of the Popular Front electoral victory, reactionary and Monarchist officers were planning a military rising. They knew that the Army was not ready to seize power, but they were absolutely convinced that Spain would go communist within a matter of months. Like military men everywhere, they felt that in troubled times they carried the ultimate responsibility for the safety of the nation as a whole. In their simplified view of events, the Army had saved Spain from communism in 1917, and it was its patriotic duty to do so again. Many of them were members of the Unión Militar Española (UME), founded by Major Bartolomé Barba Hernández late in 1933. They were men who had been offended by the Azaña reforms and thrown into confusion by the failure of the Sanjurjo revolt. The UME was not exclusively a reactionary organization. It included at one time a number of officers who later fought for the Republic during the Civil War, such as General José Miaja and Major Vicente Rojo. But its leading spirits were royalists like Goded, Fanjul, Valentín Galarza, Orgaz, and Barrera, all of them involved in the Sanjurjo affair and all of them plotting for a future, better-organized attack on the Republic. Major Barba himself was obsessed by his hatred of Azaña, against whom he had concocted the slanderous story of an order to take no prisoners and to "shoot them in the belly" in the Casas Viejas affair.

Active preparations for a rising began with several Madrid meetings in March, arranged principally by officers who had been intimate collaborators of General Sanjurjo in the 1932 uprising.[8] Sanjurjo himself was living in Portugal. His per-

---

[7] My picture of the situation in Extremadura is based on two by-line articles by Pedro Perdomo in *El Sol,* July 16 and 17, 1936; and on conversations with friends of the then Minister of Agriculture, Mariano Ruiz Funes. I owe the figures on land occupation to the courtesy of Professor Edward Malefakis of Columbia University, who kindly permitted me to read his unpublished doctoral thesis.

[8] Unless otherwise specified, I have depended, in summarizing the conspiracy, on two well-documented biographies of the leading

sonal prestige and his seniority made him once again the natural chieftain, and as in 1932, the detailed planning on his behalf was done principally by Colonel Valentín Galarza. Generals Franco and Mola were present at the Madrid meetings, but Franco adopted a completely noncommittal attitude, whereas Mola rapidly became the active head of the conspiracy.[9]

General Emilio Mola Vidal had been the last Director General of Security under the Monarchy. He was among those who had advised the King to leave Spain, and the Monarchists held against him the many unflattering details he had revealed in his published memoirs. Early in 1932 it looked as

---

generals, written by officers who had worked with them: Jorge Vigón, *General Mola* (Barcelona, 1957) and Emilio Esteban-Infantes, *General Sanjurjo* (Barcelona, 1958). There is much fascinating detail in the memoirs of secondary, but very active, figures such as Antonio Lizarza and Juan Antonio Ansaldo. But one must tread warily when Carlists, Falangists, and UME men all claim passionately to have been the "real" initiators of the *movimiento*. On the basis of both reading and interviews, I am convinced that the significant planning was done by the officers, with Mola in the lead; that many of the claims by right-wing political figures reflect their anger at not having been fully trusted by the military and their frustration at the political results of the Civil War, from which they had hoped for something different than the dictatorship of General Franco.

[9] According to Manuel Goded, *Un faccioso cien por cien* (Zaragoza, 1939), pp. 26–7, General Goded, José Antonio, and Gil Robles also attended the Madrid meetings. His statement illustrates the impossibility, at this date, of getting the full truth. He was writing to justify his father, who had been bitterly criticized for surrendering in Barcelona on July 19. Hence he had every motive to claim a role for him in the early preparations. Neither Vigón nor Esteban-Infantes speak of Goded as a leader in the plot, but this may well be explained by the fact that Goded has been in semi-official disgrace since his death. Mention of José Antonio would also help the author to associate his father's memory with the patron saint of the *movimiento*. As for Gil Robles, this is simply one more reference to his part, all of which references he denies. No places and dates are specified. No one can prove who attended or did not attend.

though the government would pass him to the reserve. However, he had a reputation for keen intelligence and for relative liberalism, and he was not involved in the Sanjurjo rising; thus he appeared to be one of the more loyal of the senior generals.

In the spring of 1936 he was moved from the command of the Moroccan army to that of the Pamplona military district. With Sanjurjo still in Portugal, Goded in the Balearics, and Franco uncommitted, Mola's new assignment was a stroke of luck for the plotters. For while the General was no Monarchist, he had conceived a violent hatred of Azaña on account of the latter's military reforms. Now he was military commander in the heart of the Carlist country, the one portion of Spain where the conspirators could count on a degree of public support. Through the spring months, Mola held the main threads in his hands. Valentín Galarza was his link with Monarchist officers and with Sanjurjo. Lt. Colonel Yagüe, of the Foreign Legion, was his link to Falangist-minded officers, and potentially to General Franco, who had been Yagüe's idolized superior in the African campaigns of the 1920's. D. Raimundo García (editor of the *Diario de Navarra*) and D. Agustín Lizarza were his civilian emissaries to the Carlists. The Unión Militar Española were eager to help, and contacted General Sanjurjo on their own. Santiago Martín Báguenas, chief of police in Madrid, kept Mola well informed of attitudes inside the government and among the general staff officers.

Mola enjoyed the atmosphere of conspiracy, but he was beset by numerous problems. General Gonzalo Queipo de Llano, an old Republican, and a relative by marriage of Alcalá-Zamora, joined the conspiracy after the President was so unceremoniously ousted from office. But Queipo de Llano was a loud mouth who invited the most unlikely people, such as Miguel Maura, to join the conspiracy. The professional officers, especially those of the UME, wanted the rising to be handled by the military alone. But Calvo Sotelo, the leading Monarchist deputy, and the various Carlist leaders who were supplying much of the money, had to be consulted. Certain generals who were in the conspiracy from the beginning, and who were old comrades of Sanjurjo, nevertheless revealed extreme pessimism about the chances of success. Generals Villegas and Fanjul, assigned to prepare the way for the rising in Madrid, were especially conscious of their isolation, not only from the troops under them but from many of their fellow officers. Mola's brother sent pessimistic reports from Barcelona during the spring. According to the memoirs of his Carlist contacts, during much of June Mola himself was depressed over the prospect of a terrible civil war if the coup should for any reason not succeed immediately. José Antonio, in contact with Mola from his prison cell, approved an Army rising if it were supported by the people.[10] No one knew better than Mola that this was a utopian condition to attach to his approval. The Carlists were difficult because they demanded that their troops be organized separately and that the Monarchist flag be flown. They were Mola's strongest civilian supporters and he could not afford to break with them. But he knew that outside Navarre it would be fatal to rise against the Republic in the name of the Monarchy.

In spite of these difficulties, the conspiracy was well organized by the end of June, and the commanding generals had been assigned for each military district. Sanjurjo had approved Mola's plans. The UME and the Falange were pushing their own demands, but there was no doubt that they would participate. General Franco remained uncertain, but, much as the conspirators desired his collaboration, they intended to proceed with or without him. The rising was to occur sometime between July 10 and July 20. Calvo Sotelo had ratified the plans and was scheduled to have lunch on the 14th with Gil Robles to see whether the latter could at the last minute be brought in along with those Carlists and Monarchists who were already committed.

During its first two months in office, the Azaña government proceeded cautiously to redistribute a number of key military commands. After shifting Generals Goded and Franco to the Balearics and the Canaries respectively, Azaña decreed that the Minister of War could alter commands on his own initiative without following the usual rules of seniority.

[10] J. M. Iribarren, *Con el General Mola*, p. 15.

As Minister Azaña appointed General Masquelet, a devoted Republican who had served both himself and Lerroux as Chief of Staff. General Sebastián Pozas, the military investigator who had recognized Azaña's innocence after the Barcelona events of October 6, became Inspector General of the Civil Guard. General José Miaja (assigned to Madrid), Generals Molero and Batet (assigned respectively to Valladolid and Burgos), and General Nuñez del Prado (in charge of the small Air Force) were all staunch Republicans. By quietly appointing known Republicans to key posts, the government hoped to counteract possible plots without making a general purge of the officer corps. With the fatal exception of Mola, the appointments were shrewdly made.

From early April onward, the government received ample warning from both military and civilian sources. As a riposte to the activities of the UME, Republican officers had formed the Unión Militar Republicana Antifascista (UMRA). Prominent in this organization were General Nuñez del Prado, Colonel José Asensio Torrado, one of the most brilliant officers of the general staff, and Major Pérez Farras, the Catalan who had led the brief resistance of the Generalitat in October 1934. Many younger general staff, artillery corps, and Assault Guard officers belonged to the UMRA. In the late spring it was common knowledge in Madrid that the UME had undertaken a campaign of assassination against the UMRA and that the latter had sworn to reply in kind.

UMRA officers of the general staff kept the government informed of the efforts of General Fanjul, and their activities were the principal reason for the General's pessimism concerning a quick success in Madrid. Alonso Mallol, Director General of Security, communicated his strong suspicions of General Mola, and Prieto warned the government publicly in his Cuenca speech. Some of the conservative deputies approached by Calvo Sotelo informed the cabinet of the latter's efforts to enlist them. The alcalde of Estella, a Basque Nationalist, warned Casares specifically of Mola's meeting with the Carlist leaders at the nearby monastery of Irache on June 16.[11] And

[11] A. de Lizarra (pseud. of Andrés María de Irujo), *Los vascos y la república española* (Buenos Aires, 1944), pp. 33–6.

227

on June 23 General Franco wrote to the Prime Minister to warn him that the frequent shifting of assignments for high officers constituted a threat to the good discipline of the Army.

But in June, Casares was an ill man, preoccupied by the construction strike and pathetically anxious to woo the friendship of the Army. He brushed off Prieto's warnings as "fantasies of the male menopause," and publicly proclaimed his confidence in General Mola. Hearing that a group of cavalry officers who had hoped to participate in the Berlin Olympic Games had been unable to go for lack of funds, he had the Ministry of War pay their expenses to Germany, from which country they returned to the Insurgent zone in late July after the start of the Civil War. Left Socialists talked of arming the people to protect the government against a military coup, but this was the last thing a Republican cabinet would consider, with Madrid construction workers practicing *comunismo libertario* at the expense of their local grocers, and the Unified Socialist Youth calling for the formation of a Red Army.

In the Palacio del Oriente President Manuel Azaña assured both politicians and journalists that the present effervescence would pass rapidly, and occasionally he appeared at concerts and arts exhibits, imperturbable and dignified. As for the urban middle class, and the mass of Republicans and Socialists, they certainly did not act as though they anticipated war or revolution. In early July thousands of wives took their children to summer homes while their husbands remained in Madrid, Barcelona, Bilbao. Thousands of children left for summer camps, some under private auspices, some under labor union or Church auspices. These families were to be separated immediately by the geographical accidents of the Civil War. Had the parents, or the Catholic social workers, or the UGT camp directors anticipated war, these camps would never have been opened in the first week of July; nor would the cavalry officers have gone off to Berlin, nor would Largo Caballero have attended a labor conference of the Second International in London, during this first week of July, had any of them anticipated war. Quite possibly the majority of Spaniards were not worried about a prononciamiento in July because none had occurred in February, when a military rising had been widely anticipated after the elections.[12]

Among the younger military, however, tension remained acute. During the afternoon of Sunday, July 12, a Lieutenant José Castillo of the Assault Guard was shot dead by a posse of four Falangists. The victim had been a prominent member of the UMRA and an instructor of the Socialist Youth militia. His comrades decided in a matter of hours to enact a spectacular vengeance. Without reference to any political party or program, and without reflecting on the wider implications of their act, they resolved to assassinate an important leader of the Right.

The government itself, during the spring, had begun to supply armed guards to the prominent deputies of all parties. José Calvo Sotelo was among those who suspected, early in July, that some men in his escort were untrustworthy. He had aired his suspicion to Gil Robles, who advised him to speak to the Minister of the Interior, Juan Moles. The latter had immediately replaced the two guards of whom Calvo Sotelo was suspicious, the replacement taking effect on July 12 itself. That evening, when the Assault Guard friends of Castillo set out to kill a prominent Right politician, they first sought Antonio Goicoechea, the head of *Renovación Española,* and not finding him, sought Gil Robles, who was in Biarritz for the weekend. They then went to the apartment of Calvo Sotelo in the Calle Velásquez.

The police on guard at the door challenged their intent, but as they had come in an official police car and showed Civil Guard papers calling for the arrest of Calvo Sotelo, the police permitted them to enter. Calvo Sotelo himself, though immediately suspicious, nevertheless consented to leave after

[12] Jesús Pérez Salas, *Guerra en España,* pp. 75–6, 79, claims, in contrast with all other writers, that Azaña and Casares were aware of military plotting. He was a staunch Catalan republican and career officer who enjoyed the personal confidence of Azaña. His conversations with Azaña and with friends of Casares took place, however, in late March. They may thus constitute one more piece of indirect evidence that by July Azaña and Casares thought the danger had passed.

seeing the papers, not without telling his wife that he would telephone shortly if his brains were not blown out. A brave and strong man who suspected treachery, and who psychologically was prepared to accept martyrdom, walked off between the friends of Lieutenant Castillo, for whom he represented the Spanish fascism which had assassinated their comrade. They shot him, and before dawn dumped the body, with its marks of violent struggle, in the public morgue of Madrid, where it was not identified until late the following morning.

The government immediately condemned this brutal assassination of a major opposition leader. Martínez Barrio, President of the Cortes, announced that he had on that very day signed an order for the release of Calvo Sotelo, in case he had, as rumored, been arrested. The Minister of the Interior announced the arrest of fifteen Assault officers of Castillo's company and promised their immediate trial in the civil courts. There would thus be absolutely no "hush-up" by the government nor protection of its own members by a military force. But the Right was not to be mollified. Remembering the exchange between Calvo Sotelo and Casares Quiroga during the debate on public order, many accused the government of outright collusion in the murder.[13] Less violent opponents considered that the government should have shot the obviously guilty *Asaltos* without fussing over legal procedure. For everyone not blindly partisan of the Left, it was intolerable that a chief of the opposition should be murdered by officers in uniform driving a government car. For believers in democratic, civilian government, it was equally intolerable that the Falange and the UME should conduct in impunity a campaign of terror against leftist officers. The July 12 assassinations of Lieutenant Castillo and of José Calvo Sotelo shocked public opinion far more deeply than had any of the numerous disorders and occasional deaths since February.

[13] *El Sol,* July 17, 1936. Practically the entire issue was devoted to the Cortes debate concerning the Calvo Sotelo assassination.

13

THE PRONUNCIAMIENTO OF JULY 17-20

||||||||||||||||||||||||||||||||||||||||||||||||||||||||||||||||||||||||||||||||||||||||||||||||||||||||||||||||||||||||||||||||||||||||||||||||||||||||

THE assassinations of Lieutenant Castillo and José Calvo Sotelo coincided with the final stages of General Mola's planning. The generals and colonels who were to take command in each district had already received their assignments, and they all knew that the rising was to occur between July 10 and 20.[1] The Carlists were still holding out for the royal flag, the dissolution of all political parties, and a corporative state. General Mola, at Irache, had submitted a plan which, under an all-military directory, included the retention of the Republican regime and the separation of Church and state, with liberty for all religions. The bitter debate was submitted to the arbitration of General Sanjurjo on July 9. Sanjurjo, whose father had been a Carlist General in the last Carlist war, was far more sympathetic to the *Comunión Tradicionalista* than was Mola. Nevertheless, in his letter of arbitration he also insisted on an all-military directory, spoke of ending the activity (not the existence) of the political parties, and avoided all mention of either a monarchy or a corporative state.[2]

In the Canaries General Franco was preparing to take his own assigned command in Morocco. The private English airplane which was to fly him to Casablanca had left London on July 11 and was at his disposition in Tenerife on July 14. The plane, and its pilot, Captain Bebb, had been arranged for by Luis Bolín, *ABC* correspondent in London.[3] General

[1] Vigón, *Mola*, pp. 98–103.

[2] Antonio Lizarza Iribarren, *Memorias de la conspiración, 1931–1936*, 3d ed. (Pamplona, 1954), pp. 104–111. Sr. Lizarza was the courier between the two generals. Also Hugh Thomas, *The Spanish Civil War* (New York, 1961), pp. 118–19, a concordant version based on Carlist documentation belonging to Fal Conde.

[3] Reynolds and Eleanor Packard, *Balcony Empire* (New York, 1942), pp. 38–40.

Franco was thus assured of transport without being dependent on the Spanish Air Force, most of which was opposed to the rising. At the eastern extremity of Spain a last minute shift of command was necessary. General Goded had been assigned to the Balearic Islands and Valencia, but he now asked to be shifted from Valencia to Barcelona.

The murder of Calvo Sotelo precipitated the fixing of a precise moment for the rising: 5 p.m. on Friday the 17th in Morocco, to be followed within 24 hours by all the principal garrisons in the Peninsula. Morocco was indeed the Achilles' heel of the Spanish Republic. Left Socialists had intermittently urged an end of the colonial regime. Azaña in 1931, and again in 1936, had appointed both military and civilian chiefs of great integrity and known Republican loyalty. But virtually nothing had been done either to improve the condition of the masses or to break the hold of the career officers, colonial administrators, and arms and tobacco smugglers who had flourished in Morocco for decades. Most of the middle-rank officers, captains and majors, were either partisans of the rising or had been effectively intimidated by those who were. The garrison seized the main public buildings, including the radio station, in Melilla and immediately proclaimed the estado de guerra. The Foreign Legion seized the Casas del Pueblo of Melilla and Tetuán, shooting the union officers and all persons found with arms or those suspected of planning to resist. At the airbase the aviators resisted the rising for some hours, after which many were shot and the rest jailed.

The rising took the top Republican officials, as well as the Madrid government, by surprise. In response to their telephone calls, Casares Quiroga urged them to resist, promised reinforcements of loyal troops, and insisted that the revolt was a purely local affair. Generals Gómez Morato and Romerales and the High Commissioner Plácido Alvarez Buylla were loyal to the government; they were individually courageous but completely isolated from the real levers of power. They were arrested the first day, and later shot. On the 18th, the workers of Tetuán and Melilla attempted a general strike, which was easily broken by the Insurgent garrisons and the natives.[4]

[4] Pierre Broué and Emile Témime, *La révolution et la guerre*

Meanwhile, General Franco declared the *estado de guerra* in Tenerife and went on the radio to explain the motives of the military rising. He stated that anarchy and revolutionary strikes were destroying the nation; that the Constitution was for all practical purposes suspended; that neither liberty nor equality before the law could survive in such circumstances; that regionalism was destroying national unity; and that the enemies of public order had systematically slandered the armed forces. The Army could no longer idly watch these shameful developments. It was rising in order to bring justice, equality, and peace to all Spaniards. The Army would not reverse the social gains recently won by the people; it would not act in a spirit of vengeance. It would guarantee to Spain "for the first time, and in this order, the trilogy fraternity, liberty, and equality."[5] The General then flew to Casablanca, in French Morocco, refueled, received news of the complete and rapid success in the Spanish zone, and on July 19 flew in to take supreme command of the Army of Morocco.

On Saturday the 18th, a series of swift, successful risings took place in Navarre, Aragon, Old Castile, and southern Andalusia. In Pamplona the Requetés poured into the street, rousing wild enthusiasm among the Catholic and Carlist elements and smothering in blood the brief resistance at the Casa del Pueblo. The local head of the Civil Guard, Rodríguez Medel, refused to rise, and was shot. In Saragossa General Miguel Cabanellas proclaimed the estado de guerra in the name of the Republic. Though he had been connected with the conspiracy for months, Cabanellas, as an old Republican, a Mason, and something of a liberal, was suspected of indecisive sentiments; thus, the younger officers ardently committed to the rising arrived in his office armed, to make sure that he went through with the rising as planned. In the streets, Assault Guards led by Falangist officers dispersed the little worker

---

d'Espagne (Paris, 1961), pp. 82–4. This thoroughly admirable book has excellent sketches of the first days in many parts of Spain, (pp. 82–102), details of which I have incorporated in the following paragraphs without additional footnoting.

[5] The text of the radio address is printed in Iturralde, *El catolicismo y la cruzada de Franco*, ii, 22–6.

resistance in the center of the city. The civil governor, an Azaña Republican who had earned an excellent reputation in the city for minimizing both Falangist and leftist disorders, was arrested.[6] Madrid had immediately dispatched Air General Nuñez del Prado, a personal friend of Cabanellas, to confer with the latter. He was arrested as he stepped off his plane in Saragossa, and later shot.

The commanding general of the military district in Burgos was Batet, loyal to the Republican government. On July 16 Batet had, upon his own initiative, met Mola and had asked the latter point-blank whether he was involved in plans for a pronunciamiento. The interview had been disagreeable and had produced no tangible result.[7] General Batet had also arrested General González de Lara and sent him to Madrid for disciplinary action. The majority of top officers at Burgos, however, belonged to the conspiracy. At 2 a.m. on Sunday morning July 19 General Dávila declared the *estado de guerra* in the presence of the civilian officials convoked for the purpose. He stated that the Army was rising in order to save the Republic, and the majority of those present, regardless of their inner thoughts, appeared to take him at his word. General Batet was already under arrest and was later to be executed.[8] The same fate awaited General González de Lara on the other side, where he was taken off the train at Guadalajara by Popular Front militia.

In Valladolid on the afternoon of the 18th, Generals Saliquet and Ponte, members of the conspiracy, arrested and later shot their commanding officer, General Molero. Valladolid had important railway repair shops staffed by militant Socialist workers. A combination of Assault Guards and

[6] Vigón, *Mola*, pp. 121–27, for the quick successes in northern Spain. I also had opportunities in Saragossa, Valladolid, and Salamanca to question several persons who were lifelong residents and who had lived through the first days of the war in those cities.

[7] Vigón, *Mola*, pp. 108–109.

[8] Antonio Ruiz Vilaplana, *Burgos Justice* (New York, 1938), pp. 17–24. The author was a lawyer and municipal official in Burgos at the time of the rising. He emigrated to France in June, 1937; the original Spanish edition of his book was entitled *Doy Fe*.

Falangists captured the main Socialist leaders when they occupied the Casa del Pueblo that evening. There was sporadic firing during the night, but on Sunday the 19th the city was firmly in the hands of the Insurgent military.[9] In Salamanca, on Sunday morning, the military set up machine guns in the center of the municipal square and declared the *estado de guerra* in the presence of the hundreds of Salamantines who were strolling under the arcades. Someone shouted "Viva la República," at which the soldiers were ordered to fire. Some half-dozen people were killed and an undetermined number wounded. The square emptied immediately, and the city came quickly under military rule. In the other provincial capitals of Castile—Palencia, Zamora, Avila—the estado de guerra took the population by surprise, and in each instance the swift occupation of the Casa del Pueblo and the shooting of known Left personalities brought the towns under control.

In Old Castile the rural population were generally conservative or apolitical. The sparseness of industrial development made it easy in advance to pinpoint the Casa del Pueblo and the "red" suburbs where resistance would be likely. In Andalusia, however, while the Insurgents won equally quick victories through surprise and audacity, the pacification was more difficult, for the population here was heavily anarchist, anti-military, and anticlerical.[10] In Algeciras and Córdoba the workers demanded the distribution of arms as soon as the news of the Morocco rising arrived. The civil governors refused, giving as their reasons the pledges of loyalty received from the local military commanders and the lack of authority for any such move in the absence of orders from Madrid. Hours later, the military rose, establishing control quickly by means of machine-gun fire; nonetheless, they were forced to kill

[9] Francisco de Cossío, *Manolo* (Valladolid, 1939), pp. 115–28, gives a vivid picture of the emotions and acts of the young Falangists in the taking of Valladolid. The book as a whole gives a literate, moving account of the reactions of the conservative middle class of Old Castile to the Republic.

[10] Vigón, *Mola*, pp. 141ff., for the first days in Andalusia and Extremadura. I also had conversations with Nationalist officers who took part in the actions at Algeciras and Cádiz.

hundreds of *canalla* who insisted on resisting modern arms with knives and bare chests.

In Cádiz a general strike began on the 19th, and elements of the Assault Guards distributed arms. The governor guaranteed the loyalty of the local officers in order to prevent their being lynched. The next day the garrison rose and in a few bloody hours established control of the city. In Málaga the opposite sequence occurred. On the evening of the 17th, before any other Peninsular rising had begun, General Paxtot had his troops quietly occupy the center of the city. The next morning, however, he returned them to the barracks. During the afternoon and evening of the 18th, he heeded the telephone pleas of Madrid to hold his fire while the government desperately sought an understanding with the generals which would pull Spain back from the brink of civil war. On the 19th, the workers surrounded the barracks. By means of dynamite and the threat to set the barracks on fire, they obtained the surrender of the garrison to a detachment of loyal Assault Guards.

In Huelva and Granada the rising was successful, at the cost of heavy slaughter among the proletariat; Jaén remained in Republican hands. But the key to the control of Andalusia was Seville, whose capture the conspirators had assigned to General Gonzalo Queipo de Llano. Queipo was at this time the head of the *carabineros* (the frontier police), and he appeared in Seville late on the afternoon of the 17th, ostensibly on a tour of inspection. On Saturday afternoon he quickly and quietly arrested the division commander, General Villa-Abrille, the civil governor, and the chief of police. The Assault Guards were expected to be loyal to the government, and so Queipo's first military move was to neutralize them by the use of some 200 troops whose company officers were members of the conspiracy. He had disarmed the *asaltos* and occupied the municipal government buildings before the city as a whole knew that anything was happening.

Early in the evening the workers called a general strike. During that night, and for several days following, Queipo established control through a combination of audacity, terror, and propaganda. His soldiers, dressed in baggy pants and daubed with walnut juice so as to look like Moors, made lightning machine-gun raids from the backs of trucks driving rapidly through the working-class districts. Meanwhile, the General went on the radio frequently, to tell the Sevillanos that the rising had triumphed everywhere, that he was entirely favorable to the social accomplishments of the Republic, and that he would not hesitate to shoot anyone foolish enough not to accept the new regime immediately.[11] Admiring journalists, at the time, and Nationalist historians ever since, have written eloquently of Queipo's extraordinary victory over one of the most "red" cities in Spain. Since he enjoyed the advantage of his surprise arrests, and since his troops had the only trucks and modern arms available, his military accomplishment does not seem particularly outstanding. But in the logistics of the war as they developed in the following weeks, the quick capture of Seville was one of the greatest advantages enjoyed by the Insurgent forces.

The most crucial events of the first few days occurred in the two largest cities, Madrid and Barcelona. In Madrid, the conspirators had planned that General García de la Herrán should win over the Army camp at Carabanchel and General Fanjul should take the inner city from the Montaña Barracks, located close to the Plaza de España and the upper end of the Gran Vía. When news of the Moroccan rising arrived on Friday evening, the UGT and the CNT immediately demanded the distribution of arms. Throughout Saturday, the government was unable to make up its mind on the question, but during Saturday afternoon a group of younger officers, led by Lt. Colonel Rodrigo Gil of the artillery corps, distributed some 5,000 rifles. Meanwhile, for reasons not entirely clear, the conspirators hesitated; though without doubt, one general reason was the evident hostility of a large proportion

[11] Antonio Bahamonde, *Memoirs of a Spanish Nationalist* (London, 1939), pp. 27–31; Harold Cardozo, *March of a Nation* (London, 1937), pp. 11–15. Bahamonde was a civil servant under Queipo and emigrated in 1938. His *Memoirs* are marked by haste and by the sense of revulsion at what he had lived through, but his details were amply confirmed by my interviews in Seville. Cardozo was an English journalist favorable to the Insurgents from the start.

of their own troops and fellow officers. Early Sunday, General García attempted to rally the *campamento*, failed, and was shot before he could leave the grounds with the few officers ready to follow him to Madrid. At Getafe and Cuatro Vientos loyal artillery and Air Force officers defeated the rebels. Inside the Montaña Barracks General Fanjul was unable to decide on a consistent course of action. He ordered that machine guns fire on the workers beginning to surround the building, but he did not try to break out of the siege. He suspected that many of his officers were not favorable to his declaration of the estado de guerra. He kept hoping for reinforcements from Carabanchel, from Getafe, from Cuatro Vientos—all points at which the rebellion had been suffocated.[12]

At 5 a.m. on Sunday, July 19, General Fernández Burriel brought several battalions of the 4th Division into the streets of Barcelona on behalf of the rising. The Insurgents quickly dominated the main squares (the Plaza de Catalunya, Plaza de España, and Plaza de la Universidad), capturing the Telephone Building and several university halls to the cry of "Viva la República, compañeros." But Generals Llano de la Ecomienda and Aranguren, together with most of the Civil and Assault Guards, and the Air Force, remained loyal to the government.[13] At 8:45 a.m. General Burriel telephoned his superior, General Goded, who had enjoyed a quick triumph in Palma de Majorca, and who was scheduled to fly to Barcelona to take command. Burriel spoke with great optimism, thereby arousing uneasy suspicions in Goded, who had heard the Barcelona radio proclaiming the failure of the rising and listing the loyal military units in the city.

---

[12] Concerning Madrid, I depended on Vigón's *Mola*, on Julián Zugazagoitia, *Historia de la guerra en España* (Buenos Aires, 1940), pp. 42ff., and on the living memory of many Madrileños. Zugazagoitia was the editor of *El Socialista*, and knew personally all the leading actors of the Left in the Montaña drama.

[13] J. Pérez Salas, *Guerra en España*, pp. 83–4, details the changes in police and troop commands made by the Generalitat in June, 1936. Pérez was one of those advising the changes, and feels that they were an important factor in the Republican triumph in Barcelona.

General Goded nevertheless flew to the Catalan capital in the Savoia hydroplane which had been waiting for him in the harbor of Palma. In the air over Barcelona he did not receive the expected salutes for an arriving general, but landed hurriedly in the harbor and proceeded at once to 4th Division headquarters. During the afternoon, Catalan *mossos* and loyal Civil Guards besieged the Hotel Colón (in the Plaza de Catalunya) with the few artillery pieces available. Anarchist workers rushed the building, at tremendous cost, while loyal troops destroyed machine-gun nests at various points along the main thoroughfares. From the recaptured Plaza de Catalunya, the guns were dragged into position before General Goded's headquarters. At 5 p.m. the fighting was over. Lieutenant Pérez Farras, who had led the Catalan troops on the night of October 6, 1934, commanded the troops which now received the surrender of Goded and his staff. The Insurgent officers were quickly escorted out to prevent their being massacred. At the request of Companys, and in order to avoid useless bloodshed, General Goded went on the radio at 7 p.m., saying: "Destiny has been adverse, and I have fallen prisoner, for which reason I release from their obligations towards me all those who have followed me."[14]

In Madrid, during Sunday afternoon and evening, the

[14] Manuel Goded, *Un faccioso cien por cien,* pp. 37–49 for the details of the General's role. "Remembrança, 19 de juliol del 1936," *Butlleti D'Informació,* n.d. (mimeographed organ of the Generalitat-in-exile), and Jesús Pérez Salas, *Guerra en España,* pp. 97–101 for the events in Barcelona.

The words I attribute to General Goded are those given in *Un faccioso,* pp. 58–9. The version given in "Remembrança" is practically the same except for an additional phrase: "to avoid the continued shedding of blood." The surrender of Goded is a sensitive point in Spanish memories. Many Nationalists regard him as having been a coward and traitor, while Republican veterans believe that he regretted the rising from the moment that he realized how little popular backing it enjoyed. His son explains the radio speech as the only move his father could make to prevent various air and naval reinforcements from leaving Insurgent Palma for Barcelona, in which latter city they would have been captured without in any way affecting the outcome of the struggle.

workers prepared to storm the Montaña barracks. The next morning, advancing with their 5,000 rifles and two pieces of field artillery, they absorbed tremendous losses from the accurate and heavy machine-gun fire coming from within. Loudspeakers broadcast the victorious news from Barcelona, culminating in repeated readings of General Goded's surrender address. Differences of opinion among the defenders led to the hoisting of the white flag and then to renewed firing at the besiegers as they came forward, presumably to receive the surrender. Around noon the crowd, thoroughly maddened by the white flag incidents, broke through the main gate. Inside, a group of young rebel officers sat down at a council table, took leave of one another, cocked their own pistols, and committed collective suicide. Lieutenant Moreno of the Assault Guards, preceding the angry mob, whisked General Fanjul away to prison. Dozens of other officers were killed on the spot. The crowd carried off the arms captured during the assault, and loyal soldiers removed to the War Ministry some 50,000 rifles and large quantities of ammunition which had been stored in the Montaña.

In the northernmost provinces events during these first days took still another course. In Bilbao, when the news of the Moroccan rising arrived, the government took the precaution of routing all military telephone calls through the office of the civil governor. Consequently, when General Mola in Pamplona called military headquarters in Bilbao with the order to rise, the call was received by the civil governor, and there was no military revolt. At the Loyola Barracks in San Sebastián the officers were ready to rise, and the left wing of the Popular Front wished to rush the barracks, but the Basque Nationalists arranged for a peaceful surrender.[15]

At Oviedo, capital of the Asturias, the military commander was Colonel Aranda, reputed to be a Mason and a Republican, a man who got on well with Left Republican civil officials,

[15] G. L. Steer, *The Tree of Gernika* (London, 1938), pp. 68–70; A. de Lizarra, *Los vascos y la república española* (Buenos Aires, 1944), pp. 20–6, 41–57. Lizarra was a Basque Nationalist deputy, and his book makes liberal use also of the unpublished memoirs of his colleague and cousin, Manuel de Irujo.

and who was distrusted by the Falange. When, on July 18, the workers called for the distribution of arms, the colonel temporized, giving the impression that he favored the idea but that he could not act without a signed order from the Minister of War. He also cooperated with the Popular Front organizations, forming trainloads of armed miners to depart for the defense of Madrid. Simultaneously, he ordered the several Civil Guard units in the province to come to Oviedo, and as they marched out of their barracks, they gave the clenched fist salute.

By early morning of July 20 both the civil governor and the various union officials strongly suspected that they had been hoodwinked by the colonel, and their grumblings forced him to declare the estado de guerra earlier than he would otherwise have chosen. But since the most militant miners were off to Madrid, taking the rifles and dynamite they had been hiding since October 1934; and since the entire Civil Guard and most of the Assault Guard were under his orders, the Colonel was able quickly to take control of the inner city while the revolutionary miners took over the villages. Meanwhile, the triumphant military at Valladolid, alerted by Aranda, met the miners' trains and liquidated, without hesitation, these "rebels" caught with arms in hands.[16]

On Friday afternoon the 17th, in strongly Republican Galicia, the news from Morocco led to immediate mass meetings calling for support of the government and distribution of arms. During the 18th and 19th, the province waited tensely. Generals Salcedo and Caridad Pita, and Admiral Azarola assured the civil governor, Pérez Carballo, of their loyalty. During the 19th, Popular Front leaders in Vigo obtained similar pledges from the officers of the Civil and Assault

[16] Oscar Pérez Solís, *Sitio y defensa de Oviedo* (Valladolid, 1938), pp. 39–41; G. Carrascal, *Asturias* (Valladolid, 1938), pp. 50–4. Both these works are highly laudatory eyewitness accounts of the leadership of Colonel Aranda. Pérez Solís was a former communist and during the Civil War became a leading ideologist of the *movimiento*. See also Fernando Solano Palacio, *La tragedia del norte* (Barcelona, 1938), pp. 23–33, for an anarchist version of the first days in Asturias.

Guards, and in the light of these pledges they decided, in a long, night meeting on the 19th, not to press for the distribution of arms. On Monday morning they joined in the general strikes which were presumably occurring throughout Spain as a means to check the military rebellion. That same morning Insurgent officers arrested Generals Salcedo and Caridad Pita. An engineer officer, Colonel Cánovas de la Cruz, occupied the center of La Coruña with his troops shouting "Viva la República" as they marched. While he set up artillery to bombard the civil governor's office if necessary, the Assault and Civil Guard wavered, then came over to the side of the rebellion.

In Vigo Captain Carreró Vergés led his infantry company into the streets. A suspicious crowd, and nervous soldiers, exchanged greetings of "Viva la República" and "UHP." In the Puerta del Sol the Captain began to read the proclamation of the estado de guerra. "Death to the traitors" cried a few voices. The soldiers raised their rifles, the crowd moved forward, and the Captain gave the order to fire. The unarmed crowd fled, leaving their handful of dead and wounded in the street. Barricades were thrown up in the suburbs, but the military controlled Vigo on Monday the 20th, and the suburbs a day or two later.[17]

During these same days, high officers of the Navy attempted to bring their ships to the support of the rising. In the drydock at El Ferrol loyal sailors and rebels fought between the decks of the cruiser *Almirante Cervera*. The Insurgents took control of nearby La Coruña on Monday, whereupon the loyal sailors, whose ammunition was almost exhausted, radioed Madrid for advice. The rebel-held radio station at El Ferrol heard the message. Broadcasting on Madrid's wave length and simulating the lesser power of a distant transmitter, El Ferrol answered the appeal with advice to surrender in order to avoid useless bloodshed. At the naval base, then, as in the province of

[17] *Lo que han hecho en Galicia* (Paris, 1938), pp. 11–28, 160–75; Luis Moure-Mariño, *Galicia en la guerra* (Madrid, 1939), pp. 34–7. The first is a detailed account by two refugees; the second is the work of one of the founders of the Falange in Galicia. Their descriptions of the first days tally with each other.

Galicia generally, the rising triumphed on Monday. On the other hand, at Cartagena, the great naval base in southeastern Spain, the sailors rose over the weekend, murdering their officers and capturing the battleship *Jaime Primero,* some three cruisers, a dozen destroyers, and ten unseaworthy submarines. Under elected sailors' councils, they then prepared to weigh anchor for the straits of Gibraltar, with the purpose of preventing the Moroccan Army from being ferried to Spain.

The pronunciamiento of July 17 caught the government completely by surprise, since neither President Azaña nor Prime Minister Casares Quiroga had credited the many warnings they had received from Popular Front personalities and from loyal military men. Casares' first impulse was to suppose that the rising was a purely local affair in Morocco, which could and should be suppressed by loyal Army units. He was opposed to publishing the news for he feared it would excite public opinion unduly. But in the predawn hours of July 18 the government was receiving anguished telephone calls from provincial officials in Castile and the entire north. Casares urged all such callers to resist; he promised armed aid if necessary, but he did not want them to compromise desperate peace efforts by distributing arms to the people. During the day of the 18th in Madrid, the unions clamored for arms, and in the afternoon, rifles were distributed by young officers deliberately disobeying the consigns of the Casares government.

On the morning of July 18th President Azaña proposed a government of national concentration to include the elements and effect the kind of program put forward by Miguel Maura in his *El Sol* articles of June.[18] Largo Caballero, the entire CNT, UGT, and Socialist Youth leadership firmly vetoed the plan. That evening Casares Quiroga resigned and Azaña asked Martínez Barrio to form a government. The latter represented the most conservative element of the Popular Front. He managed to get certain Insurgent officers, notably General Paxtot in Málaga, to hold off in the hope of a compromise that would satisfy the military without civil war, and his

[18] Information from a conversation with Miguel Maura.

proposed cabinet included Felipe Sánchez Román and General José Miaja. But the announcement of his government brought predawn protest demonstrations in the streets of Madrid, which were rapidly coming under the control of the newly armed workers. On the 19th the intimate collaborator of Azaña and professor of chemistry, José Giral, formed an all-Republican cabinet which explicitly accepted the *fait accompli* of the arms distribution and proposed to checkmate the military rebellion in cooperation with the armed masses. Even this government, however, did not order the provincial governors to distribute arms.

During the afternoon of the 19th, Luis Companys sent a teletype message to Azaña saying that the Insurgent officers in Barcelona were disposed to negotiate with the government. Some days earlier, General Goded had sent his friend the Marqués de Carvajal to see Azaña. Goded was a Monarchist and was deeply disturbed when he had learned of the plans to receive aid from Italy and Germany. The Marqués was to ask Azaña to telegraph Goded in Palma de Majorca, ordering him to come to Madrid. In a first interview he merely hinted at Goded's feelings, for he had planned to suggest the telegram in a second conversation; but in the meantime, the Madrid police sacked his hotel room and he left the city. On Sunday afternoon the 19th, after the armed workers had refused a Martínez Barrio cabinet, and before anyone could be sure whether Giral would fare better, Azaña decided it would be utterly useless for himself or Companys to treat with the Insurgent generals.[19]

All did not go according to plan on the Insurgent side either. General José Sanjurjo, titular chief of the rising, was killed in an airplane accident on his way from Portugal to take command in Spain. At Badajoz the loyal General

[19] See the article of Indalecio Prieto in *El Socialista,* July 19, 1956. In a letter to me, Prieto added that the Marqués himself had confirmed his information in 1948, and named two foreign statesmen who had received the same version of the incident. Azaña's reception of the teletype message was described to me by an intimate friend of the President who was with him at the time.

Castelló prevented a rising. Consequently, despite the rapid success in the Navarre-Castile area and in lower Andalusia, the two main areas won by the rebellion remained cut off from each other. The sailors' revolt meant that instead of having naval vessels ready to escort the Army of Africa across the straits, it was now likely that these ships would interfere with the crossing. Also, Spain's small Air Force had remained loyal to the Republican government.

But the most serious limitation of all was the failure to take the large cities. In Madrid and Barcelona the armed people defeated the rising. In Bilbao no rising occurred. In Valencia multiple confusions of command, purpose, and allegiance prevented any rising from occurring during the first days. Catalonia, New Castile, and the entire Mediterranean coast, from the French frontier almost to Gibraltar, remained in the hands of the Republicans. While the Insurgents won all of Galicia and much of Andalusia, the hostility of the population in those areas was evident.

The balance of the four-day pronunciamiento was mixed. The Insurgents controlled perhaps one-third the national territory, including the principal wheat-growing districts of Castile. They were therefore well able to feed both their troops and the civil population. But the major industrial cities and the economically most advanced portions of the country were in Republican hands. The generals would thus be obliged to import armaments and machine-made goods of all kinds. Careful planning, surprise, and audacity had won a number of stunning victories at relatively little cost, but everywhere there had been high-ranking military men who opposed the rising, and in a great many instances it was evident that the Civil Guard, the Assault Guard, and the Army units were waiting to see who would win before committing themselves. In Navarre the Requetés shouted "Viva Cristo Rey," but in Galicia the soldiers shouted "Viva la República." The weak reaction of the Madrid government had been a great boon. Many civil governors and many local regimental commanders might have distributed arms on Saturday and Sunday if the Madrid government had ordered them to do so.

In the last analysis, many of the victories resulted only from confusion and terror. If the Leftist workers in Seville, Cádiz, and the Galician ports had been aided by energetic professional officers, the rebellion would not have triumphed in those areas. Similarly, if no Republican-minded professional officers had aided the Left masses in Madrid and Barcelona, the rebellion might have triumphed in the form intended— as a pronunciamiento. In many rural areas the population had no inkling of what had occurred over the weekend until refugees or soldiers from the provincial capitals appeared in the villages. Thus many "red" villages in Andalusia were lost to the Republic because Seville was lost, and many reactionary villages in the Levant and Catalonia remained with the Republic because Valencia and Barcelona remained Republican.

At the end of four days it was clear to Generals Mola and Franco that the pronunciamiento which had succeeded in limited areas of Spain could only be extended to the rest of the country by means of a war of conquest.

14

THE BEGINNINGS OF INTERNATIONAL INTERVENTION

WITH the Insurgents holding one-third of Spain, and with no prospect of compromise, both sides appealed immediately for foreign aid, for neither had the supplies and arms necessary to conduct even a brief civil war. From the beginning, the military plotters had counted on the armed aid of Italy, the assistance of Portugal, and the friendly neutrality of English and American interests in the Peninsula. In particular, Mussolini had undertaken to arm and train the Monarchists. In March 1934 a four-man delegation representing both the Alphonsine and Carlist wings had obtained from the Italian dictator personally a commitment to supply 20,000 rifles and 200 machine guns. No date for an anti-Republican rising was set, and Mussolini had seemed mildly amused that the two Monarchist parties could not agree on a candidate to the throne. During the following months, he had arranged for the training of young Carlists, who came to Italy in the guise of "Peruvian officers."[1] It does not appear, however, that Mussolini supplied arms in any quantity before the actual outbreak of the Civil War. The Carlists were busy purchasing arms during the spring of 1936, most of which were confiscated in the port of Antwerp, but the 150 machine guns which they managed to smuggle into Spain before July had been bought through private channels in Germany.[2]

General Sanjurjo had lived in Portugal throughout the period of preparation. Mola's emissaries had at all times communicated freely with him, and Portuguese frontier police, from the first moment aided in arms deliveries and turned

[1] Lizarza, *Memorias de la conspiración*, pp. 24–7, 35.
[2] Hugh Thomas, *The Spanish Civil War*, p. 101.

over fleeing Republicans to the Insurgents. In the days preceding the revolt, the American colonel who headed the Telephone Company had placed private lines at the disposal of the Madrid plotters for their conversations with Generals Mola and Franco. General Kindelán, who was in charge of the rising in Algeciras, asked British officers at nearby Gibraltar if they could supply him with ships. The Englishmen regretted their inability to help directly, but offered to obtain for him a few unregistered ships lying in Portuguese harbors. They also placed at his disposition Gibraltar telephone lines, which made it possible for Kindelán to talk with Morocco and later with Rome and Berlin, without the calls passing through any Spanish exchange.[3]

As of July 19, Republican warships were effectively patrolling the waters between the mainland and Morocco, thus preventing General Franco from ferrying his Moorish troops across the straits. In these difficult circumstances a Nazi businessman who had been established for some years in Tetuán, one Johannes Bernhardt, offered his services to General Franco. He was well known among Spanish officers, having sold supplies of all kinds to the Army in Morocco. In June he had offered Junkers transport planes on credit to General Sanjurjo, but the then titular chief of the rising had not considered that German planes would be necessary.[4]

On July 21 General Franco accepted Bernhardt's offer. The latter interviewed Hitler on July 26 at Bayreuth, where the Chancellor was attending the Wagner festival. After consultation with Hermann Goering, chief of the German Air Force, Hitler authorized the immediate dispatch of some 20 JU 52 heavy transports. They were to be flown, unarmed, by German crews. As of July 28 these planes had established an air ferry between Tetuán and Seville, each machine crossing the straits four times daily, carrying about 30 completely armed soldiers on each trip. By August 5 the Insurgents were

[3] Information from an interview with General Kindelán, Madrid, 1960.

[4] Charles Foltz, Jr., *The Masquerade in Spain* (Boston, 1948), pp. 46-8.

thus able to place some 15,000 troops in Seville despite the Republican naval blockade.[5]

Italy also acted promptly, sending about 12 bombers, 3 of which were unfortunately obliged, on July 30, to land in French Morocco for lack of fuel. Their logbooks indicated that they had been reassigned as of July 15, two days before the rising at Melilla—a fact which strongly suggested that Mussolini had known of the plans for a pronunciamiento sometime between 10 and 20 July.[6] At the end of the month, the German airlift was encountering heavy anti-aircraft fire from the cruiser *Jaime Primero*. The JU 52 had been designed as a transport plane which could readily be converted for use as a bomber. During the first week of August, a converted Junker put the *Jaime Primero* out of action with direct hits by two 500-pound bombs, and the Italians developed successful tactics for harassing the smaller naval vessels sufficiently so that they could no longer prevent the passage of troop ships. As of August 6, ships began to cross the straits under the protection of some nine Italian tri-motored bombers.[7]

The Republican Navy lost control of the narrow waters between Europe and Africa partly through air attack, partly through inefficient handling of the ships by crews which had killed many of their officers and distrusted the remaining ones, and partly through the hostility of the political authorities

[5] Werner Beumelberg, *Kampf um Spanien* (Berlin, 1940), pp. 22–6. This work is an unofficial history of the Condor Legion. Its published data were all confirmed by the German Foreign Office documents published after the Second World War. I have therefore counted on its general reliability in writing of German intervention.

[6] Pierre Cot, *The Triumph of Treason* (New York, 1941), pp. 341–42.

[7] Beumelberg, *Kampf*, pp. 28–9, and Guido Mattioli, *L'aviazione legionaria in Spagna* (Rome, 1940), pp. 14–24. Also Georges Oudard, *Chemises noires, brunes, vertes en Espagne* (Paris, 1938), pp. 190–94. Oudard was a veteran-journalist of the First World War, generally favorable to the Nationalists, but very temperate and factual in his reporting.

and the business community in both Gibraltar and Tangier.
British oil companies at Gibraltar, and the American-owned
Vacuum Oil Company in Tangier, refused to sell to the Republican ships.[8] Tangier was an internationalized port city
within Spanish Morocco. Several Spanish naval vessels and a
number of Spanish merchant ships had been in the harbor
on July 17. The International Commission which governed
the city ruled that continued use of the harbor by the Republican Navy was contrary to the neutrality guaranteed in
the Statute of Tangier. At the same time, however, it laid no
restrictions on the passage of goods and persons between
Spanish Morocco and Tangier. The German planes ferrying
Moors to Seville bought aviation gasoline, without hindrance,
from a Portuguese firm in the international city.[9]

The Insurgents were well supplied with petroleum products
from the beginning. In July 1935 the Texas Oil Company had
signed a long-term contract to supply the Spanish government oil monopoly, CAMPSA. On July 18, 1936, some five
tankers were at sea. The chairman of the board of Texaco,
Thorkild Rieber, decided immediately to send the oil to
Franco-controlled ports, and the Texas Company continued to
supply gasoline on credit until the war's end.[10]

Generally speaking, the Insurgents could count from the
start on the good will of the international financial community.
For generations, England had been the most important market
for quality Spanish wines. Spanish and English capital shared
control of many mining and steel-producing enterprises in
the Basque country. Wealthy Spaniards mingled with English
summer residents at San Sebastián and Biarritz. Luca de Tena
and other Monarchists had arranged and paid for the English
plane which carried Franco to Morocco and then transported
Franco's emissaries to Rome. By July 25, Juan March and

[8] F. Jay Taylor, *The United States and the Spanish Civil War*
(New York, 1956), p. 66. Robert Garland Colodny, *The Struggle
for Madrid* (New York, 1958), pp. 150–51.

[9] Beumelberg, *Kampf*, p. 28. Toynbee, *Survey of International Affairs,* 1937, II, 231.

[10] Herbert Feis, *The Spanish Story* (New York, 1948), p. 269.

Gil Robles had established headquarters in Lisbon. The former owned a controlling interest in the Claiworth Bank in London, through which he financed purchases of material for the Insurgent army. Gil Robles and Nicolás Franco, older brother of the General, coordinated the efforts of other wealthy Spanish backers of the rising. The Portuguese government treated them rather than the Republican ambassador (the medieval historian Claudio Sánchez Albornoz) as the effective representatives of Spain.

Meanwhile, the Republican government appealed to France. One of the first acts of the new Prime Minister, José Giral, was to telegraph an appeal, on July 20, for arms to the French Socialist Prime Minister, Léon Blum. Blum represented in France the same left-of-center democratic ideals as did Giral and his cabinet in Spain. In addition, Spain had, during 1935 and early 1936, negotiated a commercial treaty which included clauses concerning the sale of military supplies to Spain; and the government counted on its legal right to seek the aid of other governments in suppressing internal rebellion.

Blum's initial reaction was entirely positive. However, a trip to London on July 22 made him strongly aware of English cabinet sympathies toward the rising. On July 25 the right-wing press in Paris printed news of the Spanish request, and worried members of the Radical Party asked Blum to desist. It was clear that open aid to the Spanish Republic would alienate England, with whom relations were already strained, and would split the Popular Front within France. The cabinet itself was divided. The Air Minister, Pierre Cot, strongly favored aid to the Giral government, whereas the Defense Minister refused absolutely to permit French military pilots to fly the planes which Cot was preparing to deliver. Cot hurriedly arranged the fake sale of about 50 aircraft to Hejaz, Finland, and Brazil; these machines then found their way to Spain "en route" to their fictitious destinations. Altogether, by the first week of August, Cot had dispatched some 30 reconnaissance and bombing planes, 15 pursuits, and 10 transport and training planes—all of them obsolete in 1936.[11] During the same period, hundreds of volunteers crossed the border, mostly into Catalonia, with few or no questions asked by the French police.

The forced landing of the Italians in French Morocco had strengthened Blum's diplomatic position, but he was under increasing pressure not only from England, but from the Polish and Belgian governments. Above all, four months after Hitler had marched unopposed into the Rhineland, Blum could not afford the prospect of French isolation in the face of rearmed Germany. Neither, of course, could he afford an ally of Italy and Germany on his southern frontier. He therefore proposed the formula of nonintervention, to which he hoped that all the powers would adhere, and which would rapidly end the war for lack of armament. He closed the French frontier to military traffic on August 8, without waiting to know the precise intentions of the powers backing the Insurgents.

The transformation of a pronunciamiento into a civil war caught the European powers by surprise. All of them had strategic interests in the western Mediterranean. The Insurgent conquests of Algeciras, La Línea, and Spanish Morocco had occurred within earshot of Gibraltar, and the Republican Navy was operating in waters which had been subject to British control ever since Britain had acquired Gibraltar during the War of the Spanish Succession (1701–1713). Late in the nineteenth century, England, France, and Spain had all developed imperialist interests in the turbulent kingdom of Morocco. In 1904 an Anglo-French convention recognized the primacy of French military and political interests in Morocco. But the Kaiser had precipitated a war scare the next year by landing at Tangier and publicly affirming the independence of the Sultan. The Spaniards were also dissatisfied with the Anglo-French arrangements, inasmuch as Spain had sent several military expeditions into Morocco since 1859; and particularly after the Spanish-American War of 1898,

[11] Pierre Cot, *The Triumph of Treason*, pp. 338–55; and the testimony of Léon Blum during the French Chamber of Deputies investigation of foreign relations for the period 1933–1945, testimony of July 27, 1947.

Spain had come to consider Morocco as her rightful province for expansion.

The international congress of Algeciras in 1906 pledged an open door in Morocco for the merchants of all nations and gave considerable, if vaguely defined, police powers to France and Spain. In 1912 Morocco was, in effect, partitioned between France and Spain, with Spain, as the weaker of the two powers, occupying the area across the straits from Gibraltar. The "pacification" of Morocco required many years, and the Moroccans ably exploited the many misunderstandings between French and Spanish officials. The rebellion of Abd-el-Krim forced the two powers to cooperate for the defeat of this most powerful of the nationalist leaders in 1926. But as late as 1934 there were still "police actions" occurring in both the French and Spanish zones. Throughout these decades of sporadic military action, private financial interests in England, France, Germany, and Spain had invested in the development of the Riff iron mines.

The status of Tangier had also been a matter of lengthy negotiation among the powers. Relatively speaking, French commercial interests were paramount at the turn of the century. In 1906 the international character of the city had been recognized at Algeciras, partly as a concession to German and Spanish interests, partly to make sure that the city would never become a French base capable of rivaling Gibraltar. In 1912 there were inconclusive negotiations aimed at giving Tangier an international charter, but not until 1923 was an agreement reached, whereby England, France, and Spain were to share in the administration of the neutral port. In 1927 the Italian dictator Mussolini sent three warships to Tangier at a time when the Statute of 1923 was being revised. The assembled commissioners saw the point of this delicate gesture and invited Italy henceforth to share in the administration.

Thus, strategic interests in the western Mediterranean, and a complex of military, economic, and imperialist interests in Morocco, involved all the major European powers as soon as the *status quo* was threatened. Economic motives, and fraternal relations with the officers of the Spanish Army go far to explain why, on the whole, the authorities at Gibraltar and Tangier reacted definitely, if discreetly, in favor of the Insurgents. But the prospect of a bitter, and perhaps protracted, civil war aroused powerful emotions throughout the entire European and Western world.

Of all the European nations, France was most deeply affected, and bitterly divided, by the outbreak of the Civil War. All labor, both Socialist and Communist, demanded the immediate dispatch of arms to the Giral government. The liberal middle class, those who had struggled for the vindication of Dreyfus and who were now alarmed by the blatant anti-Semitism of the Nazis, those who had favored the separation of Church and State, those who had fought German militarism at the Marne and at Verdun—all such persons instinctively favored the cause of the Spanish Republic. At the same time, the royalists and clericals, those who supported *Action Française* or the *Croix de Feu* of Colonel de la Rocque, those who had applauded the pro-fascist riots in February, 1934—such persons instinctively favored the Insurgent cause. The latter group were the minority, but they included a high proportion of the most wealthy families as well as many military officers and civil officials who had served the French Empire in North Africa.

Technical as well as political considerations checked the impulse to provide military aid. From a strictly objective standpoint, all officers recognized the potential danger to France of an aggressive, authoritarian government across the Pyrenees. But the state of France's own defenses hardly permitted her to supply arms to Spain while Hitler, who had just remilitarized the Rhineland in March 1936, continued his feverish course of rearmament. While France of the Popular Front declared its overwhelming sympathy for the embattled Popular Front of Spain, the government was virtually paralyzed by the menace of civil war at home, the German danger abroad, and the weakness of her own defenses. In addition, French security depended upon Briitsh action, and the British had warned immediately that they would not consider themselves bound to come to France's defense in case her involvement south of the Pyrenees should lead to military action by Germany.

English reaction to the Civil War was less emotional than the French, but since England was stronger than France militarily, and more deeply involved in the Spanish economy, her attitude weighed more heavily in the international balance. Labor was pro-Republican, albeit disturbed by the "infantile leftism" of the Caballero Socialists and the anarchists. A Parliamentary delegation had visited Spain in 1935 to investigate the repression of the Asturian miners' revolt. The men who had brought the Moors and the Foreign Legion into Oviedo were now leading figures in the Insurgent zone; those who had espoused social reforms and had sought amnesty for the miners were now prominent in Madrid.

But the Prime Minister, Stanley Baldwin, and the majority of the naval and consular officials from whom he received his first reports, were instinctively favorable to the Insurgents. British Conservatives tended to assume that the volatile Spaniards needed a strong hand. The pro-fascist wing, commonly referred to as the "Cliveden set," favored dealing with the Spanish generals as with Mussolini and Hitler. Financial London had heavy investments in both zones. The Río Tinto and Riff mines were quickly occupied by the Insurgents, and they also dominated the Andalusian zone from which the most commercially important wines were exported. But the Basque mines and iron foundries and the English-owned electrical installations of Catalonia were in the Popular Front zone. Englishmen of all viewpoints were shocked by the atrocity reports, though whether they lent greater credence to stories of "white" or "red" terror depended upon their political outlook. The Baldwin government, in contrast to that of Léon Blum, enjoyed the support of the wealthy classes and was thus free to make its decisions without the threat of civil disturbances at home. Official policy during the first weeks was one of noninvolvement, coupled with a quiet desire for the quick and not too cruel victory of the generals.

Across the Atlantic, the attitude of the United States was dominated by the twin desires for isolation and neutrality. In his personal sympathies and in his domestic policies President Roosevelt was far closer to Giral, Azaña, and Prieto than he was to the Insurgent generals. His ambassador, Claude Bowers, remained a firm friend of the Republican government. But on August 7 the State Department sent a circular to all consular officials recommending strict impartiality. The Neutrality Act of 1935 did not apply to civil wars, and there was no question of withdrawing recognition from the Republican government; but when the Glenn L. Martin Company asked for an advisory opinion as to whether it should sell aircraft to the Spanish government, the State Department replied on August 10 that such a sale would be contrary to the spirit of American policy.

Roosevelt and Bowers, as well as Secretary of State Cordell Hull, favored complete noninvolvement, so much so that Bowers recommended during the second half of August that the United States not join in the mediation proposals of either the Argentine or the Uruguayan embassies. In the summer of 1936 newspaper attention showed that Americans recognized the potential importance of a civil war in Spain, but relatively few Americans, conservative or liberal, Catholic or Protestant, thought that the United States should make an effort to influence its outcome.[12] At the same time, since oil was not considered a war material under the Neutrality Act (any more than it had been in the League of Nations sanctions against Italy during the Ethiopian War), the government made no effort to interrupt the flow of Texaco products to Insurgent Spain.

Thus, of the three Western democratic powers, France was the only one prepared even partially to aid the Spanish Republic to defeat the military rebellion. And when it was made clear to Blum, almost from the day that he had received Giral's anguished telegram, that the British government and the French Right were strongly opposed to such aid, he sought —by the proposal of Non-Intervention on August 2 and by the closing of the Pyrenean border to military traffic on August 8—to place some degree of pressure on the fascist

[12] Taylor, *op. cit.*, pp. 57ff.

powers to keep them from intervening increasingly on behalf of the Insurgents.

In Italy and Germany, public opinion willingly followed the lead of the governments. Neither country possessed a free press, and in neither country were the people conscious, as in France, of the complex historic and social issues involved. Italy was intoxicated by its military romp in Ethiopia, and the Germans were proud that the *Diktat* of Versailles had been overthrown by the reintroduction of conscription, the beginning of rearmament, and the remilitarization of the Rhineland. In the first weeks of the war the Insurgents needed only small units of airplanes, tanks, and communications teams. The Italian and German specialists who were assigned to Spain went willingly, with high morale and a naïve sense of adventure, to serve their *Duce* and their *Führer* in the battle against Bolshevism.[13] In Portugal, under the dictatorship of Antonio Salazar, the silent masses would have welcomed the victory of the Popular Front as a step toward their own liberation. But the government and the military had given every facility to the Insurgents during the preparation of the revolt, and from the first day of the Civil War, Portugal was a thinly disguised base of supply for the Insurgents.

Among the major powers, it was only in the Soviet Union that popular feeling and government policy coincided in favoring the cause of the Republic. The controlled press could present an essentially truthful, if oversimplified, version of the uprising as an international fascist attack upon the legitimate, peace-loving, democratic government. By the hundreds, separate factories and collective farms held mass meetings, and by August 6 over $2 million had been donated to send food and medical supplies to Spain.[14] The government was pleased to permit the expression of genuine emotion among the Russian people, especially at a time when Hitler's rearmament was forcing the Russians to postpone butter in favor of guns, and when the arrest of the Old Bolsheviks Zinoviev and Kamenev had shocked many a loyal citizen.

[13] Mattioli, *L'aviazione legionaria* and Hellmut H. Führing, *Wir funken für Franco* (Breslau, 1941), *passim*.

[14] Cattell, *Communism and the Spanish Civil War*, pp. 70–71.

The Soviet government itself moved cautiously. Since 1931, Republican Spain and the Soviet Union had not even exchanged ambassadors, though they had been on the point of doing so just before the Center-Right victory in the elections of November, 1933. After the Popular Front victory of February, 1936, the diplomatic machinery was once again set in motion, but not until the end of August did Marcel Rosenberg reach Madrid as the first Soviet ambassador to the Spanish Republic. The Soviets had no direct economic or strategic interests in Spain. Russia had not been a party to the occupation of Morocco or the internationalization of Tangier, and the Russian navy had never operated in the western Mediterranean.

But the outbreak of war in Spain, under present conditions, was immensely important as a test of the twin policies of Popular Front and collective security which the Soviet Union and the world Communist parties had launched in 1935. Spain was the first country in which a Popular Front government had achieved power. If the Western nations, seeing themselves threatened by the spread of fascist power, could be brought to cooperate with the Soviets in defense of a legitimately elected democratic government, such collective action might halt the uninterrupted series of fascist triumphs since the rise of Hitler. With this in mind, all Soviet and world communist literature emphasized the entirely bourgeois composition of the Republican cabinet and the very small total representation of the Communists in the Cortes (16 out of about 473 deputies elected in February, 1936). The Soviets also ostentatiously refrained from sending arms during the months of August and September, when it seemed even faintly possible that the Non-Intervention scheme would curb the aid of the fascist powers to the Insurgents. On August 30, however, the chief of their intelligence service in Western Europe, General Krivitsky, received orders to create dummy firms which could buy arms in Germany and several small European countries and then ship them to Spain in Scandinavian bottoms, with false destination papers for Latin America or the Far East.[15]

[15] P. A. M. Van der Esch, *Prelude to War* (The Hague, 1951), p. 44, based on the memoirs of General Krivitsky. *Prelude* gives

Behind these sophisticated calculations lay intangible but important sentiments. Lenin had once remarked that Spain was the European country in which conditions most closely resembled those of Russia, and that she might well be the next country to follow the Soviet lead. The Asturian revolt had stirred memories of 1905 in Russia and of the Paris Commune of 1871. A number of miners, perhaps several hundred in all, had gone to the Soviet Union in 1935 and returned home after the Popular Front election with glowing tales of the Moscow subway, the collective farms, and the excellent, free medical care. The popular victories of July 19 and 20 in Barcelona and Madrid were reminiscent of the storming of the Winter Palace in the November Revolution of 1917—and the storming of the Bastille in 1789.

The glowing memories of 1917 would also rekindle the bitter memories of the years since: of defeat in Hungary and Germany in 1919; of defeat in China in 1927; of the triumph of fascism in Germany and the destruction of the German Communist Party in 1933. The interrupted movement toward world revolution, as well as the security of the Soviet Union, might well be advanced by a Republican victory in Spain. For the moment it was essential not to frighten the middle classes or the Western governments. No Soviet statesman expected Spain to adopt communism in the near future. But the cause of Spain was, in a wider perspective, the cause of the worldwide "people's revolution" with which Soviet leaders hoped to identify themselves.

One country alone reacted without fear, and with great generosity, toward the plight of the Spanish Republic. Mexico supported fully and publicly the claims of the Madrid government as the legitimate, democratically chosen government of Spain. From the first days of August, she sent small arms and food supplies; she accepted Republican pesetas in payment. No black market, no intermediaries, and no Bank of Spain gold were necessary where Mexican purchases were concerned. Mexico refused to follow the French-British Non-Intervention

---

the best general account available of the diplomacy and foreign intervention in the Civil War.

proposals, recognizing immediately the great advantage they offered the Insurgents.[16] Contrary to the United States, Mexico did not feel that neutrality between an elected government and a military junta was a proper policy. At the same time, the Mexican embassy in Madrid, like those of the other Latin American states, sheltered priests and Spanish conservatives endangered by the revolutionary anarchy of the first weeks of the war.

There were several reasons for this unique policy. The Mexican revolution had been struggling for a quarter of a century to raise health and literacy standards, to distribute land to the landless, and to reduce clerical control of education. Mexican laborers, students, and intellectuals understood the Marxist and anarchist influences at work in Spain. They, too, were capable of admiring the Soviets without intending to imitate them slavishly. President Lázaro Cárdenas was working for rapid land reform, a mixed economy, and the fuller utilization of the nation's natural resources through irrigation and electrification. At the same time, he had ended the sporadic civil war between Church and State in Mexico. It was therefore natural that such a man would support the Spanish Republic diplomatically and materially, and at the same time give asylum to the victims of political and religious persecution.

Mexico's attitude gave immense moral comfort to the Republic, especially since the major South American governments—those of Argentina, Brazil, Chile, and Peru—sympathized more or less openly with the Insurgents. But Mexican aid could mean relatively little in practical terms if the French border were closed and if the dictators remained free to supply the Insurgents with a quality and quantity of weapons far beyond the power of Mexico.

Within several weeks of the pronunciamiento, the European and New World powers had all indicated what were to be, in fact, if not in legal prose, their policies toward the developing Civil War. Italy, Germany, and Portugal aided the Insurgents; England hoped the Insurgents would win with a

[16] Lois Elwyn Smith, *Mexico and the Spanish Republicans* (Berkeley, 1955), pp. 190–91.

minimum of fighting. The United States placed isolationism and neutrality before its democratic sympathies, while Russia moved cautiously toward countering the Axis intervention. France deliberately refrained from aiding the Republic after the first ten days, and Mexico supported the Republic to the best of her very limited ability. The smaller European powers, and most South American governments, played no active role, but tended to prefer an Insurgent victory.

15

MILITARY DEVELOPMENTS,
AUGUST–OCTOBER 1936

WITHIN Spain, during the first months of the war, Generals Mola and Franco still hoped for a rapid victory, which would be achieved by simultaneous drives on Madrid: one from the Navarre-Castile territories controlled by Mola, the other from southern Andalusia—when the Army of Africa had been transported across the straits. Mola drove rapidly for the passes of the Somosierra and the Sierra de Guadarrama, the keys to an invasion of Madrid from the north. He had perhaps 10,000 Requetés, and several thousand Falange and miscellaneous troops. He had a good supply of trucks and gasoline, and he had broken a partial railway strike by the threat of the death penalty. But he had little ammunition. The Basque Nationalists, supporting the Republic, threatened his rear; Galicia and León were full of guerrillas, although nominally in Insurgent hands. Much of the Asturias, and the provinces of Gijón and Santander, were controlled by forces of the Popular Front. Mola's advance units reached the passes at the end of July, but his drive was stalled through most of August until arms and ammunition in quantity began to arrive in German planes flying from Portugal and Morocco.[1]

The Republicans also had rushed for the mountain passes north of Madrid. Each of the Popular Front parties and the Unified Socialist Youth (JSU) formed militias. Professional officers who were loyal to the government distributed the arms of the several military bases around Madrid and gave elementary instruction in handling of rifles, digging trenches, and using cover. In the Sierra itself the war consisted of isolated engagements between small units: patrols probing each other's lines or digging in along the mountain crests. The more

[1] Foltz, *Masquerade in Spain,* pp. 43–4; Vigón, *Mola,* pp. 200–201.

politically conscious militia groups established trench systems, and command and communications posts. But during August, the majority came out daily by truck from the city. The weather was beautiful, the mountain air bracing, and the trees gave a sense of security against hostile observation. War involved adventure and raw courage, not science. On the one side were Mola's Requetés and Falangists, with bases at Avila and Segovia; on the other were the left-wing militias of Madrid. When they met head-on, they fought with equally reckless bravery. When an occasional bomber attacked them, they fired back at it with their rifles and died willingly of wounds they could have avoided by taking cover. When cut off from their lines, they would fight for days without food or water—until the last cartridge had been used. Mola's troops were the more disciplined and skilled, but their lack of numbers and armament prevented them from doing more than defend the high ground they had seized in the first days. The Madrid militia, brave in frontal engagements, would panic at the unexpected and many strong positions were lost because of a surprise flank attack. The few professionals, like Lt. Colonel Moriones and Colonel José Asensio Torrado, rushed from one danger spot to another to stem panic and restore confidence through their knowledge of military tactics.[2]

Meanwhile, in Catalonia the triumphant anarchists set out to conquer their spiritual home, Saragossa. Cheerful, intoxicated by their success in Barcelona, inured to physical hardship, and insouciant of death, they worked their way, village by village, into the hills of eastern Aragon. It was a war without artillery, without plans, without reconnaissance, without definable fronts. On each side prisoners were shot, and deserters, to avoid the same fate, had to identify themselves by syndicate or political party. At Huesca, which was held by

[2] José Martín Blázquez, *I Helped Build an Army* (London, 1939), pp. 175–82, and Pietro Nenni, *La guerre d'Espagne* (Paris, 1960), *passim*, contain much interesting material on the war in the Sierra. Martín Blázquez was a professional officer of Republican sympathies. Pietro Nenni, the Italian Left Socialist, was among the first anti-fascist *émigrés* to enter Spain, and he became one of the leaders of the International Brigades.

the Insurgents and besieged by the Catalans, Falangists and anarchists exchanged foulmouthed insults preparatory to fighting grenade and bayonet battles in the city cemetery. Yet, at the same time, everyone observed the afternoon siesta. As in Madrid, the militia was organized in columns of variable size according to the different parties of the Popular Front. The anarchists were numerically the most important, but there were columns also of the anti-Stalinist *Partido Obrero de Unificación Marxista* (POUM), of the *Esquerra,* and of the newly unified Catalan Socialist and Communist parties (PSUC). Lack of arms and discipline forced these columns to stop far short of Saragossa, but in terms of Catalan revolutionary politics, it was important for each party to participate in the presumed conquest of the Aragonese capital.

In Valencia, capital of Levantine Spain, the situation remained tense and ambiguous for some weeks. Valencia was a major port and the center of a very productive agricultural district. It was strongly republican in sentiment, but also the local farmers and merchants were intensely conservative. The province had split its vote almost evenly between the Right and the Popular Front. On July 18 the Left Republican civil governor refused the demand of the CNT and UGT unions for the distribution of arms. The attitude of the local military commander, General Martínez Monje, was doubtful. He pledged his loyalty while confining his troops to the barracks. The workers, profoundly suspicious of both the governor and the general, called a general strike for the 19th and formed a CNT-UGT committee which demanded that the government take the barracks, distribute arms, and form mixed militia units, using workers and loyal soldiers.

The Giral government, hoping to avoid bloodshed and to establish its authority, sent to Valencia a *junta delegada* composed by Martínez Barrio and several Left Republicans. For a week the CNT collected arms, the troops remained in their barracks, General Martínez Monje reiterated republican loyalty while refusing to recognize the revolutionary committee, and the Madrid junta tried to calm spirits on both sides. In the city streets, virtually empty of soldiers and police, Falangists shot workers and workers attacked convents. Hearing that the CNT intended to burn the *Virgen de los Desamparados* (the helpless), the patron saint of Valencia, the Left Republican mayor rushed to the church and removed the Virgen to a safe hiding place in the municipal archives, where she spent the war.[3] On the 25th a mixed column of workers and apparently loyal Civil Guards set out toward Insurgent-held Teruel. In Puebla Valverde the Civil Guards turned their guns on the militia, killed as many as possible, and crossed to the Insurgent lines.

The next day a Sergeant Fabra of the engineer corps led a revolt against the officers within the barracks, and a number of soldiers fled to the city with their arms. The CNT-UGT committee determined once and for all to take the barracks. Led by Lieutenant Benedito and loyal Civil Guards, the workers rushed the barracks on July 31. The officers of several regiments attempted to rally their troops to the Insurgent cause, but the victory of the revolutionary soldiers and militia was complete. Madrid accepted the *fait accompli*, recognizing the CNT-UGT committee as the effective government of Valencia.[4]

In northern Spain the Insurgents were preoccupied during the first weeks with securing their early victories. Partial strikes continued in the Galician cities until mid-August. Oviedo, though captured by Colonel Aranda on July 20, was besieged by revolutionary miners. In the port of Gijón the Insurgents had coordinated their rising with that of Colonel Aranda, but workers armed with pistols and dynamite had besieged the barracks and on August 17 forced their surrender. The fishing center of Avilés and the port city of Santander also remained in Republican hands. Meanwhile, guerrilla bands were formed by port workers who had fled from El Ferrol and Vigo, by Asturian miners, and by railroad workers who had fled from Valladolid, Alsasua, and Miranda de Ebro.[5] Insurgent supply trains moved at a walking pace through the hills of Galicia

[3] Information from conversations in Valencia, 1960.

[4] Vigón, *Mola,* pp. 161–63. Broué and Témime *La révolution et la guerre d'Espagne,* pp. 100–101, 116–20.

[5] G. Carrascal, *Asturias,* pp. 66–7. Solano Palacio, *La tragedia del norte,* pp. 41 and *passim.*

and León. The engineer watched the track for mines, and on the platform of each carriage and freight car stood two armed guards. At the Portuguese border, however, the Insurgent authorities could count on the frontier police to hand over both guerrillas and civilian refugees.

Throughout August and September, the most important fighting occurred in Andalusia and Extremadura as the Army of Africa, holding the initiative all the way, marched north from Seville to Mérida and Badajoz, and then up the Tagus valley toward Toledo and Madrid. From the 5th of August on, General Franco controlled the straits of Gibraltar by means of his Italian planes, the friendly neutrality of the British, and the obsolescence and incompetence of the Republican Navy. Nearly 20,000 Moors and *Legionnaires* were ferried across during the late summer. They were organized in "columns" of 500 to 1,000 under Spanish officers—General Varela; Colonels Yagüe and Carlos Asensio; Lt. Colonels Barrón, Delgado, and de Tella; Majors Castejón and Mizzian. The officers shared the pride of service in the crack Foreign Legion created by General Francisco Franco. They carried in their wallets pictures of their comrades killed at the Montaña Barracks or in Barcelona on July 19. Relations with their own troops were excellent. Spanish officers flying between the front and Melilla wrote and carried letters for the soldiers, and delivered to their families the rings, gold teeth, and watches taken from the corpses of the "reds." Each soldier carried a 60-pound pack, 200 cartridges, and the long curved knives with which the Moors killed the wounded or silently murdered opposing sentries at night. The columns traveled in trucks, enjoying the camaraderie of small elite units and living off a countryside far richer than that of the Riff in which they had fought their earlier battles.

The trucks would stop perhaps 100 yards short of a village, and the men would advance cautiously on foot. If there were signs of resistance, light artillery would bombard the walls or the stone buildings likely to be strong points. The town would be taken by bayonet charge and loud-speakers would order that all doors be opened and white flags displayed. Anyone caught with arms in hand, or with a shoulder bruised from the recoil of a fired rifle, would be shot. According to the legal concepts of the Insurgent officers, the men of the Popular Front militia not in uniform were the "rebels," and their lives were forfeit as such. While their ammunition lasted, and while they enjoyed the cover of buildings and trees, the militia would fight desperately, and often the Army of Africa paid in heavy casualties for its scorn of the enemy. When threatened by a flanking movement, or dislodged by artillery fire, the militiamen would flee along the roads, having no idea of the advantages of spreading themselves thin in the fields. Insurgent machine guns, trained on the road, would slaughter the fugitives like jack rabbits; the corpses would be piled up, sprinkled with gasoline, and burned. A platoon would be left behind to assure communications—and the tranquility of the village. The column would then drive north to the next objective.

In Guareña, where the revolutionary committee had established an anarchist "republic," the English reporter Cecil Gerahty had a rare opportunity to interview one of some ten peasants about to be shot. The local loud-speaker system, which this man referred to as the "radio" and which he evidently considered a kind of supernatural oracle, had convinced him that killing the landlords would automatically produce a happy Spain. He realized now that he had "bet on the wrong horse," and thus, without the sacraments and without grumbling, he was about to go off to his death.[6]

[6] Concerning the march of the Army of Africa, I depended principally on Harold Cardozo, *March of a Nation* (London, 1937); H. R. Knickerbocker, *The Siege of the Alcázar* (Philadelphia, 1936); and Cecil Gerahty, *The Road to Madrid* (London, 1937). Cardozo and Knickerbocker were excellent journalists with considerable war reporting to their credit before 1936. Knickerbocker's book, despite the title, is largely a diary of his experience with the victorious columns in Andalusia and Extremadura. Gerahty was less skilled as a reporter, but had many social connections which enabled him to observe more freely than most other foreigners. Incomplete as they are, I trusted these sources more fully than the multi-volume official history *Cruzada,* or Manuel Aznar's *Historia militar de la guerra de España* (Madrid, 1940). The latter con-

Some miles further north, at Almendralejo, about 100 militiamen retreated to the church tower as the Insurgents entered the town. In June the landlords had announced that they would not give a day's work to the anarchist proletariat and had threatened to shoot any landlord who did. The soldiers in the church tower resisted a week of shelling, even though they had no water for the entire time; 41 survivors surrendered on the eighth day, to be marched off and shot.

The best known incident in this savage campaign occurred when Badajoz was captured on August 14. A city of some 40,000, close to the Portuguese border, its fall to the Insurgents was especially significant because it enabled them to link their northern and southern armies without having to use Portuguese roads. Badajoz was also the capital of the province in which the peasant revolution was occurring on the eve of the Civil War, and in which the Republic had begun its largest single irrigation project. The city was fiercely defended by some 4,000 militiamen equipped with a few mortars and more rifle and machine gun ammunition than the African columns had faced thus far. The defenders had mounted machine guns on the city walls and sandbagged the gateways through which the trolley tracks ran. The English reporter Harold Cardozo saw the Insurgent engineers dynamite a gate, through which the *Legionnaires* then poured to attack the defenders from the rear. On the first rush they lost 127 men in 20 seconds of machine-gun fire, but the survivors of this desperate assault took the barricade at bayonet point. Inside the city, Colonel Yagüe released some 380 rightist prisoners and heard tales of the shootings of priests and landlords.

---

tains excellent sketch maps, and much order of battle information. But it lists only the losses of the "rojos"; the third edition, in 1958, is nearly identical with the first on major points which I checked in the hope that Aznar's access to the archives would, twenty years later, have produced real history. Several officers who fought on opposite sides in the Civil War considered Aznar mostly propaganda, whereas they confirmed the information I had drawn from Cardozo and Knickerbocker. Since no one but Aznar and his collaborators have seen the archives, and since *Cruzada* is obviously deformed by its propaganda intent, the journalistic materials of the time remain the best sources.

Several French and Portuguese journalists, and the American, Jay Allen, witnessed the taking of the city and the repression which followed. The Portuguese were indiscreet in their reporting of executions, perhaps because they were no more aware than were the Insurgent officers of the impression that such techniques made upon public opinion outside the battle area. Jay Allen was horrified by a style of warfare no American had seen in the twentieth century, and his report of mass shootings in the bull ring electrified world opinion. Unquestionably he exaggerated in using the figure 4,000. Colonel Yagüe told a Portuguese reporter that perhaps even 2,000 was a slightly high figure. No one can say with certainty whether the colonel knew exactly how many had been shot, whether he meant to say that in fact slightly less than 2,000 had been shot, or whether he was content to have the journalist suppose that he might have shot that many men in a perfectly matter-of-fact fashion. But there was no doubt of the nightly ceremony, which had occurred in other towns besides Badajoz, without foreign reporters being present. And there was no doubt that Spanish officers were crossing the border to Elvas, arresting refugee militia and civilians, taking their enemies from hospital beds, and shooting all those caught with the telltale bruises on their shoulders.[7]

During August and September the Republican militia re-

[7] The reports of the French and Portuguese journalists are quoted at length in Arthur Koestler, *L'Espagne ensanglantée* (Paris, 1937). Jay Allen's dispatch of August 25 to the Chicago *Tribune* was printed in many newspapers and pamphlets. The *New York Times* on September 16, 1936, carried the story of the French photographer René Bru, who had filmed an estimated thousand prisoners awaiting execution at the bull ring of Anandaleja, as well as piles of bodies being burned. He was arrested and held in Seville. Two weeks later he was released at Tangier, having left his films with the Insurgent authorities.

See also J. T. Whitaker, "Prelude to War. A Witness from Spain," *Foreign Affairs*, October, 1942, pp. 104–106, for frank statements of mass terror by several Spanish officers and by the German Captain Ronald von Strunk, who was accompanying the Army of Africa. See H. Thomas, *The Spanish Civil War*, p. 247, for a skeptical view of what the author calls the "massacre" of Badajoz.

treated steadily. Now and again, a heroic stand would delay the conquerors for a day or two and cost them a few dozen extra lives. An occasional Breguet bomber, flown by a Republican or a French volunteer aviator, would harass the truck convoys and enable the Madrid government to follow

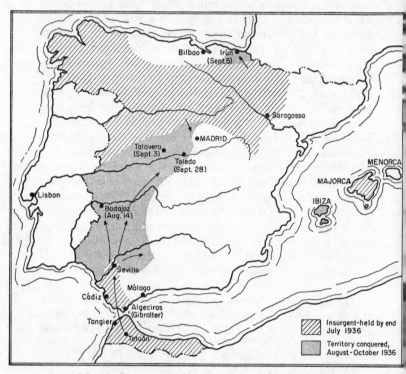

MAP 3. Insurgent Advances, August–October, 1936

the rapid progress of the Insurgent forces. But there were virtually no professional staff officers, no barbed wire, no artillery, no shovels, little ammunition. The loyal officers were needed to prepare the eventual defense of Madrid. The lack of qualified pilots and the scarcity of spare parts and gasoline kept most of the planes on the ground; in addition, the

15-year-old Breguets, which had no nose guns and traveled slowly, were an easy mark for the Italian fighter planes.

At the city of Toledo a unique situation developed. There had been many instances in which barracks had been isolated or particular sections of a city besieged for several weeks after July 18. In Toledo, after three days of seesaw combat in the narrow streets of the medieval city, about 1,000 Civil and Assault Guards, Falangists, and a handful of infantry cadets, retreated into the Alcázar. They took with them a few hundred women and children, many of them the families of known leftists.[8] Under the leadership of Colonel Moscardó, they prepared to withstand a siege while awaiting the triumph of the military rising.

The Alcázar was a stone fortress set on high ground over-looking the Tagus River. The Republicans controlled all the surrounding buildings. Besiegers and besieged could shout to each other without benefit of megaphones. When it was clear that the pronunciamiento had failed, the Republicans hoped that the fortress would surrender. As the Army of Africa began its swift march through Andalusia, the defenders took heart and the attackers began to wonder whether the shortage of food and water would suffice to force a capitulation before outside help arrived. No one was sure just how many persons were in the fortress and what supplies Colonel Moscardó disposed of to feed them. The government possessed virtually no heavy guns capable of making an impression on the stone walls which were at many points several feet thick. Until August 24 they did not shell the fortress at all, partly for lack of projectiles and fuses, partly because the militia were con-scious of the presence inside of their own families. At the end of the month, they were firing a single 155 and a few 75's and were digging tunnels with the intention of blowing up the cellars in which the besieged garrison and its hostages lived.

On September 9, Lt. Colonel Vicente Rojo, who had been an instructor at the military academy in the Alcázar, who came of a rightist family, and who had several personal friends among the defenders, entered the fort under a flag of

[8] Arthur Koestler, *Spanish Testament* (London, 1937), pp. 149–57, including affidavits by persons escaping from the Alcázar.

truce to try to obtain its surrender, and failing that, the release of the hostages. On the 11th, a Madrid priest, Father Vásquez Camarasa, tried to persuade Moscardó to release the women and children. The colonel sent for one of the women, who in his presence assured the padre that the women of the Alcázar wished to share the fate of their men. Two days later the Chilean ambassador, dean of the diplomatic corps, came to Toledo for the same purpose. Colonel Moscardó sent his aide-de-camp to greet the ambassador by loud-speaker and to tell him that the defenders would listen most respectfully to any message he wished to send them via the "national government at Burgos." At the phrase "national government," the Republican militia began shouting insults, and the dialogue went no further.[9] On September 18 the attackers exploded three subterranean mines which did some damage to the building, but not to its occupants. On the 26th General Varela camped across the river from the Alcázar. The majority of the demoralized militia were already retreating toward Madrid. Some hundreds made a desperate stand in the cemetery the next morning, but it was shelled heavily and then taken, stone by stone. The men then moved on to the barracks and the hospital, where the wounded were killed in their beds. Late in the afternoon, the famished occupants of the fortress came out into streets now dominated by Moors and *Legionnaires*. A thin and heavily bearded Colonel Moscardó reported to General Varela the next day: *Sin novedad* (all quiet). The defenders had suffered some 80 casualties in the 10-week siege. The Insurgent army and the defenders of the Alcázar celebrated a fervent mass, and the former prepared after brief rest to set out for Madrid.

In the following weeks Colonel Moscardó became the personal symbol of the Insurgent cause. Wide publicity was given to the story concerning the militia commander of Toledo who called the Alcázar on July 23. Among his hostages was a son of Moscardó, whom he brought to the telephone to

[9] Aurelio Núñez Morgado, *Los sucesos de España visto por un diplomático* (Buenos Aires, 1941), pp. 214–21 for the Ambassador's account. *The Red Domination in Spain* (Madrid, 1946), pp. 325–37 for Colonel Moscardó's account.

explain to his father that he would be shot if the fortress did not surrender. The colonel told his son to commend his soul to God, and to die bravely. The son was executed a month later. The text of the conversation has been printed in many languages on the cellar wall of the Alcázar, now one of the principal monuments to the Nationalist victory. People in Spain still argue passionately about whether the conversation could have taken place.[10] But factual accuracy in this case is less important than symbolic meaning. In the Spanish Civil War there were fathers on both sides who would have done exactly what Colonel Moscardó testifies he did; and there were sons who would have died willingly after such an injunction from their fathers.

The victory at Badajoz enabled the Insurgents to regain the initiative in the north. At the end of July, they controlled the Pyrennean border from the western edge of Lérida province to within perhaps 20 miles of the Bay of Biscay. Now they were anxious to close the border at Hendaye and eliminate the troublesome Basque threat to their rear. After Badajoz, General Franco was able to release some 700 *Legionnaires* and send a battery of 6-inch guns to reinforce the Carlist commander, Colonel Beorlegui, in his campaign to capture Irún. By August 26, the Junker transport-bombers had brought these new units to Beorlegui's headquarters. The week-long struggle for Irún involved somewhat over 2,000 men on each side, with the superior military training and armament being clearly on the side of the attackers. Colonel Beorlegui's troops included roughly equal proportions of *Legionnaires,* Carlists, Falangists, and Civil Guards. He took the mountain ridges overlooking the town by night, and his troops communicated by hunting horn. On the first daylight attacks toward the city he sustained heavy losses, due to overconfidence and steadier machine-gun fire than he had anticipated.

The militiamen defending the city were reinforced by several hundred Catalans who had come across southern France and then reentered Spain at Hendaye. Prime Minister

[10] H. Thomas, *op. cit.,* p. 203, gives convincing details to support the authenticity of the story.

Léon Blum had ordered the frontier closed on August 8 as a first step toward establishing the nonintervention policy. As a result, the defenders of Irún were unable to touch a half-dozen carloads of ammunition in the freight yards of Hendaye; but national policy did not prevent the local population from aiding the Republicans, with whom in large majority they sympathized. French farmers in the hills across from Beorlegui's troops signaled to Irún the position of his guns and the general preparation of his daily moves. Border police made virtually no effort to prevent armed Catalans from going to Irún, or to keep militiamen from crossing the border each night to eat and sleep in safety and to return the next morning with as much rifle and machine-gun ammunition as they could carry.[11]

Between August 26 and September 4, superior organization, skill, and armament produced complete victory for Colonel Beorlegui. At the last moment, fleeing anarchists burned the city they could no longer defend. A few hundred militiamen crossed into France, but the majority retreated under Basque leadership to San Sebastián. In the latter town the Basque Nationalists, determined not to see the city uselessly destroyed, arranged for an orderly retreat to more defensible positions, and by agreement with the advancing Insurgents left a skeleton government to control the situation until the entry of General Mola's forces on September 12.

This northern campaign was not characterized, militarily speaking, by the ferocity that marked the Andalusian warfare. Neither the Carlists nor the Basque Nationalists shot their prisoners. Both took pride in the correct behavior of their troops. The anarchists and the *Legionnaires* were the minority elements in their respective camps and did not set the standards of conduct. Spaniards are wont to say, and with much justification in certain contexts, that they are free of

---

[11] Concerning the fall of Irún and San Sebastián, I depended principally on G. L. Steer, *The Tree of Gernika* (London, 1938), pp. 32–58. Steer enjoyed the confidence of the Basque Nationalists. His book shows little knowledge of the rest of Spain, but is highly informative on both the military and political aspects of the war as seen by the Basques.

the race prejudice that marks the Germanic and Anglo-Saxon peoples. But the contrast between military behavior in Andalusia and in the north reflected deeply embedded racial feelings. Spaniards of all political persuasions are liable to speak of Andalusians as an inferior breed and of the Basques and Navarrese as the best "stock" in Spain. In Andalusia the professional officers frequently acted as though they were conducting a chemical exterminating operation. In the north they regarded their enemies as fellow human beings—as disciplined, as Catholic, and as honorable as themselves, despite the bitter difference of political views.

16

REVOLUTION AND TERROR
IN THE POPULAR FRONT ZONE

THE agitation of the spring months had seriously undermined
the authority of the Republican government, and the pronunciamiento of July 17–20 temporarily destroyed the remaining authority of the state. The police virtually disappeared
from the main cities during the first days of the rising. The
most active elements of the Army and the Civil Guard supported the Insurgents, and the government was hesitant, often
with good reason, to trust many of the apparently loyal units
and officers. After the surrender of General Goded, Luis
Companys had called to his office the principal anarchist
leaders. He told them that they had saved Catalonia from the
military rebellion; he acknowledged that they were the masters
in Barcelona, and that they could dispose of their power as
they saw fit. At the same time, he hoped that they would
remember his and the Esquerra's services to the working
class, and that they would take advantage of his governing
experience in the battle against fascism and for further social
advances.[1] Companys, as a labor lawyer, had defended many
of the men to whom he spoke. In Madrid, Prime Minister José
Giral, a professor of chemistry, had had no such contact with
the working-class leaders, but he might have spoken similarly,
for the situation in the two capital cities was the same. The
workers had defeated the rebellion, and they disposed of the
effective political power.

[1] Carlos M. Rama, *La crisis español a del siglo XX* (Mexico, 1960),
pp. 249–50, based on the article of García Oliver in *Solidaridad
Obrera*, July 18, 1937. Though I cite it in this instance for information on the Civil War, this book is primarily a detailed and
extremely thoughtful study of the political forms and political
thought underlying the Civil War.

In the second half of 1936 the most profound social revolution since the fifteenth century took place in much of the territory remaining in the hands of the Popular Front.[2] The main characteristics of that revolution were a passion for equality, and the affirmation of local, and collective, authority. In Barcelona, felt hats, the symbol of bourgeois status, disappeared from the streets. Luxury restaurants and hotels were either collectivized or *incautados* (requisitioned) by their staffs. Salaries remained the same. Waiters wore white coats

[2] The problem of vocabulary raises difficult questions in dealing with the Civil War. Such terms as "Reds" and "Whites," "Fascists" and "Marxists," I rejected as general headings, not because of their emotive associations but because they are not accurate terms for more than a small proportion of the forces in presence. "Rebels" and "Loyalists" are slightly more inclusive, but if used as names for the two camps they imply a degree of legal deliberation which I do not think was very important in the choice of sides made by most of those who were in a position to choose. During the first 3 to 4 months of the war, the Madrid government enjoyed only a nominal authority in its zone. It therefore seemed to me that "Popular Front zone" would be an accurate term to use for the territory declaring itself loyal to the Republican government during this period. Similarly the Burgos junta had not, during this period, achieved full internal organization or international recognition. Thus the term "Insurgents" appeared to me reasonably accurate and neutral for the forces commanded by Generals Franco, Mola, and Queipo de Llano. After about November, 1936, the Largo Caballero and later Negrín governments increasingly asserted their authority in the Republican zone, and General Franco increasingly established his personal authority and the international standing of his government. In these conditions, the terms "Republicans" and "Nationalists" appeared to me the best available. "Republicans" is justified by the fact that the revolutionary forces were in steady retreat, and that the government repeatedly affirmed the aims and program of the liberal, reformist Republic. "Nationalists" is justified by the fact that the Burgos government steadily affirmed the primacy of Castile over the regions, and governed with the aid of the most conservative economic and religious forces of Spain. It goes without saying that in the complex circumstances of revolution and civil war any single term applied to either side will be open to some legitimate objection.

and served with the same courtesy and finesse as before, for the same prices—but the clients dined in shirtsleeves, and the worker management abolished tipping. All the workers carried arms, and, in a country long dominated by brutal police, these arms—often completely unserviceable—were more important as symbols of emancipation than as weapons. Rent and public utilities were controlled by neighborhood committees which included one member for each party of the Popular Front, but were nevertheless completely dominated, in the early days, by the anarchists. Spacious private homes of the wealthy who had fled to France were converted for use as schools, orphanages, hospitals. Pablo Casals gave 10,000 pesetas for war relief and organized free concerts (as he had before the war) in the industrial suburbs.

Most factories were taken over by their workers. Some owners were shot, some fled the city, and some continued to work in their own requisitioned industries, at the salary being paid to top administrators and engineers. The workers did not lose their sense of practical realities. Tramways, buses, light and water services operated normally. Machine shops and garages carried on business as usual, some of them preparing also to manufacture grenades, shell fuses, and armor plate for cars and trucks going to the front. The hatmakers petitioned the Generalitat to inform the people of Barcelona of the crisis in their industry. The technical personnel of textile factories sent salesmen to France and hoped to arrange for Russian markets also. The Cordoniu Champagne workers did likewise. Wages went up about 15 per cent and rents were cut by 50 per cent in low-cost apartments. Everyone was taxed 10 per cent of his salary for the war effort. There was a boom in the sale of berets, red ties, other war souvenirs, and pornographic literature. But savings bank accounts also rose rapidly through the autumn. The workers took pride in the quick reestablishment of industrial activity after the revolutionary weekend of July 19. They looked with sympathy upon the Soviet Union, but at the same time insisted on local rather than central control of the collectivized factories and emphasized the intimacy of the predominantly small units of Catalan industry. Most individual retail businesses were untouched. Walter Duranty, the *New York Times* correspondent who had witnessed the several phases of the Russian revolution, compared the spirit of Barcelona in the fall of 1936 with that of the New Economic Policy in Soviet History.[3]

In Madrid, the unionized cabinetmakers, shoemakers, and barbers collectivized their shops. The Palace Hotel was converted into an orphanage, and during August it was filled to overflowing with children who had lost their parents in retreat from Andalusia and Extremadura. All foreign businesses were confiscated at first. Many of them had been incorporated as purely Spanish firms in order to evade the taxes on foreign-owned businesses, and these were permanently lost to the owners; many of the others were restored in the course of the fall. Unions here, as in Barcelona and Valencia, abused their sudden authority to place the sign *incautado* on all manner of buildings and vehicles, but the urge to collectivize the entire economy was not nearly so strong in Madrid as in Barcelona. And well-dressed, undisguisedly bourgeois women, as well as shopgirls, walked the streets in pairs, soliciting pesetas for medical aid in the same manner as formerly they had collected for foreign missionary work.

Throughout the rural areas of Popular Front territory, a corresponding revolution took place, yet one that varied greatly from village to village. Once again, social equality and local control were the guiding impulses rather than any organized conception of the new society to be created. Almost everywhere, rents were abolished and property records burned. In some instances the entire village land was collectivized, while in others, the land belonging to owners who had fled or been shot was distributed among the peasant majority. Sometimes the confiscated land was collectivized while other property relations remained untouched. In some villages no property changes occurred. Almost everywhere, the former municipal governments were replaced by committees including one member for each party of the Popular Front. In some cases this meant little change—if, for example, the former alcalde (mayor) had been a Socialist or Left Republican, he would

[3] The *New York Times,* September 17, 1936.

simply become head of the village committee and continue business as before. However, where the CEDA or the Lliga Catalana had won the February elections, the alcalde and the Civil Guards would likely have fled or been imprisoned or assassinated, and new men dominated the committees.

Generally speaking, work methods and wages tended to be frozen. The peasants desired land and social equality, but they were not theorists. On the whole, in the summer of 1936 production was not upset by the revolution, but neither was there much initiative toward a change of existing economic practices. The committees controlled wages, and the sale of the harvest. They converted the church, whose altar had frequently been burned in the first days, into a market, or, if close to the front, a hospital. Some of them abolished money and declared a "republic" within their own municipal boundaries. The anarchist peasants considered money second only to the Church as a source of corruption. In Catalonia long traditions of commerce and industry kept them from going to excessive lengths, but in Aragon, the Levant, New Castile, Murcia, and Andalusia, dozens of villages proudly abolished the use of money within their territory. Local commerce was conducted in chits or in kind. Wages were revised in accordance with the size of a man's family rather than the skill or quantity of his work. Money, still a necessary evil in dealing with the outside world, was confiscated by the committee and given to the villagers for specific purchases or travel needs. The anarchist peasant's feeling about money was analagous to the prohibitionist's feeling about liquor. It was tempting, it was sinful, it was necessary in particular circumstances. But its use should be strictly controlled, and ideally speaking it should some day be eliminated entirely.[4]

[4] My principal sources of information on the revolution in Catalonia, the Levant, and Castile were: H. E. Kaminski, *Ceux de Barcelone* (Paris, 1937); Anton Sieberer, *Katalonien gegen Kastilien* (Vienna, 1936); Franz Borkenau, *The Spanish Cockpit* (London, 1937); and José Peirats, *La C.N.T. en la revolución española,* 3 vols. (Toulouse, 1951–1952). I also used Rama, *op. cit.,* ch. 5; Broué and Témime *La révolution et la guerre d'Espagne,* Part I, chs. 5 and 6; and José Martín Blázquez, *I Helped to Build*

In Republican-held Guipúzcoa and Vizcaya, the Basque Nationalists were the strongest element in village politics. The traditions of local autonomy and cooperation in the use of machines and in harvesting were strong. But there was no wave of collectivizations and no such flourishing of anarchist propoganda as in the east and south. In the Asturias the traditions of October 1934 were renewed. Village committees collectivized all commerce, served meals by chit in public kitchens, and abolished money for all local purposes. The fishermen of Avilés and Gijón collectivized their equipment, the docks, and the canning factories.[5] They had owned their boats collectively ever since the Middle Ages and had disposed of much of the catch by barter. The fishermen of Catalonia, some of the mountain villagers of Aragon and the Maestrazgo, and the farmers of Valencia all had similar collective traditions, but these features were survivals of a medieval economy and were as often accompanied by reactionary as by leftist political emotions.[6]

In the Asturias, however, local tradition coincided with contemporary political consciousness. The miners and the fishermen had for years debated the course of the Soviet

---

an Army (London, 1939). In Saragossa, Barcelona, and Valencia, I had the opportunity to speak with several persons who had experience both with the social experiments and the revolutionary terror.

[5] Solano Palacio, *La tragedia del norte,* pp. 73–87. There is very little printed information concerning the Republican-held parts of the Asturias in 1936–37, as the area was cut off from the rest of the Republican zone. Solano Palacio was an anarchist, and I have trusted what he has to say about the collectives, since his reports on military action jibe well with those of foreign journalists and Nationalist historians.

[6] Joaquín Costa, in his monumental *Colectivismo agrario,* revived Spanish interest at the end of the 19th century in the varied local collectivist traditions of the Peninsula. J. Langdon-Davies, *Behind the Spanish Barricades* (London, 1936), describes the Catalan fishing collectives. I treated the relationship of these medieval-born traditions to the revolution of 1936 in an article: "The Origins of Spanish Anarchism," *The Southwestern Social Science Quarterly* (Sept., 1955), pp. 135–47.

revolution, the theories of both Bolshevik and Trotskyite, as well as anarchist, writers. The revolutionary forms of Marxist thought had enjoyed more influence, proportionately speaking, among the Asturian proletariat than anywhere else in Spain. Finally, in the dry farming districts of central and southern Spain, the Land Workers Federation of the UGT ran about 100 collective farms consciously patterned on Soviet models. Some of these had been established as early as 1934, and most of them operated until the end of the Civil War.[7]

The psychological reactions of the people were as varied and original as the forms of collectivism. In one of the Aragonese villages where the local landlord had been well liked, he stayed on unmolested after the expropriation of his estate. The revolutionary committee established by the Durruti column abolished money and took charge of all wages and the sale of the harvest. They employed the landlord in their administration, and the peasants secretly asked him to keep conventional accounts so that they would know where they stood in terms of pesetas in case the situation changed again.

The anarchists preached the equality of the sexes, but continued to feel that human dignity required separate dining rooms for men and women workers. Despite outward appearances, they were often more conservative in their social instincts than the *bourgeoisie*. Federica Montsény, the leading woman anarchist in Catalonia, confirmed to a foreign visitor that the anarchists were indeed opposed to conventional marriage. She went on to explain that they favored *unión libre*. Instead of having fathers virtually sell their daughters to a husband whom the brides promised forever to *obey*, the anarchists favored an unión libre to be founded on mutual consent and on shared responsibilities. Sra. Montsény did not believe in easy divorce; she would permit the practice of birth control, but did not think that Spanish women would want to avoid having children; and she thought that children were often better educated at home than in school. She was asked her opinion of *piropos*, the vigorous and often crude compli-

[7] Gerald Brenan, *The Spanish Labyrinth* (Cambridge, England, 1943), p. 275; and *Claridad* for July 13, August 17 and September 14, 1935, and for April 7, 1936.

ments which were addressed to girls by strangers in the streets. She thought that women would always enjoy compliments, even in an egalitarian society, and smiled incredulously when her visitor said that the women of some countries would be insulted by the piropo.[8]

The practical results of the collectivizations varied too greatly for any general judgment to cover them accurately. Where raw materials continued to be available, where workers were proud and skillful in the maintenance of their machines, where a reasonable proportion of the technical personnel sympathized with the revolution, factories operated successfully. Where materials ran short, where replacement parts could not be found, where UGT-CNT rivalries embittered the workers and placed political considerations ahead of operating efficiency, the collectivized factories failed. Similarly in the countryside—there were collectives where machines were intelligently used and human problems tactfully handled; and there were collectives where the absence of intelligent direction led to the demoralization of the peasants and greatly reduced production. In the villages where money had been abolished, there were committees which showed great acumen in the sale of the harvest and distributed money for all reasonable outside expenses; and there were committees which simply burned or stole the cash resources of their village. The common denominator of all these situations was the energy with which the common people formed committees, gladly substituted for a central authority they had rarely respected, and ran their own affairs along collectivist and egalitarian lines. It was a phenomenon which had occurred before in Spanish history, notably during the resistance to Napoleon, in the Carlist communities during the 1830's, and in the "cantonalist" and "federalist" revolts of 1873.

These varied urban and rural revolutions were accompanied in different areas by varying degrees of terror. In Madrid and Barcelona the workers shot as many of the Insurgent officers as they could find. The leading officers faced court-martials which handed down numerous death sentences for

[8] Kaminski, *op. cit.*, pp. 68–74 for the interview with Federica Montsény.

military rebellion. It was the unpleasant duty of the all-Republican Giral cabinet to confirm or commute these sentences. They confirmed those against Generals Goded and Fanjul and commuted most of the others.

The main purging in the big cities was done on the initiative of the left-wing elements of the Popular Front. In Madrid the CNT, the UGT, and the Communist Party all had their lists of suspects. *Claridad, Mundo Obrero,* and the anarchist press daily "exposed" the machinations of local "fascists" and called for vigilance against "class enemies." It was more dangerous to be a known partisan of Lerroux or Gil Robles than to be a Monarchist. The latter had never pretended to accept the Republic. The former were looked upon as traitors whose chieftains had sabotaged the social gains of the Republic during the *biennio negro* (the "two black years," 1934–35) and had now appeared in Lisbon, offering their services to General Franco.

The standards of the self-constituted purge committees were inevitably very crude. No lawyers were involved. It was up to the accused, who were considered guilty until proven innocent, to gather convincing witnesses within a matter of hours. If a man shines a flashlight at night, how does one determine whether he was looking for his cigarettes or signaling to an enemy plane? If he listens to Radio Seville with the volume turned up, is he trying to demoralize the neighborhood with news of Insurgent victories? Does he enjoy the salaciousness of General Queipo de Llano? Is he trying to circumvent the ridiculous censorship of news in the Madrid press? Or is he simply hard of hearing? People's lives depended on the way such questions were answered. The committees took their work seriously. CNT, UGT, and Communists frequently consulted each other and compared lists. If a name appeared on all three, there was a heavy presumption of guilt. If it appeared on only one, the accused would get a sympathetic hearing, and if declared innocent, might be treated to a round of drinks and given a guard of honor to return home. The committees were capable of shooting false informers.[9]

While in Madrid the revolutionary organizations generally

[9] Borkenau, *op. cit.,* pp. 125ff.

cooperated with each other, in the other main cities their mutual rivalries were an important element in the terror. In Barcelona a few prominent labor leaders died as a result of UGT-CNT warfare on the waterfront. The Trotskyite POUM and the Communist-dominated PSUC directed their fire at one another as well as at the reactionary bosses. In Valencia and Málaga the internecine warfare of UGT, CNT, and Communist factions resulted in a number of deaths.

Prominent individuals were the victims of revenge for real or imagined offenses. A group of Asturians went to the Madrid military hospital to kill General López Ochoa, who had headed the military forces in Oviedo in October, 1934. Actually he had done much to limit the severity of the repression, but the Asturians held him responsible for their sufferings. On August 23, after a mysterious fire in the Model Prison, the guards decided to shoot some fourteen prominent prisoners. Among those selected were Melquiades Alvarez, one-time deputy for Oviedo, who had praised General Sanjurjo' after the latter's unsuccessful revolt in 1932, and who had in public speeches referred to the Socialists as "traitors." They also shot Fernando Primo de Rivera, brother of the founder of the Falange; J. Ruiz de Alda, a Falange founder; Rico Avello, who had been Minister of the Interior in 1933 when the Left lost the elections; General Villegas and the former Madrid police chief Santiago M. Báguenas, both of whom had taken part in the Madrid rising, but whom the Giral government had not executed. In each of these cases the guards thought they were carrying out revolutionary justice, a justice which the government had been too weak and indecisive to exact. Later in the autumn an international incident was created by the assassination of Baron Borchgrave, the Belgian chargé d'affaires in Madrid. The assassins were never identified. But Baron Borchgrave had in 1934 been the representative of Mercedes autos in Spain, and the car driven by the Falangists who had killed Juana Rico was a Mercedes belonging to Sr. Merry del Val. There were tens of thousands of Madrid workers who remembered the incident, and who could on that account easily have placed the name of the Baron on their list.

Many executions were motivated by reprisals for enemy

raids. Some 50 prisoners were shot in Málaga after the air raid of August 23.[10] When the Insurgent Navy threatened to shell San Sebastián, the city officials announced that they would shoot two prisoners for each victim of such shelling. The *España* and the *Almirante Cervera* made a raid which caused 4 deaths, and 8 hostages were shot. Two air raids on the city of Bilbao on September 25 and October 2 led to the shooting of about 100 prisoners.[11] On both sides, prisons were likely to be rushed after air raids, and aviators liable to be lynched if they were forced to bail out over enemy territory.

The first three months of the war were the period of maximum terror in the Republican zone. Revolutionary passions were at their height and the authority of the government at its nadir. In the main cities gangs of juvenile delinquents requisitioned automobiles, gave themselves dramatic titles such as the Lynxes, the Red Lions, the Death Battalion, and the Godless, and conducted an average of ten to fifteen *paseos* each night. Originally the cars had been seized as part of the struggle to suppress the rebellion. The victims were theoretically important fascists, and the revolutionary committees had presumably sentenced them to death as such. But many of the victims never received even the crudest form of revolutionary trial.

On February 22 the amnesty had released thousands of common criminals along with the political prisoners, and in the spring months many of these pistoleros had appeared before judges who were afraid to convict them no matter what the evidence. After July 19 they could add to their habitual criminality the luxury of "serving the revolution" while driving cars and playing older brother to teen-age revolutionaries. The most readily identifiable, and in the cities the most hated "class enemy," were the priests. Between 5–6,000 priests and monks were killed in the big cities, and proportionately speaking, they were the main victims of sheer gangsterism.[12]

[10] Toynbee, *Survey,* 1937, II, 86–87.

[11] G. L. Steer, *The Tree of Gernika,* p. 139. Javier Ybarra y Bergé, *Mi diario de la guerra de España* (Bilbao, 1941), pp. 31–48.

[12] A Montero, *La persecución religiosa,* pp. 762–64 for detailed figures.

Revolutionary violence in turn gave an easy opportunity to counter-revolutionary violence. The Falange in Madrid and Valencia eliminated a number of Republican and moderate Socialist personalities. The capital cities, Madrid and Barcelona, provided an anonymity which covered all types of crime and which also enabled the killers to feel quite impersonal about their work. In southern cities like Málaga and Alicante the traditional ignorance and misery of the population lent itself to the crudest instincts of both revolutionaries and disguised fascists.

The government knew very well that unbridled terrorism would destroy everything for which the Republic stood. Over the radio it repeatedly advised the people not to open their doors at night, and to call the police immediately if gangs visited a block of apartments. In many instances the arrival of an Assault Guard, or simply the firmness of a janitor, dispersed a shamefaced group of teen-agers who might otherwise have committed murder. Thousands of persons who felt threatened by their right-wing political associations took refuge in the embassies, with the consent of the government, which permitted a number of legations to rent neighboring buildings to which they could extend their extraterritorial status. Juan Negrín, Manuel de Irujo, and other officials visited the prisons at night to protect the inmates from mob assault. On August 10 Prieto went on the air to excoriate the paseos as sheer criminality, and after the killing of the fourteen prominent prisoners in the *Modelo,* he made the point more powerfully by beginning his address with the words: "Today we have lost the war."

The revolutionary forces after July 19 had set up *tribunales populares* in the main cities. The government exercised a restraining influence on these courts through the appointment of moderate, courageous, professional lawyers to preside over them: men such as Mariano Gómez in Madrid and Rafael Supervía in Valencia. They could not checkmate class hatred, nor impose impeccable procedure on untrained prosecutors and juries; but they could prevent flagrant errors in the treatment of evidence, protect witnesses, increase the proportion of prison sentences, and decrease the proportion of death penalties. Many Radicals and Cedistas felt safer in prison than at home, for there was much less danger of a capital penalty from the courts than from a paseo.[13]

It would be impossible to state quantitatively how many innocent persons suffered imprisonment, violence, robbery, or death and how many were saved by the courageous intervention of citizens, government officials, or a sense of justice on the part of the revolutionary committees. With badly driven cars careening through the streets, machine guns protruding from the windows and revolutionary slogans painted on the doors; and with thousands of Madrileños hearing the nightly shootings on the outskirts of the city and seeing the bodies in the road the next morning, everyone was conscious of the terror. Resistance to it was in the nature of things less publicized. Early in August the CNT and UGT threatened to shoot false informants. Employers were being reported as "fascist spies" by vengeful employees. Priests were being accused of firing shots from churches by people for whom anticlericalism was a religion. There are known instances in which, after releasing the accused person, the committee then hailed in the informant and shot him for false testimony.[14]

Early in August an anarchist squad entered one of the Augustinian *colegios* of Madrid. The government had just published a decree forbidding searches of private homes. One person present showed a copy of the decree to the somewhat confused visitors while another called the Ministry of the

---

[13] Jesús de Galíndez, *Los vascos en el Madrid sitiado* (Buenos Aires, 1945), pp. 58, 87, and *passim*. This book is the best single source of information on paseos, prisons, justice, and the operations (good and bad) of the revolutionary committees in Madrid. Concerning the creditable, courageous work of the Valencia Tribunal Popular, see *The Times*, London, Oct. 15, 1936.

[14] *Red Terror in Madrid* (London, 1937), a highly circumstantial anonymous account by a refugee from the city, describes on pp. 59–61 the release of the prebendary of the Cathedral of Madrid and the shooting of the person who had falsely denounced him. I heard similar stories in both Barcelona and Madrid from persons of the most conservative social and political ideas.

Interior. In a few minutes Assault Guards appeared and sent the anarchists on their way. At his own request, the man who had talked with them at the door went off to prison for several days as a protective measure against the possibility of a revenge paseo. The Augustinians remained in their building unmolested throughout the war. At the Colegio de Salesianos in the Ronda de Atocha, the government quartered a Communist Party regiment, La Joven Guardia. The regiment and the friars lived side by side throughout the war. It is worth noting in the second instance that the Salesianos enjoyed a sympathetic reputation with the public, due to their large number of scholarships and concern for the education of the poor. A number of nunneries were also taken over as hospitals, and many of the nuns continued to serve as nurses, with the Republican officers making it a point of honor that they be well treated.

In Barcelona during the first three months of the war the situation was similar to that in Madrid. The unions had their purge lists, gangsters and juvenile delinquents with anarchist vocabularies carried out paseos, and revolutionary courts handed down frequent death sentences; these courts also released many an innocent defendant who had the presence of mind to fight the uphill battle against jurors who assumed him guilty until proven innocent. The Generalitat could not openly confront the anarchists, but it granted passports freely to thousands of threatened middle-class families. The anarchists controlled the trains and the French border posts, but there were several foreign ships in the harbor, and the government quietly helped refugees to get passage on them.

Anticlerical fury was greater in Barcelona than in Madrid. The Carmelite church in the Calle Lauria had been one of the strongholds of the Insurgents on July 19. After the surrendering soldiers had come out, the crowd set fire to the building in order to dislodge the priests. A machine gun was set up commanding the entrance to the church, and as the terror-stricken priests emerged they were shot down.[15] Virtually every

[15] For the surrender of the Carmelite Church see Megan Laird, "A Diary of Revolution," *The Atlantic Monthly* (November, 1936), pp. 513–33.

church in the city was burned. There were occasional macabre scenes of dancing around corpses and breaking open the coffins of deceased nuns.

The ferocious persecution of the Church had many causes. In both city and village the average priest was careful to flatter the "best families" and to share the political opinions of the small, tightly united, ruling circles. The Spanish people had never accepted as normal the rule of celibacy, and in many villages they would not permit their daughters to go to confession unless the priest had a "niece" or a "housekeeper," who was in reality, with the approval of the village, his common-law wife.[16] The Church, like the Spanish Army, had been accustomed for centuries to dealing with colonial populations, masses of Indians or Filipino tribesmen who could be charmed and frightened by rather simple means. The Spanish people were often illiterate, but they resented deeply the condescending priestly manner, especially when they knew that the Church had steadily opposed the extension of public education.

Within the Spanish people there welled up a mortal hatred of that condescending Church. Several times in the nineteenth century, churches had been burned, as they were also in 1931 and in the spring of 1936. Stories of cupidity, and of sexual orgies and perversions, were always easily believed among all classes of the population. On July 18 the rumor swept Spain that priests were firing at the people from church towers. With very few exceptions this was absolutely untrue except in the Carlist country. The military had no more taken the Church into confidence on their plans than they had the conservative republican parties. It is probable that the military seized the church in the Calle Lauria as a fine stone fortress, counting at the same time on the complacency of the priests toward the rising. The important point is that public esteem of the Church was so low that people easily believed that priests were shooting at the workers. And, of course, there was no doubt of the overwhelming conservatism of the Church.

The Generalitat sent loyal Civil Guards with cars to evacuate the bishops of Tortosa and Gerona. They offered

[16] Brenan, *Spanish Labyrinth,* p. 49.

a similar service to the Bishop of Barcelona, but the latter decided to remain in the city incognito. Cardinal Vidal of Tarragona, who had been discreetly friendly to the Republic, was arrested by anarchists in Poblet. As he sat in the back seat of the car, composing himself to meet a sure death, he heard his two captors in the front ruminating regretfully to the effect that they didn't really feel happy about killing a man of his character and age. Fortunately the youths did not have to go through with their assignment. The Generalitat had already sent a police car which rescued the Cardinal from the anarchists; the police officials then hid him in a government office in Barcelona. The Cardinal wanted to shave, put on a clean collar, and leave via the French or British consulate so as not to provide a propaganda opportunity to speak of a prince of the Church fleeing in rags via a fascist consulate. But in the circumstances of the moment only the Italian consulate was available.

In the early weeks of the war each competing authority challenged the validity of the others, and there were numerous cases like that of professor García Morente, dean of the faculty of philosophy at Madrid. Threatened with a paseo in September, he had sought the help of his friend the Minister of Communications, Bernardo Giner. The latter had given him a bed in the government office while he obtained for him a passport to leave Spain via Barcelona. On his arrival in Barcelona, the professor saw the posters in the railway station stating that no documents issued in Madrid would be honored. He then went to his friend Professor Bosch Gimpera, dean of the faculty of letters in Barcelona, who obtained for him a Generalitat passport which enabled him to get to France. He had had to leave his family in Madrid, and he now wrote his old colleague, Professor Juan Negrín, Minister of Finance, asking him to expedite the emigration of his family. Negrín sent a squad of carabineros (the frontier police who were attached to the Ministry of Finance) to accompany the García Morente family to the French border.[17]

The village revolutions also were accompanied by varying

[17] My accounts of Cardinal Vidal and Professor García Morente are based on interviews with close personal associates of conservative political convictions.

degrees of terror. In southern Spain particularly, priests and Civil Guards were practically always shot if they had sided with the Insurgents; occasionally they were shot even if they had made no move on July 18. Throughout the Popular Front area, the village committees acted on their own initiative, and generalization concerning the results is impossible. Some villages took pride in deciding not to shoot any "class enemies" at all, but to "reeducate" them as long as they did not sabotage the revolution. Some villages warned the priest and the landlords to leave, for a time at least, lest uncontrollable elements decide to lynch them. Some villages shot the priest, the Civil Guards, the main landlords, and professional persons such as notaries and pharmacists, known or assumed to favor the old order. In villages with populations of several thousand, the death toll might run between 4 or 5 and 35 to 40, with the casualties tending to be higher in Andalusia and the southeast than in the Levant and Catalonia. Sometimes the executions were carried out by the local committees, sometimes by outside anarchist squads. In Aragon the Durruti column, on its way toward Saragossa, earned an evil reputation among the generally conservative peasants. On the other hand, there are also many testimonials to the intervention of Durruti personally to prevent the killing of landlords who had not aided the rising, but who were condemned simply as known Catholics, monarchists, or partisans of Lerroux. The anarchists had an almost superstitious respect for teachers and doctors, and spared many such even when the individuals in question were known to be reactionary.[18]

[18] Borkenau, *op. cit.*, pp. 97–8 speaks of executions in rural Aragon organized by the Durruti column. But in separate conversations with two monarchist landlords, one of them a university professor and the other a lawyer, I heard a strong defense of Durruti's active opposition to assassinations.

17

AUTHORITY AND TERROR
IN THE INSURGENT ZONE

IN THE territory controlled by the Insurgents no such revolution took place as in Popular Front Spain. The military were accustomed by their profession to respect hierarchies and obey central directives. They counted from the first moment on the support of conservative social and propertied interests, for whom, also, order and hierarchy were accepted principles. After the failure of the pronunciamiento, the generals and their civilian supporters knew that the most strict mobilization of resources would be necessary for the conquest of two-thirds of Spain. In the Popular Front zone the *estado de guerra* was not declared until practically the end of the Civil War. In Insurgent Spain, the *estado de guerra* was proclaimed on July 18 and maintained without exception thenceforward.

Transportation, public utilities, and food distribution were efficiently handled. Businessmen in the main towns formed committees which assessed financial contributions from the professional, administrative, and business personnel, and which collected clothes, food, and medical supplies for the front. The military had been victorious in the less populous, agricultural provinces. Their zone was easy to feed, but suffered from a constant shortage of labor, aggravated by the flight of thousands of workers and peasants to the Republican lines or to the inaccessible mountains. Prices and wages were frozen, sometimes at the July 18 level (relatively advantageous to the workers), sometimes at the February 16 level (advantageous to employers). Inflation was thus partially checked, though, as in all such situations, a black market arose, and many of the great fortunes of postwar Spain were founded upon fruitful wartime speculations. A large proportion of labor leaders were shot; strikes were forbidden; and all business was obliged to remain open regardless of the wishes of the owners.

In the portions of Spain immediately dominated by the Insurgents, the military governor of monarchical times (the "captain general") had always in reality exercised a higher authority than the civil governor. One of the most fundamental, if little mentioned, reasons why the officer corps hated the Republic, was that the Republicans intended to establish civilian supremacy in Spanish government for the first time. On July 18 the generals became the supreme civil as well as military commanders, and traditional lines of authority remained in force. The majority of judges, notaries, Civil Guards, and businessmen willingly served the military. Popular Front officials were imprisoned, civilian supporters of the rebellion were named in their stead, and virtually no other changes of administrative routine were necessary.

Nevertheless, the organization of a central government presented difficulties. While the military had planned and executed the rebellion on their own, they were eager to associate civilians in the governing responsibility as rapidly as possible. But Calvo Sotelo, who had been their principal civilian collaborator, had been assassinated. Lerroux and Gil Robles were ready to serve, but had either of them entered Insurgent Spain in late July or August 1936 he would have been shot by Falangist or Carlist fanatics. In Carlist Pamplona, General Mola had found the civil governor unenthusiastic and had given him a safe conduct to leave town. The Bishop of Pamplona, Marcelino Olaechea, had been appointed by the Republic and was known to be concerned for the material as well as spiritual condition of the working class. When Mola first appeared in Burgos, the civil officials came to greet him, but prudently left at home their insignia of office.

In these circumstances the generals decided on July 24 to form a temporary junta of military men only. It included the main figures who had risen in the northern zone of the Peninsula: Mola, Saliquet, Ponte, Dávila, and Miguel Cabanellas. Queipo de Llano was already establishing an independent principality based on Seville, and Franco joined the Burgos junta early in August. General Cabanellas was chosen as chairman. Well known to the public for his long white beard, a man of mild character behind whom others could easily maneuver, a long-time Mason and declared Republican, he was an excellent public-relations choice at a time when, in various corners of the country, officers were still trying to bring their soldiers to the side of the Insurgents with the slogan "Viva la República!"

In the months of August and September, however, real political power lay in the hands of three generals: Mola, Queipo de Llano, and Franco. The only question was which of these would become the supreme chief. Mola had directed the conspiracy and ruled in the provinces where the rebellion enjoyed a measure of popular approval. He was a foxy man of great intelligence and energy, but he was condemned by his past. The Monarchists, though they worked with him in preparing the rising, remembered resentfully his attitude toward Alfonso XIII. Also, he had been the Director General of Security. Among his peers he had therefore the reputation of a "policeman" rather than of a "soldier," and generally speaking, authoritarians of both the Right and the Left have never wished to hand supreme power to the head of the police. General Queipo de Llano had conspired against the Monarchy in 1930. He was related by marriage to Alcalá-Zamora and had headed the presidential military household. He was a colorful figure, "the very model of a modern major general" in his bearing, attractive to the masses, but with a coarse streak that made him doubly despised by the aristocracy: for his political past and for his personal manner.

General Franco stood head and shoulders above his rivals as a soldier's soldier, the man who had trained the most redoubtable military force in Spain: the Foreign Legion. There were endless anecdotes concerning his coolness under fire and his cruelty as a disciplinarian. Literally true or not, they formed the basis of an incomparable prestige within the officer corps. During the planning stages, Franco had been cautious, noncommittal to the last, and had not entered Spanish Morocco until assured of the success of the local rising. Romantics and *exaltados* hated him for his calculations, but for this very characteristic the financier Juan March, the German and Portuguese, and later the Italian, business representatives, looked upon him as the most able of the Insurgent leaders. Companions of General Sanjurjo did not forget that Franco had withdrawn from the 1932 rising at the last moment, but they also had to admit that his judgment of political realities had been much keener than theirs. Franco was neither a Monarchist nor a Republican; but he had been appointed the youngest general in the Spanish Army by the personal favor of Alfonso XIII, and the Monarchists hoped that he might incline toward them in organizing the future state.

The rapid march of the Army of Africa added to Franco's military prestige. By late September the Insurgents were talking about entering Madrid for the *Día de la Raza* (Day of the [Spanish] Race, October 12) and it became urgent to form a more substantial government than that of the Burgos junta. On September 29 the junta adopted a decree naming General Franco "Head of the Government" and military operations. On October 1 General Franco promulgated his first *law*, in which he referred to himself as "Head of the State." In time of war few persons dwelt upon the slight change of phraseology. Generals Mola and Cabanellas protested violently, in private.[1] The observant were put on notice concerning General Franco's limitless ambition, and with his brother Nicolás as principal civilian aide, all documents continued to refer to Franco as Head of State—if not by the choice of his peers, then as he later engraved it on Spanish coins, *por la gracia de Dios* (by the grace of God).

The establishment of military authority was everywhere accompanied by the massive exercise of terror. In Andalusia, General Queipo de Llano carved out a semi-independent

---

[1] Alfredo Kindelán, *Mis cuadernos de guerra* (Madrid, 1945), pp. 47–59. Kindelán was a monarchist general who had developed the Spanish Air Force under Alfonso XIII and who headed the Nationalist Air Force during the Civil War. Regarding the manner in which Franco took upon himself the title "Head of the State," my source is Joaquín Satrustegui, Speech at the Hotel Menfis, Jan. 29, 1959. Satrustegui is a prominent leader in the monarchist opposition, and the speech has circulated widely in mimeographed form.

principality of his own, in the manner of the Cid or the Italian *condottiere*. With canny business instinct, he assured absolute continuity in the export of sherry, olives, and citrus fruits, thereby earning the admiration of the English business community and maintaining the flow of foreign exchange to the Insurgent treasury. He established connections with Lisbon for overland commerce and came to rapid understandings for the import of Fiat motors and German chemicals. Loyal followers received the necessary import licenses, and everyone remembered to be generous with the chief. He smilingly advised the workers, over whom he exercised an undeniable personal fascination, to put on the *salvavida,* as he dubbed it —that is, the blue shirt of the Falange.

On July 23 he announced the death penalty for strikes. On the 25th he requisitioned nine-tenths of the available automobiles of Seville in a simple, expeditious manner by means of the following order: "I address myself exclusively to the taxidrivers of Seville to inform them that this afternoon, at 5 o'clock sharp, they shall be in the Paseo de la Palmera, with full equipment, in order to make an exact accounting . . . . After the accounting we shall proceed to release the president of the taxi syndicate, and the vice-president as well, who at present are both under arrest." Meanwhile on the 24th he had decreed the death penalty for *marxistas* in any town where crimes occurred. On the 28th came the death penalty for hidden arms, and on August 19, for the export of capital.

In the city the Moors tore up shrubs in the park to cook their rations, and everyone, Moors included, wore religious medallions as a sign of conformity with the new order. Methodically, night by night, all persons of Republican or Left connections were rounded up. There being no room in the prison, overflow prisoners stood for several days under guard in the courtyard of a Jesuit school. It was more dangerous to be a Mason than a Socialist. The death lists were read off between 1 and 3 a.m. and the executions took place on the edges of the city, but within full hearing of everyone on the hot summer nights. Parallel to a more or less orderly purge of political and professional persons by list was a less formal repression of the workers, most of whom had belonged to CNT, UGT, or Communist unions. The immediate head of the repression was Colonel Díaz Criado, by all testimonies an alcoholic and a sadist. Girls could sometimes save the lives of their brothers or sweethearts by sleeping with the colonel or his assistants, and Colonel Díaz had worthy compeers in other Andalusian cities: "Don Bruno," the Civil Guard colonel in Córdoba; and in Granada the Captain Rojas of the Casas Viejas affair.

In the towns surrounding Seville the Popular Front authorities had responded to Queipo's seizure of the city by arresting priests and landlords. In some such cases the entire town council was shot, although the released prisoners had testified to the incoming soldiers that they had not been mistreated. Officers, troubled by having priests intercede for the lives of "reds," would order the town leaders shot before anyone had time to reach them with a plea. Throughout the campaign in Andalusia and Extremadura, the Insurgents faced the problem of their small numbers in a hostile countryside. The reasoning concerning a thinly held front shaded over into legalistic arguments that the militia were guerrillas not entitled to be treated according to the laws of war, and these arguments in turn justified summary executions of the type carried out in Eastern Europe and Russia by the Germans in the Second World War.

Meanwhile, Queipo de Llano's picture appeared in all public buildings and the general began the series of astounding radio addresses that were to make him world-famous. After commenting on the war news, he would chatter amiably about life in Seville, invite the lily-livered "reds" to send their women to Andalusia, where men were men, and boast in salacious, and doubtless imaginative, detail about the sexual exploits of the Moors. In the Nationalist zone he was regarded as a "card," a bluff, hearty soldier with perhaps a trace too much of the barracks in his vocabulary. In the Republican zone he was regarded as the epitome of militarist and fascist degeneracy.[2]

[2] Concerning Seville, I depended largely on Antonio Bahamonde,

In Castile the authorities were more discreet than in Andalusia, and the general population more docile; but a similar system of terror prevailed. In the villages the military established committees consisting normally of the priest, the Civil Guard(s), and a leading landlord. Condemnation of a suspect by all three meant death; in cases of disagreement, a lesser penalty; and, if given a clean bill of health, the Republican or Socialist could show his gratitude by making a large financial contribution, by enlisting, or by persuading his sons to enlist in the Nationalist Army. Castile had ruled a world empire during three centuries; its traditions of bureaucracy, hierarchy, and obedience were highly developed. In the large towns the judges presided over mass court-martials in which the main charges were Marxism and complicity with the Popular Front government. In most cases no specific crimes or acts of violence were alleged. Confiscation of property was virtually automatic from the moment of arrest.

Most convictions carried prison sentences, but night after night, squads of Falange and Civil Guards visited the jails, called out by list ten, fifteen, perhaps twenty prisoners, put them in trucks, drove to the outskirts of town, and shot them, leaving the bodies on the highway so as to be seen by everyone traveling to and from work the following day. Sanitary services placed notices in the press calling for the aid of all doctors and pharmacists to help bury the corpses, and reminding the public not to place the graves near wells. General Mola addressed a peremptory telegram to the authorities at Valladolid, ordering them to choose less conspicuous spots for the executions and to bury the dead more rapidly. Problems of identification were practically insoluble and in many cases, families feared to come forward to identify their own dead. A particular Falange signature on their killings was a pistol

---

Memoirs of a Spanish Nationalist (London, 1939); Julio de Ramón-Laca, *Como fué governada Andalucía* (Seville, 1939); and portions of Arthur Koestler, *Spanish Testament* (London, 1937). Bahamonde had served on Queipo's publicity staff, and was writing as a refugee. Ramón-Laca's book is a semi-official account by an ardent admirer of the general.

shot between the eyes. Long-trusted doctors found their patients' families unwilling to open the door, fearing that he had come in the service of the police.

In the city of Salamanca, Miguel de Unamuno, the rector of Spain's most famous university, had welcomed the military rising which would end the disorder and the regional fragmentation of the nation. Soon friends began arriving from Granada with news of the assassination of the poet García Lorca and of several university professors; others told of how they had fled their Andalusian villages in which the revolutionaries had killed four or five persons, only to learn in horror of the tenfold reprisals taken by the Army of Africa. Bodies were appearing in Salamanca ditches, though not nearly in such numbers as at Zamora and Valladolid.

On October 12—the Día de la Raza, honoring Columbus' unique discovery and the worldwide expansion of Hispanic civilization which followed from it—there was a ceremony at the university. On the platform sat the university officials, the Bishop of Salamanca, and Señora Carmen Polo de Franco, wife of the recently appointed Generalissimo. At this ceremony General Millán Astray, first commander of the Foreign Legion, and a man who had lost an eye and an arm in Morocco, was the speaker. While he glorified the role of Castile and its conquering armies, his followers in the back of the hall punctuated his phrases with the Legion slogan *Viva la Muerte* (Long Live Death). Unamuno, the chairman, could not contain himself. Referring scornfully to the phrase "Long Live Death," he turned to the general and told him in his best didactic manner that the military movement needed not only to conquer (vencer), but to convince (convencer). He did not think they were fitted for the latter task. Only the intervention of Señora Franco prevented the enraged Millán Astray, now shouting *Muera la Inteligencia,* from striking Unamuno.[3] The next day, when Unamuno entered the casino for his morning coffee, he was informed of his expulsion, and he was shortly removed as rector of the university. Sitting

[3] My knowledge of Unamuno's attitude comes principally from friends of his still living in Salamanca, supplemented by the article of Luis Portilo in *Golden Horizon* (London), 1953.

at his favorite café in the middle of town, he continued for some days to shout his defiance of the barbarians, but his friends no longer dared sit with him. He retired to his home, to die of chagrin in December.

The case of Unamuno was doubly tragic. He was an intellectual liberal who had always protested incursions on individual rights. But in various literary contexts he had also glorified the austerity, the militance, the authoritarianism of historic Castile. Hating the relatively mild dictatorship of Primo de Rivera because of its censorship and its lack of dignity, he had befriended the Left, and in the first year or two of the Republic he had frequently spoken in the Casa del Pueblo. But by the time of the election of November, 1933, he was already saying that only fascism could save Spain.[4] Beneath varying forms of rhetoric, he was a man who believed in elites, in heroes, and who scorned parliaments with their muddy compromises, their "deals." The greatest prose writer, and one of the greatest poets of modern Spain, he had inadvertently fostered the type of impatience, scornful rhetoric, and rolled-up-shirt-sleeves attitude which was characteristic of the young Falangists. In his Cortes interventions, and in his public speeches, he often lacked the moderation and spirit of compromise which is absolutely essential to democratic politics. At the end of his life the grand old man was the victim of the vicious antiintellectualism which he had not immediately recognized as part of the warp and woof of the Insurgent movement.

In strongly Republican Galicia the blood purge began more slowly than in the neighboring provinces. Partial strikes, and hesitant negotiations between Republican officials and military men, continued for several weeks. Carlism was practically nonexistent, and the Falange had numbered less than 1,000 in the spring. The first paseos did not take place until August 5, and not until mid-September were large numbers taken from the prisons. In the beginning, wives were able partially to frustrate the executioners by mounting a 24-hour

[4] Reported by Anita Brenner, the *New York Times Magazine,* October 8, 1933. The general interpretation of his political conduct is my own, based on the Cortes *Diario* for 1931–1933.

vigil at the prisons. A particular feature of the Galician purge was the ferocity in regard to teachers and doctors. Everywhere in Spain these professions were thought of as being leftish, whereas lawyers and professors of humanities were generally thought of as conservative. Galicia was the most Republican of the provinces initially controlled by the Insurgents, and this perhaps explains the particular persecution of those professionals considered by definition to be "reds." In the cities the families of victims did not dare wear mourning. In certain villages practically all the men had been killed or had fled to the mountains, and Galician draftees throughout the war saw villages in which practically every family was in mourning.[5]

In Navarre the triumph of the rising released the long-repressed enthusiasm of the Carlists. Carlism had been defeated three times in the nineteenth century, and in the twentieth century it had appeared to be merely a historic curiosity. On July 18 the Carlists descended from their villages to begin the *Reconquista* of Spain in the name of a traditional, Catholic monarchy. At the same time, both the Carlist chiefs and General Mola were aware of the strength of the Basque Nationalists in many a Navarrese town. Mola told the assembled mayors of Navarre that he would not hesitate to shoot anyone caught sheltering "reds" for any reason whatever. The press in Vitoria reminded its readers that hostages sitting in the provincial jail would have to pay with their lives for any sentimental foolishness toward the enemy.

Carlist fervor, and hatred of the Basque Nationalists, stamped a particular character on the purge in Navarre. When Colonel Beorlegui approached the town of Beasaín, he was maddened by the fact that the sole resistance came, of

[5] My principal printed sources on Castile and Galicia were, respectively, Antonio Ruiz Vilaplana, *Burgos Justice* (New York, 1938), and *Lo que han hecho en Galicia* (Paris, 1938), both works cited previously for ch. 13. In the matter of the purges in Seville, Salamanca, Valladolid, and Galicia, however, my reading notes were less important than the oral testimony of some fifteen persons who had lived through the first months of the Civil War in those provinces.

all groups, from the fourteen Civil Guards. He had them all shot for "rebellion," and then rounded up several dozen "suspicious" characters. Night by night, a few of these disappeared, and the local priest, embarrassed but helpless, would say to their families, as one says to children, that the departed had gone on a long journey.

Religion played a conspicuous role in the purge of the Carlist country. The 15th of August was annually celebrated in Pamplona as the festival of the Virgen del Sagrario. In the late afternoon a parade, whose marchers carried the images and relics of the Virgen, began to wind its way through the streets of the city to the Cathedral. At about the same time, two firing squads, one composed of Falangists and one of Requetés, took a group of 50 to 60 political prisoners from the city jail. Most of the captives were Catholic, and several priests were brought along. The victims were handcuffed and hobbled, but not tied together in a single chain, and thus had relative privacy for their confessions. The squads waited impatiently for the unusually long confessions to be made. As the first victims were shot, a hysterical panic seized the remainder. Men began running, only to be shot down like animals. With darkness falling, the Falange and Requetés quarreled violently, the former shouting that the "reds" didn't deserve a chance to confess, the latter insisting on the opportunity of practicing Christians to make their peace with God. To settle matters the priests gave mass absolution to the remainder, the executions were finished, and the trucks regained Pamplona in time for the Requetés to join the procession entering the Cathedral.[6]

An equally macabre persecution took place on the island of Majorca, under the auspices of an Italian fascist functionary calling himself Count Rossi. The arrangements for Mus-

[6] Iturralde, *El catolicismo y la cruzada de Franco,* vol. ii, part i, ch. 8; and Marino Ayerra Redín, *No me avergoncé del Evangelio* (Buenos Aires, 1959). This work, by the former parish priest of Alsásua, first appeared in 1956 under the title *Desde mi parroquia.* Also Inaki de Aberrigoyen, *7 mois and 7 jours dans l'Espagne de Franco* (Paris, 1938), pp. 120–26, the diary of a Basque Nationalist priest.

solini's aid, which had caused the last-minute misgivings of General Goded, included wartime Italian control of the Balearics. Rossi arrived by air a few days after the rising and removed from office the military governor left behind by Goded. He drove his own racing car, wore a black shirt decorated with a white cross, confided to society ladies in Palma that he needed at least one woman a day, and announced the "crusade" in the villages, flanked by the mayor and the priest. Neither Catalan nationalism nor anarchism was strong in Majorca, but as in Extremadura, it was necessary on at least one occasion to burn the large pile of bodies remaining from one night's work.

In August the Catalans tried to reconquer Majorca, and for six weeks they held a small bridgehead near Porto Cristo. During this period, they had obliged a group of nuns who ran a private school in the town to use their building as a hospital and to act as nurses. After the Catalans had reembarked, the Palma newspapers carried a long interview with the voluble matron. She recalled humorously a South American giant who had appeared, brandishing a revolver, and saying: "Sisters, I am a Catholic and a Communist and I'll blow the brains of the first man who treats you disrespectfully." For two days he had made himself useful making beds, preparing bandages, and getting food supplies, during which time he carried on a running theological argument with the matron. When the Nationalist troops arrived, they killed all the wounded, and lastly, the South American. The French Catholic novelist, Georges Bernanos, a long-time resident of Majorca, discussed the article with its author, who then published a further note in which he stated: "Certain generous souls believe it their duty to be revolted by the necessities of the holy war. But whoever makes war must conform to its laws."[7]

However, the virulence of the purge in Insurgent Spain is not to be explained by the laws of war, even when those "laws" deliberately omit the humane treatment of wounded

[7] Georges Bernanos, *Les grands cimetières sous la lune* (Paris, 1938), pp. 138–40, for the Porto Cristo incident; *passim* for other details of the Majorcan repression.

and prisoners. The Spanish Insurgents were fighting to preserve traditional privileges of the Army, the Church, and the landlords—groups which had been mortally frightened by the five years of Republican rule. After the revolution in the Asturias, their desire for a repression that would wipe out once and for all the liberal, Marxist, and anarchist Left had been frustrated. The military rising of July 18 appeared to be their last chance to preserve a Spain in which their privileges would be secure. No category of human beings are more cruel than a threatened ruling class, which feels itself on historical, economic, and cultural grounds to be a natural "elite," and which finds itself challenged by an inchoate mass which will no longer recognize its privileges. The war was not only a civil war, but a colonial war. The Insurgent leaders felt as did the European ruling minority in Algeria before 1962, and as do the white rulers of South Africa. The Popular Front zone was the rebellious colonial area to be reduced.

The executions in Nationalist Spain were not the work of revolutionary mobs taking advantage of the breakdown of the Republican state. They were ordered and approved by the highest military authorities. In certain provinces, such as Segovia, relatively few persons were shot, and this fact was attributable in part to the lack of resistance to the rising, in part to the decency of the local commanding officer. In Alsásua the parish priest, a social Catholic appointed there precisely for his known sympathy with the working class, went to General Solchaga in an effort to improve conditions for the condemned men in the local prison. After pretending that he did not know what the priest was talking about, the general ended the interview with the point-blank statement that no one in this prison was being shot, absolutely no one.[8] Such men as this, not Falangist and Requeté teen-agers, were responsible for the vast killing behind the Nationalist lines. In early November the failure to take Madrid roused the military authorities to a fury, and at this time many Republican officers who had been under arrest since July were shot.

In all areas there were a large number of persons for

[8] Ayerra Redín, pp. 89–90. See appendix D for an effort to evaluate the total deaths from all causes in the Civil War.

whom the shootings were an emotionally satisfying spectacle. Requetés in Pamplona joked about the aristocratic women who rose at dawn to be present at an execution. On September 25, 1936, the civil governor of Valladolid published a letter in *El Norte de Castilla*. Referring to the sad necessity for the organs of military justice to carry out death penalties, and granting that the executions were legally open to the public, he nevertheless reminded his readers that their presence at such acts "says very little in their favor and the considering as a spectacle the mortal torment of a fellow human being, however justified, gives a poor impression of the culture of a people." In this letter, and in press notices appearing in Galicia in October, officials deplored particularly the presence of young women and small children.

The situation of the Church in the Insurgent zone was entirely different from that in the Popular Front zone. There was nothing specifically religious in the first public pronouncements of the military authorities. However, the slogans of hierarchy and tradition indicated that the Church would hold a strong position in the new regime, and the generals assumed the Church's cooperation. The Bishop of Salamanca was embarrassed to have General Franco requisition his palace as headquarters, not because he did not sympathize with the rising, but because the Church had to consider how immeasurably worse its situation would be all over Spain if the Insurgents were to be defeated.

On the whole, the Church cooperated willingly. The bishops and archbishops appeared in the company of the military officials at all manner of public ceremonies. They blessed the troops and provided confessors for the prisons. Occasional parish priests pleaded for the lives of particular individuals under sentence of death, but none questioned the principle and the general extent of the purge itself. Village priests were expected to serve on the local purge committees, and they were neither more cruel nor more generous than their fellow members in voting penalties.

When in early November the people of a Navarrese town lynched 50 political prisoners, Bishop Olaechea of Pamplona, speaking to a local branch of Acción Católica pleaded with his hearers: shed no more blood than that decreed by the tribunals.[9] It is difficult also to picture Cardinal Ilundáin of Seville truly approving the regime of Queipo de Llano. But the Bishop and the Cardinal, and their peers throughout the Nationalist zone, ratified all the public acts of the Insurgent regime by their presence and never voiced open criticism.

For sensitive Catholics, the fate of the Church was almost worse in the Insurgent zone than in the Popular Front zone. In Madrid and Barcelona, Catholics lived through an experience like that of the catacombs. But sacrifice, and even martyrdom, had spiritual compensations. In the Insurgent zone power and prestige were on the side of the Church. When a woman of the Salamanca aristocracy decided to work in the Falange children's dining rooms, in order to feel that she was doing something humanly rewarding, Cardinal Gomá asked her smilingly why she associated with the *canalla*. In some parishes lifelong Catholics ceased going to mass because they could not stand the weekly fulminations from the pulpit against the "reds." Georges Bernanos, realizing that the Archbishop of Palma knew everything that he, Bernanos, knew, about the regime of "Count" Rossi, wrote vitriolically of "the personage whom convention obliges me to name the Archbishop of Majorca."

Certain elements were common to the terror in both zones. Both anarchists and professional officers could "kill without hate," convinced that their enemies were not human in the same sense as themselves, ready also to sacrifice freely their own lives and often those of their families. Among less exalted participants, envy was a powerful motive. Many people had sensed the approach of the Civil War, not because of an insoluble economic or political crisis, but because of the palpable hatred with which class-conscious workers regarded well-dressed women, or peasants the town notary. Revolutionary and Insurgent purge committees, if at all scrupulous in their operations, were constantly discovering the wildest

[9] *Ibid.,* pp. 138–39.

accusations based on pure spite. Among the business and professional middle class, some of the most financially successful were prominent Republicans. Just because they were intelligent, self-made men, they wished to create a society more open to change and more equal in opportunity of all kinds. Many of the leading purgers in the Insurgent zone were the less successful, the envious second-raters who would destroy a competitor by purging a "red."

Juvenile delinquency flourished in both zones in the conditions of the purge. What could be more intoxicating than to drive requisitioned cars, use firearms, see mortal terror in the eyes of a well-dressed victim, and kill without any sense of personal responsibility, in the name of a "surgical operation" to cleanse society of a "gangrenous member"? In the Insurgent zone the more conservative supporters of the rising referred to the Falange as the "FAIlange" and as "our reds." Among the newly enrolled Falangists there were indeed a considerable number of anarchists and Communists who had "changed shirts." In the Popular Front zone left-wing terrorist squads were easily infiltrated by the Falange.[10] Some of the chauffeurs of paseo squads in the Levant turned out to be Falangists, and a number of Republican and Socialist personalities were assassinated in the Popular Front zone by Falangists.

Some of the vocabulary of the paseo, particularly in the Insurgent zone where it was officially conducted, indicates a fanaticism bordering on insanity. Occasional theologians offered doctrinal justifications of the paseo. The magazine *Mundo Hispánico* spoke of purging the rear areas "a cristazo limpio," with a blow of the crucifix, as fanatical priests had sometimes finished off the Liberal wounded during the Carlist wars. The purge must also eradicate the *semilla,* the seeds of Marxism, laicism, and so forth. It was sarcastically referred to as the *reforma agraria* whereby the *rojoseparatistas,* the red separatists, received finally their piece of earth. The Greek tragedian Euripides would have seen armed bands like those

[10] See the anonymous article in *Living Age,* October, 1936, by a young Englishman who had spent a few adventurous months in Valencia with right-wing terrorists cruising the streets in CNT and UGT cars.

in his *Bacchae* ravaging Spain in the summer and fall of 1936; self-intoxicated fanatics murdering their presumed enemies with the illusion that they were performing a cleansing operation of religious purity. Without a doubt, these execution squads contributed greatly toward establishing the unquestioned authority of the Insurgent leaders over a largely hostile population.

18

THE ASSAULT ON MADRID

THE rapid advance of the Army of Africa and the continuing disorganization of the Popular Front zone permitted the Insurgents, in September and October, to hope for a quick victory based on the early capture of the national capital. Using their limited, but unopposed, Air Force, they bombed Málaga and other Republican harbors, thereby destroying much of the equipment and dock facilities of the Republican Navy. On September 29 the *Canarias* and the *Almirante Cervera* sank one Republican destroyer and forced a second to take refuge at Casablanca. From that time on, the Insurgents held uncontested control of the waters of southern Spain. During late August and September, Majorca also became, with Italian equipment and under Italian control, a major air and naval base.

Meanwhile, the Burgos junta gathered supplies for the march to Madrid. Some 50 German planes arrived during August, and two freighters, the *Kamerun* and the *Wigbert,* unloaded military equipment of all types in Lisbon, the overland transport of which was facilitated personally by Prime Minister Salazar.[1] Heinkel fighters were reported by Republican pilots as of September 5. In late September Italy turned over two small submarines to the Insurgent Navy and landed in southern ports its first armored cars, artillery and antiaircraft units.[2] During early October the Junker and Caproni

[1] *Documents on German Foreign Policy, 1918–1945,* Series D, Vol. III, Germany and the Spanish Civil War (Washington, 1950), 53. Referred to as *DGFP* in future notes.

[2] *Foreign Policy Reports* (published by the Foreign Policy Association, New York) issue of Dec. 1, 1936 and "Hispanicus", *Foreign Intervention in Spain,* vol. I (London, 1937), pp. 200ff. and *passim* for the arrival of German and Italian supplies. The Foreign Policy Report is based largely on The *New York Times,* and the "His-

bombers began frequent raids on airports and supply points along the road to Madrid.[3]

In the Popular Front zone it was imperative to install a government enjoying much wider popular support than that of Professor Giral and to make an army out of the miscellaneous militias. Francisco Largo Caballero was the one figure who might conceivably unite the many factions of the Left. He was the idolized leader of both the UGT workers and the younger intellectuals of the Socialist party. The Communists were worried about his "infantile leftism," but they were also building him up as the "Spanish Lenin." The anarchists were still overwhelmingly opposed to participation in the government, but Largo was the one leader of national stature with whom they would be likely to cooperate. Left Republicans had shared prison cells with him in 1917 and 1930 and had known him as a colleague in the Azaña cabinet. Largo Caballero would have liked to form an all-labor government, based on the UGT and the CNT. But the latter were not yet willing to enter the government; he could not ignore the moderate wing of his own party without splitting it irrevocably; and above all, the Republic would have lost all hope of support from the democratic powers if a "proletarian" government were named.

The first Caballero government, formed on September 4, included 6 Socialists, 4 Republicans, 2 Communists, and 1 representative each of the Catalan Republicans and the Basque Nationalists. The principal moderate Socialists, Prieto and Negrín, were present along with the followers of Largo Caballero. The cabinet was thus distinctly more representative of the fighting forces than had been the Giral ministry. But during

---

panicus" volume consists largely of excerpts from the leading British newspapers. It is interesting to note that all the Axis aid which has been confirmed by the publication of the *DGFP* and the Ciano Diaries was reported at the time by the English language press.

[3] Oloff de Wet, *Cardboard Crucifix* (London, 1938), *passim*. The author was a mercenary piloting the old French Potez machines for the Republicans in September and October, 1936. His book contains many interesting details on the performance of both Insurgent and Republican planes during those months.

his first two months in office, Caballero succeeded no better than had Giral in his efforts to solve the immense problems of organization and supply. The city of Madrid, and its military front, were controlled by the party militias. Since the authority of the government was an unknown quantity, each group hoarded arms with which to protect itself against a possible *putsch.* The fusion of the Socialist and Communist Youth in April, and the comradeship of shared battles in the Sierra, helped to produce a spirit of unity on the Left. But the JSU was an organization only of students and the more alert and politically conscious younger workers.

The powerful bureaucracy of the UGT, and the combative CNT chiefs, could not in a few months forget the bitter rivalry of years, and both scorned the Communists as virtual new-comers to the labor movement. Caballero found that old friends in the building-trades unions refused to urge their members to build trenches after working hours. Militiamen stationed within reach of Madrid considered that the weekend at home was one of a soldier's rights. UGT units were accused of hoarding arms seized at the fall of the Montaña barracks, and anarchists hid the few high-quality French and Czech machine guns which their comrades had appropriated at the Catalan frontier.[4]

Largo himself had been a strong partisan of the militia sys-tem. All Spanish labor leaders looked upon the professional Army as the natural enemy of the masses, and indeed, one of the factors which greatly retarded the preparation of Madrid's defense was the government's reluctance to use the services of many officers who had declared themselves loyal. During September the Prime Minister became convinced of the in-sufficiency of the militia system. He had greatly admired the role of Colonel José Asensio Torrado in the Sierra battles and now appointed him to command the central front. In October he issued a series of decrees looking to the disbandment of the militia and the formation of "mixed brigades." The new units would include the former party militiamen, soldiers who had been doing their military service on July 18, and new recruits.

[4] Louis Fischer, *Men and Politics* (New York, 1941), pp. 372–77. Martín Blázquez, *I Helped Build an Army,* pp. 214–15.

They would be trained by professional officers, and later led by a combination of these professionals and the more able leaders who had emerged in the first skirmishes on the Madrid front.

The most important party unit at this time was the famous Fifth Regiment, organized and led by the Communist Party, but incorporating many nonpolitical youth, who were attracted by its superior spirit, and not a few anarchists, who had recognized the weakness of their own undisciplined units. The Fifth Regiment practiced military discipline. It had chosen its name because Madrid, before the war, had theoretically possessed four regiments, and the Communists now founded the "fifth" as their contribution to the capital's defense. It was the largest and most efficient component at the Madrid front. In mid-October it offered to disband in favor of the newly announced mixed brigade system, and Largo Caballero found himself in the strange position of receiving better cooperation from the Communists than from the Left Socialists and the anarchists upon whose loyalty he had hoped to base his power. But almost no progress was made in the reorganization of the militia before the Insurgent armies reached Madrid.

The Prime Minister's personal limitations hindered the improvement of conditions in the Popular Front zone. The most able executive in the Socialist Party was clearly Prieto, but Caballero's long-standing jealousy and distrust were such that he assigned Prieto to the virtually nonexistent Navy and Air Force and insisted on combining the Ministry of War with the Prime Ministership in his own person. All the leaders knew that the paseos were rapidly discrediting the Republic both at home and abroad, but Caballero could apparently find no one better than the very mediocre Angel Galarza to serve as Minister of the Interior. A few of the worst gangs claimed to be Caballero adherents, and he was unable or unwilling effectively to disavow their crimes. Intellectuals and professional men who had declared their loyalty to the Republic on July 18 were still departing for France or taking refuge in the embassies.

During these same months the revolutionary tide began to ebb in Catalonia. In August the anarchists had forced the

Unified Socialist-Communist Party of Catalonia (PSUC) not to enter the Generalitat cabinet, and in early September they had refused Largo Caballero's invitation. But accumulating food and supply problems, and the experience of administering villages, frontier posts, and public utilities, had rapidly shown the anarchists the unsuspected complexity of modern society. Their naïveté left them sufficiently flexible to change their minds, and on September 26 a new government took office, with the Esquerra and the anarchists holding three seats each. The commissioner of public safety belonged to the Esquerra, and *La Vanguardia,* organ of the Generalitat, now called for a campaign against informers and terrorists. The commissioner of public services, Juan Comorera, of the PSUC, immediately took steps to end barter and requisitioning, and became the defender of the peasants against the revolution. The commissioner of justice was the POUM leader Andrés Nin, who early in September had announced that the dictatorship of the proletariat *existed* in Barcelona. On the 27th the anarchist organ *Solidaridad Obrera* justified the end of "dual powers" in Catalonia, and the POUM organ, *La Batalla,* spoke of a necessary transitional period of cooperation with the liberal *bourgeoisie.*

These beginnings of change in the internal political picture were, however, overshadowed by the international situation. On August 8 France had closed the border to the passage of military supplies, hoping by that gesture to speed acceptance of the nonintervention scheme by the powers friendly to the Insurgents. By August 24, Germany and Italy had accepted the notion "in principle." On September 9 the Non-Intervention Committee held its first meeting. England, France, Russia, Germany, and Italy were represented, but Portugal had not yet named a delegate. The Spanish government was immediately ready to present evidence of Italian, German, and Portuguese intervention. However, neither the Madrid government nor the Burgos junta had been invited to join the Committee, and one of the first procedural rules adopted was a requirement that allegations could be heard only if presented to the Committee by a member thereof. In the course of several further meetings during September, it was decided that all discussions were to be considered confidential until a mutually agreed upon communiqué was published, that all charges must be submitted in writing to the accused governments, and that their answers in writing should be awaited before further discussion ensued.

Meanwhile, the Republican government turned in desperation to the League of Nations, whose General Assembly was to open on September 21 in Geneva. However, the League refused to place the Spanish affair on its agenda at this late date. The Spanish Foreign Minister, Alvarez del Vayo, addressed the Assembly on September 25, but in the light of the pro-Insurgent sympathies of the Assembly chairman, Carlos Saavedra Lamas of Argentina, he was careful not to make specific charges against the three intervening powers. On September 30, Spain published its evidence of the presence of Italian and German planes in the Insurgent zone, and of the unloading of German war materials in Lisbon during August.

In London a Portuguese delegate had at last arrived on September 28, and the Committee had chosen as its permanent chairman the British Conservative Lord Plymouth. The Committee took umbrage at the action of the Spanish government in appealing to the League instead of awaiting the orderly, confidential procedure which it was elaborating. During October it undertook to examine the Spanish charges. Most of the evidence referred to incidents prior to August 28, the date on which the fascist powers had committed themselves, albeit with reservations that deprived their notes of any binding force, not to send war supplies to Spain. The pre-August 28 data was therefore regarded as beyond the Committee's competence. The rest of the evidence was considered insubstantial, since it was based principally on newspaper reports. In addition, the three fascist powers declared that the charges were without foundation, so that acceptance of the evidence would have involved branding the accused governments liars.[5]

The Soviet Union had supported the Republican position

[5] Toynbee, *Survey,* 1937, II, 246–52 for the first Non-Intervention Committee meetings. In this and subsequent chapters my main sources on the Committee are the *Survey;* P. A. M. Van der Esch,

both in Geneva and in London. While agreeing to join the Non-Intervention Committee, it had never hidden its belief that its rules and procedures were simply intended as a screen for fascist intervention and that the proper policy would be the open support of the legitimate government faced with military rebellion. Until October, it shipped only food and medical supplies. But on October 7, and twice thereafter in the same month, Soviet statesmen warned that the Soviet Union would consider itself no more bound by the Non-Intervention Agreement than were the other signatory governments. In the course of the month, some dozen Soviet vessels carried to Spain approximately 400 trucks, 50 planes, 100 tanks, and 400 flyers and tank drivers.[6]

The narrow passage through the Dardanelles and the long voyage across Italy's *Mare Nostrum* made it impossible to conceal the Soviet traffic. Espionage and newspaper reports came before the London Committee by mid-October. It was instructive to observe how much more convincing the members found these reports than they had the similarly derived evidence in the Spanish government charges of September

---

Prelude to War (The Hague, 1951); and the following articles: N. J. Padelford, "The International Non-Intervention Agreement and the Spanish Civil War," *American Journal of International Law,* October, 1937; and N. J. Padelford and H. G. Seymour, "Some International Problems of the Spanish Civil War," *The Political Science Quarterly,* September, 1937.

[6] My figures are those of R. G. Colodny, *The Struggle for Madrid,* p. 161, based in turn upon The *New York Times* reports of Russian arms arrivals at Spanish ports. In Madrid in 1960 I had two fairly detailed conversations concerning both Russian and Italo-German intervention with officers at the *Archivo Militar.* They insisted forcibly that all foreign estimates were incorrect, that Russian intervention had been much greater than pictured, and Italo-German much smaller. They said that much material in their archive would bear out their statements. However, I was not able in the course of ten months to get permission to see those materials, and since my interlocutors did not specifically contradict the sources on which I have based my work I feel reasonably confident of the estimates I offer.

30. Lord Plymouth and the British Foreign Minister, Anthony Eden, spoke of a country more guilty than Germany or Italy. As for Portugal, the Committee exonerated her on October 28, several days after it had solemnly found evidence of one Italian and three Soviet violations.

The unequal treatment of the evidence did not surprise anyone. By late October, Italy, Germany, Portugal, and Russia had all openly flouted the accords. The fascist powers knew that England shared their sympathies, inasmuch as a German diplomat in Spain reported on October 16 that the British at Gibraltar were supplying ammunition to the Insurgents, and information on Soviet shipments to him.[7] But neither France nor Russia walked out of the Committee. The former was paralyzed by the fear of offending England. The Soviets still hoped to achieve the policy of collective security, and in any event were determined to avoid a diplomatic break with the Western powers. Thus the Non-Intervention Committee continued to meet, providing a sounding board and a face-saving device for powers all of which, with the exception of France, pursued their national interests as they understood them in relation to the Civil War.

In Popular Front Spain the arrival of the first Soviet arms produced a tremendous moral impression and created a sense of gratitude which temporarily swept away all suspicion of possible ulterior motives. But there was nothing sentimental in Stalin's action. Payment for Russian arms was guaranteed when the Caballero government, in the last week of October, shipped more than half the gold reserve of the Bank of Spain in four unescorted Russian freighters from Cartagena to Odessa.

The Premier and his Finance Minister, Juan Negrín, had several motives for this act. By mid-September the government was assuming the likelihood that it would lose the city of Madrid. The international financial community had backed the Insurgents. The Republic had no financial power except its gold reserve, and no allies except Mexico and the Soviet Union. It might have been possible to deposit this treasure (at

[7] David T. Cattell, *Soviet Diplomacy and the Spanish Civil War* (Berkeley, 1957), p. 46.

$35 per ounce the shipment was worth $578,000,000) in French or Swiss banks, but that would include the risk that at any moment the officials of those banks might recognize the Franco government, or at the very least, impound the Spanish gold until the end of the war. Stalin's insistence on guaranteed payment thus coincided with the practical situation of the Republic. Neither President Azaña nor the cabinet majority were happy to send the Spanish gold to Russia. Their feelings at the time were spared by the fact that officially they had only authorized the Prime Minister to do whatever he felt necessary to protect government control of the gold. The responsibility for the specific decision belonged to Caballero and Negrín.[8]

In September Largo had rejected the suggestion of the Italian republican Randolfo Pacciardi to form a brigade of Italian anti-fascists. At that time the Prime Minister had opposed the use of foreign troops, but by mid-October the government was desperate and willing to use any trained men it could find.

The second half of October witnessed feverish activity on both sides. Some 8,000 to 10,000 foreign volunteers had crossed the French border since July 19. On October 17 Caballero established a training base for them at Albacete under the administration of Martínez Barrio. The Italian Communist chief Togliatti (known by the name Ercoli in

[8] There have been many discussions of the gold transfer. I believe the most enlightening was that between Luis Araquistáin and Indalecio Prieto. It began with an article by Araquistáin in *Cuadernos del Congreso por la Libertad de la Cultura,* March, 1958. Prieto commented thereon in *El Socialista* of November 13, 1958; Araquistáin replied in the same paper on November 27; and Prieto commented once more on December 18. I have adopted the essential of Araquistáin's view that Azaña and Prieto could not possibly have been entirely unaware of the plans of Caballero and Negrín. On the other hand, I accept Prieto's statement that the Republic could not, as Araquistáin argues, have just as well deposited the gold in Switzerland. Given the attitude of the various governments and financial groups in October, 1936, the Republican government could not have counted on any foreign powers except Mexico and Russia, assuming the gold were to leave Spain at all.

Spain) and the French Communist André Marty were the effective organizational heads of the new International Brigades. During the last ten days of the month, several dozen high-ranking Russian staff officers arrived to help organize the defense of the capital. On the 24th the first Russian tanks had seen action near Aranjuez, and on the 29th they took part in a briefly successful counterattack along the Insurgent flanks at Illescas. As always, the Russians had a mania for secrecy, from their allies as well as their enemies. No one was to know the precise identity of the Russian officers, and when two anti-Nazi Germans gleefully took photos of the Soviet tanks at Aranjuez, the Russian crews not only confiscated the film but later tried unsuccessfully to have the two men expelled from Spain through the good offices of the GPU.[9]

The columns racing toward Madrid from the southwest met stiffening resistance. The militia made all the mistakes they had made in Andalusia, but while they had ammunition, and buildings to defend, they fought to the death. Behind them,

[9] Louis Fischer, *Men and Politics,* p. 383, for the photography incident. The fascinating question of identities is discussed by Fischer, by Walter G. Krivitsky, *In Stalin's Secret Service* (New York, 1939) and several others. The conflicting information is summarized by Colodny, 162–65, concerning the general most commonly known as "Goriev" (possibly General Berzin); and pp. 179–80 for Emil Kleber, who Colodny believes was General Gregory Stern of the Red Army. I had the opportunity to discuss the latter identification with two former Republican officers who had known Kleber intimately. One of them had seen Kleber treated most casually at headquarters and the other had been present when most of the shells fired by Kleber's orders turned out to be duds. Neither believed for a moment that he could have been a Red Army general. It seems well established that Marshals Konev and Malinovsky served in Spain and highly likely that Marshal Zhukov did also. The problem of identification arises not only from the Russian penchant for secrecy, but from the fact that many of the officers who fought in Spain were shot in the purges, and that later promotions or disgraces affect all official biographies. We will probably never have the full truth. The important point is perfectly clear, however, that many top-ranking Russian officers were in Spain during the Civil War, and in the highest advisory capacities.

clogging the roads to Madrid, were thousands of peasant families fleeing from their villages. Food and transportation problems in the capital were aggravated by the arrival of the refugees, who camped in the parks, in the subway stations, and in the confiscated palaces of the wealthy. On October 20 General Franco issued the general order for the capture of the city. At the same time, the government was debating how and when to leave without causing panic. President Azaña departed on October 22, for what was described as a tour of the fronts. The majority felt it would be wiser to leave in relative dignity than to flee at the last moment, but the Prime Minister could not make up his mind. On October 23 the Junkers bombed the city, and on November 1 an army of roughly 25,000 men began arriving in the western and southern suburbs. Italian planes dropped leaflets asking the citizens to help them take the city, "otherwise the National aviation will wipe it off the earth."

In reality the Insurgents had no desire to destroy Madrid. It was the capital of Spain, and they wished to establish their own regime in it as soon as possible. But neither did they wish to fight for it. The militiamen had always shown their greatest skill when fighting among buildings. Madrid was located on high ground, and any invasion from the southwest to the northwest would have to fight uphill into the city. Of the approximately 25,000 troops under General Mola's command, roughly 5,000—organized in five "columns" as in the Andalusian-Extremaduran march—constituted the attacking force. The rest were needed to handle supplies and to guard the long flanks facing Republican territory. Mola over-estimated the danger to his flanks, and this fear was probably the most important practical result of the several Russian tank attacks launched by General Asensio as the invaders approached the capital. Acting on German theories of war, Mola attempted to terrorize the city into surrender by indiscriminate bombing. But he did not have an air force comparable to those which flattened English and German cities during the Second World War, and his raids, made by about a dozen planes each day, killed less than 50 persons on each occasion.[10] On November 2 Russian fighter planes appeared for the first time, and on the fifth, they forced the Junker bombers to turn back, so that in fact these first raids reinforced the fighting morale of Madrid.

Earlier in the autumn, General Mola had spoken of his "four columns" which would march to Madrid and of the "fifth column" of his partisans waiting within the city. As the ex-Director General of Security, Mola possessed detailed dossiers on the political, business, and labor personnel of Madrid. Simply from the election returns of February 1936 he knew that 45 per cent of the city had voted for the Right; in addition, a large proportion of those who had voted for the Popular Front would have been disgusted and frightened by the paseos. It must have seemed reasonable to suppose that the majority of the population would welcome the Insurgent Army and that a determined minority would actively help them take the city.

However, thousands of refugees from all classes of the population had filled the capital with tales of the ferocious repression in each town occupied by the advancing troops. General Queipo de Llano had advertised the Moors over the Seville radio, and in Spain, the country of the eight centuries' *Reconquista,* the use of Moorish troops constituted not only a confession of the unpopularity of the rising but a challenge to the deepest emotions of the population. The Portuguese and Jay Allen dispatches concerning Badajoz were also present in all minds.

The generals hoped, through their reputation for terror, to paralyze the will to defend Madrid. They made the same psychological miscalculation as the Germans who had fostered their reputation for *Schrecklichkeit* on the eve of the First World War. Before the German invasion of Belgium no one

[10] Figures vary very widely for the air-raid casualties in October and November. My "less than fifty" is based upon municipal police reports of Madrid which I had occasion to examine for the period October 20–November 20. It is more than likely that the police figures are incomplete. On the other hand the number of planes and the weight of bombs reported would not produce heavy casualties, with the exception of the massive raids of November 17 and 18.

would have characterized Belgian opinion as pro-French. On the contrary, the Flemish majority were pro-German in outlook. But the scorn, the deceit, and the brutality which the Germans thought would overawe the people and then be quickly forgotten, aroused an indomitable will to resist. The same characteristics on the part of the Burgos generals aroused a similar will to resist among the vast majority of the populace of Madrid.

On the southern and western edges of the city, which were largely working-class districts, the people tore up the stone pavements to build barricades, and mounted machine-gun and sniping nests in apartment windows. Workers in the metal trades manufactured hand grenades instead of andirons. The building workers who had refused Largo Caballero's appeal to dig trenches in September, now braved sporadic artillery fire to build a line of fortifications on the western approaches to the city. Working-class wives prepared to carry hot meals to the barricades manned by their husbands and the young men of the JSU. Middle-class women ran soup kitchens for the peasant refugees and first aid stations for the victims of bombing and the sniping done by the "fifth column." Artillery officers placed their few batteries in position to shell the bridges where the Manzanares river flowed close to the western edge of Madrid. Workers trained feverishly under the dozens of loyal professional officers whom they had earlier refused to trust. While the Nationalist army prepared to storm the capital, and hoped that resistance would be minimal, the population prepared to defend it street by street and house by house.[11]

The government, however, did not believe that the city could be held. On November 4, under pressure of the climactic crisis, the anarchists finally consented to join the Madrid cabinet. When the four new CNT ministers attended their first cabinet meeting the next day, they were to hear

[11] Antonio López Fernández, *Defensa de Madrid* (Mexico, 1945), pp. 135ff. This book is an adulatory biography of Miaja by his aide-de-camp. It is highly factual, however, and a good corrective to the overemphasis found in most French and English books on the role of the International Brigades.

the decision to evacuate to Valencia. On the afternoon of the 6th, Largo Caballero placed General José Miaja in full command of the defense of Madrid. General Miaja had enjoyed a normal, and in no way militarily distinguished, career. His unique value at this moment appeared to be his tested Republican loyalty and the absence of qualities that would make him essential to the future operations of the Republican army. He had been promoted in August 1932 in recognition of his loyalty at the time of the Sanjurjo revolt. Martínez Barrio had placed him in charge of the Madrid military district in October 1933 when the prospect of Cortes elections made it important to appoint a moderate, firm, and loyal officer. In the spring of 1936 he was again the division general in Madrid, and during the months of evident conspiracy he had cooperated with the younger staff officers who were loyal to the Republic. The government had sent him to the Córdoba front in late July, and then to Valencia—both of these ungrateful assignments in view of the situation in each area, but assignments which could be given only to an absolutely loyal officer.

When Largo Caballero appointed him on November 6, his first reaction was to conclude that the government wished upon him the privilege of surrendering Madrid, and from that moment there was to be no love lost between the Prime Minister and the General. Rumors of the government's flight brought the city close to panic. But in a matter of hours the psychological situation changed completely. At 7 p.m., after the government had already left the city, General Asensio, now Under-Secretary of War, handed to Generals Miaja and Pozas two envelopes with sealed orders, not to be opened until dawn. The two generals decided to open the orders immediately, whereupon they discovered that each had been handed the other's assignment. At an all-night meeting in his office, Miaja organized what everyone considered then to be a desperate suicidal stand in order to gain time for the building of a real army in the Levant. Lieutenant Colonel Vicente Rojo, one of the most brilliant of the younger general staff officers, assisted by Major Manuel Matallana Gómez, a lawyer as well as professional officer, was to organize the communications, the supplies, and the chain of command for the defense. General Miaja told the several dozen assembled officers that most of them would probably die, and the officers later repeated the news to their troops. The sole general order was to resist all along the front, and not to retreat an inch.[12]

The attacking columns were commanded by General Varela. On the morning of the 7th they moved into the Casa de Campo and drove forward toward the several Manzanares bridges. A few *Legionnaires* reached the Frenchman's bridge, just west of the University City, but were thrown back by artillery firing from the Retiro Park. At the Toledo bridge, and at Ferraz Street near the Model Prison, isolated patrols penetrated but were cut down by machine-gun and rifle fire.[13] All day, officers called Miaja to report that their lines were holding, but that they were out of ammunition. The General answered reassuringly that reserves and ammunition were on the way. In reality he had no reserves, but the young officers were ready to forgive what they knew was probably a lie. On November 7 the high morale and combativeness of the Republican commanders was fully equal to that which animated the field chieftains of the Army of Africa. But the basis of comradeship in this case was loyalty to the Republic. Most of these officers were university as well as military men. They had approved the broad lines, if not the details, of Azaña's reforms. Many had belonged to the UMRA, had fought at the Montaña barracks and in the Sierra. They had shared the experience of training the militia, and the exhilara-

[12] For military and logistic information on the assault of Madrid, and also in later pages on the battles of the Jarama and Guadalajara, I have depended heavily on the excellent study of Robert G. Colodny, *The Struggle for Madrid*. Its factual material, if not its interpretation, always checked out with my other sources.

[13] John T. Whitaker, "Prelude to War. A Witness from Spain," *Foreign Affairs*, October, 1942, p. 115. Whitaker accompanied the Moors to the edge of the Manzanares, hoping to be the first correspondent to enter the city with Franco's troops. The battery in the Retiro was popularly known as "el abuelo" (grandpa) and its shots as "tosidos" (coughs). Galíndez, *Los vascos*, p. 64. Its presence was one of the Nationalist justifications for the bombs which dropped near the Prado in November.

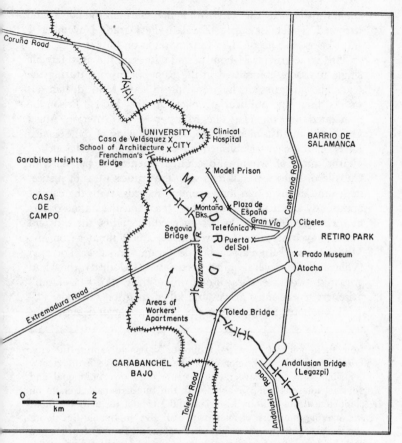

Coruña Road

UNIVERSITY
Casa de Velásquez X
School of Architecture X CITY
Frenchman's
Bridge

X Clinical
Hospital

BARRIO DE
SALAMANCA

Garabitas Heights

CASA
DE
CAMPO

M A D R I D

X Model Prison

X
Montaña
Bks.

X Plaza de
España

Gran Vía

Segovia
Bridge

Telefónica X

Castellana Road

Cibeles

RETIRO PARK

Puerta X
del Sol

Manzanares R.

X Prado Museum

Atocha

Areas of
Workers'
Apartments

Toledo Bridge

Extremadura Road

CARABANCHEL
BAJO

Toledo Road

Andalusian Bridge
(Legazpi)

Andalusian Road

0   1   2
km

MAP 4. The Madrid front, end of November 1936

tion of seeing the whole population turn out to help with
food, communications, and medical supplies.[14] General Miaja
gave his orders to the civil population over the radio, and the
speed with which they were obeyed was the measure of popular
involvement in the defense. Meanwhile, the Russian fighter

[14] Nationalist historians have exaggerated the role of the Russians
and the International Brigades at Madrid in an effort to explain,

planes protected the city from the German bombers and dropped leaflets saying: "Emulate Petrograd. November 7 must be as glorious on the Manzanares as on the Neva."

This same crucial 24-hour period witnessed the most terrible single massacre committed in the Republican zone during the war. The government, in preparing to leave Madrid, had left orders that the political prisoners in the Model Prison be evacuated to Valencia. The Minister of the Interior, Angel Galarza, himself a member of Caballero's wing of the Socialist Party, had never established effective control of the prison guards, most of whom also counted themselves partisans of Caballero. They were all men with the crudest ideas of justice, and some of them had long criminal records. With the capital apparently about to fall, they interpreted the evacuation orders in their own fashion. On two succeeding nights, the 6th and 7th of November, they removed nearly 1,000 inmates from the Model Prison.[15] In Paracuellos de Jarama and near Torrejón (villages lying several miles northeast of Madrid) they had prepared wide trenches. They drove their "Fifth Column" prisoners to the mass graves and killed them on the spot.

Throughout the day of the 7th, the Republican defense lines

---

from their point of view, the failure of Varela to capture the city. Foreign reporters and veterans of the Brigades have inadvertently contributed to the exaggeration because their own emotional and political interests were involved with the Internationals. I claim no competence as a military historian, and I cannot list names without endangering numbers of men who still live in Spain. But I am convinced, from the geography of the Madrid front (of which the part held by the Internationals was a very small, though vital, fraction) and from a number of interviews with Republican officers, that some 30 to 50 professionals, commanding up to 40,000 semi-armed militiamen, played an absolutely crucial role in the ten-day battle which stopped the Nationalist army at the gates of the capital. They were not the sort of men to seek publicity at the time, and circumstances have made silence advisable since.

[15] The nature of the incident is well known from many sources, but estimates of the number of victims vary widely. I have accepted, as roughly accurate, the figure of 1,020 given by Jesús de Galíndez, *Los vascos en el Madrid sitiado,* p. 66.

had held. Morale was high; supplies and reserves of fighting men were low. At 9 p.m. an Italian tank was blown up on the Extremadura road. On the body of one of the officers killed was a copy of General Varela's operational order for the conquest of Madrid. Originally it had been intended for November 7. Due to the stiffening resistance it had been postponed for the 8th. Colonel Rojo gambled on the notion that in any case the order was too complex to be altered at the last minute, and he moved all his best troops to the Casa de Campo and the University City, in which, according to the captured order, the main assault would take place. On the morning of the 8th telegrams arrived in the War Ministry congratulating General Franco on his victorious entry. Outside began the supreme test of wills between Generals Varela and Miaja, between the elite Army of Africa and the aroused populace of Madrid. Wave after wave of Varela's troops braved the machine-gun fire of desperate defenders who had only limited ammunition but knew exactly where to expect their enemies. The Germans bombed the University City in preparation for the infantry assault, while Varela's men fought their way up the Garabitas heights from which they would be able to observe, and shell, the city. Once again forward patrols reached each of the main bridges, to be cut down by machine guns. Colonel Rojo had ordered the unarmed reserves to wait under cover, and as hundreds of militiamen died at their posts, replacements came forward to pick up their rifles. When the Moroccans broke through in the direction of the Model Prison, General Miaja himself drove to the threatened sector, drew out his pistol, and shouted at the retreating soldiers: "Cowards, die in your trenches. Die with your General." The gap was closed and the Moroccan vanguard killed while Colonel Rojo dragged Miaja back into the relative safety of his car.

Meanwhile, on the afternoon of Sunday, November 8, the first units of the International Brigades formed at Albacete arrived in Madrid. Some 3,000 men, mostly Germans and Italians, many of them veterans of the First World War and of fascist concentration camps, marching with absolute precision and singing revolutionary songs, paraded across the embattled capital. Varela's most dangerous thrust of the moment was the partial conquest of the Garabitas heights. The first few hundred Internationals were ordered into the Casa de Campo, where they were fused in the proportion of roughly one to four among the militiamen, who immediately followed their examples in the digging of foxholes, the use of cover, and the economy of ammunition. The next day the major portion of them bore the brunt of the Nationalist effort to breach the capital's defenses via the University City.

For ten days the battle continued without pause. Madrid became suddenly the center of the world. Ace journalists of all countries followed the fighting in the Casa de Campo and the University City through binoculars from their hotel rooms near the Plaza de España. In the streets they tasted the humor, the verve, and the dignity which were to convert almost all of them into lifelong champions of the Spanish *pueblo*. For the Nationalists, regardless of heavy losses and the danger to their flanks, the supreme effort was worthwhile because upon the capture of Madrid hinged diplomatic recognition by the major powers and a military success that would mean quick victory in the war. For the Republicans the successful defense was the first good news, militarily speaking, since July 18. To the oppressed populations in Galicia, Asturias, Andalusia, it meant that the Republic would not be defeated; and all over the world antifascists who had watched Mussolini and Hitler move from success to success without challenge, launched the slogan: "Madrid will be the tomb of fascism." From the trenches, and over the radio, came the phrase made famous in 1916 at the defense of Verdun: "No pasarán," they shall not pass.

The Madrileños returned in kind the admiration of the foreign soldiers and journalists. The cafés were a babel of languages, and Spaniards, hearing an unfamiliar tongue, would come over and embrace the unknown guest. "Vivan los rusos" served as a toast to cover the 20-odd nations represented in the International Brigades. And if a Czech or a Pole, knowing not a word of any romance language, lost his way, a dozen Spaniards would triumphantly accompany him to his hotel or dugout. For the first time, during this week, Catalonia sent large numbers of men—Esquerra and anarchist columns—who carried the French and Czech automatic weapons which had been transported freely across the border until August 8, and had continued to be smuggled in in variable quantities since then. In the War Ministry the Russian advisers, quickly appreciating the thinness of the Nationalist lines and the approaching exhaustion of their elite troops, urged Miaja and Rojo to launch flank attacks. But the defenders of Madrid had seen too many militiamen uselessly killed in open field fighting for which they had no training, and such militia would have been completely incapable of the coordinated tank and infantry advances recommended by the Russians.

On November 14 the famous anarchist chieftain Buenaventura Durruti arrived with his 3,000-man column. They had left the Saragossa front and temporarily forgotten their regionalism, and their grievances against the Socialists and Communists. They asked General Miaja for a tough assignment and demanded a sector which they would hold alone, in order to establish their prowess beyond doubt. They were assigned to a portion of the University City, where, by chance, General Varela was preparing a concentrated local attack for the next day. For several hours the anarchists held their ground, but when the enemy broke into the Hall of Philosophy and the School of Architecture, the column turned and fled.[16] Internationals and Fifth Regiment men stemmed the advance, but could not prevent Varela's men on the 17th from entering the Clinical Hospital.

For several days, in the partially destroyed university buildings, the opposing units held different floors, shouting insults through the walls and hurling hand grenades through windows and down stair wells. Durruti, enraged at the disgrace of his

[16] Ludwig Renn, *Der Spanische Krieg* (Berlin, 1956), pp. 70–72 and *passim* for observations on the state of training, morale, and efficiency of the different militias. Renn, whose real name was Arnold Friedrich Vieth von Golssenau, was a Communist of aristocratic background. He had been a captain in the Imperial German Army during the First World War. He judged both the Spanish and the international troops with a professional eye. Of all the memoirs by members of the International Brigades, this is the most competent as a military commentary on the events lived through.

men, demanded of them the sacrifices that would wipe out their shame. On November 21 he died in mysterious circumstances, close to the front, but apparently shot from behind. His friends conducted a house-to-house search for the fifth columnist or disgruntled anarchist who might have shot him. Meanwhile, his body was returned to Barcelona for a hero's funeral, the cortege of which was led by the Generalitat government.[17]

The entry to the Clinical Hospital represented the maximum advance of the invading army. That same day, the 17th, Moroccans once again broke through in the direction of the Plaza de España, and once again General Miaja rushed to the front to rally the defenders. But on the 17th the offensive power of Varela's columns was exhausted. The Nationalists combined their last advances with a supreme effort to break the city's resistance by bombardment. That afternoon some 2,000 shells an hour landed in the center of Madrid. Hospitals and subway entrances were hit. Shrapnel shells exploded in wide squares such as the Plaza de España. Incendiary shells set the working-class and residential quarters afire, and that night, bombers coming over ten to twelve at a time, guided by the fires, dropped cargo after cargo. Madrid had no air-raid shelters and almost no anti-aircraft artillery. The Russian fighter planes could not be used as effectively against night raids as during the day. It is possible that up to 500 persons were killed that night, but in a city of a million inhabitants these deaths produced anger and the will to resist; they strengthened rather than weakened the morale of the defenders.

On November 18 Italy and Germany announced their recognition of the Burgos regime as the legitimate government of Spain. Originally, the announcement was to have

[17] Kaminski, *Ceux de Barcelone,* pp. 60–65. The speakers at the funeral were García Oliver, who two weeks earlier had become the first anarchist to enter the government, as Caballero's Minister of Justice; Vladimir A. Antonov-Ovseenko, "Old Bolshevik" Consul in Barcelona, who was to be shot in the Soviet purges during 1937; and Luis Companys, who was to be handed over to the Franco government by the Gestapo and shot, in 1940.

coincided with the expected entry of the Nationalists into Madrid. Coming on the 18th, it constituted simultaneously a pledge of all necessary aid to General Franco and a confession that the war would be long. It was, above all, a tonic to heavily depressed Nationalist morale. In late July the Insurgent generals had received friendly aid from British and American business interests and from Gibraltar officials. In August and September their elite African columns had marched from Seville to the upper Tagus valley. Their allies had supplied planes, guns, and tanks, but the ground troops which had reached Madrid all were units of the Spanish Army, and Carlist and Falangist volunteers. (For the Nationalist officers, the Moors were not foreigners.)

At Madrid they found world opinion against them. Conservative as well as liberal foreign papers accused them of *Schrecklichkeit*. If English industrialists and naval officers were their friends, how was it that the English government embargoed the shipment of war materials and that English public opinion condemned them? As military men, they did not understand the complexity of a democratic industrial society and were angered at what they considered to be hypocrisy and double-dealing. At Madrid they also met an enemy who for the first time possessed foreign equipment comparable to their own. They found volunteers of twenty nations fighting them. The Moors, superb warriors during the advance from village to village, were disoriented by the streets and buildings of a modern city, and by opponents not only as brave as themselves, but skilled in the lessons of the First World War and the Russian Revolution. Though they dominated Madrid with their artillery on the hard-won Garabitas heights, though they had pushed a salient deep in the University City, though they could shell and bomb the capital almost at will, they had lost their forward momentum, and they felt morally isolated.

The assault on Madrid was suspended. For moral and prestige reasons, General Franco decided to maintain his forces in the most forward positions they had reached rather than withdraw them to superior siege lines. Both armies created a labyrinth of trench and barbed wire defenses. Fifty feet apart along the western perimeter of the city, they hurled insults and grenades, fired short machine-gun bursts, and trained mortars on the opposing trenches. But from late November, 1936, until the end of the Civil War, the lines at Madrid never varied more than one hundred yards in any sector.

19

POLITICS AND WAR IN EARLY 1937

FROM the first days of November 1936 until the end of March 1937, Madrid remained the principal front. With rare exceptions, the Nationalists held the military initiative throughout. In December they conducted only small probing operations, but on January 5 launched an all-out attack northwest of the city. Variously known as the Battle of the Fog and as the Battle of the Coruña Road, it cut the highway and won for the Nationalists a number of tactically advantageous positions, but ended, after heavy casualties on both sides, in temporary exhaustion. General Franco's main concern during this period was to equip a new offensive force to replace the African and Requeté units which had suffered most heavily in November.

At a meeting of the Non-Intervention Committee on December 4, Germany and Italy rejected two Franco-British suggestions: one looking toward mediation, and the other proposing to have Non-Intervention cover foreign volunteers as well as arms shipments. In this manner they served notice frankly that they intended both with arms and men to aid the Nationalist cause. A first major shipment of 3,000 Italians left the homeland on December 18. Between this date and late April 1937, the Italian navy and merchant marine transported about 100,000 troops to Spain, of which up to 70,000 were Italians and the rest North Africans recruited mainly in the mountainous districts of Morocco.[1] During the month of

---

[1] The figure of 100,000 transported comes from the Italian naval journal *Forze Armate*. It has been quoted in many accounts and is perhaps the basis of some claims that 100,000, or even more, Italians served in Spain. Since the article was published in June, 1939, I have assumed that the author was not inclined to minimize the Italian contribution. At the same time, it is known that Mussolini sent 4 full divisions with their supply and transport services, and miscellaneous other troops. The 4 divisions would come to

November Germany assembled the so-called Condor Legion: 5–6000 specialized troops intended to act autonomously under German command. The basic units were 4 bomber squadrons (48 planes), 4 fighter squadrons, a reconnaissance squadron (12 planes), a seaplane squadron, 4 batteries of 20 mm. artillery (4 guns per battery), 4 batteries of 88's, and 4 tank companies totaling 48 tanks.[2] Volunteers were recruited openly at training bases; diplomats and journalists, if not the Non-Intervention Committee, were well aware of the departures from Hamburg; by late December the Condor Legion had arrived in its entirety at Seville. A final foreign unit, more important for reasons of morale than of military strength, was a battalion of 6–700 Irish volunteers who assembled at the end of 1936.[3]

Within Nationalist Spain the authorities counted on 30,000 Carlist troops in early 1937 and had recruited up to 120,000 Falangist militiamen.[4] After the failure to take Madrid, and with the prospect of a long war, General Franco gave attention also to the future. Speaking on January 19, the six-month anniversary of the military rising, he told his audience that Spain had suffered through mistaken intellectualism, and the imitation of foreign ways. He did not define the future

---

roughly 60,000, and this consideration, plus an allowance for aviators, tank crews, and technical services, leads me to say "up to 70,000." I assume that the rest of the 100,000 were Moors because on the one hand, *Forze* does not say that all the troops it shipped were Italian, and on the other, several Foreign Legion officers told me that they had recruited heavily in North Africa after the first check at Madrid.

[2] Beumelburg, *Kampf um Spanien,* p. 56. Also declarations of General Jaenecke, who had been Hitler's chief of staff for the Spanish operation, quoted in Colodny, *The Struggle for Madrid,* pp. 166–67.

[3] Eoin O'Duffy, *Crusade in Spain* (Clanskeagh, 1938), p. 155 for their numbers, and *passim* for their military role at the Jarama front.

[4] These were the estimates of General Monasterio, in charge of all Nationalist militia at the time, and quoted to me by a Falangist official who had worked with the General.

form of government, but stated that universal suffrage and regional autonomy were to end. Spain needed schools, sanatoria, and more just relations between capital and labor. She would be a Catholic state, with respect for the religious beliefs of others. The General evoked the great periods in Spanish history: the *Reconquista* and the Habsburg era through the reign of Philip II; the period of the Carlist wars, seen as a struggle to maintain Spanish traditions against Liberal and Europeanizing influences; and the Primo de Rivera dictatorship, which he saw as a precursor of his own regime.[5] He took considerable pains to indicate that his inspiration lay in these Spanish precedents rather than in contemporary fascism. His proposals represented a dexterous combination of the ideas of his most active supporters, the Falange and the Carlists. At the same time, he made no demagogic concessions to the hopes of the leftist masses. During these same months the Falange waged a strong propaganda campaign in favor of eventual land reform and separation of Church and state. Their idealistic impulses were expressed principally in the creation of children's restaurants and orphanages, and in sending nurses and medical supplies to the front.[6]

The main task of the Nationalists at this time was to create military unity. The Germans thought the attack on Madrid had been poorly managed and were pressing Franco in January to accept a combined general staff including 5 German and 5 Italian officers.[7] The Germans and Italians, however, had their own differences. Franco and the Germans favored a plan to launch a pincers attack against the capital from both the northwest and southwest, thereby preventing the defending army from transferring its best troops to a single threatened area. The combined attack, however, would have

[5] E. Allison Peers, *Spain in Eclipse* (London, 1943), pp. 101–106.
[6] Douglas Jerrold, in *Nineteenth Century,* April, 1937, published a detailed article on the civilian aims and accomplishments of the Nationalist regime in early 1937. See also the official handbook of the *Sección Femenina* of the Falange for information on restaurants and hospitals.
[7] DGFP, pp. 124, 137–39, 155–56, 236, and *passim.*

placed the newly arrived Italians under German authority, and the Italians demanded a front of their own. Feeling was not improved by the fact that in November Russian tanks had proved superior to the Italian ones and Russian fighter planes superior to the Heinkels. Both fascist powers were now sending their latest equipment, and both intended to control the use of that equipment.

After the Battle of Madrid, the Republic also reorganized its military forces. The Fifth Regiment, numbering around 60–70,000, of whom about half were Communists, was disbanded, as was a 30,000-man CNT force. These two units became the basis of a half-dozen "mixed brigades" whose outstanding leaders were the Communists Lister, Modesto, and Valentin González ("El Campesino"), and the anarchist Cipriano Mera. The mixed brigades accepted centralized supply and pay systems, and came under the hierarchical command of General Miaja's defense junta. However, Socialists, Communists, and anarchists retained their mutually guarded attitudes toward each other. While they accepted formal reorganization at the top, they successfully resisted the breakup of their individual battalions and companies. The Madrid army did not become in any sense a true "melting pot" of its different political components.

At Albacete the Marty administration formed two more International Brigades with effective strengths of perhaps 3,000 each.[8] The volunteers arrived by the hundreds from all parts of central and western Europe, from England, Canada, and the United States, and in smaller numbers from Latin

[8] A wide variety of both Republican and Nationalist sources place the total number of the Internationals between 30–40,000 for the war. There is much disagreement about the numbers in action at any given time, and the significance of their contribution. I have followed Colodny's analysis of their composition. There were 5 brigades, numbered 11 through 15 (one of the sources of confusion about their total numbers) with effective battle strengths of 2–3,000 each. Used as shock troops or to save key positions, they naturally suffered very heavy casualties. It is thus reasonable to estimate that as many as 40,000 foreigners, most of them volunteers in a cause, and a fraction of them mercenaries, fought in 5 brigades whose strength varied between 10–15,000. Of the tremendous memoir

336

America. Many of them had sacrificed professional positions to the all-important task, as they saw it, of defeating fascism. Most of them came of bourgeois background, though many had deliberately chosen to live as sailors or industrial workers in order to escape the limitations of a bourgeois existence. In coming to Spain most of them defied the wishes, if not the laws, of their governments, and many traveled on false passports. The complexity of their personal motives is clearly reflected in the following passage by one of the American veterans of the International Brigades: "Men went to Spain for various reasons, but behind almost every man I met there was a common restlessness, a loneliness. In action these men would fight like devils, with the desperation of an iron-bound conscience; in private conversation there was something else again. I knew, myself, that the historical events of Spain had coincided with a long-felt compulsion to complete the destruction of the training I had received all through my youth. There were two major reasons for my being there; to achieve self-integration, and to lend my individual strength (such as it was) to the fight against our eternal enemy—oppression; and the validity of the second reason was not impaired by the fact that it was a shade weaker than the first, for they were both a part of the same thing. It was necessary for me, at that stage of my development as a man, to work (for the first time) in a large body of men; to submerge myself in that mass, seeking neither distinction nor preferment (the reverse of my activities for the past several years) and in this way to achieve self-discipline, patience and unselfishness—the opposite of a

---

literature on the brigades, I found especially useful the following: Tom Wintringham, *English Captain* (London, 1939) for information on the training and the inner politics of the brigades, and their role at the Jarama; John Sommerfield, *Volunteer in Spain* (London, 1937), the work of a romantic British Communist who fought in November at Madrid; Alvah Bessie, *Men in Battle,* (New York, 1939) concerning the disastrous retreat in early 1938, and the battle of the Ebro; Pietro Nenni, *La guerre d'Espagne* (Paris, 1960, originally published in 1958 in Italy under the title *Spagna*) for the experience and interpretation of a politically active, non-Communist anti-fascist exile.

long middle class training—and the construction of a life that would be geared to other men and the world events that circumscribed them. There is much truth in the old saw—for a desperate disease, a desperate cure."[9]

These ardent idealists, often unsettled in their personal as well as professional lives, saw in the defense of Spanish democracy a cause worthy of all their energies. Most of them were not Communists, but practically all of them admired the Communist role in organizing international aid to the Republic. In Paris and Marseilles they were grateful to the French Communist Party, and to its Socialist and liberal allies, for arranging the adventurous border crossings, via mountain passes and fishing vessels. In Spain they shared with the Socialist and Communist Youth the conviction that the era of the *bourgeoisie* was drawing to a close and that the international proletariat was destined to lead humanity to a better future. With such faith and such idealism, they asked no questions when their passports were confiscated at Albacete. They accepted eagerly the iron rule of the very proletarian André Marty, who as a sailor had led the mutiny of the French naval units sent to intervene in 1919 against the Bolsheviks. And when comrades mysteriously disappeared from the training base, most of them accepted, with whatever regretful qualms, the explanation that "fascist spies" were being rooted out of the ranks.[10]

[9] Alvah Bessie, *Men in Battle*, p. 181.
[10] Many writers have tried to estimate the proportion of Communist Party members in the Brigades. In his introduction to Gustav Regler's widely read novel concerning the defense of Madrid, *The Great Crusade* (New York, 1940), Ernest Hemingway wrote that the majority of the 11th Brigade were Communists (mostly Germans) and that in the 12th "some were Communists, but there were men of all political beliefs" (p. viii). The secret nature of Party membership, and the fact that under certain circumstances the Party itself preferred not to have particular persons be Party members, make it absolutely impossible to give accurate figures. More important in any case is the fact that the great majority of the Internationals, and of the JSU, acted as fellow-travelers, for reasons of their own. They saw the Communists as the most efficient organizers of the anti-fascist resistance in Europe. When the Hitler-Stalin Pact was signed in August, 1939, the fellow

During these same months, the Finance Minister, Juan Negrín, reorganized the carabineros, making an elite corps (humorously known as the "hundred thousand sons of Juan Negrín" but actually numbering more like 20,000) out of the Civil Guards, Assault Guards, and carabineros who had remained loyal to the Republic. The Generalitat had its own army, starved for equipment by a combination of Russian policy and the requirements of the Madrid front.[11] Local militias retained control in much of the Levant and the southeast; and the government in late December recognized the anarchist-dominated *Consejo de Aragón* in the area where the CNT columns had established *comunismo libertario* in August 1936.

A prominent victim of the political disunity of both zones in the early months of the war was José Antonio Primo de Rivera. The Azaña government had jailed him, along with the other principal Falangist leaders, in March 1936. Transferred to Alicante, he had corresponded freely with General Mola before the rising. During the first weeks of the war, the civil governor of Alicante had looked the other way when middle-class personalities had fled to the Insurgent zone. One such refugee was convinced that he would be able personally, if given facilities, to arrange for the unofficial release of José Antonio. General Franco and his German advisers were lukewarm to the proposal, on both political and technical grounds. However, they permitted the Alicante refugee, accompanied by several intimate friends of José Antonio, to visit the port on a German naval vessel. The civil governor was invited aboard, but instead of permitting the Spaniards to plead their cause with him, the German officer in charge locked the Spaniards in a cabin and did the talking himself. The governor rejected out of hand the notion of turning over his prisoner to the German navy.[12]

---

travelers stepped off the train. But that was five months after the end of the Civil War.

[11] Krivitsky, *In Stalin's Secret Service,* 91 and *passim.*

[12] Many highly embroidered stories circulate in Spain concerning efforts to rescue José Antonio. I remained entirely skeptical until told the above story by an evidently down-to-earth professional man who had been one of the participants.

By early November, Alicante had a new civil governor, this time a Communist, and the bombardment of Madrid had produced public demands for the execution of the long-held Falangist chief. Tried on November 13, he defended himself by reading editorials from the party organ, *Arriba,* which clearly differentiated the Falange from both the far Right and the generals. He also noted that the Insurgents had made no effort to free him and had not named him for any future governing post. The evidence concerning his role in the rising reflected the contradictions of his own spirit. At times he offered Falangist troops to Mola—as he had to Lerroux on the occasion of the Asturian revolt. But he had condemned the rising in the form in which it actually occurred, probably because he had always dreamed of a true "movimiento nacional" led by the military but based on wide popular approval. He was condemned to death on the 17th, while the local press lauded the dignity of his behavior during the trial.[13] The provincial governor carried out the sentence on the 20th, without awaiting, as he knew he was legally obliged to, the confirmation of sentence by the cabinet. The execution angered Largo Caballero, for its political stupidity as well as insubordination. The young man left a testament in which he named his ideal government of national union, including a majority of Republicans and moderate Socialists. His death was not officially announced in Nationalist Spain until late in 1938, by which time he had been transformed into the patron saint of a cause he had never approved in his lifetime.

The reorganization of the Republican zone was greatly hampered by both ideological and personal factors. Largo Caballero had come to power as the hero of the masses. He wished to base his authority on the UGT and the CNT, and when the anarchists consented to participate in his second government, named on November 4, he considered this to be his greatest personal triumph as an educator of the people.

[13] Payne, *Falange,* pp. 132ff. For the leftward evolution of José Antonio's thought, compare his proposed government of 1935 (Payne, p. 283), with the government named in his testament (Payne, p. 135).

But the CNT as a whole, and the UGT in large part (precisely among those most devoted to Largo personally) considered their own participation in the government to be the guarantee of the decentralized, collectivist revolutionary changes of the first weeks of the war.

Caballero, on the other hand, had no sooner become Prime Minister than he realized that it was absolutely necessary to rebuild the authority of the Republican state and to work in close cooperation with the middle-class liberals. The masses of the left considered Martínez Barrio a virtual traitor for his effort to form a compromise government on July 18. Caballero placed him in charge of the newly formed Albacete base for foreign volunteers. The workers continued to believe, as the Prime Minister once had, that the militia were preferable to a regular army. Largo appointed General José Asensio Torrado to command the central army. When the anarchists complained about discipline, about prohibitions on political propaganda, about punishments for ridiculing religious images, Caballero backed Asensio. While some of his presumed followers continued to conduct paseos, Caballero approved the private efforts of his Republican ministers—Ruiz Funes, Giral, Irujo, Negrín, Bernardo Giner de los Ríos—to help threatened people leave the country.[14] Either Caballero was not sufficiently articulate to explain his intentions to the public or he was too preoccupied with daily problems to make the effort.

As part of rebuilding the Republican state, Caballero insisted punctiliously on the recognition of his authority. Both that authority and his personal pride had suffered a terrible blow when the government had fled from Madrid on November 6. He was intensely jealous of the undistinguished general whom he had left behind to defend the doomed capital as best he could—and who had become overnight the toast of anti-fascists throughout the world. In mid-November he obliged Miaja to make a militarily useless journey to Valencia, in order to satisfy himself that the head of

[14] Burnett Bolloten, *The Grand Camouflage* (London, 1961), p. 227, Martín Blázquez, *I Helped Build an Army,* pp. 316ff.; Francisco Largo Caballero, *Mis recuerdos* (Mexico, 1954), pp. 182ff. Also conversations with Manuel de Irujo in Paris, 1961.

the Madrid junta knew that he was still a subordinate of the civilian premier. Neither Philip II nor the viceroys who ruled in Lima and Mexico were more concerned than Francisco Largo Caballero with proper accounting. A *fraile sindical* (syndicalist monk) as he was described by more than one bourgeois colleague, he wanted receipts for every cartridge issued to the desperate defenders of Madrid. When the Internationals decided to cut the "red tape" and supply themselves with blankets at Albacete, the Prime Minister, through Martínez Barrio, had the blankets returned to the warehouse—after which they were duly reissued. Comrades Togliatti and Marty probably wondered whether they were dealing with "the Spanish Lenin" or with an old schoolmaster. For Largo, the question was one of honesty, decorum, and governmental authority. Fortunately for the Republicans, their most able officers did not permit jurisdictional squabbles to interfere with their principal business. Colonel Rojo in the Madrid area and General Asensio for the Valencia government, created in the months of December and January the first Republican infantry capable of open-field fighting.

In the Nationalist zone, the difficulties of coordinating Italo-German cooperation led General Franco to concede the Italian demand for a separate front. The new Moorish troops and the Condor Legion would be assigned for the eventual resumption of the offensive at Madrid. The first Italian infantry would meanwhile participate in the capture of Málaga, in coordination with the Spanish and Moorish troops of General Queipo de Llano. The city was not important strategically, and it had long since been rendered useless as a naval base, but the campaign would provide training for the Italians and a sure victory to offset the stalemate at Madrid.

The situation in Málaga epitomized all the worst conditions existing in the Republican zone. In the second week of June, labor violence had cost three lives through assassination: those of a Communist city councilor, a Socialist labor delegate, and the child of a CNT leader accidentally killed instead of his father. In the weeks after July 18 the city's shops were looted and the best residential quarters burned. Perhaps 600 hostages were held on a prison ship in the harbor, and groups of them were shot in reprisal for the several air raids over the port. The sailors' committees in the fleet and the city administration were divided in mortal rivalry between CNT and Communist adherents. Valencian and Almerian truck drivers' syndicates could not agree on the division of labor between them for the delivery of supplies to Málaga, and one of the bridges on the main coastal road remained unrepaired for five months preceding the city's fall. Like all the Republican cities, it lacked anti-aircraft defense. Its militiamen, mostly anarchists, built no trenches or road blocks. In January the government assigned a dependable professional officer, Colonel Villalba, to organize the defense; but without guns to place on the heights, without ammunition to give his soldiers, and without the slightest possibility of controlling the bitter political rivalries within the city, there was virtually nothing he could do.[15]

The invading force consisted of some 10,000 Moors, 5,000 Requetés, and 5,000 Italians, with plentiful supplies of Italian trucks and artillery, and the small numbers of tanks and planes which could be used with maximum effectiveness in the virtual absence of opposition.[16] The militiamen re-

[15] On the June struggles see *El Sol,* June 12, 1936. On the terror in Málaga see The *New York Times,* July 26–27 and September 19, 1936; and *ABC, Sevilla,* March 3 and 5, 1937. Concerning general conditions of the defense of Málaga see the previously cited Koestler, *Spanish Testament,* pp. 186–99, and Borkenau, *The Spanish Cockpit,* pp. 216–28.

[16] There are wide differences in the estimates of numbers and composition of the force which took Málaga. Reynolds Packard in *Balcony Empire* speaks of 40,000 troops, at least half of whom were Italians. I rejected this because so large a force for so small an objective, with Nationalist forces strained to the utmost near Madrid, did not make sense. General Kindelán in his *Cuadernos* speaks of 25,000, two-thirds of whom were Spaniards. I doubted this on several grounds. First, Kindelán's writings are very valuable for qualitative insights concerning strategy and equipment, but he constantly played down the German and Italian aid to the Nationalists. His statement would also mean that Franco had 16,000 Spanish troops to spare for the Málaga campaign after the terrible

sisted rifle and grenade fire, but broke at the totally unfamiliar sight of tanks. On February 6 about 100,000 persons began a disorganized mass exodus along the coastal road to Almería. The invaders waited on the heights for three days and then entered the city practically without firing a shot. They brought with them an interminable list of persons to be executed: for leadership in the Popular Front, for looting, for responsibilities on the prison ships, for participation in strikes of past years.

The prisoners were crowded into the municipal court, to be tried without testimony by three military judges and to be sentenced to death for military rebellion. Hands bound with cords, they shuffled out to the street to be loaded into trucks and carried to the city outskirts.[17] Italian and Spanish firing squads shared the labor. The Italian military authorities were horrified at the number of executions and at the mutilations practiced on the corpses and on those who were wounded. Consul Bianchi was able to save some persons from execution since he enjoyed the good will of the conservative community for having protected many prominent individuals during the Communist-anarchist domination of the city. General Roatta wrote to the Italian Ambassador, Roberto Cantalupo, saying

---

attrition of the Battle of Madrid and while he was preparing a more important offensive at the Jarama. On the other hand, a possible explanation consistent with the figures I have quoted in the text is that Kindelán, like many a Spanish officer, might use the term "Spaniards" for Moorish troops, since of course the Moors formed a large part of the Army of Africa. The figures I used are those of R. Sencourt, *Spain's Ordeal* (New York, 1940), p. 227, the work of an English reporter of monarchist sympathies and long personal knowledge of Spain. They seemed to me the most consistent with the logistic needs of the campaign and with the type of troops that General Queipo de Llano would have available. On the other hand, there is no doubt the Italians could have contributed more than 5,000. Ambassador Faupel, in a dispatch of Jan. 18, 1937, referred to 20,000 Italians ready for action near Seville (DGFP, p. 229). There is thus no numerical certainty, and I have supplied this detailed note to illustrate the kind of guesswork repeatedly necessary in judging military statistics.

[17] Foltz, *Masquerade in Spain*, pp. 77–78.

that the Italians had orders to treat their prisoners humanely and were afraid to turn them over to the Spaniards. Meanwhile, for some two weeks along the coastal highway the Nationalist Navy and Air Force bombed the refugee columns at will. German warships also took part in the shelling, sometimes in the presence of English naval vessels which did nothing. Twenty years later, truck drivers were still finding the skeletons of those who had fled Málaga in February 1937.

On March 2 Ambassador Cantalupo received instructions to discuss the Málaga executions with General Franco as a moral question affecting the reputations of both Spain and Italy. In their subsequent conversation the General recognized that Málaga was a heavily "red" city, and that the tribunals had functioned rigorously. He intimated that he was not in a position to control the local courts easily and suggested that only the clergy could moderate the vengeful passions being vented at Málaga.[18]

The triumphal march to Málaga coincided with a strategically far more important offensive south of Madrid. Both sides had been concentrating troops in the valley of the Jarama during January. The Valencia government had chosen that area to launch a counterattack against the right flank of the army besieging Madrid. The Nationalists were planning an action to cut the main Madrid-Valencia highway, so as to tighten the siege and prepare the final encirclement of the capital from the north. The Madrid junta was well aware of the Nationalist plan, but the Jarama area came under the authority of the central, rather than the Madrid, army, and Largo Caballero felt that until the Republican government could successfully take the military initiative it would be unable to solve its political problems. Due to the continuous tension between Madrid and Valencia, there was no coordinated plan either for offense or defense, and even the boundary between the Madrid army (Miaja) and the central army (Pozas) was not clearly defined.

General Orgaz, in tactical command of the Nationalist force, had by late January concentrated some 40,000 troops

---

[18] Roberto Cantalupo, *Fu la Spagna* (Milan, 1948), pp. 131–37.

(preponderantly African), supported by anti-tank artillery, by two battalions of German-operated heavy machine guns, and by tanks and planes of the Condor Legion. The Jarama terrain was mostly flat. In dry weather it would lend itself to speedy motorized actions, but rains forced Orgaz to wait from January 23 to February 5 for the launching of his attack. The new Republican infantry failed to fortify their high ground, and since they were thinking in terms of their own forthcoming offensive, they did not mine the Jarama bridges until after the Nationalist attack began. The hills were quickly lost, and the two principal bridges, though blown, had been mined in such a way that one fell back into place and the other was merely weakened by the loss of a few heavy timbers.

Russian tanks slowed the advance for brief periods, but the Nationalists quickly concentrated heavy artillery fire and forced their withdrawal. For five days it looked as though the Nationalists would fully achieve their objective. But after the first losses due to ignorance of military technique, the Republican army, fortified by the 14th and 15th International Brigades, blunted the Orgaz offensive. The hard, flat ground afforded no cover, and gave the opportunity only for shallow trenches. But in three months of intensive training, the soldiers had learned to keep low, move swiftly, fire short bursts, and keep in communication with their officers. They now handled rifles, mortars, and machine guns as well as their Moorish opponents. To the Spaniards' traditional stoicism, and resistance to cold and hunger, they added the courage which animates an army conscious of the cause for which it fights.

On February 12 some 40 new Russian planes (15 ground-strafers and 25 fighters) gave the Republicans air supremacy. The strafers could dive to 1,000 feet to machinegun the enemy infantry, and the "Chatos" (thus nicknamed for their "snub-nose" fuselage) proved superior to the Italian Fiat fighters and consequently forced the Condor Legion bombers to retreat.[19]

[19] On the performance of Russian planes both at the Jarama and Guadalajara there is much interesting detail in an article by Eugene Finick, "I Fly for Spain," *Harper's*, Jan. 1938. My accounts of these two battles as a whole are drawn from Colodny and from Tom Wintringham, *English Captain* (London, 1939).

That night (February 12) General Orgaz committed all his reserves, and several companies of British, Poles, and Spaniards were cut to pieces when they attempted to hold the key positions which still prevented the Nationalists from cutting the Valencia highway. By the 15th the force of the offensive

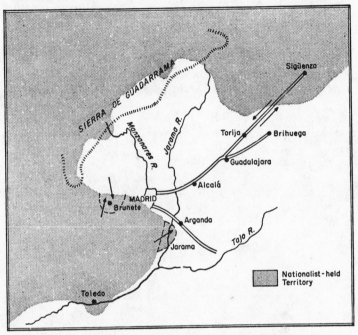

MAP 5. The Battles Near Madrid, 1937
Jarama, February—Guadalajara, March—Brunete, July

had spent itself. As in the Battle of Coruña Road, the Nationalists had gained ground, but strategic victory had escaped them.

The Jarama casuality list was the longest thus far for any given ten days' fighting. In addition, the recently recruited Moors had brought malaria with them. For weeks the hospitals of Madrid and Talavera were to be filled with the wounded and the feverish of both sides. But now more than

347

ever, time was important to General Franco. From early November to the Battle of the Jarama, the combined losses of the Foreign Legion and Moors were such that these crack units would never again be able to spearhead a Nationalist offensive. The Republicans, too, had lost the cream of the International Brigades, but the brunt of the Jarama struggle had been born by Spanish troops which would be stronger with each passing week.

GUADALAJARA AND THE
UNIFICATION OF NATIONALIST SPAIN

AFTER the stalemated Battle of the Jarama, General Franco was under pressure from his allies to strike again quickly, and to win, without obliging them to constantly greater investments and international risks. It was just as true in March as in the previous November, that only the capture of Madrid could end the war quickly. The largest mass of fresh troops and equipment available in March came from Italy. Málaga had been celebrated in the fascist press as an Italian victory, and on March 2 the Fascist Grand Council sent a message of encouragement and solidarity to the *Corpo Truppe Volontarie* (CTV) in Nationalist Spain. Some 50,000 troops were concentrated at Siguenza, in the hills northeast of Madrid. Thirty thousand were Italians under Generals Roatta and Mancini; the remainder were a combination of *Legionnaires*, Moors, and Requetés commanded by General Moscardó. The plan was to advance to Madrid via Brihuega and Guadalajara, moving generally downhill along fairly good roads. The attacking force included 250 tanks, 180 pieces of artillery, 4 motorized machine-gun companies, about 70 planes (mostly fighters), and some 20 trucks per battalion of 650 soldiers. Altogether it was the most heavily armed and best-equipped force yet to enter battle.[1]

The Madrid junta expected a major offensive from the north, and defense plans were better coordinated than in February, because the authority of General Miaja had been extended to cover both the Jarama and Guadalajara sectors. The attack, however, achieved tactical surprise. On March 8 the Italians broke the front quickly, and by the end of the day, dominated the heights from which they could

[1] Colodny, *Struggle for Madrid,* pp. 129–30 and *passim.*

349

literally roll downhill to Madrid. Overconfidence led them to move too rapidly for their units to preserve communication and supply lines. A sudden turn in the weather caught the Italian trucks in a snow and sleet storm, just as the Republicans were beginning to hold firm south of Brihuega and Trijueque. The weather also grounded the Italian planes at their bases west of the Sierra Guadarrama, whereas the Republican planes, albeit at considerable risk, could operate from airfields east of Madrid. Colonel Hidalgo de Cisneros committed his entire force. Low-flying Russian fighters machinegunned the stalled truck columns while vintage 1918 Breguets, which had survived the summer air battles, ran bombing missions.

Meanwhile, the political leaders of the Garibaldi battalion, the Communists Vittorio Vidal (Carlos Contreras) and Luigi Longo, and the Socialist Pietro Nenni, mounted a propaganda campaign intended to destroy the morale of the CTV. Pulling loudspeakers up to the lines, and dropping leaflets from the air further back, they exhorted the Italian soldiers not to fire on their brother workers, and guaranteed them immunity if they would desert to the Republican lines with their arms.[2] On the other side General Mancini reminded his troops that "Italy of the Year XV" (of the fascist era) would be judged by their performance. The Garibaldis, he said, were only the brothers of the Marxist rabble which the fascist squads had smashed in Italy.

For five days (March 12–17) the Italians continued to launch minor attacks and to contain Republican counterattacks, with very few desertions occurring. On several occasions when fascist strong points were completely surrounded, and the anti-fascist loud-speakers invited their "brothers" to surrender, several dozen Italians were happy to become prisoners under the circumstances. But the evidence does not suggest that the Garibaldi propaganda played a large role in the battle.[3] The Italian soldiers were by no means

[2] Luigi Longo, *Die Internationalen Brigaden in Spanien* (Berlin, 1958), pp. 220ff. Renn, *Der Spanische Krieg,* pp. 201–40, valuable not only on the role of the Internationals but for tactical military comments and sketch maps.

[3] The loud-speaker episode, and its crucial meaning for the foreign

volunteers in the same sense as were the International Brigades. They were neither intellectuals, who had suffered in concentration camps, nor democrats and Marxists, who had sacrificed good jobs in order to fight for a noble cause. They were uniformed soldiers performing regular military service, but they also enjoyed seeing the world and having adventures. Most of them had embarked for Spain with enthusiasm. They were well fed and well equipped, their *Duce* was proud of them, and all those with special skills were earning bonus pay.

However, they had come to Spain anticipating easy victories. Lacking the individual motives that animated their fellow Italians in the Garibaldi battalion, they were easily demoralized by the destruction of their truck columns and the absence of effective aid from their allies. Disagreement between the Germans and Italians had prevented General Franco from launching the coordinated offensive from both south and north that might have captured the capital. The Jarama offensive had exhausted itself while the Italians flexed their muscles in the Málaga romp. At the end of February General Orgaz had renewed the Jarama push; but he had suffered punishing losses, so that when the desperate Italians once again asked for pressure to relieve their own units near Guadalajara, there was no response. On March 18 General Mancini was in Salamanca seeking Moroccan reinforcements, while the troops of Lister, El Campesino, and Cipriano Mera, spearheaded by 70 Russian tanks, pursued the CTV along the road north of Brihuega.

Actually the rout stopped short of the bases from which the advance had started. Once again the Nationalists had achieved a net gain in terrain. But the Battle of Guadalajara was far more than another defensive victory for the Republicans. Mussolini had openly staked the prestige of Italian arms on victory at Madrid. His army, fully motorized, and equipped

---

anti-fascists, Communist and non-Communist alike, is powerfully evoked by Gustav Regler, in fictional guise, *The Great Crusade*, pp. 374–78, and in his autobiography, *The Owl of Minerva* (New York, 1960), pp. 283–312 *passim*.

with an abundance of the most recent weapons, had been defeated by a Spanish Republican army which had not even existed four months earlier, and by some thousand anti-fascist Italian exiles. European and American newspaper readers, uneasily accustomed to read only of fascist victories, welcomed eagerly the *New York Times* dispatches of Herbert Matthews, and the articles of Ernest Hemingway. Both men were experienced war reporters, neither of them a man of the Left, and both celebrated Guadalajara as a military and moral turning point in the struggle against a boastful, previously undefeated fascism. General Franco was to be occupied for some weeks mollifying the Italian officers who were all too conscious of the satisfaction felt by many Spaniards at their discomfiture. In the café conversation of both zones, CTV was translated laughingly as "Cuando Te Vas?" (When are you going home?).

During the retreat, the Republicans had captured large stocks of equipment, about 300 prisoners, and a mass of documentary evidence showing that Italy's tens of thousands of "volunteers" were in fact drafted soldiers. The government hoped first to lay this evidence before the London Committee. The latter, adhering firmly to its own procedural rules of September, 1936, declared itself incompetent to receive material from any source not represented on the Non-Intervention Committee. Thereupon the Spanish Foreign Minister, Alvarez del Vayo, exhibited the documents before the League of Nations Assembly.[4] To make sure that no one would have any illusions about a possible change in Italian policy, Count Grandi on March 23 told the Non-Intervention Committee that not a single Italian soldier would be withdrawn until the Nationalist victory had been assured. The French kept their frontier tightly closed. The English, as always, found the evidence inconclusive.

The Battle of Guadalajara, however, had dramatized the increasingly international aspect of the Civil War. Far from denying charges of intervention, as he had directed his

[4] *The Italian Invasion of Spain* (Washington, 1937). French and Spanish editions were also published by the Madrid government and widely distributed in world capitals.

delegates to do at the early meetings of the Non-Intervention Committee, Mussolini was bellowing with wounded indignation and vowing that Italian arms would avenge the humiliation of Guadalajara. The balance of British sentiment had shifted slightly also since the autum of 1936. The decline of anarchist power, the virtual end of assassinations, and the staunch Republican loyalty of the Basques impressed even a considerable sector of Conservative opinion. At the same time, the Foreign Minister was at loggerheads with some of his cabinet colleagues. On November 17, 1936, just as Germany and Italy were about to recognize the Nationalist government, the British Navy was instructed not to accompany merchant vessels up to the three-mile limit. While England had pressed British shipowners from the beginning not to carry arms to either side, the Navy had nevertheless protected freighters in international waters, if only to maintain England's prestige as a sea power. With Madrid apparently about to fall, the First Lord of the Admiralty, Sir Samuel Hoare, favored granting belligerent rights to the Nationalists, and Eden had difficulty convincing the cabinet majority that such a policy would be mistaken.

On January 8, 1937, Eden proposed that the British Navy patrol the entire Spanish coastline in order to prevent arms from reaching either side. He was incensed by the information that some 4,000 Italian troops had landed in Spain since the signature, on January 2, of a "Gentlemen's Agreement" to preserve the Anglo-Italian *status quo* in the Mediterranean. The Admiralty pointed out the technical difficulties of such an operation and Prime Minister Baldwin did not support the Eden proposal.[5]

During January and February there was much talk in the Non-Intervention Committee of establishing a system of neutral land and sea observers to check on the effectiveness of the agreements. The Russians proposed that the naval teams include vessels of all the signatory powers. This was completely unacceptable to the fascist states, and after several months' discussion, a scheme was agreed upon whereby the Republican

[5] Anthony Eden, *Facing the Dictators*, vol. 2 of the *Memoirs of Anthony Eden* (Boston, 1962), pp. 464–65, 487–90.

coast would be patrolled by the Italian and German navies and the Nationalist coast by the French and British navies.[6] By April 19, when the agreement was to take effect, the excitement over Guadalajara had subsided. Italy had all the troops in Spain that she wished to have there for the time being. Italo-German surveillance of the Republican ports would greatly hamper Soviet aid, whereas the British and French navies were unlikely to trouble ships bound for Portugal or Nationalist Spain. While France accepted international supervision of her land frontier, Portugal would permit only British observers along her land frontier, and she expected them to act in the spirit of the historic Anglo-Portuguese alliance.

Neither the Battle of Madrid nor the Battle of Guadalajara had altered American policy as established in the first days of the Civil War. In late November the French Foreign Minister, Yvon Delbos, had sounded out Ambassador Bullitt as to the possibility of a joint Anglo-French-American appeal to the intervening powers. On November 30 Bullitt and the State Department agreed that such an action would not be appropriate for the United States. The Neutrality Act of 1935 said nothing about civil wars, and in the absence of specific law, the government had relied successfully on moral suasion to prevent the sale of arms to Spain. But on December 28 the State Department felt obliged, however reluctantly, to issue an export license for a $2,777,000 cargo of aircraft engines destined for Bilbao. Congress now acted swiftly, passing a joint resolution on January 6, 1937, forbidding the export of arms to Spain. The resolution came a few hours too late to prevent the sailing of the *Mar Cantábrico*, whose well-publicized voyage ended with capture by the Nationalist navy. On January 11 the government tried to inhibit the enlistment of Americans in the International Brigade by ruling American passports invalid for travel in Spain. On May 1 the Neutrality

[6] Besides the previously cited Toynbee *Survey* and Van der Esch *Prelude to War*, the diplomacy of the major powers is treated in detail in David T. Cattell, *Soviet Diplomacy and the Spanish Civil War* (Berkeley, 1957), and Dante Puzzo, *Spain and the Great Powers, 1936–1941* (New York, 1962).

Act of 1937 became law, and this Act applied specifically to civil wars as well as to wars betwen states. On the other hand, like the previous law, it did not apply to oil or to nonmilitary vehicles. The passport ruling was also amended to permit

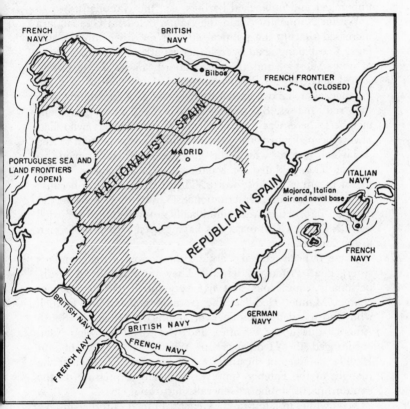

MAP 6. Non-Intervention Naval Patrol Assignments,
April–June, 1937

doctors, nurses, and ambulance drivers to go to Spain.[7] Thus it may be said that government-approved American participa-

[7] F. Jay Taylor, *The United States and the Spanish Civil War*, pp. 76–89, 133.

tion in the Spanish Civil War in 1937 amounted to volunteer medical aid, most of which went to the Republicans, and to the sale of oil and trucks, most of which went to those who possessed credit and who could receive merchant ships in unbombed and unblocked harbors, i.e., the Nationalists.

Within Nationalist Spain the Italian defeat at Guadalajara increased sharply the political effervescence beneath the surface. The Falange had been leaderless after the imprisonment of José Antonio, and the vast majority of its members had joined since July 18. The military had always conceived of the Falange as a handy organization to aid them in dominating the "red" masses. But among the older and more prestigious members there was a strong core of left-wingers who had always been dissatisfied by the indefinite postponement of the social reforms to which the generals occasionally paid lip service. They agitated for a national socialist ideology, in the literal meaning of those words. They hated Marxism because it was atheist and internationalist. But they believed in agrarian reform and were emotionally pro-labor; they regarded the CNT and UGT masses as having been misled by foreign propagandists.

These radicals gathered around the person of the founder's sister, Pilar Primo de Rivera. They were led by a brash, personally courageous, but not very intelligent former mechanic, Manuel Hedilla. The German ambassador, Faupel, who had headed a number of military missions in South America during the twenties, and who was a left-wing Nazi, encouraged the Hedilla group. Whether he really thought Hedilla capable of heading a government, or whether he thought of the Falange simply as a means of pressure on the extraordinarily stubborn Generalissimo, is not clear.

Meanwhile, in late March, General Franco's brother-in-law, Ramón Serrano Suñer, arrived in Salamanca. In 1931 Serrano Suñer had been a young lawyer of recognized ability and monarchist convictions. He became the chief of the Youth Section of Catholic Action (JAP) and one of the parliamentary leaders of the CEDA. He was also a personal friend of José Antonio, but had not joined the Falange. An admirer of Mussolini and Dollfuss and a frank enemy of democracy, he had spent the month of August, 1936, in the Model Prison, where he witnessed the killing of Ruiz de Alda and José Antonio's brother. Two of his own brothers were the victims of paseos. In early 1937, he escaped from Madrid with the help of the Asturian Socialist leader Belarmino Tomás and of foreign diplomatic personnel.[8]

His arrival in Salamanca coincided with the rising Falange agitation. He imparted to his brother-in-law his long-held conviction that neither the Falange nor the Carlists possessed leaders of real stature. The Popular Front experience had roused in him a deeply nationalist, traditionalist reaction. He compared the current chaos, physical insecurity, and threat to the unity of the nation with the situation at the beginning of the reign of the Catholic Kings. There was no royal Isabella available, however, and General Franco himself would have to be God's instrument for restoring order and unity in Spain.[9]

Early in April the General was planning to fuse the Carlist and miscellaneous remaining Catholic and JONS youth groups with the Falange in order to form a unique political party under his own absolute control. He intended to name a *Secretariado Político*, giving a majority influence to the less radical fraction of the Falange. Hedilla attempted to head off this development by naming a *Junta Política* of his own, composed of left wingers like Pilar Primo de Rivera and the poet and propagandist Dionisio Ridruejo. Enmities within the Falange led to a gang fight one night in Salamanca between the adherents of Hedilla and those of his arch-rival Agustín Aznar.[10] Franco took advantage of the disorders to break Hedilla completely. The left-wing chief was court-martialed and condemned to death; his sentence was commuted, but nevertheless he spent the years 1937–41 in solitary confinement. On April 19 Franco unilaterally announced the

[8] Foltz, *Masquerade*, p. 83.

[9] Ramón Serrano Suñer, *Entre Hendaya y Gibraltar* (Madrid, 1947), pp. 23–9 and passim. Serrano strongly implies that the ideas were his, and that he was molding his brother-in-law's thought. He may, like many persons, have underestimated Franco's ability to think for himself.

[10] Payne, *Falange*, pp. 164–66.

unification of the several parties as the *Falange Española Tradicionalista y de las JONS*. The decisiveness and ease with which he defeated the Hedilla faction confirmed his absolute political control of Nationalist Spain and also notified Faupel as to who was master in Salamanca.

By the spring of 1937 General Franco had acquired full confidence in himself as the predestined master of the new Spain. On April 18 he talked for over an hour with Ambassador Cantalupo, who was about to return to Rome. Relations between the two men had been marked by mutual respect, but not by cordiality. The Ambassador's most recent interviews had dealt with two unpleasant subjects: the mass executions in Málaga and the Italian debacle at Guadalajara. The General was well aware of the long war ahead, and of the undercurrent of disapproval among his allies concerning both military and political policy.

Speaking partly in Spanish, partly in French, he explained that the Civil War was one of the many internal wars in Spanish history. He would do what he could not to have it last a day longer than necessary. But he could not hurry matters by destroying the cities, railroads, farms, and population of Spain. This was a war of Reconquest against the foreigners and foreign influences which had poisoned the Spanish mind with Bolshevik ideas. The Nationalists must not only "liberate" (liberare) the Reds in the Popular Front zone, they must liberate the Reds under the authority of Salamanca as well. The process would take a long time. It would require both patience and sternness. The General said he knew that the Italians thought he was restoring only the old Spain. He insisted that he would create a new Spain, and he asked the Ambassador to report this fact clearly in Rome. Over and over he insisted: "Mr. Ambassador, Franco is not making war against Spain; he is only liberating Spain."[11]

The iron will, the idealism, and the absolute centering of the cause in his own person were clear to Cantalupo. They became increasingly clear to all Spaniards and many foreigners in the further course of the Civil War. No Falangist leader,

[11] Cantalupo, *Fu la Spagna,* pp. 230–34.

no other general, and no figure of the traditional Right compared remotely with Franco in power and determination. The unification of the Falange and the Carlists into a single party with himself as head simply confirmed the fact that by April 1937 the Nationalist cause was completely embodied in the person of General Francisco Franco y Bahamonde.

THE FALL OF LARGO CABALLERO

THE successful defense of Madrid, the creation of a disciplined army, and the performance of that army at the Jarama and Guadalajara were all factors of strength in the over-all situation of the Republican government. But between December 1936, and May 1937 a bitter struggle was occurring in the background. The most important single development in that struggle was the astonishing growth of the Communist Party. On July 18 it had counted between 20,000 and 30,000 members. By January 1937 it had grown to about 200,000 and by mid-1937 claimed 1,000,000.[1] Gratitude for Russian aid was a powerful motive for the Party's growth. In November Madrid had been hung with portraits of Marx, Lenin, and Stalin. Tens of thousands had flocked to see *Chapayev* and other movies and documentary films of the Russian Revolution, and everyone compared the defense of Madrid with that of Petrograd. General Mola had said he would enter Madrid on the 7th in order to celebrate the anniversary of the Russian Revolution, and the Madrileños accepted the challenge in his terms. Also, as was the case with all the Western countries, many liberals and Socialists had visited the Soviet Union in the past few years. Whatever their reservations about dictatorship as a type of government, they had been deeply impressed by the atmosphere of enthusiasm and construction, and by the absence, in sharp contrast with the capitalist world, of unemployment.

But gratitude for military aid was only one of a number of factors. In the defense of Madrid the Communists had given the most notable examples of efficiency. Their precinct directors had organized the best communications posts, kitchens, first aid stations, and their troops had shown the best discipline

[1] Broué and Témime, *La révolution et la guerre d'Espagne*, pp. 208ff.

under fire. Their orators explained tirelessly, without rhetoric, the political and military significance of the defense of Madrid. The Communist woman deputy Dolores Ibarruri spoke repeatedly over the radio to deny defeatist rumors and stem potential panic. Married to an Asturian miner, simple and warm in speech, she dressed austerely in black; to thousands of soldiers and citizens who saw her at the front lines and heard her on the air she was known as "La Pasionaria."

From the moment of the Popular Front electoral victory, the Communist Party had presented itself as the advocate of loyal cooperation between the middle-class liberals and the working class. At the outbreak of the war, they had opposed the local, collectivist revolutions and made themselves the champions of small bourgeois property against anarchist and left Socialist confiscation. In Catalonia, when the PSUC entered the Cabinet in late September, their minister of supply, Juan Comorera, ended requisitions, restored money payments, and protected the Catalan peasants against further collectivization. At Valencia the Communist Minister of Agriculture, Vicente Uribe, had difficulty explaining to the grateful farmers, many of whom were Catholics, and not a few Carlists, that one must study and become a convinced Marxist before joining the Party.

The Communists, in the very name of Marxist principles, defended the rights of the small middle class who were threatened by the "infantile left," composed principally of anarchists and left Socialists. Their new recruits were not, for the most part, proletarians, and their expansion made no dent on the loyalties of the UGT and CNT workers. They became a party of functionaries, army officers, young intellectuals, and small *bourgeoisie*. In the course of time, the Communist Party counted among its members General Miaja, head of the Madrid defense junta, General Pozas of the central army, and Colonel Hidalgo de Cisneros, head of the Air Force. These men, and many other Republican officers, joined the Party not on the basis of Marxist doctrine, but on the basis of the efficacy of the Communists in the defense of Madrid.

The Communist expansion caused considerable misgivings

within the Caballero wing of the Socialist Party. Leading intellectuals like Luis Araquistáin, and most of the long-time UGT union officers, feared the Communists as a Trojan horse which would destroy the truly Spanish revolutionary program in favor of a Stalinist bureaucracy and a foreign policy geared purely to the interests of the Soviet Union. But Santiago Carrillo, of the JSU, and other younger leaders who had been ardent "Caballeristas" until late in the summer of 1936, now saw the Communist Party as a more "advanced," sophisticated organization. Margarita Nelken, left Socialist deputy, troubled by the passivity of the Socialists in comparison with the energy of the Communists, joined the latter party in early 1937.

The attitude of the Communists, and of the JSU chiefs, toward Caballero mingled admiration with condescension. The Party had the discipline, the clear "dialectical" understanding of the significance of the war, and the prestige of Russian arms. But it had no distinguished national chief, no great personality to compare with Largo Caballero. They hoped the old man would "evolve" politically to the point where he would see the correctness of the demand for a fusion of the two parties under his own leadership.

Alvarez del Vayo, as Foreign Minister, not only acted as interpreter for Ambassador Rosenberg in the latter's daily visits to the Prime Minister, but consulted Rosenberg and the Russian military advisers as though they were unconditional allies who could not possibly have motives and interests different from those of the Spanish Republic.[2] The Argentine Communist Victor Codovila (also known as Medina) several times visited Caballero to urge the union of the parties, and at one point, the Republican ambassador to the Soviet Union returned to Valencia with a personal demand from Stalin to know whether or not Caballero proposed to go through with the fusion.[3]

Equally important in the struggle was the constitution of a corps of political commissars, modeled on that of

[2] Prieto in *El Socialista* (Toulouse), Dec. 18, 1958.
[3] Largo Caballero, *Mis recuerdos,* pp. 224–26.

the Red Army during the Russian Revolution. The commissars were supposed to serve the dual function of orienting the political consciousness of the troops and checking on the loyalty of professional officers. In fact, they also had considerable influence over promotions and the distribution of supplies. In the hands of a single, disciplined party, they would obviously constitute a hierarchy of their own parallel to the military command under the War Minister. Caballero had named Alvarez del Vayo to head the war commissariat, and the latter appointed mostly Communists to these key posts, doubtless counting on the expected evolution of the Prime Minister toward closer collaboration with the Party.[4]

Largo Caballero personally had maintained a stiff, guarded attitude toward both Rosenberg and the Spanish Communists. Without openly challenging them, he nevertheless resisted their efforts to dominate the War Ministry. The first public clash came just after the fall of Málaga, when the Communists demanded the removal of General José Asensio, whom they stigmatized as the "organizer of defeat." In September, when Largo had appointed him to command the central front, the Communists had enthusiastically praised him. But Asensio had offended both them and the anarchists by his efforts to eliminate all party propaganda in the training of the Republican Army. The Communists had then demanded his removal from the central front, and Largo had demonstrated his continuing confidence by appointing Asensio Under-Secretary of War in the cabinet of which he was himself the Minister of War.

Since Asensio was responsible for the training of the

[4] Burnett Bolloten, *The Grand Camouflage*, pp. 226ff. Throughout the present chapter, I have drawn heavily on this carefully documented study of the Communist Party in 1936–37. It is unrivaled in its coverage of the wartime press, of which Bolloten, himself a UP correspondent in Spain, made a large collection. J. Pérez Salas, *Guerra en España, passim,* has much valuable material on the Army staff appointments in relation to both Communist vs. non-Communist and professional vs. militia rivalries.

infantry which gave so excellent an account of itself at the Jarama, the Communists could not logically accuse him of incompetence. Instead, they implied that there was something treasonable in his failure to supply Málaga with weapons. This made no impression on the Prime Minister since it was fully evident that the Republic did not have the resources simultaneously to defend Málaga and fight at the Jarama. Finally they attacked on personal grounds, charging that his drinking prowess and known fondness for women were dangerous characteristics, to which Largo Caballero, according to his memoirs, retorted that he understood there were homosexuals in the Communist Party, and referred also to rumors of a Masonic plot to assassinate Asensio.

A few days after the fall of Málaga, Rosenberg, accompanied by Del Vayo, visited Caballero to demand flatly the removal of Asensio. The old man threw Rosenberg out of his office, and then angrily asked Del Vayo why he made himself so readily the spokesman of Soviet wishes. Del Vayo replied that unfortunately the question was one of public confidence. The Republican and anarchist press were also attacking Asensio, and if so many groups considered him a traitor, this fact alone made it necessary to replace him. No argument could more deeply have wounded the 69-year-old Prime Minister, so scrupulous concerning his own integrity, and so certain of Asensio's. He held out for a week before admitting that the latter's usefulness had in fact been destroyed by the press campaign.[5]

On February 21 he accepted the general's resignation. At the same time he replaced him with Colonel Cerón, a

[5] For the climax of the Asensio affair, Caballero, *Mis recuerdos,* p. 193; Julio Alvarez del Vayo, *Freedom's Battle* (New York, 1940), p. 126. The *Recuerdos* consist of letters written by Caballero at the end of World War II, without access to documents. Their extreme bitterness, and their dependence on memory, limit their usefulness when he is talking of other people's reactions. However, they give an honest and revealing view of his own outlook, and in the present instance Del Vayo's account accords with Caballero's except as to the motives.

one-time monarchist and personal secretary of the Count
Jordana who was serving in the Nationalist Army.[6] He retained as chief of operations Colonel Sigismundo Casado,
who had been appointed by Asensio. He removed three of the
most important Communists from the Valencia staff, assigning them to the front, and appointed six trusted Socialists as
inspectors of the War Commissars. He demanded the recall
of Rosenberg to Moscow.

These moves indicated Caballero's determination to stop the
growth of Communist influence, but they did nothing to solve
the problem of unifying the war effort. In Catalonia the CNT
factory committees dragged their heels on war production,
claiming that the government deprived them of raw materials
and was favoring the *bourgeoisie*. On the Teruel front the
so-called "Iron Column," composed largely of anarchists and
some convicts released from the San Miguel de los Reyes
penitentiary, refused to obey the long-standing government
order for all militia units to be incorporated into the regular
Army. In Valencia, the capital of Republican Spain since
November 6, crack units of the Assault Guards and part of
the 13th International Brigade were held in readiness during
the winter to defend the government against threatened
anarchist efforts to seize control of the city. The ports of
Alicante and Cartagena (at which most of the Russian ships
docked) and the supply bases at Murcia and Albacete were
administered by the Communists who had unofficial prisons
of their own in which to handle recalcitrant anarchist workers
or occasional International Brigaders who showed marked
antipathy to the Party. At Madrid the Communists were the
preponderant influence within the defense junta, but by no
means in absolute control. The anarchist press complained of
Communist control of the prisons. Socialist and Communist
journals replied with lists of comrades liquidated by the
anarchist "chekas"; and the Socialists, while generally supporting the defense junta, nevertheless complained of favor-

[6] Martín Blázquez, *op.cit.*, pp. 319–21, considers Cerón the best
professional appointment Caballero could have made in the
circumstances.

itism toward Communist units in the distribution of military supplies.[7]

Largo Caballero had been chosen Prime Minister in the hope that his immense personal prestige in all sectors of the working class would create a more unified war effort. But this hope rapidly diminished in the continuing presence of bitter regional and ideological tensions. A realignment of forces gradually took place between December and March. The Republicans generally drew closer to the Communists. The fifteen years' rivalry between the Socialist and Communist parties was of little consequence to them, and they saw in the Communists the defenders of the small *bourgeoisie*. Prieto and Negrín, both much abler men than the Prime Minister, were frustrated by his slowness, his bureaucratic outlook, his pathological jealousy of any potential Socialist candidate for the premiership, his insistence on running the military aspect of the war. Negrín habitually napped at cabinet meetings, head down on his folded arms, coming to life only when financial projects were mentioned, and then generally saying no. Prieto despaired of making concrete suggestions, knowing that the very fact that they came from him would cause Caballero to propose something else.

Thus an alliance of circumstance brought together the middle-class Republicans, the moderate Socialists, and the Communists. The alliance was based on the all-out defense of Madrid, the restraint of proletarian revolution, the need for a strongly centralized war government, and the growing conviction that Largo Caballero must at the very least give up the war portfolio. On the other side were the "Caballeristas," and the bulk of both the UGT and the CNT, united in fear of the Communists and in defense of the regional collective authorities established in the first days of the war. As against the Communist call for cooperation with the *bourgeoisie*, they insisted that the war could not be won unless the proletarian revolution were won also. In the center stood the Prime Minister, anxious to rebuild the authority of the state, but unable to choose between or to dominate the opposing forces.

In late March, after the Battle of Guadalajara, the struggle

[7] Broué and Témime, *op.cit.*, pp. 249–50.

again came into the open in Madrid. The CNT prison delegate, Melchor Rodríguez, published precise accusations of torture in unofficial Communist prisons, the victims of which were often released prisoners who had been kidnapped by the Communists. Rodríguez was an autodidact, a philosophical anarchist, absolutely fearless personally, and absolutely opposed to terrorism. Prisoners of all political affiliations had benefitted from his humanity, and the scandal was enormous when he not only cited the practices but named as responsible the Communist councilor of public order, José Cazorla.[8] The incident enabled Largo simultaneously to strike a blow at political terrorism and to reestablish the authority of the Valencia government in Madrid. The defense junta accepted Cazorla's resignation, and on April 23 the junta itself was dissolved.

Caballero also proposed at this time to break the power of the political commissars, hundreds of whom had been appointed by Del Vayo without his signature.[9] On April 17 he published a decree stating that all future nominations would be made directly by the Prime Minister, and that all current commissars must have their appointments validated by his signature before May 15. A bitter press debate followed. *Adelante,* the Caballero organ, accused the commissars of political pressure, favoritism, and occasional assassination. *Frente Rojo,* the Communist organ, saw the decree as the work of "fascist elements" and urged the commissars to stick to their posts. *El Socialista,* organ of the Prieto wing, which had previously confined itself to occasional complaints of favoritism, now published a list of party militants who had been tortured in private Communist prisons in Murcia.

The Communists were now determined, in defense of their own acquired positions, to get rid of Caballero. A few days

[8] A. Nuñez Morgado, *Los sucesos de España visto por un diplomático,* pp. 285–88 and Galíndez, *Los vascos, passim,* concerning Melchor Rodríguez. The CNT prison delegate became a legend among Madrid political prisoners, as I had occasion to learn from the number who asked me what had happened to him after the war.

[9] Caballero, *op.cit.,* pp. 223–24.

of virtual civil war within the city of Barcelona in early May provided them with the perfect occasion, one which involved many issues besides the Party's enmity toward the Prime Minister. Ever since July 18, Barcelona had been the mecca of unorthodox revolutionary groups. French Proudhonians, English utopian socialists, Italian and Balkan anarchists, Russian menshevik intellectuals—all saw in the Catalán revolution the beginnings of a non-Stalinist, "pure" revolution. The Communists had no such prestige in Barcelona as in Madrid, and in any case the "front" to most Catalans meant eastern Aragon, where the drive to Saragossa and the siege of Huesca had long since lost their momentum.

Among the proletariat, the naïve optimism of the revolutionary conquests of the previous August had given way to feelings of resentment and of somehow having been cheated. The cost of living had doubled since July 18, while wages had risen only about 15 per cent. Women spent hours each day waiting for bread, and the police were as brutal with complainers as in times of the Monarchy. The POUM and the anarchist press simultaneously extolled the collectivizations and explained the failures of production as due to Valencia policies of boycotting the Catalan economy and favoring the *bourgeoisie*. They explained the loss of Málaga as due in large measure to the low morale and the disorientation of the Andalusian proletariat, which saw the Valencia government evolving steadily toward the right. Evoking the importance of the Moorish contingents in the Nationalist Army, they urged the government to offer independence to Morocco, a gesture which would have been highly appreciated in Paris and London.

Meanwhile, the government slowly pursued its aim of reestablishing central control of the state apparatus. The Communists, the JSU, and the PSUC in Catalonia called for a strengthened alliance of all the "healthy" social forces in Spain against "Franco, the Trotskyites, and the uncontrollables." In Catalonia the anarchists had, ever since July 18, controlled the customs stations at the French border. On April 17, 1937, the reorganized carabineros, acting on orders of the Finance Minister, Juan Negrín, began to reoccupy the frontier. At least eight anarchists were killed in clashes with the carabineros. A prominent UGT official, Roldán Cortado, was murdered, probably by CNT elements, and his funeral in Barcelona was the occasion of a massive demonstration against the anarchists.

At the end of March the "Iron Column" had finally been militarized, at the cost of dozens of desertions and several clashes between its members and Valencia troops.[10] Caballero made clear his intention also to militarize the remaining worker militias of Catalonia. In the last days of April the anarchist and POUM press sounded the alarm. Militarization, for them, was simply a euphemism for disarmament and repression of the class-conscious revolutionary workers. Tension was such that the Generalitat canceled the scheduled May Day celebrations, fearing pitched battles between the police and the anti-Communist Left.

Among the public services still jealously controlled by the anarchists was the Telephone Company, administration of which enabled them to listen in on government conversations with Valencia or Madrid, and to monitor all foreign calls originating from or directed to Barcelona and Valencia. On May 3 Rodríguez Salas (councilor for public order in the Generalitat and a member of the PSUC) intended, peaceably, he hoped, but by force if necessary, to take control of the Barcelona telephone central. He arrived with a company of Assault Guards and was met by fire from within the building.

This skirmish led to three days of sporadic fighting all over the city. POUM and anarchist troops assembled at Barbastro and prepared to march to Barcelona in order to defend their brothers from the "counter-revolutionary" *putsch*. Luis Companys, the anarchist ministers in the Caballero government, and *Solidaridad Obrera* all appealed for an immediate cease-fire. The revolutionaries were deeply divided as to tactics. All of them instinctively hated the Assault Guard, and all of them demanded the removal of the principal PSUC councilors,

[10] Besides the previously cited Bolloten book, see the article by Lawrence Fernsworth in *Foreign Affairs*, July, 1937, pp. 666ff. for the "Iron Column" and other details on the government's reassertion of police power.

Rodríguez Salas and Juan Comorera. The CNT and the POUM officially ordered their followers only to "defend" themselves, but this settled nothing, since the whole question was whether the government or the separate political parties were going to control the public services of Catalonia. Small but vehement anarchist groups, the Libertarian Youth and the Friends of Durruti, encouraged armed resistance in the name of the revolutionary conquests which alone made worthwhile the maintenance of the Popular Front.

On May 5, Companys obtained a fragile truce, on the basis of which the PSUC councilors were to retire from the regional government, and the question of the Telephone Company was left to future negotiation. That very night, however, Antonio Sesé, a UGT official who was about to enter the reorganized cabinet, was murdered. In any event, the Valencia authorities were in no mood to temporize further with the Catalan Left. On May 6 several thousand *asaltos* arrived in the city, and the Republican Navy demonstrated in the port. Caballero named General Sebastián Pozas, a professional officer who had recently become a Communist, to command the Army of Aragon. The Left militia were disarmed, and military discipline was established on the Aragon front. The Prime Minister pledged himself against political reprisals, but in the following few days a dozen anti-Communist Left leaders were the victims of assassinations motivated in part by revenge for the UGT deaths of the recent past, in part by Communist determination to liquidate physically the anti-Stalinist leadership in Barcelona.[11]

In Valencia the Communist ministers insisted that Largo remove the Minister of the Interior, Angel Galarza, for failure

[11] Broué and Témime, *op.cit.*, pp. 258–66, give the best short account of the Barcelona events. Pietro Nenni, *La guerre d'Espagne*, pp. 75, 177, names a number of anti-Stalinist victims of Spanish, Italian, and Russian nationality. Nenni is, on the whole, friendly to, but not uncritical of, the Communists. George Orwell, *Homage to Catalonia* (London, 1938) gives a vivid, sympathetic picture of the situation as seen by the POUM militia, but the reader should bear in mind Orwell's own honest statement that he knew very little about the political complexities of the struggle.

to uncover the "Trotskyite plot" in Barcelona, and demanded the suppression of *La Batalla,* the POUM organ, as having incited to rebellion. The Prime Minister saw no evidence to justify either demand. On May 13, at a cabinet meeting, they demanded the suppression of the POUM; when Caballero refused to take up the question, they walked out, thereby precipitating a cabinet crisis.[12]

The many-faceted struggle between the Prime Minister and his enemies now came to a head. The Communists attacked him because of his threat to their control of the commissars and because of their pathological hatred of the POUM. But both Republicans and anarchists had opposed him in the Asensio case, and the anti-Communist Left would hardly rise to his defense after the Barcelona events. The moderate Socialists, in turn, were by no means averse to the political (as against the physical) liquidation of the Trotskyites, anarchists, and "Caballeristas."

Disagreements on military strategy also played a role. In April Largo Caballero wished to activate a long-discussed plan for an offensive in Extremadura. If the Republicans struck hard to recapture Mérida and Badajoz, they would be able to cut off the Burgos zone from its supplies and communications with Andalusia. The Nationalist lines were known to be thinly held, and the population to be pro-Republican; thus the government would strike the Nationalists in an area where they were weak both militarily and politically. Generals Asensio and Martínez Cabrera had drawn up the first plans before Asensio's resignation. The operational plan in the spring was prepared by Colonel Sigismundo Casado, and Colonel Hernández Sarabia had begun in strict secrecy to concentrate troops near Ciudad Real.

However, the Russian advisers, the Madrid general staff, and the Prieto Socialists all opposed the Extremadura plan. The Spaniards were afraid to uncover the Madrid front, and the strategic value of the operation, even if successful, was doubtful since the Nationalists were welcome to use Portuguese roads, air bases, and telephone facilities. The Russian advisers

[12] Caballero, *op.cit.,* pp. 218ff.

favored an offensive near Madrid. In their view, since General Franco had concentrated his best troops before the capital, and since he had little popular support, the way to win the war was to destroy the army besieging Madrid. With Russian backing, Miaja refused in late April to transfer central army units to Ciudad Real, and the Russian air officers made clear to Colonel Casado that practically no aviation would be available.[13]

When the Communists precipitated the cabinet crisis on May 13, they did not wish to appear responsible for the overthrow of Caballero. During the presidential consultations for the formation of a new government, they told Azaña that they would continue to collaborate with him providing he gave up the war portfolio, which latter office should be filled by Prieto. Azaña communicated these conditions to the Prime Minister. But Caballero's pride, his view of his own responsibility in the creation of the new army, and his old rivalry with Prieto would not permit him to accept this solution. He also refused to bow to obvious Russian pressure on military planning, but at the same time, he did not want to weaken the

[13] Luis Araquistáin, in *El comunismo y la guerra de España* (Carmaux, Tarn, France, 1939) speaks of Largo as having been preparing the Extremadura offensive "for months," and Colonel Sigismundo Casado, in *The Last Days of Madrid* (London, 1939), pp. 71–4, speaks of Russian sabotage of these plans and of Miaja's resistance to the idea of transferring troops from Madrid. In an extended conversation concerning Largo's government, Rodolfo Llopis, who had been his cabinet secretary, emphasized to me the importance of the Extremadura plan; and Julio Just, the Left Republican Minister of Public Works in the Caballero government, told me that he had prepared dozens of portable bridges and dispatched numerous supply trains to Ciudad Real. On the other hand Prieto told me flatly that upon taking office as Minister of Defense on May 17, he found absolutely no practical dispositions looking toward an offensive in Extremadura, and this statement was confirmed by a Madrid general officer now living in Spain. Thus the evidence concerning the practical importance of this affair is contradictory, but its political import is clear: the lineup of those following Russian lead against those following the orders of Largo Caballero as Prime Minister and Minister of War.

war effort by bringing the struggle into the open. He resigned, as his enemies hoped he would.

The fall of Largo Caballero did not have any immediate spectacular repercussions, but it was a major spiritual crisis in the history of the Spanish Left. He was the first representative of the working class to become the Prime Minister of what the Constitution of 1931 declared to be a "Republic of workers of all categories." In early 1936 he had indeed been an "infantile leftist," seduced by the Marxist imagery concerning the will of History. The Spanish middle class in September 1936, had feared a Soviet revolution when he became Prime Minister. But in office he had devoted his energies to the reconstruction of the democratic state. He had gladly backed Manuel de Irujo in the latter's campaign to improve court procedures and prison conditions. Hating the atmosphere of innuendo, he had fought to retain General Asensio. When, later in the spring, it was discovered that General Miaja and Colonel Rojo had been members of the UME, their political enemies wanted them arrested. Caballero refused to consider UME membership in itself as evidence of disloyalty, though he had been forced to drop Asensio for less cause. In the case of the POUM he had taken a similar stand.

But Caballero was an inarticulate man, unable to explain to his followers the need for discipline, for cooperation with the middle class, for subordination to central authority. He had doubtless forgotten his own revolutionary growlings of early 1936. He did not think to claim credit for a policy of tolerance toward all political factions in Republican Spain because it had never occurred to him, once in office, to institute any other policy. With the defection of close collaborators like Alvarez del Vayo and Santiago Carrillo, he felt his growing isolation. He never seemed to appreciate either the manifold appeal of the Communist Party, in the particular circumstances, or the discredit cast upon him in the summer of 1936 by Left Socialist chekas using his name.

Caballero also failed to appreciate the importance of "public relations." In the autumn of 1936 the Communists created the image of him as the "Spanish Lenin," and in the spring of 1937 they portrayed him as a cacique dictating to his colleagues of the Popular Front.[14] The old man himself made no efforts to woo the press, Spanish or foreign. The Communists launched clear slogans, and made sure that all the grateful Madrileños were acquainted with the images of Lenin and Stalin. Largo had no such publicity machine. He was blamed for the disunity of the Republican zone and for the loss of Málaga. He received no credit for the victories at the Jarama and Guadalajara. His own wartime education had been too rapid and too recent for him to clarify the difference between the "infantile leftist" of early 1936 and the Prime Minister of 1937. During his later months in office he had defended Republican liberty better than many a lifelong Republican. He resigned in great bitterness, silently, so as not to cause further disunity. But the Spanish people never gave to his successor, Juan Negrín, the confidence they had originally given Largo Caballero. They recognized in Largo a man of great courage and inner nobility and knew that he had been defeated, not for his shortcomings as an executive, but for his resistance to the demands of the Communists and the Russians. Technically and administratively the Republic gained by the change. Spiritually it lost ground.

[14] The manner in which the Communists first built up Largo and later undermined his reputation can be followed very vividly in the autobiography of Jesús Hernández, published simultaneously as *La grande trahison* (Paris, 1953) and *Yo fuí un ministro de Stalin* (Mexico, D.F., 1953). Several writers on this period have depended principally on Hernández for their description of Largo's fall. I preferred for several reasons not to rely on him for specific data. Hernández as a young Communist had taken part in an unsuccessful attempt to assassinate Prieto. In 1936–38 he was successively assigned to undertake the character assassination, in public speeches, of Asensio, then Caballero, and finally Prieto. After the war he was expelled from the Spanish Communist Party. His cabinet colleagues, Prieto and Manuel de Irujo, with whom I discussed a number of points in his book, were of the opinion that he was *trying* to tell the truth. I therefore used his work only in corroboration of other sources. The reader should also beware of a bowdlerized Spanish edition even more sensational in tone than the genuine article, and published under the title, *Yo, ministro de Stalin en España.*

22

THE WAR IN THE NORTH

FROM the moment of the military rising until late October 1937, a separate war was being fought in the northern coastal provinces. In Santander and the Asturias, left-wing Popular Front forces dominated, but in the highly important industrial region around Bilbao, power rested in the hands of the Basque Nationalists, a fact which impressed a special character on both the military and political history of the northern campaigns. On July 18 the firm reaction of the civilian authorities had prevented any rising from occurring in Bilbao. The Basque Nationalist organ *Euzkadi* announced that in a struggle between civilian republican government on the one hand and monarchism and fascism on the other, it supported the Republican regime.

The Carlists and the Insurgent military immediately regarded the Basque Nationalists as traitors. The very fact that they were prosperous, bourgeois Catholics made it all the more incomprehensible—and unpardonable—that they should take the side of the Popular Front government against the rising by the "forces of order." As the Carlist troops swept through the villages of Alava and Guipúzcoa, they purged the Basque municipal authorities before turning their attention to Socialists and anarchists. They were angered also by the unenthusiastic attitude of leading prelates. In Pamplona Bishop Marcelino Olaechea deplored the outbreak of the war and refused to give his unconditional blessing to the troops. In Vitoria, Bishop Mateo Múgica was quickly remembered for his statement during the last electoral campaign, to the effect that Basque Nationalism was in no way incompatible with the obligations of a good Catholic. The Bishop of Pamplona came from a working-class family and was well known for his interest in social questions. The Bishop of Vitoria was a vehement Monarchist who had served as the confidential courier of Cardinal Segura in the summer of 1931. But both men knew that the Basque Nationalists, in spirit and in works, were the best Catholics in their diocese. Both feared the primitive fanaticism of the Carlists. In the last days of July, Bishop Olaechea was being stigmatized as a "Socialist," and Bishop Múgica was subjected to a series of petty gestures and threats by General Millán Astray and by the Carlist deputy for Vitoria, José Luis Oriol.[1]

Cardinal Gomá, primate of Spain, had come to Navarre for reasons of health some days before the outbreak of the Civil War. He, too, avoided public gestures during the first days in Pamplona; he was favorably disposed toward the Insurgents but sensed the delicacy and importance of the Basque question. Hoping to avoid a fratricidal struggle between Catholics, he urged the two bishops to issue a pastoral letter condemning the Basque Nationalist opposition to the rising. He composed the letter himself, but it was much too strong for Bishop Olaechea, who made corrections and additions to the draft before signing it. In Vitoria, Bishop Múgica wished to communicate with persons of his confidence in Bilbao before signing, and thought that he had received the permission of the military to do so. But on the same day, August 6, the letter was read over the Vitoria radio, without the Bishop of Pamplona's corrections and without the voluntary assent of the Bishop of Vitoria. As there was no real front yet—the Basques on both sides of the line were in constant communication—the circumstances surrounding the pastoral letter were well known in Bilbao. Thus the letter was never accepted as a genuine pastoral, despite a radio statement by Bishop Múgica himself in September denying all the stories of pressure exerted upon him.[2]

The Basques never varied from their initial position of defending civilian republican government against the military rising. They hoped, of course, that their personal and commercial connections with England would stand them in good stead, and not until the fall of Irún on September 4 could they

[1] Juan de Iturralde, *El catolicismo y la cruzada de Franco*, II, 279–89.

[2] *Ibid.*, II, 300–303.

truly believe that the French border was permanently closed. On September 7, they decided to form their own government, and they opened negotiations with the new Largo Caballero cabinet concerning the official status of the Basques. Prime Minister José Antonio Aguirre wanted Caballero to recognize the Basque cabinet by immediate decree. Caballero replied that passage of the long-pending autonomy statute by the Cortes would provide a firmer legal basis. He also asked the Basques to supply a minister for the Madrid government. On October 1, those members of the Cortes loyal to the Republic, and able to get to Madrid, unanimously passed the statute. Manuel de Irujo entered the cabinet as Minister without Portfolio. His presence served both to symbolize Basque co-operation and to support Caballero's eventual efforts to improve prison conditions and reestablish the rule of law in the Republican zone.

During August and September, dozens of priests suspected of being Basque Nationalists were arrested in the Insurgent zone, and many Basque political leaders were imprisoned, if not shot. In Vitoria their wives and daughters had their hair cut off as a sign of shame. A short tuft was left on top—enough to be tied with a ribbon of the colors of the old monarchist flag. The women were marched to Mass on Sunday morning by Falange and Requeté guards, and afterward they were paraded through the streets of the city.[3] Bishop Múgica's friends were convinced that the military planned to assassinate him and then give the act the appearance of an accident or "red atrocity" on the road to Burgos. The Bishop of Valencia, who was summering in Burgos at the outbreak of the war, inter-vened with the military to prevent such an enormity. In early October one of the first acts of the new Burgos government under General Franco was to demand the expulsion of Múgica who, despite his efforts to ingratiate himself, remained for the local military a Basque *rojoseparatista*. Cardinal Góma came to Victoria to urge the Bishop's compliance, and together they covered appearances by announcing that Múgica was going to Rome in connection with his duties as president of the

[3] Letter of P. Luis Ramírez, sent from Vitoria to a fellow priest in Belgium, Oct. 17, 1936, cited in Iturralde, ɪɪ, 439–40.

Unión Misional del Clero. In the last weeks of October the
military authorities executed some dozen Basque priests on
grounds of their political activities. At the request of the
Vatican, Cardinal Gomá intervened with General Franco,
and the latter ordered, as of November 6, the suspension of
such executions.[4]

Meanwhile, the Basques prepared to fight, establishing their
defensive front along the heights which formed, generally
speaking, the provincial border between Guipúzcoa and
Vizcaya. They had 30–40,000 militiamen of their own, and
several thousand anarchist and UGT militiamen who had retreated with them from San Sebastián. But they were virtually
without arms. On September 26 they unloaded 5,000 Czech
rifles and a large supply of ammunition which they had bought
from contraband sources in Hamburg. In October one Russian
ship arrived in Bilbao bringing 12 aircraft and 25 armored
cars which mounted 47 mm. cannon and heavy machine guns.
These enabled the Basques to establish excellent communications and reconnaissance posts near the front, but the total
was much too slight for any but defensive use. Bilbao was the
center of the Spanish steel industry, with iron mines in
Vizcaya and coal available in Asturias. But no practical
arrangement was ever worked out for getting Asturian coal to
Bilbao. Insurgent command of the air, and of the city of
Oviedo, with its railheads, of course made the task difficult.
But the principal barrier to cooperation was the permanent
state of mutual rancor between the Basque authorities and
the revolutionary leadership in the Asturias. The Catholic
bourgeoisie and the atheist proletariat were enemies on both
religious and class grounds. They also had totally different conceptions of the way to fight. The revolutionary militia fled
the open country and fought heroically in the cities. If the
latter could not be defended, let them be burned so as not to
benefit the enemy. The Basques considered it criminal when

[4] *Ibid.*, 425–28 for the shooting of the Basque priests. On
the situation of the Basque Nationalist clergy, see also Inaki de
Aberrigoyen, *7 mois et 7 jours dans l'Espagne de Franco,* the work
of a priest and member of the Catholic labor organization *Solidaridad de Obreros Vascos.*

the anarchists burned Irún, and the anarchists (and some Socialists and Communists as well) considered the Basques traitors when they evacuated San Sebastián without a fight.

The Basque military plan was to defend the heights at the provincial border while constructing a belt of fortifications around the city of Bilbao. Their militiamen were tough, resourceful, and disciplined. In late September the Insurgents had thought they would walk to Bilbao in three weeks, but the Basques held them at the border of Vizcaya until April 1937. Meanwhile, Asturian miners and Bilbao building workers constructed the "Iron Ring" according to the plans of Basque engineers, one of whom crossed the lines in January with the blueprints in his pocket. Whether out of defeatism, inertia, or lack of materials and labor with which to begin all over again, construction continued along the lines of the betrayed plans, and was in fact never completed. The utter lack of confidence between the Basques and their Santander and Asturian allies hampered the entire defense effort. On September 26, and again on January 4, after German air raids on the city, militiamen had rushed into the prisons and lynched large numbers of political prisoners. After the second set of incidents, the Basque government decided to guard the prisons with their own militiamen only. They were thus able absolutely to end prison raids; but the workers on whom they depended for transportation and construction, and the revolutionary authorities from whom they hoped to receive Asturian coal, looked upon them as "fascists."

In the early months of 1937 the Basques had pinned all their hopes on aid from England and from Madrid. The Insurgent Navy declared Bilbao under blockade. Since the Burgos government was not internationally recognized, the declaration did not carry even the very mild force of international naval custom, and the English, for reasons both of commerce and sympathy, did not recognize it. The Basque government had converted some 24 fishing trawlers into mine sweepers, and they also patrolled the mouth of Bilbao harbor with a half-dozen motor boats protected by coastal guns which reached beyond the three-mile limit. They converted deep-sea trawlers into blockade runners, armoring them as best they

379

could; they used these boats to bring in food and supplies of all sorts and also to assure the continuing export of iron ore.

The attitude of the English varied with circumstances. Some dozen British food ships, occasionally escorted by the British navy up to the three-mile line, entered Bilbao. Sympathetic captains would risk their companies' properties to bring in food or take out refugees, old people, and undernourished children. The British navy did not want to fight the Nationalists, but neither did it wish to grant them the belligerent rights which would empower them to search neutral ships bound for Spanish harbors. Humanitarian considerations played an important role. Conservative as were most British officers, they had been horrified by things they had seen and heard in picking up refugees at Galician ports during the first days. They assumed that the fall of Bilbao would occur sometime in the spring, and were determined to be able at least to carry off political refugees who otherwise were likely to be shot.

On April 6 the *Almirante Cervera,* intending to enforce the blockade, stopped the British freighter *Thorpehall* some five miles off the coast. When two British destroyers appeared, the *Cervera* yielded, but England then ordered its merchant ships not to head for Bilbao, on the grounds that the harbor was heavily mined and effectively blockaded. On the 20th another British freighter, the *Seven Seas Spray,* heeding Basque claims that the harbor was open, brought in a cargo of food from Valencia without being challenged by the Nationalist navy, after which the British government withdrew its earlier order. Until the fall of Bilbao, occasional food ships continued to enter the harbor, and a few ore ships departed, but nowhere could the Basques buy arms legally, or in quantity.[5]

Until after the Battle of the Jarama, the Nationalists marked time at the Vizcaya border, and the occasional engagements in the hills convinced them that a serious buildup would be necessary before Bilbao could be taken. During the month of

[5] Concerning the armament and politics of the Basque government, I depended principally upon G. L. Steer, *The Tree of Gernika.* Further information on naval aspects from the *Survey of International Affairs,* 1937, II, and from Hugh Thomas, *The Spanish Civil War,* 407–11.

March General Mola concentrated roughly 40,000 troops in Guipúzcoa and Alava with Navarrese and Moroccans in the lead and Italians in reserve. The northern campaign was also the most important operation thus far involving German equipment, and the Condor Legion worked as an independent unit, with its own telephone and radio network, German gun crews, mechanics, and pilots. Since the Basques had no anti-aircraft artillery and only a few planes, the Germans operated in virtual laboratory conditions.[6] Bombing raids on the trench systems in the hills caused very few casualties, due to their inaccuracy. But they often caused untrained troops to desert advantageous positions and eventually wore down the nerves even of disciplined soldiers. Most strong points were taken by outflanking movements rather than by assault. A general fault of the Basque trenches was that they were rectilinear, facing the front but not providing flank protection. Once the planes or artillery had dislodged one company, the whole line would tend to crumble, lest the others be attacked from the side or surrounded. The mountain passes were slowly and methodically taken in this manner during April, with small losses on both sides.

On the 26th the Condor aviators made what became one of history's most famous calculated experiments in terror. Choosing market day in Guernica, a town without defenses, without military objectives, and not on the line of march to Bilbao, they first dropped high explosive bombs, then practiced machinegunning the civilians fleeing from the town, and finally set it afire with incendiary bombs. The whole procedure took 2 hours and 45 minutes, with time in between the stages to judge the effectiveness. The town was located in a wide valley. The weather was good, and visibility excellent.

Guernica was not only well chosen from the point of view of the military experiment. It was the traditional, medieval capital of *Euzkadi,* and there was no more effective way to symbolize the Nationalist intent to destroy Basque autonomy than to destroy the city of Guernica. Reacting to the wave of

[6] Hellmut H. Führing, *Wir funken für Franco* (Breslau, 1941), pp. 171–87 and *passim*. Also Reynolds and Eleanor Packard, *Balcony Empire*, pp. 52–6.

international indignation which followed immediately upon the news, Hitler insisted that the Burgos authorities state clearly that Germany was not responsible for the bombing. On the 29th Burgos announced that the city had been burned by the "reds," a myth which some Spanish spokesmen have tried to maintain to the present day. But the eyewitness-account came from Canon Alberto Onaindia, a Basque priest of unchallengable veracity, and all the essential points were confirmed by the testimony of several German officers during the Nüremberg trials in 1946.[7]

The bombing of Guernica, and similar raids on Eibar and Durango, highlighted the Basques' desperate need for aviation if they were to continue to defend themselves. Madrid was willing to supply several Russian fighter planes in spite of the risk which this would entail for the capital's defense. The problem was how to deliver the planes since, even with the most favorable weather conditions, they barely had the range to fly nonstop from Madrid to Bilbao. Prieto, Minister for Navy and Air, and Hidalgo de Cisneros, operational chief of the Air Force, hoped that the French would permit the planes to cross their territory. On May 8 fifteen planes landed at Toulouse, claiming that headwinds and fuel shortage had forced them to alter their course. Non-Intervention officers permitted them to refuel on condition that they return to Barcelona. On the 17th a dozen planes landed at Pau, with the story that they had come from Santander and gotten lost in the fog. Non-Intervention officers disarmed the machines, held them five days, and finally premitted them to leave for Barcelona with a warning to the Republican government that any more flights of that sort would be confiscated. A week later, Cisneros took the risk of sending ten fighters directly to Bilbao; seven arrived safely.[8] For a couple of weeks, boys playing on the outskirts of the city would count "our aviation"

[7] Victor Montserrat, *Le drame d'un peuple incompris* (Paris, 1937), pp. 70–5 for the account of Onaindia; Steer, *Tree of Gernika,* pp. 246–50 for the corroboratory evidence by other journalists visiting the town after the Nationalist announcement that the "reds" had burned it.

[8] Steer, *op.cit.,* pp. 278–81. J. Zugazagoitia, *Historia de la guerra en España,* pp. 254 and *passim.*

as the planes rose—one, two, three, four, five; then a day or so later— one, two, three, four; until on June 6, a week before the final offensive, there were none left.

During the second half of May the Nationalists closed the siege ring around Bilbao. On the 18th, at Amorebieta, the local priest crossed the lines on what he hoped was a mission of conciliation. The Nationalist military authorities court-martialed and shot him, on grounds that he had been the head of the "cheka" in Amorebieta. Then they told the townspeople that he had been shot by the "reds."[9] During the first days of June, the Condor planes and artillery bombarded the so-called "Iron Ring." Since they had the plans in hand, their fire was extremely accurate. In terms of quality, the 37mm. and 88mm. antiaircraft guns were the best weapons the Germans tried out in Spain. Their mobility and accuracy made them very useful as light field artillery in the absence of any need for air defense. They pulverized the enemy trenches with tracer shells and forced the abandonment of many strong points without a fight.

Over and above the fact that the plans of the Iron Ring had been betrayed, it had the same general weakness as the other Basque fortifications. The trenches formed a thin perimeter in the hills outside the city, and in most areas there were only two lines, perhaps 200 to 300 meters apart. They stood on the crests, with the generally uncamouflaged concrete visible to the enemy, without any positions in depth on the counterslope, and without protection on the flanks. A few energetic commanders, seeing the uselessness of the prepared defenses, built other trench systems closeby, zigzagged to permit crossfire, and camouflaged with pine branches. They were able to hold such positions for a number of days, but the men were eventually demoralized by the sight of tracer shells landing directly in the trenches of the Iron Ring.[10] Both political and military commentators at the time suspected treason in the

[9] Iturralde, II, 425–26.

[10] On the failure of the Bilbao defense see in particular the article by Wing Commander A. W. H. James in *The Journal of the United Service Institute* for Feb., 1939; also the observations of the Swiss war correspondent Eddy Bauer, *Rouge et Or* (Neuchâtel, 1938), pp. 71–2.

entire planning of the defense of Bilbao. Undoubtedly a large proportion of the Basque Nationalists were defeatist from the start, in a strictly military sense; but the errors they made in planning their fortifications may just as well have arisen from the fact that as architects and engineers they had devoted their entire previous careers to civilian tasks. It is difficult to suppose that they purposely planned a trench system which would be untenable for their own sons and brothers.

The defense ring was pierced on June 12. For a week thereafter, Asturian, Santander, and Basque militia units retreated westward. The Basque police prevented any desperate gestures at the prisons and protected the factories and unbombed docks from sabotage. As at San Sebastián, they intended to preserve the city rather than practice a scorched-earth policy. At night, motor boats and fishing launches, packed to the gunwales, slipped away—some with refugees headed for San Jean de Luz, others with men intending to carry on the struggle at Santander and Gijón. Altogether perhaps 200,000 persons fled the immediate area in one fashion or another. On the 19th the Nationalist Army entered without opposition and began immediately to distribute food to thousands of women lining the streets.

A few days later Burgos announced the abrogation of the *concierto económico* for the provinces of Guipúzcoa and Vizcaya. In 1840 the absolute royal government had punished the Basques for their part in the Carlist uprising. Now, a centralizing military dictatorship punished them for having taken the side of the Republic in behalf of regional autonomy and democratic government. The concierto remained in force for Alava and Navarre, the provinces which had rallied to the Nationalist cause. On the other hand, the physical purge of Bilbao was relatively lighter than in other areas. Franco was anxious to revive Basque industry as rapidly as possible and to resume the export of iron ore. He was ready to act moderately in order to be assured the cooperation of the Basque industrialists.

The war in the Basque country had worldwide repercussions of its own. Many people who had wasted no sympathy on the Popular Front regimes of Madrid and Barcelona, or who had hoped for an enlightened dictatorship at the start of the military rising, were stirred by the fate of the Basques. The treatment of Bishop Múgica and the shooting of the Basque priests were quickly known in French Catholic circles. The Catholic intellectuals Jacques Maritain and François Mauriac not only presided over a relief committee for the Basque refugees, but published the strongest condemnations of the Nationalist regime. Since Bilbao was an industrial rather than a food-producing region, the food shortage had been acute throughout the winter and spring. Englishmen, Belgians, and Dutchmen, regardless of their politics, were quick to understand the cruelty of a naval blockade which included food on the contraband list.

Basque children placed in French and English foster homes rushed to cellars or had fits of hysterical fear when single airplanes appeared in the sky, thereby teaching their anguished foster parents the meaning of war. The exiled Bishop Múgica joined Cardinal Gomá to plead that the refugee children be placed in Catholic homes, a condition not easily met in England, where readiness to provide foster homes was more widespread among Protestants. In the United States the hierarchy objected vehemently to the plans of a predominantly Protestant committee to bring 500 Basque children to America for the duration of the war. It was not that Catholics in the two countries were less sympathetic to the children's sufferings, but the great majority of their spokesmen were angered by the implication that the children would not be well cared for by the victorious Nationalist government in Spain.[11]

Cardinal Gomá stepped forward as the spokesman of the Spanish Church. A man of forceful character, well able to keep his own counsel, he had generally avoided making statements of a specific political nature during his tenure as Cardinal-Archbishop of Toledo. He was, however, a man of fundamentally conservative, and frequently fascist, views. Speaking in Buenos Aires on the Día de la Raza, October 12, 1934, he had invited his audience to look toward the Old

[11] F. Jay Taylor, *The United States and the Spanish Civil War* (New York, 1956). Chapter 7 treats in detail the attitude of U.S. Catholics toward the war. See also the editorial in *Commonweal,* June 18, 1937.

world where, "over the sea which has interred the democracies, stand forth the summits of the dictatorships."[12] Back in Spain a few weeks later he shared the rightist view that the government had been too mild in the repression of the Asturian revolt. At the time of the Popular Front electoral victory, he recognized, in a very acute analysis of the results, that the sufferings of the workers had certainly not been intelligently or generously dealt with by the Center-Right governments. However, faced with the rising tide of anticlerical and revolutionary agitation late in the spring of 1936, he felt that quite possibly only a military dictatorship could protect the Church.[13]

His first public pronouncement of the war was a radio address from Pamplona on September 28, 1936, celebrating the relief of the Alcázar. He explained that the Nationalists were fighting against the Anti-Spain, the "bastard soul of the sons of Moscow," the Jews and Masons who had poisoned the ingenuous *pueblo* with Tartar and Mongol ideas, and who were erecting a system manipulated by the Semitic International. In December, in his first wartime pastoral, entitled *The Case of Spain,* he repeated similar charges, and attributed Spain's sufferings also to the servile imitation of foreign ways, the farce of parliamentarism, the falsehood of universal suffrage, and the insensate liberties of university teaching and the press. On January 10, 1937, he published an open letter to President Aguirre of the Basque government, in which, while he deplored the executions of the Basque priests he deplored equally the "aberration" which had led to the regretted incidents. He asked the Basques how it was that they could unite with the Marxist hordes to fight against brother Catholics because of a "nuance of political forms."[14]

[12] Quoted in Iturralde, I, 429.

[13] *Ibid.,* I, 403–406. Cardinal Gomá had left Toledo shortly before the outbreak of the Civil War. His papers and correspondence were eventually recovered by the Basques. These papers are the principal documentary source of Iturralde's first volume.

[14] Iturralde, II, 264–66 for the radio address; for the pastorals, Cardinal Isidro Gomá y Tomás, *Pastorales de la guerra de España* (Madrid, 1955).

Neither Cardinal Gomá, nor the Nationalist leadership, nor Spanish conservatives generally, ever understood why the Basques had fought on the side of the Republic. They attempted to explain it away as a result of overwhelming "separatist" sentiment, charging that only because of the October 1936 autonomy statute did the Basques cooperate with the Republic. But the Basques took the side of the Republic on July 18, and never varied from that position. Their ministers served in both the Largo Caballero and Negrín governments, and regardless of wide discrepancies of criterion, they always honored the intentions of both Prime Ministers.

Between the Basque Nationalists and their Carlist and Castilian enemies there was a tremendous gulf in attitude concerning the human treatment of human beings. The Basques assigned as many of their own militia as necessary to protect the political prisoners in their possession. They welcomed eagerly, and gave every facility to, the International Red Cross efforts at prisoner exchange. When they caught priests attempting to cross the Nationalist lines, they tried them in regular courts where they were defended by conservative lawyers of their own choosing. Within the Republican government they concentrated particularly on the protection of political prisoners and Catholics, and would never have remained in the government had they not felt that the Prime Ministers fully approved their efforts. At home they practiced political democracy and were engaged in a land reform on behalf of the many tenant farmers; and their debates never resounded with fulminations concerning Masons or Jews. On the other side of the battle lines their enemies shot their political opponents, including priests, publicly humiliated their wives and children, exalted dictatorship, authority, and tradition against all democratic values, and refused categorically the principle of equality in the proposed prisoner exchanges.

In the half-century preceding the Civil War the Basques had assimilated the finest ideals of the eighteenth-century Enlightenment and had seen the prosperity of the French Basques under a regime of religious tolerance and universal education. In their dealings with the English they had admired not only the economic progress but the constant extension of democracy

and the spirit of "fair play." Finally, they had interpreted the
social pronouncements of Leo XIII not as mere counter-
propaganda to the spread of Marxism but as a program of
social and economic democracy within a Christian framework.
In Burgos and Pamplona the authorities both spoke and acted
each day their scorn for the humane values of the Basques.
Cardinal Gomá perhaps did not realize how similar his pronouncements sounded to those of the neopagan, racist rulers of
Nazi Germany. For him, the Basque dissidence resulted from a
"nuance of political forms." For the Basques, as indeed for
liberal elements throughout Republican Spain, the Burgos
regime represented that retrograde Castile of which the great
poet Antonio Machado had sadly written:

> Castilla miserable, ayer dominadora,
> envuelta en sus andrajos desprecia cuanto ignora.

(Miserable Castile, yesterday an imperial power, wrapped in
its rags despises everything of which it is ignorant.)

After the fall of Bilbao the Republican soldiers retreated
westward. The Basques set up an administration of their own
in the coastal towns of Laredo and Santoña. The local militias
of Santander and Asturias prepared to defend their home
provinces. Everyone knew that it was only a matter of time
before the Nationalists would have conquered the entire north.
To the strong current of defeatism was added a growing
resentment against Valencia, which the central government
tried desperately to counter by small but spectacular deliveries
of arms, either by plane or by eluding the naval blockade. And
in early July the central army launched an offensive at
Brunete, one of whose objectives was to relieve the pressure
on the northern front. Throughout late June and July there
were many desertions. Soldiers retreating through their home
districts would contact peasants, on behalf of themselves and
their friends, and the peasants would arrange with the
Franquist officers for the deserters to cross the lines. The
victors advanced slowly so as to benefit as fully as possible by
this attrition of the retreating enemy.

The triumphant offensive against Santander in August was
the principal Italian military operation of the war. Defeated

at Guadalajara, and held in reserve during the Bilbao campaign, the Italian divisions, numbering perhaps 60,000 with their supporting artillery, armored cars, and airplanes, took the lead. They found few trenches, and no lines of fortifications. The Republicans fought in their separate militia units, not as an army. They had virtually no planes and tanks. Occasionally they made desperate stands from a machine-gun nest perched on the heights or at the bend of a mountain road, but the main obstacle to the Italians was the mountainous countryside.[15] They threw themselves enthusiastically into the logistic exercise of moving a complex, motorized army through narrow passes, and practiced at rapidly zeroing-in their artillery against the successive machine-gun nests. On August 26 they paraded before the awe-struck populace of Santander, complete with giant portraits of Mussolini.

At this same time the Basque authorities at Santoña negotiated a separate surrender with General Mancini. Mancini had seen the fierce repression at Málaga, and like many of the Italian officers, he was shocked at the quantitative aspect of the shootings which took place in each conquered province. The Basques proposed to surrender their arms to the Italians, to maintain public order, and to guarantee the lives of their hostages.[16] In return General Mancini undertook to guarantee the lives of the Basque soldiers, to authorize the emigration of their officials, and to use his influence to protect the Basque population against political persecution. It is completely understandable that in their desperate circumstances the Basques should have attempted to surrender to the Italians, and General Mancini was doubtless flattered to receive their appeal. But he had no authority whatever to accept such a surrender. Nationalist officers, hearing of the move, dispatched troops immediately, and arrived in Santoña just as the first boatloads of Basques were preparing to weigh anchor. They

[15] Though Santander was primarily an Italian objective, German fliers also assisted. One of the most vivid testimonials of air action in the mountains is that of Major Handrick in Wulf Bley, ed., *Das Buch der Spanienflieger* (Leipzig, 1939), pp. 146ff.

[16] R. Cantalupo, *Fu la Spagna*, pp. 226 and *passim*. Steer, *Tree of Gernika*, pp. 386–94.

were all arrested, and the situation of the Basques in general was perhaps worsened by this attempt to avoid surrendering to the Nationalist Army.

September and October were occupied with mopping-up operations in the Asturias. Here, with the memories of 1934 still fresh, the villages emptied in terror at the approach of the conquerers. The miners practiced a scorched earth policy, and from the ruins of their houses fought to the death with dynamite charges. As their military situation became more and more hopeless, many fled to the maquis operating in the most inaccessible mountains. Others, hearing that their village had fallen, decided that for them the war was over. On October 21 Gijón and Avilés fell, and the remaining besiegers of Oviedo surrendered. In the latter city hardly a house remained with an undamaged roof. In both Santander and Gijón the Nationalist authorities found large stores of unused supplies: underwear, stockings, wine, powdered milk, canned fish. No precise explanation can be given for this phenomenon, which was to occur repeatedly at the surrender of other cities. Hoarding and inefficiency each played their part. In any event, the Nationalists, who brought food with them and established relief kitchens in each town, impressed the hungry population by the contrast between this apparent hoarding and their own largess.[17]

At the end of October the northern war was over. The docks and mills had already been repaired in Bilbao, and iron ore was being exported after only about a month's interruption. Roads, railroads, and docks were being rebuilt by the militiamen, who were now prisoners of war. The most ardent

[17] For many details of the northern war, I drew on the accounts of two excellent journalists who accompanied the Nationalist forces: Georges Oudard, *Chemises noires, brunes, vertes en Espagne* (Paris, 1938) and O. Treyvaud, *Les deux Espagnes* (Lausanne, 1937); also upon the very human, nonideological memoirs of a young Argentine doctor who served the Nationalist Army in the north throughout 1936–37: Hector Colmegna, *Diario de un médico argentino en la guerra de España* (Buenos Aires, 1941); and upon the factual military account of an Italian journalist: Emilio Faldella, *Venti mesi di guerra in Spagna* (Florence, 1939).

fighters had swelled the ranks of the guerrilla bands, but the majority of the populace, undernourished and morally depressed by their isolation from the main Republican zone and by the never-settled internecine quarrels of the Popular Front committees, accepted passively the new regime. The Navarrese and Italian troops were ready for transfer to another front.

THE INITIATIVES OF THE
NEGRÍN GOVERNMENT

ON MAY 17, Largo Caballero stepped down, to be replaced as
Prime Minister by Juan Negrín, the moderate Socialist who
had been Minister of Finance. Juan Negrín came from a
merchant family in the Canary Islands. At the University of
Madrid he had been one of the most brilliant students of the
Nobel prize-winning physiologist, Santiago Ramón y Cajal. He
had done graduate work in Germany and had profited as much
from the stimulating artistic and political atmosphere of the
early Weimar Republic as from his laboratory studies. He had
succeeded Ramón y Cajal in the chair of physiology at
Madrid. In 1929 he became chairman of the faculty committee
in charge of building the new University City, and at this time
he also joined the Socialist Party.[1]

Negrín was a man of great generosity and unselfish enthusiasm who used his personal income to equip the laboratory and library of the Medical School (where his collection
of German scientific periodicals remains available to this day).
He combined a passion for work with an almost equal passion
for personal unobtrusiveness, aiding students to publish their
research instead of exploiting their results to build his own
reputation. He brought expensive German cameras to his
children, but refused to let them take his picture. He deliberately avoided the limelight on ceremonial occasions
marking the various stages of expansion in the University
City. In August 1936, when many men of the moderate
Left had been completely demoralized by the anarchic terror
of the paseos, Negrín had walked the streets of Madrid at
night and had braved the chekas to speak in favor of arrested

---

[1] Arthur Rosenblueth, writing in *Cuadernos Americanos*, March,
1957, concerning the early career of Negrín.

suspects. He had helped several colleagues send their families abroad, but he himself had two sons at the front.

In the prewar Cortes Negrín had worked generally with the Prieto wing of the Party and was particularly active in defense of the Socialist deputies arrested in the summer of 1934, at the time of the peasants' strike. As Minister of Finance during late 1936, he had rebuilt the carabineros into an elite, dis- ciplined corps, had managed, relatively speaking, to restrain inflation, and had gotten along particularly well with the Russian trade representatives with whom he dealt constantly. He did not hold a high opinion of Largo Caballero, and he unhesitatingly cut cabinet meetings without informing the Prime Minister. This minor deficiency did not lower his stand- ing with the moderates in the cabinet. Azaña, Giral, and the Republicans generally were relieved to have this genial, immensely able bourgeois replace the dour, bureaucratic trade- union chief who had been Prime Minister for almost nine months. In addition to his other abilities, the new Premier spoke fluent German, considerable French and English, and a little Russian. Foreign journalists could easily picture him as a British Premier or American President. He cultivated good relations with them, and was to enjoy a better international press than had Largo.

Negrín chose able, democratic-minded collaborators: Giral as Foreign Minister, Prieto as Defense Minister, Irujo as Minister of Justice, and Julián Zugazagoitia as Minister of the Interior. Irujo consented to serve only on condition that he be free, not only to continue the work he had done under Largo in connection with prisons, but to restore professional court procedures and standards as they had existed before the Civil War. Zugazagoitia as the editor of *El Socialista* had written courageously against the paseos in the first terrible weeks of the war and had on several occasions exposed anarchist, and later Communist, chekas. Now he would pre- sumably have the opportunity to end these abuses once and for all.

But the most important task was to win the war, and, to do this, the Republic must take the initiative. In the spring and summer of 1937 the Nationalist forces were committed to the reduction of the northern provinces. An offensive on the central front would strike them from behind and would relieve the pressure on the remaining northern territories. It would prove to the Russians a spirit of military initiative which their advisers had found lacking thus far. A Republican victory would also encourage the French to open the border once more, and this was in itself a matter of vital necessity, for the Russians had had several freighters sunk during the spring and had notified the Valencia authorities that they must in the future provide their own transportation facilities. There was much Russian and miscellaneous war material lying in French warehouses, already paid for with the gold of the Bank of Spain but unavailable as long as the French observed scrupulously the Non-Intervention accords.

The sector chosen was less than fifteen miles west of Madrid, an area which had been quiet since the January struggle at the Coruña highway. The opposing lines faced each other from east to west. The plan was to drive due south to the village of Brunete, an important road junction; from this village the attackers would be able to envelop the besieging army from behind and thus lift the siege of Madrid. The total Republican army consisted by this time of perhaps 600,000 men, of whom about 50,000 were concentrated for the Brunete offensive. The most battle-hardened units of that army were present: the divisions of Líster and El Campesino, and three of the International Brigades. They were well supplied with machine guns and grenades of Verdun vintage, and with Vickers Armstrong artillery manufactured for the Tsarist army in 1916. They were supported by about 100 Russian tanks, and by perhaps 100 Russian planes, flown now mostly by Spanish pilots.

The plans for the Brunete offensive were the work of the Russian advisers and the Madrid general staff. The decision to attack Brunete rather than mount an offensive in Extremadura had been one aspect of the struggle between Largo Caballero and his opponents. Besides this political factor, which was well known in Madrid, a Captain Luján of Miaja's staff had crossed the lines with an early version of the Brunete plan. However, when the Republicans attacked on

July 6, they achieved a surprise breakthrough, advancing some five miles to surround and then storm Brunete on the first day. Republican historians have suggested that this illustrates the poor quality of Nationalist military intelligence. It more likely illustrates the constant truth that on both sides the lines were very thinly manned outside the immediate battle areas. Neither the Republicans nor the Nationalists ever had sufficient manpower to hold long fronts, and Nationalist power at this time was concentrated in the north.

Within two days, General Varela had moved up the necessary armor and infantry to stem the offensive tide. On flat ground—and at temperatures of over 100° in the shade—the two armies fought what doctors and nurses on both sides remembered as the most sanguinary battle of the entire war. Neither Lister nor El Campesino counted the casualties as they fought to hold the ground won in the first four days. Both armies mistakenly rained shells on their own forward lines; communications failures and cowardice led to near mutiny and to executions on the battlefield in several Republican units. Overhead, as many as 200 airplanes appeared on July 10 and 11 while the Republicans tried to retain their initial superiority in the face of Nationalist reinforcements.

Until July 19 the Republicans, at terrible cost, held the bulge they had created in taking Brunete. By this time, however, the Nationalists had concentrated an overwhelming weight of artillery and air power, drawing upon the supplies which had been accumulated for the Santander offensive, whereas Republican reserves of both men and weapons had been entirely committed. During the week from July 19 to July 26, the Republicans retreated almost to their starting positions. German pilots exulted in their virtually unchallenged command of the air and marveled at the tenacity of the defenders who could be dislodged from their trenches and gun positions only by repeated direct hits. Hundreds of brave men who could have saved their lives by earlier retreat, died running under the machine-gun fire of Heinkels and Messerschmidts.[2] Elsewhere, in the infantry encounters, the retreating Republicans exacted the same terrible toll of casu-

[2] *Buch der Spanienflieger*, pp. 94–105.

alties as their own advance had cost.[3] In Navalcarnero and San Martín de Valdeiglesias young girls from convent schools, who had been sheltered from all knowledge of human biology, silently treated the delirious, blaspheming wounded. Penicillin had not yet been discovered, and the young doctors learned experimentally that gangrene would not set in so frequently after amputations if the wounds were left open. On both sides, buses went out each night to bring back the wounded who could not be reached under shell fire during the day. A lightly wounded Russian colonel, seeing the offensive broken, committed suicide.[4]

The Battle of Brunete retarded the fall of Santander, but it did not raise, or even threaten to raise, the siege of Madrid. In the summer of 1937 the lost equipment could not be replaced, and trained men too were precious, although the raw manpower potential remained high. Nevertheless, Negrín and Prieto were determined to maintain the initiative. The Aragon front had been quiet since the first two

[3] Regarding the Battles of Brunete and Teruel, I depended principally on Manual Aznar, *Historia militar de la guerra de España* (Madrid, 1940) and Vicente Rojo, *España heroica* (Buenos Aires, 1942). Comparison of Aznar on specific points with the work of foreign journalists and with the *DGFP* indicates that he consistently exaggerated the numbers and the equipment of the Republicans in order to highlight the prowess of the Nationalist Army. I have thus not accepted his unverified figures when he writes, for example, that the Republicans had 128 tanks and 150 planes at Brunete, that they suffered more than 25,000 casualties (more than half the attacking force), etc. Rojo discusses the tactics and the nature of the fighting without trying to specify numbers closely. In respect to the course of the battles, the two accounts are quite consistent with each other. Also extremely valuable for technical observations and clarity of detail are the pages on Brunete in Renn, *Der Spanische Krieg,* pp. 299–318.

[4] By coincidence, my conversations in Spain included separate meetings with a monarchist nurse, an official of the *Sección Femina* of the Falange, and an apolitical doctor who had worked in Nationalist hospitals during the battle of Brunete; and with a nurse and a doctor who had been stationed in different Madrid hospitals at the same period.

months of the war. Anarchists and Catalan nationalists had long complained of the government's neglect of their front, and the low morale of their troops was doubtless in large measure to be explained by the absence of activity. On August 24 the Republic launched a series of small actions intended to envelop and then capture Saragossa. The most important attacks were carried out against the towns of Belchite and Quinto, which covered the southeastern approaches to Saragossa through the Ebro valley.

Only about 10,000 men, including several hundred American Internationals, and a few planes, could be alloted to the Belchite-Quinto area. The combined Nationalist garrisons amounted to perhaps 7,000 all-Spanish troops. The attackers benefited by surprise, and in the quickly surrounded towns both armies fought with great courage. Like their brothers in the Republican zone, the Nationalist militia were fanatically brave and resourceful in defense of buildings. The towns had to be taken block by block, in fighting which lasted for a week. As each individual house was surrounded, its defenders would at the last moment escape by the back door to join the defenders of the next one. The *New York Times* reporter, Herbert Matthews, described parapets made of corpses heaped eight high, and characterized Belchite after its capture as a "fetid mass of wreckage." The Republican offensive capability was completely exhausted by the struggle in the two towns.[5]

Local attacks mounted north of the Ebro made virtually no headway, for coordination, supplies, and military intelligence were all lacking. General Kleber had been assigned to advance along the Barcelona-Saragossa highway, but when he asked for information at the headquarters of the army of Aragon, he was met by sullen statements to the effect that there was no enemy along the road. Advancing cautiously, with largely anarchist troops, he found the highway indeed quiet until he was suddenly caught by crossfire from two heavily fortified hills at a narrow point in the road. He brought the heights under fire of his light artillery, but half

[5] Herbert Matthews, *Two Wars and More to Come* (New York, 1938), pp. 301–310. Rojo, *España heroica*, pp. 115–127.

the shells either were not the right size or turned out to be duds. He then ordered an anarchist battalion to storm one of the hills. They got half way up and then retreated before a hail of machine-gun bullets. He sent them up again, accompanied by 100 cavalrymen who had been assigned to his column without horses. The combined force took the hill. Kleber then proposed to move on, using his cavalrymen to pace the advance and leaving the captured heights in the hands of the anarchists. When the cavalrymen descended, the anarchists did likewise, and the Nationalists retook the hill without a struggle. At no other point did Kleber meet resistance, but what was the use of trying to advance with such troops, such guns, and such lack of information concerning the location of fortifications on a front which had been stationary for eight months?[6] Various Republican units conducted short attacks until mid-September, but the expensive capture of Quinto and Belchite was the only tangible result of the Aragon offensive.

After the Nationalist capture of Gijón in late October, it was obvious that General Franco would soon concentrate his forces for an offensive either on the Aragon front or at Madrid. Prieto, working with Colonels Hernández Sarabia and Rojo, rushed preparations for a new offensive which would permit the Republicans to choose their own battleground and throw the Nationalist plans off balance. They chose the city of Teruel, located on high, rocky bluffs, above the Guadalaviar river, known to be lightly held, and constituting a salient approximately two-thirds surrounded by existing Republican lines. For this offensive they gathered 90–100,000 troops, all the First World War Russian and European field guns which they had been able to ship themselves from Marseilles or buy from contrabandeers, all the rifle and machine-gun ammunition, the grenades, fuses, shells, and trucks-remodeled-as-armored-cars which had been produced in 1937 by Catalan factories. Franco's decision to storm Madrid on December 18 was known to them. They planned to attack Teruel a week earlier, postponed the action four days because of

[6] Information concerning Kleber in Aragon from one of his staff officers.

a locomotive strike in Barcelona, and finally launched the offensive on the bitter cold, windy morning of December 15.[7]

They achieved complete surprise, and forced the postponement of the Nationalist assault of Madrid. Morale was excellent, despite frostbite and deadly accurate mortar and artillery fire from the defenders. Snow had begun to fall during the 15th, and a veritable blizzard on the 17th cut communications between headquarters and the advancing troops. Planes were grounded, and trucks stranded on the icy roads, but the Republican infantry moved forward, lightly wounded men rising from the snow to rejoin the advancing march. On December 21 they began to enter the city itself, fighting their way from building to building. Machinegunners covered windows and doors while dynamiters advanced to blow up strong points. The invaders seized the lower floors of buildings whose upper stories were defended to the death. As in the University City in November 1936, grenades and oaths were hurled down stairwells, water pipes and wiring were destroyed, soldiers wrestled and bayoneted one another in the darkness.

The Nationalists rushed reinforcements from the Madrid zone, and on the 29th General Varela, once again the operational commander of a lightning counterattack, struck from the northwest, supported by the aviation of the Condor Legion. On New Year's Eve panic seized the Republican soldiers, and for about four hours the city lay completely open to Varela's advance. But the Nationalists did not learn of their opportunity in time, and by morning the troops had returned and discipline had been reestablished. The counterattack had

[7] Concerning the strike, see the article of Indalecio Prieto in *Adelante* (Mexico, D.F.) for May 4, 1942; on Catalan war production, *De Companys a Indalecio Prieto* (Buenos Aires, 1939), the text being a letter of December 13, 1937, written in answer to criticisms of the Catalan war effort. Concerning the battle, I used, besides Aznar and Rojo, Herbert Matthews, *The Education of a Correspondent* (New York, 1946), pp. 97–117, and his dispatch to The *New York Times* of January 8, 1938. There is also an excellent account based on British and German newspaper reports in the *Survey of International Affairs*, 1938, I, 260–63.

captured La Muela, a piece of high ground outside the city, while within, the Republicans resumed their street-by-street advance.

The greatly reduced garrison under Colonel d'Harcourt was isolated in the cellar of one of the main buildings, cut off from water, and encumbered by several hundred civilian refugees, including the Bishop of Teruel and the chairman of the local Red Cross. The latter came out under a white flag to ask permission to evacuate the wounded from the Assumption Hospital, which had been isolated, but not touched, by the entering Republicans. Prieto seized the opportunity to humanize the conduct of the war on one of the rare occasions when the Republicans held the upper hand militarily. He guaranteed the evacuation of the hospital, and also promised security against reprisal for all persons of non-military age who had taken refuge with the garrison. On January 7, 1938, after the old, the women, and the children had left the cellar, the famished garrison demanded of the Colonel that he surrender their militarily hopeless position.

During the following six weeks, the Republicans defended their hold on most of the city against increasingly heavy air and artillery attacks. But to the north, motorized troops under Colonel Aranda pushed the Republican lines eastward, inexorably threatening the city with encirclement. Late in January, International Brigaders were brought in to stiffen the defense. The Republicans, however, did not have the reserves to counterattack outside the city. They held on as long as possible, for morale and prestige reasons, taking terrible punishment, but were forced to evacuate Teruel hastily on February 21 lest the entire besieged garrison be cut off. Last to leave was El Campesino's division, which had literally to fight its way through the closing Nationalist lines in order to join the retreating Republican Army. According to the German ambassador, the Nationalists took some 14,500 prisoners, of whom only a handful were foreigners, which latter fact General Franco asked him to keep secret.[8]

In the second half of 1937 the Republican Army had made three significant attempts to take the offensive. They

[8] *DGFP,* p. 615.

had proved the discipline and combativeness of their soldiers. They had achieved tactical surprise and forced the Nationalists to fight on ground of their choosing. Both armies had fought heroically and had consented to heavy sacrifices for prestige reasons—the Nationalists in order to regain every inch of ground lost, regardless of its strategic value, the Republicans in order to achieve victories, however costly and however temporary. The material superiority of the Nationalists became increasingly obvious in these campaigns, as in the northern battles. In mid-1937 the supply of Russian tanks and planes fell off sharply, whereas the weight of Italian and German supplies, and the availability of Italian soldiers, steadily increased. The Republican Army, conscious of the material superiority of their opponent, was hampered by an entirely defensive psychology; they prepared excellent trenches and made the enemy pay heavily for every inch of ground gained, but were unable to exploit their own breakthroughs, as in the first days at Brunete and Teruel.

Intelligence specialists of all the European armies were watching the performance and the tactics of the Russian, Italian, and German tanks. The low-silhouetted, heavily armored Russian tanks moved forward accompanied by infantry. At both Brunete and Teruel the infantry for one reason or another did not follow closely enough. The tank crews, cooped up with hot, clanking machinery, did not enjoy good visibility, and their machines were easily isolated and captured intact. General von Thoma, in charge of the Condor Legion tanks, claimed in 1938 to have added some 60 Russian tanks to his forces, most of them captured by Moors who had been rewarded with 500 pesetas per vehicle. The Germans insisted that their tanks, which were somewhat lighter and faster than the Russian tanks, be used in groups to punch through the enemy front; these tanks were accompanied by armored cars and motorcycles for communication, but were not immediately dependent upon the infantry.[9] The German tactic, predecessor of the World War II blitzkrieg, was the

[9] B. H. Liddell-Hart, *The German Generals Talk* (New York, 1948), pp. 91–3; and the report based on English and French military observations in *The Journal of the United Service Infantry*, February, 1939, pp. 91–9.

more successful, not entirely, however, because of its inherent superiority. The Germans had thousands of their own trained technicians in the field, and the over-all material superiority of the Nationalist army contributed not a little to the success of the tank tactics. At Brunete, where their influence was paramount, the Russians were prodigal of men and guns in an effort to exploit a breakthrough on a narrow but important front. They were to spend guns and men similarly in the Finnish War and in World War II, and their tactics had many a precedent in such slaughters as the three Battles of Ypres in World War I.

During these same months the Republican government took a number of political initiatives. From the beginning of the war, Prieto had preached that the winning side would be the one with the healthier rear guard. In this, as in most other matters at the time, Negrín was of the same mind, and he gave full support to Irujo and Zugazagoitia. The Minister of Justice decreed the restoration of the toga and the biretta in the courts, made certain that career judges sat as chairmen of all the *Tribunales Populares,* and arranged for the unpublicized release of all priests held in prison merely as such. No flag except the Republican was to fly over any prison, and seniority within the prison staff, rather than political allegiance, was to determine the naming of prison directors. In cooperation with the Minister of the Interior he established a system whereby, at the discretion of the director, and upon the oath of the inmate, political prisoners could be temporarily released for important family crises or celebrations. No escapes occurred under this system.[10]

In August the government decreed the right of private Catholic worship, although the churches remained closed, and in Catalonia the Generalitat facilitated the necessarily unpublicized contact of Cardinal Vidal, resident in Rome, with his diocese. The Communists urged upon Negrín, as they had upon Largo Caballero, the desirability of fusing the

[10] Information on the courts and prisons from Manuel de Irujo.

Socialist and Communist parties. Negrín replied courteously but firmly that the proposal was not appropriate to a democratic country, and on October 1 the Socialist Party, acting at the behest of both Prieto and Negrín, decided formally against fusion.[11]

Militarily and diplomatically, however, the government remained completely dependent upon the good will of the Soviet Union. Stalin's paranoid purges were at their height in the spring and summer of 1937. The Russian dictator did not hesitate to extend his police activities to Spain, where he was represented principally by Colonel Orlov of the NKVD and by Erno Gero, the Hungarian Communist working in Barcelona under the name of "Pedro." On June 16, at the demand of the Communists, some 40 leaders of the POUM were arrested, and on the 22nd the government announced the creation of a new Tribunal of Espionage, before which they would soon appear.

The strongest personality of the POUM, Andrés Nin, was separated from the other prisoners and secretly taken to a private Communist prison in Alcalá de Henares, near Madrid. There he was tortured and interrogated by Orlov, probably in the attempt to extort from him the kind of spectacular oral confessions which had marked the Moscow purge trials. Nin was a well-known figure, both in Spain and abroad. He had been one of the founders of the Third International and had rallied to Trotsky shortly after the latter's exile. He had been councilor of justice in the Generalitat in the fall of 1936 and was one of the chief theoreticians of the Catalan collectivist revolution.[12]

[11] *Survey of International Affairs,* 1937, II, 112–13; Cattell, *Communism,* p. 169; Zugazagoitia, *Historia de la guerra, passim.* The chapters by Katharine Duff in the *Survey* for both 1937 and 1938 are especially excellent concerning the internal development of both Republican and Nationalist Spain. Her work shows that a careful newspaper reader, with some background knowledge of Spain, could appreciate both main characteristics and nuances at the time of the struggle itself.

[12] Julián Gorkín, *Caníbales políticos* (Mexico, D.F., 1941), pp. 247–50. Gorkín was a POUM leader, and through personal knowl-

After his disappearance, Irujo and Zugazagoitia publicly tried to maintain that he was in government hands while within the cabinet they threatened to resign at this flagrant violation of the government's authority by the Communists. Negrín demanded of the Party ministers to know the whereabouts of Nin. They insisted on their ignorance of the matter, perhaps quite honestly, but no one believed them. Nor did Negrín and Irujo place much stock in the documentary proofs which the Communists claimed to have, linking the POUM leaders with the secret services of the Nationalists.

Meanwhile Orlov was unable to obtain the desired confession from Nin, and so it became necessary quite simply to do away with him. The Colonel arranged for a simulated kidnapping, using German International Brigaders whom he and the Communists explained afterwards were Gestapo agents. In early August they were claiming that Nin had thus escaped to Salamanca or Berlin, whereas in fact they had assassinated him.

The Nin case was a terrible moral blow to the credit of the Negrín government. Two months after taking office with strong pledges for the restoration of personal security and justice, the Prime Minister had been forced to tolerate the Communist outrage or to fight back, at the risk of being destroyed as Largo Caballero had been destroyed. He chose to swallow his anger, and he was able to convince Irujo and Zugazagoitia that his government would find means in the future to control entirely its own internal affairs. He removed as Director General· of Security Colonel Ortega, a man he had himself appointed in May, and who had evidently cooperated with Orlov. In mid-August he announced the creation of the *Servicio de*

---

edge of the many Left political groups was better able than anyone else to piece together Nin's story. At the time, the world Socialist and Trotskyite press told the story essentially as given here. The Communists labeled the account slander, and Popular Front liberals maintained a troubled silence. Jesús Hernández' autobiography, *La grande trahison* (*Yo fuí un ministro de Stalin*) confirmed the story in detail.

Inteligencia Militar (SIM), headed by a Prieto Socialist, with the function of protecting the war effort against fascist or counter-revolutionary activities. Meanwhile, the Russian advisers were being replaced with increasing frequency, and it was an open secret that many had been shot after their return home.[13] The supply of Russian arms was also falling off rapidly, for practical as well as political reasons, and the government was putting up discreet posters in Valencia and Barcelona asking the people not to speak badly of Russia and to remember that the Soviet Union was the only great power which had aided the Republic.

Whatever his inner thoughts about Soviet methods, Negrín did not permit himself to be discouraged either by the Nin case or the failure of the Brunete offensive. He worked steadily to affirm the authority of his government against all forms of regional and political dissidence. On August 11 the government announced the dissolution of the *Consejo de Aragón*, the anarchist-dominated administration which had been recognized by Largo Caballero in December, 1936. The peasants were known to hate the Consejo, the anarchists had deserted the front during the Barcelona fighting, and the very existence of the Consejo was a standing challenge to the authority of the central government. For all these reasons Negrín did not hesitate to send in troops, and to arrest the anarchist officials. Once their authority had been broken, however, they were released.[14]

On August 16 political meetings were forbidden in Bar-

---

[13] Ilya Ehrenburg, in memoirs serially published in *Novy Mir* (May, 1962) and excerpted in the *Current Digest of the Soviet Press,* Sept. 5 and 12, 1962, states flatly that virtually all the Russians sent to Spain died either there, or upon their return to the Soviet Union. It is also of interest, though I do not cite Ehrenburg as an authority in political matters, that he referred to the POUM in these memoirs as an anti-fascist force.

[14] José Peirats, *La CNT en la revolución española,* 3 vols. (Toulouse, 1951–52), II, 360–64. This is the official anarchist history of the war, poorly written and edited, but containing valuable documents. The present testimony to the government's leniency comes from an author who was violently anti-Negrín.

celona, where the mixture of regionalism, "infantile leftism," and defeatism, constituted a steady drain on the war effort. On October 1, Negrín achieved control of the Socialist Party by engineering the removal of Largo Caballero as head of the UGT and installing Ramón González Peña, unconditionally devoted at this time to Negrín, as head of the Party executive. At the same time, the Party voted against fusion with the Communists. Largo was permitted in a public speech on October 17 in Madrid to explain the circumstances of his resignation as Prime Minister, but he was prevented from making a series of speeches thereafter.[15] At the end of October the government moved from Valencia to Barcelona, the better to control Catalonia. Government control of the press was tightened when the principal Caballero organ, *Adelante*, and the Generalitat organ, *La Vanguardia*, became Negrín mouthpieces.

Meanwhile, in the Ministry of Defense, Prieto faced constant Soviet interference. Behind the fiction of Spanish general staff hierarchies, the Russians maintained direct control of their tanks and planes. The location of some of their airfields was unknown to the Spanish generals. They bombed Valladolid against Prieto's orders, and failed to bomb a Córdoba electric plant in accordance with his orders. Anticipating the fall of Gijón, on October 19, Prieto prepared a telegram ordering the *Ciscar*, the best destroyer in the Republican navy, to sail for Casablanca. One of the Russian officers asked him to change the order. When Prieto refused, the officer said no more, but his telegram was delayed five days without his knowledge, by which time the *Ciscar* had been sunk by Nationalist aviation in the harbor of Gijón.

The Party also continued both to maintain its own police and to infiltrate the government's. When the SIM could not locate a certain Communist whom Prieto had ordered arrested, the Party informed him that they had arrested the individual in question and were handling the case. On another

[15] The contradictory desires of the government to silence Largo Caballero without mistreating him personally, show through very clearly in his account of an effort to keep a speaking engagement in Alicante: *Mis recuerdos,* 235–38.

occasion Prieto removed the Madrid head of the SIM because the latter had named a number of Communist agents without obtaining the Minister's consent (as had happened to Largo Caballero with the naming of political commissars). In November Prieto was able to remove a few political commissars to whom he particularly objected, and to have Alvarez del Vayo removed as Commissar General.[16] Negrín's attitude in all these matters was that the government's authority should be affirmed wherever possible. But Russian supplies were indispensable, and the Communists produced the best field commanders in the army; thus Negrín would not back anyone in an open clash with the Communists where military matters were involved.

The Battle of Teruel had exhausted the resources of the Republican Army. At the same time, the Nationalists had transferred the bulk of their forces eastward, and they prepared to follow-up the recapture of Teruel with a general offensive toward the Levant and Catalonia. Along a north-south line, running roughly between Saragossa and Teruel, they were able to concentrate at least 100,000 men, with highly combative Spanish and Moroccan units in the lead. During the course of 1937 they had amassed over 700 Italian and about 250 German planes, some 150 to 200 tanks, and thousands of trucks of varying sizes. The greater part of these facilities was available for the new offensive. In the airdromes planes were lined up wing tip to wing tip, and at the supply bases Ford, Studebaker, and Italian trucks stood hub to hub without fear of air raids.

The attack was launched on March 9. Belchite and Quinto fell within the first 24 hours, and in a week the Nationalists had advanced an average of 60 miles all along the line. Tanks employing the German panzer tactics broke the front at selected points and encircled the entrenched Republican troops, who were then bombed and strafed as they retreated from their fixed positions. Desperate stands could arouse the admiration of the victorious enemy, but his speed in most areas

[16] Indalecio Prieto, *Cómo y por qué salí del Ministerio de Defensa Nacional* (Paris, 1939), the author's detailed explanation to the Socialist Party.

depended more on the state of roads and communications than upon enemy action. In Saragossa exultant Nationalists bought images of the Virgin of Pilar mounted in shell casings, and young women of the *Auxilio Social* accompanied food trucks into the recently conquered towns. During this same week, Hitler marched into Austria and a second Léon Blum cabinet was formed in France. Prime Minister Negrín flew to Paris to plead for the reopening of the border, which Blum granted immediately, and long-held Russian supplies began rapidly to pass from Bordeaux, Marseilles, and Perpignan to Barcelona.

Mussolini, acting on his own, replied to the French with a series of mass bombing raids on the city of Barcelona, beginning on the full-moon night of March 16.[17] The Italians employed delayed-fuse bombs designed to pass through the roof and then explode on the inside of the building; they also used a type of bomb which exploded with a strong lateral force, so as to destroy things and persons within a few inches of the ground. The number of planes and the weight of bombs dropped was considerably greater than during the November 1936 raids on Madrid, but, as in the latter case, the military damage accomplished was very minor. On the other hand, coming after 20 months of war, and striking at a slowly starving city, the raids contributed to the steadily sinking morale of the general population.[18] As in the cases of Madrid and Guernica, the Western powers protested what was clearly to be the fate of civilian populations in any future war. According to his malicious son-in-law and Foreign Minister, Count Ciano, Mussolini was delighted that the Italians should acquire a reputation for *Schrecklichkeit*.

The victorious offensive continued. In the first days of April the Nationalists' northern wing had captured Lérida and established a line north into the Pyrennees along the Segre River, occupying also the town of Tremp, whose water-power

[17] Galeazzo Ciano, *Ciano's Hidden Diary* (New York, 1953), pp. 91–2.
[18] H. Matthews, *Education of a Correspondent*, pp. 122–28; Virginia Cowles, article in The *New York Times*, March 16, 1938.

generators supplied Barcelona with most of its electricity. The central units rushed down the Ebro valley and on April 15 reached Viñaroz on the coast, thereby cutting off Catalonia from the central and southern provinces remaining in Republican control. Thereafter, in the Pyrennees and the Maestrazgo, among mountains and olive groves where tanks were not so effective, the advance met stiffening resistance; but by the end of April the Nationalists held a strip of the Mediterranean coast running some 50 miles southward from the mouth of the Ebro river.[19]

The military disaster of the Republican Army brought about a crisis within the Negrín government. During the second half of March, the Prime Minister was determined to fight on, whereas Azaña and Prieto regarded the war as lost. The Communist Minister of Education, Jesús Hernández, using the pseudonym Juan Ventura and overriding the censorship, attacked Prieto in *La Vanguardia*. While the cabinet met at the Pedralbes Palace, Azaña's residence, the Communists organized a demonstration which broke into the palace grounds with cries of "Down with the traitor ministers." Negrín was not averse to frightening the President, whom he had once greatly respected, but whom he had come to consider a coward. He wanted, however, to retain Prieto in the cabinet, despite his own mounting annoyance at what he considered to be unnecessary pathos in Prieto's manner of describing the military debacle. But on March 27 the French ambassador asked Negrín whether he shared the opinion of his Defense Minister that the war was lost. Having just gotten the border reopened, Negrín was in no mood to leave a defeatist in charge of the Army. A few days earlier, he had told the Socialist Party executive meeting that he would not wish to continue as Prime Minister without Prieto as Defense chief. But after the incident with Ambassador Labonne, he

---

[19] Particularly valuable on the Aragon offensive are the observations of a Swiss journalist favorable to the Nationalists but writing without any propaganda intent: Eddy Bauer, *Rouge et Or* (Neuchâtel, 1938). I also benefitted from conversations with two Nationalist officers.

sent Julián Zugazagoitia, a mutual friend, to ask for Prieto's resignation.[20]

The Prieto affair aggravated the continuing disunity within the Republican camp. The Socialist Party had been split by the fall of Largo Caballero; it ceased to function as a Party

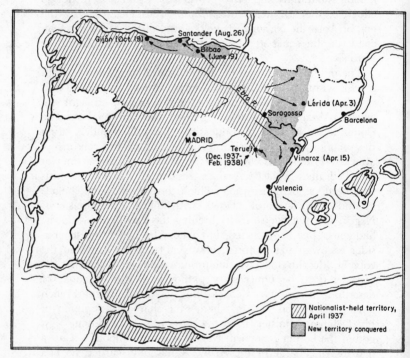

MAP 7. Northern Conquests, April–October, 1937
Advances Toward the Mediterranean Sea, March–June, 1938

after the forced resignation of Prieto. It is impossible to say precisely whether Negrín worked in collusion with the Communists to discredit Prieto after the loss of Teruel. Regardless

[20] Prieto and Negrín, *Epistolario* (Paris, 1939), gives the full detail of their political differences while showing Negrín's extreme reticence about his personal feelings.

of whether he knew in advance of the Pedralbes demonstration and the Juan Ventura articles, he had long since decided that the Communists were his only dependable, energetic allies in the conduct of the war. The democratic unity of May 1937 was consciously sacrificed to satisfy the group which most consistently supported the war. In the reorganized government of April 5, 1938, Del Vayo replaced Giral as Foreign Minister. Irujo and Zugazagoitia, associated with the improved court and police practices, yielded the Ministries of Justice and Interior to the less qualified, but strongly pro-Negrín Socialists Ramón González Peña and Paulino Gómez. Negrín added the Defense portfolio to his tasks as Prime Minister.

The parting of the ways between Prieto and Negrín was also an emotional crisis in the lives of both men; they had been friends and collaborators for the past eight years, and unquestionably were the ablest wartime leaders produced by Republican Spain. For Prieto it had always been axiomatic that only with the aid of England could the Republic finally triumph. In early 1938 Anthony Eden, an anti-fascist, had been replaced in the Foreign Office by Lord Halifax, champion of appeasement, and the English were actively seeking an arrangement with Mussolini in the Mediterranean. At the same time, Russian aid was greatly diminished—and always accompanied by political blackmail. The reopening of the French border could not outweigh these somber facts.

Prieto also lacked the proper temperament for a war leader. It was one of the duties of the cabinet to confirm all death sentences. Negrín and the majority of ministers of all parties regularly voted for the execution of these sentences, which were never numerous. Prieto and Irujo generally voted against execution. In preparation for Teruel, Prieto had performed prodigies in the way of supply, and in the first days he had been elated not only by the success, but by the relatively light casualties. After the collapse of the front in March, adolescent peasant boys were being called up, the food situation in the rear areas was disastrous, and Barcelona was being destroyed from the air. Always a man of dramatic manner, he gave way increasingly to outbursts of pessimism. When, in late March, General Rojo and Colonel Hidalgo de Cisneros talked of surrendering themselves to General Franco, Prieto thought the action would not soften the fate of the defeated army but insisted on joining them if they decided to go ahead.[21]

Negrín, intellectually, was aware of every problem and shortcoming known to Prieto. But he chose to believe that England and France would somehow change their policy, and in contrast both with Azaña and Prieto, he drew emotional strength from adversity. He saw himself as the incarnation of the will to resist, to die on one's feet rather than to live on one's knees, as Pasionaria had said during the first siege of Madrid. It was his job to maintain an army in the field, and to maintain the morale of that army's leaders. He knew the suffering and the low morale of the rear guard, but these things, terrible as they were, must not interfere with the defense of the Republic. The difference between the two men was a difference in the weight which they gave to different factors within their total thinking.[22]

The resignation of Prieto did not lead to a complete breakup of the governing coalition. Giral and Irujo rejoined the cabinet as ministers without portfolio, and Prieto and Zugazagoitia remained at the disposition of the Prime Minister. Rojo and Hidalgo de Cisneros served the new Defense Minister as they had served Prieto. But the narrowing base of Negrín's support was perfectly clear.

[21] Incident reported in Zugazagoitia, *Historia de la guerra en España.* This work is unique for the inner history of the Negrín governments and for the personal relationships among Azaña, Prieto, and Negrín. Zugazagoitia, writing rapidly and from memory, but with years' experience as an editor and a long intimate knowledge of Republican and Socialist circles, succeeded in giving a more balanced account of Republican zone politics than many a later writer.

[22] My judgment of Negrín's personality and of his differences with Prieto is based principally on the *Epistolario,* supplemented by the views of Negrín expressed by the journalists Louis Fischer, Herbert Matthews, and Lawrence Fernsworth, by conversation with the Spanish Socialist engineer in whose home several efforts were made after the war to reconcile the two men, and by the above cited work of Julián Zugazagoitia.

THE DEVELOPMENT
OF NATIONALIST SPAIN

FROM the moment that they had successfully transported the
Army of Africa across the straits of Gibraltar, the Nationalist
leaders had never doubted their final victory. The defense of
Madrid, and the Battles of the Jarama, Guadalajara, Brunete,
and Teruel, had severely strained the morale of the troops;
they postponed the victory by months and made it far more
costly in men and materials than originally anticipated. But
Republican military success was purely defensive; at no time
did it interfere with the construction of a new state in the
steadily increasing proportion of the national territory controlled by General Franco.

The confidence of the Nationalists was shared not only by
their major allies, Italy and Germany, but by the British financial community, which had the largest stake of any foreign
power in Spanish mineral and agricultural exports. Whereas
revolutionary ideology and experiments in the Republican
zone aroused the hostility of businessmen, the Nationalist
leaders not only maintained an orderly economy but turned
out to be very capable administrators and shrewd negotiators
in everything relating to Spain's trading position.

Until almost the end of the war, Andalusia was the personal fief of General Gonzalo Queipo de Llano. He made
sure in the first instance that the port facilities of Seville,
Cádiz, Algeciras, and shortly afterwards Huelva, should
operate virtually without interruption. Olives, oranges, sherry,
and iron pyrites were shipped to England and northern Europe
in their normal quantities. The fact that the Burgos junta was
not internationally recognized freed the military of government obligations existing on July 18. Burgos fixed an exchange
rate of 42 pesetas to the British pound. The actual quotation
in London was closer to 70, and the confiscatory rate made it

difficult in isolated instances to buy machinery, but the exporters accepted it in return for the advantages of labor peace, continuity, and good relations with those whom they were convinced would win the war. Through export licenses and this artificially maintained exchange rate the Nationalist treasury acquired millions of pounds.

Queipo de Llano distributed seed to the grain farmers and extended the cultivation of rice in the marshlands. Andalusia fed Morocco and the Balearic Islands as well as contributing to the food supply of Castile, and was able to do this without rationing or significant price increases until well into the year 1938. Queipo enjoyed a reputation as the "social general." In his radio talk of March 4, 1937, he announced to the peasants a system of loans on which they would pay 5 per cent per annum instead of having to go, as he put it, to loan sharks who charged "only 5 per cent per month." On several occasions he decreed moratoria on the payment of mortgages and protected tenants against eviction for nonpayment. Over the radio he appealed for funds to buy land on which to settle the families of needy "soldaditos." The money was used to buy estates at confiscatory rates from landowners whose Republican sympathies made them easy targets for blackmail. No accounts were kept. A certain number of Potemkin villages were built, and an unknown quantity of cash and land became the booty of the General and his friends. Queipo also launched a highly publicized housing project in Seville in March 1937 and on June 19, 1938, delivered the keys of the first 124 houses completed to owners who had been chosen by lot among worker and soldier families. Titled aristocracy contributed land which was to be used for family garden plots. Of his more than 35,000 acres, the Duke of Alba turned over 40.[1]

The payment of Italo-German aid posed problems. Mussolini was much less exacting than was Stalin with the Republic or Hitler with the Nationalists. As the Ciano diaries reveal him, Mussolini was overwhelmingly concerned with his, and Italy's, reputation for virility. He was proud to be involved in the anti-Communist crusade, proud of the terror sown by

[1] Julio de Ramón-Laca, *Como fué gobernada Andalucía* (Seville, 1939), and *ABC*, Seville edition.

Italian planes, proud of his infantry's role in the northern war. He dreamed of a new Roman Empire, of ousting England from the Mediterranean and France from Tunis and Algiers. He was often angered by Franco's slowness and stubbornness, but whatever their conflicts, he was committed to the cause for the duration, and his vanity would not permit him to haggle over finances. A mixed Italian-Spanish trading company, SAFNI, was organized in August 1936 to handle the pyrites, olive oil, and woolens which Spain was to exchange for military supplies. Reports in mid-1937 indicated that the Italians were getting little in return for the arms delivered thus far.[2] The Spaniards in turn were annoyed to learn that Spanish olive oil was being packaged and sold in world markets as Italian oil. After the conquest of the north, Italy operated some of the fish canneries in Gijón. At times Mussolini threatened to curtail exports to Spain, but he did not carry out such threats, nor did Italy ever recover any sizable proportion of her investment in the Nationalist victory.

Payment for German aid was placed on a strict business basis within ten days of the start of the Civil War. A binational trading company, HISMA/ROWAK, was established, with HISMA (Compañía Hispano-Marroquí de Transportes) arranging for Spanish exports to Germany and ROWAK (Rohstoffe und Waren Einkaufsgesellschaft) facilitating German exports to Spain. The principal economic organizer of the company was Johannes Bernhardt, the German businessman who had long been established in Tetuán and who had communicated Franco's first request for aircraft to Hitler.[3] The Riff mines were requisitioned from their French and British owners in August 1936 and HISMA, as of January 1937 held a contract to deliver to Germany 60 per cent of the Río Tinto production at 42 pesetas to the British pound—the exchange rate set by General Franco. For cash transactions HIMSA maintained a large peseta credit, and ROWAK had a mark balance in Berlin. The company held a monopoly

[2] J. R. Hubbard, "How Franco Financed His War," *The Journal of Modern History*, December 1953, p. 397.

[3] H. Feis, *The Spanish Story*, p. 281. *DGFP*, pp. 230, 234 and *passim*.

under the supervision of the two governments. In addition to ore, it dealt in wheat, hides, and vegetables.

The Germans were even more concerned with postwar economic advantages than with immediate payment. Until late 1938 General Franco very cannily resisted their efforts, reiterating in all conversations that his was only a provisional government which could not dispose of the national patrimony. Existing Spanish law limited to 25 per cent the share of foreign capital in Spanish enterprises. In March 1938, he conceded a new upper limit of 40 per cent, but without making any specific engagements. However, on December 19, 1938, when he needed massive quantities of arms for the projected Catalan offensive, and after Hitler had won his greatest peacetime victory at Munich, Franco consented to the creation of MONTANA, a consolidation of five peninsular mining companies, in the three largest of which the Germans held 75 per cent of the capital. The Germans also obtained control at this time of the Mauretania Mining Company of Tetuán.[4]

With this important exception, the Generalissimo maintained his economic independence throughout the war. After the fall of Bilbao, in June 1937, he unabashedly directed the lion's share of Biscayan ore to its traditional English market, despite the displeasure of the Germans. Finding American vehicles more to his taste than German and Italian ones, he used his foreign exchange earnings to buy 1,200 Fiat trucks, 1,800 German trucks, and 12,000 Ford, Studebaker, and GM trucks. Nothing better illustrates the independent and successful trading policies of the Nationalists than the fact that in 1937 they exported $60,000,000 worth to the sterling area and $31,000,000 worth to Germany through HISMA, for a total of $91,000,000, whereas the entire exports of undivided Spain in 1935 had amounted to only $115,000,000.[5]

The English companies which held the majority of stock in the Río Tinto and Peñarroya mines lodged no official complaints during the war about the confiscatory exchange rates or the export of roughly half their ores to Germany. They

[4] Hubbard, op.cit., pp. 398–403. Also the article of J. Berthet, L'Europe Nouvelle (edited by "Pertinax"), Feb. 26, 1938.

[5] Hubbard, op.cit., p. 404.

were convinced that Franco's victory would serve their long-term interests, and their attitude led the various French, Belgian, and American interests to judge likewise. In his dealings with foreign interests, General Franco profited from the financial backing and the connections of particular individuals. In early 1937 Juan March was reported to have contributed £15,000,000 before the rising, as well as to have financed much of the Italian occupation of Majorca. The former King Alfonso XIII gave $10,000,000, and his son Don Juan (the present pretender) fought in the Nationalist Army. Latin American, English, and American sympathizers were reported to have contributed £1,000,000. Franco benefitted also from the able diplomacy of the moderate, generally pro-British General Jordana. But the Generalissimo himself was second to none as a businessman-diplomat, and many knowledgeable persons who disliked his political regime took pride in the hard bargains he drove with Spain's trading partners.

The Nationalist economy also enjoyed the advantages of strict public order and the cooperation of the business community. Strikes were forbidden and wages frozen, generally at levels close to those of February 15, 1936, before the Popular Front victory and the subsequent wage raises of the spring. There were shortages of fabrics, since most of the textile factories were located in Catalonia, and the maintenance of railroads and machinery suffered from the fact that a high proportion of skilled labor fled to the Asturian maquis or to the Republican zone. But those few observers who traveled in both zones (largely consular personnel and Swiss journalists) all noted that farms in Nationalist Spain were as carefully cultivated as in peacetime, whereas neglect was frequently evident in the Republican provinces. The cost of living rose only about 50 per cent in the Nationalist zone during the war itself. The time of serious shortages and inflation came afterward.[6]

The political character of the new state combined the superficial features of fascism with an intensely personal, traditional,

[6] The 50 per cent estimate is given in the Royal Institute *Survey of International Affairs*, 1938, I, 292–94; on economic conditions generally in the Nationalist zone see also the articles by Harold Callender in The *New York Times*, April 2, May 14 and 15, 1938.

military dictatorship. Like the Communist Party in Republican Spain, the Falange in Nationalist Spain underwent a phenomenal growth: from about 5,000 in February 1936 to perhaps 60,000 late in the spring, to 1,000,000 in August 1936 and to upwards of 2,000,000 during the war years. Like the Communist Party, it felt itself predestined to guide the development of its less politically mature allies, and like the Communist Party, it lacked leaders of national stature. There, however, the analogy ends, for the Falange was not a Party of technicians, and it did not have any coherent, consistent program.

There were at least four distinct groups within the Falange of the years 1937–38. There was a small, but eloquent, group which preached a syndicalist revolution—the creation of a decentralized economy in which the labor syndicates would have an equal voice with management in the control of industry and in which the great estates would be distributed to the peasants actually working the land. Most of the Falange intellectuals, and the surviving close associates of José Antonio and Ramiro Ledesma Ramos, belonged to this group. The second group was comprised of a small but important nucleus of reactionary terrorists—those who had attempted to assassinate liberal and Socialist deputies, and who had sprayed bullets at political meetings and funeral processions in the spring of 1936. Then there was a mass of Catholic youth and university students, many of whom had belonged to the JAP before the war. Finally there was a mass of former anarchists and Communists, particularly in Andalusia, where the demagogic General Queipo de Llano had urged them to don the blue shirt as a *salvavida* (life jacket), and where the sophisticated monarchist aristocracy referred smilingly to "our reds" and to the "FAIlange."

These heterogeneous groups were united by one common aspiration: that the Civil War should lead to a revolutionary transformation of Spain. None of them felt inspired to fight in defense of the landed aristocracy or for the restoration of clerical privilege. They were emotionally as antibourgeois and anticapitalist as they were anticommunist. They talked about blood and race, imitating the Nazis, but without any practical object in view. They talked of the imperial destiny of Spain, occasionally embarrassing the government by publishing maps of "Iberia" from which the Portuguese border was notably absent, and occasionally serving the government by making threatening gestures in the direction of Gibraltar. Falange editorials picked up Mussolinian phrases about the need for heroic violence, and the tempering of virile nations through war. They rejected schematized, intellectual solutions and defined politics as the art of directing people through intuition and improvisation.[7]

The Falangists were also ardent hero-worshippers. The "old shirts" talked of José Antonio and of Mussolini in personal, emotional terms which almost no Communists employed toward Stalin, let alone toward José Díaz. The mass of troubled, unsophisticated youth had no outstanding leader. José Antonio, Onésimo Redondo, Julio Ruiz de Alda all were dead. Hedilla and Aznar, the faction leaders of early 1937, were mediocrities. Raimundo Fernández Cuesta, exchanged from Madrid prison in October 1937, and one of the original associates of José Antonio, became Secretary General of the Falange, but only after Serrano Suñer had refused the post; and he never enjoyed any large influence on policy.[8]

The Falange was extremely useful to the Caudillo, precisely because it had neither a coherent program nor an outstanding leader. Its fascist phraseology constituted an escape valve for pressures which might otherwise have taken a truly revolutionary direction, and General Franco sprinkled his own speeches with the adjectives national-syndicalist, social, unitary, imperial, and missionary. He did not spend his time on balconies nor attempt to mesmerize mass audiences with his voice. It was fine to have Falange hero worship focus on the

---

[7] See Javier M. de Bedoya, *Siete años de lucha* (Valladolid, 1939) for a series of editorials reprinted from the Valladolid Falange organ *Libertad*. I also had the opportunity to discuss the composition and aims of the wartime Falange with three "old shirts," two of whom had been personal friends of José Antonio and the third of whom had been a disciple of Onésimo Redondo. See also the earlier cited Payne, *Falange*.

[8] Payne, *op.cit.*, pp. 179, 186–87.

image of "the absent one," and one of the established rituals of the Falange was to begin its meetings by invoking the mystic presence of the founder with the choral shout: *"José Antonio, Presente!"* Curiously enough for an organization which talked so much of virility, the most important practical work of the Falange during the war was that of the *Sección Femenina*. Pilar Primo de Rivera, sister of the founder, and Mercedes Sanz Bachiller, widow of Onésimo Redondo, were the leading spirits in developing a network of hundreds of children's dining rooms, organizing nursing service both at the front and in the rear areas, and distributing food in newly conquered territories.[9]

Meanwhile, General Franco governed Nationalist Spain in the military, personal, arbitrary, and nonideological manner of such great nineteenth-century Hispanic dictators as Narváez in Spain, Rosas in Argentina, and Porfirio Díaz in Mexico. He leaned heavily on the advice of Serrano Suñer, whose influence gave rise to numerous jokes about *cuñadismo* (brother-in-lawism) as a form of government, and about himself as *cuñadísimo* (to fit with *generalísimo*). At no time, however, did anyone manipulate General Franco, who, in the civilian life of a democratic country, would have enjoyed a very successful political career.

On January 3, 1938, he formed his first regular cabinet, the composition of which reflected accurately the various political currents within Nationalist Spain. There were two Monarchists who had held important offices before the coming of the Republic: General Gómez Jordana, the Foreign Minister, and Andrés Amado, Minister of Finance. There were two Carlists: the Count of Rodezno as Minister of Justice and Pedro Sáinz Rodríguez as Minister of Education. There were two Falangists: the "old-shirt" Raimundo Fernández Cuesta as Secretary General of the Party, and the less prestigious González Bueno as Minister of Labor. General Dávila, unconditionally devoted to Franco within the military, became Minister of the Army. General Martínez Anido, who had repressed the CNT in Barcelona in the early 1920's, and who had been Minister of

[9] Merwin K. Hart, *America Looks at Spain* (New York, 1939), pp. 103–110.

the Interior under Primo de Rivera, became Minister of Public Order. Serrano Suñer served as Minister of the Interior, and Juan Antonio Suances, a boyhood friend of Franco's and a successful industrialist, served as Minister of Commerce and Industry. It was a carefully balanced group of experts representing the major political tendencies. They took their oath of office in the centuries-old monastery of Las Huelgas, near Burgos, in a ceremony described by Serrano Suñer as "intimate, fervent, and devout, like a vigil in arms," after which the nuns served sherry in the cloister, accompanied by traditional wafers made with egg yoke.[10] The moment was solemn, and the appropriate imagery, for the Generalissimo, was not that of modern fascism, but of the Catholic Kings.

This cabinet elaborated several fundamental laws in the course of 1938. On March 9 came the Labor Charter, governing wages and working conditions in industry and protecting the leases of tenant farmers; however, it did not apply to wage laborers on the great estates. In April the government created the *Servicio Nacional de Reforma Económica Social de la Tierra*. The Republic had distributed some half-million acres to the peasants before the war, and several million additional acres were being operated as cooperative or collective farms by early 1938. The task of the new Servicio would be to return the property to its rightful owners and to substitute for Republican and revolutionary land reform an unspecified form of "colonization."

On April 5 the Catalan autonomy statute of 1932 was officially abrogated, and on April 22 a press law was published which stated clearly the government's responsibility for the press and the establishment of censorship. On May 3 the Jesuits, referred to as a particularly Spanish Order, were welcomed back to Spain, and their property, most of which had been held for them by other Orders and by fictional corporations since 1932, was restored. On July 19 General Franco became "Captain General of the Army and Navy,"; this action, while it did not increase his effective authority, was significant because the title had been held in the past only by

[10] Ramón Serrano Suñer, *Entre Hendaya y Gibraltar* (Madrid, 1947), pp. 64–5.

the King. On December 15 the deposed King Alfonso was restored to citizenship and his family properties returned to him. These laws confirmed existing trends toward a centralized state, a government-controlled economy, and the restoration of the vested religious and economic interests of the pre-Republican era. The Labor Charter alone paid mild lip service to the ideals of the Falange left.[11]

The first statements justifying the military rising had said nothing about religion, but the influence of the Church increased steadily in the Nationalist zone.[12] In early 1937, primary school teachers were specifically directed to have an image of the Virgin in the classroom, and crucifixes were to be hung in all secondary and university classes. Religious services were held regularly at the front, and attendance at them was required of all military and civil officials. At Easter in Majorca the Church announced a census. Forms were distributed for parishioners to say where and when they had performed their Easter religious obligations. Only 14 per cent of the population had observed Easter in 1936, but compliance was almost universal in 1937.[13]

The government decreed that religious instruction in both primary and secondary schools would be obligatory except for Moroccans. All schoolteachers were examined as to their religious beliefs, and many schools were closed for lack of instructors with satisfactory religious background. The Church organized orientation courses for all teachers on the role of Christianity in teaching methods and ethical doctrine. These several laws gave the Church a degree of control it had never exercised in modern times, since under the Monarchy it had always been possible for parents to withdraw their children from religious instruction, and there had been many private schools and university classrooms which were laic in practice if not in theory. In March 1938, the Republican divorce law,

[11] Concerning legislation see E. Allison Peers, *Spain in Eclipse, 1937–43* (London, 1943) and Carlos M. Rama, *La crisis española del siglo XX* (Mexico, D. F., 1960).

[12] Iturralde, *El catolicismo y la cruzada de Franco*, I, 99–104, for the laicism of both Franco and Mola.

[13] Georges Bernanos, *Les grands cimetières sous la lune* (Paris, 1938), pp. 141–43.

already abrogated in practice, was officially repealed. The middle-class women who supervised hospitals and dining rooms also strove to re-Catholicize the masses, as the belief was widespread among them that Spain's social troubles were principally traceable to a lack of Christian charity among the rich and a lack of Christian faith among the poor.

On July 1, 1937, the prestige of the Nationalist cause was greatly enhanced by the publication of the Collective Letter of the Spanish bishops, composed by Cardinal Gomá and signed by all Spain's prelates, with the significant exceptions of Bishop Múgica of Vitoria and Cardinal Vidal of Tarragona. The Spanish hierarchy took the position that the rising of July 18 had been a "civic-military" rising on the part of the healthiest and best qualified civilian elements of the nation as well as of part of the army. The Church had been the victim of laic legislation which infringed upon its rights and liberties. It had counseled respect for the constituted authorities while the constituted authorities had permitted the burning of churches, the criminal revolt in Catalonia and the Asturias, and the general chaos of the spring of 1936. The Church had not wished the war, but it was grateful for the protection which the Nationalists had afforded, while in the Republican zone priests were being martyred by the thousand. Cardinal Gomá quoted Saint Thomas concerning the right of legitimate self-defense and referred to "irrefutable" documentary evidence to the effect that the rising had forestalled a long-planned Soviet Revolution in Spain. The Collective Letter, published just after the fall of Bilbao, ranged the Church officially on the side of the Nationalists, and in October Pope Pius XI sent a nuncio to Salamanca.[14]

The diplomatic repercussions of the war were favorable to the Nationalists from the start. The initial impulse of France to aid the Republic had been checked by fear of Hitler, British pressure, and the possibility of civil war within France. The flow of Italian and German aid was in no way hampered by the actual operation of the Non-Intervention scheme, and if, in the fall of 1936, Russia hastened to give the Republic roughly equivalent aid, Russia was geographically much further from Spain than were the fascist powers and

[14] Cardenal Gomá, *Pastorales de la guerra,* pp. 147–90.

was not willing to incur the open displeasure of the Western powers. After November 1936, there was a steadily increasing gap between the extent of Russian aid and that which reached the Nationalists.

In February 1937 Republican diplomats hinted to England and France that the government would consider revising the status of Morocco if the Western governments would consider revising their policy toward the Civil War. Since Franco depended heavily on the recruitment of Moroccan soldiers, he was undoubtedly relieved when the London *Times* published news of these feelers on March 18, together with the indication that the British had refused the proposition. March 18 was also the day on which the Republican army captured from the retreating Italians a mass of documentary evidence proving that over 50,000 Italian soldiers, belonging to regular, uniformed military units, had arrived in Spain. When the Western powers refused to act on this evidence, General Franco could be absolutely certain that they would do nothing to prevent his victory.

For some months the Non-Intervention Committee discussed a neutral land and sea patrol. On April 19, 1937, they inaugurated a scheme whereby the British and French navies would patrol the Nationalist coasts and the German and Italian navies would patrol (as "neutrals") the Republican coasts. The sentry vessels were authorized to board ships in order to "verify" their destination, but they were not authorized to search or seize. British observers were also stationed on the French and Portuguese land frontiers. No aerial supervision was attempted.

In the course of April and May about 35 ships of 7 nationalities were "subjected to belligerent action" in the neighborhood of Republican ports.[15] Neither Burgos nor Valencia had recognized the legality of the patrol, and the Republican

[15] Different sources give somewhat different totals for the number of incidents and the seriousness of the damage. It is obviously impossible to report accurately in time of war every attack on single ships. I have taken my figures from N. J. Padelford and H. G. Seymour, "Some International Problems of the Spanish Civil War," *The Political Science Quarterly*, September, 1937.

government warned that in any event it would feel free to attack Italian or German warships within territorial waters. A few such incidents occurred in late May, the most critical being the bombing of the *Deutschland* in the harbor of Ibiza on May 29. The *Deutschland* took its revenge by shelling the city of Almería on the 31st. On June 15 Germany announced that the *Leipzig* had been attacked by torpedo on the high seas. The Valencia government coupled its denial with an offer for the British navy to investigate the alleged incident, which offer the Germans refused, for in reality they were only seeking a plausible pretext to withdraw from the patrol. On June 23 Italy and Germany announced their withdrawal, made necessary, as they put it, by the piratical conduct of the Valencia government. The Portuguese, who had most reluctantly agreed to have a few British observers on their frontier, now also withdrew authorization at the end of June. On July 12 France withdrew the observer facilities on her border.

The British and French patrols had not interfered in the least with shipments to Nationalist Spain, and now even the annoying shadow of control was removed. The conquest of the north freed the Nationalist navy to concentrate its power in the Mediterranean. The outbreak of the Sino-Japanese war, taken together with the loss of perhaps a dozen freighters through sinking, led the Russians to reduce drastically their military aid.[16] The French were afraid to draw British displeasure by reopening their frontier, even though, as a matter of diplomatic pride, they had withdrawn observer facilities after Portugal had done so.

The Republic was thus virtually isolated in mid-1937 by the combination of diplomatic and naval acts. Mussolini, however, pressed his advantages too far. "Unknown" submarines attacked British and other neutral freighters in the Mediterranean during July and August, and so the British, concerned by an immediate threat to their control of the seas, called a conference at Nyon, in Switzerland, to deal with "piracy." Germany and Italy responded to the invitation with the sug-

[16] D. Cattell, *Soviet Diplomacy and the Spanish Civil War,* pp. 115–16.

gestion that the matter be taken up by the Non-Intervention Committee. On this occasion the British indicated that life was earnest by refusing to be sidetracked. The invitations had been sent on September 6 and the conference convened on the 10th. In one week of deliberations Britain, France, Russia, and several smaller Mediterranean powers agreed to sink on sight any submarine attacking a non-Spanish vessel, and they arranged for a British-French naval patrol of the western Mediterranean. The mysterious torpedo attacks ceased. Italy even joined the new patrol upon her own request.[17]

This rare example of British firmness with the fascist powers was by no means unfavorable to the cause of Nationalist Spain. The ships being attacked were not the ones carrying supplies to her ports, and the Nyon agreements did not interrupt Italian or German shipping. They merely showed that the British could and would react to an Italian naval challenge. Furthermore, while the Nyon agreement ended the torpedoing of non-Spanish ships, Italy continued frequently to bomb ships of all nationalities in, or en route toward, Republican ports. In the autumn of 1937 she delivered 4 destroyers and 2 submarines to the Nationalists.[18] The sole further blow to the combined Italo-Nationalist navy was the spectacular sinking of the Nationalist cruiser *Baleares* by Republican destroyers on the night of March 5, 1938.

The major unresolved issue between Franco and the British concerned the question of belligerent rights. The English had from the beginning refused to grant such rights to either side, since the recognition of belligerency would confer the right to confiscate merchant cargoes on the high seas. The British government wanted the Nationalists to win the war, but it wanted also to retain control of the seas and to avoid incidents which could threaten to spread the fighting beyond the territory of Spain itself. After the fall of Bilbao in June 1937, British trade with Nationalist Spain rose steeply, and Franco threatened to discriminate against the British if not granted belligerent rights. It also looked as though the war would

[17] John C. DeWilde, *Foreign Policy Reports,* April 1, 1938. Anthony Eden, *Facing the Dictators,* pp. 515ff.
[18] *Survey of International Affairs,* 1938, I, 272–74.

soon end, and the British were concerned at the large number of Italians in the Peninsula and the possible military, naval, and commercial commitments that the Nationalists might have made to Italy.

In the summer of 1937 they spoke of granting belligerent rights in return for the withdrawal of the Italian troops. On November 4 the Non-Intervention Committee voted to re-establish the land frontier patrol in order to supervise the withdrawal of foreign volunteers from both sides. Belligerent rights would be awarded when a "substantial" number had been withdrawn. There followed ten months of complete deadlock as to the manner of supervising the withdrawal. Meanwhile, the British negotiated a naval agreement of their own with Italy, whereby they were assured directly that Italy had no territorial designs on the Balearic Islands and would also repatriate all her troops as soon as the Nationalists had won. The agreement was announced on April 16, 1938, the day after General Alonso Vega had reached the sea at Viñaroz, thereby isolating Catalonia from the central zone of the Republic. The specific clauses of the treaty were to come into force when a "substantial" number of Italians had been repatriated, and again, in April 1938, it looked to the British as though the war would be over very shortly.

Since Italian and Nationalist planes unhesitatingly attacked merchant shipping headed for Republican ports, the continued refusal to grant belligerent rights had no great practical importance. The main inconvenience to General Franco was that the coupling of belligerence with the withdrawal of foreign troops obliged him to show his open dependence on those forces. In addition, during 1938 the British several times submitted damage claims for British ships which had been bombed. The Nationalists could barely conceal their scorn for a government which obviously desired their victory but which simultaneously demanded compensation for the damage done to British ships trading with the Republic.

Thus from the middle of 1937 the internal political and economic situation, and the international diplomatic conjuncture, all evolved in a manner highly favorable to General Franco. From time to time there would be reports of unrest in southern Andalusia, of guerrilla activity in the Asturias, of street brawls between Falangists and Carlists, or between Spanish and Italian officers. But these were isolated incidents. There were, under the surface in Nationalist Spain, almost as many conflicting ideological currents as in Republican Spain, but they had no organization and no leadership. General Franco was simultaneously an authoritarian leader of immense personal prestige and a skillful politician who harnessed the contradictory forces within his camp and made good use of the diplomatic and administrative talent at his disposal. Diplomats in Valencia and Barcelona frequently did not know who was making policy and where authority lay. In the case of Salamanca, the spokesman might be Serrano Suñer, or General Jordana, or the Duke of Alba, but the listener always knew that the policy was General Franco's.

The great weakness of Nationalist Spain was that it lacked support among the people. Middle-class and Catholic youth had rallied to the cause. Indeed, their German instructors in the officer training camp had great trouble restraining their enthusiasm for romantic tactics. They considered it cowardly to sit in a trench and to remain silent instead of shouting insults and then charging directly at the enemy. They proved at Brunete, at Belchite, and at Teruel that they had the same courage and physical resistance as the Republicans, and they shed their blood just as generously for a cause they honored. But in the autumn of 1937, when both armies likely attained their maximum size, General Franco had about 250,000 such Spanish troops in Carlist and Falangist militia units, whereas the Republican Army numbered about 600,000 anti-fascist Spaniards. Hence Franco's complete dependence upon the 100,000 Moors, the 70,000 Italians, and the several thousand Germans and Portuguese.[19] Only with foreign troops and

[19] In the classification of the Nationalist forces, I have used the figures of the Swiss journalist, O. Treyvaud, *Les deux Espagnes* (Lausanne, 1937), pp. 161–62. He conducted an inquiry on this particular subject in September, and both his reasoning and his totals were consistent with my other scattered information. The Republican Army in late 1937 was estimated at 600,000 by the usually well-informed London *Times*.

superior armament could he in fact win the war, despite all the political and diplomatic factors favoring his cause.

This situation strained his relations with Germany and Italy. The governments of those countries had suppressed liberty and put thousands of opponents in concentration camps, but they still rested upon a high degree of popular support. They would never have had to say, as Franco told the German ambassador in May 1938, that 40 per cent of the population was "unreliable.[20]" They were not entirely pleased to be sacrificing blood and treasure in a long-drawn-out war to impose an unpopular regime. Italian officers openly criticized the fierce repression occurring in conquered zones, and the Germans thought that only major social reforms could win over the people. Ambassador Faupel, who had flirted with the Falange left, was replaced by the more conservative, and correct, Von Stohrer in May 1937. But the reports of both men, and of the Italian diplomats as well, all agreed as to the unpopularity of the regime. At the height of the Battle of Teruel, Von Stohrer thought that the opposing forces were equally balanced and that time would work for the Republicans. Early in the spring of 1938, when one of the many mediation proposals was being aired, he wrote that mediation must be prevented because any referendum as to the future government would be won by the Republic.

Thus it was necessary for Franco constantly to renew his requests for aid both in men and arms, and to forego any diplomatic concessions which would have depended upon the withdrawal of Italian troops. He also refused to consider mediation, from whatever quarter and in whatever circumstances. He was determined to enjoy a total victory over the Republic, no matter what the cost. In this, as in all political and economic decisions, the iron-willed Generalissimo had his way.

[20] *DGFP,* pp. 657–63 for the extended analysis by von Stohrer of the internal weaknesses of the Franco regime.

EFFORTS TO LIMIT
SUFFERING AND DESTRUCTION

From the very beginning of the war, attempts were made to limit the suffering of noncombatants. British and French warships took several thousand persons aboard at Barcelona, with the Generalitat government facilitating their emigration.[1] In Madrid several thousands entered the Latin-American embassies, whose diplomatic practice recognized the right of political refuge in foreign legations. Several European embassies also opened their gates, and the Giral government allowed them to rent extra buildings for the purpose of housing refugees. At Gibraltar the British permitted hundreds to cross the line in the first days, and in Galician ports English captains embarked the few persons who could get to their ships.[2] When the Nationalist army approached Madrid, General Franco defined an area, principally the middle-class residential district, which would not be shelled, and this limitation was strictly observed. Similarly, at the fall of Bilbao, the Nationalist artillery had orders not to bombard the portion of the shore where noncombatant families were being taken aboard rescue ships under the supervision of foreign consuls. Generally speaking, both sides respected the Red Cross on hospitals. There are specific instances in which aviators bombed hospitals, but they appear to have done so on their own. No nation has ever succeeded in teaching all its soldiers to fire only at military objectives.

The International Red Cross immediately offered its services to exchange noncombatants and hostages, and attempted to get both Madrid and Burgos to recognize the standards of the

[1] Lawrence Fernsworth, the *New York Times,* Jan. 2, 1938, and the testimony of a number of conservative Catalans now living in Barcelona.

[2] Alfonso Camín, *España a hierro y fuego* (Mexico, 1938), *passim.*

Hague Convention of 1907 and the Geneva Convention of 1929 regarding the treatment of prisoners. The Hague rules had been observed by both the Central Powers and the Allies during the First World War. The rules did not apply to civil wars, but the IRC looked upon the Spanish conflict as an excellent occasion for extending humane practices as widely as possible. In August Dr. Marcel Junod obtained from Prime Minister Giral a verbal commitment to permit the emigration of women and children, a process which was already occurring at the Catalan and Levantine ports controlled by the government. In Burgos Junod was received by Generals Cabanellas and Mola. The latter stated brutally the main problem of all future negotiations when he asked the doctor how he could propose to exchange *caballeros* (gentlemen) for *rojos* (reds). It was also Mola's opinion that the "reds" had already shot everyone worth saving, and he argued that if rumors began concerning a general exchange, they would shoot their remaining hostages.

On September 3 the Giral government gave the IRC a written statement offering to exchange groups of noncombatants, particularly women and children. On September 15 the Burgos junta offered similarly to exchange women and children who expressed the desire to leave the Nationalist zone, but prefaced the declaration with the claim that it had absolutely no hostages, military or civil. This preface made it difficult to suppose that the Nationalists would negotiate seriously.

Nevertheless, in mid-September Dr. Junod made several trips between Burgos and Bilbao. In the Basque capital the chief of police was ready to hand over all the inmates of the prison ship lying in the harbor. At each Nationalist raid on the city there had been lynchings, and the Basque authorities were eager to effect a solution which would be both humane and practical. Dr. Junod obtained authority from Burgos for the exchange of 130 women and children. On September 27 the Basques loaded 130 of their prisoners aboard the British ship *Exmouth,* during the night, so as not to attract public attention. After safe passage to St. Jean de Luz, and a dinner in his honor at Burgos, the doctor asked for the 130 persons to be returned to Bilbao in exchange. He was told that the Basque women had already been freed and did not wish to return to Bilbao. He presented the list prepared by the Basque government, and received a flat refusal.

After a month of further effort, he was given a dozen adults and the promise of 40 children who had been vacationing near Burgos on July 18. The children were to be at St. Jean on October 25, and the *Exmouth* was waiting, when a telegram arrived from Burgos stating that they would not arrive. Dr. Junod sailed for Bilbao, and attempted to explain the situation against a background of cries of "Down with the Red Cross." He promised a final effort through Carlist friends, and was able ten days later to deliver the forty children. The incident was closed just as General Mola's army reached the gates of Madrid, and the story, quickly known throughout the Republican zone, may well have bolstered middle-class loyalty to the Republic.[3]

From early November 1936 until late February 1937, circumstances were not propitious for the negotiation of noncombatant exchanges. The Republic was fighting for its life and the Nationalists were anticipating a swift, total victory. However, after the Battle of the Jarama, it was evident that the war would continue for many months, and also that any acceptable exchange policy would have to cover prisoners of war as well as civilians. In March 1937 Dr. Junod asked Largo Caballero to permit the exchange of military prisoners, in particular of aviators, who were hated by the civilian populace of both zones and who were being regularly condemned to death and not infrequently lynched. Reproaching the IRC with its failure to obtain equal exchanges from Burgos in the past,

[3] For the negotiations with both sides see Marcel Junod, *Le troisième combattant* (Paris, 1947), pp. 83–104. My other information on the conditions in which the IRC worked came from interviews in Geneva with the late Dr. Junod and two other delegates of the time. On the news service, prison conditions, and the exact number of exchanges, see *Rapport Général du Comité International de la Croix-Rouge sur son activité d'août 1934 à mars 1938* (Genève, 1938). The IRC offices in Geneva very kindly facilitated also a mimeographed *Rapport Complémentaire . . . relatif à la guerre civile en Espagne . . . et à ses suites,* prepared in 1948.

the Prime Minister refused to commit himself on general policy, but granted a two-week postponement of several pending executions. Meanwhile, Dr. Junod hoped to reopen negotiations with the Nationalists through the good offices of Ramón Serrano Suñer, whom he had helped to escape from Madrid.

There followed some eighteen months of painful bargaining, since the widely differing criteria of the Republicans and the Nationalists permitted only minimal agreements to be carried through. One source of inevitable misunderstanding was the differing legal treatment of combatant prisoners. On April 9, 1937, the Caballero government decreed that prisoners henceforth were not to be court-martialed except by specific order of the cabinet. Only two such orders were issued by Caballero during his remaining tenure of office, and not more than a few dozen in all were issued by Prime Minister Negrín. However, prisoners in the Nationalist zone were regularly court-martialed, with considerable numbers being condemned to death and a large proportion receiving twenty- and thirty-year sentences. When the two governments bargained over their lists of captives, the Nationalists insisted that they could not exchange men convicted of serious crimes for *simples detenidos* (simple prisoners).[4] On this point the gap in attitudes was unbridgeable, and it effectively prevented any mass exchange of prisoners.

In mid-December 1937 it seemed briefly as though some 200 prisoners held in Barcelona might be exchanged for 200 Basques captured during the conquest of the north. The Nationalists had drawn up both lists, and in communicating

[4] José Giral, *Año y medio de gestiones de canjes* (Barcelona, 1938), pp. 5, 41. Sr. Giral was Prime Minister in August, 1936, when the first IRC delegates arrived in Spain. In March, 1937, Largo Caballero asked him to represent the Republican government in all negotiations regarding prisoner exchange, and he continued this function under Negrín until late 1938. *Año y medio* includes much of the correspondence relative to the exchange efforts, together with dozens of case histories of both successful and unsuccessful negotiations. I am indebted to the family of Sr. Giral for a microfilm copy of this important source.

433

them to the IRC they had insisted that these lists be accepted without change. Those they offered were militiamen of no professional training; those they asked for were career officers, notably artillery specialists. The Republican government was loath to accept an exchange in which the military value of the two lists was so unequal and in which, moreover, the enemy demanded the prerogative of naming those to be exchanged by both sides. Meanwhile, on December 27 the Valencia authorities received a telegram from the Basque delegation in Bayonne reporting some 140 recent executions of captured Basque militiamen. On December 29 the Republican government agreed to begin with an exchange of 25 men from each list. At the same time, they informed the IRC that as long as progress continued on the exchanges they would suspend all pending executions, providing that the Nationalists agreed to do likewise. The Salamanca authorities did not respond directly to this proposition, but during the ensuing weeks some 16 further exchanges were made. On January 28, 1938, the Nationalists informed the IRC of their readiness to suspend death penalties against the remaining 159 (200 minus 41) Basque militiamen and against prisoners taken recently on the Teruel and Aragon fronts. This concession, covering only a very limited proportion of the prisoners in Nationalist hands, was not sufficient in the eyes of the Republican government, and no further exchanges occurred from these two lists.[5]

Throughout the war there were several general factors limiting the effectiveness of IRC work. The delegates explained tirelessly that they were not concerned with the guilt of prisoners, but only with their treatment up to the moment of release or death, and that whatever information they acquired about prisons would remain absolutely confidential, indeed that lack of publicity was a fundamental condition of their work. In the Republican zone the authorities were ready to recognize the humane principles, but their pride forbade them to acknowledge the existence of uncontrolled prisons like those of the Communist Party. All the delegates, in accordance with the constitution of the IRC, were of Swiss

[5] *Ibid.*, pp. 55–68.

nationality. The organization was completely autonomous, but the Republicans could not entirely overcome a certain distrust based on the fact that the Swiss government, and most of the Swiss press, seemed to anticipate with satisfaction the eventual victory of the generals.

In the Nationalist zone the delegates faced strong prejudice because they were Protestant. The representative in Burgos, chosen for his known conservatism, and for his school-day friendships with several monarchist personalities, never succeeded in obtaining a long-sought interview with Cardinal Gomá. The aristocracy generally resented the very presence of the Red Cross, a presence which implied that there might be conditions which needed checking by an outsider. The delegates stayed close to their offices in order not to be accused of espionage, and many military authorities were convinced that the Red Cross was just as "red" as the enemy. Both sides demanded guarantees that the exchanged combatants not fight again, guarantees which of course the IRC was unable to give.

Although negotiations began in April 1937, the first actual exchanges did not occur until October. Almost all the agreements involved individuals or small groups only, and by the end of the war only 647 prisoners had been handed over to the IRC by each side.[6] In late 1936 the Republicans permitted the IRC delegates to aid the widows of men who had been assassinated in the Popular Front zone during the first weeks of the war, and throughout the conflict they facilitated the emigration of noncombatants. These policies were never reciprocated in the Nationalist zone. Nor were the Hague and Geneva rules concerning exchange of medical personnel, regular visits to prisons, and the submission to the IRC of complete lists of prisoners ever accepted by either party to the Civil War. On the other hand, both sides permitted the IRC to establish a message service whereby families could learn whether their sons and brothers were still alive. Some three million requests for information and two million responses were transmitted via Geneva in the course of the war. A final

[6] *Revue Internationale de la Croix-Rouge,* May, 1939, p. 435.

unfortunate aspect of the IRC efforts, in terms of Spanish public feeling, was the fact that the vast majority of those exchanged were foreigners: Italian and German aviators, Russian sailors and pilots, and International Brigaders. Both sides wished to avoid embroiling themselves unnecessarily with foreign powers, and the non-Spanish prisoners also enjoyed a better prison regime than did the Spaniards.

The presence of thousands of refugees in the Madrid embassies posed one of the most difficult human and political problems of the war. On July 18, 1936, most of the ambassadors accredited to the Spanish Republic were either summering at San Sebastián or were at home on leave. The senior diplomat in Madrid at the time was the Chilean Ambassador, Aurelio Núñez Morgado. The right of political refuge in foreign embassies was a time-honored custom in Latin America, and its practice had been specifically reaffirmed at the Inter-American Conferences of 1928 in Havana and 1933 in Montevideo. Sr. Núñez undertook immediately to form an emergency organization of the diplomatic corps which, under his chairmanship, met several times weekly through the months of August and September.[7]

The Madrid situation was virtually unique in diplomatic history. The right of asylum as practiced in Latin America was understood to apply to leaders of governments overthrown by revolutions or to prominent personalities belonging to persecuted political parties. None of the persons seeking refuge in the Madrid embassies were leaders of an overturned regime, and only a small minority of them were leading figures in anti-government parties. The diplomats themselves held a wide variety of views concerning the rights and wrongs of the Civil War. Núñez, and the Peruvian and Cuban ambassadors, clearly favored the Insurgents and held that a thorough Communist revolution was occurring in the Popular Front zone. The ambassadors of Argentina and El Salvador held more moderate views and were ready to grant asylum up to the physical limit of their premises. But when Núñez talked of

[7] A. Núñez Morgado, *Los sucesos de España,* p. 192. Also pp. 200–40 for detailed summaries of the discussions among the diplomats, on which the following paragraphs are based.

having the diplomatic corps withdraw from Madrid in a body, they took the position on both humane and political grounds that the corps should remain in Madrid in order to bolster the authority of the legitimate, and still internationally recognized government. The Mexican consul told his colleagues that his country had undergone a similar revolution, that his embassy would grant asylum, but that it favored the victory of the Republic.

There was broad agreement among all the Latin American and European diplomats to do whatever lay in their power to aid the victims of political and religious persecution. But implementing that agreement involved many difficult legal questions. Contemporary European diplomatic practice did not include the right of embassy asylum for opponents of a recognized government. Both the British and American consuls had instructions not to open their embassies to refugees of Spanish nationality, on the grounds that such action would constitute intervention in the internal affairs of a friendly power. The Russian Ambassador, arriving in Madrid at the end of August, refused to attend the meetings. The Soviet Union did not recognize the right of embassy asylum nor the right of the Chilean Ambassador to speak for the diplomatic corps as a unit. There were serious questions arising from the temporary breakdown of governmental authority. Should the diplomats recognize identification papers and safe conducts signed by the delegation of the autonomous Basque government? Most were willing to do this. Should they deal with the militia committees? The Peruvian Ambassador expressed his amazement that the British consul had done so. Should the principle of extraterritoriality apply to the apartments inhabited by consuls and embassy secretaries, as well as to the premises leased by the ambassadors? The most pro-Insurgent diplomats would have liked to state such a claim, but the corps as such did not.

The Madrid press and radio were hostile to the embassies from the beginning, alleging (incorrectly) that only fascists were seeking refuge. Among others, the wife of President Azaña, the daughters of Indalecio Prieto, and the families of numerous Republican deputies of both Right and Left parties, left Spain via the Argentine embassy and the Argentine cruiser *25 de Mayo*. The Foreign Minister of the Giral government, Augusto Barcía, provided government cars on several occasions to transport threatened persons to the Chilean embassy. When rumors reached Geneva in September that the embassies might feel obliged to close their Madrid offices, the Spanish delegate Ossorio y Gallardo stated that the Republican government recognized the right of refuge and would guarantee the lives of the embassy refugees. In mid-September the new Prime Minister, Largo Caballero, privately asked Ambassador Núñez to protect the nieces of the Dukes of Veragua (descendants of Christopher Columbus) who had been assassinated in Madrid.[8] Largo also welcomed enthusiastically the Chilean ambassador's offer to visit Toledo in an effort to have the women and children evacuated from the Alcázar.

On October 13, however, Foreign Minister Del Vayo sent Núñez a note concerning the right of asylum, in which he referred to the presence of "political delinquents" in the embassies. From that day on, the embassy question was complicated by the strong mutual antipathy of the two men.[9] The government appeared to be acting at cross purposes, but the situation was extremely complex. On the one hand there were the genuinely humane impulses of both the Giral and the Caballero governments, and their readiness, within limits, to use the embassies in order to protect innocent persons from the anarchists in the fall of 1936 and from the Communists in early 1937. But the clearly pro-Nationalist attitude of Ambassador Núñez constituted a steady provocation to the Madrid government. In addition, a number of European embassies, in particular the Turkish, Polish, Finnish, Dutch, Norwegian, and Belgian, greatly expanded their facilities by renting extra buildings.

Both the letter and spirit of political asylum were much abused. The Peruvian and Cuban legations were known centers of espionage, but untouchable because of their diplomatic immunity.[10] The Dutch and the Norwegian chargés

[8] *Ibid.,* p. 229.

[9] *Ibid.,* pp. 230–32. J. Alvarez del Vayo, *La guerra empezó en España,* pp. 241–42.

[10] J. de Galíndez, *Los vascos,* pp. 103, 115, 168–69.

d'affaires were both German citizens, able to serve Germany in Republican Spain after the Germans had recognized the Franco government in November, 1936. At night, shots were fired from embassy buildings. Both food and luxuries entered duty-free. In 1937 the inmates were eating far better than were most Madrileños, and some of them were engaged in a highly lucrative black market. With order having been restored in the streets, friends and families could visit freely, bringing information of military value which could then be sent to Salamanca in the diplomatic mail sacks—or broadcast with impunity from the transmitters located in the legations.[11]

The spectacular abuses of course did not cancel the genuinely humane work. The population of the Chilean embassy included many completely honorable conservatives such as the engineer Manuel Lorenzo Pardo. The German Hospital, when placed under the Chilean flag, provided essential services to children and old persons without political distinction. The Dominican Ambassador harbored reactionaries but also organized a home for Republican children evacuated from their villages or otherwise separated from their families by the war.[12] The Dutch chargé d'affaires, despite his Nazi connections, aided the Basque delegation in its work on behalf of moderate Republicans and nonpolitical victims of cheka persecution. But the obviously fascist sympathies of the most active diplomats would have taxed the patience of any democratic regime. At the same time, the Madrid government could obtain absolutely no counterpart for its own policy of tolerance. The foreign consulates of Seville and Coruña were forbidden to refugees, whose very existence the Burgos government refused to acknowledge.

The Caballero government wanted the embassies emptied as completely as possible. The major difficulty, as with prisoner exchanges, was the question of guaranteeing that the released

[11] Segismundo Casado, *The Last Days of Madrid* (London, 1939), pp. 87–93; article on the embassies by Indalecio Prieto in *El Socialista,* December 27, 1951. There are numerous references to "fifth column" activities in Claude Bowers, *My Mission to Spain* (New York, 1954).

[12] Galíndez, *op.cit.,* p. 97.

refugee would not take arms against the Republic. Alvarez del Vayo negotiated separate agreements with France, Holland, Turkey, Czechoslovakia, and Cuba, whereby Spain agreed to evacuate the refugees and the contracting governments undertook to keep those persons from emigrating again to Nationalist Spain.[13] Under these agreements about 1,000 persons of military age left Republican Spain early in 1937. Most governments honored their pledges, but the Belgians released their contingent unconditionally as soon as they stepped on French soil, thereby delaying considerably the arrangement of further such evacuations.[14]

Ardent debates took place among the legation populations as to the desirability of leaving, especially during the months from November 1936 to April 1937, during which period it seemed reasonable to suppose that the Nationalist army would be entering Madrid shortly.[15] Why risk an unpleasant journey and temporary exile if the war was about to end? Yet for many officers it was important not to be found in the embassies by the victorious army. The Burgos authorities had nothing but scorn for military men who had gone to the embassies instead of fighting at the Montaña barracks or making their way to Insurgent lines in the first days of the war. Such officers might partially rehabilitate themselves by leaving Republican Spain and offering their services at Burgos, but in order to do so they would also have deliberately to break their word to the Republican authorities permitting them to leave.

The entire question was never resolved. Altogether some 15–20,000 persons sought refuge at one moment or another, the great majority of them in the first three months of the war. The government announced in late June, 1937, that 4,000 persons had been evacuated from the embassies, but this figure gives only a minimal indication since all kinds of entries and

[13] *Survey of International Affairs,* 1937, ii, 388–90.

[14] Galíndez, *op.cit.,* p. 101.

[15] In this connection see the semi-fictional, but also highly documentary account of life in the embassies and hospitals: Javier Martín Artajo, *"No me cuente Ud su caso"* (Madrid, 1955). The author, a future Foreign Minister of the Franco government, spent a considerable portion of the war in the Mexican Embassy.

exits were made without record. Toward the end of the war the total refugee population stood between 2–3,000.[16] The publicity arising from the embassy question was generally unfavorable to the Republic. The origin of the problem was a constant reminder of the government's helplessness in the first weeks of the war. The letters and newspaper interviews, widely published both in Europe and Latin America by the refugees, naturally highlighted the ugly situation within Madrid and reinforced conservative preference for the Nationalists as the "forces of order."

It was obvious to everyone that the longer the war lasted, the more its outcome would depend upon foreign intervention, and the more it would destroy the physical and moral fiber of Spain. Almost all the Republican leaders hoped at one time or another for mediation as a means to end the struggle. The moderate Socialist Julián Besteiro had taken a pacifist position, practically speaking, from the start. President Azaña had passed from black despair in the first months of the war to a position of moderate optimism when, in early 1937, legal authority was being reinforced and the Republican Army was giving a favorable account of itself. But he never for a moment believed that the Republic could win the war. Everything should be done to use the Republic's limited bargaining power to achieve a negotiated peace.[17]

With this end in view he asked Besteiro to represent Spain at the Coronation of George VI in May 1937. World opinion had been aroused by the evidence of the massive dispatch of Italian troops to Spain, and the Non-Intervention Committee

[16] Estimates on the total number of embassy refugees vary from 5,000 to 20,000. I have followed the reasoning of Burnett Bolloten, who, in *The Grand Camouflage*, gives an estimate of close to 20,-000, noting that Núñez Morgado estimated 15,000, Del Vayo 20,000, and that the unimportant Norwegian legation alone had 900 at one time. The lower estimates may well have been based on information for 1938. Thus I accept as probably correct the IRC figure of 2,500 for close to the end of the war.

[17] Manuel Azaña, *Discurso en el ayuntamiento de Valencia,* Jan. 21, 1937.

had been discussing proposals for the withdrawal of foreign "volunteers" from both sides. Azaña saw in these proposals the best opportunity for a truce and a mediated peace. As President he had no constitutional authority to take the initiative, but like many statesmen before and since, he was willing to violate the letter of the law for vital cause. More than any other principal figure in the government, he felt personally the weight of misery and destruction occasioned by the war. He had no confidence in Del Vayo as Foreign Minister, and he seized the opportunity to reach the British Foreign Office via Besteiro.

He, as well as the Prime Minister, came to the Valencia airport to see the special envoy off to London. Since Besteiro and Largo Caballero were not on speaking terms, it did not seem extraordinary to either man that Azaña should closet himself privately with D. Julián. Azaña asked Besteiro to press the question of volunteer withdrawal and to sound out the willingness of the English to mediate. Apparently he gave Besteiro the impression that he was speaking for the Prime Minister as well as for himself. By the time Besteiro returned, Largo Caballero had been replaced by Juan Negrín. The specific results of his London conversations are not clear, because the new Prime Minister would not consent to hear the report. The misunderstanding within the government was complete, due to Azaña's secretive behavior. Since Caballero had known nothing of the diplomatic aspect of the Besteiro journey, and since such initiatives were constitutionally the prerogative of the Prime Minister, Negrín, who intended to intensify the war effort, did not propose to begin by treating with a "defeatist" who mistakenly believed he had had the authority to seek mediation.[18]

[18] Despite the fact that Besteiro's mission had no practical consequences, it was an extremely important moral event, because it determined in advance the misunderstanding between Besteiro and Negrín. My conviction that Besteiro thought he had been empowered to seek mediation is based on separate conversations with three of his friends in Madrid, plus the article of José del Río in *El Socialista,* September 24, 1959. I owe to D. Pablo Azcárate, the Republican ambassador in London, the information that

From the middle of 1937 on, moreover, Republican personalities were constantly putting out feelers. Prieto, with many
friendships among Basques on both sides of the line, and with
multiple personal contacts at St. Jean de Luz among the diplomatic corps, tried several times to sound out a possible readiness for negotiation. In contrast with Besteiro, however, he
realized that he was not empowered to make proposals, and
he did not try to. But he knew that there was no unanimity
under the surface in Nationalist Spain, and it was difficult for
anyone of humane instincts to believe that General Franco
would sacrifice tens of thousands of extra lives rather than
accept any form of compromise.[19]

Generalitat representatives in France and Belgium apparently sought mediation also. It is impossible to know exactly what they did, since everything took the form of hints,
feelers, tones of voice, and since neither they nor their interlocutors could make the error of considering them authorized
to negotiate. All these activities contributed to a sense of weakness and lack of structured authority in the Republic.[20] No
one from Salamanca dropped any hints about negotiation,
and the contrast in spirit and authority was clear for all to see.

However, even if the Republicans had been thoroughly
discreet in their diplomacy, it is extremely doubtful whether
they could have achieved mediation. On numerous occasions,
diplomats friendly to the Nationalists mentioned the possibility in Salamanca. General Gómez Jordana gave them a consistent and fixed reply: mediation was unthinkable, because if
the Republic were not crushed entirely, the Civil War would
have to be fought over again in a few years. If England, with
her control of the seas and her position as Spain's chief trading partner, had wished to exercise pressure for a compromise

---

Besteiro was to emphasize the question of withdrawing volunteers.
The airport meeting and the anger of Besteiro after his return are
described briefly in Largo Caballero's *Mis recuerdos,* pp. 199–200,
and I had the opportunity also to discuss the whole question with
Rodolfo Llopis, who was Caballero's secretary.

[19] Prieto in *El Socialista* (Toulouse), March 5, 1959.
[20] Zugazagoitia, *op.cit.,* pp. 418–23.

peace, such pressure might have altered the Nationalist stand. But the Chamberlain government was staking everything on the appeasement of Hitler and Mussolini. The resignation of Anthony Eden as Foreign Minister in February 1938 indicated, if proof were still necessary, that Chamberlain preferred the victory of General Franco as part and parcel of his understanding with Mussolini in the Mediterranean.

Throughout the war noncombatants were constantly retreating before the advancing armies and passing across the lines at thinly held points. Those crossing into the Nationalist zone were usually persons of some means, and they were not large in number. They were also moving into the area in which the food situation and general economic organization were far superior, so that their arrival created few problems. However, tens of thousands of persons, mostly without economic means, fled to the Republican zone in which the food situation went from bad to worse.

During the autumn of 1936, thousands of peasants from Extremadura and Andalusia inundated Madrid. They lived in subway stations, football grounds, the Retiro Park, and the deserted palaces. The men joined the Army, and the government, after November, tried to evacuate their families to the rear. But the latter preferred to remain, the more especially as they could thus share, however slightly, in the distribution of military rations. After the Battle of the Jarama, the perimeter of Madrid itself remained quiet. The Army organized literacy courses in the trenches, and the peasant children could join their fathers in receiving the rudiments of an education. Older civilian elements of the city population also resisted the idea of evacuation, for different reasons. Many of them hoped that the Nationalists would soon enter Madrid, and they had seen how frequently empty apartments were looted. They took a purely fatalistic attitude toward the bombings and shellings, which were in any case infrequent after the first all-out attack on the city. Altogether, the population of Madrid increased by well over 50 per cent during the war.

The archivists and librarians of the capital took the initiative, in August, 1936, to save the national art treasures

444

from destruction. Under the nominal direction of the Ministry of Public Instruction, they formed the *Junta delegada de in-cautación, protección y conservación del tesoro artístico na-cional*. With the aid of enlightened UGT and CNT elements they printed illustrated leaflets explaining to the refugees and soldiers the value of the art objects among which they were moving in the palaces. They went through abandoned and sacked convents with moving crews to transfer the valuable items to the Prado, and saved many a building from looting by the simple process of placing on it a "requisitioned for the use of the government" sign. In the palaces they interrupted refugee families cooking their meals on the parquet floors, and asked their help in piling the art treasures in one or two rooms. Then they fixed on the door a large sign *incautado* stamped like a passport with the seals of a dozen unions, committees, and Popular Front political parties. As trucks became available the art was then moved to the Prado, but in more than one case the owner of the palace returned in 1939 to find the insignia of the junta still protecting the paintings where they had been hastily stored in late 1936.[21]

The city of Barcelona had been the mecca of Spain's landless peasants ever since the beginning of industrialization in the nineteenth century. The provinces of Alicante, Murcia, and Almería had traditionally supplied large numbers of unskilled workers to Catalonia. The war and the blockade quickly disorganized their always weak economies, and whole families migrated north. Quaker representatives in January 1937 estimated that there were already 25,000 children wandering the streets of Barcelona; by October 1937 there were about 500,000 refugees in the Catalan capital. At the end of the year they numbered 800,000, including a contingent of more than 50,000 refugees from the northern war who had been evacuated to France, and then, partly by choice and partly at the request of the French government, been repatriated at the Catalan frontier. After the successful Nationalist offensive

[21] A former member of the junta described to me its activities and proudly showed me his collection of leaflets and posters written in the campaign to educate the refugees in the Madrid palaces. See also Galíndez, *op.cit.*, pp. 130–32.

in Aragon in the spring of 1938, well over a million home-less persons were crowded into the provinces of Tarragona, Barcelona, and Gerona. It is impossible to estimate even with approximate accuracy how many such persons were wandering about in the area south from Valencia to Almería. Also by early 1938 there were perhaps 90,000 refugees in Nationalist Spain, frequently Basque and Asturian children separated from their families. The occupation of the northern coast in late 1937, coupled with the Aragon offensive, added huge numbers of distressed persons to the population of the Nationalist zone. For the first time, food shortages were felt, and the *auxilio social* was unable adequately to cope with the situation in Lérida and along the Mediterranean coast.

In Barcelona the Quakers established canteens which were staffed by refugee women. In March 1937 they distributed milk according to the following theoretical rations: 1 pint 3 times weekly for infants up to nine months of age; $1\frac{1}{3}$ pints daily from nine months to 6 years. But most of the time no milk was available for those over two years of age. A half-pound of sugar and a package of biscuits were distributed twice weekly, and there was some cod liver oil available on medical prescription. In Murcia, where they found the worst overcrowding and undernourishment, but where transporta-tion difficulties were infinitely greater than in Catalonia, they fed thousands of children on bread and cocoa, with occa-sionally a few prunes for those under six years of age.

During the first year of the war, the population of Barce-lona gave the refugees a sympathetic welcome. A children's relief organization, *Pro Infancia Obrera,* with representatives of all the Popular Front parties, helped the Quakers to place children in homes, and when this soon became impractical, to run camps in the stadia and school grounds of the many in-dustrial suburbs of Barcelona. To the extent possible, they maintained school instruction and gave manual training to adolescents. In March, 1938, the Nationalists captured the Pyrennean power stations on which Catalan industries and public utilities depended. In the absence of transportation, and with the food shortage ever more acute, all other activities yielded to the search for food and the effort to avoid physical

446

exertion other than the miles of walking necessary to obtain a minimum of nourishment.[22]

Scabies, symptomatic of unsanitary living conditions, and pellegra, due to vitamin deficiencies, appeared early among the refugees. For the resident population most foods were available until early 1938, but by the summer, meat and fats were unobtainable except on the black market, and normally well-off people considered themselves lucky if they had bread and lentils in reasonable quantity, plus an occasional egg from the farm of the janitor's cousin. Persons up to about the age of fifty who had previously enjoyed good health could generally maintain their necessary activities. City children sickened more quickly than did their cousins from the villages. One of the first dramatic symptoms of malnutrition was the collapse of a person's legs, and incidents of the sort were common occurrences on bread lines and among factory workers who had long distances to cover before reaching their shops. According to Barcelona hospital reports, deaths from malnutrition, mostly among children and old people, more than doubled from 1936 to 1937, and doubled again in 1938. Nor do such statistics tell the whole story, because they refer principally to the local population—those who came to be treated in hospitals in the first place[23].

The problems of civilian suffering could never be separated from the issues of the war itself. Various governments and church and charitable societies raised their voices against the

[22] On the number of refugees, and on Quaker efforts in Catalonia, I depended principally on Noah Curtis and Cyril Gilbey, *Malnutrition* (London, 1944), pp. 46–71. The book contains a great deal of technical information on the organization of food relief, and compares Quaker experience in Austria from 1919 to 1924 with the experience in Catalonia, 1936–1939. See also Grace Rhoads, "The Quakers in Spain," *The Christian Century*, August 24, 1938; and the article by Alfred W. Jones in The *New York Times Magazine*, April 3, 1938.

[23] A. Pedro Pons, *Enfermedades por insuficiencia alimenticia observadas en Barcelona durante la guerra* (Barcelona, 1940). The author was professor of clinical medicine at the University of Barcelona.

bombing of cities like Madrid, Bilbao, Barcelona, and Valencia. The Nationalist authorities replied by listing the military objectives located in those cities, and by listing the raids carried out by the Republican Air Force. Most of these produced very few casualties. The danger came more from the spent anti-aircraft shells returning to the ground than from the bombs dropped. However, there were a number of raids on major Nationalist cities which cost a dozen or more deaths each, and in strict logic there was no moral distinction between the raids of one side and those of the other.[24]

The British objected repeatedly to the blockade of food-ships. The Nationalists replied that the Republic had sent Spain's gold reserve to Russia in order to buy arms, and that the entrance of food relief ships to Republican ports would constitute in effect a subsidy to the war effort.[25] Only in February 1939, when the war was clearly about to end in the unconditional surrender of the Republic, did General Franco direct his navy to permit food ships to enter the Levantine ports.

In Nationalist Spain the Quakers, like the Red Cross delegates, were suspect as Protestants. Most of them were personally sympathetic to the Republic, and their political ideas were indeed those which the Falangist press stigmatized as "red-masonic-international." They were permitted to aid in the relief of Oviedo and Gijón in late 1937, and to distribute supplies in Saragossa, Teruel, and Lérida in the spring of 1938, but they could never establish relations of trust and cordiality with the *auxilio social*. Latin-American doctors volunteered their services on both sides, and the well-known American surgeon Dr. Edward Barsky established a field hospital in Republican Spain. In these instances the political ideals of the individual doctors frankly determined their choice of side.

Similar difficulties applied to the efforts of the various national Red Cross societies. In proportion to their population and resources, the Latin-American Red Crosses made the

[24] Unofficially I received an opportunity to see the complete listing by the Nationalist Air Ministry of Republican air strikes against Nationalist territory.

[25] *Survey of International Affairs*, 1938, I, 386–87.

largest contributions. Their national committees were composed, on the whole, of well-to-do conservatives whose sympathies were engaged on the Nationalist side. In Europe, where the British, Swedish, and Swiss governments made particularly large contributions to the Red Cross, the International Committee in Geneva was able roughly to equalize the total distribution of Red Cross aid to the two sides, with more clothes and medicines going to the Nationalist zone, and more food to the Republican. Questions of pride and efficiency also hampered distribution. At the end of the war there was a complete, unpacked mobile hospital in Burgos which had arrived from Geneva a year earlier. The army had refused to accept the condition that it be publicly acknowledged as a Red Cross hospital, and the IRC was unwilling to let it be, in effect, confiscated. At the end of the war, Quaker and Red Cross representatives found quantities of canned food, medicines, and clothing lying untouched in warehouses in both zones.

The significance of these endeavors to lighten human suffering is extremely difficult to measure. The number of persons who escaped to Gibraltar, to British and French ships, and to the Madrid embassies were but a tiny fraction of the population which would very willingly have dispensed with the entire war. To their friends committed to either side, they appeared to be opportunists fleeing from their political responsibilities at a crucial moment. And in the embassies, certainly, a high proportion were in reality belligerents who took advantage of the protection afforded by a foreign flag. Doctors and ambulance drivers who reported either to Madrid or to Burgos, national Red Cross societies which earmarked their contributions, were indeed relieving human suffering, but not without making a political choice. Governments which protested aerial bombing were not prepared to give up the weapons and the ambitions which had led them in the past and would lead them in the future to commit similar acts. The number of prisoners exchanged was less than 1 per cent of the total number taken, and the food relief provided by the Quakers reached, on a temporary basis only, perhaps 10 per cent of those in dire need.

However, the significance of these efforts must not be

judged purely on a numerical basis. The Civil War began with a terrible lust for the extermination of the absolute enemy. As the months passed, more and more people desired only the return of peace and a degree of mutual conciliation. But an increasing proportion of the human and physical resources of the nation were being thrown into the war, and the probable victor had set his face against all compromise. In these circumstances every act of peace had an absolute value: each prisoner exchanged, each refugee hidden, each child fed, each work of art preserved was important. Prisoners took hope of eventual freedom from the mere fact that exchanges were being negotiated. Young middle-class women in the auxilio social could feel that their acts of mercy would nourish the future of Spain. The presence of the Quakers testified that there were human beings capable of sacrificing their own immediate comfort to aid other human beings with whom they had had no previous personal, sentimental, or historical ties. The IRC delegates were working to widen the area in which the civilized treatment of military and political prisoners would apply. The Republican officials who sought mediation showed their readiness to lay aside old animosities and accept compromise in order to end the bloodshed. The sum of all these actions was small in practical effect, but they aided a silent, suffering population to maintain a minimal faith in human decency.

26

THE EBRO
AND THE FALL OF CATALONIA

ON APRIL 15, 1938, the Nationalists had reached the sea at Viñaroz. They had severed Catalonia from the central zone of the Republic, and they had deprived Barcelona of electric power. They had enjoyed overwhelming material superiority and suffered only light casualties. They had taken thousands of prisoners, and the disorganization of the Republican defense in many sectors suggested demoralization as well as material shortages. The Nationalist Air Force freely bombed its chosen objectives, and the people of the Republican zone sardonically referred to their own planes as *el arco de iris,* the rainbow which appears after the storm has passed.

Yet in moral and political terms the Nationalist victory was by no means decisive. In Lérida they found only a few hundred old people, and in Barbastro none but women and children.[1] As in Andalusia in the autumn of 1936, the population fled before the invader, burning, or attempting to burn, villages and fields. The officers of the Army of Africa, accustomed to the conditions of colonial warfare, had been little affected by such suffering. But the Nationalist Army in Aragon now included thousands of young officers who had left the universities and volunteered to serve in what they considered to be a national rising against conditions of intolerable chaos and the threat of communism. These officers were depressed by the flight of the villagers. They reacted angrily to rumors of the Italian bombings of Barcelona— bombings which were never mentioned in the Nationalist press. Street brawls occurred between Italian and Spanish officers, and General Yagüe created a sensation in Burgos on April 19 with a public speech extoling the bravery of

[1] See the detailed dispatches by William Carney to The *New York Times,* April 4 and 5, 1938.

Spaniards on both sides and suggesting that the Falange extend the hand of reconciliation to the "reds."[2] French border officials, polling the men of military age who had retreated to the Pyrenees frontier, found that less than 5 per cent desired to be repatriated to the Nationalist zone. The overwhelming majority chose to reenter Catalonia.[3]

In Republican Spain the sheer willpower of Prime Minister Negrín had staved off panic in the first days of April. Arms, oil, and food, pouring over the reopened French border and rapidly delivered to the Army, enabled it to mount increasingly stiff resistance to the Nationalists in the last days of the month. The Republican Navy convoyed supply ships between Barcelona and Valencia, and serious air-raid preparations were made in the coastal cities. The arms workers of Sagunto stayed on the job despite repeated heavy bombing of the city.[4] The Prime Minister visited the front constantly, infusing the troops with his own renewed energy and optimism. No occupations were more highly respected by Spanish workingmen than those of doctor and professor. Juan Negrín was both, and in addition, a man whose warm personality inspired the individual loyalty of both troops and officers. The soldiers referred to themselves proudly as *hijos de Negrín* (sons of Negrín), to their plentiful, if not particularly varied, rations as *lentejas de Negrín* (lentils), and to his thirteen-point political program as *puntos de Negrín*. For the majority of men not committed to a particular political line, his image effaced those of Azaña, Prieto, and Largo Caballero.

Fortified by the increase in his personal authority and the renewal of French aid, Negrín on May 1, 1938, publicly defined the position of the Spanish Republic. In the form of thirteen points, he proposed the maintenance of Spain's political and economic integrity against all foreign penetration; affirmed both liberty of conscience and the regional liberties; called for agrarian reform with respect, at the same time, for small property and for foreign property of firms not involved in the military rebellion; and proposed a general

[2] Harold Callender in The *New York Times,* June 5 and 6, 1938.
[3] *Survey of International Affairs,* 1938, I, 394.
[4] Vincent Sheean, *Not Peace but a Sword* (New York, 1939), pp. 140–48.

political amnesty and withdrawal of all foreign troops. He reaffirmed his country's attachment to the League of Nations and to the principle of collective security.

The speech was a direct reply to the several recent Nationalist laws abolishing the reforms and liberties enacted between 1931 and 1936. It also presented to world opinion the image of a regime whose aims and methods were similar to those of the Western democracies. It was a supreme effort to convince the Western governments of their own stake in the survival of the Republic. The absence of international response was a bitter disappointment to Negrín. The United States did not budge from its neutrality, nor England from its policy of appeasement. In France, Daladier, who had succeeded Blum on April 3, was pro-Republican, but even more timid than the latter in the face of fascist threats and British pressure. In late May the border was again closed. ostensibly as a step toward winning fascist consent for the withdrawal of foreign volunteers from Spain.[5]

Outside the Army Negrín's position was not strong. The more he saw himself as the incarnation of Republican resistance the more the diverse elements of the Popular Front feared him as a potential dictator. As Defense Minister, he appointed his only unconditional supporters, the Communists, as sub-secretaries for the Army, Navy, and Air Force. Jesús Hernández headed the corps of war commissars in the central zone, and the Communist press built up the image of Negrín as it had that of Largo Caballero in late 1936. In the spring of 1938 there was a perceptible increase in arrests and death penalties among civilians. The SIM was also controlled in large part by the Communists.[6] Its terror reflected the growth

---

[5] *Survey*, 1938, I, 314–16. The *New York Times*, March 23 and 27, April 13 and 17, May 19 and 20, June 21, July 3, 1938.

[6] Gabriel Avilés, *Tribunales Rojos* (Barcelona, 1939) gives a sober, detailed account of the courts and prisons of the SIM. The author was a liberal lawyer and a personal friend of Luis Companys. He belongs to the small, and too little known, group of lawyers who devoted all their energy and courage to the struggle for the maintenance of legal standards in Republican Spain. See also the informative articles of Lawrence Fernsworth in The *New York Times*, April 20–24 and May 25, 1938.

of defeatism after the Nationalist victories and the cruder standards of justice consequent upon the elimination of Prieto, Irujo, and Zugazagoitia from all posts of real authority. A vicious circle had developed, from which the Prime Minister was never to escape. He himself was a patriot, a bourgeois, and a democrat; but the international situation forced him to depend increasingly upon the Communists, and with the growth of their power, he inevitably alienated the non-Communist Left and made less likely than ever a change in the foreign policy of the Western powers.

When the Thirteen Points speech failed to alter the diplomatic situation, Negrín decided that only a spectacular military action could save the Republic from slow asphyxiation. Because of its material inferiority, the Republican Army could not hope to take the offensive on a broad front or in open country. But Brunete and Teruel had both proved that General Franco felt compelled for prestige reasons to regain every inch of ground taken from him by enemy action. Working in intimate collaboration, Negrín and his chief of staff, General Vicente Rojo, sought a field of battle which would strike at the communications of the Nationalist Army, place the fighting in hill country so as to minimize the enemy's material superiority, and yet enable the Republic to concentrate its reserves and supplies. They chose the bend of the Ebro river, between Fayón and Benifollet, an area held by only one Nationalist division. North of this bend they concentrated perhaps 100,000 men, about 100 operational planes, somewhat over 100 heavy guns, and several dozen light anti-aircraft pieces. In early July the troops were rehearsing the use of pontoon bridges and small boats. Their battle training anticipated the fact that communications with the rear would be extremely difficult, and that machine guns and mortars would have to do most of the work usually assigned to field artillery.

The Republicans began to cross the Ebro on the night of July 24. The maneuver achieved complete surprise, and in the course of a week some 50,000 men occupied the hills south of the river. During the day, the Republicans used their entire anti-aircraft artillery to force the Nationalist planes to fly high, and this fact, together with the thinness of the target, protected the bridges. Most of the supplies and men, however, crossed at night. The Nationalists opened the dams along the Pyrennean tributaries of the Ebro, and when

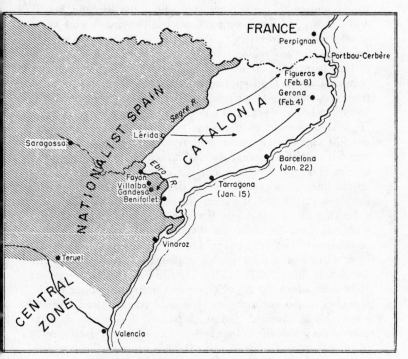

MAP 8. The Ebro, July–November, 1938
Catalonia, December 1938–February 1939

these flood waters descended to the battle area they temporarily destroyed the pontoons. Meanwhile, General Franco rushed reinforcements to the area, with the result that by August 1 the Republican advance had been stopped just short of the towns of Gandesa and Villalba de los Arcos. The army established its lines, using wells for command posts and stone parapets for cover. The country was hilly, but with few trees, and the ground was too hard in many parts for the digging of fox holes. Food and ammunition could be brought up, and the wounded evacuated, only at night—and only by means of small boats. Nationalist artillery kept the Republican troops pinned to the ground throughout the daylight hours and destroyed all land communications. The orders were very simple, as in the November 1936 defense of Madrid: no retreat anywhere, for any reason.[7]

The launching of the Ebro offensive did not produce political unity in the Republican zone. After Prieto's departure from the Defense Ministry, President Azaña feared what he judged to be the dictatorial tendencies of Negrín's personality. He shared the widespread belief that after the crushing Nationalist victories of March and April the war was lost. He also felt, as had President Alcalá-Zamora before him, that his role as Head of State implicitly gave him a right of veto on crucial lines of policy even though the Constitution emphasized the limits rather than the prerogatives of the President.

In Madrid Julián Besteiro regarded Negrín as an adventurer who was gambling with the lives of millions of his fellow countrymen. The resentment dated from Negrín's refusal to hear Besteiro's report of his diplomatic conversations in London in May 1937. Madrileños traveling to Barcelona in 1938 were struck by the evidence of Communist power in all branches of the government. When old friends asked Negrín about this he laughed, as though hearing a silly rumor, and assured his interlocutors that he was a bourgeois to the marrow of his bones, and that he was nobody's catspaw. To Besteiro such reports signified that Negrín was deceiving either himself or the Spanish Republicans, and that, whichever was the case, he was a dangerous man. In June Besteiro gave an interview to an Australian editor in which he declared himself

For the Battle of the Ebro I depended principally on Vicente Rojo, *España heroica* (Buenos Aires, 1942), pp. 168–90; and Alvah Bessie, *Men in Battle* (New York, 1939), pp. 275–90. I had the opportunity in Spain to consult officers of both the Republican and Nationalist armies on questions of supply, tactics, and morale.

ready to form a mediation government. In Barcelona Azaña talked of a truce and the withdrawal of all foreign troops as the first and most essential step toward restoring peace. Despairing of any real comprehension on the part of foreign powers, he acted on the inner conviction that if a truce was once achieved, no matter how temporary in form, neither side would be able to resume fighting.[8]

The initial success of the Ebro crossing raised the prestige of Negrín, but when the advance was stopped on August 1, and it became evident that the bulk of the Republican Army might now be trapped and annihilated in a pocket with its back to the river, criticism of the Prime Minister became stronger than ever. Knowing that Azaña wished to call upon Besteiro, he precipitated the crisis himself with a decree placing all Catalan military factories under the jurisdiction of the sub-secretariat of armament. The Catalan and Basque representatives in the cabinet resigned. Telegrams poured in to Azaña's office from the front demanding the retention of Negrín. The Air Force demonstrated over the city in a manner reminiscent of the technique used to impress the President during the crisis of late March. His personal friends urged him to resign. But Azaña thought of a mediated peace as the one service he might still perform for the Spanish people by remaining in office, and with the Army backing Negrín, he would not risk a civil war within the Civil War in order to oust the Prime Minister. On August 16 Negrín formed his third cabinet, merely replacing the Catalan and Basque members, neither of whom had held an important post.[9]

In the hills above Gandesa the Nationalists now held the initiative. They prepared their counterattacks with all-day artillery barrages from guns lined up hub to hub as in the great western-front battles of the First World War: and they

[8] Zugazagoitia, *Historia de la guerra en España*, pp. 430–32, 438–40.
[9] On the August crisis and its background, see Zugazagoitia, *op.cit.*, pp. 430–65 *passim* and Prieto y Negrín, *Epistolario*, p. 105. I received confirmation of Zugazagoitia's interpretation of the attitudes of Besteiro and Azaña from surviving friends of both men.

supplemented the artillery with relays of bombers. But when the infantry charged, the defenders knew just where to expect them and concentrated a murderous fire from machine guns and mortars. The battle continued in this manner for 90 days, during which time the Nationalists achieved a maximum penetration of some 5 miles along a 20-mile front. General Franco was impatient at the slow progress of the counter-offensive. The Nationalist Air Force protested the use of its bombers as artillery, and the Italians sulked in their tents.[10] The eager young officers who had paraded through eastern Aragon in the spring now died leading gallant charges against the stubborn units of a Republican army which by all the rules had been beaten, but which did not know it.

The performance of the Republican Army reminded the world of Verdun, and Madrid. But in contrast with the situation of November 1936, the Republican zone had a government which not only spoke the language of bourgeois democracy but had long since reduced the "uncontrollables" to order. The SIM employed torture against the political enemies of the Communists, but it also protected some 2,000 priests who were conducting private services in Barcelona homes.[11] Widely respected journalists such as Herbert Matthews, Vincent Sheean, Lawrence Fernsworth, Louis Fischer, and "Pertinax" all reported the moderate, Western orientation of the Negrín government and wrote admiringly of both the military recovery and the civil administration. Prominent conservatives in the Anglo-Saxon world, notably Winston Churchill and the former U.S. Secretary of State, Henry L. Stimson, declared themselves favorable to the Republic in the summer of 1938. The French military attaché, who had already advised Blum in March to aid the Republic, flew home from the Ebro front in a fruitless effort to convince General Gamelin that France should intervene directly. In early September Negrín flew to Switzerland, ostensibly to attend an international medical

[10] Alfredo Kindelán, *Mis cuadernos de guerra,* pp. 150ff.

[11] Lawrence Fernsworth, in The *New York Times,* March 23, 1938, reported his personal findings concerning the renewed activity of an estimated 2,000 priests in Barcelona. I learned from private Catholic sources that the SIM protected these priests.

congress, in reality to make a supreme effort to achieve a compromise peace at a secret meeting with the Duke of Alba.[12]

But General Franco would have no compromise, and the military fate of the Republic was soon to be settled as the by-product of a larger international crisis. In March 1938 Hitler had occupied Austria, and within a matter of weeks he had demanded that the border areas of Czechoslovakia be handed over to Germany, on the grounds that the majority of the population were German. Czechoslovakia had mutual assistance pacts with both France and the Soviet Union. She possessed a line of heavy fortifications along her German frontier and an army reputed to have the highest fire-power per man on the European continent. England sent Lord Runciman, a personal friend of Chamberlain, to "mediate" between the Sudeten German minority and the Czech government. Runciman pressed the Czechs to yield on every important point, but they refused ultimately to accept what would have been a simple surrender under British auspices. The Germans prepared for war, and in September the flow of supplies to Nationalist Spain was drastically cut because of the needs of the German Army itself.[13]

On September 15 Prime Minister Chamberlain flew to meet Hitler, received the latter's minimal demands, and in the next few days wrung a bitter consent from the Czechs. But when he brought that consent to Germany on the 22nd, Hitler presented a series of new demands. Chamberlain himself was shaken, and did not protest when the Czechs decreed general mobilization. Construction of air-raid shelters was rushed in Hyde Park. Moscow assured the Czechs that she would honor the mutual assistance treaty, and it appeared that war was inevitable. In the last week of September General Franco hastened to assure London and Paris that he would be absolutely neutral in case of war. To his infuriated allies he explained that Spain would be in no condition to help them effectively, and he retorted to German criticism with com-

---

[12] H. Thomas, *The Spanish Civil War*, p. 554, information based on the State Department Papers for 1938. See also Prieto in *El Socialista* (Toulouse), Feb. 19, 1953.

[13] Thomas, *op.cit.*, p. 553.

plaints that Hitler had kept him completely in the dark as to German plans. Meanwhile, French and Italian diplomats were multiplying last-minute efforts to avoid a war which neither of their governments could contemplate. As a result the Prime Ministers of England, France, Italy, and Germany met at Munich on September 28. Without consulting Russia or Czechoslovakia, they forced upon the latter virtually the entire list of Hitler's maximal demands.

The Munich Pact was a deathblow to the diplomatic hopes of the Spanish Republic. If war had come in September 1938, Russia and the Western democracies would have been allies in the military struggle against fascism, as were the Communist and democratic forces within Spain. The Republican Army would have been actively engaged from the first moment in holding down Italian and German troops, and the Western governments would surely have accepted the Spanish Republic as an ally in the circumstances.[14] The Munich Pact, on the contrary, not only proved the determination of Chamberlain to maintain the appeasement policy. By its deliberate snub to Russia, it obliged that country inevitably to protect its own security through an arrangement with Hitlerite Germany.

Munich momentarily worried the Nationalists. General Franco feared that the same four powers which had settled the fate of Czechoslavakia might try to impose on Spain a settlement which would fall short of total victory for him. He need not have been anxious. Mussolini had spoken to Chamberlain of repatriating some 10,000 of his veterans; the two statesmen had agreed that this action would be the appropriate signal for the Anglo-Italian agreements of April 16 to take full effect. Chamberlain was unlikely to do anything in the meantime to ruffle Italian feathers. Indeed, Italian planes resumed their attacks on British and other neutral shipping, after a brief pause for the Munich negotiations.

On October 2 Prime Minister Negrín asked in a public speech how long Spaniards would go on killing one another.

[14] From an intimate friend of Negrín I learned that the Prime Minister received a personal message from Winston Churchill in November, 1938, saying, in effect: "Keep doing what you are doing."

On the same day, the German ambassador reported terrible war weariness in Nationalist Spain and warned his government that a major effort in armament would still be necessary to assure Franco's victory.[15] In San Sebastián the Falange newspaper *Unidad* stated editorially: "The Caudillo should know that Spain will not become the cemetery of patriots."[16] Munich may have crushed the diplomatic hopes of the Republic and caused fear of an unwelcome compromise in Salamanca. But the proud Republican army hung on grimly in the Sierra de Gandesa and the Generalissimo maintained his resolve to fight on for total victory. By the end of October he had gathered supplies and a corps of 30–40,000 fresh troops under General García Valiño. In the first two weeks of November the Nationalists forced the Republican army to evacuate the entire salient won at the end of July. Each army had suffered perhaps 40,000 casualties in the most grueling single battle of the war.[17] The Republicans had committed virtually all their armament and all their experienced combat units. The Nationalists had expended most of their best young officers. Tanks and trucks were in dire need of repair, for the lack of careful oiling, the absence of spare parts, the punishing sandstorms of eastern Aragon, and the rocky hillsides of the Ebro battlefield had taken their toll.

But the Generalissimo still had his hundreds of planes, guns, and motor vehicles. He asked the Germans for large new supplies of ammunition of all types and for men and machines to refurbish the Condor Legion. Germany's price was a more favorable agreement on mining rights, and on November 19 Salamanca agreed for the first time to give the Germans a majority interest in five important mines, to pay the bills of

[15] *GDFP*, pp. 754ff.

[16] Quoted in *The Nation*, December 31, 1938, with the information that the newspaper in question had been confiscated.

[17] This is the casualty estimate of *The Times*, London, November 19, 1938. I submitted it to the former General Rojo and to several other officers of the time, all of whom found it decidedly more reasonable than the estimate of 100,000 casualties for the "reds" alone given by Aznar. General Rojo thought even the *Times* figures might perhaps be on the high side.

the Condor Legion, and to import German mine machinery which would be paid for in ore.[18]

In hungry Barcelona the government persevered in the restoration of Spanish democracy. Negrín negotiated privately with a committee of Catalan Catholics, including the Bishop of Lérida, an agreement to restore public Catholic worship. During the summer, masses had already been celebrated on the Ebro and Madrid fronts. The Prime Minister wanted the churches themselves reopened, but the committee did not wish to give the appearance that all was normal when in fact Catholics still suffered persecution from some elements of the Popular Front. They agreed instead to have public services in some 30 garages and warehouses which would be designated by the government and protected by the police.[19] The plan, however, had barely been put into effect when the city fell to the Nationalists.

In October the government also brought to trial the long-imprisoned leaders of the POUM. They had been accused, in Moscow purge style, of receiving Nationalist subsidies and planning to assassinate important public figures, the best known of whom were Prieto and Colonel Modesto. In contrast with the Moscow trials, these unsupported accusations were quickly rejected. The court handed down five prison sentences for acknowledged participation in the May 1937 Barcelona uprising. There were no death penalties, and all the prisoners were freed before the Nationalist army arrived.[20] Similarly in October the government disbanded the International Brigades and on November 15, in Barcelona, paid tribute to the thousands of European and American anti-fascists who had fought to defend world democracy in Spain.

On November 16 about 10,000 Italian veterans reached home, and the Anglo-Italian Mediterranean agreement took effect. On the 19th the new mining agreement between Berlin and Salamanca was signed. Supplies flowed rapidly to the

[18] *GDFP,* pp. 769–71.

[19] Information from Barcelona personalities involved in the negotiations.

[20] The *New York Times,* Oct. 12, 14, 18, and 30, 1938. Gorkín, *Caníbales políticos,* pp. 260ff. Gorkin was one of the defendants.

Nationalists, and they were able on December 23 to launch the final, decisive offensive against the Republican Army. Some 350,000 men attacked along the entire Segre-Ebro front from Lérida to Tortosa. They possessed an absolute superiority in supplies and weapons of all types, with a field gun for every ten yards of front, unchallenged control of the skies, and sufficient transportation facilities to allow the advancing troops to be relieved every 48 hours in any sector where strong resistance occurred. In their path lay 90,000 semi-armed men whose morale and supplies had been exhausted by the Battle of the Ebro. Only the crack Communist-led units of Lister, Galán, and Tagüeña opposed serious resistance. On January 15 the Nationalists entered Tarragona without a fight.[21]

The government talked halfheartedly of turning Barcelona into a second Madrid, but an irresistible panic seized the population of Catalonia, and one-half million human beings began trudging toward the French border. The government released its political prisoners. Those of the Left joined the retreating masses; those of the Right were protected by the police and the Red Cross delegates. However, their protectors were unable to prevent a few isolated lynchings. The majority of the population, and most of the municipal officials, passively awaited the arrival of the Nationalists. On the 22nd General Yagüe's troops began to occupy the city, virtually without firing a shot. The doctors of the Nationalist Army found the hospital patients unfed for two or three days past, and did their best to protect wounded military men from victorious soldiers who wished to finish them off. The Moors entered empty apartments, collecting rugs and silverware which they then naïvely tried to sell to neighbors in the same building. Shops were closed and shuttered. The troops received four days of "liberty," after which discipline was restored quickly, and the Nationalists began to administer the city with the cooperation of most of the municipal employees. Their aviation bombed the roads leading to France. The League for

[21] For the Battle of Catalonia, I depended upon Vicente Rojo, *Alerta los pueblos!* (Buenos Aires, 1939); the *Survey of International Affairs*, 1938, i, 274–78; and Herbert Matthews, *The Education of a Correspondent* (New York, 1946), pp. 144ff.

the Rights of Man wished to cover the highways with Red Cross flags, but the IRC refused the request as a clear violation of the Geneva Convention. It would in any case have been a useless gesture, since the aviators knew perfectly well what and whom they were bombing.[22]

The government had retreated to Figueras, the last town of any importance on the road to France. On February 4 the Nationalists occupied Gerona. On the 6th, the leaders of the Republic—Azaña, Negrín, Companys, Aguirre, and Martínez Barrio—crossed the frontier together, on foot. On February 8 the Nationalists reached Figueras, and on that same day the British navy arranged the transfer of Minorca from Republican to Nationalist authority, thereby earning diplomatic credit with General Franco, satisfying themselves that Mussolini would not dominate the Balearics, and evacuating several hundred persons who would otherwise have suffered imprisonment or death.[23] During the afternoon of February 9 the Nationalists occupied the frontier from Perthus to Port Bou, and by the 12th practically the entire border was sealed.

[22] The American, English, and French journalists who had been stationed in Barcelona all left before the Nationalist entry. My account is based on interviews with several civilians, a Republican officer charged with maintaining order in the retreat, two Nationalist officers and a doctor who entered with General Yagüe's troops, and an International Red Cross delegate who was present. The question of the use of the Red Cross flag is discussed in the earlier cited (mimeographed) *Rapport Complémentaire* of 1948 concerning IRC activity in the Spanish Civil War.

[23] *Survey*, 1938, I, 301.

THE END OF THE WAR

During the first two weeks of Feburary 1939, the main concern of Prime Minister Negrín was to end the war on a nonreprisal basis. At the last meeting of the Cortes, on February 1, in Figueras, he announced the three conditions on which he hoped to make peace: the independence and territorial integrity of Spain were to be guaranteed (against possible Italian control of the Balearics and German control of mines); the people were to be free to choose their own future form of government; and Republican soldiers and officials were to be guaranteed against reprisals. A few days later, at the village of Agullana, he met the British chargé d'affaires Stevenson and the French ambassador Henry. Hoping for their mediation in Salamanca, he intimated that in reality the third condition, the guarantee against reprisals, was the only one which the government would feel absolutely obliged to insist on before downing arms. After crossing the frontier on the 6th, he established headquarters at the Spanish consulate in Toulouse.[1]

Between January 27 and February 10 approximately one-half million Spaniards retreated into France. Families of three generations, pushing two-wheeled carts piled high with mattresses, utensils, and dolls, covered the roads from Barcelona to Port Bou. The French had counted 170,000 of them by February 5, up to which time they had permitted only the civilians to cross. From the 5th to the 9th they allowed 300,000 soldiers to enter on condition of surrendering their arms at the border. As the gendarmes herded the refugees toward impromptu camps on the beaches near Argelès and

[1] Zugazagoitia, *op.cit.*, p. 509; Broué and Témime, *op.cit.*, pp. 483, 487–90. The latter authors are particularly well informed on Republican activities on French soil during the last weeks of the war.

St. Cyprien, the French peasants watched, some with tears in their eyes, others muttering "sales rouges" (dirty reds). The soldiers, for the most part, had maintained discipline throughout the retreat. They proudly formed ranks and marched across the frontier in military order. Thinking of themselves as the defenders of the legitimate Republican government and of world democracy, they were indignant to have French gendarmes frisk them as though handling a horde of criminal suspects. General Rojo and his staff exerted every effort to minimize the ill will between the police and the disbanded army.

The French, with their long tradition of granting political asylum and their knowledge of the reprisals carried out in conquered territory by the Nationalists, did not hesitate to offer refuge. But they were completely unprepared for such numbers and loath to complicate their future relations with the victors. Burgos representatives, accompanied by French officers, visited the camps to invite the ex-Republican soldiers to repatriate themselves. They promised that no one would be persecuted for mere opinions or membership in political organizations. On the other hand, General Franco on February 13 published a decree covering the political responsibilities of all those who had opposed the *movimiento nacional* in action or "by grave passivity" since October 1, 1934. This meant clearly that all civil servants, officeholders, party leaders, and militia volunteers who had supported the Popular Front would have to answer for their activities. The veterans weighed their chances while trucks and hot coffee waited for those who would choose repatriation. In late February and March perhaps 70,000 men crossed southern France to reenter Spain at the Hendaye-Irún border.[2]

In Toulouse, Negrín, Del Vayo, and Uribe attempted to convince Azaña and their cabinet colleagues to return to the remaining Republican territory, either to aid in an orderly surrender and evacuation of that territory, or to fight on, depending upon circumstances. Negrín's three points drew

[2] My figures on the number of refugees and on the number of soldiers returning to Spain come from the *Rapport Complémentaire* of 1948 concerning IRC activity in the Spanish Civil War.

no response whatever from the Nationalists. General Franco stated repeatedly to British and French representatives that the war was over and that he had no intention of negotiating with Negrín or anyone else. By about February 22, Negrín concluded that there was nothing to do but fight on. General Rojo had already resigned, in refusal, as he put it, to ask the Spanish people to commit suicide.[3] Martínez Barrio, President of the Cortes, José Antonio Aguirre, head of the Basque government, and Luis Companys, head of the Generalitat, took the same stand as Azaña.

Negrín, accompanied by Del Vayo and the Communists, flew to the central zone. On February 26 at Los Llanos airport near Valencia, he met with the commanding officers of the remaining armies. He told them he had been seeking an honorable peace through negotiation, not only since the Figueras meeting of the Cortes, but on several occasions since the spring of 1938. He concluded that the Republic had no choice but to resist. The professional officers who had been loyal to the Republic since July 18—Generals Matallana, Escobar, and Menéndez—all took the position that further military resistance was impossible.[4] Meanwhile, on February 24, General Franco, sure of victory, made an agreement with the Quakers whereby the Nationalist navy would permit food ships to enter the Republican ports.[5]

On February 27 France and England announced their recognition of the Nationalist government. Hours later, Manuel Azaña resigned, and Martínez Barrio, his constitu-

[3] Zugazagoitia, op.cit., p. 522.

[4] My principal sources on the Los Llanos meeting, and later on the Casado coup, were Segismundo Casado, The Last Days of Madrid (London, 1939) and Edmundo Domínguez, Los vencedores de Negrín (Mexico, D. F., 1940). These are highly detailed accounts, but I have tried to limit my summary to points which are corroborated by other sources. Casado's work is motivated by an almost hysterical desire for self-justification. Domínguez wrote his in Oran during the spring of 1939, at which time he was passionately convinced that the War had not been lost militarily and that Negrín had been "betrayed."

[5] Kershner, Quaker Service in Modern War, pp. 43-6.

tional successor, refused to take office. The structure of the
Second Spanish Republic had collapsed. The vast majority
of both its civilian and military leaders believed that there
was nothing more to be done than to end the shooting and
hope that the Nationalists would be merciful to the population
after the defeated leaders had effaced themselves. In the
central zone Negrín saw his responsibility in entirely different
terms. Regardless of the action of Azaña (always a defeatist),
the Prime Minister who had willed the Battle of the Ebro
could not surrender Republican Spain to an enemy who
refused all guarantees. In response to pessimism from the
officers, he talked of Russian artillery and machine guns
waiting in Marseilles, and a rumor spread widely among the
troops of American aircraft engines supposedly on the way.

In desperation, on March 2, he announced a number of
appointments which he hoped would enable him to retain
control of the central zone. The Communist officers who had
led the only concerted resistance during the Battle of Catalonia
were promoted: Colonel Modesto became the General in
charge of the central army (in replacement of Miaja), Majors
Líster and Galán were given the rank of colonel. Communist
officers were appointed to command the ports of Alicante,
Murcia, and Cartagena. At Madrid Negrín gambled on holding the loyalty of Colonel Casado, a non-Communist professional officer who had served both Largo Caballero and himself, and whom he now named a general.

Negrín's appointments served only to precipitate his down-
fall. The non-Communist elements reacted immediately, not
so much to the militarily well-earned promotions of the Communist officers as to the prospect of Communist control of
the ports through which any evacuation must take place. On
March 4 a confused rising took place at Cartagena, involving
both Falangist and Left groups, and the fleet sailed for French
North Africa. Jesús Hernández, commissar general for the
central-southern zone, sent troops under Communist officers
to repress the rising.[6]

The main event, however, occurred at Madrid. Colonel

[6] Broué and Témime, *op.cit.*, p. 491.

468

Casado had made clear at Los Llanos and in subsequent telephone conversations that he was not in accord with Negrín's policy of resistance at all costs. During the last days of February, he was negotiating within Madrid the formation of a *Consejo Nacional de Defensa* which would seize power for the purpose of ending the war on the best terms possible, if Negrín persisted in his effort to continue the struggle. The resignation of Azaña and the March 2 promotions (Casado refused to accept his when Negrín first addressed him as "General") hastened the decision of the Prime Minister's enemies.

The mood of Madrid had altered greatly since the heroic days of November 1936. Until well into the spring of 1937, the populace had believed in victory, and had been exhilarated by the sense that their city was the center of events having world-wide significance. Then came the fall of Largo Caballero, the loss of Bilbao, and the horrible, useless carnage at Brunete. The war became a nerve-racking stalemate, with the principal theaters of action far from Madrid, but with the enemy camped at the gates, and with hunger and cold wearing down the morale of the citizens within. Galloping inflation signified the deterioration of the Republican economy. The Burgos radio broadcast the serial numbers of the bank-notes the Nationalists would honor at their entry into the capital, and merchants frankly refused to accept others. The working class in Madrid was overwhelmingly Socialist or anarchist, the middle classes were largely moderate Republican. In November 1936 they had both welcomed Russian arms and officers, and toasted the health of Joseph Stalin. The united front of democratic and far left elements against fascism had been a flesh-and-blood reality. By the end of 1937 the population were no longer "fellow travelers." Communist influence in the army naturally aroused the resentment of the other parties. Most Socialists considered Negrín a renegade, and Republican liberals, while greatly admiring his ability and his personal intentions, considered him the front man for the Communists.

The most admired civilian personality in Madrid was undoubtedly the moderate Socialist Julián Besteiro. Besteiro had been born in Madrid, had been a professor of philosophy and a dean at the university. He had served as a municipal councilor in Madrid, and had sat in the Cortes from 1918 until the Primo de Rivera coup. In 1931 his fellow deputies had chosen him to preside over the Constitutional Cortes. A product of the *Institución Libre de Enseñanza,* he was a frequent lecturer there and at the *Casa del Pueblo.* He had been an intimate associate of Pablo Iglesias, and several times president of the UGT. He had thus for decades participated actively in the best liberal, intellectual, and Socialist phases of Madrid life. During the war he was particularly beloved for his intense loyalty to the city itself. He had remained in Madrid when the government and Cortes had moved to Valencia. He had been offered the ambassadorship to Argentina in early 1937. An ill man, he might honorably have seized the opportunity both to serve the Republic and escape from the war.[7] But as a city councilor he was occupied with the housing problems and general living conditions of the refugee population, and he stated that he did not wish to leave while the city was besieged. After his disappointing mission to London in May 1937, he immediately returned to Madrid, saying that he would not leave the city again except to perform a major service to the Spanish people—by which he meant, and everyone knew that he meant, to head a peace-making government.[8]

Besteiro's pessimism was political as well as military. In his opinion the Republic had come a generation too early, before a liberal, tolerant cultural attitude had taken root in the Spanish masses, and before the UGT had had time to prepare a generation of politically educated workers with the necessary

[7] *ABC,* Madrid, Feb. 20, 1937, carried his statement that the offer honored him, but that he had lost those dearest to him in the city, and that he was resolved in present circumstances not to leave it.

[8] On Besteiro's career see the moving article by Rodolfo Llopis, *Cuadernos del Congreso por la Libertad de la Cultura,* Dec., 1961. Llopis had been a bitter enemy of Besteiro within the Socialist Party during the war.

administrative and self-governing experience. As chairman of the Constituent Cortes he had naturally not taken personal part in the debates. It was nevertheless well known that he disliked the floods of anticlerical oratory and the dogmatic attack on the entire role of Church schools. In 1933 he regarded the leftward evolution of Largo Caballero as a political disaster. He spoke openly against the revolutionary line, and in the party caucus he voted against the planned rising in October 1934. At the same time, he shared entirely the Left's distrust of Gil Robles and determination to resist fascism by force if necessary. Therefore he unhesitatingly favored the Republic on July 18. But soon, horror at the paseos, and later the steady rise of Communist power, kept him passive, apolitical, in his relation to public authority. His loyalty was to the Republic of 1931–36, and to the traditions of Francisco Giner de los Ríos and Pablo Iglesias, not to the Republic of Largo Caballero or Juan Negrín.

Besteiro's personality, like those of many Spanish liberals and Socialists, included a profound religious element. As a professor of philosophy, he taught logic without a trace of mysticism, and in economic discussions he espoused an orthodox Marxism. As with many intellectuals in Catholic countries, his religious feelings were unexpressed since he refused the Catholic Church without desiring to fight it or to substitute another church. For years he had guarded himself against latent tuberculosis. Now, working intensely and living without adequate food or heat, he became increasingly ill. In March 1939 he was prepared to make any sacrifice to alleviate the suffering of those who were younger, in good health, and towards whom he felt the responsibility of a leader whose cause had failed. In the back of his mind lay the notion of vicarious sacrifice, the hope that his imprisonment and death might lighten the burden of reprisals against others.[9]

The junta, as organized by Colonel Casado, represented

[9] My view of Besteiro was greatly influenced by conversations with several of his close friends in Madrid and with one of the Basque priests who knew him—indeed almost worshipped him— during their imprisonment together at Carmona after the war.

practically all the non-Communist elements of the Popular Front in the Madrid zone. Casado held the Defense portfolio, and Besteiro served as Minister of State in anticipation of negotiations with Burgos. A Caballero Socialist, Wenceslao Carrillo, acted as Minister of the Interior. General Miaja, who had become a Communist during the defense of Madrid, and who as commander of the central-zone armies had favored resistance even up to the time of the Los Llanos conference, joined the conspiracy at the last moment. His prestige made him the natural choice for the presidency of the junta. The nonpolitical and highly respected professional generals Matallana and Menéndez supported the junta, as did Cipriano Mera, the principal anarchist officer at the Madrid front, and as did practically all the UGT and CNT leaders in the city.

The junta seized power on March 5, and Besteiro in a radio broadcast explained its purposes to the people of Madrid. He accused Negrín of attempting to maintain himself in office despite the resignation of Azaña and his extreme minority position within the government after the loss of Catalonia. He held Negrín guilty of deceiving the people with false hopes of renewed armament and of a world war which would merge the Spanish struggle into a victorious war against the fascist powers. He urged the people to obey the Casado junta and to show their valor by the manner in which they accepted defeat.

Negrín did not react immediately to the Madrid coup. The Communist military chiefs in Madrid and Ciudad Real, after a day or two of uncertainty as to their own attitude, rose against Casado, thus bringing about a civil war within the two cities. The troops of Cipriano Mera in the capital and of General Escobar in Ciudad Real quickly gave the upper hand to the Casado junta. The much more difficult problem was to convince the rank-and-file Communists of their ghastly error and to reestablish some degree of moral authority for the Consejo. On March 9 Edmundo Domínguez, a Negrín Socialist, went on the air to insist that Negrín had had absolutely no desire to sustain himself in office by force, that he had offered no resistance to Casado, and that he had "neither given the lie to nor disavowed (ni desmentido ni desautorizado) the Consejo Nacional de Defensa." The next

472

day General Matallana spoke over the radio to reason simply and calmly that no one had overthrown the Negrín government; it had fallen apart.[10]

The contradictions of Negrín's personal position, together with physical exhaustion, culminated in his surprising passivity. A year and a half of wartime leadership had revealed a degree of executive ability, and a taste for power, whose existence Negrín himself had perhaps barely suspected before 1937. He had found Azaña demoralized. As for Prieto, his admired political mentor was a brilliant analyst and organizer, a loyal and tireless collegue, but easily upset by bad news and increasingly dependent upon Negrín's equanimity and power of decision. From the beginning of his Prime Ministership he had worked equally well with the most important professional soldiers, such as Rojo and Matallana, and with the leading Communist officers produced by the war itself, such as Lister and Modesto. Amidst military and diplomatic disappointments he saw himself as the man upon whom even his strongest collaborators depended for courage in difficult moments. He had saved the Republic from collapse in April 1938, and without his spirit the miraculous resistance at the Ebro would have been inconceivable.

In viewing the general situation of the Republic, he was not burdened by the bad memories and the scruples of the earlier leaders. Besteiro wondered whether the Republic had not come too soon to succeed. Azaña could not help asking himself whether his own anticlericalism of 1931–33 had not in some measure made him responsible for the frenzy of 1936. The rivalry between Prieto and Largo Caballero had paralyzed the Socialist Party, and both men had scruples which reduced their effectiveness as war leaders. Prieto hated death sentences, and Largo Caballero would leave office rather than connive at the suppression of the non-Communist Left. The leading

[10] The radio speeches of Besteiro, Domínguez, and Matallana were printed in *El Socialista,* Madrid, March 7, 10, and 11, 1939, respectively. Further confirmation of Negrín's passivity may be found in the account of J. García Pradas, *Como terminó la guerra de España* (Buenos Aires, 1940), pp. 72–6. The author was the editor of CNT, Madrid, and a member of the Casado junta.

moderate Republicans, such as Giral, Martínez Barrio, Bernardo Giner, and Julio Just, were men of pacifist temperament, as were the Basque leaders Aguirre and Irujo, and the Catalans Companys and Tarradellas. They were all men whose energies were to a greater or lesser extent absorbed in asking themselves questions about their past errors and in trying to minimize suffering during the war. Negrín, too, was fundametally a civilian and a man of peace, but individual deaths did not weigh upon his mind, and he had virtually no political past over which to ruminate. He admired courage, tenacity, willpower. Scruples which he did not share were apt to appear to him as cowardice.

He considered that the significant forces in the Republican zone were the Communists and the anarchists, and that the significant Nationalist forces were the Falange and the Requetés. His opinion reflects the great weight he gave to those who *act,* and his relative unconcern for the moderate Republicans and the Socialists shows his detachment from the labors and the preoccupations of the great majority of the Spanish Left. He viewed himself outside the context of political parties, as the leader of civilian, democratic Spain, just as General Franco (also a man with very little political past) was the leader of military, reactionary Spain. He once confided to General Rojo that he felt more in common with some of the less sectarian Nationalists than with many of the Popular Front leaders.[11] He must have considered, right down to the first days of March 1939, that he could somehow arrive at an understanding with his opponents whereas they would, of course, show no respect to the old party politicians for whom he had little enough regard himself.

Until the fall of Catalonia, Negrín was absolutely certain of his mission. He knew that his army was well disciplined and ably led. He maintained the cooperation of the ablest officers regardless of their political affiliations. He had no illusions about the motives of the several European powers. On the other hand, his distaste for party politics probably kept him

[11] On the character of Negrín as wartime Prime Minister see particularly Vicente Rojo, *¡Alerta los pueblos!,* pp. 222–25, and Zugazagoitia, pp. 408–16, 480.

from realizing the extent to which civilian morale had crumbled, and the complete collapse in early February may have surprised him. In any case, after the Battle of Catalonia, he lost the certainty which had carried him through his 18-month ministry. His critics have taxed him with hypocrisy because in mid-February 1939 he would at one moment say that he was planning the evacuation of the central zone and at another moment say that the only thing to be done was to resist, resist, resist. He felt equally responsible for one-half million refugees on the beaches south of Perpignan and for upwards of 250,000 Republican soldiers in the central zone. His actions in the last few weeks of the war were not decisions, they were reflexes. In the face of the Nationalist refusal to negotiate, a reflex to fight on; in the face of the Casado coup, a reflex to yield, to avoid the worst evil of all, a civil war within the Civil War.

On March 5 he flew from Valencia to Dakar, and then to France, without taking any public position on the establishment of the Casado junta. By March 13 the Communist resistance had been defeated, at the cost of several hundred deaths in the fighting and the execution of two Communist officers in Madrid. The Casado government now hoped to negotiate an end of the war with the Nationalists. The Madrid press began to refer to the "forces under General Franco" rather than to "the fascist hordes." Besteiro spoke over the Madrid radio of arranging an "honorable peace." Serrano Suñer spoke over the Saragossa radio of a "victorious peace." On March 14 Burgos announced the establishment of a Court of Political Responsibilities which, under the presidency of Serrano Suñer, would judge the acts of those who had opposed the National Movement in the period since October 1, 1934.

Like Negrín before them, Casado and Besteiro hoped to achieve one essential point: a guarantee against political reprisals. They asked that in the case of trials full civil court procedure and the rights of the defense be accorded as in peacetime. They asked that the liberty of both professional soldiers and militiamen be respected unless they were guilty of *delitos comunes* (common crimes). The Nationalists answered as they had spoken to the demobilized soldiers in the French camps and as they had replied to the English diplomats who asked them their intentions toward the defeated enemy. They would be generous "with those who, having committed no crimes, had through deception been drawn into the struggle." "Neither mere service in the red forces nor having simply acted in political parties unconnected with the movimiento nacional would be considered motives of political responsibility."[12] But as to specific procedures and guarantees, the defeated would have to throw themselves on the mercy of the victors. At no time in the past had the Spanish Right ever been willing to guarantee Western standards of justice. It was chimerical to suppose that they would do so at the close of a civil war in which they had fought to preserve Spain from the evils of Western liberalism.

Nevertheless the comedy was played out. On March 23 two officers representing Casado flew to Burgos to negotiate. They were met with a demand for the surrender of the Republic aviation between 3 p.m. and 6 p.m. on March 25. The time seemed impossibly short, and the Madrid officers explained that their request for delay was motivated partly by uncertainty as to whether all the pilots would obey orders to bring their machines to Burgos. Their interlocutors seemed to understand this point and granted a new meeting for the 25th itself. The editing of peace terms was apparently going well, when at 6 p.m. sharp the Nationalist representatives received the order to break off negotiations since the air force had not been delivered as stipulated. The Republican officers were to return to Madrid forthwith.

On the morning of the 26th Madrid offered to deliver the planes the next day. Receiving no reply, they offered a few hours later to deliver the planes that afternoon. The Nationalists now replied that an advance was scheduled to start on all the fronts, that the troops should be sure to raise the white flag and send hostages to the Nationalist commanders. Julián Besteiro went on the air once more to urge the soldiers and

[12] The cited phrases are drawn from Nationalist statements printed by *El Socialista*, March 28, 1939, in its detailed account of the negotiation efforts. This newspaper, during February and March, is an indispensable source for understanding the end of the war.

the populace to go out to meet the Nationalists as brothers, in sign of reconciliation. Burgos had indicated that it would permit the junta officials to leave Spain, and in his office in the basement of the Ministry of the Interior Besteiro urged his younger colleagues particularly to take advantage of the opportunity. He himself had decided to remain in Madrid. The entry of the victors was delayed another 24 hours by the task of removing the mines which had been placed along the entire western edge of the city more than two years earlier. Even so, several persons were hurt walking out to meet the entering army on March 30.

During the period March 28–31, the Nationalists received the surrender of the Republican garrisons throughout the central and southern zones, almost without incident. The last motor boats and fishing vessels set sail from Valencia, and small groups of refugees, both military and civilian, continued to slip across the mountainous Aragonese border. At Alicante the Italian General Gambara was prepared to permit the evacuation of political refugees waiting in the Argentine consulate. On March 31 a French cruiser appeared offshore, but turned back in view of the mined waters and the uncertain reception. Later in the day the Foreign Legion arrived and took over jurisdiction from Gambara.[13] On April 1, 1939, the war had ended with the complete and unconditional victory of General Franco.

[13] Zugazagoitia, pp. 580–83.

THE SPANISH TRAGEDY

ONE of the recurring historic traits of the Spanish people has been the occasional sudden outpouring of energy in an idealistic cause. In the mid-thirteenth century, with the reconquest of Andalusia, the people of Spain made a tremendous effort to assimilate the political, cultural, and religious values of the Moslems and the Jews, thereby providing a virtually unique example of constructive coexistence among the three great religions: Judaism, Christianity, and Islam. After the discovery of America, the Spaniards, animated largely by a messianic ideal, depopulated the homeland in order to convert to Christianity the peoples of America and the Philippines, and poured their blood and treasure into the effort of Charles V to maintain the religious unity of Europe. In 1808, considering Napoleon the Anti-Christ, they resisted the French armies as did no other people in Europe.

The period which culminated in the Second Republic and the Civil War was also one of these great bursts of energy motivated by primarily idealistic causes. But this time the great aim was not the conquest or the assimilation of other cultures, nor an effort to impose imperial and religious unity as in the case of the Counter-Reformation. It was an effort to assimilate the Spanish past and to raise the cultural and economic level of the long-neglected homeland. For half a century before 1930, the middle class had been admiring the prosperity of Western Europe and the working class had been absorbing the concepts of socialism and anarchism. A generation of writers and philosophers had, from widely differing emotional and ideological standpoints, attempted to synthesize the best of the Spanish heritage with the best of European nineteenth-century culture. Modern industry had begun to develop in the northern provinces.

When the Republic arrived in 1931, taking many of its

leaders by surprise, Spaniards wanted to do everything at once; separate Church and state, create primary and secondary schools, reform the universities, cut numbers and increase efficiency in the civil service and in the Army, achieve legal equality for women, distribute the great estates to the peasants, improve the system of justice as it applied both to individuals and to political and labor organizations, build roads, dams, and electric power stations, grant autonomy to the major cultural minorities, the Catalans and the Basques. They wanted to give Spain quickly the political and religious liberties, and the high quality public educational system, which France had achieved in more than a century of experiment and conflict since 1789. They wanted Spain as a nation, and also the peoples of Spain separately considered, to enjoy that affirmation of cultural autonomy and uniqueness which was one of the generous ideals of the nineteenth century. They also wanted Spain to enjoy those benefits, real or imagined, which they saw emerging from the first dozen years of the Soviet revolution. There were enormous differences among the middle-class political groups, and within the Left parties, in the evaluation of what constituted the desirable heritage of the French and Russian revolutions, and of nineteenth-century liberalism and nationalism. But in 1931 all the political energy of Spain was devoted to realizing these several European ideals.

It is easy to say, as many commentators of both Right and Left sympathies have said, that the Republic tried to do too much, too fast. By simultaneous attacks on the entrenched privileges of the Army, the Church, and the landlords, the new regime roused the combined hostility of all the powerful conservative forces in the country. In attempting to electrify railroads, build dams, schools, and secondary roads all at once, it created deficits and invited technical errors and financial corruption. Through plans to dispose of the clerical budget and close the Church schools within two years, it worked hardship on the priests and diminished the available educational facilities. Such are the major criticisms from a pragmatic point of view.

Bitter critics from the Right have charged that the Republic sought to destroy the traditional fabric of society. For them the separation of Church and state, the army reform, the divorce law, and the laic school system were not forms of progress bursting old shackles. They were attacks on the concept Spain as they understood Spain, and the Europeanizing Republic for them represented the "Anti-Spain." Marxist critics, on the other hand, have waxed sarcastic at the timidity of the new regime. In their view the Republic limited itself to Platonic threats without really touching the power of the Church, the Army, and the landlords. Hence the impatience of the working class and the landless peasants, who by 1934 were rapidly detaching themselves from the Republic, while leftist critics joked about the Republican leaders as a generation of politicians with "a brilliant future in the past."

While recognizing a degree of truth in these several criticisms, I do not accept the conclusion that because of these errors the failure of the Republic, and the coming of the Civil War, were inevitable. Until the summer of 1934, all the conflicts arising out of Republican legislation were fully susceptible of parliamentary solution. In the case of the Church, for example, the Constituent Cortes clearly underestimated the strength of Catholic feeling in defense of the Orders and the schools. The elections of 1933 made clear this miscalculation, and the schools and convents continued to operate as in the past. In the case of the New-Deal-type public works program of Prieto, the debate was exactly like that which took place in all the Western countries in the 1930's concerning deficit financing and government sponsorship of industrial projects in capitalist countries. There was much hue and cry when Marcelino Domingo imported wheat and when he bought for the government otherwise unsaleable Asturian coal. The regime of General Franco has done both things on many occasions. The high officers of the Army felt persecuted when Azaña enacted the army reform laws. The succeeding government retained the main structural reforms while promoting the officers of greatest corps prestige, and there is no reason to suppose that in circumstances of peace the civilian government and the professional Army could not have arrived at a new understanding of the role of the Army in the Republic. Conflicts of overlapping authority between the central and regional governments were similarly amenable to negotiated solutions. Of the main problems facing the Republic, it seems to me that land reform was the only one truly incapable of moderate, legislative solution.

My conclusion concerning the chances of the Republic during its first three years are based upon my having followed, in a day-to-day manner, the legislative work of the Cortes and the administration of major laws and departments. Within the anticlerical and antimilitary majority there were always candid and dignified defenders of the best elements in the Church and the Army. Within the Center-Right majority elected in 1933 there were always defenders of the public school program, of the hydraulic works, and of the new social legislation. If the problem of land reform defied even the beginnings of a viable solution, this was not merely due to the timidity, the ideological fears, or the selfishness of the deputies. The enormous variety of geographical and social conditions, the technical ignorance of the peasants, the questions of payment for the land and investment in the better use of it, the primitive political consciousness and long-repressed hatreds of the peasantry, the sabotage by landlords and Civil Guards of any mild effort on their behalf—all these factors interfered, and interfere to this day, with the solution of the land question.

The crisis of the parliamentary Republic occurred in the summer and autumn of 1934. Under the Republican, as well as the Monarchical, Constitution, the Minister of the Interior received wide discretionary powers for the preservation of public order. Miguel Maura, Santiago Casares Quiroga, and Diego Martínez Barrio had all, as Interior ministers, been obliged to use armed police to repress anarchist risings; but they had been scrupulous to employ the minimum force compatible with the preservation of public order and were careful not to confuse problems of public order with political and social questions.

In the spring of 1934 the new Interior Minister, Rafael Salazar Alonso, took the position that strikes were not simply economic conflicts, and that the Republic must be defended by all available means against the oncoming "Marxist Revolution." In June the newly organized peasants of Extremadura and Andalusia threatened a general strike which, if they had gone through with it, might well have crippled the harvest. Some of their local leaders were semi-literate demagogues who produced leaflets exalting the burning of harvests and the murder of landlords. The responsible national leaders called off the strike. The Minister of the Interior nevertheless chose to punish sporadic local stoppages by the deportation of hundreds of landless workers to Castilian jails and by the arrest of several Socialist deputies in defiance of parliamentary immunity. In defending himself before the Cortes, he insisted that both the peasant unions and the Socialists were preparing the Revolution, and that parliamentary immunity did not include the right to make revolutionary propaganda. His action punished ideas and affiliations far more than deeds. The parliamentary Right applauded him, and Prime Minister Samper, while anxious to appease liberal opinion, did not disavow the abuse. The Socialists, both moderate and revolutionary, warned that they would not let themselves be gagged and muzzled as in Germany since January 1933, and Austria since February of 1934.

Regional issues came to a head in the summer of 1934 at the same time as did the political abuse of police power. The Companys government refused to accept the Tribunal of Guarantees decision annulling the Catalan *ley de cultivos,* and the Basque municipalities defied the government on questions of taxation and local elections. In each case Prime Minister Samper was negotiating compromise solutions which he hoped to present to the Cortes in the autumn. Meanwhile, the arms landings in the Asturias were discovered, and the CEDA announced in advance that it would withdraw its support of Samper on the grounds that his concessions to the Catalans and Basques were unacceptable.

A parliamentary crisis therefore occurred immediately at the October 1 Cortes meeting. The CEDA was the largest single minority in the chamber. It had supported the Center-Right coalition without entering the cabinet, but it now demanded its legal right to hold several portfolios. In normal parliamentary circumstances Gil Robles should long since have joined the government. But he was profoundly distrusted, not just by the Socialists and the liberal Republicans, but by the conservative Catholic President Alcalá-Zamora. Gil Robles had always insisted that he would respect established legality, but he had no word of criticism for Salazar Alonso's treatment of the peasants and the Socialist deputies. He had publicly distinguished his movement from fascism and nazism, but he was an admirer of Dollfuss and never disavowed the Austrian dictator's methods of crushing the opposition. When asked whether he was loyal to the Republic, he would explain that the form of government was "accidental." It was well known that his party depended on Monarchist financial backing.

In these circumstances the moderate party leaders Azaña, Martínez Barrio, Felipe Sánchez Román, and Miguel Maura all warned the President against permitting the CEDA to enter the government, and they all publicly broke with him when he announced that Lerroux would form a cabinet with three CEDA ministers. A divided Socialist Party voted for a general strike which, for the UGT mine leaders, would mean an armed rising in the Asturias. In Barcelona the Companys government tried a species of civilian pronunciamiento, declaring the Catalan state within the "federal" Spanish Republic, and inviting a democratic "government in exile" to establish itself in Barcelona. In the district centered on Oviedo the miners created a commune based upon the cooperation of Left Socialists, Communists, anarchists, and Trotskyites. The more primitive among them committed several dozen murders and a certain amount of looting. In Catalonia the revolt yielded quickly before the firmness and common sense of General Domingo Batet. In the Asturias the government, afraid to depend upon drafted troops, used the Moors and the Foreign Legion to "pacify" the province. Two weeks of fighting, followed by two months of ruthless repression, created an international scandal. Constant censorship prevented the Spanish public from knowing what had happened during the armed struggle and in the police stations and prisons afterwards.

Several hundred municipal governments were suspended, and government appointees exercised their functions throughout the year 1935.

Taken as a sequence, the peasants' strike, the October risings, the long-continued suspension of local elected governments, and the heavy Asturian repression came close to destroying the Republic. A democratic government could not operate if the Minister of the Interior felt free to arrest political opponents at will. It could not operate if the leader of the largest single party in the Cortes refused to declare his loyalty to the Republic. It could not operate if a portion of the Socialist Party prepared and participated in an armed rising against the constitutionally chosen cabinet. It could not operate if the regional government revolted against Madrid. It could not operate if the armed forces and the police were a law unto themselves in restoring order. It could not operate if month after month newspaper censorship was to be extended and hundreds of elected municipal councils were to remain suspended because their members belonged to the same political party as some of the revolutionary leaders. These were not, like the earlier-mentioned controversies, problems which, given experience, compromise, and increasing political maturity, could be solved within a democratic Republic. They were abuses which attacked the basis of the regime.

In the twenty months from October 1934 to July 1936 the terrible lessons of the Asturian revolution might have been learned. But in fact the October revolt seemed to both the Right and the Left to have been *mal liquidado*. The former held that the death sentences should have been executed, and that the investigations of torture constituted an intolerable attack on the armed forces which had saved Spain from communism. The latter refused to recognize the responsibility of those who had risen, arms in hand, against the constitutional government. They pictured the miners (and the Catalan government) as the completely innocent victims of "fascist provocation." The arbitrary suspension of hundreds of municipal councils and the frenzied effort to smear Azaña then created a defensive alliance between the moderate Republicans and the entire Left. Spanish political opinion in 1935 was dominated by two completely negative emotions: fear of fascism and fear of communism. In the presence of continued censorship and parliamentary sterility, direct action groups of both the Right and the Left prepared for a coming test of strength.

At the same time, it is important to emphasize that there was nothing inevitable or irreversible about the degradation of the situation. A historian must deal strictly with what happened rather than with what might have happened. But if he does not mention the factors which could have produced a different course of events, he runs the risk of giving a false impression of "predestination." Within the Center-Right coalition there were men like Manuel Giménez Fernández, ready to work for effective land reform, men like Filiberto Villalobos, determined to continue the construction of public schools, men like Joaquín Chapaprieta, ready to cut administrative waste and redistribute taxes more equitably. The Radical ministers of public works were not nearly as able as Indalecio Prieto, but they intended to continue hydraulic development. A large fraction of the governing coalition backed Portela Valladares when he successfully resisted Gil Robles' efforts to have the Civil Guard placed under the authority of the Minister of War. If the wounds of the Asturian revolt had been healed, these constructive elements of the moderate Right would have carried greater weight. In the fall of 1935 some of these leaders were urging the reestablishment of the suspended municipalities and the Catalan Generalitat, and the amnesty of the thousands of political prisoners, *before* the coming electoral campaign. An amnesty alone, at the end of 1935, would have altered the entire nature of that campaign, and it is therefore perfectly reasonable to say that the entire course of events culminating in the Civil War might well have been avoided. This possibility has been obscured by polemical writings. Most Left interpreters have indiscriminately identified the Cortes majority of 1933–35 with reaction and fascism. The Franquist interpreters have been pleased for their own reasons to claim that the Nationalist cause in the war was the cause of the moderate Right.

The Left victory in the February 1936 elections brought

Manuel Azaña to power once more. In terms of the Popular Front program and the new Cortes majority, the government would now resume the construction of a reformist, laic Republic whose foundations had been laid during the 1931–33 period. Several circumstances, however, made it absolutely impossible for Azaña to govern as he, and the majority of the people who voted for him, had hoped. The stability of his earlier governments had depended upon the cooperation of the Socialists. The latter were always internally divided as to the wisdom of sharing power with the bourgeois liberals. During the period of the Constituent Cortes they had steadily supported Azaña. But disappointments as to land reform, bitterness over the Asturian repression, the progress of revolutionary theory among the younger membership, and the conversion of Largo Caballero to the revolutionary position, altered radically the posture of the Socialists. They now intended to spur the reformist government from the left rather than share responsibility with it in the enactment of a gradual program.

The radicalization of the Socialist Party reflected the revolutionary intoxication developing among the masses. This intoxication did not answer to any specific program or party, nor was it controlled by either the UGT or the CNT. It was positively embarrassing to the Communists. I have known several Caballerist intellectuals in exile, all of them admirers of Hugh Gaitskell and Paul Henri Spaak. I have known Caballerist workers in Spain, whose main concern was, and is, with complete freedom of union activity, be it under a monarchy or a republic. (They were the "accidentalists" of the Left just as the CEDA majority were the accidentalists of the Right.)

Largo Caballero was a bricklayer, a trade-union bureaucrat, and a recently converted Marxist. But the "Caballerist" phenomenon can be understood only in terms of the peasant question. It had the same roots as the Zapatista movement in Mexico and the Castrist revolution in Cuba. For decades, anarchist missionaries had been preaching the dignity of labor and the absolute equality of man to peasants whom the landlords treated as domestic animals. The first two years of the

Republic had brought substantial political and economic benefits to the peasants, and a vast increase in both anarchist and Marxist propaganda. From the beginning of the Lerroux period, a species of "cold war" in the countryside had reduced wages to pre-Republican levels. Then the peasants' strike and the Asturian revolt had given the government the opportunity to repress the Casas del Pueblo in the villages. Disappointed hopes, and starvation wages, produced a revolutionary mood in the rural masses, and many a young Marxist intellectual, who would have been a Social Democrat in northern Europe, became a revolutionary in anger at the fate of the peasants.

The Caballerist current ran strongest from the summer of 1934 until the end of 1936. Emotionally it was motivated by an overwhelming desire to achieve full comradeship between the liberal middle class and intellectuals on the one hand, and the industrial and agricultural proletariat on the other. It assumed without question that the proletariat was the class which would guide human destinies in a future free of exploitation. The Caballerists had no dogmatic program, nor were they hero-worshippers. Largo Caballero was not looked upon as a *Duce* or a *Führer*. He had no motorcycle escorts and no songs dedicated to him. He symbolized the best that the Spanish working class had produced in the way of self-education and absolute dedication to the economic and spiritual liberation of the masses.

Largo was not alone, of course, in the leadership of the Socialist Party. Julián Besteiro was every bit his equal in dedication, honesty, and absence of all worldly ambition. However, in the international context, Besteiro was the precise equivalent of the generous but ineffectual Italian, German, and Austrian professors who had constituted no obstacle whatever to the triumph of fascism in their countries. Indalecio Prieto was a more earthy, practical politician than Besteiro, but again, in the world context, he looked like a Ramsay Mac-Donald who was more admired outside his party than within, and who would be capable of presiding (as MacDonald had done in the England of 1931) over a government of "national union" which would in reality simply turn the country over to the reactionaries. In Spain Largo was the only Socialist chief who could be counted on not to "sell out" to the *bourgeoisie,* and he was the only leader of any party who could find willing collaborators in all sectors from the liberal Republican camp to the Communists and anarchists.

The Caballerist movement also included certain temporary illusions. *Claridad* writers had visited a few chosen collective farms in the Soviet Union and had assumed that what they saw in these Potemkin villages was the truth, or would very soon be the truth, concerning rural life all over Russia. Stalin published in 1935 a constitution which not only guaranteed the main "bourgeois" liberties won in the French revolution, but included the right to work and promised the construction of a completely classless society. The listed guarantees and liberties had not, of course, all been translated into practice. But Spaniards were accustomed to constitutions which formulated a future framework rather than a present reality. Their own constitution was of that type. Being completely honest in their own intentions, they assumed as much for Joseph Stalin. The blood purges, which were to make a complete mockery of Soviet liberty, did not start until August 1936—after the beginning of the Civil War in Spain.

In thinking that Spain was ready for proletarian government, the UGT leaders and workers also made optimistic assumptions about the automatic benefits of socialization. Prieto knew from his experience with the nationalized railroads that government control and higher wages do not for a moment guarantee efficient operation and do not in themselves lead the workers to take a more sympathetic view of management problems. Most of the UGT were not ready to recognize this fact. For decades the moral optimism of the class-conscious workers, and their sense of the injustice of the capitalist system, had nourished itself on the idea that the proletariat were the ones who "really" did the productive work, and that they should therefore govern. They greatly underestimated the complexity of the organizational and administrative functions performed by those whom they could see only as exploiters.

The practical effect of these several hopes and illusions was that instead of supporting the Azaña government in the early spring of 1936, the Socialist majority anticipated the

frustration of the bourgeois liberals and confidently expected
to achieve power for the proletariat in the foreseeable future.
At the same time the antidemocratic Right frankly prepared
to overthrow the Republic. The Falange expanded rapidly.
The prestige of Calvo Sotelo rose while that of Gil Robles fell.
Activist officers plotted a pronunciamiento and the Carlists
prepared for an armed crusade. Lerroux's Radical Party had
been destroyed by his steady appeasement of the Monarchists
and the Church, and finally by the straperlo scandal. By June
1936 the men of the liberal Republic—Azaña, Casares
Quiroga, Martínez Barrio, Felipe Sánchez Román, Miguel
Maura—were completely isolated between the military, Monarchist, fascist Right and the revolutionary, Marxist, anarchist
Left. After the Asturian revolt, statesmanship could still have
saved the Republic. In mid-1936 the parliamentary democratic
forces could no longer control the situation.

Considering the entire five-year peacetime history of the
Republic, I think there were several important factors hobbling
the regime from the very beginning. One of the most important was that the new government could never count on the
loyal aid of the established corps of civil servants. In twentieth-
century Spain, public-service careers were open to talent. Men
of modest background (Pedro Segura in the Church, Francisco
Franco in the Army, Niceto Alcalá-Zamora in law and civil
service) distinguished themselves through merit. But the
highest appointments remained the gift of the King. Of the
men occupying high state offices in 1931, many were genuinely
grateful to Alfonso XIII. Most of them, regardless of their
feelings toward the King, prized the aristocratic connections
which their professional success had procured for them. They
immediately stigmatized as "ungrateful" the minority of judges,
bishops, and generals who publicly favored the new regime,
and like the German civil servants under the Weimar Republic,
they displayed their disdain for a "Republic of workers of all
categories."

There was also, from the first days, a problem of political
discipline graphically symbolized by the much-used adjective
desbordado. One after another, responsible leaders found themselves either swamped, or forced to extreme positions, by their

more radical followers, or by groups which threatened to detach their followers. Alcalá-Zamora was *desbordado* by a mass of anticlerical deputies who found an able leader in Manuel Azaña. The moderate Socialist Prieto was *desbordado* by the Largo Caballero who took the leadership of the revolutionary Socialists, and Caballero in turn was threatened by the extremism of CNT positions to his left. Lerroux was *desbordado* by the militant stands in favor of the Church, the Army, and the financial-social aristocracy taken by Gil Robles. Gil Robles was *desbordado* by the Nazi phraseology of some of his followers, and eventually by the reactionary Monarchism of Calvo Sotelo.

A closely related weakness is succinctly stated by the phrase *gastado por el poder* (worn out by the exercise of power). The deputies were ebullient, rhetorical, inexperienced, and desirous of enjoying the fruits of public office. As with the deputies of the Third and Fourth Republics in France, the overthrow of the existing ministry was a favorite indoor sport. The Prime Minister and his leading collaborators constantly had to exercise their persuasive talents to hold their parliamentary majority in line. A wide variety of motives, from the most highly principled to the most capricious or sordid, could influence the deputies' votes. It was indeed true that after each round in office the leading ministers were *gastado por el poder*.

Many analysts have concluded from these phenomena that Spaniards are incapable of political democracy. But it must be remembered that the Republic followed upon a seven-year dictatorship, and that the preceding Constitutional Monarchy had regularly falsified the election returns and the operation of the Cortes. Democracy can only be learned through experience, and free political agitation always includes a good deal of "pie in the sky." Also, if one were to judge solely on the basis of the Cromwellian Commonwealth or of the Continental Congress, one would be likely to conclude that neither the English nor the American people were capable of self-government.

The Republic also suffered from what Nationalist historians have called a constant state of disorder, but which I think should be more accurately labeled a state of intranquillity. Ever since the Napoleonic era, and especially after the start of the Carlist wars, middle-class opinion in Spain has been preoccupied with the question of *orden público*. The surest way to discredit a government was to demonstrate that it could not control the Masons, or the Carlists, or the students, or the anarchists, as the case might be. The *Guardia Civil*, founded in 1844, quickly became known as *La Benemérita* because it freed the rural highways and the mountain passes of the semi-Robin Hood, semi-gangster bands whose membership was also the human material of the Carlist guerrillas and the anarchist jacqueries.

The Republic knew that it must maintain public order if it were to win the lasting consent of the middle classes. The anarchists, opposed on principle to political participation, felt that the threat of disorder was their best weapon for obtaining concessions from the *bourgeoisie*. The monarchists, often on friendly personal terms with anarchists in the rural areas, found it easy to subsidize and provoke anarchist activities as a means of discrediting the new regime. Until late in the spring of 1936, anarchist disorders were local and sporadic, and they were easily put down. But their repeated occurrence, and the wide publicity given them in conditions of complete political liberty, engendered a state of intranquillity which went far to undermine both the stability, and the nerves, of the Republican cabinets.

In proportion as public order appeared to be threatened, the danger of military intervention increased. In all the Hispanic countries the armed forces tend to see themselves, rather than the civilian governments, as the ultimate guardians of legality. Generally speaking, these countries have small, politically timid and inexperienced middle classes, militant and desperately poor working classes, and traditions of intellectual liberty which result in a large measure of freely conducted political agitation without there being adequate constitutional expression for that agitation. When any given regime, be it conservative or liberal, honest or corrupt, threatens to be *desbordado* by rising social agitation, the Army takes upon itself the duty of restoring public order.

The Spanish Republic began the work of endowing Spain with institutions that would respond to the democratic expression of public opinion. The government and the Army looked distrustfully at one another from the first moment, the former knowing the tendency of military men to consider themselves the arbiters of national policy, the latter knowing that one of the main aims of the Republic would be to reduce the political power of the Army. In August 1932 General Sanjurjo pictured himself as the defender of the Nation against an "illegitimate" Cortes and exaggerated concessions to regional liberty. In October 1934, the Army found it natural and correct that the government should bring African troops to put down the Asturian commune, and they were flattered in the course of 1935 to be consulted by politicians as to the advisability of a military coup in case of new revolutionary agitation. At the moment of the Popular Front victory in February 1936, Army elements offered their services to Portela Valladares to annul the elections, and in the course of the spring they repeatedly warned Azaña concerning "insults" to the Army and the developing state of disorder.

Meanwhile, they prepared a *putsch* which was to enjoy the backing of the governments of Italy, Portugal, and Germany, and the aid of powerful private interests in England. They intended a pronunciamiento which would oust the weak Republican government in the name of law and order and thereby check the possibility of either parliamentary or revolutionary rule by the militant Left. The resistance of the people in the large cities, and the manifest absence of popular support everywhere, except in Navarre and parts of Old Castile, rapidly converted an unsuccessful pronunciamiento into a civil war.

In the Popular Front zone the defeat of the pronunciamiento animated the revolutionary fervor of the masses, who immediately inaugurated a wide variety of local collectivist experiments of semi-anarchist, semi-Marxist inspiration, and who conducted a fierce purge of priests, police and military forces, and civilian personalities judged to be the accomplices of the Insurgents. In the Insurgent zone, Carlist and Falangist fanatics competed in the physical purge of both the moderate and the far Left in northern Spain, while the Army of Africa scourged Andalusia in the manner characteristic of colonial armies of all ages. The particular savagery of the war during the first year is explained only in part, however, by the colonial psychology of the professional officers and the ideological fanaticism of both Right and Left militiamen. The Spanish people were largely ignorant of the destructiveness of modern arms. The Carlist wars of the nineteenth century had been fought by small, rifle and musket armed detachments. Spain had seen nothing like the carnage of the Crimean War, the Austro-French battles in northern Italy in 1859 (those which had inspired Henri Dunant to found the International Red Cross), and the American Civil War. Spain had not lived through the Prussian siege of Paris and the Commune of 1871, nor through the First World War.

The Civil War came as the climactic release of the political passions of a century. Carlists and liberals had been struggling to control the nation ever since the era of the French Revolution. All the earlier engagements had been indecisive, and both parties recognized immediately the high stakes in the summer of 1936. On the Left, Marxism and anarchism had contributed equally to a feeling of "manifest destiny" among the proletariat. Among the military, the humiliations of the Spanish-American War and the frustrations of the Moroccan War had created a caste of officers eager to establish colonial rule over the population of the homeland. On the Right, generally, fascism and nazism appeared as forms of "manifest destiny" capable of checking the rise of the proletariat. Attitudes toward the entire heritage of the French and Russian revolutions reinforced the emotional commitments on both sides.

Perhaps at no time in the history of any nation (including revolutionary France of 1789–99 and revolutionary Russia of 1917–28) has so large a proportion of the people acted out of intimate, conscious political conviction as did the Spanish people during the years 1931–39. The rituals of the bull fight, and the heritage of the Inquisition, were also dramatic ingredients of the cruelty displayed in the war. But the conjuncture of political and ideological passions is certainly

493

the main explanation. Those who expound the supposed natural cruelty of the Spaniards tend to forget the tarring and feathering of loyalists in the American Revolution, the campaigns in the Vendée during the French Revolution, the nature of World War II in Eastern Europe, the fanatical slaughters occurring in the past few years in Algeria, Angola, and the Congo. Wherever men look upon their enemies as not belonging to the same privileged portion of the human species as themselves, the same savagery occurs.

By the spring of 1937 the worst passions had sated themselves. In the Republican zone the Caballero government worked steadily to restore the authority of the state and permitted as wide a degree of political liberty as have most mature democratic regimes in time of war. In the Nationalist zone the conservative, personal dictatorship of General Franco steadily imposed its authority on the Carlists and the Falange. The regime remained as cruel and repressive as in the early days, but its power was exercised through more "normal" channels. In the eyes of most Spaniards, the issue lay between a democratic, Left Spain and a military, reactionary Spain. Foreign forces were heavily involved from the start. Only the aid of several powers had enabled the Insurgents to recover from the failure of the pronunciamiento, and the timely arrival of Russian arms had saved the Republic in November. But in psychological terms, at least, the majority of Spaniards felt until the spring of 1937 that their fate was being resolved primarily by Spanish forces.

The longer the war lasted, however, the more evidently decisive became the foreign interventions. The Condor Legion and the Italians were decisive in the northern war from April to October 1937. Stalin determined the fall of Largo Caballero and the suppression of the POUM. The Russian advisers chose Brunete as the site of the first Republican offensive. The reopening of the French border in March 1938 made possible the continued military resistance of the Republic. Increasing British favor toward the Nationalists, appeasement of Italy and Germany, and finally the Munich Pact, settled the fate of the Republic. After mid-1937 the war was an extended agony. In neither zone did governmental policy respond to the political forces as they had existed in 1936. The military capacity of both sides depended almost entirely on the actions of the major European powers.

The international situation throughout the 1930's had developed in a manner unfavorable to the Spanish Republic. The peacetime years coincided with the worst phase of the world economic depression. The Republic had undertaken New-Deal-type public works expenditures at a time when the United States, England, and Germany all had conservative governments for whom balanced budgets and private enterprise were the sole economic virtues. Every major nation was attempting to solve the depression through autarchy rather than expanded trade, and the Bank of France was the only foreign institution willing to help the new regime protect the peseta.

The electoral victory of the Right in 1933 responded to the movement of public opinion within Spain. But it also coincided with the consolidation of fascist regimes in Germany and Austria. For two and one-half years preceding the outbreak of the Civil War, the Right was confident that fascism represented the "wave of the future," and the Left was determined not to be defeated in the manner of the German and Austrian Left. The peasants' strike and the Asturian revolt would in all likelihood not have occurred, and surely would not have had such disastrous consequences, if Germany and Austria had still enjoyed political liberty in 1934.

During the war, public opinion in all the Western countries was, for the most part, favorable to the Republic; but except in terms of medical aid and the supply of International Brigade volunteers, this opinion was of no practical use to the Republic. For the United States, neutrality and isolation outweighed the President's acknowledged personal sympathy for the Republic. England's government favored the Nationalists, and France felt it was impossible to challenge both the fascist powers and England by aiding the Republic. During the Second World War, the United States army applied to those who had fought in the International Brigades the expressive phrase "premature anti-fascists."

The war itself constituted the bitterest of political educations for the Spanish people. They learned what military rule will do to the fabric of civilian life, and they suffered the shallow boastfulness of the fascist mentality. They were the first European people to experience mass aerial bombings, and the only Western European people to suffer directly the cynical Communist exploitation of the Popular Front ideal. They learned the dangers of infantile leftism, in both the political and economic aspects of the collectivized economy. They learned that a civil war places a small nation at the mercy of the great powers.

In terms of the development of Spain itself, the most important result of the Civil War was the total defeat of the liberals and the Left. The Church and the Army held greater power than under any conservative royal government or military dictatorship of the entire nineteenth century. The landlords regained their property and authority, and the gap between their standard of living and that of the peasants remained as great as before 1931. The Institución Libre and its several affiliates were suppressed. Censorship of the press, of books, of the theater and films became far more severe than under Primo de Rivera. (Such censorship had existed under the Monarchy only at moments of particular social tension.) In sober truth it may be said that General Franco built the most powerful and repressive regime to exist in Spain since the reign of Philip II.

The Civil War was also followed by a massive political repression. General Franco did not follow the example of a Lincoln who ended the American Civil War "with malice towards none" and of a General Grant who told Lee that the demobilized confederate soldiers were welcome to take home their mules and begin the spring plowing. Tens of thousands of Republican veterans were to be shot, with or without benefit of some form of court-martial. Other tens of thousands were to perform years of hard labor, repairing roads and railroads, being hired out at peon wages to private contractors, or building the gigantic mausoleum of the Caudillo, *El Valle de los Caídos* (The Valley of the Fallen).

However, despite the total victory and the massive repression, nothing was settled by the Civil War. Neither

496

General Franco nor the powerful classes supporting him had anything to offer in the way of a social program which could resolve the country's historic problems. The crowning tragedy of the war was the utter lack of imagination or magnanimity on the part of the victor. The mass of the people, exhausted by eight years of instability and struggle, would gladly have cooperated in a program of national recovery. But such a program could only have been accomplished with the aid of the democratic powers, and at the expense of the ruling classes which had supported the Nationalist cause. It would have required democratic rather than Axis sympathies during the war, and a return to political and intellectual liberty after it, such as occurred in Italy. It would have required the building of thousands of schools, a meaningful redistribution of wealth, a drastic reduction of the power wielded by the landed and financial aristocracy. The temperament of the dictator, and the nature of the forces on which his regime depends, combined to keep such changes to a bare minimum. Increased industrialization, the example of European postwar prosperity, and the influence of American money and methods aided the gradual economic recovery of Spain through the 1950's. But ideologically and politically the regime retains to this day its original character as a reactionary military dictatorship.

Regarding the years 1931–36, historical interpretation up to now has been rather harsh on the Republic. In effect, Franquist and liberal-left historians have partially coincided in their criticisms. The former explain that the Republican leaders were *tímidos* and *resentidos,* if not homosexuals. The latter treat ironically those scrupulous intellectuals who their critics think should have acted like the Jacobins of 1793, but who tried instead to distribute land and build schools without shooting their opponents. The first interpretation is dominated by fascist myths about virility, and the second by exaggerated analogies with the French Revolution.

The efforts of the Spanish Republic should be placed in a wider context. In the last half-century, the privileged Western world has become conscious of the many "underdeveloped" nations, first in Eastern Europe and the Balkans, then in the Middle East, Asia, Africa, and Latin America. Between the late nineteenth century and the present day, there have been a multitude of political movements attempting to bring some measure of liberty and prosperity to those many countries. The Spanish Republic bears comparison with the best of those movements: the Republic of Czechoslovakia (also destroyed by fascism), the Mexican Revolution, and the Republic of India. No progressive foreign government has initiated more beneficial projects than did the Spanish government in the years 1931–34. No Spanish government has done as much for the people since the time of Charles III in the eighteenth century.

The Civil War, too, had a positive meaning which with time will transcend the suffering and destruction which were its immediate consequences. It is a terrible, and repeated, human dilemma that at times men have no choice between submission to tyranny and a war which will in all likelihood destroy many of the institutions they set out to defend. In July 1936 the Spanish people faced the alternatives of submission or resistance. They chose to resist, and like Spaniards over the past two thousand years, they fought magnificently. But the Spanish Republican army was not fighting to expel Moors, or to subjugate unwilling Dutchmen or Indians. The minority of Spaniards who continued the traditions of imperialism and intolerance were in the ranks of the Nationalist Army. The majority fought to preserve Spain, and Europe, from tyranny. They were conquered, but they were not humiliated in their souls. The moral grandeur of a generous Republic and a titanic struggle for liberty will serve their spirit well in the future.

APPENDICES
BIBLIOGRAPHY AND INDEX

CHRONOLOGY

1875–1923	Constitutional Monarchy
1898	Spanish-American War, end of the empire
1909 25–30 July	Semana Trágica in Barcelona
1917 13–17 August	Revolutionary strikes led by Besteiro and Caballero
1921 20 July	Anual disaster, suicide of General Silvestre
1921–22	Anarchist terrorism and governmental repression in Barcelona, Saragossa
1923 13 September	Primo de Rivera pronunciamiento
1930 28 January	Primo de Rivera dismissed
17 August	San Sebastián meeting of republican leaders
10 October	Socialist Party joins revolutionary committee
12 December	Abortive Jaca rising (Galán and García Hernández)
1931 14 February	Berenguer government resigns
18 February	Aznar interim government formed

1931

14 March	Ledesma Ramos founds National Syndicalist Weekly, *La conquista del estado*
12 April	Municipal elections, republican victory
14 April	Republic proclaimed and King leaves
28 April	First Términos Municipales decree
7 May	Segura pastoral letter
10–11 May	Quema de conventos
30 May	Ambassador Zulueta refused at Vatican
31 May	*ABC* and *Debate* suspended
May–June	Decrees on laic education, rural rents, and compulsory cultivation
3 June	Convocation of Constituent Cortes
12–15 June	Incognito return and expulsion of Segura
13 June	Foundation of *Libertad* in Valladolid (Onésimo Redondo)
16 June	First series of Azaña Army reform decrees
28 June	Elections for Constituent Cortes
4 July	Telephone strike (CNT)
14 July	Opening of the Cortes; closing of *Academia General* (Saragossa)
20–27 July	General strike and martial law, Seville
18 August	*Dictamen proyecto* of Constitution to Cortes
9–14 October	Article 26 debate; resignations of Alcalá-Zamora and Miguel Maura; Azaña Prime Minister
20 October	Law for Defense of the Republic
14 November	First issue of *Mundo Obrero* (CP organ)
19 November	Ex-King Alfonso condemned in absentia by Cortes
9 December	Promulgation of Constitution
December	First issue of *Acción Española;* JONS founded

1932

1 January	Castilblanco murder of Civil Guards
5 January	Arnedo (Logroño) workers clash with Civil Guards
7 January–30 November	*Mundo Obrero* suspended
20–27 January	Llobregat rising; CNT general strikes

January	Dissolution of the Jesuits; divorce law enacted; cemeteries secularized
April	Isidro Gomá y Tomás named Cardinal-Archbishop of Toledo
April-May	Wheat imports by Marcelino Domingo
28 July	Ley de Orden Público
10 August	Sanjurjo rising; *Acción Española* suspended
September	Catalan Statute and Agrarian Reform laws

1933

January	Anarchist riots in Cataloniaj Casas Viejas
1 March	Founding of *Renovación Española*
April	Municipal elections go against Azaña government
May	Law of Congregations
July	Repeal of Law for Defense of the Republic; pastoral condemning Law of Congregations
Summer	Misiones Pedagógicas begun
August	Burning of fields in Extremadura
4–5 September	Tribunal of Guarantees elections defeat government
9 October	Martínez Barrio cabinet; dissolution of Constituent Cortes
29 October	Falange founded in Madrid by José Antonio Primo de Rivera
5 November	Basque statute plebiscite
19 November	Right electoral victory; Lerroux Prime Minister
8–11 December	Anarchist risings in Catalonia and Aragon

1934

| February | Falange—JONS fusion; formation of Alianza Obrera; Martínez Velasco Agrarians declare selves republican; Austrian Parliament closed and Socialist Party suppressed. |
| 3 March | Salazar Alonso replaces Martínez Barrio in Gobernación; 4-week general strike (Durruti), Zaragoza |

1934

31 March	Quirinal agreement; Mussolini and Monarchists
April	Ifni occupied; fusion of Domingo and Azaña parties; Ley de haberes del clero
11 April	Rabassaire law passed by Generalitat
22 April	Escorial mass meeting, Gil Robles
25 April	Lerroux cabinet resigns; Sanjurjo amnesty crisis; Samper Prime Minister
3 May	Acción Española reopens (closed since 10 August, 1932)
16 May	Martínez Barrio-Lerroux split
9 June	Tribunal of Guarantees voids Rabassaire law
5–11 June	Strike of campesinos, Andalusia and Extremadura; Socialist deputies arrested
19 July	Military forbidden to join parties or syndicates
9 September	Covadonga rally, Gil Robles
13 September	*Turquesa* arms landing and discovery
1 October	Samper resigns; Lerroux cabinet with 3 CEDA ministers
6 October	Rising in Catalonia and Asturias; *estado de guerra;* African troops and Foreign Legion to Asturias

---

1935

1 February	Oviedo executions of Vásquez and Argüelles
1 March	Giménez Fernández agrarian law
13 March	Marcelino Domingo speech calling for Left unity
21 March	*Responsabilidades* debate over Azaña; founding of *Política,* organ of Izquierda Republicana
30 March	Crisis over *indulto* of Asturian Socialists; Lerroux government with 5 CEDA ministers
12 April	Unity announcement of Azaña, Martínez Barrio, and Sánchez-Román parties
7 May	Gil Robles War Minister; Portela in Gobernación

23 June	Tribunal of Guarantees condemns October 6 Catalan government
1 July	Dissolution of Patronato of Jesuit property
13 July	First issue of *Claridad* (Caballero Left Socialists)
20 July	Failure of second Cortes effort to condemn Azaña
20 October	Azaña mass meeting, Campo de Comillas
29 October	Lerroux forced to resign over straperlo; Chapaprieta government
late November	Denuncia Nombela
14 December	Portela forms cabinet
20 December	SP votes coalition with Republican Left; Caballero resigns from executive committee

1936	
2 January	Reappearance of *Mundo Obrero;* press censorship ended
7 January	Dissolution of Cortes
15 January	Popular Front electoral pact and platform
16 February	Popular Front electoral victory
19 February	Azaña cabinet, amnesty of Asturian prisoners
23 February	Suspension of rent payments in Andalusia
26 February	Companys-Generalitat government reestablished
11 March	Azaña warns Largo Caballero, gets pledge of no more victory demonstrations
13 March	Attempted assassination of Jiménez de Asúa
15 March	Falange outlawed; José Antonio arrested; Army ultimatum to Azaña on disorders; Martínez Barrio speaker of new Cortes; Internationale sung at opening
16 March	Decree confiscating returned estates in Andalusia
22 March	Oviedo assassination of Rightist deputy Martínez

505

1936

1 April	Fusion of Juventudes Socialista y Comunista
3 April	Postponement of municipal elections at request of Right
7 April	Cortes deposes Alcalá-Zamora
9 May	Assassination of Captain Faraudo
10 May	Azaña President of Republic
12 May	Casares Quiroga Prime Minister after Prieto refusal
June	Building trades and elevator strike, Madrid
10–15 June	Syndicalist struggles in Málaga, Tangier, Cádiz
16 June	Calvo Sotelo-Gil Robles speeches on disorder in Cortes
12 July	Assassination of Lt. Castillo
13 July	Assassination of Calvo Sotelo
17–20 July	Pronunciamiento in Morocco and Peninsula
20 July	Giral cabinet formed; government appeal to France; Franco emissaries to Italy and Germany
27 July	Seville under insurgent control; reinforcement by air from Morocco
28–30 July	Italian and German planes arrive Morocco and Seville; obsolete French planes dispatched to Madrid
6 August	Múgica-Olaechea pastoral on Vitoria radio
8 August	French border closed; unilateral start of Non-Intervention
14 August	Insurgents take Badajoz
24 August	Italy, Germany, Portugal accept Non-Intervention "in principle"
End August	Antonov-Ovseenko in Barcelona, Rosenberg in Madrid
3 September	Insurgents take Talavera
4 September	Largo Caballero cabinet of republicans, Socialists, Communists
5 September	Insurgents take Irún; city burned by anarchists

7 September	Basque government formed under Aguirre
9 September	Non-Intervention Committee first meeting, London
12 September	Insurgents take San Sebastián
27 September	Generalitat government with Esquerra, PSUC, POUM, anarchist participation
28 September	Insurgents take Toledo; Non-Intervention Committee refuses to hear charges against Portugal
1 October	Cortes passes Basque Statute; Franco named Generalissimo
6 October	Soviets state they will not be more bound by Non-Intervention than Portugal-Italy-Germany
17 October	Insurgents take Illescas
24 October	First Russian tanks in action, Russian officers arriving in Madrid; German-Italian bombers over capital
2 November	Insurgents in Manzanares valley; Russian fighter planes over Madrid
4 November	Anarchists join Caballero government
6 November	Government moves to Valencia; Miaja chairman of Madrid Defense Junta
8 November	All-out assault on Madrid; arrival of International Brigades
18 November	Madrid assault suspended; Germany and Italy recognize Burgos
20 November	José Antonio executed in Alicante
December	Condor Legion assembled in Seville
18 December	First Italian infantry units leave Naples
23 December	Consejo de Aragón recognized

1937	
10 February	Nationalists take Málaga
6–15 February	Battle of the Jarama
21 February	Asensio resigns; Rosenberg recall requested
8–18 March	Battle of Guadalajara
6–22 April	English accept blockade of Bilbao
19 April	Merger of Falange and Carlists under Franco; Non-Intervention land and sea patrol inaugurated

1937

23 April	Dissolution of Madrid junta de defensa
26 April	Bombing of Guernica
3–8 May	Barcelona civil war
17 May	Negrín cabinet named
31 May	*Deutschland* shells Almería
3 June	Death of General Mola in airplane accident
16 June	POUM leaders arrested
19 June	Fall of Bilbao
23 June	Germany and Italy withdraw from naval patrol
30 June	Portugal ends Non-Intervention frontier patrol
1 July	Collective letter of Spanish Bishops
12 July	France ends Non-Intervention frontier patrol
7–26 July	Battle of Brunete
28 July	Catalan cabinet without anarchists
7 August	Private Catholic worship permitted
10 August	Consejo de Aragón dissolved
15 August	SIM created; political meetings in Catalonia forbidden
17 August	SP-CP unity pact (in default of merger)
24 August– 15 September	Belchite-Quinto campaign
26 August	Fall of Santander
14–17 September	Nyon agreements on piracy
1 October	Caballero out as UGT president
7 October	Papal nuncio arrives in Salamanca
19 October	Nationalists take Gijón
31 October	Negrín government moves to Barcelona
18 November	Del Vayo resigns as Commissar General
14 December	Teruel offensive launched

1938

30 January	Burgos government with civilian members
22 February	Nationalists recapture Teruel
9 March	Nationalist offensive launched in Aragon
11 March	Hitler occupies Austria
13 March	Blum Prime Minister in France; frontier opened

5 April	Negrín government reorganized; Prieto resigns
April	Burgos laws repealing divorce, Catalan autonomy, agrarian reform
15 April	Nationalists reach the Mediterranean
mid-June	French frontier closed
24 July	Battle of the Ebro launched
9 September	Negrín-Alba secret peace talks (without result)
30 September	Munich agreement
late October	Barcelona trial of POUM leaders
15 November	Retreat from the Ebro; farewell parade for International Brigades
19 November	Burgos mine concessions for final German arms buildup
23 December	Nationalist offensive into Catalonia

1939	
15 January	Nationalists take Tarragona
26 January	Occupation of Barcelona
4 February	Occupation of Gerona
5–9 February	Mass flight over French frontier; Nationalists complete occupation of Catalonia
9 February	Minorca transferred to Nationalists
13 February	Nationalist Law of Political Responsibilities
27 February	Franco-British recognition of Burgos; resignation of Azaña
2 March	Negrín military promotions; war to continue
5 March	Council of National Defense formed; Negrín cabinet flies to France
7–11 March	Communist revolt in Madrid
15 March	German occupation of Czechoslovakia
23–26 March	Unsuccessful negotiation efforts of Casado junta
28 March	Nationalist entry to Madrid
1 April	Surrender of Republican armies completed
May–June	Repatriation of German and Italian troops

THE BLACK LEGEND
OF THE SPANISH REPUBLIC

ONE of the leading themes of the official histories of the period is that the Republic was born of a Masonic plot and was at all times controlled by the forces of "International Masonry." The charge is a fantastic distortion built upon a moderate basis of truth. Many of the important Republican leaders were Masons. Melquiades Alvarez, the leader of the very conservative, unitary Reformist Party; Manuel Portela Valladares, leader of a small "center" party; and Diego Martínez Barrio, first a follower of Lerroux and later the leader of the small liberal party *Unión Republicana,* were thirty-third degree Masons. A number of other important figures such as Marcelino Domingo and Luis Companys were Masons of lesser hierarchical standing. The Radical leaders Alejandro Lerroux and Rafael Salazar Alonso were members until about 1932. A number of liberal military men belonged to the order, notably Generals López Ochoa and Sebastián Pozas. A few of the Socialist intellectuals, such as Jiménez de Asúa and Fernando de los Ríos, were Masons, as was the Communist deputy Dr. Cayetano Bolívar, using the organizational pseudonym "Lenin." President Alcalá-Zamora was persistently rumored to be a Mason, but far from joining them, he shared many of the exaggerated fears of Masonry that were common among Spanish Catholics. Manuel Azaña became a Mason late in 1931. Indalecio Prieto remembered with gratitude and amusement the few eccentric and philanthropic Masons he had known as a working-class boy, but he never joined the society.

The Spanish lodges thus included a wide variety of Republican politicians. Those most important in grade were socially conservative, middle-class, anticlerical Republicans.

The Gran Logia Española, meeting in Madrid 23–25 May 1931 (after the church burnings and the departure of Cardinal Segura, and before the Constituent Cortes elections), adopted a declaration of principles which included the following items: freedom of thought, expression, and religion; equality before the law; universal suffrage; separation of Church and state; civil marriage and divorce; expulsion of non-Spanish Orders and control of the others through a Law of Associations; abolition of the death penalty; a volunteer Army; laic and free education, including instruction in the universal language, Esperanto; the usufruct of the land to those who till it; and a "federal" state, respecting the municipalities, the regions, and other "international and intercontinental groups." The Masons thus advocated a federal republic, guaranteeing the liberties associated with the French and American revolutions, and they espoused such idealistic hopes of the early twentieth century as the adoption of Esperanto and the abolition of conscript armies and capital punishment.

Masonry may have played a small role during the Azaña period in facilitating unity among the Republicans. The multiplicity of small *personalista* parties could be counteracted by the fact that many of the leaders were Masons. In 1932 and 1933 Lerroux, Salazar Alonso, and their friends withdrew from Masonry as part of their evolution toward the Right. In order to qualify to govern on behalf of monarchists and clericals, they proved their change of heart by dropping their anticlerical connections. When Martínez Barrio split with Lerroux, a substantial number of the Radicals who were also Masons followed the former. In *La pequeña historia* Lerroux interprets the break as a Masonic plot. But since Martínez Barrio was protesting against the clerical and police policies of his chief, it is perfectly natural that Masons should have sympathized with him. Similarly, when Portela Valladares, as Minister of the Interior, resisted the efforts of Gil Robles to have the Civil Guard transferred to the Ministry of War, conservatives saw a Masonic plot.

There is also evidence that Masons helped brother Masons, and other victims, to escape at moments of severe repression. I have no documentary evidence on the point, but a number of obviously well-informed persons told me that the Masons organized a species of "underground railway" whereby Andalusian Republicans escaped to Gibraltar during the first months of Queipo de Llano's rule. Also, on the basis of personal intervention with General López Ochoa in Oviedo the Masons may have saved a number of people from imprisonment or death during the Asturian repression.

It is clear that many anticlerical Republicans were Masons, and that Masonic political principles coincided in large measure with the outlook of the Republican-Socialist coalition of 1931–33. Official Spanish historians, however, have pictured the Republic, and during the war the Popular Front, as mere puppets in the hands of a Masonic International. Their conclusions are based principally on the works of Eduardo Comín Colomer, specialist in questions of Masonry and communism, among whose books are *Lo que España debe a la Masonería* (Barcelona, 1956) and *Historia secreta de la segunda república* (Barcelona, 1959). Comín lists not only the vast majority of liberal Republican deputies as Masons, but also dozens of left Socialists (including Largo Caballero, whom he places, however, in a French lodge), anarchists, and Communists. I showed his list to several former Spanish Masons in France and to a group of Masons in Spain. The latter passed it around the table and argued for several hours about certain names after having struck more than half of them from the list. In all these discussions it was clear that the crossed-off names were those of men who had rejected feelers or invitations from the Masons. Now, for many years after the Civil War the Franco government maintained in Salamanca a veritable archive of Masonic activity. It was the duty of the archivists to send a certain number of index cards to Madrid each month with the names of newly discovered Masons. Whoever was mentioned in the letters of known members, or in supposed lodge memoranda, eventually was indexed as a Mason. The listing of all the friends and associates of known Masons explains very simply the fantastic gazetteer produced by Sr. Comín.

In many documents treating the influence of the Masons,

the "Masonic International" is hyphenated with one or more of the adjectives "Jacobin," "Jewish," and "Communist." The obsessive fear of the Masons has historical roots in Spain. In Italy, Spain, and Austria they were often the collaborators of the French revolutionary armies. Much of the propaganda for the independence of Mexico and the South American colonies of Spain was produced and distributed in their lodges. Officials of the Franco government told me that the Masons have always been the agents of Spain's national enemy, England. As for the adjectives "Jewish" and "Communist," they have exactly the same emotive force and disregard for truth as when used by reactionaries all over the Western world. On page 443 of *Historia secreta,* for example, Comín quotes approvingly another book in which Alcalá-Zamora is referred to as a "crypto-Jew," Portela as a degenerate and a "crypto-Jew," and Francisco Cambó (wealthy conservative Catalan) as "enriched by the sinister and Machiavellian chief of European Jewry, Walther Rathenau." All the specific data adduced to prove that the Spanish Republic was the puppet of the Masonic International is of the same character.

A second *leitmotiv* in the black legend is the charge, twice rejected in Cortes investigations, that Prime Minister Azaña had ordered the police to take no prisoners and to "shoot them in the belly" at the time of the Casas Viejas anarchist rising in January 1933. Captain Manuel Rojas of the Assault Guard launched this accusation when journalists found out that he had just shot 14 prisoners. The accusation was supported by one other person, Captain Barba Hernández of the General Staff. In May 1934 Captain Rojas was tried for murder in Cadíz, and the main testimony appeared in *El Sol* for May 23, 24, and 27.

Captain Rojas charged that in an interview where no other persons had been present, the Director General of Security, Arturo Menéndez, had ordered him to take no prisoners or wounded; and that weeks later, when he was already in prison, Lt. Colonel Hernández Sarabia, whom he thought of as an older brother, had offered him a million pesetas to keep quiet. No other persons were present at this interview either. In face-to-face confrontations, Rojas maintained his accusations while Menéndez and Hernández Sarabia flatly denied them. Menéndez then explained to the court that any police officer had the right to ask a written copy of his orders if he felt that they contravened the law. The court waited for an explanation on this point from the defendant, but he did not offer any.

The next day Captain Barba Hernández testified that one of Azaña's military aides had used the phrase "shoot them in the belly," also in an interview where no one else had been present. The prosecution pointed out that no other officers had received such orders, and that the several anarchist risings that week in different parts of Spain had been suppressed without the shooting of prisoners. Captain Barba, who, only a short time before, had said that military duty required the strict fulfillment of orders as given, now explained the leniency in other areas by saying that he had "softened" the cruel orders in transmission.

It was clear to the court that Rojas and Barba were lying in order to support each other. With all the other evidence against Rojas, he was sentenced to 21 years in prison. Nevertheless, the Monarchists reintroduced the Casas Viejas charge against Azaña in the Cortes in March and again in July 1935. On the second occasion, Captain Barba stated that Azaña personally had used the fatal phrase in a private interview with him. Captain Barba was one of the founders of the UME. He went on to purge Saragossa in the first weeks of the Civil War and to earn there a reputation even among reactionaries as a bloodthirsty criminal. Captain Rojas played an important role in the purge of Granada and went on to hold high military office after the Civil War. Arturo Menéndez was taken off the Barcelona-Madrid express at Saragossa on July 18 and shot by the Nationalists. Hernández Sarabia became one of the leading generals of the Republican Army during the war. Well-educated people in Spain still talk in shocked tones about "lo de Casas Viejas" and the criminal sadism of Azaña.

A third major element in the black legend is the statement that the left-wing forces of the Popular Front intended to establish a Soviet Spain under Largo Caballero, that the revolution was to occur between May 11 and June 29, that the date was postponed for unspecified reasons until August 1, and that the military rising of July 18 therefore anticipated a Soviet revolution. Practically all the Nationalist officers with whom I spoke assumed the truth of this charge, and it is contained in most Nationalist histories. However, the best-documented study made in Spain of the revolutionary Left makes no mention of this plot: Maximiano García Venero, *Historia de las internacionales en España* (Madrid, 1956–57, 3 volumes). García Venero covers in great detail the formation of the Popular Front, the journeys of Left Socialists to Russia, the personal relations among French and Spanish members of both the Socialist and Communist parties, the visits of Russian agents to Spain—but never a word about the June 1936 "Soviet." On the other hand, the English historian Hugh Thomas, having seen references to apparent documentary evidence as early as August 7, 1936, in the *Diario de Navarra,* concluded that the *Diario* documents were not forgeries (*The Spanish Civil War,* p. 108n).

These documents received wide international publicity when published in the London *Times,* May 3, 1938, and the following year in Bilbao. They state that on May 16, 1936, in the Casa del Pueblo of Valencia, a plan was adopted by representatives of the French, Spanish, and Russian Communist parties. A revolutionary movement was to be started in both countries when Léon Blum became Prime Minister in France. Following a propaganda campaign to discredit the reformists like Besteiro and Prieto, and a strike campaign to destroy the authority of the bourgeois state, the Soviet would seize power in both countries. Largo Caballero would be its chairman in Spain, and most of the commissars would be Left Socialists.

There are numerous improbabilities in the documents. The Communist International in 1936 was oriented entirely toward the establishment of an anti-fascist front of all bourgeois and proletarian forces opposed to fascism. In Spain the Communists openly criticized the "infantile leftism" of the Caballero Socialists. The Soviet-plan documents ask one to believe that Communists wished to overthrow both the French and Spanish Popular Front governments, and that a

planning committee including several Russians would prepare a commissar list with a Caballerist majority. As commissar of Justice they named Luis Jiménez de Asúa. Then
along with Thorez, José Díaz, Georgi Dimitrov, Caballero and
others, Vincent Auriol was to be one of the guiding spirits.
The anarchists David Antón, García Oliver, and Angel Pestaña
were also named.

I believe that this incredible combination of names re-
veals that the documents were prepared by not very well-
informed rightist elements. Jiménez de Asúa was a constant
supporter of Prieto and of legal, parliamentary government.
He was a principal author of the Constitution of 1931. However, as the defending lawyer for the peasants of Castilblanco
and for various Socialist leaders after Asturias, he earned the
kind of blind hatred which would lead the Right to imagine
him as a "commissar of justice." Vincent Auriol was a parliamentary French Socialist, but he had come to Spain on behalf of The International League for the Rights of Man
to ask Alcalá-Zamora and Lerroux to amnesty the Socialist
leaders condemned to death in February 1935. This action
would easily qualify him to be placed among the Soviet
leaders by a rightist propagandist. As for the anarchists
named, David Antón was one of the extremist CNT leaders
who made cooperation with the UGT most difficult. Pestaña,
on the other hand, had been converted to reformist ideals
and was equally at odds with both the CNT majority and
with the Caballero Socialists. The Right, however, would very
easily be able to picture these men working together under
Largo Caballero to build a Soviet Spain.

The plan for a Soviet is also impossible to reconcile with
the known events of June 1936. The UGT and CNT leaders
were completely absorbed in their mutual rivalries arising
from the construction strike. The Caballerist leaders in late
June were pleading with the CNT to accept mediation so as
not to destroy the authority of the Casares government. Largo
Caballero was in England and France during late June and
early July. Finally, no evidence is ever offered for the statement that the plan was postponed until August 1. But such a
statement is necessary to account for the utter lack of "Soviet"

activity between May 11 and June 29, and to justify the military rising of July 18 as a preventive measure.[1]

Spanish historians of all viewpoints have bitterly deplored the black legend concerning Spanish imperial and colonial history. The less worthy of them have lent themselves to the creation of a fantastic black legend against the Republic.

[1] See also D. Cattell, *Communism and the Spanish Civil War,* 42–43 for the same conclusion arrived at through the examination of other evidence.

THE ELECTIONS OF
THE SECOND SPANISH REPUBLIC

THERE were five nationwide elections during the Republican period; the municipal elections of April 1931, and April 1933; the elections for the Constituent Cortes in June 1931; and the two Cortes elections of November 1933 and February 1936. The first of these had the value only of a plebiscite. Outside the big cities, only Monarchist candidates were listed, but in the cities, where the choice existed, the voting was heavily favorable to the Republicans. The King himself, the leading generals, and almost all the King's personal advisers, interpreted the results of the April 12, 1931 voting as a rejection of the Monarchy, at least in the person of Alfonso XIII. Official interpretations of later years have pointed out that the returns were never fully counted, that 22,000 royalist councilors were chosen as against only 5,800 Republicans, and that the provisional government obliged the King to leave Spain on April 14. All this, however, is beside the point. At the time, and for at least three years thereafter, the King and his supporters recognized in the April 12 vote a plebiscite against the Monarchy in those electoral districts where the voting had included choice.

The election of June 28, 1931, took place under the newly decreed system which gave votes to women and which awarded 80 per cent of the seats in a given electoral district to a simple majority party; a feature which was intended to encourage the formation of coalition lists and to avoid the possibility of a Cortes with many small parties and no effective majority. These elections were free in the sense that the Minister of the Interior guaranteed complete freedom of political agitation instead of manufacturing the results (as had been customary under the Monarchy). On the other hand, the opposition had no time to organize, and the Socialist and various small Republican parties carried on their coalition lists many candidates who were virtually unknown to the leaders of the parties. As a result, the Socialists and their Republican allies were undoubtedly overrepresented in relation to public opinion. Many of the nation's leading intellectuals were elected on the basis of their personal prestige rather than as members of any party. Thus the Constituent Cortes combined the character of an "assembly of notables" with that of a popular assembly in which many new, inexperienced deputies participated, and in which the Left was numerically over-represented.

By the time of the municipal elections of April 1933, the Monarchists and the Right generally had had time to organize. Of 16,000 municipal councilors chosen, 9,800 belonged to parties which had been represented in the provisional government. Of the approximately 5,000 councilors elected by the Right, perhaps half were avowed Monarchists and half "accidentalists." It is impossible to make more than an approximate statement, because the Monarchists, the Agrarians of Martínez de Velasco, and the Catholic candidates grouped under the leadership of Gil Robles made coalition lists, and the members of the two latter parties were undecided in their attitude toward the Republic. The municipal elections thus indicated a country which was at least two-thirds solidly republican among the voters and politicians sufficiently interested to participate in local government.

These elections also indicated dissatisfaction with the Azaña government and the local strength of the Radical Party. While 9,800 councilors belonged to parties that joined the provisional government, only 5,000 belonged to the Left Republican and Socialist parties represented in Azaña's cabinet. The Radicals alone elected 2,479 councilors. It is difficult, however, to make any more detailed interpretation. The numerical results do not correspond accurately to voter preferences, both because the coalition lists were arranged by the party leaders and because in local circumstances there were often just single lists, and many individual candidacies not involving a party commitment. The President, and the conservative press, interpreted the elections as a swing to the Right. But it is equally possible that much of the vote against the governmental parties was a protest vote against police brutality at Casas Viejas rather than a vote against the general legislative and economic policies of the government. The success of the Radicals indicates that they were the party of local business and political interests in the conventional sense of the term. Nationally they were not clearly identified with any principle except that of the republican form of government. Pragmatic politicians, civil servants, notaries, and real estate men joined the Radicals—the men most actively interested in local politics.

The Cortes elections of November 1933 and February 1936 were undoubtedly the most representative elections in Spanish history. They involved national issues which were clear to the voters. The government guaranteed freedom of press, assembly, and political agitation. In each case there was a period of six weeks in which the parties negotiated their coalition lists. In both instances, Right, Center, and Left had ample opportunity to bring to bear all their economic, political, and ideological resources.

The elections of November 1933 showed that there were three sizable parties in Spanish politics: the Socialists, the Radicals, and the Catholics. When the Socialists and the Left Republican parties ran separately rather than as a coalition, it was immediately obvious that the voting mass of the former Azaña coalition consisted of Socialists. The Radicals retained the strength they had shown earlier with municipal middle-class voters. Gil Robles, with the CEDA coalition, showed that there was a mass of Catholic voters in the cities, and in the countryside of northern Spain and the Levant. Judging by the oratory of the CEDA campaign and its success at the polls, these voters were reacting principally against the anticlerical legislation of the Constituent Cortes. They were not monarchists and not fascists. Neither Antonio Goicoechea nor Calvo Sotelo nor José Antonio Primo de Rivera found any wide echo in public opinion. The Catholic masses voted against Marcelino Domingo because he was a Mason and an anticlerical, not because he had imported wheat. Nor did they vote against the public works policies of Prieto or against the tax policies of Carner.

Since the CEDA was a coalition rather than a party; since Gil Robles was young, timid, and conservative; since the monarchists had supplied most of the money for the CEDA campaign; monarchical influence was stronger within the Catholic bloc than it deserved to be. But the CEDA had the makings of a mass party which would represent the Catholic middle class and peasantry within the Republic. The very irregular pattern of coalitions in different areas, the bargaining for seats within the coalition, and the fact that sometimes the Radicals had informal agreements with the CEDA and sometimes ran against them, makes it impossible to assess in percentage terms the relative strength of the Radicals and of the Catholic bloc. The nonmonarchist parties of the CEDA received about 110 seats, the Radicals 100, the Socialists 58. But the operation of the electoral law and the coalition agreements, rather than voting power, explain those numbers. All one can conclude is that these were the three groups with a mass following, and that the several Left Republican parties, the Traditionalists (Carlists), the Alfonsine Monarchists (Renovación Española), the Falange, and the JONS, were all distinctly minor groups, numerically speaking.

The elections of February 1936 indicated a polarization of opinion around a Left coalition, of which the Socialists were the mass base, and a Right coalition based upon the Catholics. These coalitions were almost equal in voting strength, and in many cities and provinces the margin of victory was only 1 or 2 per cent. The strong Left majority in the Cortes resulted from the fact that frequent slim victories in the popular vote gave the victorious coalition 80 per cent of the seats in the province. The Radicals virtually disappeared. Those who were anticlerical, and who opposed the heavy hand in Asturias after October, voted with the Popular Front in 1936. Those who had approved Lerroux's record as Prime Minister voted with the Right. The straperlo scandal had destroyed what was left of the personal prestige of Lerroux himself. About 9¼ million votes were cast in 1936 by a population of 25,000,000. This meant the highest proportional voter participation in Spanish history, and a proportion infrequently attained in the legislative elections of many a mature democracy. Of that 9¼ million votes, roughly 4 million represented the Right, 4 million the Left, perhaps a half-million the Center (Portela and Alcalá-Zamora) and three-quarters of a million the anarchists.

Although the polarization around two coalitions makes it easy to say that Spain was almost equally divided between the Right and the Left in 1936, it is even harder than in 1933 to say precisely what the voters meant. Within coalition lists, the candidates were not identified by party. But each party ran well-known men in the big cities, and the politically conscious voter could indicate preferences by numbering, by crossing out names, and other informal devices. Where voters acted this way they often indicated their preference for the moderates. Due to the closeness of the vote in 1933 in Madrid, a second round was necessary to determine how many Socialists and how many of the Right coalition would be seated in the Cortes. In this runoff, conservative voters placed the distinguished Monarchist, Luca de Tena, at the bottom of their list. The Socialist voters in both cases gave the first and second places to Julián Besteiro and Luis Jiménez de Asúa. In the first round Largo Caballero had been third on the Socialist list, but between the first and second votes, Largo had made a number of statements to the effect that the Socialists, if disappointed by the Republic, would have to think in terms of revolutionary means to power. On the second vote Largo appeared at the bottom of the Socialist list.

In 1936 many voters acted like the philosopher Ortega who, according to reports of his friends, voted for the Popular Front—but crossed off all the names except that of Besteiro. In Madrid the Popular Front majority chose thirteen deputies in an order which makes the impression of being simultaneously a plebiscite in favor of moderation. At the top of the list, Martínez Barrio, representing the right wing of the coalition, and almost dead center politically if one considers the record of the five years of Republican government; then Julián Besteiro, particularly beloved in Madrid, but representing also the most gradualist opinion within the Socialist Party; then

Azaña, followed by several other Left Republicans and by the Left Socialists Del Vayo, Araquistáin, and Largo Caballero; and at the bottom of the list José Díaz, secertary general of the Communist Party. I did not have the opportunity to seek similarly detailed data for the victorious lists throughout the country, and in any case, vote counting was not too exact in most areas. But according to the returns sent in by the provinces on February 20, the top candidates in all but three Popular Front victories were either Left Republicans or members of the Esquerra, and with four exceptions the top candidates in the case of Right victories were members of the CEDA.

Salvador de Madariaga, analyzing the Popular Front election in his *Spain* (pp. 444–48, edition of 1958) concludes that Spaniards voted 2 to 1 against Marxism, 2 to 1 against clericals and militarists, 8 to 1 against a Socialist revolution (Largo Caballero and the Communists), and almost unanimously against military rebellion. But these proportions are based on the party affiliations of the elected deputies. Since the panels were prepared by the party leaders, one cannot attribute these proportions to the choice of the voters. On the other hand, the leaders undoubtedly gave a heavy representation to the moderates within their coalitions in order to attract the moderate voters. This tactic, taken together with the fact that moderates polled the highest individual votes, justifies the general conclusion that Spanish voters in 1936 hoped to see temperate men gain power. If one then asks why they did not vote for the Center in greater numbers, the answer is that they were afraid to waste their votes. When one compares 1933 with 1936, it is clear that Spain was in fact moving toward a two-party system. For the great mass of voters who were neither revolutionary Socialist nor fascist, the election was a contest between Azaña and Gil Robles, between the parliamentary Left and the parliamentary Right. This truth has been obscured by the fact that immediately after the election the revolutionary wing of the Popular Front, the Monarchist reactionaries, the militant youth groups, and the military, all refused to permit the parliamentary government to function.

A comparison of the 1933 and 1936 elections also indicates

very little change in the relative strength of Right and Left in different parts of the country. Making allowances for the tendency toward a two-party, or two-coalition system, and for the fact that the anarchists abstained in 1933 and voted in 1936, it appears in both cases that the Left was strong in the industrial cities, in Catalonia, in Galicia, and in Andalusia; that the Right was strong in the two Castiles and Navarre; that Valencia, much of the Levant and Aragon were divided almost equally between Right and Left.

Certain general observations can be made from the data of the five elections discussed above. First of all, the mass of Spanish opinion was favorable to the Republic, though this remark must be qualified by the fact that the further one moves to the Right the more frequently one finds men ready to resort to a military *putsch,* and the further one moves to the Left the more frequently one finds men speaking of the Republic as a temporary stage on the road to a proletarian dictatorship. The single-chamber Cortes lacked continuity, in that only one-fifth the deputies served in all three Cortes. The electoral law which was designed to produce workable legislative majorities went far, in its practical effects, to exasperate minority opinion. Neither the Left in 1933, nor the Right in 1936 were ready to accept the fact that a slight majority of votes gave their rivals a large plurality of seats.

More important than the weakness of the electoral law, however, was the fact that the most able men produced by the Republic were not the chiefs of the large parties. Azaña and Martínez Barrio led small Left Republican parties; Miguel Maura captained a tiny conservative Republican group; Joaquín Chapaprieta was an enlightened conservative without a party; Indalecia Prieto was strong within the Socialist Party executive, but the masses followed Largo Caballero.

A number of special elections deserve brief comment. The plebiscites concerning autonomy statutes in Catalonia (1931), in the Basque provinces (1933), and in Galicia (1936) all were overwhelmingly favorable to regional autonomy. A plebiscite is a crude, and often rigged, form of vote. In these instances, however, specific texts were submitted to the voters and ample public discussion preceded the votes. Also, Navarre rejected strongly the same text which the Basques approved.

Thus it seems correct to credit these plebiscites with reflecting the true state of public opinion in those provinces. In September, 1933, the first elections to the Tribunal of Guarantees showed that the municipal councilors and the lawyers of Spain were more conservative than the government. In April 1935 municipal elections were canceled, and in August 1935 Tribunal of Guarantees elections were canceled. No by-elections were ever held to fill the numerous vacancies which occurred in both Cortes, and municipal elections at first scheduled for April 1936, were canceled by mutual agreement between the Right and the Azaña government. These cancellations and the absence of partial elections indicate the fact that elections were always considered a potential threat to public order and to the prestige of the government in office.

Aside from the information they yield concerning public opinion, the elections of the Republican era are interesting to compare with those of the Spanish past and with those of other countries. Under the Constitutional Monarchy Spain enjoyed substantial freedom of the press and freedom of electoral propaganda in the big cities. But all the elections before 1931 were more or less manufactured. Since 1939 there have been minor elections within corporate bodies such as the colegio de abogados or the vertical labor unions. However, there has been absolutely no freedom of press or political agitation, and the Cortes is merely a ceremonial body appointed by the dictator and has no legislative functions.

Compared with general elections in Western Europe, Scandinavia, England, or the United States, even the most representative of the Republican elections, those of 1933 and 1936, were marked by violence at the polls and corruption in the counting. The results, however, were not known in advance and were thus more representative than the results of Mexican elections. They compare favorably with the freest elections in such countries as Argentina, Chile, and Uruguay. They were of course infinitely more democratic than elections in the Popular Democracies of Eastern Europe. All this is worth pointing out since the official propaganda in Spain for over 25 years has given many Spaniards a painful inferiority complex as to their ability to live according to the norms of democracy.

DEATHS ATTRIBUTABLE TO THE CIVIL WAR

DUE to the ensemble of conditions existing in Spain during and since the Civil War, it will never be possible to provide even approximately accurate totals for deaths of all kinds attributable to the war. However, it is possible to set credible upper and lower limits, and to judge proportionately the importance of different factors. The victorious government, anxious to impress upon the people the high cost of the war, has habitually used the phrase *un millón de muertos*. The very knowledgeable and courageous writer, José María Gironella, used that phrase as the title of a novel which described the war more objectively than any other work of fiction or non-fiction published in Spain. At the same time, in the preface, Gironella stated his belief that while the phrase *un millón de muertos* symbolized accurately the devastating quality of the struggle, actually more like one-half million persons died.

Shortly after the war, a Santander physician with some knowledge of statistics and demography, Jesús Villar Salinas, published a study entitled *Repercusiones demográficas de la última guerra civil española* (Madrid, 1942). The population of Spain had been increasing at a fairly steady rate in the decade before the war. Dr. Villar extended the average rate of increase for the period 1926–35 up through 1939 and arrived at the conclusion that without the war Spain's population would have been roughly 1,100,000 larger than the census of 1940 revealed it to be. If we subtract 300,000 to account for the *émigrés* (as of mid-1940), Dr. Villar's study leaves about 800,000 deaths to be accounted for. Any such demographic estimate can only be approximate, even for circumstances in which statistics can be carefully gathered, but the Villar study is impressive for a particular reason. In 1940, going over all the civil death and war casualty lists available to him, he estimated the total population of Spain at a figure which turned out to differ by only 17,000 from the census figure published in March 1941. Taking the three above estimates into account, I started from the hypothesis that between 500,000 and 1,000,000 persons had died, and that the round figure 800,000 for the period from 1936 to mid-1940 might be pretty close. I then tried to estimate separately the total deaths to be attributed to several causes: battles, repression on each side, air raids, and disease.

The most hard-fought battle of the war, and the one most carefully observed by experienced war reporters, was the Battle of the Ebro. On November 19, 1938, the *Times* of London estimated that in the fighting from July 25 to November 15, each side had suffered about 40,000 casualties. This estimate is consistent with the size of the forces engaged and the nature of the fighting. Thus the Republicans had concentrated 90–100,000 men, of whom about half crossed the river in the last week of July. From early August on, the combat involved artillery, machine-gun, and mortar fire comparable to the western front battles of the First World War, but along a front of only some 15 miles. Assuming that eventually some 100,000 men were engaged on each side, it is reasonable to believe that they suffered 40 per cent casualties in a battle of such intensity. In estimating the proportion of dead in a total casualty figure, it is normal to count 1 death for 5 casualties. This would mean 8,000 deaths for each side. All the accounts agree in describing the virtually suicidal bravery of both the attackers and the defenders. If we increase by 50 per cent the "normal" proportion of deaths, this might mean 12,000 for each side, and a possible (rounded off) maximum of 25,000 deaths for the battle as a whole.

The other long and sanguinary battles were those of the Jarama, Brunete, and Teruel. At Jarama, General Orgaz attacked with a maximum of 40,000 troops, and at Brunete, the Republic sent almost 50,000 men into the offensive. The Battle of the Jarama lasted about ten days, and that of Brunete three weeks. Again, journalistic and medical observer reports agree on the intensity of the fighting. The struggles ended in temporary exhaustion. If each side suffered 50 per cent *casualties,* a very high rate, of whom 20–25 per cent may be counted as deaths, this would still mean not more than about 10,000 total deaths in each case. At Teruel, almost 100,000 were eventually engaged on each side, but except for the bitter struggle in the heart of the city itself, casualties were relatively light. The Republicans advanced quickly in the first days, and at the end, after the long Nationalist buildup, they retreated eastward to avoid encirclement. Nationalist historians claim that the Republic suffered 50,000 casualties. Even if this high figure is accepted, we get roughly 10,000 deaths, and estimating that the victors in this instance suffered half the deaths of the losers, the total for the battle would come to 15,000. (Against this high figure I quote for comparative purposes the estimate of General Rojo that the Republicans suffered 6,000 deaths at Teruel.)

Casualties were also high in the November 1936 assault on Madrid, but the forces involved were still small. General Mola arrived before the capital with an army of 20,000, of which he employed about 5,000 in the attacking columns. We know more in detail about the fighting in the University City than along the western approaches. During the November fighting, possibly 2,000 Internationals died in the University City. The attackers might, at the very limit, have lost 4–5,000 on the entire front before being forced to suspend the assault. Thus it is unreasonable to suppose more than 10,000 maximum killed at this time. Both Nationalist and Republican accounts imply that the late December and January local battles near Madrid cost about as much as did the original assault, and so once again I would offer a rough estimate of 10,000 deaths.

The military cost of the rest of the war was relatively light. The Nationalists lost more men at Madrid in November than they had during the entire Andalusia-Extremadura campaign. The militia fought only sporadically, and their death totals in this period belong more in the reprisal than the military category. The northern war was also relatively light in casualties. The total Basque militia did not exceed 50,000, and they made no suicide stands. Some 80,000 Nationalist troops took Santander, and all the accounts of the march through Guipúzcoa, Vizcaya, and Santander emphasize the sporadic nature of the fighting. Large sectors of the fronts in Aragon, New Castile, and Andalusia were quiet throughout the war, and fighting was merely sporadic during the January 1939 conquest of Catalonia. Guerrilla operations in Galicia and Asturias tied down large numbers of Nationalist troops but did not involve heavy engagements. An estimate of 20,000 military deaths would cover the northern war and the quiet fronts.

On the basis of the reasoning outlined above, I arrived at an estimate of about 100,000 battle deaths, broken down as follows:

> 10,000 at Madrid in November
> 10,000 near Madrid in December–January
> 10,000 at the Jarama
> 10,000 at Brunete
> 15,000 at Teruel
> 25,000 at the Ebro
> 20,000 for the rest of the war
> ‾‾‾‾‾‾‾‾
> 100,000

I have purposely left the figures obviously approximate. I suspect, for example, on the basis of weighing all factors more closely that Brunete cost more than 10,000 and the Jarama less. I doubt whether Teruel caused 15,000 deaths, but I may be underestimating the deaths on the minor fronts.

The total of 100,000 is smaller than that of any of the military histories I have read. In the case of Nationalist versions I believe this is due to the fact that Aznar and the authors of *Cruzada* consistently exaggerated, for political purposes, the size and equipment of the Republican forces, and hence the numbers which the Nationalists killed or wounded among those forces. In the case of pro-Republican histories the desire to highlight heroism and pay tribute to the valor of the losers caused exaggeration. Thus General Rojo wrote in *¡Alerta los pueblos!* that 100,000 died for the Republic. He may have meant to include reprisal deaths in that figure, but in any event, since he estimated 6,000 Republican deaths at Teruel, and less than 10,000 for the Ebro, it is difficult to see how the battle deaths of the Republican Army could come to 100,000.

On the other hand, my estimate is consistent with the size

of the forces involved. The maximum size of the Republican Army was about 600,000, and the Nationalists had a total of some 500,000 men under arms (including the Italian, German, and Portuguese troops). It is credible in a bitter two-and-a-half-year civil war, that of 1,100,000 men, between 40 and 50 per cent would have been at least lightly wounded at some time. This would mean some 500,000 casualties, of which 20 per cent or 100,000, were deaths.

Accuracy in the matter of reprisals is even more difficult than in the case of battle deaths. One can only put together scattered information and simultaneously offer the reader the bases of the reasoning through which the estimates are arrived at. In 1943 the Ministry of Justice published a mass of testimony and documentation concerning assassinations in the Republican zone: *Causa General*. The concluding sentence of this work states that the Ministry had duly investigated 85,940 such cases—a statement which has been widely accepted by later writers, perhaps because it seems to show a spirit of moderation in comparison with the first claims which ran as high as 300,000.

The information in *Causa* is highly detailed and specific for the cities of Madrid and Bilbao, and for the religious persecution in Catalonia. It includes detailed accounts of particularly gruesome incidents elsewhere, such as the murder of priests in Ciudad Real, the assault on a prison in Jaén, and the murder of over 100 naval officers. I went through this work page by page, totaling all the numbers claimed in the text, rounding off estimated totals in an upward direction, and making no subtraction even where the context indicated that there was probably some overlap between one account and another. This total comes to 6,000. It does not, as already indicated, cover the whole of Spain. However, it does describe the main well-known incidents of mass murder, and needless to say, it does not minimize "red" guilt. It is a prosecution case without any defense. Its political notes distort so violently the history of the period that no serious student can credit its general claims without other confirmation. Hence in the absence of such other evidence, I do not for a moment accept the figure of 85,940 assassinations therein imputed to the "reds."

A much more worthy source of information in a limited field is Antonio Montero, *Historia de la persecución religiosa en España, 1936–39* (Madrid, 1961). After years of careful research, the author lists some 6,800 religious personnel as victims of terror in the Popular Front zone. The figure is high but credible, there having been some 30,000 priests and monks in Spain in 1936. Also, separating the two categories, Montero shows that 13 per cent of the secular priests and 23 per cent of the monks were killed. This would be consistent with the circumstances that individual priests could more easily hide and would be more likely to find civilian witnesses in their behalf before the revolutionary committees.

Priests, Civil Guards (in the villages), and known Falangists (in the main cities) were by all testimonies the principal classes of victim. The Guards and the Falangists were obviously more capable than priests of defending themselves physically, and would also have been better prepared psychologically to resort to violent action rather than be easy victims. In 1936 the Civil Guard numbered 32,000. Well over half of these rose with the Insurgents, and several thousand were loyal to the Republic, notably in Catalonia and the Levant. Thousands of others simply took off their uniforms (if in the Popular Front zone) and disappeared from the towns where they might have feared assassination. It would be most difficult to believe that more than 1,000 Civil Guards fell victim to revolutionary violence. Similar considerations apply to the Falange. At the time of the February 1936 elections, the Falange numbered about 5,000. It grew rapidly in the spring, reaching some 60,000 before the outbreak of the Civil War. However, the vast majority of those new members would not have been known to revolutionary committees as leaders to be held responsible for the rising. But suppose for the sake of making an estimate, that in July the revolutionaries had the names of 10,000 Falangists in the part of Spain dominated by the Popular Front. I do not think it credible that even 2,000 could have been assassinated.

Another estimated figure to which I gave great weight, because it came independently from several doctors and from a member of the Spanish Red Cross who had occupied himself with this very question from the first moment, was the total of 6,000 victims for the city of Madrid—the 6,000 including the prisoners taken from jails on November 5 and 6, and the priests and Falangists. In the other major cities, Barcelona and Valencia, similar terrorism occurred but on a smaller scale, and also with greater escape facilities for the potential victims due to the proximity of the sea. If 6,000 is a reasonable estimate for Madrid, 6,000 should also cover both Barcelona and Valencia.

In the villages the situation varied greatly, as described in the chapter on revolution and terror. But in the villages a very few persons were considered by definition to be the enemy: at most the priest, the Civil Guards, and a few hated landlords or their representatives. In Andalusia the villagers often *arrested* such persons immediately. Most of them, far from being shot, were released by the invading army. In Catalonia and the Levant the anarchists arrested many a landlord and monarchist on the assumption that he had probably backed the rising, but most of these people were released when the evidence, and the testimony of villagers who had known them for years, indicated that they had had nothing to do with the rising. Finally, it should be remembered with regard to both city and village that the vast majority of assassinations occurred in the first three months of the war.

Admittedly this is the most difficult category in which to make even limiting estimates. If, for example, 500 villages in the Popular Front zone witnessed 10 assassinations each, the total would be 5,000. I do not believe that any such number of villages actually killed any such number of persons. In large portions of New Castile and Aragon practically no revolutionary violence occurred. However, rather than underestimate the total, I made the hypothesis of 5,000 in full confidence that it was more than sufficient. By estimating high I also wished to be sure of covering such incidents as the lynching of downed aviators and the shooting of hostages after air raids.

There are a few numerically significant instances to be accounted for after the first months. The Barcelona fighting in May 1937 may have produced up to 1,000 victims who belong in the assassination or reprisal category rather than in the military. Perhaps there were another 1,000 such victims in Madrid in March 1939. The SIM in 1938 carried out numerous political assassinations, and both the Communists and the anarchists at the front, or at military bases, were guilty of political murder on a small scale: inevitably small because they had to act primarily as allies, no matter how many disputes they might desire to settle with one another after the war. At the moments of worst tension, the Communists, anarchists, and POUM might feel that the leaders of the rival groups had to be physically liquidated, but they never took such an attitude toward the general membership. I therefore reason that 1,000 would be a high estimate for the number of political murders, aside from the Barcelona and Madrid risings for which I have already made higher than likely allowances.

On the basis of the reasoning given above, I arrived at a most tentative estimate of 20,000 deaths by assassination in the Popular Front zone, broken down as follows:

6000	for Madrid	⎤ virtually all during the
6000	for Barcelona and Valencia	⎟ first 3 months of the
5000	for the towns and villages	⎦ war
1000	May, 1937 in Barcelona	
1000	March, 1939 in Madrid	
1000	SIM, etc.	
20,000		

Referring back to estimates by category rather than geographical area:

6800	priests (close to exact total)
1000	Civil Guards
2000	Falangists

In short, that roughly half of the total falls in the categories which were the obvious enemies for the revolutionaries.

The largest single category of deaths were the reprisals carried out by the Carlists, the Falangists, and the military themselves. Physical liquidation of the enemy behind the lines was a constant process throughout the war. The Nationalists had, by definition, far more enemies than the revolutionaries: all members of Popular Front parties, all Masons, all officeholders of UGT or CNT unions or of Casas del Pueblo, all members of mixed juries who had generally voted in favor of worker demands. The repression took place in three stages. At the outbreak of the war, the arrests and wholesale shootings of such persons corresponded to the revolutionary terror in the Popular Front zone; but there were a great many more victims, because such arrests and shootings were officially sanctioned and because so large a percentage of the population were considered hostile. In the second stage, the Nationalist Army, conquering areas which had been held by the Popular Front, carried out heavy reprisals in revenge for those of the revolutionaries and in order to control a hostile populace with few troops. In both Andalusian and Castilian villages there are many testimonies concerning reprisals on the order of 60 for 6, 90 for 9, and so forth. In the third stage, which lasted at least into the year 1943, the military authorities carried out mass court-martials followed by large-scale executions.

For all these stages the evidence is clear in a qualitative sense, but numbers can be estimated only very tentatively. Prison records and death registers are misleading, since it is known that certificates of release were regularly signed by or for men who were then taken out and shot, and that certificates alleging heart attacks or apoplexy were made out for corpses left on the open road. Execution techniques deliberately disfigured the corpses so as to make them unrecognizable. Officials of the time have testified that families were afraid to report missing male members, and did not come to identify the bodies of the dead.

Concerning political executions during the first months of the war, I offer the following several illustrations of the sort of estimates on which my conclusions are based. A doctor of forensic medicine, a member of one of the moderate republican parties in the 1930's, with a decade of service in the provincial government of one of the provinces concerned, gave me what he considered to be a minimal estimate for

534

the first six months: 15,000 for the province of Valladolid, 15,000 for Zamora, and 4,000 for Salamanca. (I received separate confirmation of the fact that the repression had been less severe in Salamanca than in the other two provinces.) A municipal official in Seville, jailed on July 19 as a Socialist, and who survived because one of the judges at his court-martial testified that as a mixed jury member in 1932 he had been "fair" and not always voted for the workers, estimated 6,000 executions in the city by the end of 1936. His estimate was based on the number of men taken nightly from the prison while he was there, together with similar information from friends who survived other Seville jails. Other persons with whom I spoke in the same city considered his estimate extremely modest. A notary, and former member of the CEDA, having lived his entire life in the province of Córdoba, tried in 1946 to determine as exactly as he could the number of political executions in Andalusia. He could consult other notaries, and municipal death lists. He spoke to local priests, who could name dozens of Catholic victims (whose families were not permitted to list their names on any public memorial plaque). He had numerous personal contacts among former UGT and CNT members. He estimated 26,000 for the province of Granada, 32,000 for Córdoba, and 47,000 for Seville.

In the course of a year's research, I had more than a dozen conversations with Nationalist officers who described to me the first days of the war. In one Aragonese town the workers lay low during the July 18–19 weekend. Then, hearing of the fall of the Montaña barracks, they organized a parade, complete with their hunting muskets. "We" turned the machine guns on them. Not many were killed at that moment, of course, but they fled to the Casa del Pueblo, and there the *limpia* (cleanup) was easy, and the town was quiet the rest of the war. In an Andalusian coastal town the "reds" naïvely thought that a general strike would defeat the rising. The officer who took the city described how his men, who were only a "handful," machinegunned the waves of advancing workers. More than one explained to me the procedure of shooting everyone in overalls, or everyone with a black

535

and blue mark on his shoulder. After all, the army was in a hurry, and had no time or men to waste on the rear guard. There was nothing excited, self-conscious, or defensive in the tone of these descriptions. The officers treated the matter as though it were a question of exterminating vermin. One of the strongest impressions leading me eventually to accept such large estimates for Nationalist reprisals was the fact that these officers obviously did not think of their enemies as human beings. They weren't killing men; they were cleaning out rats. If I mentioned Badajoz, they were prompt to explain the importance of the junction between the northern and southern forces. Far from considering the bull-ring executions a slander, they had memories of other such incidents not reported in the world press. In general, the descriptions given by the conquerors corresponded closely with those of the conquered, except as to viewpoints and the choice of adjectives.

By mid-1937 the military *limpias* and the passionate Carlist and Falangist executions were almost entirely ended. But court-martials and execution squads operated for more than another five years. Elena de la Souchère, in *Explication de l'Espagne* (Paris, 1962), prints the results of her own reading of official statistics for the immediate postwar period. In the category of violent deaths, the total for 1939–41 is 84,000 higher than the total for the same category for the 3 years preceding the war (the population being about 1 per cent larger in the later period). Death figures as a whole are 220,000 higher for the years 1939–41 than for the 3 years before the war. The 84,000 is undoubtedly smaller than the number of executions, many of which were listed as natural deaths. The figure of 220,000 is too large, since allowance must be made for the higher postwar death rates from disease and malnutrition. But a large part of the 220,000 can be attributed either to execution or to death from concentration-camp conditions, which latter deaths would not have occurred except as part of the mass proscription.

After the war the government maintained military prisons in each of the 50 provincial capitals and used dozens of school buildings and convents as overflow prisons in the great cities. Nearly 70,000 Republican veterans had returned to Spain through Hendaye in late February and March, 1939, and roughly 300,000 soldiers and guerrillas laid down their arms all over Spain in the last days of March. There were tens of thousands of men already waiting in Nationalist jails and prisoner-of-war camps, and there were more than 100,000 factory workers in the Levant and Catalonia who had contributed to industrial war production. Thus well over one-half million men were candidates for court-martial in the spring of 1939. All of them had, in the words of the Law of Political Responsibilities, opposed the *movimiento nacional* in the period since October 1, 1934.

The Nationalist authorities were apparently surprised at the obedience of the defeated army in reporting to the demobilization centers, and they had no personnel ready to handle them. Thousands of men were transported to their home provinces in cattle cars, and remained unfed during an eight- or ten-day journey. Other thousands waited in similar conditions of starvation in the concentration camps set up on the outskirts of the large cities.

Women brought food to their husbands and brothers, and gifts for the guards who might conceivably lighten their fate. Those without families, or away from home, subsisted on watery soups containing a bit of lentils or vegetable peelings. The men were court-martialed for "military rebellion" in groups of 20 and 30, day after day, in each of the hundreds of prisons. Drafted soldiers were assigned duty in what was euphemistically called the *servicio de ambulancia*. Their actual task was to collect the bodies of the men who had walked to their death single file across the path of a machine gun. Many draftees paid 25 pesetas to soldiers with stronger stomachs than their own in order to be excused from the *servicio*. Educated prisoners served as clerks, with the task of making out receipts for the belongings of their fellow inmates and for the pin money brought them by their families. Such clerks could not help but know that thousands of executions occurred from their prisons during the years 1939–41, and lesser numbers in 1942 and 1943. The actual extermination of the "reds" and the approaching defeat of Germany greatly reduced the number of executions by 1943. Increasingly, those who had been condemned to death had their sentences commuted to 30 years in labor camps with each day of work counting for two days of the original sentence. There is no way of knowing what proportion of the death sentences were thus commuted, nor what number of men died of dysentery, typhus, tuberculosis, or the combination of overwork and undernourishment in the labor camps.

From the type of qualitative evidence given above, and the general statistical indications of Elena de la Souchère, I consider it certain that close to 200,000 men died in the years 1939–43. A professional officer and lawyer, who had served with the Nationalists in the war and was appointed as a defense attorney for the mass court-martials, swore to me that on the basis of Ministry of Interior lists alone, he knew that more than 300,000 death sentences had been executed by the end of World War II. A former Republican deputy, who gave very low estimates for the Asturian repression, who had not himself fought in the war, but who spent the years 1939–47 in prison, was absolutely convinced, by comparing his large-city prison notes with those of friends keeping count in other prisons, that 300,000 was a minimal estimate for the postwar repression. In any event, Nationalist political executions during and after the war constituted the largest single category of deaths attributable to the Civil War.

Two remaining factors are air raids and disease deaths. The main air raids were those over Madrid in November 1936 and over Barcelona in March and May 1938. Incomplete but indicative police and journalistic records suggest that even the heaviest raids killed hundreds rather than thousands of persons. The total for the entire war might run between 5,000 and 10,000, the latter figure being truly maximal. As for disease: typhus, tuberculosis, and the various diseases of malnutrition were all endemic in Spain, but sanitary services were excellently maintained on both sides (except in the prisons), so that no epidemics occurred. It is very doubtful whether even 50,000 deaths should be attributed to the increase of endemic diseases during the war itself. I would consider also that the majority of postwar deaths were due to execution, but undoubtedly many older men, intellectuals particularly, died of prison conditions. Due to the outbreak of World War II, food and medical supplies were shorter in the period 1939–41 than they had ever been during the Civil War.

To sum up the separate estimates:

100,000	battlefield deaths
10,000	air raid deaths
50,000	disease and malnutrition deaths (during the Civil War)
20,000	Republican zone paseos and political reprisals
200,000	wartime Nationalist paseos and political reprisals
200,000	"red" prisoner deaths through execution or disease, 1939–43
580,000	

The total is on the low side, in terms of Spanish and foreign opinion, and in terms of the demographic estimate of Dr. Villar Salinas (800,000). I would emphasize once more the inevitably approximate nature of all the figures. I believe, however, that my first four figures tend toward the maximum. With regard to the last two figures a few comparisons are in order. In the two weeks following the surrender of the Paris Commune of 1871, the French army set up some 15 machine-gun posts in the squares and parks of the city and shot 17–25,000 communards. Perhaps 3,000 more persons died in prisons and on prison ships in the following year. Paris was a city of less than 2,000,000 population at the time. The repression I have been summarizing applied to a nation of 25,000,000 and continued over a period of 6 years.

During the last year of the Civil War, the Republican cabinet repeatedly discussed the question of whether it was worth continuing resistance in a war which was militarily hopeless. One of Negrín's constant arguments was that more men would die if the Republic surrendered than if it resisted. On this point he was absolutely correct. The skeptical reader

APPENDIX D

should also recall what is perfectly well known of Nazi behavior during the Second World War. The men in power in Spain were men with the same ideas, and men who more than once shocked the Germans and Italians.

When Heinrich Himmler visited Madrid in 1941 in connection with the training of the Spanish political police, he disapproved, on practical grounds, the rate of executions. The denazification of Germany and the de-Stalinization of Russia have revealed the extent of mass murder practiced by totalitarian governments in the twentieth century. The men who did such things in Spain are still its rulers. By and large they have not behaved since 1945 in the manner that they behaved between 1936 and 1945. But some day, with a change of regime, the world will learn openly of the crimes which today can only be deduced from scattered and poorly documented evidences.

BIBLIOGRAPHY

IN PREPARING this bibliography, I have been guided by several considerations. There is an extraordinary amount of ephemeral and purely propagandistic literature concerning Spain in the 1930's. Before registering a book or periodical, I therefore applied a rule of thumb: that I should have taken important factual notes from any publication I would list. The inventory is thus by no means exhaustive, but I believe that any scholar consulting the items listed below will find them truly valuable in some regard.

Sections I, II, and III contain respectively background works, studies dealing primarily with the Republic, 1931–1936, and studies of the Civil War. There is, of course, inevitable overlap in any such division. Rather than duplicate numerous entries, I have tried simply to list each book once, in the section where it had been most valuable to my research. In section I brief indications of significance are given with many of the entries. Many works in sections II and III (those listed with an asterisk) have been commented on in footnotes, and an index heading under the author's name will lead the interested reader to those comments. Sections IV and V list, respectively, newspapers of the Republican era, and miscellaneous periodicals. These entries are again briefly annotated to indicate their significance wherever the title does not speak for itself.

I

BACKGROUND WORKS

Alba, Victor. *Histoire des républiques espagnoles.* Vincennes, 1948. A well-informed Catalanist and Marxist view comparing the weaknesses of the First and Second Republics.

Baelen, Jean. *Principaux traits du développement économique de l'Espagne.* Paris, 1924.

Barcelo, José Luis. *Historia económica de España.* Madrid, 1952.

Barea, Arturo. *The Forging of a Rebel.* New York, 1946. Autobiography rich in information about the life of the working class and the lower middle class in the first decades of the twentieth century.

Bec, René. *La dictature espagnole de Primo de Rivera.* Montpellier, 1933. Stresses the problem of political indifference among the educated classes.

* Brenan, Gerald. *The Spanish Labyrinth.* Cambridge, England, 1943. Especially valuable on the anarchists, the Catalan question, and on land problems; also useful for its bibliography and notes.

Bruguera, F. G. *Histoire contemporaine de l'Éspagne.* Paris, 1953. A pioneer attempt to provide economic and demographic information from the year 1789 forward.

Deakin, Frank B. *Spain Today.* London, 1924.

* For each title carrying an asterisk, see index under author's name.

Díaz del Moral, Juan. *Historia de las agitaciones campesinas andaluzas—Córdoba.* Madrid, 1929. Unique as an objective study of both economic and political aspects of the agrarian problem; deals with the province of Córdoba for roughly the half-century 1880–1930.

Domingo, Marcelino. *¿A dónde va España?* Madrid, 1930.

Fernández Almagro, Melchor. *Historia del reinado de Don Alfonso XIII.* Barcelona, 1933.

García Venero, Maximiano. *Historia del nacionalismo vasco.* Madrid, 1945.

———. *Historia del nacionalismo catalan.* Madrid, 1944.

Jiménez de Asúa, Luis. *Al servicio de la nueva generacion.* Madrid, 1930. Vivid reflection of middle-class reformist hopes on the eve of the Second Republic.

Jobit, Pierre. *Les éducateurs de l'Éspagne moderne.* Paris, 1936. Fundamental for the understanding of Krausism.

Jupin, René. *La question agraire en Andalousie.* Paris, 1932.

López Morillas, José. *El Krausismo español.* Mexico, D.F., 1956.

Lorenzo, Anselmo. *El proletariado militante.* Mexico, D.F., 1943. Invaluable for the psychology and ideals of the self-educated leaders of Spanish anarchism in the industrial towns of Catalonia. The present edition is a reprint of the original, published in 1901 in Barcelona.

Lorenzo Pardo, Manuel. *La conquista del Ebro.* Zaragoza, 1931. The work of Spain's leading hydraulic engineer, covering accomplishments of the 1920's and future plans.

* Madariaga, Salvador de. *Spain.* New York, 1958. Rich in personal memories of liberal groups during the decades preceding the

Republic. Earlier editions of 1930 and 1943 contain the same background chapters as does the currently available book.

Marvaud, Angel. *L'Espagne au xx⁰ siècle*. Paris, 1913.

Marvaud, Angel. *La question sociale en Espagne*. Paris, 1910.

Maura Gamazo, Gabriel. *Bosquejo histórico de la dictadura*. 2 vols. Madrid, 1930.

Morote, Luis. *Los frailes en España*. Madrid, 1904.

Ossorio y Gallardo, Angel. *Diccionario político español*. Buenos Aires, 1945.

————. *La España de mi vida*. Buenos Aires, 1941.

————. *Mis memorias*. Buenos Aires, 1946.

Pabón y Suarez, Jesús. *Cambó*. Barcelona, 1952.

Reventós, Manuel. *Els moviments socials a Barcelona durant el segle xix*. Barcelona, 1925.

Rodríguez Revilla, Vicente. *El agro español y sus moradores*. Madrid, 1931.

Romanones, Alvaro Figueroa y Torres, Conde de. *Las responsabilidades políticas del antiguo regimen de 1875 a 1923*. Madrid, 1924. Able and clear defense of the Constitutional Monarchy.

Sancho Izquierdo, Miguel. *El programa mínimo de las derechas*. Zaragoza, 1919. Especially interesting as a forerunner of the CEDA program.

Santullano, Luis A. *El pensamiento vivo de Manuel B. Cossío*. Buenos Aires, 1946.

Söffner, W. *Die deutsch-spanischen Handelsbeziehungen, 1871–1926*. Eilenburg, 1929.

Spain. Resources, Industries, Trade and Public Finance. U.S. Department of Commerce. Trade Info. Bull. no. 739, 1930.

* Torrubiano Ripoll, J. *Beatería y religión*. Madrid, 1930.

Trend, J. B. *The Origins of Modern Spain*. Cambridge, England, 1934. Deals principally with liberal intellectual currents, 1860–1930.

Vicens Vives, Jaime. *Aproximación a la historia de España*. Barcelona, 1952.

————. *Els catalans en el segle xix*. Barcelona, 1958.

————. *Historia social y económica de España y América*. vol. IV, siglos xix y xx. Barcelona, 1959.

Vilar, Pierre. *Histoire de l'Espagne*. Paris, 1947. This work and the above-listed *Aproximación* of Vicens Vives are indispensable to any student of Spanish history as the most incisive brief interpretations available.

[A more extensive, critical bibliography of background works will be found in Gerald Brenan, *The Spanish Labyrinth*.]

II
THE SECOND REPUBLIC, 1931–1936

Ackermann, Georg. *Spanien Wirtschaftlich Gesehen*. Berlin, 1939.

Adams, Alexander. *Economic Conditions in Spain*. London, 1930, 1933, 1935.

Agirè y Lekube, José Antonio. *Entre la libertad y la revolución, 1930–1935*. Bilbao, 1936.

Albert Despujol, Carlos de. *La gran tragedia de España, 1931–1939*. Madrid, 1940.

Albornoz, Alvaro de. *Paginas del destierro*. Mexico, D.F., 1941.

———. *El partido republicano*. Madrid, n.d.

———. *La política religiosa de la república*. Madrid, 1935.

———. *Al servico de la república*. Madrid, 1936.

Alcalá-Zamora, Niceto. *Regimen político de convivencia en España*. Buenos Aires, 1945.

Altabella Gracia, Pedro P. *El catolicismo de los nacionalistas vascos*. Vitoria, 1939.

Alvarez, Basilio. *Dos años de agitacíon política*. Alcalá de Henares, 1933.

* Angulo, Enrique de. *Diez horas de estat català*. Barcelona, 1935.

* Ansaldo, Juan Antonio. *Mémoires d'un monarchiste espagnol, 1931–1952*. Monaco, 1952.

Aragon Montejo, José. *La revancha del campo*. Madrid, 1929.

Arrabal, Juan. *José María Gil Robles*. Madrid, 1933.

* Arrarás, Joaquín. *Historia de la segunda república española*. Vol. I. Madrid, 1956.

——— (ed.). *Memorias íntimas de Azaña*. Madrid, 1939.

Azaña, Manuel. *Discursos en campo abierto*. Madrid, 1936.

———. *En el poder y en la oposición*. 2 vols. Madrid, 1934.

———. *Mi rebelión en Barcelona*. Madrid, 1935.

———. *Una política*. Madrid, 1932.

Barcena, F. A. *Los jesuitas españoles*. Madrid, 1932.

* Barea, Ilsa and Arturo. *Spain in the Post-war World*. London, 1945.

Barrail, Henri. *L'autonomie régionale en Espagne*. Lyon, 1933.

Bazan, Armando. *España ante el abismo*. Santiago de Chile, 1937.

Bedoya, Javier M. de. *Siete años de lucha*. Valladolid, 1939.

Benavides, Manuel D. *El último pirata del Mediterraneo*. Barcelona, 1934.

Burgo, Jaime del. *Requetés en Navarra antes del alzamiento*. San Sebastian, 1939.

Camín, Alfonso. *Le valle negro*. Mexico, 1938.

* Canel, José (pseud.). *Octubre rojo en Asturias*. Madrid, 1935.

Carbo, Eusebio C. *Reconstrucción de España*. Mexico, D.F., 1945.

* Carrión, Pascual. *Los latifundios en España*. Madrid, 1932.

Casona, Alejandro (pseud. of Alejandro Rodríguez Alvarez). *Una misión pedagógica-social en Sanabria*. Buenos Aires, 1941.

Castillejo, José. *War of Ideas in Spain*. London, 1937.

* Comín Colomer, Eduardo. *Historia secreta de la segunda república*. Barcelona, 1959.

Conze, Edward. *Spain Today*. London, 1936.

* Cossío, Francisco de. *Manolo*. Valladolid, 1939.

Dalmau, E. Isern. *Política fiscal de la república*. Barcelona, 1933.

Díaz-Ambrona, Domingo. *Panorama*. Madrid, 1933.

Diez Vicario, V. de. *¿Laica España?* Toledo, 1933.

Domingo, Marcelino. *La experiencia del poder*. Madrid, 1934.

* Esteban-Infantes, Emilio. *General Sanjurjo*. Barcelona, 1958.

—————. *La sublevación del General Sanjurjo*. Madrid, 1933.

Fábregas, Joan P. *La crisis mundial y sus repercusiones en España*. Barcelona, 1933.

—————. *Factors econòmics de la revolució*. Barcelona, 1937.

Fernández Almagro, Melchor. *Catalanismo y república española*. Madrid, 1932.

—————. *Historia de la república española*. Madrid, 1940.

Fernsworth, Lawrence. *Spain's Struggle for Freedom*. Boston, 1957.

Fuentes Irurozqui, Manuel. *Sintesis de la economía española*. Madrid, 1946.

—————. *Viaje a traves de la España económica*. Madrid, 1948.

* Galindo Herrero, Santiago. *Los partidos monárquicos bajo la segunda república*, 2d ed. Madrid, 1956.

* García Venero, Maximiano. *Historia de los internacionales en España*. 3 vols. Madrid, 1957.

González-Blanco, Pedro. *Ordenación y prosperidad de España*. Madrid, 1934.

Gordón Ordás, Félix. *Una campaña parlamentaria, el artículo 26 . . . y los haberes pasivos al clero*. Madrid, 1934.

* Grossi, Manuel. *La insurrección de Asturias*. Barcelona, 1935.

Gual Villalbi, Pedro. *Política económica*. Barcelona, 1936.

Guixé, Juan. *¿Que ha hecho la república?* Madrid, 1933.

A slightly abbreviated French edition appeared as *Le vrai visage de la république espagnole* (Paris, 1938).

Hidalgo, Diego. *¿Por qué fui lanzado del ministerio de la guerra?* Madrid, 1934.

* Iniesta Corredor, Alfonso. *Educación española*. Madrid, 1942.

* Iturralde, Juan de (pseud. of Padre Juan de Usabiaga.) *El catolicismo y la cruzada de Franco*. 2 vols. Vienne, France, 1955 and 1960.

Jato, David. *La rebelión de los estudiantes*. Madrid, 1953.

* Jiménez de Asúa, Luis. *Castilblanco*. Madrid, 1933.

———. *La constitución política de la democracia española*. Santiago de Chile, 1942.

———. *Proceso histórico de la constitución de la república española*. Madrid, 1932.

Ledesma Ramos, Ramiro. *Discurso a las juventudes de España*. Madrid, 1935.

Lefaucheux, Charles. *La peseta et l'économie espagnole depuis 1928*. Paris, 1935.

* Lerroux, Alejandro. *La pequeña historia*. Buenos Aires, 1945.

———. *Trayectoria política*. Madrid, 1934.

Lesaffre, Jean. *Le problème national de la Catalogne et sa solution par le statut de 1932*. Montpellier, 1934.

Lindner, Elli. *El derecho arancelario español*. Barcelona, 1934.

* Lizarra, A. de (pseud. of Andrés María de Irujo). *Los vascos y la república española* . . . . Buenos Aires, 1944.

Llopis, Rodolfo. *Hacia una escuela más humana*. Madrid, 1934.

———. *La revolución en la escuela*. Madrid, 1933.

* Lubac, André. *Le tribunal espagnol des garanties constitutionnelles*. Montpellier, 1936.

Madden, Marie R. "The Church and Catholic Action in Contemporary Spain," *The Catholic Historical Review*, xviii, 19–60.

Madrid, Francisco. *Film de la república comunista libertaria*. Barcelona, 1932.

———. *Ocho meses y un día en el gobierno civil de Barcelona*. Barcelona, 1932.

Manning, Leah. *What I Saw in Spain*. London, 1935.

Manrique, Gervasio. *Sistema español de organización escolar*. Madrid, 1935.

Manuel, Frank E. *The Politics of Modern Spain*. New York, 1938.

* Martí, Casimir; Nadal, Jordi; and Vicens Vives, Jaume. "El moviment obrer a Espanya de 1929 a 1936 en relació amb la crisi econòmica," *Serra D'Or*, February, 1961.

Martínez Aguiar, Manuel. *¿A dónde va el estado español?* Madrid, 1935.

Maurín, Joaquín. *Hacia la segunda revolución*. Barcelona, 1935.

* Mendizábal, Alfred. *Aux origines d'une tragédie*. Paris, 1937. Published in English as *The Martyrdom of Spain*. London. 1937.

Miguel, Antonio. *El potencial económico de España.* Madrid, 1935.

Minlos, Bruno R. *Paysans d'Espagne en lutte pour la terre et la liberté.* Paris, 1937.

Miravitlles, Jaume. *Critica del 6 d'Octubre.* Barcelona, 1935.

* Moch, Jules, and Picard-Moch, Germaine. *L'Espagne républicaine.* Paris, 1933.

* Mola Vidal, Emilio. *Obras completas.* Valladolid, 1940.

* Montes Agudo, Gumersindo. *Vieja guardia.* Madrid, 1939.

Mora, Constancia de la. *In Place of Splendor.* New York, 1939.

Mori, Arturo. *Crónica de las cortes constituyentes de la segunda república española.* Madrid, 1931–1934.

Ortega y Gasset, José. *Rectificación de la república.* Madrid, 1931.

Ossorio, Angel. *Vida y sacrificio de Companys.* Buenos Aires, 1943.

* *Patronato de misiones pedagógicas.* 2 vols. Madrid, 1934 and 1935.

* Payne, Stanley. *Falange, A History of Spanish Fascism.* Stanford, 1961.

Peers, E. Allison. *Catalonia Infelix.* London, 1937.

———. *Spain, the Church and the Orders.* London, 1939.

———. *The Spanish Tragedy, 1930–1936.* London, 1937.

Peiró, Francisco. *El problema religioso-social de España.* Madrid, 1936.

* Pildaín y Zapiaín, Antonio de. *En defense de la Iglesia y de la libertad de enseñanza.* Madrid, 1935.

Plá, José. *Historia de la segunda república española.* 4 vols. Barcelona, 1940–1941.

* Prats, Alardo. *El gobierno de la generalidad en el banquillo.* Madrid, 1935.

Rama, Carlos. *La crisis española del siglo xx.* Mexico, D.F., 1960.

Ramos Oliveira, A. *Politics, Economics and Men of Modern Spain, 1808–1946.* London, 1946.

———. *La revolución española de Octubre.* Madrid, 1935.

Requejo San Román, Jesús. *Los jesuitas.* Madrid, 1932.

Romanones, Conde de. *Las últimas horas de una monarquía.* Madrid, 1931.

Salazar Alonso, Rafael. *Bajo el signo de la revolución.* Madrid, 1935.

Schveitzer, Marcel N. *Notes sur la vie économique de l'Espagne en 1931–1932.* Alger, 1933.

Sedwick, Frank. *The Tragedy of Manuel Azaña.* Columbus, Ohio, 1963.

* Sender, Ramón J. *Viaje a la aldea del crimen.* Madrid, 1934.

Sieberer, Anton. *Katalonien gegen Kastilien.* Vienna, 1936. A

French edition appeared as *Espagne contre espagne* (Geneva, 1937).

* Smith, Rhea Marsh. *The Day of the Liberals in Spain.* Philadelphia, 1938.

* Souchère, Eléna de la. *Explication de l'Espagne.* Paris, 1962.

Spain. *Diario de sesiones de las Cortes Constitýuentes, 1931–1933.* 25 vols. Madrid, 1933.

Spain. Instituto de Reforma Agraria. *Agrarian Reform in Spain.* London, 1937.

Spain, Laws, Statutes, etc. *Reforma agraria.* Madrid, 1932.

Spain. Ministry of Labor. *Anuario español de política social.* Madrid, 1934.

Una poderoso fuerza secreta. San Sebastian, 1940.

* Venegas, José. *Las elecciones del frente popular.* Buenos Aires, 1942.

Ventosa y Calvell, Juan. *La situación política y los problemas económicos de España.* Barcelona, 1932.

Vicens, Juan. *L'Espagne vivante.* Paris, 1938.

Villanueva, Francisco. *Azaña (El Gobierno).* Mexico, D.F., 1941.

Xirau, Joaquín. *Manuel B. Cossío y la educación en España.* Mexico City, 1945.

Young, Sir George. *The New Spain.* London, 1933.

[For further bibliography on the republican period, in particular the development of both the monarchist and fascist movements, see Stanley Payne, *Falange.*]

III
THE CIVIL WAR, 1936–1939

Abad de Santillán, Diego. *La revolución y la guerra en España.* Havana, 1938.

———. *Por qúe perdimos la guerra.* Buenos Aires, 1940.

* Aberrigoyen, Inaki de. *7 mois e 7 jours dans l'Espagne de Franco.* Paris, 1938.

Acier, Marcel (ed.). *From Spanish Trenches.* New York, 1937.

Alvarez del Vayo, Julio. *Freedom's Battle.* New York, 1940.

———. *The Last Optimist.* New York, 1949.

* Avilés Gabriel. *Tribunales rojos.* Barcelona, 1939.

* Ayerra Redín, Marino. *No me avergoncé del evangelio.* Buenos Aires, 1959. Second edition of work whose original title was *Desde mi parroquía.*

Azaña, Manuel. *Discurso . . . en el ayuntamiento de Valencia,* 21 January, 1937.

———. *Discurso . . . en el paraninfo de la Universidad de Valencia,* 18 July, 1937.

———. *Discurso . . . en el ayuntamiento de Madrid,* 13 November, 1937.

———. *Discurso . . . en el día 18 de julio de 1938 en Barcelona.*

———. *La velada en Benicarló.* Buenos Aires, 1939.

* Aznar, Manuel. *Historia militar de la guerra de España.* Madrid, 1940.

* Bahamonde, Antonio. *Memoirs of a Spanish Nationalist.* London, 1939.

* Bauer, Eddy. *Rouge et or.* Neuchâtel, 1938.

Beltrán Güell, Felipe. *Preparación y desarrollo del alzamiento nacional.* Valladolid, 1939.

———. *Rutas de la Victoria.* Barcelona, 1939.

* Bernanos, Georges. *Les grands cimetières sous la lune.* Paris, 1938.

* Bessie, Alvah. *Men in Battle.* New York, 1939.

* Beumelburg, Werner. *Kampf um Spanien.* Berlin, 1940.

* Bley, Wulf (ed.). *Das Buch der Spanienflieger.* Leipzig, 1939.

* Bolloten, Burnett. *The Grand Camouflage.* London, 1961.

* Borkenau, Franz, *The Spanish Cockpit.* London, 1937.

Bowers, Claude G. *My Mission to Spain.* New York, 1954.

Brereton, Geoffrey. *Inside Spain.* London, 1938.

* Broué, Pierre, and Témime, Emile. *La révolution et la guerre d'Espagne.* Paris, 1961.

Buckley, Henry. *Life and Death of the Spanish Republic.* London, 1940.

Camín, Alfonso. *España a hierro y fuego.* Mexico, 1938.

Cantalupo, Roberto. *Fu la Spagna.* Milan, 1948.

* Cardozo, Harold G. *March of a Nation.* London, 1937.

Carrascal, G. *Asturias.* Valladolid, 1938.

Carreras, Luis. *The Glory of Martyred Spain.* London, 1939.

* Casado, Segismundo. *The Last Days of Madrid.* London, 1939.

* Cattell, David T. *Communism and the Spanish Civil War.* Berkeley, 1955.

———. *Soviet Diplomacy and the Spanish Civil War.* Berkeley, 1957.

Cavero y Cavero, Francisco. *Con la segunda bandera en el frente de Aragón.* Zaragoza, 1938.

Chamson, André. *Rien qu'un temoinage.* Paris, 1937.

Ciano, Galeazzo. *The Ciano Diaries, 1939–1943,* edited by Hugh Gibson. New York, 1946.

———. *Ciano's Hidden Diary, 1937–1938,* translation and notes by Andreas Mayor. New York, 1953.

* *Le Clergé Basque*. Paris, 1938.

Clérisse, Henri. *Espagne, 1936–1937*. Paris, 1937.

* Colmegna, Hector. *Diario de un médico argentino en la guerra de España*. Buenos Aires, 1941.

* Colodny, Robert G. *The Struggle for Madrid*. New York, 1958.

Cot, Pierre. *The Triumph of Treason*. New York, 1941.

Cox, Geoffrey, *The Defense of Madrid*. London, 1937.

* Curtis, Noah, and Gilbey, Cyril. *Malnutrition*. London, 1944.

* *De companys a indalecio prieto*. Buenos Aires, 1939.

Delaprée, Louis. *Mort en Espagne*. Paris, 1937.

Deschamps, Bernard. *La vérité sur Guadalajara*. Paris, 1938.

Diego, Capitán de. *Belchite*. Barcelona, 1939.

Documents on German Foreign Policy, 1918–1945. Series D, vol. iii, Germany and the Spanish Civil War. Washington, 1950.

* Domínguez, Edmundo. *Los vencedores de Negrín*. Mexico, D.F., 1940.

Dundas, Lawrence. *Behind the Spanish Mask*. New York, 1943.

Eden, Anthony. *Facing the Dictators*. Vol. 2 of the *Memoirs of Anthony Eden*. Boston, 1962.

* Ehrenburg, Ilya. Memoirs of the pre-war era, excerpted in *The Current Digest of the Soviet Press*, 5 and 12 September, 1962.

* Faldella, Emilio. *Venti mesi di guerra in Spagna*. Florence, 1939.

Feis, Herbert. *The Spanish Story*. New York, 1948.

Fischer, Louis, *Men and Politics*. New York, 1941.

Fonteriz, Luis de (pseud.). *Red Terror in Madrid*. London, 1937.

Führing, Hellmut H. *Wir funken für Franco*. Breslau, 1941.

Gabriel, José. *La vida y la muerte en Aragón*. Buenos Aires, 1938.

* Galíndez, Jesús de. *Los vascos en el Madrid sitiado*. Buenos Aires, 1945.

García Mercadal, J. *Aire tierra y mar*. 3 vols. Zaragoza, 1939.

García Morato, Joaquín. *Guerra en el aire*. Madrid, 1940.

* García Pradas, J. *Como terminó la guerra de España*. Buenos Aires, 1940.

Garibaldini in Spagna. Madrid, 1937.

* Gerahty, Cecil. *The Road to Madrid*. London, 1937.

Gillain, Nick. *Le mercenaire*. Paris, 1938.

* Giral, José. *Año y medio de gestiones de canjes*. Barcelona, 1938.

* Goded, Manuel. *Un faccioso cien por cien*. Zaragoza, 1939.

Gomá y Tomás Isidro, Cardenal. *Pastorales de la guerra de España*. Madrid, 1955.

Gomá y Tomás, Isidro, Cardenal. *Por Dios y por España*. Barcelona, 1940.

Gómez, Carlos A. *La guerra de España*. 2 vols. Buenos Aires, 1940.

Gómez Oliveiros, Benito. *General Moscardó*. Barcelona, 1956.

Gonzálbez Ruíz, Francisco. *Yo he creído en Franco*. Paris, 1937.

* Gorkín, Julián. *Canibales políticos*. Mexico, D.F., 1941.

Gutiérrez, Ricardo. *Memorias de un azul*. Salamanca, 1937.

Hamilton, Thomas J. *Appeasement's Child, the Franco Regime in Spain*. New York, 1943.

Hanighen, Frank C. (ed.). *Nothing But Danger*. London, 1940.

Hart, Merwin K. *America Looks at Spain*. New York, 1939.

* Hemingway, Ernest, "The Spanish War," *Fact*, 15 July 1938.

Henríquez Caubín, Julián. *La Batalla del Ebro*. Mexico, D.F., 1949.

* Hernández, Jesús. *La grande trahison*. Paris, 1953. The original Spanish edition was published as *Yo fui un ministro de Stalin* (Mexico, D.F., 1953). A bowdlerized propaganda version was published in Spain under the title *Yo, ministro de Stalin en España*.

* "Hispanicus," *Foreign Intervention in Spain*, vol. i. London, 1937.

Hubbard, John R. "How Franco Financed His War." *The Journal of Modern History*, December, 1953.

International Red Cross. XVIᵉ Conférence internationale de la Croix-Rouge, *Rapport général du comité internationale de la Croix-Rouge sur son activité d'août 1934 à mars 1938* (Geneva, 1938).

————. XVIIᵉ Conférence internationale de la Croix-Rouge, *Rapport complémentaire sur l'activité du comité internationale de la Croix-Rouge relative à la guerre civile en Espagne (du 1ᵉʳ juin 1938 au 31 août 1939) et à ses suites*. Mimeographed. (Geneva, 1948).

* Iribarren, José María. *Con el General Mola*. Zaragoza, 1937.

* Junod, Marcel. *Le troisième combattant*. Paris, 1947.

* Kaminski, H. E. *Ceux de Barcelone*. Paris, 1937.

Kershner, Howard E., *Quaker Service in Modern War*. New York, 1950.

* Kindelán, Alfredo. *Mis cuadernos de guerra*. Madrid, 1945.

* Knickerbocker, H. R. *The Siege of the Alcázar*. Philadelphia, 1936.

* Koestler, Arthur. *Spanish Testament*. London, 1937.

Krivitsky, Walter G. *In Stalin's Secret Service*. New York, 1939.

Lacruz, Francisco. *El Alzamiento, la revolucion y el terror en Barcelona*. Barcelona, 1943.

Langdon-Davies, John. *Behind the Spanish Barricades*. London, 1936.

————. *The Spanish Church and Politics*. New York, 1938.

* Largo Caballero, Francisco. *Mis recuerdos*. Mexico, 1954.

Last, Jef. *The Spanish Tragedy*. London, 1939.

Lent, Alfred. *Wir kämpften für Spanien*. Berlin, 1939.

Liddell-Hart, B. H. *The German Generals Talk*. New York, 1948.

* *Lo que han hecho en Galicia*. Paris, 1938.

* Lizarza Iribarren, Antonio. *Memorias de la conspiracion, 1931–1936*, 3d. ed. Pamplona, 1954.

* Longo, Luigi. *Die internationalen brigaden in Spanien*. Berlin, 1958. The Italian original appeared as *Le brigate internationali in Spagna* (Rome, 1956).

* López Fernández, Antonio. *Defensa de Madrid*. Mexico, 1945.

Lowenstein, Prince Hubertus Friedrich of. *A Catholic in Republican Spain*. London, 1937.

Lozoya, Marqués de (Juan de Contreras). *La iniciación en Segovia del movimiento nacional*. Segovia, 1938.

Lunn, Arnold. *Spanish Rehearsal*. New York, 1937.

MacNeill-Moss, Geoffrey. *The Epic of the Alcázar*. London, 1937.

* Martín Artajo, Javier. *"No me cuente Ud. su caso."* Madrid, 1955.

* Martín Blázquez, José. *I Helped to Build an Army*. London, 1939.

Matthews, Herbert. *The Education of a Correspondent*. New York, 1946.

———. *Two Wars and More to Come*. New York, 1938.

Mattioli, Guido. *L'aviazione legionaria in Spagna*. Rome, 1940.

McCullagh, Francis. *In Franco's Spain*. London, 1937.

Merin, Peter. *Spain Between Death and Birth*. New York, 1938.

* Montero, Antonio. *Historia de la persecución religiosa en España, 1936–1939*. Madrid, 1961.

* Montserrat, Victor (pseud. of Catalan Padre Tarragó). *Le drame d'un peuple incompris*. Paris, 1937.

* Moure-Mariño, Luis. *Galicia en la guerra*. Madrid, 1939.

* Nenni, Pietro. *La guerre d'Espagne*. Paris, 1960. The original edition appeared as *Spagna* (Rome, 1958).

* Núñez Morgado, A. *Los sucesos de España visto por un diplomático*. Buenos Aires, 1941.

O'Duffy, Eoin. *Crusade in Spain*. Clanskeagh, 1938.

* Orwell, George. *Homage to Catalonia*. London, 1938.

* Oudard, Georges. *Chemises noires, brunes, vertes en Espagne*. Paris, 1938.

Packard, Reynolds and Eleanor. *Balcony Empire*. New York, 1942.

Padelford, Norman J. *International Law and Diplomacy in the Spanish Civil Strife*. New York, 1939.

———. "The International Non-Intervention Agreement and the Spanish Civil War," *The American Journal of International Law*, October, 1937.

Padelford, N. J., and Seymour, H. G. "Some International Problems of the Spanish Civil War," *The Political Science Quarterly,* September, 1937.

* Pedro y Pons, A. *Enfermedades por insuficiencia alimenticia.* Barcelona, 1940.

Peers, E. Allison. *Spain in Eclipse.* London, 1943.

* Peirats, José. *La CNT en la revolución española.* 3 vols. Toulouse, 1951–1952.

Pemán, José María. *Un soldado en la historia.* Cadiz, 1954.

* Pérez Salas, Jesús. *Guerra en España.* Mexico, D.F., 1947.

* Pérez Solís, Oscar. *Sitio y defensa de Oviedo.* Valladolid, 1938.

Prats y Beltrán, Alardo. *Vanguardia y retaguardia de Aragón.* Buenos Aires, 1938.

Prieto, Indalecio. *Cómo y por qué salí del ministerio de defensa nacional.* Paris, 1939.

———. *Confesiones y rectificaciones.* Mexico, 1942.

———. *Palabras al viento.* Mexico, 1942.

* Prieto y Negrín. *Epistolario.* Paris, 1939.

* Puzzo, Dante A. *Spain and the Great Powers, 1936–1941.* New York, 1962.

* Rama, Carlos M. *La crisis española del siglo XX.* Mexico, 1960.

* Ramón-Laca, Julio de. *Como fué gobernada Andalucía.* Seville, 1939.

Regler, Gustav. *The Great Crusade.* New York, 1940.

———. *The Owl of Minerva.* New York, 1960.

* Renn, Ludwig (pseud. of A. F. Vieth von Golssenau). *Der Spanische Krieg.* Berlin, 1956.

Rieger, Max. *Espionnage en Espagne.* Paris, 1938.

* Rojo, Vicente. *¡Alerta los pueblos!* Buenos Aires, 1939.

* ———. *España heroica.* Buenos Aires, 1942.

Romancero de la résistance espagnole, edited by Dario Puccini. Paris, 1962. Originally published as *Romancero della resistenza spagnola* (Milan, 1960).

* Ruiz Vilaplana, Antonio. *Burgos Justice.* New York, 1938. The Spanish original appeared as *Doy Fe* (Paris, 1937).

Saint-Charmant, Jean de. "Le problème religieux en Catalogne," *Revue des Deux Mondes,* 15 February 1939.

Sánchez Guerra, Rafael. *Mis prisiones.* Buenos Aires, 1946.

* Sencourt, Robert. *Spain's Ordeal.* New York, 1940.

* Serrano Súñer, Ramón. *Entre Hendaya y Gibraltar.* Madrid, 1947.

Sevilla Andrés, Diego. *Historia política de la zona roja.* Madrid, 1954.

Silva, Carlos de. *General Millán Astray.* Barcelona, 1956.

Smith, Lois Elwyn. *Mexico and the Spanish Republicans.* Berkeley, 1955.

* Solano Palacio, Fernando. *La tragedia del norte.* Barcelona, 1938.

Soler, Juan M. (pseud. of Máximo Silvio). *La guerra en el frente de Aragón.* Barcelona, 1937.

* Sommerfield, John. *Volunteer in Spain.* London, 1937.

Somoza Silva, Lázaro. *El General Miaja.* Mexico, D.F., 1944.

Spain. Estado Mayor Central del Ejército. Servicio Histórico Militar. *Guerra de minas en España, 1936–9.* Madrid, 1948.

Spain. *Foreign Intervention in Spain,* collected and edited by "Hispanicus," vol. 1, July 1936–January, 1937. London, 1937.

Spain. Ministry of Justice. *The Red Domination in Spain.* Madrid, 1946. This volume is the official translation of *Causa General.*

Spain. Spanish White Book. *The Italian Invasion of Spain.* Washington, 1937.

Spanish Relief Committee, San Francisco, 1937. *Spanish Liberals Speak on the Counter-revolution in Spain.*

* Steer, G. L. *The Tree of Gernika.* London, 1938.

Tarradellas, Josep. *The Financial Work of the Generalitat of Catalunya.* Barcelona, 1938.

Taylor, F. Jay. *The United States and the Spanish Civil War.* New York, 1956.

* Thomas, Hugh. *The Spanish Civil War.* London and New York, 1961.

* Toynbee, Arnold (ed.). *Survey of International Affairs,* 1937. Vol. ii. London, 1938; and 1938, Vol. i, (London, 1941).

Trabal, Josep A. *Final d'etapa.* Barcelona, 1937.

* Treyvaud, O. *Les deux Espagne.* Lausanne, 1937.

* Van der Esch, P. A. M. Prelude to War. The Hague, 1951.

* Vigón, Jorge. *General Mola* (subtitle "El Conspirador"). Barcelona, 1957.

* Villar Salinas, Jesús. *Repercusiones demográficas de la última guerra civil española.* Madrid, 1942.

Volunteer for Liberty. Limited edition by the Veterans of the Abraham Lincoln Brigade. New York, 1949.

Whitaker, John T. "Prelude to War. A Witness from Spain," *Foreign Affairs,* October, 1942.

* Wet, Oloff de. *Cardboard Crucifix.* London, 1938.

* Wintringham, Tom. *English Captain.* London, 1939.

* Ximénez de Sandoval, Felipe. *José Antonio.* Barcelona, 1941.

Ybarra y Bergé, Javier. *Mi diario de la guerra de España.* Bilbao, 1941.

* Zugazagoitia, J. *Historia de la guerra en España.* Buenos Aires, 1940.

[For further bibliography and discussion of sources for the Civil War, see in particular Broué et Témime, *La guerre et la révolution d'Espagne;* R. G. Colodny, *The Struggle for Madrid;* and Hugh Thomas, *The Spanish Civil War.*]

IV

PRINCIPAL NEWSPAPERS OF THE REPUBLICAN ERA

DURING the years 1931–1936 every faction and interest group published its own journals. The study of the press for this period would merit a book in itself. I have limited the following list to those which I used, and which are available in the municipal newspaper archives (*Hemerotecas*) of the principal Spanish cities.

ABC, Madrid and Seville (leading monarchist journal).

Arriba, Madrid (organ of the Falange).

La Batalla, Barcelona (organ of the POUM, most important of the non-Communist Marxist press in Catalonia).

Claridad, Madrid (organ of the revolutionary, Largo Caballero wing of the Socialist Party in 1935–1936).

El Debate, Madrid (organ of Acción Católica and Gil Robles).

El Diario de Navarra, Pamplona (Carlist journal).

Euzkadi, Bilbao (organ of the Basque Nationalists).

La Gaceta del Norte, Bilbao (representing conservative business interests).

El Liberal, Bilbao (personal organ of Prieto).

El Liberal, Madrid (anticlerical republican journal).

Mundo Obrero, Madrid (principal Communist Party paper).

La Nación, Madrid (personal organ of Calvo Sotelo).

El Pueblo, Valencia (moderate republican journal).

El Socialista, Madrid (official Party organ, of Prietist tendency).

El Sol, Madrid (may be characterized as *The Manchester Guardian* or *Le Monde* of Spain).

Solidaridad Obrera, Barcelona (leading organ of the CNT).

La Vanguardia, Barcelona (representing conservative business interests and offering more detailed economic news than any other newspaper in Spain).

[In my study of the Civil War I made relatively little use of Spanish newspapers. There is a particularly valuable bibliography of the wartime press in Burnett Bolloten, *The Grand Camouflage.*]

555

V

PERIODICALS AND SERIALS

Adelante, Mexico, D.F., 1942–1945. Contains valuable discussions, polemics, and memoirs of the exiled republican leaders.

Anuario estadístico de España, 1914–1934 (published by the Instituto Geográfico, Catastral y de Estadística).

Boletín de Información, joint publication of the CNT, AIT, and FAI (Barcelona, 17 September, 1936 — 1 March, 1938). One of the most detailed sources on anarchist collectives and anarchist interpretation of the Civil War. Available in the Library of Congress.

Boletín del Centro de Investigaciones Especiales o Laboratorio de Estadística. Published irregularly, 1933–1935; contains studies of development problems in particular areas, and statistics not previously collected, on such matters as the use of libraries.

Boletín de la Institución Libre de Enseñanza, Madrid, 1877–1936. Contains a wide variety of information on educational and scientific trends both in Spain and abroad.

Boletín del Ministerio de Trabajo y Previsión Social, Madrid, 1929–1936. Information on the cost of living given monthly, province by province, and detailed coverage of strikes and application of labor laws.

Bulletin of Spanish Studies (edited by E. Allison Peers, University of Liverpool, 1923———). Though primarily a literary bulletin, it contains monthly news chronicles useful for following the reactions of Spanish intellectuals during the years of the Republic.

Bulletin périodique de la presse espagnole, published by the French Ministry of Foreign Affairs. Valuable day-to-day coverage of Spanish press and radio sources of both zones throughout the Civil War. The Library of Congress file runs from May, 1936 to May, 1940.

Butlletí D'Informació, Neuilly sur Seine. Mimeographed organ of the Generalitat-in-exile, contains frequent articles of historical interest.

Caudernos Americanos, Mexico, D.F., 1941———.

Cuadernos del Congreso por la Libertad de la Cultura, Paris, 1953———. Both *Cuadernos* contain important biographical, philosophical, and cultural articles bearing on the history of the Republic and the Civil War.

Economía Española, Madrid, 1933–1936. Organ of the Unión

Económica Española, carrying articles of high professional caliber, generally conservative and critical of Republican policies.

Hora de España, Madrid, 1937–1938. Published by young intellectuals representative of all the tendencies within the Popular Front.

Ibérica, New York. Carries much biographical and political commentary concerning both the Republic and the Civil War.

Information télégraphique, published by Agence Espagne and containing daily dispatches from the Republican zone, September, 1937–January, 1939. Available in the Library of Congress.

Journal of the United Service Institution (for the years 1936–1938). British military journal carrying quarterly technical reports on the performance of armament in the Civil War.

The *New York Times* (for the years 1931–1939).

Revista Nacional de Economía, Madrid, 1916–1935.

Revue Internationale de la Croix-Rouge, Geneva, 1936–1939.

El Socialista, Toulouse, 1944———. Contains valuable articles by liberal republicans as well as Socialist *émigrés.* An almost complete file is available at the headquarters of the Partido Socialista Obrero Español in Toulouse.

The Times, London (for the years 1931–1939).

INDEX

559

INDEX

Chilean Ambassador, 437
church burnings (May 11, 1931), 32–35
Church and State, separation of, 48–52; attitude toward Republic, 106–107; budget, 124; internal divisions (1935), 188; schools (spring 1936), 215; in Insurgent zone, 306–307; influence in Nationalist Spain, 422–423
Churchill, Winston, 458
Ciano, Count, 408
Círculo Monárquico, 31
Ciscar, 406
citrus export problem (1932), 88–90
Ciudad Real, 472
Civil Guard, 27, 30, 32, 68, 70, 99, 123, 150, 172, 531; and Castilblanco incident, 69; and arrest of Socialist deputies, 137–138
Civil War, main issues for Spaniards, 494; outcome dependent on foreign influence, 494–495; results in Spain, 495–496; positive significance of, 498
civilian refugees, Barcelona, 445; Nationalist Spain, 446
Claridad, 180, 181, 206–209 *passim,* 284
Los Clásicos Olvidados, 181
Le clergé basque, 142
Clinical Hospital, 329, 330
"Cliveden set," 255
CNT, *see Confederación Nacional de Trabajo*
CNT-UGT Committee, Valencia, 264, 265
coal crisis of 1932, 87–88
Codovila, Victor, 362
colegio de abogados, 99
Colegio de Salesianos, 289
Collective Letter of the Spanish Bishops, 423
collective security, 258
Colmegna, Hector, 390

Colodny, Robert G., 324, 336
Comín Colomer, Eduardo, 512
comités paritarios, 29
"Committee of Reconstruction," 112
Communist International, 185, 186; press, 453; officers, 468; in 1936, 515
Communist Party, 111, 179, 186, 258, 284, 313, 373, 406, 434; role in spring, 1936, 207–208; and Caballero government, 360–362
Communists, 153, 284, 360, 402–404, 407, 411, 418, 467, 474; and fall of Largo Caballero, 363–367, 371–372; and attack on Prieto, 409; importance of in Negrín government, 453–454
Comorera, Juan, 314, 361, 370
Companys, Luis, 28, 72, 132, 151, 239, 244, 276, 467; and *ley de cultivos,* 133; and May 1937 incidents in Barcelona, 369–370
comunismo libertario, 100, 220, 339
concierto económico, 140, 384
Concordat of 1851, 48, 57, 188
Condor Legion, 334, 346, 381, 383, 390, 401, 461
Confederación Nacional de Trabajo (CNT), 19, 111, 237, 284, 341, 370, 445, 472; in Asturias, 153; factory committees of, 365
Confederación Patronal Española, 102
Confederation of Autonomous Right parties, 115
Consejo de Aragón, 339, 405
Consejo Nacional de Defensa, 469
Conservative Party, 5
conservative republicans, 41
Constituent Cortes elections, of 1931, 39–42; of 1933, 118–

Partido Social Popular, 116
paseo, vocabulary of, 308
paseos, 286, 313
"La Pasionaria," 361, 412
*Patronato de misiones pedagó-
gicas,* 110
Paxtot, General, 243
Payne, Stanley, 136, 179, 194
peasant refugees, Madrid, 444
Peasants' strike (June 1934),
134–135; Cortes debate over,
136–140
Pedralbes demonstration, 409,
411
Pedregal, Manuel, 201
Pedro y Pons, A., 447
Peirats, José, 405
pellegra, 447
Peñarroya Mine, 416
Pérez Farras, Major, 161, 164,
227, 239
Pérez Salas, Jesús, 150, 229, 238,
363
Pérez Solís, Oscar, 241
"Pertinax," 458
Peruvian Ambassador, 436, 437
Pestaña, Angel, 28, 125
Pich y Pon, 176
Pildaín y Zapaín, Antonio de,
49, 58
"piracy," 425
pistoleros, 100, 112, 213
Pita Romero, 188
Pius IX, 14
Pius XI, 49, 116, 423
Plan de Badajoz, 92
Plaza de Catalunya, 93
Plymouth, Lord, 315, 317
Política hidráulica, 91–92
political commissars, 362, 367,
407
political prisoners, literature read,
181–182
political violence (1932), 98–
100; spring 1936, 197–198
Ponte, General, 76, 234, 294
Popular Front, 167, 258; ante-
cedents of, 185–186; pact,
186–187; electoral victory of,

192–193; celebrations and dis-
orders, 196–197
Portela Valladares, Manuel, 172,
184, 185, 189, 192, 195
Porto Cristo, 304
Portugal, military intervention of,
257; and British observers, 425
Portuguese public opinion, 257;
journalists, 269
POUM, *see Partiso Obrero de
Unificación Marxista*
Pozas, General Sebastián, 166,
195, 227, 323, 361, 370
Prado, 445
Prats, Alardo, 153
President of Republic, powers
and functions of, 46–47; power
to dissolve Cortes, 201
Presidential election (May 1936),
206
press, Casas Viejas, 101
press censorship, 148, 167, 185,
197
press, election of 1936, 189–192
priests killed, in Popular Front
zone, 531
Prieto, Indalecio, 38, 78, 125,
137, 182, 186, 201, 203, 208,
209, 227, 313, 366, 382, 393,
443, 462; financial and economic policies of, 90–92; and
Asturian arms landing, 144–
145; Cuenca speech (May 1,
1936), 204–206; denounces
paseos, 287; opposes Extremadura offensive, 371–372;
and Battle of Teruel, 398, 400;
as Defense Minister, 402–412,
443, 462
Prieto and Negrín, 410, 412, 457
Primo de Rivera, Fernando, 285
Primo de Rivera, José Antonio,
118, 119, 138, 205, 266, 419;
personality of, 178–179; trial
and death of, 339–340
Primo de Rivera, General Miguel,
6, 16, 22–24, 29, 75, 116
Primo de Rivera, Pilar, 356, 357,
420

575